Fodor's

BASEBALL VACATIONS

Great Family Trips to Minor League and Classic

Major League Ballparks Across America

D1304309

BY BRUCE ADAMS AND MARGARET ENGEL

Fodor's Travel Publications
New York • Toronto • London • Sydney • Auckland
www.fodors.com

Second Edition

ISBN 0–679–00189–1

ISSN 1527–4861

Fodor's Baseball Vacations

Editor: Lauren A. Myers
Editorial Contributors: Nancy van Itallie, Matthew Lombardi, Anto Howard
Design: Fabrizio La Rocca, *creative director*; Guido Caroti, *art director*; Jolie Novak, *photo editor*
Cover Design: Guido Caroti
Cartographer: David Lindroth
Cover Photograph: Mickey Pfleger

About the Writers

Margaret Engel, co-author of *Food Finds: America's Best Local Foods and the People Who Produce Them*, is a former reporter for the *Washington Post*. She runs the Alicia Patterson Journalism Foundation. Her husband, Bruce Adams, is a lifelong baseball and history fan and the co-author of two books on political issues. He founded Bethesda Community Base Ball Club, which built Shirley Povich Field, home of the Bethesda Big Train baseball team. He also coaches their son's Little League team.

Authors' Dedication

We dedicate this book to our children, Emily and Hugh. Without their unquenchable enthusiasm for baseball and extraordinary energy and endurance, there would be no book.

Editor's Note

Although all prices, opening times, and other details in this book are based on information supplied to us at press time, changes occur all the time in the travel world, and Fodor's cannot accept responsibility for facts that become outdated or for inadvertent errors or omissions. So **always confirm information when it matters,** especially if you're making a detour to visit a specific place.

Fodor's wants to hear about your travel experiences, both pleasant and unpleasant. Send your letters to: Editor, *Baseball Vacations,* 201 East 50th Street, New York, NY 10022. Also check out Fodor's Web site at www.fodors.com. We look forward to hearing from you, and have a wonderful trip!

Special Sales

Contents

Introduction *iv*

What's in the Book *iv*

Tips for Your Ballparks Trip *vi*

1/ Durham Bulls and Other Tar Heel Treats Durham, Greensboro, Winston-Salem, Coastal Plain League *1*

2/ Blue Ridge Baseball Bluefield, Lynchburg, Shenandoah Valley League *10*

3/ From Rails to Trails Asheville, Chattanooga *17*

4/ Antebellum Baseball Atlanta, Columbus, Macon *25*

5/ The Opry and Elvis Nashville, Memphis, Little Rock *35*

6/ Bourbon Street to Birmingham New Orleans, Mobile, Birmingham *47*

7/ Plantations and Palmettos Myrtle Beach, Charleston, Savannah *59*

8/ Grapefruit League Spring Training Orlando/Disney, Vero Beach, Lakeland, Tampa, St. Petersburg *70*

9/ Historic Virginia Norfolk, Richmond *84*

10/ Star-Spangled Banner Weekend Baltimore, Frederick, Hagerstown, Delmarva *93*

11/ Pennsylvania Dutch and Little League World Series Harrisburg, Reading, Williamsport, Scranton/Wilkes-Barre *108*

12/ Big Apple Baseball Trenton, New York, New Haven *125*

13/ The Urban Renewal League Bridgeport, Newark, Atlantic City *139*

14/ Seafood, Ships, and Fenway Pawtucket, Boston, Cape Cod League, Lowell, Portland *148*

15/ Baseball Across the Border Burlington, Ottawa, Quebec City *166*

16/ Cooperstown and the Hudson Valley Fishkill, Oneonta, Cooperstown *176*

17/ Buffalo Wings, Red Wings, and Blue Jays Buffalo, Rochester, Toronto *186*

18/ Buckeye Baseball Cleveland, Akron, Toledo *197*

19/ Lugnuts and the Motor City Lansing, Detroit *209*

20/ Stables and the Speedway Louisville, Indianapolis *216*

21/ Chicagoland Chicago, Geneva, Kane County *223*

22/ Wild and Outside St. Paul, Duluth *232*

23/ Field of Dreams Cedar Rapids, Des Moines, Davenport *240*

24/ Heartland Baseball Kansas City, Omaha and the College World Series, Wichita *252*

25/ Big Sky Baseball Helena, Butte *265*

26/ Wild West Baseball Idaho Falls, Boise *272*

27/ Evergreen Baseball Seattle, Tacoma *278*

28/ The Emerald Cities Portland, Eugene *287*

29/ Joltin' Joe and Mighty Casey Stockton, San Francisco, San Jose *294*

30/ Disneyland and Hollywood Los Angeles, Rancho Cucamonga, San Bernardino, Lake Elsinore *309*

31/ The Cactus League and Desert Baseball Phoenix, Tucson, Arizona Spring Training *321*

32/ Rocky Mountain Baseball Denver, Colorado Springs, Albuquerque *335*

33/ Cowboys and Oil Wells San Antonio, Arlington *347*

34/ Sooner Baseball Oklahoma City, Tulsa *356*

Baseball Teams in the United States and Canada *364*

INTRODUCTION

The four members of the Adams family, Bruce, Peggy, Emily, and Hugh, have traveled almost 50,000 miles—nearly twice the distance around the world—to help you plan your baseball vacations. They have been in 45 states, seen baseball games in more than 110 different stadiums, gotten 17 foul balls, and seen three rainbows. As Larry King said, "If you have to have an obsession, make it baseball."

What's in the Book

The Ballparks

This is a great time to be a baseball fan who likes to travel. Fabulous new stadiums are being built all across America for major- and minor-league teams alike. Not since the golden age of major-league stadiums, in the early 20th century, and the bumper crop of municipal stadiums built by the Works Progress Administration in the 1930s, have baseball players and fans been so blessed.

After decades of concrete and steel bowls and artificial turf at the major-league level and neglect and mediocrity at the minor-league level, there has been an extraordinary turnabout in the quality and fan-friendliness of baseball-stadium architecture. Each year's new ballparks seem better than those of the year before. Fans are the big winners.

Something for Everyone in the Family

Baseball is a wonderful way to see and experience America. We saw it all—from the extraordinary beauty of our country to the shameful neglect of our downtowns.

One of the first things we saw in every small town we visited was a baseball field. The sport is a basic part of America's fabric, and its tentacles reach into all parts of life. In Memphis, patrons got free admission if they brought in a bulletin from any house of worship. No matter how many times we witnessed it, it was hard not to get teary when teams would let Little Leaguers stand next to the players for the "Star Spangled Banner."

We wrote this book to help families plan realistic vacations that include baseball. It's a departure from the usual "guy trip" books that emphasize steak houses, baseball trivia, and sports bars. Hey, we love those guys, but it's nice to know a restaurant with milk and apple juice. We've included kids' entertainments, from hands-on science museums to water parks, and history stops that, for the most part, kids will want to see, like Indian pueblos, battlefields, and a corny Boston tea party.

We divided the book into trips that could be accomplished over a long weekend. They can be stretched into a week, taking advantage of all the sights and entertainments in each town. Our interest is in economy, so we tried to keep lodgings to under $60 a night for four people, except in large cities, where we aimed at a $125-a-night limit. Lodgings $60 and under are listed by a $ symbol; those $60–$125 are $$; those over $125 have $$$.

In most cases, we listed the hotels used by the visiting baseball clubs first, as staying there gives you a chance to run into the players. Otherwise, we listed the hotel closest to the ballpark first. Please realize that visiting team hotels change frequently, as ball clubs switch whenever they get a better deal. So if it's important to you to stay at a team hotel, call the club and check which one they're using this season.

We chose restaurants that are high on charm and regional flavor and low on price. We listed the restaurant closest to the ballpark first. Nearly every restaurant listing ends with a $ symbol, which means meals are under $10 per person. Many are under $5 per person. Those few that are more expensive have the $$ symbol.

In the information box for each team, you'll find seven different designations that indicate the level of play. The top level is the *Major Leagues*. Next, there are five designations for the members of baseball's National Association, the organization of the minor leagues. Top among the minors are the two *Triple A leagues*, where many of the players are heading to the major leagues or have already been there. Each major-league team has only one Triple A affiliate. Players in the three *Double A leagues* have distinguished themselves at the lower levels and are attempting to show they have major-league talent. In the seven *Single A leagues*, major-league teams affiliate with more than one team. Two Single A leagues play a *Short Season* beginning in June. Most of the players are just out of college and recently drafted to play professional baseball. The game's youngest, rawest recruits play at the *Rookie* level.

Independent professional leagues do not belong to the National Association and their members are not affiliated with major-league teams.

The College World Series, in Rosenblatt Stadium in Omaha, Nebraska, held in the second week of June, determines the best college baseball team in the country. Many of the stars from this competition immediately join one of the summer *college-level leagues*.

Why Did We Do It?

This all began a very long time ago. Bruce's dad, Tinsley, was a young baseball fan with a very famous neighbor. Walter Johnson, the greatest right-handed pitcher of all time, lived nearby in Bethesda, Maryland. While managing the Washington Senators from 1929 to 1932, after his pitching days were over, Johnson took his son, Eddie, and Tinsley to Griffith Stadium to sit in the dugout. Bruce grew up going to Griffith Stadium for Saturday ball games.

In the Engel household, the sound of Herb Score announcing the Indians game on the radio was a summertime constant. The late, lamented *Cleveland Press* used to give students 16 pairs of Indians tickets if they got straight A's the last marking period. Peggy and her twin sister, Allison, would turn on the juice for the last 10 weeks. It was safe enough for 12-year-old girls to ride the rapid transit downtown to watch a

game in cavernous Municipal Stadium on Cleveland's Lakefront.

Bruce rediscovered baseball after a 25-year lapse in 1983 watching "Orioles Magic" bring a World Championship to Baltimore. By August of 1991, Bruce was completely hooked and went off for a classic "guy baseball trip"—four guys in a van going 3,000 miles to 11 major-league games in 10 cities in 9 days. Soon Peggy and the children joined the road trips. Our friends with young children would marvel: That sounds like fun, but how do you know where the teams are? How do you know when the games are? From those questions, this book was born.

Emily and Hugh's Excellent Adventure

The key to fan attraction to the minor leagues, especially for children, is the small scale and the resulting intimacy. In the minor leagues, you are right near the action. At most of the parks we visited, you could talk with the players before the game and kibitz with the guys in the bullpen during the game. The kids could run around and be semi-independent in a way you would never allow in a major-league stadium.

Before, during, and after the games, there were balls—well-worn practice balls and pristine official league balls. Many minor-leaguers find smiling young kids with dirty caps and beat-up mitts irresistible. Emily and Hugh collected 60 balls and countless autographs in our first cross-country adventure. There were tons of giveaways and endless contests. We came home with enough backpacks to supply half the students in an elementary school class.

We were awash in community spirit in the many stadiums where the fans enthusiastically sing "Take Me Out to the Ball Game." There's no denying the magic of the perpetual game on "The Field of Dreams" in Dyersville, Iowa. As for the games, we will never forget the thrilling finishes of the Northern League game at Saint Paul and the Babe Ruth League 16-year-old World Series in Jamestown. We doubt we will soon see three runners score on a wild pitch as we did in Idaho Falls or a mascot hip-hop dancing with the home plate umpire as we did in Stockton, California.

There were some special personal moments as well. Watching Hugh, in the awkward scrawl of a 5-year-old, write his name on a ball over and over again, Bruce asked, "Hugh, what are you doing?" "Practicing," he responded with the confidence of a kid who thinks he has a big-league future. Our 8-year-old daughter Emily's column on her summer vacation for our community newspaper ended in a way that should bring a tear to any parent: "This was the best summer of my life because my mommy and daddy were with me every day of the whole summer. The end."

Share Your Favorites with Us

When you travel, please remember that baseball leagues shift constantly. Each season brings new mascots, new logos, new management, and sometimes new teams. Do call in advance and make sure the team is still playing in its customary stadium and check on the home games.

Please share your favorite mascots, stadiums, attractions, lodgings, and restaurants with us. We are especially interested in learning of child-friendly activities near the ballparks. Write to us: Bruce Adams and Peggy Engel, 7211 Exeter Road, Bethesda, MD 20814.

One of the dangers of visiting so many ballparks is that you might get an idea to run your own baseball show. It happened to us. After four summers on the road researching this book, we helped create the Bethesda Community Base Ball Club to raise money to improve youth baseball and softball fields. With the support of an extraordinary group of friends, local businesses, and baseball fans, our organization built a small baseball jewel. We named our 750-seat ballpark Shirley Povich Field, after one of the nation's great sportswriters. Our team, the Bethesda Big Train (named after the incomparable Walter Johnson), plays in the summer wooden-bat Clark C. Griffith Collegiate Baseball League. If you are in the Washington, D.C. area in June or July, come visit us at Povich Field, which is in Cabin John Regional Park, at the junction of I-270 and I-495 (Washington Beltway). *10614 Westlake Dr., Bethesda, MD, tel. 301/983–1006, or www.bigtrain.org.*

Acknowledgments

Thanks to Emily, to Hugh, and to our still-perky 1993 Dodge Caravan for incredible adventures over four summers and spring vacations that went amazingly well.

Our thanks also are due to many people who helped us along our big baseball adventure. Three stand out. Brother-in-law and baseball aficionado Sandy Horwitt had the idea of our spending an entire summer on the road in our van. Glenn Orlin, an otherwise sane and mild-mannered government policy analyst, years ago set for himself the goal of visiting every single ballpark where professional baseball is played. Glenn was a constant source of information and encouragement. Our friend Ira Lechner joined us for 13 of the games from Rancho Cucamonga to Harrisburg and cheered us on every step of the way.

Our special thanks to Julian Bach and Carolyn Krupp, our agents, and Lauren Myers and Nancy van Itallie, our editors at Fodor's/Random House. Kevin Nealon is the brains behind our computers. Our thanks to all the owners, general managers, public relations staffs, reporters, players, and fans who took the time to share their insights and stories with us.

To all the people who went to games with us, helped get us tickets, gave us tips, let us stay a night at their homes, fed our cat while we were away, and told us stories, we are grateful to you.

Tips for Your Ballparks Trip

Travel Tips

The words "long car trip" evoke fear in many families. We found a few ingredients are key in making trips enjoyable.

A mechanical lifesaver for long trips was the 9-inch combination TV/VCR that a neighbor lent us. It plugs into the cigarette lighter and we lashed it with a bungee cord on top of the driver and passenger's armrests. A towel covered it as a rustic anti-theft device when we parked. The children never watched the TV, but the VCR worked miracles in reducing the sniping and complaints during six-hour drives. Carry the tapes (and any cameras and film) in an empty insulated cooler, so summer heat doesn't ruin them. What were the favorites? Baseball tapes, of course:

- *A League of Their Own* (1992, Columbia)—Emily and Bruce

- *Field of Dreams* (1989, Universal), *Pride of the Yankees* (1942, The Samuel Goldwyn Co.)—Peggy

- *The Sandlot* (1993, Twentieth Century-Fox), *Angels in the Outfield* (1994, Disney), *Rookie of the Year* (1993, Twentieth Century-Fox)—Hugh

A molded fiberglass roof luggage carrier was useful for the bats, balls, programs, and extras we collected. Two warnings—the extra height may put some parking garages out of reach, and you must have sufficient weight in the carrier to prevent it from bouncing. We also kept the kids' sleeping bags and pillows up top and used them during late-night and early morning drives.

You are going to stop every hour and 45 minutes or two hours if you have children under 10. Insist on bathroom visits at each stop. Bring a baseball, Frisbee, or football to throw during rest stops to burn off energy.

Carry a container of baby wipes and a roll of paper towels. Both will be well used.

In addition to a first-aid kit, carry scissors, can opener, flashlight, tape, and stapler. We used them all.

Join AAA. You'll get significant savings on family admissions at many museums, zoos, amusement parks, even restaurants. The AAA rate at motels is usually the best discount, and there are special family AAA rates at many lodgings. Always ask. Serious money can be saved at DisneyWorld and Disneyland with the AAA discount, but you must buy the passes from AAA, not at Disney ticket windows. Use the AAA trip-tickets and ask for maps of the cities you'll be visiting, too. Buying AAA traveler's checks on the road is not as easy as advertised. In many cities, you pay an extra fee for your out-of-town check. You'll have no trouble using them—AAA checks are accepted everywhere as cash.

Consider joining your hometown zoo, as the 60-plus members of the American Zoological Society extend free admission to members of other zoos. This can be a real savings if you visit more than two zoos a year. America's science centers also have an association that's following the zoo's reciprocity plan. Many museums have a free day or evening each week.

Call or write to each city's visitor's bureau before traveling; kids often like to do this so as to receive packages addressed to them in the mail. Most visitors' bureaus have coupon books with decent savings on lodging, food, and attractions.

Ballgame Tips

After you pass through the turnstiles, you may want to pin your child's ticket to a jacket or pocket, so that if you become separated, children or ushers can find you. Always instruct children to go to the game-announcing booth if they can't find you—ushers also will help.

In the Southeastern leagues during early summer, carry Avon's Skin-So-Soft or children's-strength bug deterrent to ward off chiggers and other bugs. Keep clear of the dugouts, as players often spray them with near-toxic doses of DEET-based bug repellent.

Always take a baseball hat or sun visor and sunscreen to games.

Take a sweater or jacket to night games, no matter how hot the afternoon sun was when you left for the park. Once the sun is down and winds pick up, many ballparks can be chilly. We carried a canvas bag of sweaters, sweatpants, and socks, as many times the kids would wear shorts and sandals until the late innings.

If you don't always pay attention to the game, sit behind the screen behind home plate to avoid foul balls.

Children 3 and under may be frightened by baseball mascots. Don't force them to say hello or be photographed. There's always next year.

In major-league parks, write down where you parked the car. In the excitement of arrival, you can forget. Watch kids carefully in the parking lots. Don't park in the surprisingly vacant spaces close to minor-league stadiums unless you want a cracked windshield. The spaces are empty because they're foul-ball heaven. Check with locals in the parking lot if you're unsure where balls frequently land.

Weather Tip

Don't worry about the weather. You can't do anything about it, and the odds are there will be a game. Of more than 100 games, we had only six rain-outs. New parks have incredible drainage systems, and even old parks get tarps on the field pronto.

Fun Tips

A large measure of the success of minor-league baseball in the 1980s and '90s was the result of aggressive promotions, give-aways, and constant between-innings contests.

Buy a program and enter the crazy games. Some stadiums have a very visible table soliciting contestants near the entrance, but at most parks this process is obscure. So, don't be bashful; ask how to enter.

Get there early. The minor leagues are where the players still enjoy talking with the fans and signing autographs. There's no telling what will happen before the game. Five-year-old Hugh spent 10 minutes warming up a Warthog catcher from the bullpen mound in Winston-Salem before the game with an entire team of uniformed little leaguers looking on with envy.

Hugh and Emily's Tips on Getting Foul Balls

1. Don't ask the bat girl or ball boy for a foul ball. It is their job to keep the ball. You'll just make them feel bad, and you won't get one.

2. It's sort of hard—and sometimes danger-ous—for five- and eight-year-olds to catch foul balls.

3. The very best place to go for a foul ball is near the bullpen. At many stadiums, you can stand right behind where the pitchers and catchers sit just past first and third bases. Lots of kids go there and ask the players for balls. Here's some of what does not work: "Hey, number 28, give me a ball!", "Smith, may I have a ball?" "Gimme a ball!" The players aren't supposed to give away their practice balls. They are profes-sionals at work. Respect them. Here's what does

work: Between innings, go up behind one of the players and say: "Sir, if you get a foul ball, may I have it?" Then sit patiently until a ball comes. This might take a few innings. When it does come, stand and remind the player of your interest: "Sir, may I have the ball?"

4. Always say "Thank you."

Motel Tips

When packing, consider bringing some of the following items, which can smooth the way:

• a night-light, or better yet, a night-light attached to a 16-ft extension cord. Turning the bathroom light on for middle-of-the-night illumi-nation is not an option in many motels, as the light also activates an aged, raspy ceiling fan.

• a roll of quarters. For tolls, newspaper vend-ing boxes, telephone calls, coin laundries.

• a box of laundry soap, in a plastic bag with a twistie, so you're not at the mercy of the over-priced soap vending machines.

• an oversized safety or diaper pin, to hold together the curtain edges of the drapes that let in the dawn sunlight.

• a separate bathroom bag for each family member, with his or her name on it.

• a six-pack-size cooler for drinks and/or medicines.

• children's pain-relief medicine, cough syrup, Band-Aids, creams, and a bottle of ipecac (for accidental poisoning) in your bathroom bag.

• a watch with a luminous dial that lets you tell time in the dark, without having to rely on the absent or broken motel clock radio. Do check the motel's alarm clock or radio. We've had early morning wake-ups set by the previous guest.

• a flashlight, to discern the user-unfriendly air-conditioning and heating apparatus, which often goes awry in the middle of the night.

On arrival, make a quick sweep of the motel room, removing any matches, ash trays, drinking glasses, and so on, that could be a problem for children. For children who aren't totally reliable in the wet-bed department, bring a rubber-backed flannel crib pad to place on the mattress.

If you need an all-night pharmacy and the Yellow Pages and front desk staff of your hotel aren't helpful, call the emergency room of a local hospital. The nurses there will know.

Consider joining Super 8 Motel's VIP club. It costs $3 and allows you to hold reservations without tying up your credit card. (You are on the honor system to cancel any unneeded rooms 24 hours in advance.) Super 8 Motels were the unexpected find of our trip—clean, inexpensive, and surprise-inspected four times yearly by management. Don't expect landscaping or interesting surroundings, but the rooms were equal or superior to chain motels charging $20 more a night.

Hotels and motels are slowly getting family-friendly, but you're still going to find rickety cribs with no baby linens. The Westin chain has taken the lead and offers potty seats, bed railings, and night-lights. Most of the Radisson hotels are "Family Approved," which includes cots, cribs, playpens, family movies, and child-proofing kits. You'll have to haul your own baby and safety equipment for most stays. Most lodging chains' efforts toward encouraging children are financial (no extra charge or free meals) or promotional (lots of cheap travel games or playing cards). Arranging baby-sitting through the front desk is no longer the rarity it once was, but it's still expensive. Some motels and hotels will give a discount on adjoining rooms if your children are old enough to sleep separately. These usually aren't advertised, so ask.

Ask in advance if your hotel or motel gives free or discounted tickets to the ball game. Several team hotels do this. Saving $18 on admission is a powerful persuader to use that hotel.

Also ask ahead about microwaves and refrigerators; some hotels and motels have them in the rooms, or provide them for a fee.

Choose lodgings with pools. There will be moments of meltdown, as there always are on long family vacations. It is amazing what a quick swim will do to revive children for a night of baseball. Carry a bag of swimsuits and towels so you can get in and out quickly.

If quiet is a concern, ask for a room away from the soda and ice machines, away from the eleva-

tor, away from the train tracks. Motels usually block-book rooms to help the cleaning staff. Ask for the quietest part of the motel. In a two-story motel, the top rooms are quieter, but you must haul luggage up and down stairs.

800 NUMBERS OF FREQUENTLY USED HOTELS AND MOTELS

Best Western 800/528-1234
Courtyard by Marriott 800/321-2211
Days Inn 800/325-2525
Econo Lodge 800/553-2666
Embassy Suites 800/362-2779
Hampton Inn 800/426-7866
Hilton Inn 800/445-8667
Holiday Inn 800/465-4329
Howard Johnson's Motor Lodge 800/446-4656
Hyatt Hotel 800/233-1234
La Quinta 800/531-5900
Quality Inn 800/228-5151
Radisson Hotel 800/333-3333
Ramada Hotel 800/228-2828
Super 8 Motel 800/800-8000
Travelodge 800/578-7878

Restaurant Tips

Kids' menus usually have the same four items, all heavy on the fried food. Discover the world of appetizers and a beverage for children—it's usually the right amount of food. Encourage children to try soup.

On long driving days, skip dessert and make an ice-cream stop two hours later.

Remember, peanuts, hot dogs, and grapes all pose problems for children under 5. Avoid Popsicles and lollipops if your kids are going to be running around a ballpark.

Non-soda beverages aren't as obvious in ballparks, but they are there. Fruit juices often are in barrels holding cans of beer. Bottled water is everywhere. Don't automatically get soda in kid's meal specials in ballparks and elsewhere—even McDonald's will substitute orange juice or milk if you ask.

We avoided fast-food chain restaurants and chose diners, cafeterias, Mom and Pop restaurants, and city markets' cafés instead. The service is nearly as fast and you have a much better chance of getting a fruit or vegetable into your child's mouth. The surroundings are more interesting and reflect the region.

Reading Resources

Any and all of the books on roadside America by our friend John Margolies, the premier photographer of Main Street America (*Signs of Our Time, Ticket to Paradise, Pump and Circumstance,* and *Hitting the Road*), are excellent background. We've dog-eared three copies of Jane and Michael Stern's *Roadfood* (HarperCollins, 1992) and would eat anywhere they recommend. Other important books include *Historic Black Landmarks, A Traveler's Guide,* by George Cantor (Visible Ink, 1991); *The Book of America: Inside Fifty States Today* by Neal R. Peirce and Jerry Hagstrom (Norton, 1983); *America's Heritage: Capitols of the United States* by Willis J. Ehlert (State House Publishing of Madison, WI, 1994). Also vital was *The Amusement Park Guide,* by Tim O'Brien (Globe Pequot, 1997).

Baseball America's Directory (Baseball America, Box 2089, Durham, NC 27702, tel. 800/845–2726; $13.95) is the indispensable guide for baseball travelers. It comes out in March each year. In addition to schedules, the Directory includes phone numbers, addresses, and directions to the ballparks.

The best guide to spring training each year is *Spring Training* magazine. Available in late January, it covers all teams training in Florida and Arizona. For information, contact Vanguard Sports Publications, Box 667 Chapel Hill, NC 27514, tel. 919/967–2420, www.springtraining-magazine.com.

The Minor League Baseball Book, by writers associated with *USA Today* (published by Macmillan, 1995), is a great book for what we call "guy trips," with a heavy dose of baseball trivia and sports bars. *Mud Hens and Mavericks* by Judith Blahnik and Philip S. Schulz (Viking Studio Books, 1995) profiles the 116 full-season minor-league teams. They've been useful to us in our travels, but changes in minor-league ballparks have dated them. *Ballparks of North America* by Michael Benson (McFarland & Company, 1989) is a comprehensive reference book on baseball yards and stadiums since 1845 in almost 400 cities.

Diamonds: The Evolution of the Ballpark From Elysian Fields to Camden Yards, by Michael Gershman (Houghton Mifflin, 1993); *Green Cathedrals: The Ultimate Celebration of All 271 Major League and Negro League Ballparks Past and Present,* by Philip J. Lowry (Addison-Wesley, 1992); *Lost Ballparks: A Celebration of Baseball's Legendary Fields,* by Lawrence S. Ritter (Viking Studio Books, 1992); and *Take Me Out to the Ball Park,* by Lowell Reidenbaugh with illustrations by Amadee (The Sporting News, 1983), are also valuable.

David Lamb's *Stolen Season: A Journey Through America and Baseball's Minor Leagues* (Random House, 1991) was an inspiration to us to make the journey as well as a source of things to explore that we might have missed. Two other baseball trip books made our journey more fun—Bob Wood's *Dodger Dogs to Fenway Franks* (McGraw-Hill, 1988), taking you to all the major-league stadiums, and Ernest J. Green's *The Diamonds of Dixie* (Madison Books, 1995), a trip through the Southern minor leagues.

For an overview of baseball history, we suggest: *Baseball: An Illustrated History,* by Geoffrey C. Ward and Ken Burns (Knopf, 1994), and two superb, readable, and elegantly illustrated histories by Bruce Chadwick—*Baseball's Hometown Teams: The Story of the Minor Leagues* (Abbeville Press, 1994) and *When the Game Was Black and White: The Illustrated History of Baseball's Negro Leagues* (Abbeville Press, 1992). *Away Games: The Life and Times of a Latin Ball Player"* (Simon & Schuster, 1999) tells the stories of the Latin players, past and present, first to break baseball's color line.

Books about specific minor leagues include: *Slouching Toward Fargo,* by Neal Karlen (Spike, An Avon Book, 1999), *Wild and Outside: How a Renegade Minor League Revived the Spirit of Baseball in America's Heartland,* by Stefan Fatsis (Walker and Company, 1995), about the Northern League; *Separating the Men From the Boys: The First Half-Century of the Carolina League,* by Jim L. Sumner (John F. Blair, 1994); and a series of league histories by Bill O'Neal on the American Association, International League, Pacific Coast League, Southern League, and Texas League (all published by Eakin Press).

The Ballplayers, edited by Mike Shatzkin (Arbor House, 1990), provides brief biographies of more than 6,000 ballplayers; *The Negro Leagues Book,* edited by Dick Clark and Larry Lester (Society for American Baseball Research, 1994), is the most complete record of the Negro Leagues ever published; *The Minor League Register,* edited by Lloyd Johnson (Baseball America, 1994), provides the year-by-year records of more than 800 top minor-leaguers; *The Encyclopedia of Minor League Baseball,* edited by Lloyd Johnson and Miles Wolff (Baseball America, 1993), is the definitive minor-league record book; and *Great Baseball Films,* by Rob Edelman (Citadel Press, 1994), covers that subject thoroughly. To follow minor-league baseball on a regular basis, subscribe to *Baseball America* (baseballamerica.com) and *USA TODAY Baseball.* Other good web sites are minorleagueball.com and John Skilton's Baseball links (www.baseball-links.com). *Minor Trips Newsletter* (Minor Trips, Box 360105, Strongsville, OH 44136; $8) is a superb resource for baseball travelers and is modestly priced.

DURHAM BULLS AND OTHER TAR HEEL TREATS
DURHAM, GREENSBORO, WINSTON-SALEM, COASTAL PLAIN LEAGUE

North Carolina is a mecca for baseball fans, with 10 minor-league teams and some of baseball's best stadiums and favorite mascots. You can combine baseball with three of the state's extraordinary science centers in Durham, Greensboro, and Winston-Salem.

Aim first for Durham, where the 1980s minor-league revival began, thanks to the hit movie *Bull Durham*. In 1995 a new baseball cathedral opened, a $16 million beauty with a hand-operated scoreboard and a trademark snorting bull. The original stadium is now home to the Durham Braves of the Coastal Plain League.

After a night in the Durham/Chapel Hill area (with its many colleges to visit), drive 55 mi west to Greensboro, where the stadium is ancient and character-laden. There's classic barbecue in this city, too, and the state's sprawling zoo is but 26 mi south, near Asheboro.

As you continue west, you may succumb to the lure of the country's epicenter for home furnishings in High Point, 20 mi southwest of Greensboro. Winston-Salem is another 20 mi northwest of High Point, with its home-run hitters' ballpark, Wally the Warthog mascot, and exceptional science center. Staying overnight gives you the time to visit Old Salem, a Moravian village that has a new children's section and a living history center.

Coastal Plain League games are played in eight North Carolina towns. The Kinston Indians, Carolina Mudcats in Zebulon, and the Burlington Indians are among Carolina's many other attractions for vacationing baseball fans. (We visit Asheville in Chapter 3.)

DURHAM BULLS

League: International • **Major League Affiliation:** Tampa Bay Devil Rays • **Class:** AAA • **Stadium:** Durham Bulls Athletic Park • **Opened:** 1995 • **Capacity:** 10,000 • **Dimensions:** LF: 305, CF: 400, RF: 327 • **Surface:** grass • **Season:** Apr.–Labor Day

STADIUM LOCATION: 409 Blackwell St., Durham, NC 27701

TEAM WEB SITE: www.dbulls.com

GETTING THERE: From I–85, Downtown Durham/Mangum St. exit 2 mi and follow signs. From I–40, I–40 W. to Durham Freeway (Hwy. 147). 8 mi on Durham Freeway to Mangum/Roxboro St. exit and follow signs to ballpark.

PARKING: Get to game early. Limited free parking on street near ballpark. Two $2 lots on Jackson Street. A ballpark trolley serves three free garages downtown.

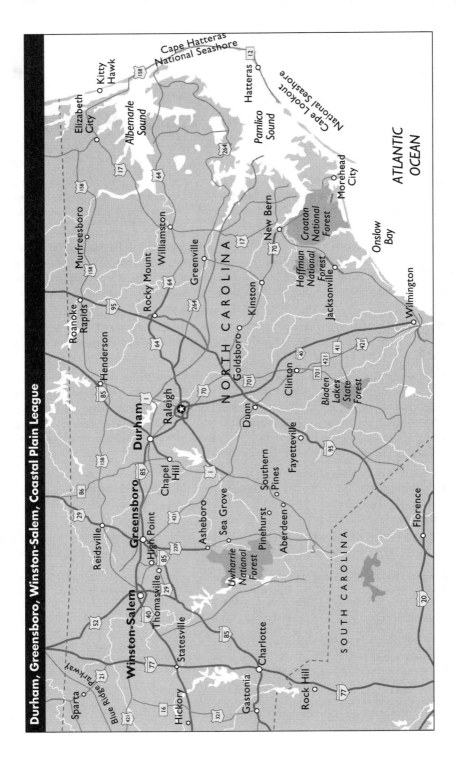

Durham, Greensboro, Winston-Salem, Coastal Plain League

TICKET INFORMATION: Box 507, Durham, NC 27702, tel. 919/687–6500, fax 919/687–6560.

PRICE RANGE: Field and club seats $6.50; reserved seats $5.50; gallery, diamondview, and lawn seats $4.50 adults, $3.50 children, senior citizens, and students. Under 6 on lap or in lawn seating, free.

GAME TIME: Mon.–Sat. 7 PM, Sun. 5 PM.

TIPS ON SEATING: All seats have good views with ample leg room and cup holders. Call ahead and buy box or reserved seats. 2,300 seats are under cover. Only 25% of 8,340 permanent seats are general admission. Best are down foul lines at first and third.

SEATING FOR PEOPLE WITH DISABILITIES: Down first- and third-base lines and behind home plate.

STADIUM FOOD: This park has some of the best food in baseball. **Dillard's BBQ** sells good pork barbecue and fried chicken. Other highlights are caramelized pecans and almonds, sold in cones for $3; an excellent steak and onion sandwich for $3.75; and hand-rolled cinnamon pretzels for $2.50. There's great ice cream, a bakery stand, and espresso carts. Try the **Flying Burrito Brothers** stand, but stick to the standards. Picnic areas adjoin each foul line.

SMOKING POLICY: Smoking prohibited in seating areas and on concourse; permitted in designated areas.

VISITING TEAM HOTEL: Durham Marriott at the Civic Center (201 Foster St., Durham, NC 27701, tel. 919/768-6000 or 800/228-9200).

TOURISM INFORMATION: Durham Visitors' Information Center (101 E. Morgan St., Durham, NC 27701, tel. 919/687–0288 or 800/446–8604).

Durham: Durham Bulls Athletic Park

Every baseball fan knows of the Durham Bulls, made famous by the 1988 baseball movie classic *Bull Durham,* starring Kevin Costner, Susan Sarandon, and Tim Robbins.

The Bulls—named for a popular brand of tobacco—first played professional baseball in Durham in 1902. Legend has it that the term "bullpen" was coined here. Pitchers would warm up in the shade of the "Genuine 'Bull' Durham Smoking Tobacco" signs that sported huge replica bulls in many turn-of-the-century ballparks.

The Carolina League, founded in 1944, has been a significant part of the roller-coaster ride that has been the history of the minor leagues these last 50 years. Durham, Greensboro, and Winston-Salem were three of the eight original teams. The golden age of minor-league baseball after World War II ended abruptly in the early 1950s when television brought the major leagues into the living rooms of fans across the nation. The minor leagues hit bottom in the 1970s. Durham was not immune, and the team folded after the 1971 season.

Baseball entrepreneur Miles Wolff paid $2,500 for the franchise rights to bring baseball back to Durham in 1980 and helped lead a national minor-league renaissance. Wolff, who sold the Bulls in 1990 for several million dollars, looks like a genius. Not so, he says—"Minor-league baseball was dead. But it was what I did for a living. It was the only team I could buy. I was buying the right to lose money." Eight years later *Bull Durham* was a hit, and Wolff had to open a store to handle the national demand for Durham Bulls memorabilia. Within a few more years, minor-league baseball was approaching the attendance records of the late 1940s as the baby boomers rediscovered baseball.

If the 1980s were the years baseball fans rekindled their appreciation for the minor leagues, the 1990s will be remembered for the return to classic stadium architecture. The highly praised redbrick Oriole Park at Camden Yards in Baltimore triggered a move to build stadiums like they once were and to locate them downtown, where they belong.

Many of us fell in love with the Durham Athletic Park we saw in *Bull Durham.* First constructed in 1926 and rebuilt after a 1939 fire, the DAP is a national symbol of baseball nostalgia. The 1988 movie crew installed a huge smoking, snorting bull in right field complete with a HIT BULL WIN STEAK sign. It was a wonderful place to see a game, but it was hopelessly unsuited for the huge crowds that came in response to the hit movie. The choice between staying in the DAP with all its faults or building a soulless aluminum and concrete stadium like Five County Stadium, built in nearby Zebulon for the Carolina Mud-cats, would be easy. Durham, to its credit, chose a third path—a modern facility with a traditional brick and steel feel.

In *Bull Durham*, Kevin Costner's character, Crash Davis—the real Crash Davis led the Car-olina League in doubles in 1948—remarks from his time in the majors: "The stadiums are like cathedrals." In 1995, a new baseball cathedral opened in Durham. The Durham Bulls Athletic Park, with a view of downtown Durham over the left-field fence, is a $16-million masterpiece designed by the architects of Camden Yards, HOK Sport of Kansas City. A tobacco ware-house à la Camden Yards runs parallel to the third-base line. Durham's "Blue Monster," the 32-ft-high left-field wall, and hand-operated scoreboard evoke memories of Boston's Fen-way Park. The attractive navy-blue seats are roomy with plenty of legroom, complete with a cup holder for every fan. The Bulls' owners pressed hard for a grandstand roof and they got a beauty, the largest cantilevered roof in the minors, covering 2,300 seats without an obstructed view. To complete the new-old feel, there is a human organist playing baseball tunes.

We usually buy general admission seats for minor-league games, but we made an exception here. We recommend calling ahead and buying reserved seats. Come early and eat at the park. The food is excellent, the music first-rate, and the parking limited. Walk along the concourse and find the three brick murals—including one of Hall of Famer and former Bull Joe Morgan— among the many tributes to the illustrious his-tory of baseball in Durham.

This ballpark is made for kids. Birthdays are announced, and there is a children's playground in the park's northwest corner beyond the third-base line. Take your kids to visit the mechanical bull beyond the left-field fence. Your children can wag the bull's tail if the Bulls make a good play or they can turn on the blazing red eyes and smoking snout if a Bull hits a home run.

More Durham Baseball

Durham Athletic Park. The ballpark where the movie *Bull Durham* was filmed is not far from the new stadium. The Durham Braves, of the Coastal Plain League, play 25 games in the old ballpark each summer. The park is also used for competitive women's softball games. A player was married in the stadium in the movie and in real life. *428 Morris St., tel. 919/956–9555. From I–85 take Downtown Durham/Mangum St. exit and turn right at Geer St.*

Where to Stay

Visiting Team Motel: Durham Marriott at the Civic Center. Within walking distance of the ballpark, it is an impressive, nine-story down-town convention hotel. There are also free shuttle buses to the park from the nearby city parking garage. *201 Foster St., Durham 27701, tel. 919/768–6000 or 800/228–9200, fax 919/768–6037. 187 rooms. Facilities: restaurant, indoor pool. AE, D, DC, MC, V. $$*

Where to Eat

Pop's. This imaginative Italian restaurant is in a former commercial laundry. Entrées include mussels, five pastas, fish, and chicken. There's also a children's pizza and pasta menu. It's across the street from Brightleaf Square, less than a mile from the ballpark. *810 W. Peabody St., Durham, tel. 919/956–1677. Reservations accepted for lunch only. AE, MC, V. $*

Allen and Son Pit-Cooked Barbecue. Here you can get very good North Carolina–style barbe-cue, with Brunswick stew. The worn, unpainted wooden floors contribute to the homey atmo-sphere. They serve fruit cobblers for dessert. *Airport Rd. (Rte. 2), Chapel Hill, tel. 919/942–7576. No credit cards. $*

Breadman's. In this comfy restaurant, you can get breakfast all day. The blueberry pancakes and waffles are standouts. The portions are huge; children get junior-size plates and prices. *224 W. Rosemary, Chapel Hill, tel. 919/967–7110. No credit cards. $*

Entertainments

Morehead Planetarium. This former NASA training center has wonderful programs for younger children. Its projector shows nearly 9,000 stars. Films roll daily in the 68-ft-high domed theater. Exhibits of planet life and basic astronomy are free. *E. Franklin St., Chapel Hill, tel. 919/549–6863. Admission to shows: $4 adults, $3 children and senior citizens. Open Sun.– Fri. 12:30–5 and 7:30–9:30, Sat. 10–5 and 7:30–9:30.*

Museum of Life and Science. At this spectacular, fascinating science center, you can stand in the center of a tornado, cup a cloud in your hand, or try launching a rocket to Mars. The well-designed museum emphasizes aerospace, weather, and scientific theories. A small zoo and aquarium focus on Carolina wildlife, including bats, snakes, flying squirrels, and river otters. A KidLab is for younger visitors, with bubble machines and climbing apparatus. For an extra $1.50, you can ride an outdoor train through a farmyard, a nature park, and bear, lion, and wolf habitats. *433 Murray Ave., Durham, tel. 919/ 220–5429. Admission: $8 adults, $5.50 ages 3– 12, $7 senior citizens. Open Memorial Day–Labor Day, Mon.–Sat. 10–6, Sun. noon–6; Sept.–May, Mon.–Sat. 10–5, Sun. noon–5.*

Sights to See

Sarah P. Duke Gardens. Here children can run and appreciate the fountains, gazebos, and nooks and crannies of a beautiful Italian garden. It lies on 55 acres of Duke University's West Campus and includes 5 mi of paths, as well as fishponds and a Japanese pond. *Anderson St., Durham, tel. 919/684–3698. Admission free. Open 8–dusk.*

GREENSBORO BATS

League: South Atlantic League • **Major League Affiliation:** New York Yankees • **Class:** A • **Stadium:** War Memorial Stadium • **Opened:** 1926 • **Capacity:** 7,500 • **Dimensions:** LF: 327, CF: 401, RF: 327 • **Surface:** grass • **Season:** Apr.–Labor Day

STADIUM LOCATION: 510 Yanceyville St., Greensboro, NC 27405

TEAM WEB SITE: www.greensborobats.com

GETTING THERE: I–40/I–85 to Exit 125, Elm-Eugene St. North on Elm St. 2 mi, right on Market St. Left on Dudley 1 mi to corner of Lindsay and Yanceyville Sts.

PARKING: Get to game early. Limited $3 parking adjacent to ballpark and across street.

TICKET INFORMATION: 510 Yanceyville St., Greensboro, NC 27405, tel. 336/333–2287, fax 336/273–7350.

PRICE RANGE: General admission $6 adults, $3 ages 4–21 and senior citizens, under 3, free.

GAME TIME: Mon.–Sat. 7 PM, Sun. 2 PM.

TIPS ON SEATING: The box seats are first come, first served. Most food and bathroom facilities are on third-base side.

SEATING FOR PEOPLE WITH DISABILITIES: Along fence in picnic area, in Family Section, and in the Grand Stand.

STADIUM FOOD: This park sells Cheerwine, a regional cherry cola favorite. Add a chicken sandwich from the **Bats Sidewalk Cafe** behind the third-base stands. There's pan pizza for $3.75, soft-serve ice cream, and warm Vinnie's pretzels. **The Grand Stand** atop the left-field stands has a bar complete with beverages and television. A picnic area down the left-field line is called **Lefty's Grove.**

SMOKING POLICY: Alcohol and smoking prohibited in small Family Section with general admission seats and 2 rows of box seats.

VISITING TEAM HOTEL: Travelodge (2112 W. Meadowview Rd., Greensboro, NC 27403A, tel. 336/ 292–2020 or 800/578–7878).

TOURISM INFORMATION: Greensboro Visitor Information Center (317 S. Greene St., Greensboro, NC 27401-2615, tel. 336/274–2282 or 800/344–2282).

Greensboro: War Memorial Stadium

This really looks like a war memorial—fortress architecture complete with flags atop towers and an arched concrete coliseum front. Built in 1926 for football and track, the stadium is shaped like a J, with the stem going down the left-field line to the end of the track.

Professional baseball first came to Greensboro in 1902, but the first minor-league baseball game wasn't played in War Memorial until 1930, when a roof for the grandstand, a press box, and dugouts were added. Greensboro dropped minor-league baseball for 10 years after the 1968 season, apparently in part because of the condition of War Memorial Stadium. In 1978 baseball returned, this time as part of the South Atlantic League. New York Yankee star Don Mattingly was the Sally League MVP in 1980, hitting .358 for the league champion Greensboro Hornets.

Bizarre is the only word for War Memorial's right field. A stream runs under fair territory along the first-base line, and wires hang over it. Because of the odd J shape of the stadium and the stream, the right-field foul pole was 248 ft from home plate when the stadium opened for baseball in 1930. The foul pole is now 327 ft from home, but the stream forces a short porch that is a left-handed hitter's dream.

The Old South is still in evidence at War Memorial. Take a close look at the war-memorial plaque listing Greensboro's dead from World War I on the first-base side at the front gate. Above the last six or so names something has been filed off crudely. It had said "Colored" for the separate listing of blacks who had given their lives for their country.

The owners have invested substantially in making aging War Memorial Stadium a good place to watch baseball. They funded a significant upgrade in 1993, including construction of the popular left-field bar, the Grand Stand. They moved seats originally from Yankee Stadium and Philadelphia's Connie Mack Stadium from behind home plate to the Grand Stand. The souvenir stand is called the Bats Belfry, and the bathrooms are called Bat Rooms in honor of Greensboro's distinctive Bat mascot. There is entertainment on and off the field every moment you are here.

In spite of recent renovations and improvements, War Memorial's future is uncertain. Parking is extremely limited, the plumbing old, and the lighting inadequate.

Where to Stay

Biltmore Greensboro Hotel. This elegant, European-style hotel downtown has reasonable rates and free limousine rides to the nearby ballpark. There is a vintage elevator and there are complementary afternoon beer and wine tastings as well. *111 W. Washington St., Greensboro 27401, tel. 336/272–3474 or 800/332–0303. 25 rooms. Facilities: parking (fee). AE, D, DC, MC, V. $$*

The Greensboro Hilton. This 11-story downtown hotel is the largest in town and often runs weekend specials. Child care is available in the athletic club. The rooms are good-sized and newly renovated. *304 N. Greene St., Greensboro 27401, tel. 336/379–8000 or 800/533–3944, fax 336/275–2810. 283 rooms. Facilities: restaurant, sports bar, indoor pool, hot tub, sauna, health club, parking (fee). AE, D, DC, MC, V. $$*

Where to Eat

Macado's Restaurant and Delicatessen. The overstuffed sandwiches and decor (planes suspended from ceilings, dinosaurs crashing through walls) appeal to kids. There's a sports memorabilia room with Yankee Stadium re-created on one wall, photos of Sandy Koufax and Stan Musial, and several autographed bats. It's 2 mi from the ballpark. *125 Summit Ave., Greensboro, tel. 336/373–0600. AE, D, MC, V. $*

Stamey's Barbecue. The city's premier barbecue mecca since 1930, this place serves pork and chicken cooked over axe-handle wood in 12 huge ovens. Don't miss the red coleslaw and fruit cobbler with ice cream. *2206 High Point Rd., Greensboro, tel. 336/299–9888. No credit cards. $*

Entertainments

Emerald Pointe Water Park. This 45-acre park has 22 rides, and you'll get wet on most of them. There are height restrictions on the thrill rides. Pools and slides keep younger children occupied. *3910 S. Holden Rd., Exit 121 off I–85, Greensboro, tel. 336/852–9721 or 800/555–5900 (in NC and VA). Admission: $22 adults, $15 children under 45". Open June–Aug., weekdays 10–8, Sat. 9–9; late May and early Sept., weekends 10–6. AE, MC, V.*

Natural Science Center. Another of North Carolina's good hands-on children's centers, this one has a planetarium, a zoo, and a petting barn. Kids like the dinosaur gallery and sea lab's touch tank. The adjoining Country Park has pedal boats, bicycling and hiking trails, and two fishing lakes. *4301 Lawndale Dr., Greensboro, tel. 336/288–3769. Admission: $4.50 adults, $4.50 ages 4–13 and senior citizens. Open Mon.–Sat. 9–5, Sun. 12:30–5.*

North Carolina Zoological Park. This is a natural-habitat zoo, which means lots of walking and few animals in cages for close viewing. Small children may be frustrated. African animals—like the warthog—are featured, in open fields and in a tropical rain-forest pavilion. The other major habitat, North America, has polar bears, sea lions, black bears, and cougars. Trams take you between habitats, but they run full, and you cannot see animals while riding. Shuttle buses return you to parking lots. The 300-acre park is 6 mi southeast of Asheboro. *Zoo Parkway (NC Rte. 159), Asheboro, tel. 336/879–7000 or 800/488–0444. Admission: $8 adults, $5 ages 2–12 and senior citizens. Open daily 9–5.*

Sights to See

Woolworth's Lunch Counter Sit-in. This downtown F. W. Woolworth store closed in 1994 but is still intact. Portions of the lunch counter are in the Smithsonian and in the Greensboro Historical Museum, but you can still see where four black students from North Carolina A&T State University staged a sit-in at the whites-only lunch counter. Their February 1, 1960, protest sparked civil rights demonstrations in 50 cities. There is a plaque and photo of the four young men. The side street where they exited has been renamed February One Place. *132 South Elm St., Greensboro.*

WINSTON-SALEM WARTHOGS

League: Carolina • **Major League Affiliation:** Chicago`White Sox • **Class:** A • **Stadium:** Ernie Shore Field • **Opened:** 1956 • **Capacity:** 6,280 • **Dimensions:** LF: 325, CF: 400, RF: 325 • **Surface:** grass • **Season:** Apr.–Labor Day

STADIUM LOCATION: 401 Deacon Blvd., Winston-Salem, NC 27105

TEAM WEB SITE: www.warthogs.com

GETTING THERE: Ernie Shore Field is next to Wake Forest football stadium; I–40 Business to Cherry St. exit, north through downtown, right on Deacon Blvd.

PARKING: Ample free parking.

TICKET INFORMATION: Box 4488, Winston-Salem, NC 27115, tel. 336/759–2233, fax 336/759–2042.

PRICE RANGE: Box seats $6.50; reserved seats $5.50; bleachers $4.50. Senior citizens and students 15 and younger, $1 off.

GAME TIME: Apr.–May, Mon.–Sat. 7:15 PM, Sun. 2:05 PM; June–Aug., Mon.–Sun. 6:05 PM.

TIPS ON SEATING: Reserved seats are a good buy. Sit on the third-base side to avoid sun. General admission seats are aluminum bleachers without backs.

SEATING FOR PEOPLE WITH DISABILITIES: On concourse along rail on first- and third-base sides.

STADIUM FOOD: The food is several cuts above most parks, in both variety and quality. The pizza slices are huge, with a thick crust. There are Buffalo wings, good BBQ sandwiches, and your choice of Winston Cup hard-dipped or soft-serve ice cream or frozen yogurt. For adults, there's an assortment of 12 beers, including Warthog Ale. Lemonade is fresh-squeezed for $2.50. Locally made Texas Pete Hot Sauce is available at all the condiment stands. Warm pretzels, topped with either cinnamon or Parmesan cheese, make a good snack for $2. A tree-shaded picnic area is down the left-field line. The concession stand area has plenty of space for watching the game while you eat.

SMOKING POLICY: Smoking and alcohol prohibited in Family Section of box seats.

VISITING TEAM HOTEL: Hawthorne Inn (420 High St., Winston-Salem, NC 27101, tel. 336/777–3000 or 800/777-3282).

TOURISM INFORMATION: Winston-Salem Visitor Center (601 N. Cherry St., Winston-Salem, NC 27101, tel. 800/331–7018).

Winston-Salem: Ernie Shore Field

Ernie Shore was Babe Ruth's roommate on the Yankees. They went together from Baltimore to Boston to New York. On June 23, 1917, starting pitcher Babe Ruth was ejected from a game for protesting a walk to the first batter. Shore relieved, the runner was thrown out trying to steal, and Shore pitched a perfect game, retiring 26 straight batters. He was ineffective after returning from military service in World War I. Shore moved back to his native North Carolina and served as Forsyth County sheriff from 1936 to 1970. He led the fundraising campaign to build a new baseball stadium in Winston-Salem. When it opened in 1956, the city named it for Shore.

Ernie Shore probably wouldn't know what to make of the team's mascots—Wally the Warthog and his brother, Wilbur—or all the hoopla at Warthog games, but he would be proud of this fine old stadium. The ballpark sits next to Grove Stadium, Wake Forest University's football field. There's an attractive brick-front entrance with a hall of fame and a brick wall between the bases behind home plate à la Chicago's Wrigley Field. In 1993, 2,000 seats were added and a new clubhouse built, and in 1997 a state-of-the-art scoreboard went up.

You walk through the brick arches and down into an amphitheater to your seats. Many of the seats under the grandstand are the original 1956 seats, styled after those then in use in Yankee Stadium. Ernie Shore Field is a home-run hitter's park. The prevailing winds carry balls over the fence in record-setting numbers.

The minor leagues are noted for contests and entertainment between the innings. In most parks, it is something of a mystery how people get chosen for these contests, as the forms are usually scattered throughout the program. When you enter this stadium, you are greeted by friendly staff at a table with forms that allow you to sign up for the various contests.

Wally the Warthog made his debut as the Winston-Salem mascot in 1995. Wally was an unusual choice. The fans voted for a camel, but management wisely scrubbed that choice because of the controversy over the infamous Joe Camel. Wally has turned out to be a winner. Somehow we can't imagine Ernie Shore's Yankees advertising "There's no SNOUT about it. The Most BOARing logo in baseball!"

Smoking is allowed through most of the ballpark, as this is RJR country. A massive RJR factory sits just over the right-field wall. Beyond the trees past the left-field fence is Planters, the peanut people, a subsidiary of RJR/Nabisco.

Where to Stay

Visiting Team Motel: Hawthorne Inn. A Continental breakfast is delivered to your door at this modern, 7-story downtown conference center that's 3 mi from the ballpark. *420 High St., Winston-Salem, 27101, tel. 336/777–3000 or 800/*

972–3774, fax 336/777–3282. 159 rooms, 25 with kitchens. Facilities: restaurant, outdoor pool, exercise room. AE, D, DC, MC, V. $$

Courtyard by Marriott. This pleasant motel offers free entry to a nearby Gold's gym and free greens passes at a local golf course. It is a half-mile to the ballpark. 3111 University Pkwy., Winston-Salem 27105, tel. 336/727–1277 or 800/321–2211, fax 336/722–8219. 123 rooms. Facilities: restaurant, outdoor pool, exercise room. AE, D, DC, MC, V. $$

Where to Eat

The Village Tavern. Sit outside on the patio for fresh salads, sandwiches, and pizza and marvel over the beautifully restored village and grounds of the R. J. Reynolds estate. 221 Reynolds Village, Winston-Salem, tel. 336/748–0221. MC, V. $

Mayberry Restaurant. Next door to the Old Salem Visitor's Center, this family restaurant serves breakfast, lunch, and dinner until 7 PM. Walk a bit of Old Salem and have lunch here. 201-B West St., Old Salem Village, Winston-Salem, tel. 336/721–4801. AE, DC, MC, V. $

Entertainments

Old Salem. The emphasis on artifacts and architecture may not hold children's interest through a full exploration of this German Moravian town. View 90 buildings, walk historic streets, and watch costumed staff reenact how people lived. Patronize Winkler's Bakery, circa 1800, and get a free ginger cookie. A new, interactive history museum for ages 4 to 12 has a climbing sculpture and a backward-running clock. Old Salem Rd., Winston-Salem, tel. 336/721–7300 or 800/441–5305. Two-day Village admission: $15 adults, $11 ages 5–16. Museum is $2 extra. Museum only admission: $4. Open Mon.–Sat. 9–5, Sun. 1:30–5.

SciWorks. This superlative science center is well kept, imaginative, and aimed at kids' interests. The hands-on saltwater aquariums, sea lions, and insects are a hit. You can hunt fossils, get next to a stuffed leopard and lion, and learn about chemical reactions. There's a 120-seat planetarium with laser shows and kids' programs and a play room for preschoolers. 400 Hanes Mill Rd.,

Winston-Salem, tel. 336/767–6730. Admission: $8 adults, $6 ages 6–19 and senior citizens, $4 ages 3–5. Open Mon.–Sat. 10–5.

Unusual Shopping

High Point Furniture Outlet Clearance Center. Call the High Point Convention Bureau (tel. 336/884–5255) to get a full listing and discount coupons.

Coastal Plain League

In minor-league baseball's first golden era immediately after World War II, Class D was the entry level for aspiring big-leaguers. For hundreds of small towns across America, Class D baseball was an important link to the national scene. One of the best of these leagues was the Coastal Plain Baseball League (CPL) in North Carolina. Sadly, with the advent of television and other entertainment options, this slice of Americana faded into obscurity. The league folded after the 1952 season.

Baseball entrepreneurs Jerry Petitt and Pete Bock brought the league back in 1997 as a summer college league based in some of the original towns and ballparks. College students play wooden-bat baseball in June and July, like in the Shenandoah Valley League (Chapter 2) and the Cape Cod League (Chapter 14). This is affordable family entertainment, with baseball at its most genuine.

Some of the largest Coastal Plain League crowds are in the smallest towns. The CPL packs them into Wilson's **Fleming Stadium** (tel. 919/291–8627), a 1939 treasure, where the original Wilson Tobs played in the 1940s and '50s, and the current team plays now. Also popular is Edenton's **Hicks Field** (tel. 252/482–4080), another 1930s standout that served as the home of the Edenton Colonials in 1952 and now houses the Edenton Steamers. Other Coastal Plain teams are the Asheboro Copperheads, Florence Redwolves, Outer Banks Daredevils, Thomasville Hi-Toms, Wilmington Sharks, and Durham Braves. For more information, contact the Coastal Plain League (tel. 919/852–1960, www.coastalplain.com).

BLUE RIDGE BASEBALL
BLUEFIELD, LYNCHBURG, SHENANDOAH VALLEY LEAGUE

2

The Blue Ridge Mountains are the stunning backdrop for several mountain ballparks, beginning with tiny Bluefield, West Virginia, where Bowen Field literally straddles West Virginia and Virginia. A stream and deep forest lie beyond center field. The seating is rustic, and games here are one of baseball's biggest bargains. The attractions of Bluefield are physical—its mountain beauty and a nearby coal mine in a partial ghost town that visitors can explore.

Eastward 150 mi in central Virginia is Lynchburg, a city of seven hills that wisely put its Carolina League stadium on one of them. The city has several unusual kid-friendly restaurants and a central city market. One of the wonders of the world—Natural Bridge—is nearby. Just an hour north of Lynchburg, you'll find the Shenandoah Valley League, a summer college league. The endearing stadiums have basic seating, attractive views, and a competitive level of play. In the cities you'll find vintage downtowns, plus many B&Bs in historic homes that welcome children and are near the Valley's famed caverns and river sports.

BLUEFIELD ORIOLES

League: Appalachian League • **Major League Affiliation:** Baltimore Orioles • **Class:** Rookie/Short Season • **Stadium:** Bowen Field • **Opened:** 1939/75 • **Capacity:** 3,000 • **Dimensions:** LF: 335, CF: 365, RF: 335 • **Surface:** grass • **Season:** mid-June–Aug.

STADIUM LOCATION: 2001 Stadium Dr., Bluefield, WV 24701

TEAM WEB SITE: www.ci.bluefield.wv.us

GETTING THERE: From I-77, take Bluefield exit, going west. On Route 460, take West Gate Shopping Center exit (look for sign for Bluefield College). Turn onto Leatherwood Lane. Take left at first stop light onto College Ave. and then first right onto Stadium Dr. into parking lot.

PARKING: Ample free parking.

TICKET INFORMATION: Box 356, Bluefield, WV 24701, tel. 540/326–1326, fax 540/326–1318.

PRICE RANGE: General admission $3 adults, $2 students, $1 ages 6–12, under 5 free.

GAME TIME: Mon.–Sat. 7 PM, Sun. 6 PM, doubleheaders one hour earlier; gates open for batting practice 90 minutes before the game.

TIPS ON SEATING: Come early and get one of the few folding chairs or bring a cushion or your own folding chair. General admission seats are close to action.

SEATING FOR PEOPLE WITH DISABILITIES: On walking concourse just inside dugouts on first and third.

STADIUM FOOD: This is bargain baseball fare, where you can feed the whole family for under $10. The hot dogs are $1.40, soft drinks are $1, and popcorn is 60¢. Pizza slices are only $1.50, as are nachos. Good hamburgers are $1.60, and a small ice water is 10¢. No alcohol is sold or allowed in Bowen Field, and you cannot bring in outside food.

Bluefield, Lynchburg, Shenandoah Valley League

Smoking Policy: No-smoking section designated behind screen in back of home.

Visiting Team Hotel: Ramada Inn East River Mountain (3175 East Cumberland Rd., Bluefield, WV 24701, tel. 304/325–5421 or 800/228–2828).

Tourism Information: West Virginia Tourist Information Center (I–77 and Rte. 460, Princeton, WV 24740, tel. 304/487–2214).

Bluefield: Bowen Field

This Appalachian League park is a mountain gem. Built in 1939, Bowen Field sits at the edge of a city park on West Virginia's southern border with Virginia. A ball hit to right field goes out of the state, as the state line crosses the field. A stream runs by, and a deep-green forest lies just beyond the outfield wall. This beautiful natural setting is marred only by the Marlboro Man cutout advertisement that stands near a scoreboard in center field.

Thankfully, not much has changed here in the last 50 years. This nostalgia trip back to the '40s is the perfect setting for the Appalachian League's rookie-level baseball. The park's high elevation can make for cool evenings, even in August. Bowen Field can accommodate 3,000 fans on wide concrete benches arranged in a horseshoe shape behind home plate under a rust-color roof. The seats let you see the almost-perfect arch of trees on a green hill beyond the close-in fences and give you a clear view of your wandering children. A wide wooden ramp makes the stadium accessible to wheelchairs and baby carriages, a rarity among the older minor-league stadiums.

No skyboxes here. Come early if you want to sit on one of the few metal folding chairs. Bring a seat cushion or your own folding chair if you want to be comfortable. Bowen Field is the best bargain in baseball, with $3 tickets, $2 for students, and kids 5 and under free. The policy under long-time general manager George Fanning was always "If you don't have the money, we'll let you in for free." The night we were there, a local business bought all the tickets and everyone got in free.

The best treat for children is the easy access to the dugouts before and after the game. The gates were open hours before the game for bat-

ting practice. Our children wandered through the home-team dugout before the game, getting their baseballs signed by nearly every player and coach. Club security was a kindly older man who gently shooed the children back up to the stands as game time approached. Balls fly out of the stadium during batting practice, so snag one before it lands in the stream.

For decades, this ballpark has been run as George Fanning thought a ballpark should be run—it's open, friendly, and inexpensive. You won't find the legions of recent college grads in T-shirts with team logos running around the stadium with walkie-talkies imbedded in their ears. The small staff is virtually invisible, but the job gets done. A bunch of veteran Orioles fans sit in the "Railbirds" box on the third-base side.

George Fanning and his wife, Catherine, ran the show from a small office near the entrance and the concession stands on the third-base side. When we visited shortly before Mr. Fanning's death in 1995, he reminisced about the 1920s, when the parking lot was a dirt airstrip and the miners' league played baseball right there in front of a grandstand from the old fairgrounds.

Future Hall of Famers Eddie Murray and Cal Ripken, Jr., played here in the 1980s. The field is named for Joe Bowen, a coal-company executive who bought the land and donated it to the city of Bluefield. The Fannings told us the story of the early morning call they got in the summer of 1973. Lightning had hit a transformer and set the stadium roof on fire. The wooden grandstand was quickly destroyed. For a season, fans brought their chairs and the team played without a grandstand. Then in 1975, the city of Bluefield rebuilt the grandstand with concrete and cinderblock.

A huge orange-and-black Baltimore Orioles logo with bird welcomes visitors to Bowen Field, a symbol of the longest-running affiliation in professional baseball. Local churches and civic clubs take turns at the refreshment stand. The cinderblock construction that looks tacky in the fancy new stadiums fits right in here. Bluefield doesn't promise anything very fancy—just a good, solid all-American night at a beautiful mountain ballpark.

Where to Stay

Visiting Team Hotel: Ramada Inn East River Mountain. This two-story brick hotel is nestled into a mountain. Its rooms are larger than usual but are ordinary. You are away from road noise. *3175 E. Cumberland Rd., Bluefield 24701, tel. 304/325–5421 or 800/228–2828. 158 rooms. Facilities: restaurant, indoor pool, sauna, hot tub, billiards. AE, D, DC, MC, V. $*

Holiday Inn. This standard roadside motel sits along the town's commercial strip. Its rooms are conventional and clean. *Rte. 460, Exit 1 off I–77, Bluefield 24701, tel. 304/325–6170 or 800/465–4329, fax 304/325–6170. 120 rooms. Facilities: 2 restaurants, no-smoking rooms, outdoor pool, sauna. AE, D, DC, MC, V. $*

Where to Eat

Johnston's Inn and Restaurant. Here, in a small commercial crossroads amid the mountains, you can eat country ham, homemade bread, and rolls. It's known for its coconut cream and peanut butter pies. There is a children's menu. *Oakvale Rd., Princeton, WV, tel. 304/425–7591 or 800/424–7591. Exit 9 off I–77, west on Rte. 460 to Pipestem/Bluestone exit; inn is at first stop sign. AE, D, DC, MC, V. $*

Roma III. At this Italian family restaurant, the homemade lasagna and ravioli are especially good. There is homemade cannoli. A children's menu is available. *140 Brick St., Princeton, WV, tel. 304/487–2568 or 304/425–7662. AE, MC, V. $*

Entertainments

Pocahontas Exhibition Mine. A fascinating walk-through coal mine, it has tours conducted by men who once dug coal out of its 13-ft-high seam. The work was dirty and dangerous. This prodigious mine heated homes throughout America until it closed in 1955. Wear sweaters, as it's a cool 52° inside. An adjoining education room has artifacts and a movie. Afterward, walk the streets of this old mining town and view the Opera House and log schoolhouse. Bluefield's Craft Memorial Library (600 E. Commerce St., tel. 304/325–3943) contains the history of this mine in its Eastern Regional Coal Archives. *Pocahontas, VA, tel. 540/945–2134. Admission: $6 adults, $3.50 ages 6–12, under 6 free. Open May–Oct., Mon.–Sat. 10–5, Sun. noon–5.*

The Science Center of West Virginia. Here hands-on exhibits on electricity, computers, and geology are housed in actual jail cells. Try playing basketball with Virtual Hoops. The center shares space in the city's original municipal building with an arts-and-crafts center that displays authentic mountain handwork. *500 Bland St., Bluefield, tel. 304/325–8855. Admission: $5. Open June–Aug., Tues.–Sat. 10–5; Sept.–May, Tues.–Fri. 9–3, Sat. 10–4.*

Unusual Shopping

West Virginia Tourist Information Center. One of four centers along I–77 between Princeton and Charleston, it contains "West Virginia Made" food, crafts, art, unusual jewelry, and books. *I–77 N and Rte. 460, Princeton exit, Princeton, tel. 304/487–2214.*

LYNCHBURG HILLCATS

League: Carolina League • **Major League Affiliation:** Pittsburgh Pirates • **Stadium:** City Stadium • **Opened:** 1940 • **Capacity:** 4,000 • **Dimensions:** LF: 325, CF: 390, RF: 325 • **Surface:** grass • **Season:** Apr.–Labor Day

STADIUM LOCATION: City Stadium, 3180 Fort Ave. and Wythe Rd., Lynchburg, VA 24501.

TEAM WEB SITE: www.lynchburg-hillcats.com

GETTING THERE: U.S. 29 South to Exit 4, City Stadium or U.S. 29 North to Exit 6, City Stadium. Follow signs to stadium.

PARKING: Free.

TICKET INFORMATION: Box 10213, Lynchburg, VA 24506, tel. 804/528–1144 or 804/846–0768.

PRICE RANGE: Reserved box seats $5; general admission $4 adults, $3 senior citizens and students.

GAME TIME: Mon.–Sat. 7:05 PM, Sun. 2:05 PM.

TIPS ON SEATING: Best view of Blue Ridge Mountains is from first-base visitors' side. Stadium is windy, so bring jackets no matter how warm the day.

SEATING FOR PEOPLE WITH DISABILITIES: Special ramp for wheelchairs at right field entrance gate (Wythe Rd. entrance).

STADIUM FOOD: A grill on parking-lot level mimics a neighborhood picnic—great burgers with tubs of tomatoes, lettuce, pickles, and onions. It's at the stadium entrance—watch for foul balls. Vendors carry newsboy bags, selling Cracker Jack and peanuts. At concession stands at top of seating, you can get bar-becued chicken and pork sandwiches, corn dogs, french fries, nachos, foot-long hotdogs, a "Big Cat" quarter-pound hot dog, and pizza.

SMOKING POLICY: No smoking or alcohol in section 5.

VISITING TEAM HOTEL: Best Western (2815 Candlers Mountain Rd., Lynchburg, VA 24502, tel. 804/237–2986 or 800/528–1234).

TOURISM INFORMATION: Visitors Center (216 12th St., Lynchburg, VA 24504, tel. 804/847–1811 or 800/732–5821).

Lynchburg:
City Stadium

Baseball has deep roots in Lynchburg. Professionals played ball here as far back as 1886. In 1895, the Lynchburg Tobacconists finished in second place in the 150-game Virginia State League. Since 1966, Lynchburg has played in the Carolina League. The Lynchburg Mets won the 1983 league title behind 18-year-old Dwight Gooden's 19 wins and 300 strikeouts. In 1995 the team became affiliated with the Pittsburgh Pirates and acquired a new name—the Hill-cats—and a sporty new logo.

Lynchburg's City Stadium reflects the city's long baseball tradition. With the exception of a gorgeous new coat of Camden Yards dark green paint, City Stadium must look much like it did when it opened in 1940. We asked Hillcats general manager Paul Sunwall how he could maintain this wonderful 1940s feel in the face of pressure from professional baseball to upgrade facilities. He pointed to the new foul poles and the fact that the chicken wire had been replaced behind home plate. A $5 million renovation and a name change, to Merritt Huchinson Stadium,

is scheduled to take place by the beginning of the 2001 season.

With a general admission ticket, you'll be right near the action. There are only 208 reserved seats in this cozy, scenic 4,000-capacity stadium. In this "Hill City," the stadium has the Blue Ridge Mountains as its backdrop. The best view of the Blue Ridge is from the visitors' first-base side. The ubiquitous Marlboro Man appears to be looking incredulously at a STRIKE OUT TOBACCO USE! sign among the ads for local merchants stacked two deep along the outfield wall.

Most of the concession stands are at the top of the seating, so you can get your basic food and drinks without missing any of the action. The big exceptions are the excellent grill on the parking-lot level near the stadium entrance, the souvenir stand, and the bathrooms.

Minor-league baseball provides a friendly, relaxed ambience all too absent in the high-stakes major leagues. A Hillcat player talked with five-year-old Hugh for 10 minutes before the game and gave him a ball. We saw a fast-paced, error-free game played in just over two hours. A Hillcat player hit a home run, but no one collected the $500 for hitting a ball through the basketball net in right-center field.

If you decide to explore Lynchburg after the game, be forewarned: With children it's easier to drive than to walk the city's seven hills.

Where to Stay

Lynchburg Mansion Inn. Call first to stay on historic Garland Hill in an unforgettable B&B that accepts children. The rooms, all with private baths, are large and beautifully decorated. *405 Madison St., Lynchburg 24504, tel. 804/528–5400 or 800/352–1199. 5 rooms. Facilities: outdoor spa pool, solarium. AE, DC, MC, V. $$*

Days Inn. At one of the chain's nicest properties you get free breakfast and a buy one, get one free game of bowling at the adjacent alley. Rooms are freshly decorated. The hotel is 15 minutes from the ballpark and next to the River Ridge Mall. Children under 18 stay free. *3320 Chandlers Mountain Rd., Exit 8B off I–29, Lynchburg 23502, tel. 804/847–8655 or 800/329–7466, fax 804/846–3297. 131 rooms. Facilities: restaurant, outdoor pool, playground. AE, D, DC, MC, V. $$*

Where to Eat

Spanky's. Crammed with roadside art, neon signs, and circus memorabilia, this visual fun fest is a rollicking place to eat. There's an inexpensive kid's menu (59¢ macaroni and cheese!), a separate soda fountain, and a huge menu of sandwiches and salads. *908 Main St., Lynchburg, tel. 804/846–4146. AE, MC, V. $*

Billy Joe's Ice Cream Parlor. The Wurlitzer here is filled with records from the '50s and '60s. Sandwiches, pizza, pita, burgers, and ice cream creations are on the menu. *4915 Fort Ave., Lynchburg, tel. 804/237–7825. AE, D, MC, V. $*

Entertainments

City Pest House Medical Museum and Cemetery. Walking among the 2,071 Confederate headstones brought history alive for our children. Look inside the tiny Pest House, a re-creation of the miserable quarters given to those suffering from malaria and smallpox. You can also see the former office of Quaker doctor John Jay Terrell, who worked with these shunned patients. The cemetery has artistic ironwork and old garden roses throughout. *4th and Taylor Sts., Lynchburg. Admission: Free. Open sunrise–sunset.*

Community Market. Buy flowers, cheap and beautiful produce, and wooden toys. A few stalls are open during the week, but the market comes alive on Friday and Saturday, plus a few summer Sundays. *Main and 12th Sts., Lynchburg, tel. 804/847–1499. Open Mar.–Dec., Mon.–Sat. 7–2.*

Sights to See

Poplar Forest. Fifteen minutes west of Lynchburg is the elegant, octagonal home Thomas Jefferson designed as a country retreat in 1806. It's being restored, and kids like viewing the rats' nests as archivists explain the clues the rodents hid. Tours are conducted every half hour. *Rte. 661; take U.S. 221 to Rte. 811, left on Rte. 661 to front gate; Forest 24551, tel. 804/525–1806. Admission: $7 adults, $6 senior citizens, $1 ages 2–18. Open daily 10–4, closed Dec.–Mar.*

Natural Bridge. The James River has carved 36,000 tons of limestone into a bridgelike wonder. The view is free; a nightly light show and daily cavern tours are extra. To get here, follow mansion-lined Rivermont Avenue (Rte. 501) out of Lynchburg and make a left onto Route 130. *Rte. 130, Natural Bridge, tel. 800/533–1410.*

Shenandoah Valley League

If you like the small-town, family atmosphere of minor-league baseball, you'll be taken by the endearing Shenandoah Valley League. This summer college league is even more intimate and genuine than the entry-level rookie leagues of professional baseball. Here, many of the nation's top college baseball players move in with local families, get jobs, and play baseball almost every night in June and July. The league motto is "Gateway to the Major Leagues," and there may be a major-league scout, holding a speed gun and a stat book, in the audience when you visit. The Valley League has been an officially NCAA-sanctioned league for 38 seasons.

America's community spirit is alive and well in the Valley League. The players rake, line, and water the fields before the games. Club officers walk through the crowd selling 50–50 raffle tickets (the winner splits the proceeds with the team). It's a county-fair atmosphere, complete with volunteers operating the concession stands. There aren't any big shots here. When a larger-than-expected crowd shows up on a steamy summer night and the ice cream starts to melt, the owner goes out for the ice. When a player's family and girlfriend are in town for a game, they are announced on the public address system, and the several hundred loyal fans in attendance give them a warm cheer of welcome. The players from the opposing teams still shake hands after the game, just like in Little League.

Don't come here looking for Camden Yards. In the Valley League, you will find the wonderful, scruffy little ballparks that professional baseball has tried hard to eliminate. For three bucks, you can sit right next to the baseball action. A program costs a quarter. Hot dogs are about a dollar, and the parking is free. In our trips through the minor leagues, we thought we had seen every imaginable contest until we heard of "Best Decorated Lawn Chair Night," held each year at Waynesboro's Kate Collins Field.

We enjoyed visiting all six teams in the Valley League. The league can be reached through its president, Dave Biery (tel. 540/885–8901), and its Web site: www.valleybaseball.com.

The **Front Royal Cardinals** play in Bing Crosby Stadium, named for the crooner who contributed $1,000 toward building the ballpark in 1948 when he visited as grand marshal of the Apple Blossom Festival. The cinderblock wall in center field is only 330 ft from home plate.

The **Harrisonburg Turks** play in Veterans' Memorial Stadium, an aging, ex–minor-league park. Why Turks? Harrisonburg is the self-described Turkey Capital of the World.

The home of the **New Market Rebels** is Rebel Park, a small ballpark at the old high school, with a stunning mountain view beyond the outfield fences. The crowd sings "Take Me Out to the Ball Game" a cappella in the seventh inning unless an accordion-player fan shows up. Most of the park's fences are post and rail fences.

The **Staunton Braves** play in John Moxie Stadium, adjacent to the magnificent Gypsy Hill city park. The ballpark has an unusual blue grandstand with a mansard roof. If a player hits a ball through the o in the Coke ad in center field, some lucky fan wins $3,000.

The **Waynesboro Generals** play in Kate Collins Field, at Kate Collins Elementary School, which has seats for only about 300 fans in the aluminum bleachers. Bring a lawn chair or a blanket. There's plenty of room on the hill that runs along the first-base side.

The **Winchester Royals** play in Bridgeforth Field, perhaps the best baseball facility in the league. The ballpark sits on a hill above a city park full of recreational activities.

The Shenandoah Valley is a gorgeous region of trails, rivers, and historic small towns in western Virginia, lying between the Blue Ridge Mountains to the east and the Allegheny Mountains to the west. It's a perfect place for hiking, camping, fishing, and antiquing. The 105-mi Skyline Drive runs the entire length of the Shenandoah National Park (tel. 540/999–3500). We especially like Luray Caverns (tel. 540/743–6551), Staunton's Woodrow Wilson Birthplace and Museum (tel. 540/885–0897) and Museum of American Frontier Culture (tel. 540/332–7850), and New Market's Civil War Battlefield Historical Park (tel. 540/740–3101). For travel information, contact the Shenandoah Valley Travel Association (tel. 540/740–3132).

FROM RAILS TO TRAILS
ASHEVILLE, CHATTANOOGA

Asheville, North Carolina, is home to McCormick Field—an intimate, modern stadium set into the foothills of the Blue Ridge Mountains. This resort city also has the spectacular Biltmore Estate, the largest private home in America. Its gardens, walking paths, and sumptuous architecture make it a memorable family excursion.

Southwest 150 mi lies Chattanooga; its Historic Engel Stadium was replaced in spring 2000 with a state-of-the-art park downtown, next to the impressive freshwater Tennessee Aquarium. A smoke-puffing Chattanooga Choo-Choo emerges from behind the scoreboard for home runs and game wins. The lively downtown also has train cars you can sleep in (at the renovated Beaux Arts Terminal Station) and a hundred-year-old incline railroad that speeds up Lookout Mountain.

ASHEVILLE TOURISTS

League: South Atlantic League • **Major League Affiliation:** Colorado Rockies • **Class:** A • **Stadium:** McCormick Field • **Opened:** 1924/92 • **Capacity:** 4,000 • **Dimensions:** LF: 328, CF: 406, RF: 300 • **Surface:** grass • **Season:** Apr.–Labor Day

STADIUM LOCATION: 30 Buchanan Pl., Asheville, NC 28801.

TEAM WEB SITE: www.theashevilletourists.com

GETTING THERE: From I–240, take Charlotte St. exit south. Turn left on McCormick Place just after you pass brick city government buildings on right. You'll see stadium as you turn left onto Buchanan St.

PARKING: Parking at stadium free, but lot is tiny. Additional parking up hill in front of Asheville Municipal Stadium.

TICKET INFORMATION: Box 1556, Asheville, NC 28802, tel. 828/258–0428, fax 828/258–0320.

PRICE RANGE: Box seats $7 adults, $6 children and senior citizens; general admission $5 adults, $4 children 3–12 and senior citizens.

GAME TIME: Mon.–Sat. 7 PM, Sun. 2 PM; gates open 1 hr before game.

TIPS ON SEATING: Only 835 box seats. General admission seats are aluminum benches with backs, close to action.

SEATING FOR PEOPLE WITH DISABILITIES: Behind home plate just behind box seats.

STADIUM FOOD: Two chains provide most of the food, which includes ice cream and pizza. The other offerings are ordinary: decent grilled chicken sandwiches and brats for $3 each, and burgers, fries, and chili-cheese nachos. Tropical snow cones have fruit juice instead of lurid-colored flavorings. On Tuesday, soft drinks and hot dogs are 50¢.

SMOKING POLICY: Smoking and alcohol prohibited in general admission and box-seat family sections behind home plate on third-base side.

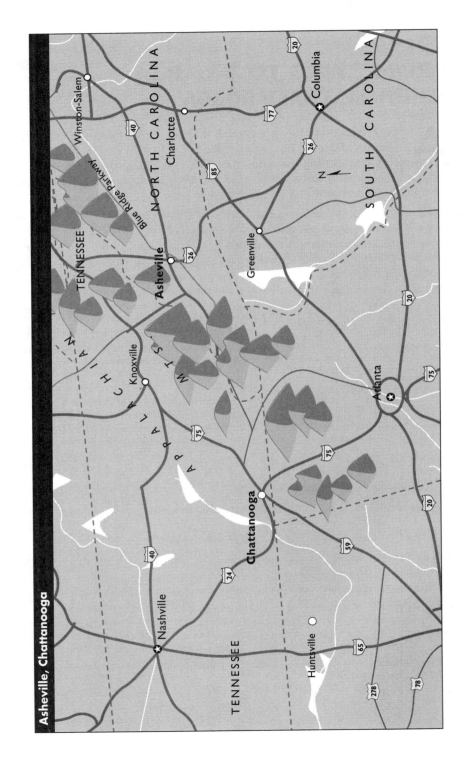

VISITING TEAM HOTEL: Days Inn (199 Tunnel Rd., Asheville, NC 28805, tel. 828/254–4311 or 800/ 325–2525).

TOURISM INFORMATION: Asheville Convention & Visitors Bureau (Box 1010, Asheville, NC 28802, tel. 828/258–6111 or 800/257–1300).

Asheville: McCormick Field

McCormick Field in Asheville, North Carolina, is one of the most beautiful little fields in all of baseball. From the grandstand, fans look out over the green outfield grass to a gorgeous stand of tall trees on the hillside beyond the outfield fence.

Built in 1924 near the city's downtown, the ballpark had no outfield fence for much of its history. A hill sloping sharply up to a city football field above served the purpose. When we visited, we heard the story of rival teams complaining that the home-team Tourists hid balls in the bushes before games. When the visitors hit a ball into the woods, the home-team outfielder would find it in short order. The visiting team outfielders never had such luck.

The Buncombe County commissioners authorized a $3 million reconstruction of the ballpark for the 1992 season, replacing the wooden grandstand with brick and steel. Local architects Bowers, Ellis, and Watson produced a baseball jewel. The new McCormick Field retains the classic feel of its historic predecessor. We fell in love with this redbrick ballpark just walking up the hill from the small parking lot below. The brick exterior is carried inside with brick behind home plate and down the base lines as in Chicago's Wrigley Field. Asheville's short right field has tempted ballplayers ever since McCormick Field's opening exhibition game in 1924. Ty Cobb hit a home run, one of six hit that day. Outfield fences were put in during the 1950s, and today the right-field fence, although only 300 ft from home, is 35 ft high. The wide concourse, with tall brick arches and a picnic and play area, fits nicely below the field level.

Babe Ruth was a big fan of McCormick Field, but his first visit to Asheville produced "the bellyache heard 'round the world!" In April of 1925, the Yankees and the Dodgers, barnstorming north from spring training, played exhibition games in Chattanooga and Knoxville. After a train ride from Knoxville, Ruth collapsed at the Asheville station. Teammates carried the unconscious Ruth to a hotel, and he missed the exhibition game against the Dodgers. The doctor reported a case of flu. Others suspected too much beer and too many hot dogs. There were even rumors that the Babe had died in Asheville. Whatever the problem, it was more than indigestion, as Ruth missed all the games in April and May. He returned to Asheville for two exhibition games in 1931 and hit a home run in each.

McCormick Field has seen more than its share of stars. In addition to Cobb and Ruth, Jackie Robinson played two exhibition games here in 1948, one year after he broke through baseball's color line. Future Hall of Famer Willie Stargel hit 22 home runs for Asheville in 1961, and Sparky Anderson managed the Tourists to first place in 1968. Future Hall of Famer Eddie Murray played here when Asheville was a Baltimore Orioles franchise in the 1970s. Cal Ripken, Sr. was the manager and Cal Ripken, Jr., baseball's iron man, was the bat boy.

In the 1988 movie *Bull Durham*, Crash Davis, the character played by Kevin Costner, needed one more home run to set the all-time minor-league record. The record-breaking home run was filmed in McCormick Stadium. Costner's signed uniform is framed and on display in the Tourists' Office at the ballpark.

McCormick Field got its name from Dr. Lewis M. McCormick, a local hero who had died two years before the ballpark opened. McCormick, a bacteriologist, arrived in town in 1904. He was horrified at the large number of houseflies in town. McCormick pushed to have the livery stables cleaned up and started a campaign in town to "Swat That Fly." His movement spread nationwide, and we've all been swatting flies ever since. Despite McCormick Field's great history, it was endangered when the region's Tri-State League folded after the 1955 season. To keep the stadium from falling down, the city leased it for weekly stock-car races for three summers. They tore out the quarter-mile asphalt track and started playing minor-league baseball in McCormick Field again in 1959, this time in the South Atlantic League.

There is a fine souvenir shop at the entrance selling all the regular baseball memorabilia plus blankets, which can come in handy. It can be cool even on an August night. Asheville's logo is a lively Ted E. Tourist bear complete with pin-striped uniform and baseball cap.

Where to Stay

Grove Park Inn Resort. This is worth seeing, even if you can't splurge to stay here. Built from local stone in 1913, it includes a massive Great Hall lobby. Rock in a wooden chair on the veranda and view the Blue Ridge Mountains. A crafts museum, mountain crafts, and an antique-car museum are next door. *290 Macon Ave., Asheville 28804, tel. 828/252–2711 or 800/438–5800, fax 828/253–7053. 510 rooms. Facilities: 4 restaurants, indoor and outdoor pools, golf, health club. AE, D, DC, MC, V. $$$*

The Log Cabin Motor Court. In this collection of rustic log cabins, some have fireplaces and living rooms and about half have kitchens. There's a two-night minimum stay. *330 Weaverville Hwy., Asheville 28804, tel. 828/645–6546. 18 cabins. Facilities: outdoor pool, coin laundry, playground. D, MC, V. $*

Where to Eat

Biltmore Dairy Bar. Famous for its ice cream (from the Biltmore herd), this sandwich-and-soup restaurant dates from 1957. Don't miss the homemade tomato soup, tipsy spiced fruit, and Dagwood sandwich. *115 Hendersonville Rd., 2 blocks from Biltmore estate, Asheville, tel. 828/274–2370. AE, MC, V. $*

Lil Pigs BBQ. Baseball and other sports memorabilia and antiques fill the walls. The delectable hickory-smoked pork is cooked for 14 hours. Half-orders are available. *1916 Hendersonville Rd., 2½ mi south of town, Asheville, tel. 828/684–0500. No credit cards. $*

Picadilly Cafeteria. This is part of a fine southern cafeteria chain. Kids can pick vegetables they like (even carrot soufflé), and there's good pink lemonade and homemade pie. *Asheville Mall, Asheville, tel. 828/298–5048. AE, D, DC, MC, V. $*

Entertainments

Old Presley Gem Mining. Travel 30 minutes from town and try your hand at finding a sapphire, a garnet, or quartz from a flume trough. Even preschoolers enjoy this. *240 Presley Mine Rd. Take I–40 west. Exit 33 to Newfound Rd., bear left on New Harmony Rd., left on Presley Mine Rd., Canton, tel. 828/648–6320. Admission: $5, plus 50¢ per bucket of ore. Open daily 9–6.*

Pack Place Education, Arts and Science Center. Take a scavenger hunt inside the body, hear a transparent woman talk, and try hands-on health and science exhibits. A Cultural Center, part of the education division, celebrates African-American life. The center also has art, gem, and mineral museums. *2 S. Pack Sq., Asheville, tel. 828/257–4500. Admission to all museums: $9.50 adults, $7.50 ages 4–15. Single passes available. Open Nov.–May, Tues.–Sat. 10–5; June–Oct., Tues.–Sat. 10–5, Sun. 1–5.*

Sights to See

Biltmore Estate. Your children will know this as the mansion in the film *Richie Rich.* You may recall Peter Sellers strolling the grounds in *Being There.* This is not a movie set but the largest private home in the United States. It's George Washington Vanderbilt's American version of a European estate. As the grandson of "Commodore" Cornelius Vanderbilt, the fabulously wealthy railroad industrialist and investor, young Vanderbilt was able to retain the finest architects and devote extraordinary resources to the task. The result is a masterpiece. In 1888, Vanderbilt commissioned Richard Morris Hunt and landscape architect Frederick Law Olmsted to design his dream estate on 125,000 acres in the Blue Ridge Mountains. An army of stonecutters and artisans labored for six years before completing the 250-room mansion. Vanderbilt himself collected much of the art, furniture, and rugs, including paintings by Auguste Renoir and John Singer Sargent. The gardens and grounds are every bit as breathtaking and meticulously kept as the main house. Look particularly at the Winter Garden, the Tapestry Gallery, and the Walled Garden. You can eat at the Stable Cafe and Deerpark restaurants. There's also a winery, with free tastings, and gift shops on the grounds. *Hwy. 25, One N. Pack Sq., just north of Exit 50 or 50B off I–40, Asheville 28801, tel. 828/255–1700 or 800/543–2961. Admission: $29.95 adults, $22.50 ages 10–15, under 10 free with paying adult. Open daily 8:30–5. Closed Christmas Day, Thanksgiving.*

Blue Ridge Parkway and Folk Art Center. The parkway entrance is 4 mi from Asheville. The center, operated by Southern Highland Handicraft Guild, has wooden toys, crafts, and demonstrations of music and dance. *Milepost 382; take I–40 to U.S. 70W, Exit 55 to parkway; follow parkway ½ mi north to Milepost 382; ½ mi north of U.S. 70; Asheville, tel. 828/298–7928. Admission: donations. Open Apr.–Dec., daily 9–6; Jan.–Mar., daily 10–5.*

Thomas Wolfe House. View the 29-room boardinghouse that the novelist's mother ran. It's "Dixieland," which Wolfe described in *Look Homeward, Angel*. Children may be amazed at how travelers lived and that, as a child, Wolfe had no room but roamed nightly to find an empty bed. *48 Spruce St., Asheville, tel. 828/253–8304. Admission: $1.50 adults, 50¢ students. Open Mon.–Sat. 9–5, Sun. 1–5.*

CHATTANOOGA LOOKOUTS

League: Southern League • **Major League Affiliation:** Cincinnati Reds • **Class:** AA • **Stadium:** BellSouth Park • **Opened:** 2000 • **Capacity:** 6,000 • **Dimensions:** LF: 325, CF: 471, RF: 318 • **Surface:** grass • **Season:** Apr.–Labor Day

STADIUM LOCATION: One Power Alley, Chattanooga, TN 37401.

TEAM WEB SITE: www.lookouts.com

GETTING THERE: The ballpark is on Hawk Hill in the heart of downtown, directly behind the Tennessee Aquarium, IMAX Theatre, and Creative Discovery Museum. From I–24, take I–27 north to exit 1C. The ballpark is immediately on your left.

PARKING: No parking at the park. The area is surrounded by surface lots and a large parking garage ($2). Free trams and shuttles to the park are available from several downtown hotels and tourist spots.

TICKET INFORMATION: Box 11002, Chattanooga, TN 37401, tel. 423/267–2208, fax 423/267–4258.

PRICE RANGE: Box seats $8; reserved seats $5; general admission $4, $2 children and senior citizens.

GAME TIME: Mon.–Sat. 7 PM, Sun. 5 PM; gates open 90 min before game.

TIPS ON SEATING: Virtually all seats are close to the action with great sight lines. The sun sets over a hill directly behind the third-base dugout and might be in the eyes of fans on the first-base side for a short time. The home-team dugout is on the first-base side.

SEATING FOR PEOPLE WITH DISABILITIES: Throughout the park at general admission prices. Valet disability parking provided at no charge.

STADIUM FOOD: Bratwursts and fries, grilled chicken sandwiches, and pizza are served, along with nachos, popcorn, slushies, and other standard ballpark fare. There's locally brewed beer. A picnic area is behind the right-field fence.

SMOKING POLICY: Smoking not allowed in the grandstand. Permitted only in designated areas.

VISITING TEAM HOTEL: Howard Johnsons Plaza (6700 Ringgold Rd., Chattanooga 37412, tel. 423/892–8100 or 800/722–2332).

TOURISM INFORMATION: Chattanooga Visitors Center (2 Broad St., Chattanooga, TN 37402, tel. 423/266–7070).

Chattanooga: BellSouth Park

We are big fans of the old parks, and no city and minor-league owners did a better job of preserving a great old ballpark, Engel Stadium. Unfortunately, the park's ongoing maintenance was causing the owners of the Chattanooga Lookouts to lose too much money. When city businesses and residents bought 1,800 season tickets, owner Frank Burke and his associates bit the financial bullet and privately financed a new $10 million ballpark right in the center of the downtown. BellSouth Park will never match Engel Stadium's charm and history. But the convenient, intimate stadium will be a lasting resource in the redevelopment of this great city.

The Chattanooga Urban Design Center worked to make the ballpark fit in with the architecture of its downtown neighbors. The 6,000-seat ballpark sits on Hawk Hill, overlooking the Tennessee Aquarium. It was built on land provided at no charge by a public-private downtown development agency, and was designed by the DLR Group of Florida, the designers of Legends Field in Tampa. The ballpark is built of concrete, brick, and exposed, galvanized steel. You can look out over the Tennessee River in straight-away centerfield. I–27 is down the left-field line with the Aquarium and the IMAX Theatre down the right-field line. Exiting the ballpark, you look out over downtown Chattanooga.

Many stadiums even at the minor-league level now set off fireworks when the home team hits a home run or wins the game. Nothing compares with Frank Burke's creation in Chattanooga. When he first bought the Lookouts in 1995, Burke installed a huge, colorful Chattanooga Choo-Choo engine behind the scoreboard. When a big moment occurred, the Choo-Choo emerged from behind the scoreboard puffing smoke and blaring its horn. Burke got the idea from his father, Daniel Burke, whose Portland Sea Dogs have an exploding lighthouse. Happily, the Choo-Choo made its move from Engel to BellSouth. So did Looie the Lookout, a red creature resembling a tomato, who has become a very popular mascot.

More Chattanooga Baseball

Joe Engel Stadium. We can't figure out why the sign out front calls this HISTORIC ENGEL STADIUM. No one doubts that this is the real thing. With $2 million of city and county money and the leadership of former owner Richard Holtzman, this fabulous stadium was restored to its 1930 look for the 1990 season. The historic brick walls remain, along with the green awnings. The wide concourse under the grandstand is beautifully restored with antique street lights and black wrought-iron frame design.

The grandstand roof goes out as far as first and third bases. The mechanical fans hanging from the grandstand roof evoke the 1930s more than they cool off those in attendance. Under the roof are wonderful old brownish-red straight-back wooden chairs that make a fearsome noise when a crowd bangs them.

The outfield is particularly interesting. Older stadiums had high concrete walls far from home plate. When the home run became popular, wooden fences were built within the concrete walls. Center field in the original Engel Stadium was 471 ft from home plate. Only future Hall of Famer Harmon Killebrew cleared the wall at the 471-ft mark. The cinderblock wall still stands, now painted with ads on a tan background.

Joe Engel's genius is celebrated in plaques at the stadium entrance. In 1929, Clark Griffith, future Hall of Fame owner of the Washington Senators, sent his top baseball scout, Engel, to take over the Chattanooga franchise he had recently acquired. Engel's first job was to oversee the construction of a new ballpark.

A sample of Joe Engel stories: On May 1, 1936, Engel drew more than 24,000 fans by raffling off a $10,000 house. It was standing room only in the outfield. Engel had another stunt—freezing baseballs before the game, which cut down their loft. This was not to protect the fans but to make sure he didn't lose too many balls. On opening day 1938, the former vaudevillian Engel staged a wild-elephant hunt. Only after the shots were fired did the fans realize that each of the falling elephants was two men inside an animal suit. He once traded shortstop Johnny Jones for a 25-pound turkey. He also fed thousands of people free meals at Engel Stadium during the Depression.

The city and county jointly own Engel Stadium and have pledged to maintain it for amateur baseball. *1130 3rd St., 4th St. exit from I–27 or I–24, Chattanooga, tel. 423/697–1300.*

Where to Stay

Visiting Team Hotel: Howard Johnsons Plaza. This three-story budget hotel offers guests a Continental breakfast and free transportation to the airport. Lookout packages also are available. It is 15 minutes southwest of the ballpark, at the I–75 and I–24 interchange, in the middle of many fast-food and sit-down restaurants. *6700 Ringgold Rd., Chattanooga, TN 37412, tel. 423/892–8100 or 800/722–2332, fax 423/499–5555. 230 rooms. Facilities: restaurant, outdoor pool, game room, exercise room. AE, D, DC, MC, V. $*

Chattanooga Choo-Choo Holiday Inn. Created in Chattanooga's Beaux Arts Terminal Station, the inn lets you sleep in a sleeping-parlor car or in a regular room. A model-train museum is part of the reuse of this 1909 train station. The hotel offers discount tickets to area attractions and a free downtown shuttle to the aquarium. *1400 Market St., Chattanooga 37402, tel. 423/266–5000 or 800/465–4329, fax 423/265–4635. 315 rooms, 48 parlor-car rooms. Facilities: 3 restaurants, indoor and outdoor pools, water slide, hot tubs, tennis courts. AE, D, DC, MC, V. $$*

Radisson Read House Hotel and Suites. This 10-floor, downtown hotel is on the National Register of Historic Places. Most of the rooms are suites with dining alcoves and sitting rooms. Parking is $6 per day. The "AAA Family Adventure" rate includes two tickets to the Tennessee Aquarium. *827 Broad St., Chattanooga 37402, tel. 423/266–4121 or 800/333–3333, fax 423/267–6447. 238 rooms. Facilities: restaurant, outdoor pool, wading pool. AE, D, DC, MC, V. $$*

Where to Eat

Big River Grille & Brewing Works. At this boisterous microbrewery you can eat family meals of shepherd's pie, salads, soups, and fish. Vegetables are good. It serves homemade root beer, ginger ale, and cream soda, as well as alcoholic brews. *222 Broad St., Chattanooga, tel. 423/267–2739. AE, D, DC, MC, V. $$*

Mt. Vernon Restaurant. At this old-fashioned family restaurant, in business for 40 years, you'll find Southern cooking with homemade pies. A children's menu is available. *3509 S. Broad St., Chattanooga, tel. 423/266–6591. MC, V. $*

Silver Diner. In a real dining car parked in the former train station, you can order pizza, baked potatoes, and nachos. The adjacent **Dinner in the Diner** is for more formal meals, dinner only. *Chattanooga Choo-Choo Holiday Inn, 1400 Market St., Chattanooga, tel. 423/266–5000. AE, MC, V. $$*

Entertainments

Creative Discovery Children's Museum. Here you'll find colorful, inviting exhibits, including an inventor's workshop, an artist's studio, and a musician's workshop. Kids can experiment with water, color, light, and motion. There's a preschoolers' section and an optics tower. *321 Chestnut St., Chattanooga, tel. 423/756–2738. Admission: $7.75 adults, $4.75 ages 2–12. Open daily 10–6.*

Lookout Mountain Incline Railway No. 2. On November 24, 1863, Union troops led by General U. S. Grant crossed Lookout Creek and began an advance up the steep slope of Lookout Mountain. Amazingly—with the help of midday clouds that covered the summit and confused the Confederates—Grant took the mountain in what has come to be called the Battle Above the Clouds. Today, we can gain this extraordinary view of the Tennessee River valley a lot easier than Grant and his men. Incline No. 2 takes you a mile up Lookout Mountain, 2,200 ft above the valley, in about 10 minutes. Chattanooga became a major trading center in 1850, when the first railroad opened from Atlanta to Chattanooga. As other rail lines opened, the Lookout Mountain area became popular with Southerners wanting to escape the hot summer. In the 1880s, an incline and a broad-gauge railroad were constructed. The present Incline No. 2 opened for business in 1895 and has a perfect safety record. It is the steepest passenger incline in the world. *St. Elmo Ave., Chattanooga, tel. 423/821–4224. Admission: $7 adults, $4 ages 3–12. Open Memorial*

Day–Labor Day, daily 8:30 AM–9 PM; Labor Day–Memorial Day, daily 9–6.

Tennessee Aquarium. An imaginative, downtown freshwater aquarium, it has child-height tanks for close encounters with gigantic catfish, piranhas, alligators, sharks, and stingrays. It's arranged by ecosystem, with two forests, a 60-ft canyon, and more than 7,000 animals. *1 Broad St., Chattanooga, tel. 800/262–0695. Admission: $11 adults, $6 ages 3–12. Open 10–6.*

Sights to See

Chattanooga Regional History Museum. A woman striking out Babe Ruth? No way, you say—you won't believe it unless you see it. The ever-enterprising Joe Engel signed 17-year-old Jackie Mitchell to a contract for the Southern Association's 1931 season. When the Yankees came through Chattanooga for an exhibition game, the left-handed Mitchell came in to the game in relief and struck out Ruth and Lou Gehrig. When Judge "Kenesaw Mountain" Landis, the commissioner of baseball, learned what Engel had done, he voided Mitchell's contract, blocking women from professional baseball. The wonderful Jackie Mitchell video is one of several in the museum's permanent collection, accessible at the touch of the screen. It lasts only about two minutes, and it's worth watching several times. The video shows all three of Ruth's strikes, with Ruth throwing the bat down in disgust after the third strike. Our eight-year-old left-handed daughter, Emily, cheered every pitch. The Chattanooga Regional History Museum displays a replica locker full of baseball memorabilia going back to 1895 in its permanent collection. The museum also contains a Chattanooga Sports Hall of Fame. *400 Chestnut St., 1½ mi from Historic Engel Stadium, just off I–27, Chattanooga 37402, tel. 423/265–3247. Admission: $4 adults, $3.50 senior citizens, $3 ages 5 and up. Open weekdays 10–4:30, weekends 11–4:30.*

Chattanooga Visitors Center. Start your day at this friendly one-stop shop with the information you need to plan your visit. The visitor center is next to the Tennessee Aquarium. A 22-minute slide presentation provides basic perspective on Chattanooga for a small fee. *2 Broad St., Chattanooga 37402, tel. 423/266–7070. Open daily 8:30–5:30.*

ANTEBELLUM BASEBALL
ATLANTA, COLUMBUS, MACON

Georgia baseball gives you diversity in a relatively compact geography. A weekend triangle trip of Georgia baseball could encompass the sold-out excitement of major-league ball in Atlanta, plus a visit to the handsomely renovated riverfront stadium in Columbus and the vintage 1929 park in the middle of Macon's fairgrounds.

Atlanta, with its historic neighborhoods and flashy new attractions, is a logical starting point. You'll want to buy tickets ahead of time for the Braves, whose wild popularity stems from their consistent success on the field and the reach of the Turner superstation.

Two hours south on I–85 and you're in Columbus, seeing a good stadium made great by renovations for the Olympics. The Olympic games for women's fast-pitch softball were held here in 1996. The Columbus Redstixx, a Class A affiliate of the Cleveland Indians, play in the pine-tree-buffered stadium.

Driving east on Rt. 80 for 100 mi puts you in Macon, where one of the nation's oldest minor-league parks is still in use. The grandstand at Luther Williams Field is completely covered and so picturesque that Hollywood used it as the backdrop for a movie. Just like the old days, you enter the park under a brick ticket-booth arch.

ATLANTA BRAVES

League: National League • **Class:** Major League • **Stadium:** Turner Field • **Opened:** 1977 • **Capacity:** 49,714 • **Dimensions**: LF: 335 CF: 401 RF: 330 • **Surface:** grass • **Season:** Apr.–early Oct.

STADIUM LOCATION: 755 Hank Aaron Dr., Atlanta, GA 30315.

TEAM WEB SITE: www.atlantabraves.com

GETTING THERE: From I-77/85 north or south, take the Fulton St. exit (No. 91). From I–20 West, take Exit 24 (Capitol Ave.). From I–20 East, take Exit 22, turn right on Windsor St. and left on Fulton St. By transit, take a MARTA train to Five Points Station, exit on the Forsyth St. side, and ride a Braves Shuttle to the ballpark. Or take a MARTA train to Georgia State Station and walk south on Capitol Ave. to the ballpark. MARTA information: tel. 409/848–4711.

PARKING: Parking is available for $8 at the stadium and nearby, where Atlanta–Fulton County Stadium once stood. Extra parking is west of I–75/85 and at the corner of Aaron Dr. and Fulton St.

TICKET INFORMATION: Box 4064, Atlanta, GA 30302, tel. 404/522–7630, fax 404/614–1391.

PRICE RANGE: Dugout $33; club $27; field and terrace $22; field and terrace pavilion $16; upper level $11; upper pavilion $5; children 2 and under, free.

GAME TIME: Weekdays 7:40 PM, Sat. 7:10 PM, Sun. 1:10 PM. The plaza at North Gate and outfield seating are open 3 hrs prior to games; rest of seating 2 hrs before game.

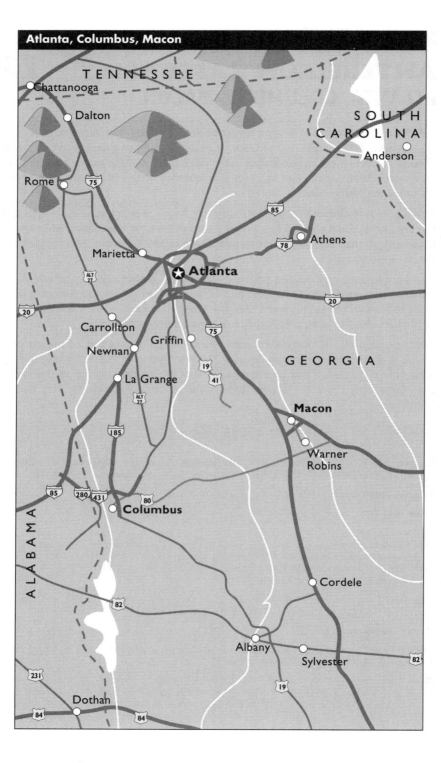

TIPS ON SEATING: Just be happy to get a seat here. The lower level seats 27,633, including 3,500 outfield bleacher seats. The upper level seats number 15,608. Skyline seats are sold for $1, three hours before game time. For sold-out games, standing-room spots are sold for $5 one hour before the first pitch. The setting sun is in your eyes down the first-base line.

SEATING FOR PEOPLE WITH DISABILITIES: Seats are throughout the stadium (tel. 404/614–1326). Disability parking is available in the south green lots east of I–75/85 on a first-come, first-served basis.

STADIUM FOOD: It's mostly routine but expensive ballpark fare here. The Braves graciously serve a food item or two that's native to the team they're playing that day—brats for the Brewers, cheesesteaks for the Phillies—and they're generally worth it. You'll find them in the lower concourse. You can't miss the Coca-Cola throughout the park. It goes well with the caramelized pecans and almonds roasting on the lower concourse. Food lines are long—try to wait until the 3rd inning or later. You may bring in food and drinks in containers that fit under seats. No bottles or cans allowed.

SMOKING POLICY: Smoking is prohibited except in designated smoking areas.

TOURISM INFORMATION: Atlanta Convention and Visitors Bureau (233 Peachtree St. NE, Atlanta, GA 30303, tel. 404/521–6600).

Atlanta: Turner Field

Atlanta–Fulton County Stadium was one of those horrid 1960s multisport stadiums built for football and baseball. Turner Field is better—much better. True, it lacks the classic architecture and the view of downtown you find in a Camden Yards. What makes Turner Field special lies outside the seating bowl and playing field. Go early and spend your time and money at the entrance plaza.

Strangely enough, this baseball-only ballpark wouldn't exist today if Atlanta hadn't needed a grand track and field stadium for the 1996 Olympic games. What does a city do with an 85,000-seat track and field stadium? Atlanta's answer was brilliant: avoid having a huge white elephant at the doorstep of downtown by removing 35,000 seats and giving the building a second life. As an added benefit, let the Olympic television money fund the construction of the $242.5 million ballpark. The $35.5 million retrofit by architectural firm Ellerbe Becket—including the elimination of the Olympic track and field equipment and the reconfiguration of the parking lot—was completed in seven months, in time for the start of the 1997 baseball season.

Don't rush in at game time and head for your seats. Take your time in entering the ballpark. Start from the parking lot to its north, the former

site of the utterly forgettable Atlanta-Fulton Stadium; Hank Aaron's 715th home run on April 8, 1974, made it famous. Aaron's awesome career is noted throughout the new baseball complex. The old stadium's playing field is outlined on the parking lot, with memorial plaques noting the location of the bases and Aaron's famous blast. Walk toward the ballpark and be greeted by statues of Hall of Famers Aaron, Phil Niekro, and Ty Cobb in Monument Grove. And there he is again as #44 in the Braves retired numbers monument along with #41 Eddie Mathews, #35 Niekro, #21 Warren Spahn, and #3 Dale Murphy.

The entrance plaza, built where the 35,000 seats once were, is the most distinctive and most entertaining part of the new stadium. There is a huge souvenir shop, as well as a museum and hall of fame. Walk along the Midway Concourse and soak up the baseball insights in Scout's Alley. Test your arm with a radar gun. And then enter the Ivan Allen, Jr. Braves Museum and Hall of Fame (at aisle 134 on the northwest side of the plaza), which showcases the team's memorabilia from its roots in Boston and Milwaukee. The museum has a 1940s sleeper railroad car, the 1995 World Series trophy, Aaron's #715 home run bat and ball, as well as an Atlanta Black Crackers jersey. There are batting cages and there's even a Tooner Field area, designed by the Cartoon Network folks, where kids can climb and play with cartoon figures.

The most memorable feature of the entrance plaza is an image, 100 ft in diameter, of the baseball Aaron hit that April night in '74. Aisle seats throughout the ballpark have an image of Aaron hitting a home run. In fact, they did everything here to honor Aaron except name the stadium after him. That honor fell to Braves owner Ted Turner.

You might get the idea that the baseball game is secondary here, but the seating at Turner Field is a vast improvement over that at the old stadium. The baseball-only design greatly reduces the amount of foul territory and allows the seats to be much closer than in the football-baseball setup. Plus, Atlanta has created a crucial fan-friendly design missing at Camden Yards: a playing field that sits below street level, making it possible for fans to watch the game while getting food and drink or walking along the wide concourse.

Tours leave from the Braves Museum every half-hour during the season and every hour during the off-season. Tours are limited to Monday through Saturday mornings on days when the Braves play at night. Admission: $7 adults, $4 ages 12 and under.

Where to Stay

Radisson Hotel Atlanta. This large, 12-story hotel has spacious rooms. There's a casual deli and a sports bar in the lobby. It's two mi north of the ballpark. *165 Courtland St., at International Blvd., Atlanta 30303, tel. 404/659–6500 or 800/333–3333, fax 404/681–5306. 747 rooms. Facilities: 3 restaurants, indoor and outdoor pool, sauna, hot tub, parking (fee). AE, D, DC, MC, V. $$*

Travelodge Downtown. Next to more expensive downtown hotels, this recently renovated three-story property has small contemporary rooms. It is two mi north of the ballpark. *311 Courtland St., Atlanta 30303, tel. 404/659–4545 or 800/578–7878, fax 404/659–5934. 71 rooms. Facilities: outdoor pool, free parking. AE, D, DC, MC, V. $$*

Where to Eat

Mary Mac's Tea Room. Four storefronts have been joined to create a 350-seat operation of efficiency and gentility, just north of the center city. This city treasure is famous for its moist fried chicken and large array of Southern side dishes. We're partial to the sweet potato soufflé, squash soufflé, shrimp Creole on rice, and the boiled custard. The cobblers and pies are delectable. There are junior plates for $4 and a bargain kid's meal for $2.50 at lunch. *224 Ponce de Leon Ave. NE, Atlanta, tel. 404/876–1800. MC, V. $*

The Varsity. The joke at this immense drive-in restaurant by Georgia Tech is that everything is fried but the Cokes. Try curb service or line up inside for sandwiches, hotdogs, and more. Busy countermen have their own lingo: a yellow streak (burger with mustard), bag of rags (potato chips). Don't miss the frosted orange drink. You can get onion rings and fried pies when it opens at 7 AM. There's a large dining room. *I–75 at North Ave., Atlanta, tel. 404/881–1706. No credit cards. $*

The Waffle House. The original restaurant is here, 15 minutes south of the city, in Avondale, looking much as it did in 1955. This yellow and brown hut turns out one of the fastest and cheapest family breakfasts in America. Have a pecan waffle for old times' sake. *2850 E. College, Avondale, tel. 404/294–8758. No credit cards. $*

Entertainments

Atlanta History Center. This 33-acre complex has a working plantation circa 1845, walking trails through lovely gardens, and a comprehensive museum containing information on author Margaret Mitchell, civil rights history, and early Atlanta manufacturing, among other things; children will enjoy the farm animals and soda fountain in the basement. The center can be found among the mansions of Buckhead, 6 mi north of downtown. *130 W. Paces Ferry Rd. NW, Atlanta, tel. 404/814–4000. Admission: $7 adults, $5 senior citizens, $4 ages 6–17. Open Mon.–Sat. 10–5:30.*

World of Coca-Cola. You are bombarded with flashing lights, billboards, radio ads, and more red and white memorabilia than seems possible. This multilevel museum opened downtown in

1990 at a cost of $15 million. (It's next to Underground Atlanta, where you'll find AtlanTIX, a half-price ticket booth for day-of-show performances.) The highlight is the tasting room, where you can try 38 flavors of soft drinks from around the world. Several are truly awful, so watch for the wise guys directing you to certain spigots. You'll look in vain for an exhibit on the New Coke fiasco. *55 Martin Luther King, Jr. Dr., Atlanta, tel. 404/676–5151. Admission: $6 adults, $4 senior citizens, $3 ages 6–12. Open Mon.–Sat. 10–9:30 PM.*

Sights to See

Martin Luther King, Jr., National Historic Site and Preservation District. Reverend King's home and Ebenezer Baptist Church are in this 12-block area known as Sweet Auburn. Visit the King Center for good visual displays of lesser-known aspects of the civil rights struggle. King's white marble tomb, with an eternal flame, is in the middle of a meditation pool. *King Center, 449 Auburn Ave., Atlanta, tel. 303/524–1956. Free. Open daily 8:30–5:30.*

COLUMBUS REDSTIXX

League: South Atlantic League • **Major League Affiliation:** Cleveland Indians • **Class:** A • **Stadium:** Golden Park • **Opened:** 1951 • **Capacity:** 5,000 • **Dimensions:** LF: 330, CF: 415, RF: 330 • **Surface:** grass • **Season:** Apr.–Labor Day.

STADIUM LOCATION: 100 Fourth St., Columbus, GA 31901.

TEAM WEB SITE: www.redstixx.com

GETTING THERE: The stadium is in the South Commons Complex just south of the city's downtown historic district. From downtown, go south on 4th Ave. (also known as Veterans Pkwy.) into the South Commons parking lot. The ballpark is on the right. From I-185, take Victory Dr. (Exit 1) west for 7 mi to Veterans Pkwy. Stadium is on left.

PARKING: Ample free parking.

TICKET INFORMATION: Box 1886, Columbus, GA 31309, tel. 706/571–8866, fax 706/571–9107.

PRICE RANGE: Box seats $7; grandstand $5, $4 children, senior citizens, and military personnel.

GAME TIME: Mon.–Sat. 7:15 PM, Sun. 2:15 PM; gates open 1 hr before game.

TIPS ON SEATING: The grandstand seats are directly behind just six rows of box seats. Get there early and get a seat with a back and arms in the front rows of grandstand seating. The original grandstand behind home plate is covered and netting protects fans from foul balls. The best view is from the third-base side, looking across the field to the handsome new clubhouse and offices. The view from the first-base side behind the home team dugout is of a three-story wall of ads, along with traffic from Veterans Parkway. The setting sun during night games is not a problem on either side.

SEATING FOR PEOPLE WITH DISABILITIES: Seats are available on the concourse behind the box seats. There are ramps on both the first- and third-base sides of the grandstand.

STADIUM FOOD: Head for a $3 barbecue sandwich, $4 chicken quesadilla, or $3.50 brat. There are decent foot-long hot dogs, with cheese and sauerkraut, for $3. A standout is the $3 funnel cake. Dill pickles are sold for $1, and burgers, pizza, and fries are on the menu. The chicken sandwiches are from Chick-Fil-A. A **Kid's Corner** stand sells slush puppies, hot dogs, pretzels, pizza, and ice cream—all for $1 to kids.

SMOKING POLICY: Smoking is allowed only in the last section of the grandstand on the third-base side (box section N and grandstand section MM) and in the two upper rows of the grandstand. Section HH is family-friendly, with no smoking or alcohol.

VISITING TEAM HOTEL: Holiday Inn Airport North (2800 Manchester Expy., Columbus, GA 31904, tel. 706/324–0231 or 800/605–8266).

TOURISM INFORMATION: Columbus Convention & Visitors Bureau (100 Bay Ave., Columbus, GA 31901, tel. 705/322–1613 or 800/999–1613).

Columbus, Georgia: Golden Park

There is a lot of baseball history along the Chattahoochee River, just south of Columbus's historic downtown. The city was a spring training site for major-league clubs from 1899 to 1920. The original Golden Park ballpark was built on this site in 1926. There is a list of the baseball greats who played here—from Shoeless Joe Jackson to Stan Musial to Cal Ripken, Jr.—on the back of the grandstand. In the 1960s, when a New York Yankees farm club played at the park, the Golden Park grandstand had a Yankees insignia and Confederate flag side-by-side. A major renovation for the 1996 Olympics dramatically changed the look of the 1926 ballpark. Golden Park played host to women's fast-pitch softball during the '96 games, and the minor-league RedStixx had to play the '96 season at a local university.

The concrete grandstand and roof are remnants of the old stadium; the 1996 renovation changed almost everything else. Fans now enter the ballpark through a handsome, well-landscaped redbrick and green-gated entryway along the river near right field. (We particularly enjoyed the sculptures of kids playing softball near the entrance.) A new redbrick clubhouse and office complex is beyond the right-field fence; the original brick outfield wall was replaced; there are flags and tall Georgia pine trees beyond right center field; and a new scoreboard sits high above a wall of ads in left center field. Walk to the top of the first-base grandstand for a good view of the river. Look for two Columbus icons—Fred Stixx, the team's friendly fox mascot, and Willie Bowman, the peanut man, who has been a Golden Park fixture for more than 50 years.

In addition to Golden Park, the South Commons Complex includes a football stadium, basketball and hockey arena, and gorgeous eight-field soft-ball complex, the legacy of the '96 Olympics. The main softball stadium, surrounded by manicured fields, was built after the Olympics, when Golden Park was restored to its hardball tradition.

Where to Stay

Visiting Team Motel: Holiday Inn Airport North. This spacious two-story motel is 33 years old, but has been updated with a new restaurant and outdoor pool. It's four mi from the ballpark and close to Peachtree Mall. *2800 Manchester Expy., Columbus 31904, tel. 706/ 324–0231 or 800/605–8266, fax 706/596– 0248. 223 rooms. Facilities: restaurant, outdoor pool, exercise room. AE, D, DC, MC, V. $$*

Columbus Hilton. This nine-story downtown hotel is built around a century-old gristmill in the Historic District. It has large rooms decorated in reproduction Federal style. *800 Front Ave., Columbus 31901, tel. 706/324–1800 or 800/445– 8667, fax 706/327–8042. 177 rooms. Facilities: 2 restaurants, outdoor pool. AE, D, DC, MC, V. $$*

Where to Eat

Country's Barbecue. The former Greyhound bus station has been retrofitted to resemble a '50s diner, with Naugahyde booths, Coke-can red tubular steel chairs, Formica counters, vintage photos, and letter jackets on the wall. There's a jukebox and a neon clock that reads "Welcome Travelers." The very good barbecue (pork, beef, ham, ribs) comes in many combos, along with smoked turkey, buttermilk-fried chicken, Brunswick stew, skillet apples, and chocolate chess pie. RC Cola is flavored with cherry or vanilla and served by the pint. *1329 Broadway, Columbus, tel. 706/596–8910. MC, V. $*

Entertainments

Heritage Corner. A sampling of Georgia's heritage is collected at the corner of Broadway and Seventh Street. A log cabin, slave quarters, and the home of Dr. John Stith Pemberton—the

Columbus druggist who originated the formula for Coca-Cola—have been relocated here. They complement Columbus's oldest house, an 1828 Federal-style cottage, and the elegant two-story, brick, 1870 Italianate town house where a one-hour Heritage Corner tour begins. The walking tour may not appeal to young children. *Historic Columbus Foundation, 700 Broadway, Columbus, tel. 706/323–7979. Tour admission: $3. Tour weekdays 11 and 3, weekends 2.*

Riverwalk and Walking Tours. A 12-mi stretch along the Chattahoochee River was designated a Riverwalk in 1992. The landscaping here is lovely and much of the walk is in the National Register Historic District. The Columbus Convention & Visitors Bureau has produced an excellent map of walking tours of the city. The only known double octagon house is included, along with the home of the "Mother of the Blues," Columbus native Gertrude Pridget "Ma" Rainey. The restored Liberty Theatre, built in 1925, featured Ma Rainey, Duke Ellington, Cab Calloway, Ella Fitzgerald, and Lena Horne. More notables, including John Philip Sousa, Will Rogers, and Franklin D. Roosevelt, appeared at the 1871 Springer Opera House, restored in 1965. *1000 Bay Ave., Columbus, tel. 706/322–1613.*

Sights to See

Callaway Gardens. Thirty minutes north of Columbus, in Pine Mountain, is a 14,000-acre nature preserve with a 45-acre butterfly center, an 800-room inn, 3 golf courses, extensive greenhouses and azalea gardens, and a man-made beach. The lake has fishing, sailing, riverboat rides and waterfront shows by Florida State's Flying High Circus. The preserve is operated by the Ida Cason Callaway Foundation, named after the mother of Cason Callaway, a farmer and industrialist who prospered by developing the muscadine grape. *Hwy. 27, Pine Mountain, tel. 404/663–2281 or 800/225–5292. Admission: $10 adults, $5 ages 6–12. Open daily 8–8.*

Jimmy Carter National Historic Site. Thirty miles southeast of Columbus is Plains, Georgia, the original and current home of former President Carter. You may take a free driving tour of Carter-related town sites. Tour booklets and rental cassettes are $1 each. *300 N. Broad St., Plains, tel. 912/824–3413. Open daily 9–5.*

The Little White House State Historic Site. Twenty miles east of Callaway Gardens is the rustic home Franklin Delano Roosevelt built in 1932, so he could bathe in nearby Warm Springs. It is now a memorial to the late President, who died here April 12, 1945. A film, museum, and memorial stone garden are available for viewing. *SR 85W, Warm Springs, tel. 706/655–5870. Admission: $4 adults, $2 ages 6–18. Open daily 9–5.*

MACON BRAVES

League: South Atlantic League • **Major League Affiliation:** Atlanta Braves • **Class:** A • **Stadium:** Luther Williams Field • **Opened:** 1926 • **Capacity:** 4,000 • **Dimensions:** LF: 338, CF: 402, RF: 338 • **Surface:** grass • **Season:** Apr.–Labor Day

STADIUM LOCATION: Central City Park, Seventh St., Macon, GA 31201.

TEAM WEB SITE: www.mbraves.com

GETTING THERE: The field is 1 mi south of the I–75 and I–16 junction. Take the Coliseum Exit (No. 4) off I–16. Cross Otis Redding Memorial Bridge and immediately turn left into Central City Park. From downtown, take Riverside Dr. to Central City Park.

PARKING: Ample free parking in front of the ballpark and beyond left field.

TICKET INFORMATION: Box 4525, Macon, GA 31308, tel. 912/745–8943, fax 912/743–5559.

PRICE RANGE: Box seats $6.50; general admission $5.50 adults, $4.50 senior citizens and military personnel, $3.50 ages 5–12.

GAME TIME: Mon.–Sat. 7 PM, Sun. 2 PM; gates open 1 hr before game.

TIPS ON SEATING: The grandstand seats are close to the action, as there are only four rows of box seats. The discount prices for children and senior citizens only apply in the grandstand. If you end up near a smoker, you can move.

SEATING FOR PEOPLE WITH DISABILITIES: There are seats on the concourse immediately behind the box seats. The ramp to the grandstand is on the first-base end.

STADIUM FOOD: You can buy peanuts roasted or boiled, along with popcorn chicken, brats, and $5 Domino's pizza. Kids get a break with $1.25 hot dogs. Adults can get a hot dog/corn dog combo for $3. There are good, bumpy french fries for $2. If you sit in box seats, waitresses will bring you a pitcher (you keep it) of french fries for $4. There's a picnic area on the third-base side, with grilled sandwiches and sausages from **Slider's Grill.** On Thirsty Thursdays, all drinks are two-for-one.

SMOKING POLICY: Watch out, you're in the Old South. There's only one smoke-free area in the entire grandstand, behind sections C and H.

VISITING TEAM HOTEL: Comfort Inn North (2690 Riverside Dr., Macon, GA 31208, tel. 912/746–8855 or 800/221–2222).

TOURISM INFORMATION: Macon–Bibb County Convention & Visitors Bureau (Terminal Station, 200 Cherry St., Macon, GA 31208, tel. 912/743–3401 or 800/768–3401).

Macon: Luther Williams Field

Luther Williams Field is a fine old ballpark set in the city park that houses the Georgia State Fair. When Universal filmed *Bingo Long and the Traveling All-Stars and Motor Kings* (1976), a film about a barnstorming group of black all-stars in the '40s, it didn't take much to re-create the period atmosphere. About all they had to do was cover the ads that lined the outfield walls.

The ballpark, one of the oldest still in use in professional baseball, was built in 1929 and named after a Macon mayor. Because of the 1991 renovation and periodic improvements since, you get the feel of an old park with sufficient modern comforts. You enter the ballpark through an arch in a small redbrick ticket booth, above which the elegant, wrought-iron letters of the stadium name appear. A large white sign hangs over the three arches in the main entrance to the redbrick grandstand. The legend, MACON BASE BALL PARK, is a throwback to the nineteenth-century style of spelling baseball as two words; it is stylishly set off with black diamonds.

The handsome, covered grandstand is shaped like a boomerang that doesn't quite reach first and third bases. Netting protects the fans in all but the end sections behind the dugouts. There is a modest aluminum bleacher on the first-base side and a small one near the picnic area on the third-base side.

For kids interested in snagging a foul ball, this is a perfect park. Balls fly over the top and beyond the ends of the small grandstand. The best place to be is on the first-base side, where there is room for a game of catch while you wait. Railroad cars travel just beyond the right-field fence throughout the game. There is a huge racetrack beyond the first-base side, big enough to house an entire complex of little league fields inside the track.

A plaque near the concession stands notes that Georgia Tech played its very first football game nearby in Central City Park, losing 12-6 to Mercer University in 1892. Macon was a founding member of the South Atlantic League in 1904, and has been in and out of the league several times over the last century. A young Pete Rose got six hits here one night in 1962 as the Macon Peaches rolled over the Greenville Dodgers, 32–5. Atlanta Braves fans can travel just 84 mi southeast from Turner Field to see their future stars perform. Chipper Jones was the first Macon Brave to make the transition to the big leagues in Atlanta.

There isn't a mascot here. As staff explained, "It's pretty hard to have a politically correct mascot when your team is named the Braves."

Where to Stay

Visiting Team Motel: Comfort Inn North. This three-story motel along a busy commercial strip is nicely landscaped and built around an attractive pool. The contemporary rooms are ordinary, however, and there's no elevator. *2690 Riverside Dr., Macon 31204, tel. 912/746–8855 or 800/ 221–2222, fax 912/746–8881. 120 rooms. Facilities: outdoor pool, coin laundry. AE, D, DC, MC, V. $$*

Super 8 Motel. The standard-size rooms are clean and nicely furnished. It's near the Macon Mall. *6007 Harrison Rd., Macon 31206, tel. 912/ 788–8800 or 800/800–8000, fax 912/788– 2327. 60 rooms. Facilities: outdoor pool, coin laundry. AE, D, DC, MC, V. $*

Where to Eat

Len Berg's. Fried oysters, homemade peach ice cream, and macaroon pie are just some of the attractions at this utilitarian downtown favorite, located in an alley behind the federal courthouse. The setting is forgettable, but the choice of fresh vegetables and meats is noteworthy. *Post Office Alley, between Broadway and Third, Macon, tel. 912/742–9255. No credit cards. Closed Sun. No dinner. $*

Fresh Air Barbeque. Don't let its location, at one end of a strip mall, fool you. This is one of the oldest barbecue restaurants in Georgia. The ribs and pulled barbecue pork are terrific. You place your order and eat at Formica tables. The side dishes aren't special, but you're too happy with the ribs to notice. *3076 Riverside Dr., Macon, tel. 912/477–7229. AE, MC, V. $*

Jeneane's Cafe. This is a weekday-only breakfast and lunch hangout for the courthouse crowd. Housed in a 19th-century downtown storefront, it's as close to a home-cooked Southern meal as you can get. The grits, oatmeal, vegetables, and homemade pies are all excellent and you'll be served huge "meat and three" portions for lunch. The decor is country clutter. *524 Mulberry St., Macon, tel. 912/743–5267. No credit cards. Closed weekends. No dinner. $*

Entertainments

Georgia Sports Hall of Fame. The brick columns of this two-level hall emulate Luther Williams Field. Opened in 1999, it honors Georgia sports heroes from golf's immortal Bobby Jones to baseball's home-run king Hank Aaron. A 15-minute film includes Ty Cobb and the Falcons winning the Superbowl. You can kick field goals and throw football passes through tires and try dunking at various basketball goals. *301 Cherry St., Macon, tel. 912/752–1585. Admission: $6 adults, $5 senior citizens, students, and military personnel, $3.50 ages 6–16, under 5 free. Open Mon.–Sat. 9–5, Sun. 1–5.*

Sights to See

Sherman didn't burn Macon, but the economic boom that so transformed Atlanta mostly missed it. Although it's not far from Atlanta, Macon seems a world and several decades apart. The city was laid out on the west bank of the Ocmulgee River in 1823 at the site of a frontier fort. In the geographic center of the state lies Macon's historic district. The city has an astonishing 48 buildings individually listed on the National Register of Historic Places. Take a walk or a drive through the Intown neighborhood. The crown jewel is the Hay House, an Italian Renaissance Revival mansion at 934 Georgia Avenue. There is a fine brochure outlining downtown walking tours available from the Convention & Visitors Bureau (*see above*).

Douglass Theatre. Macon's own Otis Redding was discovered here, and Ma Rainey, Cab Calloway, Duke Ellington, James Brown, and Little Richard performed here. This 1921 beauty was built by black entrepreneur Charles Douglass. After sitting empty for a quarter of a century, the 314-seat theater was renovated and reopened in 1997 for IMAX and other shows. The ornate ceiling and majestic furnishings are extraordinary. *355 Martin Luther King, Jr. Blvd., tel. 912/742–2000. Donations welcome. Open Tues.–Fri. 9–5, Sat. 11–5, Sun. noon–5.*

Georgia Music Hall of Fame. Opened in 1997, the Music Hall of Fame covers ragtime, soul, gospel, and country music. The museum features Georgia superstars such as Lena Horne, Little Richard, Johnny Mercer, Otis Redding, Chet Atkins, and the Allman Brothers. *200 Martin Luther King, Jr. Blvd., Macon, tel. 912/750– 8555 or 888/GA–ROCKS. Admission: $7.50 adult*

($2 AAA discount), $5.50 senior citizens, $3.50 ages 6–16, under 6 free. Open Mon.–Sat. 9–4:30, Sun. 1–4:30.

Harriet Tubman African American Museum. A large mural depicting the journey "From Africa to America" provides a powerful historical overview and reminder of the broad range of African-American achievement. The museum has African art and artifacts of daily living, such as bowls and instruments. The Convention & Visitors Bureau offers an excellent brochure listing dozens of important local black history sites— like the Cotton Avenue business district and the Ruth Hartley Mosley Memorial Women's Center—many of which are not far from the ballpark. *340 Walnut St., Macon, tel. 912/743–8544.*

Admission: $3.50 adult, $2 ages 6–12, under 6 free. Open Mon.–Sat. 10–5, Sun. 2–5.

Ocmulgee National Monument. This preserve consists of six American Indian mounds, including a burial mound and an earth lodge. Follow a driving trail or walk through the fields of the 700-acre site to learn about Creek Indian art and culture and view archaeological remains. The mounds are huge, impressive structures. The visitor center details habitations from 10,000 BC to the early 1700s. The monument is in eastern Macon. *U.S. 80 East, at Exit 1 or 2 from I–16, Macon, tel. 912/986–5441. Monument open daily dawn to dusk. Visitor center open weekdays 7:30–5, weekends 9–5.*

THE OPRY AND ELVIS
NASHVILLE, MEMPHIS, LITTLE ROCK

Three of baseball's most idiosyncratic stadiums can be visited in a tri-city sweep. Nashville is America's country music citadel: its Greer Stadium has the best scoreboard in baseball—a 60-ft-long guitar. Drive 20 minutes west of town to eat in the legendary Loveless Cafe and plan a nonbaseball night to take in the timeless and engaging Grand Ole Opry. During the day, you can spend several hours at the Country Music Hall of Fame.

Drive southwest for 206 mi to Memphis on Interstate 40 for an eye-popping visit to Elvis's mansion, a staggering number of remarkable down-home restaurants, and a game at AutoZone Park, a new $72 million park across from the famed Peabody Hotel. This 12,512-seat park is connected by walkways to a landmark building, creating a bustling alley adjoining the stadium. The city's old baseball park, Tim McCarver Stadium, is in the fairgrounds, within sight of the Libertyland amusement park, where Elvis's favorite, the Zippin Pippin wood roller coaster, still runs. You'll need to spend at least two days to do justice to the many attractions here—the gripping National Civil Rights Museum, the Beale Street Historic District, the Mud Island theme park, and the Pink Palace children's museum.

Continue southwest for 125 mi on Route 40 to Little Rock. At Ray Winder Field, there is a real organist, Alfreda Wilson, who's been playing at Travelers' games since 1970. You'll also want to see Central High School, site of one of America's most famous school integration battles. Its football stadium was used by the Travelers before Winder Field was built. At the state capitol, be certain to see the portrait of "boy" governor Bill Clinton; it was painted when he was just 27 years old.

NASHVILLE SOUNDS

League: Pacific Coast League • **Major League Affiliation:** Pittsburgh Pirates • **Class:** AAA • **Stadium:** Herschel Greer Stadium • **Opened:** 1978 • **Capacity:** 10,700 • **Dimensions:** LF: 327, CF: 400, RF: 327 • **Surface:** grass • **Season:** Apr.–Labor Day.

STADIUM LOCATION: 534 Chestnut St., Nashville, TN 37203

TEAM WEB SITE: www.nashvillesounds.com

GETTING THERE: From downtown, I-65 south to Wedgewood exit. Go west one block, right on 8th Ave. At next light, right on Chestnut.

TICKET INFORMATION: Box 23290, Nashville, TN 37202, tel. 615/242–4371, fax 615/256–5684.

PRICE RANGE: Box seats $8 adults, $7 ages 12 and under; general admission $5 adults, $4 ages 12 and under.

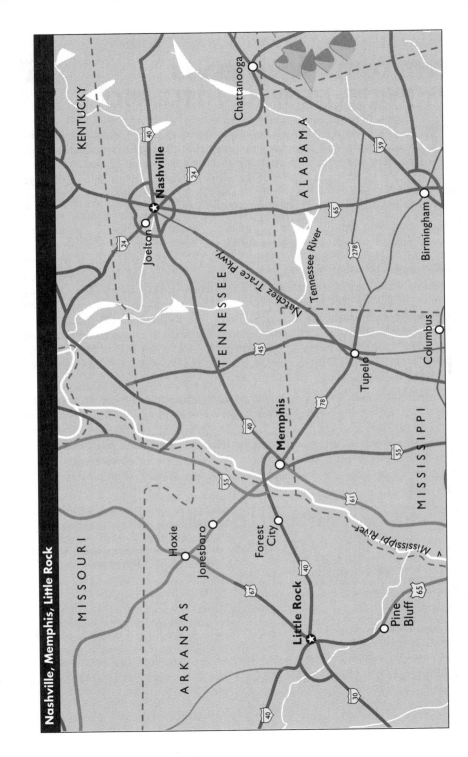

Nashville, Memphis, Little Rock

GAME TIME: Mon.–Sat. 7:15 PM, Sun. 2:05 (Apr.–May), Mon.–Sat. 7:15 PM (June–Sept.); gates open 1 hr before game.

TIPS ON SEATING: General admission seats not very good. Buy reserved seats, even though they are relatively expensive for minor leagues. $2 children's general admission seats are recommended if your children tend to roam about.

SEATING FOR PEOPLE WITH DISABILITIES: Space for 20 people in wheelchairs in box seat section L behind home plate. General admission is charged. Companions can pay for box seat in front of this section or general admission behind it.

STADIUM FOOD: The food is inexpensive, but not very good. The best bets are the $2 root beer floats and $1.50 hard-dip ice cream or frozen yogurt. Avoid the chicken sandwich. The hamburgers and cheeseburgers ($2.50) are slightly better bets. Spring water is $1. The **Stadium Club Restaurant** above the press box behind home plate is open to the public. It's worth the extra dollars to eat here.

SMOKING POLICY: Section QQ, a small box-seat section in back of grandstand on third-base side of home, is the only family section with no smoking and no alcohol.

PARKING: Ample parking, $3.

VISITING TEAM HOTEL: Ramada Inn–Governor's House (737 Harding Place, Nashville, TN 37211, tel. 615/834–5000 or 800/228–2828).

TOURISM INFORMATION: Nashville Convention & Visitors Bureau (161 4th Ave. N, Nashville, TN 37219, tel. 615/259–4700 or 800/950–4418).

Nashville: Greer Stadium

There is one reason to go to Nashville's Herschel Greer Stadium: the scoreboard. It would be the best scoreboard in baseball if it weren't, as our daughter, Emily, pointed out, dominated by eight beer ads. It is shaped like a guitar—not just any guitar, a 60-ft-long guitar that is 53 ft high. A 35,825-pound guitar. A guitar that explodes with fireworks when the home team hits a home run or wins a game. A half-million-dollar guitar. The inning-by-inning score is kept horizontally along the neck of the guitar. Balls, strikes, and outs are registered vertically on the peghead. There are two electronic scoreboards on the body of the guitar. It is spectacular.

Once you stop gawking at the scoreboard, this is a mediocre ballpark. Built in 1978 on land of the metropolitan park district (parkland south of the city), the stadium was entirely financed with private funds. It was clean and constantly upgraded. But it was too big, too heavy, too dull. With seats for 17,000 fans, it was the wrong scale for minor-league baseball, lacking the intimacy of the best old and new ballparks.

For the 1998 season, seating was reduced to 10,700 and attendance went up. The bleachers beyond the wall in right field were removed and replaced with a picnic area. Another picnic area was built down the left-field line. The uncovered grandstand forms an L shape with the long end down the first-base line.

The entryway is colorful and inviting, with pennants flying, although it lacks the grand architectural statement of the newer stadiums or the classic look of the old-time ballparks. The team's logo—a baseball player swinging a guitar for a bat—is among our favorites. The logo enhances both the entrance and the scoreboard. There is a fine souvenir shop at the entrance. Inside, a formidable structure above the seating area contains 18 large skyboxes, the press box, and the Stadium Club Restaurant. Unfortunately, from the entrance to the stadium, this complex looks like the back of a run-down 1960s motel.

Champ, the mascot, is a friendly green dinosaur who signs autographs at the end of the game. The team is named the Sounds and the music here is fine, but not as exceptional as you would expect in the capital of country music. There is a barbershop at the top of the seating area behind home plate, making Nashville one of several stadiums where fans can get haircuts. The concourse is large and serviceable, with large white baseballs honoring former players and coaches along the walls. This includes future Hall of Famer Don Mattingly, who hit .316 for Nashville in 1981. The Nashville Sounds are famous as the team Michael Jordan would have played for in 1995 had he not resumed his career as one of the greatest professional basketball players in history.

Fort Negley, a key point in the defense of the city in the Battle of Nashville on December 15, 1864, once stood just behind where the stadium was built. Railroad tracks run behind the stadium's left-field wall.

More Nashville Baseball

There is a state-government parking lot just north of the capitol where Nashville's most historic ballpark once stood. First used for baseball in 1876, the field was in the old Sulphur Spring Bottom. The famed *Tennessean* sports writer Grantland Rice named it Sulphur Dell. The ballplayers sometimes called it Suffer Hell, for the fumes from the nearby city dump. Only 440 yards from the Cumberland River, the ballpark flooded in the spring. Philip Lowry, the author of *Green Cathedrals*, said, "Sulphur Dell had the greatest and craziest right field in history." The incline in right field rose 25 ft, sometimes at an angle as steep as 45 degrees. The most successful outfielder in handling this short right-field porch was Doc Wiseman, who got the nickname the Goat for his heroic running sidehill catches.

Wilson Park, in the Trimble Bottom section of South Nashville, was named for the president of the Negro National League. Roy Campanella played here before becoming a Dodger and, later, a Hall of Famer. After the field's stint with baseball, a dog-racing track stood here and later the Paradise Ballroom, which hosted Cab Calloway, Lionel Hampton, and Sarah Vaughn.

Where to Stay

Quality Inn–Hall of Fame. This convenient downtown hotel is within walking distance of the Country Music Hall of Fame. Some rooms in the five-story property have extra sofa beds. There is a free Continental breakfast. *1407 Division St., Nashville 37203, tel. 615/242-1631 or 800/225-5151, fax 615/244-9519. 103 rooms. Facilities: outdoor pool, free parking. AE, D, DC, MC, V. $$*

Union Station Hotel/Wyndham. In the restored downtown train station, this seven-story stone hotel has a spectacular lobby. Rooms range from standard to deluxe. Parking is $9 daily. *1001 Broadway, Nashville 37203, tel. 615/726-1001 or 800/996-3426, fax 615/248-3554. 124 rooms. Facilities: 3 restaurants. AE, D, DC, MC, V. $$*

Wilson Inn. In this five-story chain hotel, many rooms have kitchens. There are some junior and regular suites. The hotel is 3 mi from Opryland. A Continental breakfast is served in the lobby. Free popcorn and punch are offered all day. Kids up to 18 stay free. *600 Ermac Dr., Elm Hill Pike exit from Briley Pkwy., Nashville 37214, tel. 615/889-4466 or 800/333-9457, fax 615/889-0484. 110 rooms. Facilities: exercise room. AE, D, DC, MC, V. $*

Where to Eat

Elliston Place Soda Shop. At this small, 1939-era fountain restaurant, you'll find good soups, fried oysters, orangeade, pie, and 14 kinds of vegetables. *2111 Elliston Pl., Nashville, tel. 615/327-1090. No credit cards. $*

Belle Meade Buffet. In a ritzy neighborhood of megamansions, 7 mi from the ballpark, you'll find a grand Southern cafeteria in a shopping center. Established in 1961, it attracts all ages and incomes. There are miniplates for children, as well as catfish, okra, mackerel, and brownie pie. *Harding Rd., Belle Meade Plaza, Nashville, tel. 615/298-5571. MC, V. $*

Loveless Cafe. One of America's best country meals is served in this former motel dining room, which is 20 minutes west of town. It's a genuine café, with oilcloths, metal chairs, and generous portions. The biscuits and preserves are to sing about. Try the spectacular fried chicken and country ham. You can even buy blackberry jam to take home. Reservations reduce your wait. *8400 Hwy. 100, Nashville, tel. 615/646-9700 or 800/-889-2432. AE, MC, V. $*

Entertainments

Grand Ole Opry. Be a part of the weekly radio broadcast by attending a show in this cavernous 4,400-seat theater. This is radio's longest-running regularly scheduled show. Write or call several weeks in advance for summer broadcasts. The box office sells walk-up tickets starting Tuesday for the weekend shows. Even small children enjoy the bouncy program, held at the Opryland complex, 9 mi northeast of downtown. River taxis (roundtrip $12.99 adults, $9.99 ages 4–11) shuttle between Riverfront Park downtown and Opryland on the half hour, 9:30 AM to 12:30 AM. *Opryland Reservations, 2808 Opryland Dr., Nashville, tel. 615/889–6611. Admission: $15–$19 evening shows. Shows: Fri. at 7:30 and Sat. 6:30 and 9:30 PM.*

Nashville Zoo. White tigers, snow leopards, pythons, giraffes, a red panda, and 600 other exotic animals are in this 135-acre zoo. Parking is $2. *1710 Ridge Rd. Circle, Joelton, Exit 31 off I–24 W, New Hope Rd. W., tel. 615/370–3333. Admission: $6 adults, $4 senior citizens and ages 3–12. Open Apr.–Sept., daily 9–6; Oct.–Mar. daily 10–5.*

Sights to See

Capitol. The Tennessee Capitol sits on a prominent site overlooking Nashville. The 206-ft-high building is modeled after a Greek Ionic temple. *Charlotte Ave., next to Capitol Plaza, Nashville, tel. 615/741–2692. Open daily 8–5.*

Country Music Hall of Fame. This is a thorough and touching museum of the hardships and triumphs of America's country music stars. Elvis's gold Cadillac is here, along with costumes from Loretta Lynn and Patsy Kline. It has many mementos, vintage photographs, and audiovisual exhibits. The Music Row area contains several studios, music company offices, the Gospel Music Association, and individual stars' museums (Hank Williams Jr., Randy Travis, Barbara Mandrell). A new $37-million hall is set to open

in spring 2001, with a 200-seat theatre, room for serious archives, and a wall with every country gold and platinum record. It will take up a city block near Ryman Auditorium. *4 Music Square E, Demonbreun St. exit (209-B) from the I–40 loop, Nashville, tel. 615/255–5333. Admission: $10.50 adults, $4.75 ages 6–11. Open June–Aug., daily 8–6; May and Sept.–Oct., Mon.–Thurs. 9–5, Fri.–Sat. 8–6, Sun. 8–5; Nov.–Apr., daily 9–5.*

The Hermitage. This huge estate is the home and burial site of President Andrew Jackson and his wife, Rachel Jackson. You can see a film of the President's life, and cassettes explain the grounds, garden, and living quarters. Tulip Grove, the home of Jackson's nephew, is also included. There are original log cabins and slave quarters. *2850 Rachel's La., 15 min from Nashville, Hermitage, 37076, tel. 615/889–2941. Admission: $8 adults, $7 senior citizens, $4 ages 6–12; free Jan. 8 and reduced fees Mar. 15. Open daily 9–5. Closed 3rd wk of Jan.*

Parthenon. If Greece is not in your travel plans, come to Centennial Park and see a full-size reproduction of the Parthenon on the Acropolis. Built for the city's centennial celebration in 1897, it has the largest bronze doors in the world. Imagine slamming 7½ tons. The interior houses the city's art collection, including a 42-ft-tall sculpture of Athena and castings from the Elgin Marbles. *West End Ave., Nashville, tel. 615/862–8431. Admission: $2.50 adults, $1.25 senior citizens and ages 4–17. Open Tues.–Sat. 9–4:30.*

Ryman Auditorium. The downtown home of the Grand Ole Opry from 1943 to 1974 has been renovated and is again used as a performance hall for bluegrass, country, jazz, and classical music. Its museum contains colorful concert posters and artifacts from its Opry years. *116 5th Ave. N, Nashville, tel. 615/254–1445. Admission: $6 adults, $2.25 ages 6–12. Open daily 8:30–4.*

MEMPHIS REDBIRDS

League: Pacific Coast League • **Major League Affiliation:** St. Louis Cardinals • **Class:** AAA • **Stadium:** AutoZone Park • **Opened:** 2000 • **Capacity:** 12,512 • **Dimensions:** LF: 319, CF: 400, RF: 323 • **Surface:** grass • **Season:** Apr.–Labor Day

STADIUM LOCATION: 3rd St. and Union Ave., Memphis, TN 38103.

TEAM WEB SITE: www.memphisredbirds.com

GETTING THERE: AutoZone Park is on the east side of downtown, just across the street from the Peabody Hotel and two blocks from Beale Street.

PARKING: The Toyota Center, next to the ballpark, has parking for 800 cars. There are 6,000 additional parking spaces within a 3-block radius of the ballpark.

TICKET INFORMATION: 1 Toyota Center, Memphis, TN 38103, tel. 901/721–6000, fax 901/527–1642

PRICE RANGE: Infield club NA; outfield club NA; lower dugout box NA; upper dugout box NA; field box NA; outfield box NA; pavilion box NA.

GAME TIME: Weekdays 7:05 PM, Sat. 6:05 PM, Sun. 2:05; gates open 90 min before game.

TIPS ON SEATING: Additional seating for 2,000 on a grass berm beyond left field.

SEATING FOR PEOPLE WITH DISABILITIES: On all levels. There are two elevators, plus a drop-off and pick-up area for disabled fans. Parking is available in the adjacent Toyota Center.

STADIUM FOOD: Barbecue is so big in this city that even the park's nachos are barbecued. You can get grilled sausages, kosher hot dogs, burgers, chicken sandwiches, Polish dogs, and yes, corn dogs. Pizza and ice cream are also available.

SMOKING POLICY: No smoking in any of the seating bowl or on the concourse. Designated smoking areas have views of the field.

VISITING TEAM HOTEL: Sleep Inn at Court Square (40 N. Front St., Memphis, TN 38102, tel. 901/522–9700 or 800/627–53367).

TOURISM INFORMATION: Memphis Convention & Visitors Bureau (47 Union Ave., Memphis, TN 38103, tel. 901/543–5333).

Memphis: AutoZone Park

Forty years ago, Russwood Park burned to the ground and with it went 60 years of baseball history. Professional baseball has been a patchwork here ever since, with most of the action at a shabby fairgrounds park (named for the not-at-all-shabby Hall of Fame catcher Tim McCarver). For lack of a decent facility, Memphis could have lost professional baseball. Happily, Memphis now has a ballpark that is a worthy successor to Russwood and another jewel in this great blues city.

Location is the key to many of the modern ballparks, and you can't get much better than this

one: directly across the street from the Peabody Hotel and but two blocks from famed Beale Street. AutoZone Park has the classic brick look of Baltimore's Camden Yards, reflecting the tradition of this historic district.

The Plaza at the main entrance on the corner of Third and Union is more than a ballpark entrance; with activities before and after the games, it's a people magnet. The historic 1913 Moore Building, adjacent to the Plaza and directly behind home plate, recently underwent a $22-million renovation and was renamed the Toyota Center. It houses the Redbirds store, offices, and the Plaza Club.

AutoZone Park was designed by the Memphis firm of Looney Ricks Kiss in consultation with

HOK Sport of Kansas City. Of the $72 million total development cost, only 12% came from the city and county. The nonprofit Redbirds Foundation covered the rest of the construction costs and owns the new stadium. Dean and Kristi Jernigan, who head the Redbirds nonprofit organization, signed on as the St. Louis Cardinals Triple A affiliate, and brought the top-quality ballpark to downtown. Profits go toward the mission of the foundation, which includes bringing baseball back to inner-city communities.

Inside the ballpark, all the seats in the main stands and the club level are real seats. The only bleacher seats are beyond the right-field wall. The upper deck has 48 club suites. The left-field corner features a game and amusement area and a baseball-theme children's play area. There is additional seating for 2,000 on a grass berm beyond left field. Rockey the Rockin' Redbird adds his own special brand of excitement to the new ballpark.

A museum of minor-league baseball is scheduled to open adjacent to the ballpark in the spring of 2002. It will have a computer database of every single player who has ever played professional baseball.

More Memphis Baseball

Tim McCarver Stadium. When the history of professional baseball is written sometime in the middle of the 21st century, Tim McCarver Stadium will be the forgettable field used between the classic old Russwood Park and AutoZone Park. Don't get us wrong—we admire Tim McCarver, the Hall of Fame catcher turned broadcaster. This stadium simply does not do him justice. Built in 1963 for American Legion baseball with a covered grandstand and 2,300 seats, it was expanded to 5,447 in 1968 and to its current capacity of 10,000 in 1980. It was home to the Memphis Chicks for 31 years.

Unfortunately, there is not a trace left of Memphis's really great baseball stadium, **Russwood Park.** Built in 1899 and expanded to hold 13,000 after the Chicks won the Southern Association championship in 1921, Russwood Park was a charming, lopsided old ballpark of the sort now in favor with fans and stadium architects alike.

A who's who of baseball stars from Babe Ruth to Stan Musial played in that park, as major-league exhibitions were often staged here before the final game on April 17, 1960, just before a fire destroyed the park. The site is now the Medical Center Complex, directly across the street from the Baptist Memorial Hospital. *Tim McCarver Stadium, 800 Home Run Lane, Mid-South Fairgrounds, Memphis.*

Where to Stay

Visiting Team Hotel: Sleep Inn at Court Square. This six-story downtown hotel is moderately priced. Guests receive a free Continental breakfast. It is four blocks from the ballpark. *40 N. Front St., Memphis, 38102, tel. 901/522–9700 or 800/627–5337, fax 901/522–9710. 124 rooms. Facilities: exercise room. AE, DC, MC, V. $$*

Hampton Inn–Medical Center. Kids stay free at this four-story brick hotel on the Medical Center campus, 2 mi north of downtown. A free Continental breakfast is served. Rooms are small and clean. There is access to a nearby health spa. *1180 Union Ave., I–240 at Exit 30, Memphis 38104, tel. 901/276–1175 or 800/426–7866, fax 901/276–4261. 126 rooms. Facilities: outdoor pool. AE, D, DC, MC, V. $$*

Where to Eat

Rendezvous. This cozy restaurant adjacent to the Peabody Hotel in General Washburn Alley offers great barbecue pork and dry, spice-crusted ribs. The Greek owners have been serving eaters hungry for Tennessee barbecue since 1948. While the waiters are gruff, the smells from the four smoking pits are heavenly. Waits can last an hour. *52 S. 2nd St. Rear, Memphis, tel. 901/523–2746. MC, V.$*

Arcade Restaurant. At Memphis's oldest lunch counter, the food has been fast and filling since 1919. It's Southern diner food for breakfast, with pancakes, waffles, and country ham. Plate lunches end at 3 PM. Light dinners of pizza, salad, and sandwiches begin at 5:30. The Arcade is at Calhoun Street, by a trolley stop. There's free parking in the rear. *540 S. Main St., Memphis, tel. 901/526–5757. AE, MC, V. $*

Buntyn Cafe. The place to eat "meat and three" in Memphis, it's along the railroad tracks. Booths and tables crowd this family restaurant and so do customers, as its fried chicken, okra, banana pudding, and cornbread are superlative. It's a small place and fills up fast. *3070 Southern Ave., Memphis, tel. 901/458–8776. No breakfast. AE, DC, D, MC, V. $*

Corky's. One of Memphis's standout purveyors of slow-smoked barbecue, it serves wet and dry ribs. Its slogan is "Bad to the bone!" There's meltingly good beef brisket, as well as Delta-style tamales, onion loaves, and fudge pie. *5259 Poplar Ave., Memphis, tel. 901/685–9744. AE, D, MC, V. $*

Leonard's Restaurant. It was for a time the world's largest barbecue drive-in restaurant and serves good ribs, slaw, and chicken. Founder Leonard Heuberger bartered a Model-T for a seven-stool sandwich place in 1922. Four decades later, Elvis was a regular customer. *5465 Fox Plaza Blvd., Memphis, tel. 901/360–1963. AE, D, DC, MC, V. $*

Wiles-Smith Drug Store. In this midtown classic, you can get great milk shakes, sandwiches, and homemade vegetable soup. Lunch ends at 3 PM. *1635 Union St., Memphis, tel. 901/278–6416. No credit cards. $*

Entertainments

Libertyland. At this amusement park adjoining the ballpark, you can ride Elvis's favorite, the Zippin Pippin wooden roller coaster. A paddle-boat and a 1909 Dentzel carousel are among the 22 rides. Get $3-off coupons at Graceland. Admission covers a show, the carousel, a train, and kiddie rides. It's in the Mid-South Fairgrounds. *940 Early Maxwell Blvd., Memphis, tel. 901/274–1776. Admission: $8; senior citizens and ages 3 and under free; thrill-ride ticket, $19; twi-light thrill-ride ticket (after 4 PM), $16. Open June–Aug., Sat. 10–9, Sun. noon–9.*

Memphis Pink Palace Museum and Planetarium. The mansion of Clarence Saunders, founder of Piggly Wiggly, the first large-scale self-service grocery, has an insect zoo, dinosaur exhibits, and the world's largest mechanical miniature circus. *3050 Central Ave., Memphis, tel. 901/320–6320. Museum admission: $6 adults, $5.50 senior citizens, $4.50 ages 3–12. Planetar-ium admission: $3.50 adults, $3 senior citizens and*

ages 3–12. Open Mon.–Wed. 9–5, Thurs. 9–9, Fri.–Sat. 9 AM–10 PM, Sun. noon–6.

Memphis Zoo and Aquarium. This huge zoo in Overton Park has 2,800 animals in Cat Country, the Primate Canyon, and Animals of the Night. Kimodo dragons are a recent addition. There's a $1 tram that stops throughout the park. There are also kiddie rides. *2000 Galloway Ave., Memphis, tel. 901/726–4787. Admission: $8.50 adults, $7.50 senior citizens, $5.50 ages 2–11; free Tues. 2–5 for TN residents. Open daily 9–5, June–July weekends until 9 PM.*

Mud Island. On the Mississippi River, this 52-acre theme park has a swimming pool, a beach, and an amphitheater. You can walk a miniature version of the 900 mi of the Mississippi along a Riverwalk, one footstep per mile. You can take a tour of the World War II bomber *Memphis Belle,* which is housed in a pavilion (donation requested), or eat in one of several restaurants. You reach the island by footbridge or monorail, the fee for which is included in admission. *125 Front St., Memphis, tel. 901/576–7212. Admis-sion to all attractions: $8 adults, $6 ages 4–11, senior citizens, and the disabled. Open daily 10–8.*

Sights to See

Beale Street Historic District. On the street where W. C. Handy established the blues, the Center for Southern Folklore (130 Beale St.) has films, tours, and exhibits. The Gibson Guitar company runs tours of its new plant, just off Beale. It adjoins a Gibson cafe and museum whose exhibit, "Rock n' Soul: Social Cross-roads," was curated by the Smithsonian Institu-tion. *Beale St. between 2nd and 4th Sts., Mem-phis, tel. 901/526–0125.*

Graceland Mansion Tour. You can save yourself an hour of waiting by calling ahead for reserva-tions, especially during Elvis Week each August. Plan to arrive 15 minutes before your ticket time. If you walk in, use a pay phone in the visi-tor center to cut the wait. Buses take you to the Presley home, which is modest in size but not in scope. It has vintage '60s furnishings, costumes, gold records, movie posters, and family pho-tographs. Many somber fans visit his gravesite and eternal flame. Touring Elvis's jets, the auto museum, and the Sincerely Elvis museum is extra. *3717 Elvis Presley Blvd., 12 mi southeast of city, Memphis, tel. 901/332–3322 or 800/238–2000. Admission: $10 adults, $9 students and senior citizens, $5 ages 5–11. Open Memorial Day–Labor Day, daily 9–6; Labor Day–Memorial Day, daily 9–5. AE, MC, V.*

National Civil Rights Museum. This spectacular, not-to-be-missed museum is in the Lorraine Motel, where Martin Luther King, Jr. was slain. It creatively tells of civil wrongs and rights throughout the South. Artifacts from the struggle include a burned-out bus, crosses, posters, and prayer books. A replica bus instructs riders to move to the back. Exhibits make a big impression on children. It ends emotionally with a view of King's room and the balcony where he fell. Beginning in fall 2000, trial evidence will be on display. An audio tape rental is $2.50. *450 Mulberry St., Memphis, tel. 901/521–9699. Admission: $6 adults, $5 senior citizens and college students, $4 ages 4–17. Open June–Aug., Wed.–Sat. 10–6, Sun. 1–6; Sept.–May, Wed.–Sat. 9–5, Sun. 1–5.*

The Peabody Ducks. To the strains of the "King Cotton March," five famous ducks waddle on a red carpet from the swank Peabody Hotel fountain to an elevator to their penthouse home twice a day. Tourists flock to the lobby at 11 and 5 for the free show. *149 Union Ave., Memphis, tel. 901/529–4000.*

ARKANSAS TRAVELERS

League: Texas League • **Major League Affiliation:** St. Louis Cardinals • **Class:** AA • **Stadium:** Ray Winder Field • **Opened:** 1932 • **Capacity:** 6,083 • **Dimensions:** LF: 330, CF: 390, RF: 345 • **Surface:** grass • **Season:** Apr.–Labor Day

STADIUM LOCATION: War Memorial Park, Little Rock, AR 72205.

TEAM WEB SITE: www.travs.com

GETTING THERE: From downtown, Markham Ave., turn south on Monroe St; stadium ½ mi away. From I–630, stadium is at Fair Park Blvd. exit (not Stadium exit; that sign is for football stadium). From Memphis, I–40 across Arkansas River Bridge to I–630.

PARKING: Stadium parking free, but not well organized.

TICKET INFORMATION: Box 55066, Little Rock, AR 72215, tel. 501/664–1555, fax 501/664–1834.

PRICE RANGE: General admission $5 adults, $3 children; box seats $2 extra.

GAME TIME: 7:30 PM, Sun. 2 PM; gates open 1 hr before game.

TIPS ON SEATING: Box seats are right at field level and amazingly close to action. 2 warnings: setting sun can shine in your eyes if you sit on third-base side; 4 poles that hold up grandstand roof can obstruct view from some general admission seats.

SEATING FOR PEOPLE WITH DISABILITIES: Spaces for wheelchairs in box-seat sections at general admission prices. Fixed seats for companions next to all wheelchair locations.

STADIUM FOOD: The menu is very limited and lines can be long. The grilled chicken ($3) is the best of the average choices. Hot dogs are better than most at $2, but there's only yellow mustard and no relish.

SMOKING POLICY: Smoking allowed throughout.

VISITING TEAM HOTEL: Little Rock Hilton (925 S. University, Little Rock, AR 72204, tel. 501/664–5021 or 800/445–8667).

TOURISM INFORMATION: Little Rock Convention & Visitors Bureau (1 State Health Plaza, Little Rock, AR 72201, tel. 501/376–4781).

Little Rock: Ray Winder Field

You won't find one of those sleek new stadiums here in Little Rock, Arkansas. Ray Winder Field is a baseball place, good ol' boy style. The entrance sits almost hidden in War Memorial Park, a complex that includes the zoo and the football stadium where the University of Arkansas Razorbacks play. The baseball stadium was built with private funds in 1932, and in many ways it seems unchanged. Almost 2,000 of the green-and-orange seats in the grandstand are the original straight-backed ones installed in 1932.

The covered grandstand forms the letter L with the stem down the first-base line. A press box hangs from the roof above home plate. Aluminum bleachers stretch down the third-base line to a comfortable bowl-like picnic area. The ballpark's most distinctive feature is a 55-ft-high chain-link fence above the outfield wall from center to right, known to locals as Screen Monster. It used to be that a player had to hit a ball 400 ft to get a home run here. That was until the mid-1970s, when the state highway department turned a residential street into a six-lane highway and took a big chunk of Ray Winder Field's right field. About once a month, someone knocks one over the screen.

The Travelers get their nickname from the legend of a 19th-century trader who rode throughout Arkansas telling yarns and selling wares. The Travelers have their own legend, Bill Valentine, the general manager since 1976. His roots are deep: "I was born eight blocks from this ballpark. I grew up here, cutting the grass and sorting the soda bottles." Valentine had been a major-league umpire until he was fired in 1968 for trying to organize an umpire's union. Valentine coined what we think is the best slogan in baseball— "the greatest show on dirt." The circus folks threatened a lawsuit, and the Travelers' slogan now reads "the greatest game on dirt."

Originally called Travelers Field, the park was renamed Ray Winder Field in 1966 after the man who led Little Rock baseball for more than 30 years. Winder was the *Sporting News's* "No. 1 Minor League Executive" in 1960. One of the two plaques to Winder at the entranceway calls him "a .400 hitter in the game of life." There is a small but fine collection of Winder and Travelers baseball memorabilia back to 1932 in a glass case next to the office on the first-base side of the entryway.

Now playing in the Double A Texas League as an affiliate of the St. Louis Cardinals, the Travelers have a long history in professional baseball. Little Rock was a charter member of the Southern Association in 1901. Future Hall of Famer Tris Speaker was the league's leading hitter at .350 in 1908. Not surprisingly, Little Rock had its problems integrating baseball in the 1960s.

We will take an old stadium with charm and history over the new stadiums almost every day, but there are some serious shortcomings here. The entranceway seemed incapable of dealing easily with the crush of the 5,000 people who showed up at the bat give-away night we attended. There were not enough concession stands to serve a large crowd. There is not a single no-smoking section in the place—and there are a lot of Travelers fans who like to smoke.

Alfreda Wilson sits way up under the grandstand roof behind home plate. She was a part-time teacher at the music shop where the team bought its first organ in 1970. The team signed her up, and she has been playing the organ at Travelers games ever since. Wilson says she gets through all 1,200 songs in her repertory during the course of each season. It was refreshing to find a Double A team that limits the contests and focuses on baseball. But we were disappointed with the nonstop commercials by the public address announcer, who pitched discount souvenirs between batters. We wanted more of Alfreda Wilson on the organ and fewer ads.

More Little Rock Baseball

Lamar Porter Field. There is a special treat awaiting baseball fans in Little Rock, a classic diamond in the rough that lies between the Capitol and Ray Winder Field. The field was used in the 1983 movie *Soldier's Story* because it so strongly evoked the ballparks of the 1940s. Alert to other movie producers: This is an absolutely enchanting, scruffy little place full of charm—

white exterior with a covered green grandstand of old wooden benches with backs. John Ross, a former minor-league umpire, gave us a tour and let the kids play on the field. According to Ross, the field was built by the Works Progress Administration (WPA) in 1936. Professional baseball was never played here. Ross was the batboy for the Little Rock Doughboys of American Legion baseball when future Hall of Famer Brooks Robinson was the shortstop. Bill Valentine, now the general manager of the Arkansas Travelers and a former major-league umpire, got his start umpiring here at the age of 14. Still in use today, Lamar Porter Field is part of the Billy Mitchell Boys Club complex of fields and recreation facilities. *7th and Johnson Sts., Little Rock. Take I–630 to Woodrow St. exit south and go left on 7th St.; field is across street from elementary school.*

Where to Stay

Markham Inn. This ordinary, inexpensive three-story brick hotel is one block from the ballpark. Its rooms are small and clean. *5129 W. Markham Ave., Little Rock 72205, tel. 501/666–0161, fax 501/666–3348. 150 rooms. Facilities: coin laundry. AE, MC, V. $*

Arkansas Excelsior Hotel. This sprawling luxury hotel faces the Arkansas River, next to the Old State House. The 20-story structure dominates the city skyline. *3 Statehouse Plaza, Little Rock 72201, tel. 501/375–5000 or 800/527–1745, fax 501/375–7320. 418 rooms. Facilities: 3 restaurants, fitness center. AE, D, DC, MC, V. $$*

La Quinta Inn–Fair Park. The rooms are small and the wooden staircases creak, but this clean motel has a cheery lobby with a free Continental breakfast. The two-story motel is four blocks from the ballpark and convenient to I–630. *901 Fair Park Blvd., Little Rock 72204, tel. 501/664–7000 or 800/551–5900, fax 501/223–2833. 122 rooms. Facilities: outdoor pool. AE, D, DC, MC, V. $*

Where to Eat

Franke's Cafeterias. This is one of three good cafeteria chains in the city, along with Wyatt's and the Dixie Cafe. Founded in 1919, it still has many classic items on the menu, such as eggplant casserole and egg custard pie. It has three

locations in Little Rock. *First Commercial Bank Bldg., 400 Broadway, downtown, Little Rock, tel. 501/372–1919; weekday lunch only. University Mall, 300 S. University Ave., Little Rock, tel. 501/666–1941. Market Place Shopping Center, 11121 Rodney Parham Rd., Little Rock, tel. 501/225–4487. AE, MC, V. $*

Catfish City. Little Rock is crazy for catfish and has two dozen restaurants devoted to this farm-raised "crop." This casual one-story restaurant in a commercial strip also serves shrimp, chicken, hush puppies, and frogs' legs. There is a children's menu with corn dogs and shrimp. *1817 S. University Ave., Little Rock, tel. 501/663–7224. AE, MC, V. $*

Entertainments

Children's Museum of Arkansas. In Union Station, this frenzied place has bubble machines, a farmer's market, and a computerized stock market. Children can make their own pretzels and peanut butter. It includes a toddler climbing area and drop-in arts area. *1400 W. Markham Ave., Little Rock, tel. 501/374–6655. Admission: $4, senior citizens $3; free parking. Open Sat.–Thurs. 10–5, Fri. 10–9.*

Little Rock Zoo. This is a small zoo of 600 animals, including 30 endangered species. A zoo train circles the waterfowl ponds. Look for the lion house, monkey island, the white tiger, giant anteaters, and the animal nursery. *War Memorial Park, Fair Park Blvd. exit off I–630, Little Rock, tel. 501/666–2406. Admission: $5 adults, $3 children under 13. Open Memorial Day–Labor Day, daily 9–5; Labor Day–Memorial Day, daily 9:30–4:30.*

Wild River Country. This pretty water park has a wave pool, a lazy river float, inner-tube rapids, and a wading pool. *6801 Crystal Hill Rd., Crystal Hill Rd. exit off I–430, at I–40, North Little Rock, tel. 501/753–8600. Admission: $17.95 adults, $15.95 ages 4–11, senior citizens free. Open June–Sept., daily 11–6.*

Sights to See

Central High School. Cross I–630 to visit this historic high school, where the most celebrated case of integration occurred. Three years after the Supreme Court in essence ended school segregation in 1954, Arkansas governor Orville

Faubus used the National Guard to turn away black students from Central High. President Eisenhower sent federal troops to Little Rock, and the nine children entered school with soldiers holding back jeering crowds with bayonets. The courage of the young students crossing through a hostile crowd to reach this imposing Art Deco building is memorable. The school is now 63% black. The fortresslike football stadium at Central High School was the site of Kavanaugh Field, home of the Travelers before Travelers Field (now called Ray Winder Field). *Park Ave. and 14th St., Little Rock.*

Old State House. What Arkansans call the Old State House is now a museum of Arkansas history. They take politics seriously in Arkansas. Here in the second-floor House chamber in 1837, the Speaker of the House killed a state representative in a knife fight during a legislative session. The Old State House is downtown, next to the Convention Center. *300 W. Markham St., Little Rock 72201, tel. 501/324–9685 Admission: $2 adults, $1 senior citizens, 25¢ ages 6–18; free Mon. Open Mon.–Sat. 9–5, Sun. 1–5.*

State Capitol. Arkansas has a traditional Greek Revival Capitol patterned after the United States Capitol. It was constructed between 1899 and 1915 on the site of the former state penitentiary. Give Arkansas credit for candor. There is a detailed display on the history of the building near the House of Representatives chamber, with every twist and turn in a bizarre 16-year story of Arkansas politics, power, and corruption. Look in the Governor's Conference Room at the portrait of the boy wonder Governor Bill Clinton, who looks impossibly young. Also, note the chandeliers in the rotunda, the legislative chambers, and the stained glass in each chamber. *W. Capitol Ave., Little Rock, tel. 501/682–5080. Open weekdays 7–4:30, weekends and holidays 10–4; guided tours, weekdays 9–4 by reservation.*

BOURBON STREET TO BIRMINGHAM

6

NEW ORLEANS, MOBILE, BIRMINGHAM

In the deep South, politics and baseball are serious subjects. Both are played to win. A visit to New Orleans, Mobile, and Birmingham is a living-history excursion with good baseball thrown into the bargain.

In New Orleans, a new $20-million stadium boosted the Zephyrs into AAA ball. Plan to spend your day walking or taking the 1920s streetcars through this magical city, eating at any of the casual restaurants serving authentic regional food. The city's aquarium is one of the nation's finest, and you can combine your visit with a riverboat excursion and tour of the impressive Audubon Park Zoo. You'll need to spend two nights minimum so you can take children for an evening of jazz at Preservation Hall, a safe and appropriate French Quarter destination.

Drive on Route 20 east to Mobile and the stadium named for its famous native son, Hank Aaron. The city, though lower profile, has much of the charm and antebellum architecture of New Orleans.

Route 65 speeds you north to Birmingham. You'll need to visit its downtown separately, as baseball has moved to the suburbs in Hoover. The 1988-era ballpark is attractive, but you may want to explore Rickwood Field, its predecessor inside the city limits and the oldest ballpark in America. Downtown also houses a superlative Civil Rights Institute, with vivid exhibits. Birmingham has a unique city landmark, a 50-ft iron figure of Vulcan, the god of fire.

Stay in Birmingham or Hoover overnight, but for history's sake, consider a 90-mi detour south on Route 65 to Montgomery, for the state capitol, the Civil Rights Memorial, Martin Luther King, Jr.'s Dexter Avenue Baptist Church, and the marked site where Rosa Parks refused to give up her bus seat.

NEW ORLEANS ZEPHYRS

League: Pacific Coast League • **Major League Affiliation:** Houston Astros • **Class:** AAA • **Stadium:** Zephyr Field • **Opened:** 1997 • **Capacity:** 10,000 • **Surface:** grass • **Season:** Apr.–Labor Day

STADIUM LOCATION: 6000 Airline Blvd., Metairie, LA 70003.

TEAM WEB SITE: www.zephyrsbaseball.com

GETTING THERE: The stadium is in Metairie, about 10 mi west of downtown New Orleans. From the city, take I-10 west to Clearview Pkwy. south. Take a right on Airline Dr. (Rt. 61); ballpark on left past cemetery.

PARKING: Ample parking, $3.

TICKET INFORMATION: 6000 Airline Blvd., Metairie, LA 70003, tel. 504/734–5155, fax 504/734–5118.

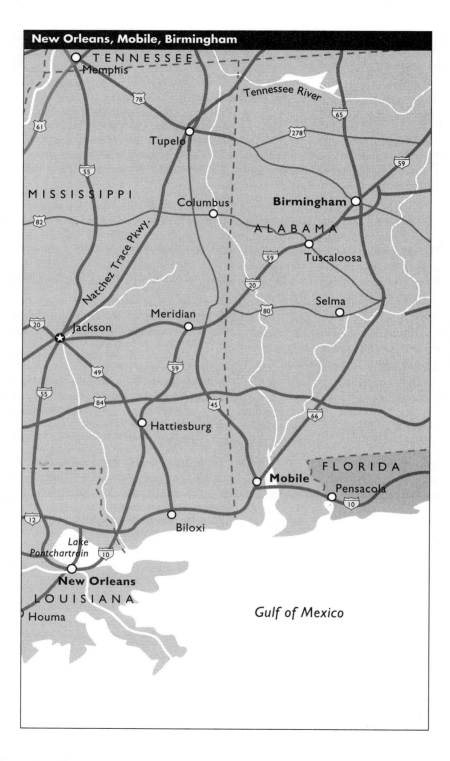

New Orleans, Mobile, Birmingham

PRICE RANGE: Reserved box $8; reserved seats $7; reserved grandstand $6; berm seating $4. $1 off all tickets for ages 12 and under and senior citizens.

GAME TIME: Mon.–Sat. 7:05 PM, Sun. 6:05 PM; gates open 1 hr before game, 90 min before Sat. games.

TIPS ON SEATING: Buy your favorite location, as price difference between seating sections is small. The view from the third-base side is of a swimming pool beyond the right-field wall, rather than Airline Drive over the left-field wall.

SEATING FOR PEOPLE WITH DISABILITIES: Seats are on the concourse just behind the reserved box seats. All fans enter the stadium by a wide ramp on first-base side.

STADIUM FOOD: This is a park that wisely emphasizes regional food specialties. It sells cups of jambalaya and Kate Latter's pralines. There is terrific fresh-squeezed lemonade and orangeade for $2. The main concession stand sells the more standard pizza, hot dogs, and soda.

SMOKING POLICY: Smoking is prohibited in seating areas.

VISITING TEAM HOTEL: Best Western Landmark (2601 Severn Ave., Metairie, LA 70002, tel. 504/885–9500 or 800/528–1234).

TOURISM INFORMATION: New Orleans Metropolitan Convention and Visitors Bureau (1520 Sugar Bowl Dr., New Orleans, LA 70112, tel. 504/566–5011). Louisiana State Visitors Center (529 St. Ann St., New Orleans, LA, tel. 504/568–5661).

New Orleans: Zephyr Field

When the Louisiana State Base Ball Association dissolved in 1873, the New Orleans *Daily Picayune* declared baseball dead. In truth, the relationship between baseball and New Orleans has been rocky ever since. New Orleans fancies itself a big-league town, but baseball here hasn't had the continuous following other cities have provided. The New Orleans Pelicans joined the Southern League in 1887 and played in the Southern Association from 1902 through 1959. Shoeless Joe Jackson was the franchise standout, leading the league in batting with a 354 average in 1910. Negro League teams played here only sporadically. Between 1960 and 1993, New Orleans had a professional baseball team only in 1977.

With new ownership, a new stadium, and a new league, baseball is alive again in New Orleans. In 1993, the Triple A minor-league team in Denver had to make room for the Rockies. The team moved to New Orleans and played at Privateer Park, a college stadium near Lake Pontchartrain. They were named the Zephyrs for the gentle breezes that blow off the lake. By 1997, the Zephyrs had a fine new stadium befitting a Triple A team. Part of a major reorganization of Triple A baseball in 1998, New Orleans joined the Pacific Coast League.

Zephyr Field is in Metairie, about 10 mi west of downtown New Orleans. The stadium cost $20 million and opened on April 16, 1997. It was built for the state by the Louisiana Stadium and Exposition District, in conjunction with a new training facility for the National Football League New Orleans Saints. The stadium was designed by Perez, Ernst, Farnet Architects and Planners of New Orleans in collaboration with HOK Sport of Kansas City.

This is a fine new Triple A stadium with seating for 10,000 fans on two levels. The wide-open concourse contains a large diversity of good foods and allows fans to continue to watch the game while they visit the concession booths. There are 16 VIP suites, two hot tubs, and a swimming pool just over the right-field wall for fans holding club seating.

New Orleans gave us an important baseball tradition. In 1887, Abner Powell came to New Orleans to manage and play for the Pelicans. Because of the frequent thundershowers in New Orleans, Powell came up with the idea of covering the infield and giving fans a rain check if the game wasn't finished.

Where to Stay

June through August are bargain months for New Orleans hotels, when rates are often half the usual cost.

Holiday Inn Chateau Le Moyne. This quaint small hotel on a quiet French Quarter street has a heated pool in a shady central courtyard. Rooms are nicely furnished. There is convenient pay parking in a guarded lot across the street. *301 Dauphine St., New Orleans 70112, tel. 504/ 581–1301 or 800/465–4329, fax 504/523– 5709. 171 rooms. Facilities: restaurant. AE, D, DC, MC, V. $$*

Avenue Plaza Suite Hotel/Eurovita Spa. This antiques-filled, 12-story hotel has charming one-bedroom suites with a living room. All contain a full kitchen. It's 2 mi west of the French Quarter. *2111 Saint Charles Ave., New Orleans 70130, tel. 504/566–1212, fax 504/525–6899. 40 suites. Facilities: restaurant, pool, sauna, hot tub, health club. AE, D, DC, MC, V. $$*

Dauphine Orleans Hotel. On a quiet French Quarter street, this hotel offers free drop-off service in the quarter and in the Central Business District (CBD). You can stay in cottages dating from the 1700s, in rooms adjoining a patio, or in the more conventional three-story main section. All rooms are well decorated. There's a free Continental breakfast. *415 Dauphine St., New Orleans 70112, tel. 504/586– 1800 or 800/521–7111, fax 504/586–1409. 111 rooms. Facilities: coffee shop, pool, hot tub, parking (fee). AE, D, DC, MC, V. $$*

Where to Eat

Mother's. Order at the grill for turtle soup, crawfish étouffée, authentic po'boys, bread pudding, and sweet potato pie. You get huge portions of genuine Creole dishes. *401 Poydras St., at Tchoupitoulas St., New Orleans, tel. 504/523– 9656. No credit cards. $*

Acme Oyster House. You can eat exquisite fresh oysters, po'boy sandwiches, gumbo, jambalaya, and bread pudding at this noisy, character-filled restaurant founded in 1910. The food is casual and served on plastic. *724 Iberville St., New Orleans, tel. 504/522–5973. AE, MC, V. $*

Café du Monde. A famous people-watching sidewalk café on Jackson Square in the French Market, it serves irresistible hot beignets covered with powdered sugar. There's chicory coffee for adults, orange juice for children. *Decatur and Saint Ann Sts., New Orleans, tel. 504/525– 4544. No credit cards. $*

Camellia Grill. At this wonderful vintage counter restaurant, cooks and waiters wear white and customers get linen napkins. The fast food, cooked before your eyes, includes heavenly burgers, salads, waffles, and turkey omelets. The "freeze" drinks resemble thin sodas, not milk shakes. There are only 29 stools, so go at off-peak hours. It's stop No. 44 (Riverbend) on the Saint Charles Avenue streetcar. *626 Carrollton Ave., New Orleans, tel. 504/866–9573. No credit cards. $*

Central Grocery. This is a storefront grocery with an expert sandwich-making counter for take-out meals. Choose from a two-item menu: stuffed artichokes or muffuletta—a filling sandwich of cold meats, marinated vegetables, mozzarella, pickles, and olives. *923 Decatur St., New Orleans, tel. 504/523–1620. No credit cards. $*

Entertainments

Aquarium of the Americas. On the French Quarter's riverfront, this aquarium is one of the nation's best. The white alligators are a big draw, but no section lets you down. Feel the shock of an electric eel. Walk through a Caribbean reef, an acrylic tunnel filled with 400,000 gallons of water and fish, and an Amazon rain forest. Combine your entry with an ecology tour on the Riverboat *John James Audubon,* departing at the aquarium's front door. *Canal St., New Orleans, tel. 504/565–3033. Admission: $12 adults, $9 senior citizens, $6 ages 2–12. Open daily 9:30–7.*

Audubon Park Zoo. Organized into ten sections, this is a lush walking zoo known for its white alligators, swamp exhibits, and World of Primates. Feed the sea lions, pat the creatures in the petting zoo, and take elephant and camel rides; or, go on a guided tram-tour (extra fee). A combination ticket is available with the aquarium and riverboat tour. *6500 Magazine St., New*

Orleans, tel. 504/861–2537. Admission: $8.75 adults, $4.75 senior citizens, $4.50 ages 2–12. Open daily 9:30–5.

St. Charles Avenue Streetcar. This is not the streetcar named Desire made famous by Tennessee Williams. That one's now a bus route. Board the streetcar anywhere along St. Charles Ave., Canal St., or the Riverwalk for a cheap way to see the city or to get to the zoo. The fare is $1 each way on the city's 35 olive-green, 1920s-era trolley cars, many with wicker seats. *Transit information, tel. 504/248–3900.*

Sights to See

The Cabildo. This Jackson Square building is a good place for children to discover the gumbo of cultures that has evolved into modern-day New Orleans. Completed in 1799 to house the governing body of Spanish Colonial New Orleans, the present structure sits on a site associated with the first official buildings of the city. The Louisiana Territory was transferred to the United States in this building on December 20, 1803. One of the most famous items in the museum is a death mask of Napoleon, one of only four in existence. For us, the most moving display was the slave auction block. Slaves sold at public auction with no regard for keeping families together. There is a Children's Visitor's Guide to the Cabildo. The Cabildo is part of the Louisiana State Museum and can be included in an admission package with the Old U.S. Mint, the Presbytère, the 1850 House, and the Arsenal. *Jackson Sq., Box 2448, New Orleans 70176, tel. 504/568–6968. Admission: $5 adults; $4 senior citizens, students, and military personnel; children under 12 free. Open Tues.–Sun. 9–5.*

Cities of the Dead. The city's cemeteries are famous for their aboveground tombs, built to avoid flooding. Lafayette Cemetery No. 1, 1400 Washington Avenue (in the Garden District), has been used since 1833. The more acclaimed St. Louis Cemetery No. 1, circa 1789, is in the French Quarter at 623 Royal Street. Tours are offered by Save Our Cemeteries and several commercial firms. *Save Our Cemeteries: tel. 504/525–3377 or 888/721–7493. Tour admission: $6 adults, $5 ages 12–18 and senior citizens, under 12 free.*

Jackson Square. In the historic heart of the French Quarter, artists of every sort—from mime to painting to balloon—set up shop around the beautifully landscaped square.

Louisiana Superdome. You may agree with us that baseball and football should be played outside on grass. That shouldn't stop you from visiting the Louisiana Superdome. As a sports facility, it may not be attractive, but as an amazing piece of architecture, it is worth a look. The Superdome opened in 1975 after four years of construction. The ceiling is 273 ft high, the roof is 9.7 acres; the stadium has 400 mi of electrical wiring and seats 63,524. It takes 40 hours to prepare the field for baseball. The Superdome is downtown near I–10. The entrance for tours is on Poydras Street at Gate A. *Sugar Bowl Dr., New Orleans 70112, tel. 504/587–3810. Admission: $6 adults, $4 ages 5–10, $5 senior citizens. 30-min tours weekdays at 10:30, noon, and 1:30.*

Old U.S. Mint. This stuffy-sounding building has some of the liveliest exhibits in the city, including "New Orleans Jazz" and "Carnival in New Orleans," which displays the costumes, masks, and crown jewels of Mardi Gras. Both exhibits come alive with music. *400 Esplanade Ave., New Orleans, tel. 504/568–6968. Admission: $5 adults; $4 students, senior citizens, active military personnel; children under 12 free. Open Tues.–Sun. 9–5.*

Preservation Hall. This is jazz in its purest form, and they make you suffer a little for it. There are no cocktail waitresses, no food, and no air-conditioning. Many of the legends who made Preservation Hall famous are dead now, but the music continues to be exceptional. Expect to wait in line, as Preservation Hall is a tiny, dingy, wonderful little place that attracts people from the world over. Unlike most of what's going on at night on and around Bourbon Street, Preservation Hall is fine for kids, and ours loved it. The music starts at 8:30 PM and ends at midnight. The sign behind the performers reads just as it has for decades: TRADITIONAL REQUESTS $1, OTHERS $2, THE SAINTS $5. *726 Saint Peter St., just off Bourbon St., New Orleans, tel. 504/522–2841 or 504/523–8939. Admission: $4. Open 8 PM–midnight.*

Walking Tours. The National Park Service Folk-life Center conducts free 1-mi tours. Sign-up opens at 9 AM. Reservations are needed for the Garden District tour, which leaves from Washington Avenue and Prytania Street at 2:30. *916 N. Peters St., New Orleans, tel. 504/589–2636.*

MOBILE BAYBEARS

League: Southern League • **Major League Affiliation:** San Diego Padres • **Class:** AA • **Stadium:** Hank Aaron Stadium • **Opened:** 1997 • **Capacity:** 6,000 • **Dimensions:** LF: 325, CF: 400, RF: 310 • **Surface:** grass • **Season:** early Apr.–Labor Day

STADIUM LOCATION: 755 Bolling Brothers Blvd., Mobile, AL 36606.

TEAM WEB SITE: www.mobilebaybears.com

GETTING THERE: From I–55, take Lakeland Dr. exit and go east for ¼ mi. Look for parking sign for Agriculture and Forestry Museum, left on Cool Papa Bell Rd. to stadium lot.

PARKING: Stadium lots cost $2.

TICKET INFORMATION: Box 161663, Mobile, AL 36616, tel. 334/479–2327, fax 334/476—1147.

PRICE RANGE: Box seats $7; reserved seats $5.50 adults, $4.50 children and senior citizens.

GAME TIME: Mon.–Sat. 7:05 PM, Sun. 2:05 PM (Apr.–May) and 6:05 PM (June–Sept.); gates open 1 hr before game.

TIPS ON SEATING: All 6,000 seats are genuine. The best 850 are on the field level and are reserved for season ticket holders and owners of the 22 field-level suites. The reserved seats in the second deck are immediately behind the box seats and are almost as good, at a lower price. Box seats have armrests; reserved seats do not. Some of the seats in the last five rows of reserved seating are obstructed by poles that hold up the roof.

SEATING FOR PEOPLE WITH DISABILITIES: Behind the field-level seats in sections MM and NN on the third-base side.

STADIUM FOOD: The best bets are huge hamburgers sold on the first-base side for $3.50. Italian ices ($2.50) are hand scooped and funnel cakes are kept hot in covered trays. Hammerin' Hank hot dogs are sold solo, or in kid's or family meal combos, which save you some change. Pan pizza, soft ice cream, and fresh lemonade are available.

SMOKING POLICY: Smoke-free facility. Sections 114 and 214, the last sections on the third-base side, are alcohol-free family sections.

VISITING TEAM HOTEL: Holiday Inn Historic District (301 Government St., Mobile, 36602, tel. 334/694–0100 or 800/692–6662).

TOURISM INFORMATION: City of Mobile Visitor Welcome Center (150 S. Royal St., Mobile, AL 36602, tel. 334/434–7304 or 800/566–2453).

Mobile: Hank Aaron Stadium

Atlanta didn't have the good sense to do it, but Mobile did. The new Mobile stadium, opened in 1997, was named after baseball's home-run king Hank Aaron, a Mobile native. It's a baseball beauty worthy of Aaron's famous name, and the great man himself threw out the first ball on opening night, April 17, 1997.

Fans enter the $8-million stadium through a handsome, redbrick building, nicely contrasted by a dark-green metal roof and dark-green awnings. The name of the stadium is spelled out in ironwork between two sets of crossed bats above the entrance. An oversized baseball with the magic number 755, signifying Aaron's extraordinary major-league home-run feat, hangs just below the stadium name in the entranceway. Flags of the other cities in the Double A Southern League fly from the top of the grandstand.

This was the first minor-league stadium we have seen with the luxury box seats on the field level. The elegant redbrick wall between the dugouts behind home plate pays homage to the great Wrigley Field. Regular box and reserved seats are in the grandstand's second deck, starting about 15 ft above the field. There is a large video scoreboard beyond the fence in right-center field and a clubhouse beyond the right-field wall. Trees frame much of the view beyond the outfield wall. Below the grandstand there is a wide concourse full of concession stands. The large restaurant past first base is reserved for season ticket holders.

Amazingly, this town that has produced four members of baseball's Hall of Fame—Hank Aaron, Willie McCovey, LeRoy "Satchel" Paige, and Billy Williams—has had a hard time keeping a professional baseball team. With the exception of a recent two-year fling with the independent Texas-Louisiana League in 1994–95, Mobile has not had a minor-league team affiliated with a major-league team since 1970. Mobile has been in and out of the Southern League and its predecessor, Southern Association, since 1887. The new team is called the BayBears in honor of the Mobile Bears teams of the 1920s, '40s, and '50s. The 1947 Mobile team won the Southern Association title with a first baseman named Chuck Connors, who became famous as television's "Rifleman."

More Mobile Baseball

National African-American Archives Museum. This new building has a collection of baseball memorabilia honoring two of Mobile's favorite sons—Henry "Hank" Aaron and pitching great LeRoy "Satchel" Paige. In addition to some Negro League material, the Archives houses the Hank Aaron Fan Club. *564 Martin Luther King, Jr. Ave., Mobile, tel. 334/433–8511. Donations welcome. Open Tues.–Fri. 9–noon and 1–4.*

Where to Stay

Visiting Team Motel: Holiday Inn Historic District. This 17-story, cylinder-style hotel has a rooftop restaurant and is adjacent to a new Holiday Inn Express. The rooms are large, with good city views. *301 Government St., Mobile 36602, tel. 334/694–0100 or 800/692–6662, fax 334/694–0160. 210 rooms. Facilities: 2 restaurants, pool, coin laundry. AE, DC, D, MC, V. $$*

Clarion Hotel. The pleasant, inexpensive rooms in this 20-story hotel are nicely decorated in paisley. Each room has Nintendo. There are sit-down restaurants plus a fast-food court in the lobby. The hotel is set back on a busy commercial strip adjacent to two malls. As you're traveling north, it's off of I-65, one exit from the ballpark. *3101 Airport Blvd., Mobile 36606, tel. 334/476–6400 or 800/252–7466, fax 334/476–9360. 250 rooms. Facilities: 2 restaurants, pool. AE, DC, C, MC, V. $*

Where to Eat

Original Oyster House. This informal seafood haven delivers tin buckets of silverware and a roll of paper towels to your polished wood table as you overlook Mobile Bay. Dig right into the rich dark-red gumbo with rice on top, or the fine crawfish po'boys, amberjack sandwiches, oyster loaves, fried crawfish tails, and other regional fish fare. Marine artifacts fill the walls and ceilings, but you'll concentrate on the authentic, Gulf Coast seafood. *Hwy. 98, ½ mi east of Battleship Park, Mobile, tel. 334/626–2188. AE, DC, MC, V. $$*

Cock of the Walk. Get your fried pickles here, along with fried catfish and tasty chicken dinners. Church buses deliver eaters to this popular, sprawling restaurant with a riverboat theme. There are no reservations, so a honky-tonk pianist plays while you wait in bent-twig chairs. Heaping pie tins of fried food are delivered to rustic wood tables, where waiters flip your cornbread in cast iron skillets. There is a standard children's menu. *4815 Halls Bells Rd., Mobile, tel. 334/666–1875. AE, MC, V. $*

Dick Russell's. Country breakfasts and barbecue are the focus of this cozy refuge between a pawnshop and a state liquor store. Fresh biscuits are made every 15 minutes, and fine peach preserves are on every green-checked vinyl table. As you concentrate on bargain plate lunches—with a multitude of Southern vegetables—bear skins, model airplanes, and other amusements hang overhead. Inexpensive eggs, hotcakes, omelets, and meats make this place popular for breakfast. There is a kid's menu for lunch and dinner. *Hwy. 90 West, Tillman's Corner, Mobile, tel. 334/661–6090. MC, V. $*

Entertainments

Battleship Memorial Park. Get a taste of World War II life by climbing throughout the huge battleship USS *Alabama*, the submarine USS *Drum*, and 21 combat aircraft at this bayside complex. The *Alabama*'s crew of 2,500 fought in Leyte, the Gilbert Islands, and Okinawa, and led the American fleet into Tokyo Bay after surrender documents were signed in September 1945. The 35,000-ton ship was an immense floating city, complete with soda fountain and bakery that produced 550 loaves daily. You'll need mobility to climb ladders and navigate high doorsills, but the main deck is handicapped accessible. Keep children close—there are many decks and routes. The hardware is impressive and a rose garden, gift shop, and concession stand allow you to spend hours here. Parking is $2. *Battleship Pkwy. (U.S. 90), at I–10 exit 27, Mobile, tel. 334/433–2703. Admission: $8 adults, $4 ages 6–11; under 6, free. Open daily 8–7.*

Exploreum. This science museum is filled with hands-on exhibits and displays on electricity, sound, water, lasers, gravity, and the like. It has two floors of controlled mayhem and learning. An IMAX theatre has a separate fee and shows four films yearly. *65 Government St., Mobile, tel. 334/208–6883. Admission (to museum or IMAX): $6.75 adults, $5.75 senior citizens and ages 3–18, $5.25 ages 2–12. Combo ticket: $10 adults, $9*

senior citizens and ages 3–18, $8 ages 2–12. *Open Mon.–Wed. 9–5, Thurs. 9–8, Fri. and Sat. 9–9, Sun. 10–5.*

Sights to See

Bienville Square. This 1850 park named for Mobile's founder, Jean Baptiste le Moyne Sieur de Bienville, has city-sponsored events for children on Thursday, and art and storytelling during the summer. The square is the site of Mobile's Mardi Gras, which began in 1703, before the larger and more famous celebration in New Orleans. While Mobile's former grandeur has faded, you can still see its outstanding 19th-century architecture, complete with cast-iron balconies and Victorian and Greek Revival details. For more architectural delights, wander down Dauphin Street, named for the son of Louis XIV, and visit Cathedral Square. *Bienville Sq., Mobile, bounded by St. Francis, St. Michael, Conception, and St. Joseph Sts.*

Fort Condé. You'll find Mobile's Welcome Center at this fort, where the flags of four nations flew during the 18th and 19th centuries. The French first claimed the area, later to become Mobile, in 1699 and set up headquarters there. They named their city after the native Maubilla Indians. The British took the fort peacefully by treaty in 1763 and ruled Mobile for 17 years until the Spanish took control during the American Revolutionary War. The United States captured the city in the War of 1812. The fort eventually fell into ruin, but fortunately it has been partially reconstructed and contains various historical exhibits, including models of the fort as it looked throughout history. Discount coupons and walking tours of historical areas are available here. *150 South Royal St., Mobile, tel. 334/434–7304 or 800/566–2453. Free. Open daily 8–5.*

BIRMINGHAM BARONS

League: Southern League • **Major League Affiliation:** Chicago White Sox • **Class:** AA • **Stadium:** Hoover Metropolitan Stadium • **Opened:** 1988 • **Capacity:** 10,800 • **Dimensions:** LF: 340, CF: 405, RF: 340 • **Surface:** grass • **Season:** Apr.–Labor Day

STADIUM LOCATION: 100 Ben Chapman Dr., Birmingham, AL 35244.

TEAM WEB SITE: www.barons.com

GETTING THERE: From I–65 or Hwy. 280, I–459 toward Tuscaloosa. Go past Galleria to Hwy. 150 exit in Hoover, turn left, ¼ mi to Stadium Trace Parkway, right to stadium.

PARKING: Ample parking, $2.

TICKET INFORMATION: Box 360007, Birmingham, AL 35236, tel. 205/988–3200, fax 205/988–9698.

PRICE RANGE: Box seats $6.50 adults, $5.50 ages 14 and under and senior citizens; general admission $4.50 adults, $3.50 children 14 and under and senior citizens.

GAME TIME: Mon.–Sat. 7:10 PM, Sun. 2 PM (Apr.–June) and 6 PM (July–Sept.); gates open 90 min before game.

TIPS ON SEATING: Box seats not expensive for such a modern facility and discounts available for children.

SEATING FOR PEOPLE WITH DISABILITIES: Near front entrance of stadium behind home plate on concourse level.

STADIUM FOOD: The best buy is soft-serve ice cream for $1 per cone, available on the third-base side. The $3.50 chicken tenders are large and come with french fries. One order may be sufficient for two youngsters. The best drinks are the frozen cherry Cokes for $3 each and the fresh lemonade for $2.50. There are chicken breast sandwiches, pizza, and Italian sausages for $3.50, but all are uninteresting.

SMOKING POLICY: General admission sections 205 (on first-base side) and 210 (on third-base side) are no-smoking/no-alcohol family areas.

VISITING TEAM HOTEL: Riverchase Inn (1800 Riverchase Dr., Hoover, AL 35244, tel. 205/985–7500 or 800/239–2401).

TOURISM INFORMATION: Greater Birmingham Convention and Visitors Bureau (2200 9th Ave. N, Birmingham, AL 35203, tel. 205/252–9825).

Birmingham: Hoover Metropolitan Stadium

Happily, the 1990s saw the return of preserved, city-center stadiums, a departure from the 1980s stadium trend—new parks in the suburbs. Unfortunately, the Hoover Metropolitan Stadium is a first-class effort of the '80s genre. It is the baseball equivalent of a suburban shopping mall—big, safe, clean, and efficient. It is a fine place to play and watch a baseball game, but, the product of white flight and suburban sprawl, almost completely lacking the character of its predecessor, Birmingham's Rickwood Field.

The Hoover Met stadium, which opened in 1988, was built a dozen miles from downtown Birmingham in a fast-growing suburb at a cost of $14.5 million. It is owned by the city of Hoover and was designed by local architects Gresham, Smith & Partners in collaboration with HOK Sport of Kansas City.

As you emerge from the tree-lined roadway of a suburban development and approach Hoover Metropolitan Stadium, the ballpark appears enormous. This place must seat 20,000 people, we thought. Well, it doesn't. It has seats for 10,800. Once you get into the stadium, you can see that the large, slanted concrete roof high above the skyboxes creates the effect of a much larger facility. It is a rather imposing place for minor-league baseball. Initial plans contemplated the possibility of a second deck for Triple A baseball.

There are a dozen luxury skyboxes, 3,202 red box seats, and room for another 7,500 general admission fans on blue aluminum benches with backs. They can squeeze more in because of seating in well-conceived grass hillsides beyond the first- and third-base lines. More than 16,000 showed up for a fireworks night the season basketball superstar Michael Jordan decided to find out if he could play a game with a smaller ball.

Here in the suburbs, the automobile is king, and there is plenty of parking right at the entrance to the stadium. There are trees beyond the out-field fence in right and center and an athletic field beyond the left-field wall.

The music is lively, and the Barons have a giant dog named Babe Ruff for a mascot. Most of the stands and facilities were built on the wrong side of the concourse, backing up to the seating area. They cannot open the concourse to the field as several of the most successful 1990s sta-diums have done.

More Birmingham Baseball

Rickwood Field. Future Hall of Fame relief pitcher Rollie Fingers—as noted for his great handlebar mustache as for his tremendous pitching—was the main attraction for the "Mus-tache Madness" game we attended at the Hoover Met. Fingers played for the 1967 South-ern League champion Birmingham Athletics with teammates Reggie Jackson and Tony LaRussa. We asked Fingers what memories he has of playing at Rickwood Field. "Getting hit in the face and being out six weeks," he said good-naturedly as he signed "Save Rickwood!" over his autograph.

A Sunday-morning visit to Rickwood Field was the highlight of our trip to the Deep South. Rodney Dalton, one of a legion of fans working to preserve Rickwood, arranged to get us into the stadium to meet with Coke Matthews, a local advertising executive who is working relentlessly as a volunteer to put Rickwood Field into its 1948 prime form. Matthews explained that in 1948 the Birmingham Black Barons had a championship season and the white Barons—shortened from the original nickname Coal Barons—won the Dixie Series Championship. The Barons set an attendance record not sur-passed until their Michael Jordan year.

What's so special about Rickwood? Everything. The stadium, listed on the National Register of Historic Places, is the oldest baseball park in America, according to the National Park Ser-vice. Nothing we have seen so evokes the spirit of baseball in its glory days of Cobb, Johnson, and Ruth. You can almost hear the organ music and smell the cigar smoke.

Birmingham industrialist Rick Woodward built the stadium in 1910; the stadium name is a con-traction of his name. Woodward was deter-mined to build a great stadium, the first minor-league park of concrete and steel. He had family friend Philadelphia's legendary Connie Mack come down and lay out the field. The lights, some of the first installed in a minor-league ballpark, hang some 20 ft out from the roof over the field.

The field evokes magnificent memories. Future Hall of Famers Hank Aaron, Ty Cobb, Reggie Jackson, Jackie Robinson, Pie Traynor, and Ted Williams all played here. It is Rickwood lore that the longest home run in history was hit here—a blast by Babe Ruth that was said to have landed in a freight train moving along the tracks just beyond the right-field wall and not to have stopped until it got to Nashville, 200 mi away.

Coke Matthews took us past the wooden out-field wall to show us the other most legendary blast in Rickwood history. Before Babe Ruth reinvented baseball, the home run wasn't a big deal. The balls were dead and the fences were deep. The concrete wall in Rickwood was 405 ft from home in left, 470 ft in center, and 334 ft in right. In many of these stadiums, wooden fences were installed within the original field. At Rick-wood, a huge scoreboard was installed in left center. In 1948, Baron Walt Dropo blasted a towering shot that went over the left corner of the scoreboard and hit the top of the concrete wall in deep center field. Beyond the trashed scoreboard and beneath the vines, there is an X painted where Dropo's shot hit the wall.

Willie Mays was discovered here. Bull Connor, before he became internationally infamous for turning dogs loose on civil rights activists, was a broadcaster for the white Barons. The white and black Barons shared Rickwood for decades, but until 1966 a city ordinance prohibited black and white players from playing together. In 1967, Reggie Jackson helped Birmingham win the Southern League championship.

The producers of the 1995 movie *Cobb* replaced the modern scoreboard with a larger, hand-operated one and painted period ads on the wooden outfield walls. Coke Matthews's Friends of Rickwood continue to work on the essential restoration and have an ambitious master plan.

We wish the investment in the Hoover Met had been made to restore Rickwood. But you should visit both and decide for yourself. Consider this: from the 1880s, big-time baseball in Birmingham was played at the **Slag Pile,** a 600-seat stadium by the railroad tracks. Adults who could not get into the small grandstand sat on the slag pile—waste from the mining process—above and outside the outfield fence. Kids cut holes in the fence to get a view. After several decades at the Slag Pile, the decision was made that the Birmingham area needed a new, state-of-the-art facility. They built it out in the then suburbs: they built Rickwood Field.

Rickwood Field is still in constant use by high-school, industrial, and senior-citizen leagues, and for an occasional movie. If you are lucky, you might find it open for a game. To get to Rickwood Field from downtown Birmingham, drive out 3rd Avenue West about 2 mi past I-65 and take a left on 12th Street West; it's a block from there to the stadium. For information, call or write Friends of Rickwood (2100 Morris Ave., Birmingham, AL 35203, tel. 205/458-8161).

Where to Stay

Visiting Team Hotel: Riverchase Inn at the Galleria. This modern two-story motel is on the edge of a shopping mall. The view is of parking lots and a gas station, but the motel is clean and convenient to the ballpark. It offers a free Continental breakfast. *1800 Riverchase Dr., Hoover 35244, tel. 205/985-7500 or 800/239-2401, fax 205/733-8122. 139 rooms. Facilities: pool. AE, D, DC, MC, V. $*

Courtyard by Marriott. This three-story hotel is modern and 1 mi from the Galleria mall. The rooms are standard size and freshly decorated. *1824 Montgomery Ave. S, Hoover 35244, tel. 205/988-5000 or 800/443-6000, fax 205/988-4659. 153 rooms. Facilities: restaurant, outdoor pool, exercise room, coin laundry, baby-sitting. AE, D, DC, MC, V. $$*

Holiday Inn Redmont City Centre. This historic downtown hotel has high ceilings, a marble lobby floor, and a sidewalk café. Ask for a room close to the top of its 14 floors for a nice city view. *2101 5th Ave. N, at 21st St., Birmingham 35203, tel. and fax 205/324-2101 or tel. 800/465-4329. 110 rooms. Facilities: restaurant, café, sauna, hot tub. AE, D, DC, MC, V. $$*

Where to Eat

John's Restaurant. This venerable seafood restaurant has long been a part of the city's history. A must-try is the unique shredded cabbage with its signature red dressing. Portions are generous, and there's a wide variety of vegetables. A children's menu is available. *112 21st St. N, Birmingham, tel. 205/322-6014. AE, D, DC, MC, V. $$*

Browdy's Fine Foods. This new, neon-filled incarnation of a 52-year-old restaurant and deli is popular before and after games. It offers New York deli food, especially corned beef, Reuben, and pastrami sandwiches. There are also po'boys on homemade buns, brownies, and cookies. Box lunches can be packed. It is 10 mi from the stadium, near the zoo and botanical gardens. *2713 Culver Rd., Birmingham, tel. 205/879-8585. Zoo exit off I-280 to Mountain Brook Shopping Center. AE, D, DC, MC, V. $*

Dreamland BBQ. This 115-seat downtown restaurant has a one-item menu—pork ribs—and the apt slogan "Ain't Nothin' Like 'Em Nowhere!" There's tea, soft drinks, or beer to wash them down and some white bread to mop up sauce, but that's it. The ribs are meaty and flavorful, and eating them on wooden tables is a happy, messy time. Nostalgic eaters can order the sauce long-distance at 800/752-0544. *1427 14th Ave. S, Birmingham, tel. 205/933-2133. AE, D, MC, V. $*

Ollie's BBQ. A huge world globe advertises this longtime restaurant from I-65. It's been selling great barbecue, baked ham, chili, six kinds of pies, and six types of Bibles since 1926. There are chicken plates or children's BBQ. *515 University Blvd., Birmingham, tel. 205/324-9485. D, MC, V. $*

Sights to See

Birmingham Civil Rights Institute. This modern, exhibit-filled museum presents a vivid description of America's civil rights movement. A 12-minute film covers Birmingham history. A "barriers gallery" includes replicas of a segregated streetcar, a classroom, a courtroom, and a church. The Confrontation Gallery illustrates the violence surrounding black liberation. Voting rights efforts, the March on Washington, Dr. King's "Letter from a Birmingham Jail," and other milestones are shown. A window overlooks the 16th Street Baptist Church, with photographs describing the four African-American children attending Sunday school who were killed here in 1963 when the church was bombed. *520 16th St. N, Birmingham, tel. 205/328–9696. Suggested donations: $4 adults, $2 college students. Open Tues.–Sat. 10–5, Sun. 1–5.*

Red Mountain Museum. Geology comes alive in a walkway carved into Red Mountain. It also houses the country's only solar telescope that's open to the public. Here's one place where you can look safely at the sun's surface. Tickets in combination with Discovery Place are available. *1421 22nd St. S, Birmingham, tel. 205/933–4104. Admission: $3 adults, $2 ages under 16. Open Tues.–Sat. 10–4:30, Sun. 1–4:30.*

Vulcan Statue. The city's landmark is a 50-ft iron figure of Vulcan, god of fire, on Red Mountain. Created for the 1904 Louisiana Purchase Expo in St. Louis, it lay in ruins on Rickwood Field until it was reassembled as a monument to the iron ore that built Birmingham. The city is currently trying to raise $11 million to renovate Vulcan and the surrounding park. In the meantime, you can no longer take an elevator to the top and view the city. There are still great photo ops with children sitting on Vulcan's sandaled foot at the base. Vulcan's torch is green normally, but it burns red for 24 hours if there's been a traffic fatality in the city. *U.S. 31, Birmingham, tel. 205/328–2863. Admission: $1 ages over 5. Open 8 AM–11 PM.*

Montgomery, Alabama

You should go the extra 90 mi to Montgomery, the Alabama capital. Here in Montgomery, the forces of white supremacy and equal rights have battled toe to toe. Both efforts are celebrated here. The Dexter Avenue King Memorial Baptist Church, where the decision to launch a bus boycott was made in 1955, is just one block from the State Capitol building that served as the first capitol of the Confederacy for three months before the move to Richmond. Martin Luther King, Jr. ended the historic 1965 Selma-to-Montgomery civil rights march on the steps of the Capitol building. Not far away, on the west portico of the Capitol, there is a bronze star that marks the spot where Jefferson Davis

took his oath of office as president of the Confederacy a little more than 100 years before.

Civil Rights Memorial. This unusual waterfall was built by the Southern Poverty Law Center and designed by Maya Lin, the architect of the Vietnam War Memorial in Washington, D.C. A stone is inscribed with the names of 40 civil rights martyrs. Water flows over black marble with a quote from Martin Luther King, Jr.: "… until justice rolls down like waters and righteousness like a mighty stream." *400 Washington Ave., near Hull St., Montgomery, tel. 205/263–3970.*

The Dexter Avenue King Memorial Baptist Church. Here, around the corner from the memorial, is the church where Martin Luther King, Jr. served as pastor. *454 Dexter Ave., Montgomery, tel. 334/263–3970. Donations appreciated for church tours. Church tours Mon.–Thurs. 10–2, Fri. 10, Sat. 10–2.*

Rosa Parks Marker. Rosa Parks and Hank Williams share a historic marker in front of the once popular and now deserted Empire Theatre. Parks, a seamstress, refused to give up her bus seat to a white man in 1955 and was arrested. The incident sparked a citywide boycott of buses for one year and launched the Rev. Martin Luther King, Jr. into leadership as chairman of the boycott committee. Williams won a contest at the Empire in 1938 that began his country music career. *Molton and Montgomery Sts., Montgomery.*

State Capitol. Montgomery became Alabama's capital city in 1846. The first Capitol was built in 1847 and burned in 1849. The present Capitol was built on the same site—known as Goat's Hill—in 1850 and 1851. The handsome Greek Revival–style building has six Corinthian columns on each facade and a distinctive clock over the front portico. The state has done an outstanding job of restoring most of the Capitol to the style of the 1870s and 1880s. Note the eight large murals just under the Capitol dome. A self-guided tour of the Capitol is available. The real legislative business of the state is now done in the Alabama Statehouse, just down the hill from the Capitol on Union Street. *Washington Ave., Montgomery, tel. 205/242–3184 or 800/252–2262. Open Mon.–Sat. 9–4, Sun. noon–4.*

PLANTATIONS AND PALMETTOS

7

MYRTLE BEACH, CHARLESTON, SAVANNAH

Begin a coastal baseball trip with a visit to the handsome new stadium in Myrtle Beach, home of the spirited Pelicans of the Carolina League. Travel 100 mi south to watch baseball in the beautiful coastal city of Charleston. In the same weekend, you can see historic Savannah, as it is only 100 mi south of Charleston. Charleston and Savannah are members of the Sally League, the South Atlantic League, and they represent the best of the new and old stadiums.

The redbrick Myrtle Beach stadium is the epicenter of the resort city's new growth of fancy theme restaurants and Broadway on the Beach, a sprawling shopping plaza built around a man-made 23-acre lake.

The Ashley River is the dramatic backdrop for Charleston's gem of a small ballpark. You can watch the sun set over the river in the early innings of a night game. Its RiverDogs have a kid-friendly mascot, Charlie, who has his own hometown ice cream at the park. During the day, you can delight your eyes and appetite at the Old City Market. It is tolerable even on steamy days to walk through the city's elegant, shady streets to the Battery at Charleston Harbor and take a boat ride to Fort Sumter.

The views are of lush, overgrown oaks along sections of Route 17 South as you head to Savannah. The Spanish moss hangs in the trees, giving a languid look to Savannah, a city you can explore in a horse-drawn carriage that takes you to many of the city's 21 squares. The entire downtown is a National Historic Landmark District, and it's easier to concentrate on the architecture and ambience if someone else is driving. The baseball field is beautiful, too, with an inspiring tree-lined entrance, a brick archway, and a pine-tree backdrop to the outfield. Savannah's City Market is lively, and the swimming is perfect for children on the Tybee Island beaches, 18 mi to the east.

MYRTLE BEACH PELICANS

League: Carolina League • **Stadium:** Coastal Federal Field • **Major League Affiliation:** Atlanta Braves • **Class:** A • **Opened:** 1999 • **Capacity:** 5,634 • **Dimensions:** LF: 328, CF: 400, RF: 325 • **Surface:** grass • **Season:** Apr.–Labor Day

STADIUM LOCATION: 1251 21st Ave. N, Myrtle Beach, SC 29577.

TEAM WEB SITE: www.myrtlebeachpelicans.com

GETTING THERE: The park is north of the Myrtle Beach airport and west of the city's Convention Center. Take the Hwy. 17 bypass (not Business 17) to 21st Ave. N. The park is a half mile on the right.

PARKING: Free parking for 800 cars adjacent to park and overflow across 21st Ave. in shopping complex.

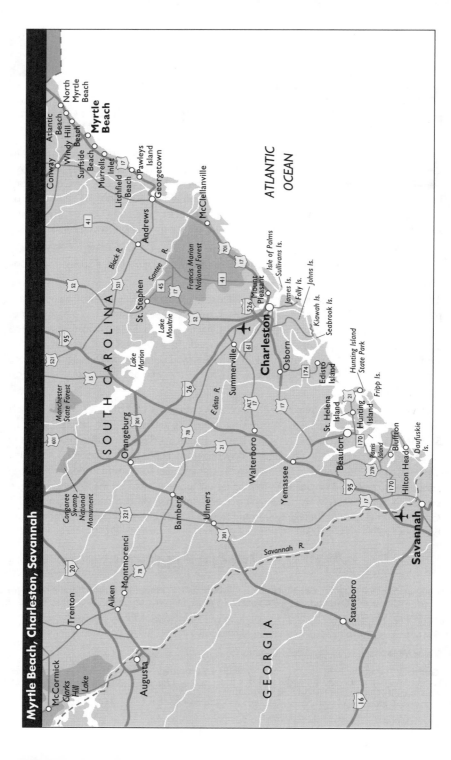

TICKET INFORMATION: 1251 21st Ave. N, Myrtle Beach, SC 29577, tel. 843/918–6000, fax 843/918–6029.

PRICE RANGE: Box seats $7.50; reserved seats $6.50; general admission $3.

GAME TIME: 7:05 PM, gates open 90 min. before games.

TIPS ON SEATING: There is only a small section of aluminum bench seating along the third-base line for general admission—most of the general admission is lawn seating. If the bench seating is full, order a soft drink at the Pelican Porch beyond first base and sit at its dark-green picnic tables. The reserved seats throughout the park have good views, and many are covered by a large green roof; all are in shade for night games except for the third-base side. Nearly all of the box seats have been sold to season ticket holders.

SEATING FOR PEOPLE WITH DISABILITIES: Top row of box seats on the main concourse along first, home, and third.

STADIUM FOOD: The hand-scooped Italian ice, in 11 flavors, is delicious, and there are $3 root beer floats. All other offerings are typical ballpark fare. Prices are good—$3 for a burger, $1.50 for a turkey dog and $2.50 for a pizza slice. Overlooking the field, there's a **Pelican Porch** picnic pavilion, but no outside food is allowed in.

SMOKING POLICY: Smoking prohibited in seating areas but allowed in two designated areas along the first- and third-base sides.

VISITING TEAM HOTEL: Hampton Inn. (4709 N. Kings Hwy., Myrtle Beach, SC 29577, tel. 843/449–5231 or 800/426–7866).

TOURISM INFORMATION: Myrtle Beach Area Chamber of Commerce (1200 N. Oak St., Myrtle Beach, SC 29578, tel. 803/626–7444 or 800/356–3016).

Myrtle Beach: Coastal Federal Field

Whether you're a hometown fan or a vacationer, you'll love Myrtle Beach's new stadium: though the food is ordinary, the beautiful setting and close-in action are not.

The $12.5-million stadium is handsome and a testament to a faithful fan, former mayor Bob Grissom, who would not let baseball die in Myrtle Beach. The city's first minor-league team, the Hurricanes, left in 1992, and Grissom led the effort for a city/county financial package. Grissom died before the inaugural season opened on April 12, 1999, but his achievement lives. The team and stadium represent a shift for Myrtle Beach from tourist stop to a thriving, year-round city.

There's a strong link to the parent team—all the new-looking seats are from Fulton County Stadium, the former home of the Atlanta Braves. A local architecture firm, Mozingo & Wallace, designed the grandstand. Redbrick columns and yellow brick accents give the facility a retro look. Palm trees line the outfield walls and a pine grove adjoins the parking lot.

The field has one of the largest scoreboard screens in the minors. The 48-ft screen has instant replay and TV, meaning fans can watch Braves games during rain delays.

This is a family-friendly park. While there are now children's play areas inside many ballparks, the one here—funded by a local Optimist group, the city, and the Pelicans—is also handicapped accessible. Every Tuesday, kids run the bases post-game. Every Sunday is family autograph night. The two pelican mascots, Splash and his mother, Pelly, stir up excitement at the games. They are joined by Dinger, a yellow Labrador retriever, who runs the bases and shags fly balls that he brings to the umpire; he's even learning to retrieve bats.

Nearly all of the seats have good sight lines. If you want to see the pitchers warm up, the far end of Pelican Porch is practically in the bullpen.

Where to Stay

Discount tickets to Pelicans games are awarded at 30 area hotels, motels, and campgrounds; ask for them at check-in.

Visiting Team Motel: Hampton Inn. This modern hotel has standard-size rooms with contemporary furnishings. It is two mi north of the ballpark and two blocks to the beach. Guests receive a free Continental breakfast. *4709 N. Kings Hwy., Myrtle Beach, SC 29577, tel. 843/449–5231 or 800/426–7866, fax 449–1528. 152 rooms. Facilities: restaurant, indoor pool, fitness room, laundry. AE, D, DC, MC, V. $$*

Fairfield Inn. This new four-story hotel is on a free trolley line that stops at the ballpark. Nicely landscaped and quiet, it is set back from the busy avenue that adjoins Broadway on the Beach. The rooms are spacious and clean, and there's a free Continental breakfast for guests. *1350 Paradise Cir., Myrtle Beach, SC 29577, tel. 803/444–8097 or 800/228–2800, fax 803/444–8394. 111 rooms, with 10 suites. Facilities: pool, hot tub. AE, D, DC, MC, V. $$*

Hampton Inn–Broadway at the Beach. This handsome eight-story hotel is tropical yellow, with a red-tile roof. Palm trees surround a large sundeck with views of paddleboats on an inland waterway. The brightly colored furnishings are Deco nautical. Guests receive a complimentary Continental breakfast in the airy lobby. Free trolleys take you to the ballpark. *1140 Celebrity Cir., Myrtle Beach, SC 29577, tel. 843/916–0600 or 888/916–2001, fax 843/946–6308. 141 rooms, 30 suites. Facilities: restaurant, pool, sauna, exercise room, game room, coin laundry. AE, D, DC, MC, V. $$*

La Quinta. This attractive four-story hotel is two blocks from the ballpark. Rooms are bright and large, with big baths. Continental breakfasts, free with stay, are served in the cheery lobby. *1561 21st Ave. N, Myrtle Beach, SC 29677, tel. 843/916–8801 or 800/687–6667, fax 843/916–8701. 128 rooms, 12 suites. Facilities: restaurant, pool, exercise room. AE, D, DC, MC, V. $$*

Where to Eat

Bullwinkle's. Look for the Frostbite Falls Water Tower built into this clever cartoon restaurant,

½ mi from the ballpark. Children can play in an arcade/gym area or watch characters like Rocky, Boris, and Natasha perform on stage or on TV screens. Meals (soups, salads, burgers) are ordered at a counter and your food is delivered to you at wooden booths or long tables. Your kids can have breakfast with the cartoon's characters. *1002 29th Ave. N, Myrtle Beach, tel. 843/626–3091. AE, D, MC, V. $*

NASCAR Cafe. Your senses go on overload, watching big screen car races and taking in the race banners, ads, helmets, and even cars suspended from the ceiling. The food is surprisingly good, with oversize plates of salads, catfish, chili, onion rings, and the like. Kids' baskets have checkered flag napkins. The overstuffed, red vinyl booth seats look like car seats, only slightly larger. Display cases focus on South Carolina racing stars. The café borders a NASCAR speed park, with 8 tracks and kiddie rides. *1808 21st Ave. N, Myrtle Beach, tel. 843/946–7223. AE, D, MC, V. $*

Entertainments

Myrtle Beach is the queen of golf, with 97 real courses and 43 miniature-golf courses. Many of the minigolf courses have wacky themes and are connected to water parks, batting cages, and other amusements. Half- and full-day fishing boats are plentiful, along with parasailing, and, of course, the clean public beaches of the Atlantic Ocean's Grand Strand. Several piers will rent to you fishing tackle and one-day licenses, and let you troll from their docks.

Family Kingdom. Substantially rebuilt after Hurricane Hugo in 1989, this amusement park has the state's only wooden roller coaster, the Swamp Fox. There are 35 other rides, including a Ferris wheel, a log flume, and a vintage carousel. There's a good arcade and a kiddie section. *Fourth Ave. S, Myrtle Beach, tel. 843/626–3447. Admission: free with pay-per-ride. All-day wrist bands $18.22. Open Apr.–Sept., weekdays 4–midnight, weekends 1–midnight.*

Myrtle Beach Pavilion. This 37-acre downtown amusement park is known for its 70-ft-tall steel roller coaster, the Corkscrew, a wood track coaster, the Hurricane, and 40 other rides, many of them thrill producing. For an extra fee you can rent go-karts and visit a large alcohol-free teen dance club. You can stroll the boardwalk for free. *812 N. Ocean Blvd., Myrtle Beach, tel. 843/448–6456. Admission: free with pay-per-ride. All-day wrist bands $21.45 for ages 6–adult, $10.95 ages 5 and younger. Open Mar.–Oct., daily 1–midnight.*

The Palace Theater. Big-name acts, like Vince Gill, Julie Andrews, the Bolshoi Ballet, Harry Belafonte, and Aretha Franklin play at this attractive new auditorium down the avenue from the ballpark. *21st Ave. N, at Hwy. 17 Bypass, Myrtle Beach, tel. 843/448–0588 or 800/905–4228.*

Sights to See

Huntington Beach State Park. Try inlet kayaking with a naturalist guide or learn about sea turtles at this 2,500-acre wildlife preserve. Knowledgeable and friendly park rangers conduct a variety of programs each day and night. Alligators are on view, and observation decks, trails, and boardwalks get you close to the wildlife. *U.S. 17, 3 mi. south of Murrell's Inlet, 17 mi south of Myrtle Beach, tel. 843/237–4440. Admission: Mar.–Nov. $3 adults, $1.50 ages 6–12. Free Dec.–Feb.*

CHARLESTON RIVERDOGS

League: South Atlantic League • **Stadium:** Joseph P. Riley Jr. Ballpark • **Major League Affiliation:** Tampa Bay Devil Rays • **Class:** A • **Opened:** 1997 • **Capacity:** 5,908 • **Dimensions:** LF: 305, CF: 386, RF: 337 • **Surface:** grass • **Season:** Apr.–Labor Day

STADIUM LOCATION: 360 Fishbourne St., Charleston, SC 29403.

TEAM WEB SITE: www.riverdogs.com

GETTING THERE: From I–26, exit at Hwy. 17S, drive to Lockwood Blvd. Right on Lockwood; ballpark is at boulevard's end. From Hwy. 17 in the downtown, exit onto Lockwood Blvd., go ½ mi to the stadium.

PARKING: Ample $3 city parking adjacent to the park.

TICKET INFORMATION: Box 20849, Charleston, SC 29413, tel. 843/577–3647, fax 843/723–2641.

PRICE RANGE: Reserved box seats $8; field reserve $6, upper reserve $5, general admission $4 adults.

GAME TIME: Mon.–Sat. 7:05 PM, Sun. 2:05 (Apr.–May) or 5:05 (June–Aug.). Gates open 90 min before games.

TIPS ON SEATING: Fans above the internal concourse in the reserved bleacher and general admission seats on the third-base side have a spectacular view of the sunset over Ashley River (behind first-base dugout). These are aluminum benches with backs. To avoid the setting sun, sit on the first-base side. Sections 104–116 are sold out to season ticket holders.

SEATING FOR PEOPLE WITH DISABILITIES: Areas designated throughout stadium; available behind sections 103, 108–112, 117, 118, 212.

STADIUM FOOD: This park really focuses on Low Country food, serving wonderful she-crab soup and popcorn shrimp, as well as fruit trays, veggies and dip, good grilled bratwurst, burgers, pizza, and lemonade. For tourists who may not get a chance to eat outside the park, this is a chance to get some regional flavor. There are also good BBQ pork sandwiches with **Sticky Fingers**, a local restaurant. Kids love to turn their mouths blue eating the purple RiverDog ripple ice cream. There are four large concession stands.

SMOKING POLICY: Smoking prohibited in seating areas but allowed in concourse.

VISITING TEAM HOTEL: Howard Johnson Riverfront (250 Spring St., Charleston, SC 29403, tel. 843/722–4000 or 800/654–2000).

TOURISM INFORMATION: Charleston Trident Convention & Visitors Bureau (Box 975, Charleston, SC 29402, tel. 843/853–8000).

Charleston: Joseph P. Riley Jr. Ballpark

Baseball fans in Charleston have a double treat—a handsome downtown stadium on the Ashley River and Mike Veeck, club president and the enthusiastic and imaginative son of baseball's premier promoter, Bill Veeck. Fans might also run into the team's chairman, actor Bill Murray, visiting the "The Joe," as the stadium's known.

The 5,908-seat stadium, Joseph P. Riley Jr. Ballpark, was designed by the HOK Sports Facilities Group. The most striking feature of the ballpark is its location adjacent to Brittlebank Park along the Ashley River. Many seats, especially those facing the left-field fence, have a spectacular view of the sunset over the river. We usually advise you to sit with the setting sun at your back, but not in Charleston!

The grandstand is J-shaped, with its long stem down the third-base line. Skyboxes and an attractive green metal roof cover more than 20% of the top rows of seats behind the dugouts and home plate. Seats have backs and are as close to the field as rules allow, providing an intimate baseball experience.

Two picnic areas overlook the field, and a wide variety of foods, including Low Country seafood, Mexican, German, and American standbys, is available.

Mike Veeck honored Hall of Famer Larry Doby by naming Joe's right-field deck after him; Veeck Sr. had hired Doby as a Cleveland Indian, thereby integrating the American League.

The berm down the right-field line is named "Shoeless Joe's Hill," after South Carolina native Shoeless Joe Jackson. Jackson, who had a career major league batting average of .356, was banned from baseball for his alleged involvement in fixing the 1919 World Series. Many dispute Jackson's involvement in the "Black Sox" scandal, citing his .375 average and six RBIs in the series.

Baseball entrepreneur Marvin Goldklang decided the Charleston Rainbows needed a spicy new nickname in anticipation of their move to a new stadium. "RiverDogs" won in a local contest, and

Charlie the RiverDog became the team mascot in August of 1993. Charlie stands 6 ft, 3 inches tall and weighs 210 pounds wringing wet. For several years he lived at the Dog House down the left-field line at College Park, where he signed autographs for the kids during the sixth inning of every RiverDogs game. Charlie moved to the new ballpark. One of the real treats of RiverDog baseball is watching Charlie boogie to "Whoop, There It Is" and other tunes before each game. Charlie's a humanitarian, too. Click on his paw at the team website and see dogs and cats at the Berkeley County Animal Shelter waiting for homes.

In keeping with Mike Veeck's motto, "Fun is good", the RiverDogs have the cleverest promotions in baseball. There are usually fireworks on Friday. One season, fans could bring their dirty laundry to the park to have it washed in a row of machines along the field. A Father's Day idea, Free Vasectomy Night, was stalled by religious protests. Ugliest Bridesmaid Dress, Salute to Seinfeld, Duct Tape Night, Fake Excuse Day, and Thomas Edison Seance Night have all come from Veeck's creative mind, so you can be assured of hilarity and crowds at his park.

The Citadel College Bulldogs share the stadium with the RiverDogs and host the Southern Conference Baseball Tournament. The old stadium gets its name—College Park—from its location next to the Citadel. If you're a ballpark aficionado, take the time to visit the classic 1930s stadium, where Elvis sang in 1956. Happily, it continues to be used as a Citadel practice field.

Make sure you bring child-strength bug deterrent to Charleston. The sand gnats are fierce in early summer. Long pants, or at minimum, socks, can help.

Where to Stay

Music and dance lovers take over the city during its Spoleto Festival (tel. 843/722–2764), from late May to mid-June. Reservations are a must then and for most other weeks during the summer.

Visiting Team Motel: Howard Johnson Riverfront. This eight-story motel is on a busy commercial road, about 1 mi from the ballpark. It is not on the water, but the waterfront is nearby and visible. The rooms are slightly larger than average. *250 Spring St., Charleston 29403, tel. 843/722–4000 or 800/654–2000, fax 843/569–1608. 151 rooms. Facilities: restaurant, pool. AE, D, DC, MC, V. $$*

Days Inn Historic. This two-story downtown hotel is within walking distance of the City Market and is on a trolley stop. Location and price make it essential to book early at this 124-room hotel. There's no charge for children under 12. *155 Meeting St., Charleston 29401, tel. 843/722–8411 or 800/325–2525, fax 843/723–5361. 124 rooms. Facilities: restaurant, outdoor pool, parking (free). AE, D, DC, MC, V. $$*

Sheraton Inn Charleston. This spacious, 13-story hotel overlooks the city park and the Ashley River. The rooms are large and light-filled. It is walking distance from the ballpark. *170 Lockwood Dr., Charleston 29403, tel. 843/723–3000 or 800/325–3535, fax 843/723–3000, ext. 1595. 333 rooms. Facilities: restaurant, outdoor pool, health club, coin laundry. AE, D, DC, MC, V. $$*

Where to Eat

Hyman's Seafood Company. One firm owns two popular Meeting Street restaurants at the same address: Hyman's is a fish feast of fresh oysters, clams, scallops, and she-crab soup. It has a large appetizer list, including shrimp and clam strips, plus a children's menu. Hyman's Half-Shell is a raw bar within the restaurant, and at Aaron's Deli, good corned beef and soups are dispensed. *215 Meeting St., Charleston, tel. 843/723–6000. AE, D, MC, V. $*

Kitty's Fine Foods. This venerable Old South restaurant serves grits, flounder, and homemade chocolate cake. With a day's notice, the cook will make banana pudding. It's a small, stand-alone restaurant with Formica tables and serious eaters. It's 1 mi from the Visitor's Information Center. *1137 Morrison Dr., Charleston, tel. 843/722–9370. No credit cards. $*

Poogan's Porch. Housed in a turn-of-the-century home with creaky floors and character, this is sufficiently casual for children. Newly rebuilt after a fire in 1991, the Porch has outdoor dining on a rear patio, not the porch. Try the Low Country soups and novelty dishes of alligator, squirrel, and rabbit. A children's menu is avail-

able. *72 Queen St., Charleston, tel. 843/577–2337. AE, DC, MC, V. $$*

Entertainments

There are several pedal-carriage companies, but it's too dangerous to be in traffic with children armed only with a modified bicycle. You can take the DASH transit to the City Market and Historic King Street areas. There are many carriage and horse-drawn wagon tours of the city, as well as organized and self-made walking tours.

CharlesTowne Landing. In this state park, 3 mi northwest of Charleston, you can watch wild animals—wolves, bobcats, pumas—in their natural habitats. You can rent bicycles or take a $1 tram through the 80 landscaped acres of Charleston's first settlement, circa 1670. There are a replica village and a 17th-century ship to explore. *Hwy. 171, 1500 Old Towne Rd., Charleston, tel. 843/852–4200. Admission: $5 adults, $2.50 ages 6–14. Bicycles $2 per hr, plus $2 deposit. Open daily 9–6.*

Magnolia Plantation. A petting zoo, a 50-acre garden, miniature horses, and a maze will interest children here. A nature train ride around the huge estate lasts 45 minutes. *Ashley River Rd. (S.R. 61), 10 mi north of U.S. 17, Charleston, tel. 843/571–1266. Admission: $10 adults, $4 ages 13–18, $3 ages 4–12, $1 under 6; train admission: $5 adults, $4 ages 13–18, $3 ages 4–12, $1 under 6. Open 8–dusk; train runs 9–5.*

Sights to See

The Battery. View Charleston Harbor at the place where the Ashley and Cooper rivers meet. Also known as White Point Gardens, this is a good place to climb on cannons and view history. *Battery Point, where E. Battery St. and Murray Blvd. meet and Meeting St. dead-ends, Charleston.*

Black History Tours. See the Battery, the Old Slave Mart Museum, Catfish Row, and the site of the Denmark Vesey Slave Uprising. One- and two-hour bus tours depart from the Charleston Visitor Center (375 Meeting St.). *Sites and Insights Tours, Charleston, tel, 843/762–0051. Admission: $15 (two-hour), $10 (one-hour).*

Fort Sumter. Boats leave from Charleston City Marina and Patriots Point (Mt. Pleasant side of Cooper River Bridge) to tour the fort where the Civil War began on April 12, 1861. Artillery captain Abner Doubleday, the man wrongly credited with inventing baseball, did fire the first

Union shot of the Civil War from Fort Sumter. The Fort Sumter tour takes 1 hour. There is a separate, 90-min tour of Charleston Harbor. *Fort Sumter Tours, City Marina, 17 Lockwood Dr., Charleston, tel. 843/722–1691. Admission: $10.50 adults, $5.50 ages 6–11. MC, V.*

SAVANNAH SAND GNATS

League: South Atlantic League • **Major League Affiliation:** Texas Rangers • **Class:** A • **Stadium:** Grayson Stadium • **Opened:** 1941 • **Capacity:** 8,500 • **Dimensions:** LF: 290, CF: 400, RF: 310 • **Surface:** grass • **Season:** Apr.–Labor Day

STADIUM LOCATION: 1401 E. Victory Dr., Savannah, GA 31404.

TEAM WEB SITE: www.sandgnats.com

GETTING THERE: Take I–16 to 37th St. exit. Turn left on 37th, right on Abercorn St., and left on Victory Dr.; 2 mi on right is Daffin Park. Stadium is on a city bus line; for schedule information, call 912/233–5767.

PARKING: Ample free parking.

TICKET INFORMATION: Box 3783, Savannah, GA 31414, tel. 912/351–9150, fax 912/352–9722.

PRICE RANGE: Reserved loge seats $6.50; general admission $5 adults, $3 children, senior citizens, and active military personnel.

GAME TIME: Mon.–Sat. 7:15 PM, Sun. 2 PM; gates open 1 hr before game.

TIPS ON SEATING: Only 500 seats are reserved. General admission seats in grandstand have backs. Bleachers are benches without backs.

SEATING FOR PEOPLE WITH DISABILITIES: In grandstand; ramps for wheelchairs on third-base side.

STADIUM FOOD: You'll find dinner food at **Big Will's Grill,** near the picnic area on the third-base side. The nicely grilled hamburgers are merely $3; brats and Polish and Italian sausages are $2.50. The meats are good; the mustard isn't. There's good pink lemonade for $1.25 and there's hand-scooped Sealtest ice cream in five flavors. There are also slush puppies and soft pretzels. A Southern specialty, boiled peanuts, is sold in brown bags for $2. They're an acquired taste and are reminiscent of black-eyed peas.

SMOKING POLICY: City ordinance prohibiting smoking is widely disregarded.

VISITING TEAM HOTEL: Holiday Inn–Midtown (7100 Abercorn St., Savannah 31406, tel. 912/352–7100 or 800/465–4329).

TOURISM INFORMATION: Savannah Area Convention & Visitors Bureau (Box 1628, Savannah, GA 31402, tel. 912/944–0456 or 800/444–2427).

Savannah: Grayson Stadium

The drive to Savannah's Grayson Stadium is one of the best in all of baseball. The approach from downtown is through a beautiful oak-tree-lined neighborhood. The Spanish moss hanging from the trees is magical for kids and parents alike. The stadium is in Daffin Park, a large city park full of ball fields and basketball courts. The magic continues as you approach the redbrick stadium's arched entranceway. GRAYSON STADIUM is etched in stone in large letters. The oak trees and Spanish moss surround the stadium.

Savannah's baseball roots are deep. The city was a charter member of the South Atlantic League in 1904. Shoeless Joe Jackson led the league in hitting with a .358 average in 1909.

Built to accommodate football as well as baseball, Grayson Stadium is the largest-capacity stadium in Single A baseball. The concrete football-stadium construction dates from 1901 and gives Grayson thousands of bleachers seats down the third-base line and beyond the left-field fence. As a result, this is a home-run hitter's park, with some of the shortest home-run alleys in professional baseball, at 290 ft down the left-field line and 310 ft down the right-field line. Center field is deep, at 400 ft. They have been playing minor-league baseball on this spot since the mid-1920s. The stadium you visit, built in 1941, is named for Spanish-American War hero General William Grayson.

Tall pine trees dominate the scene beyond the concrete left-field bleachers. There is a large scoreboard in center field. Renovations replaced an ancient press box and provided new bathrooms and bullpens. If you worry about foul balls, you'll be safe here, as the entire first-base grandstand is screened.

This setting is so perfect that the producers of *The Bingo Long Travelling All-Star & Motor Kings* (Universal), a 1976 movie with James Earl Jones, Richard Pryor, and Billy Dee Williams about black barnstormers, was filmed here.

You shouldn't have much trouble with restless kids in this stadium. There is a batting cage and a speed pitch on the third-base side. There is plenty of space for the kids to race around in the treed area beyond the picnic area. If you want a foul ball, the best place appears to be along the fence on the third-base side past the picnic area.

The atmosphere is fun and the sound system lively. The sound effects go way beyond the traditional broken-windshield-on-a-foul-ball-out-of-the-stadium gag. Listen for everything from themes from *The Wizard of Oz* to *The Three Stooges*. When an opponent got a hit, we heard the Stooges' "Oh, a wise guy, eh?!"

These folks have a sense of humor. About the only thing anyone could complain about here are the bugs. The sand gnats are ferocious in the spring and fall. During the 1996 season, the team changed its nickname. Now it's called—you guessed it—the Savannah Sand Gnats (and it has chosen the clever motto, "Baseball with a bite!"). As the temperature grows warmer, the gnats are less of a problem. But mosquitoes may appear in the summer. Wear long pants and a long-sleeved shirt. The locals swear by Avon's bath oil Skin-So-Soft, but the team does not have large quantities to sell. Plan ahead (Avon, tel. 800/858–8000). By the time you are in the stadium, it's too late to get the protection you need.

Where to Stay

Visiting Team Motel: Holiday Inn–Midtown. This ordinary two-story hotel is 5 mi from downtown and 15 minutes west of the ballpark. It's one block from the Oglethorpe Mall. Kids stay free and eat free with paying adults in the hotel restaurant. *7100 Abercorn St., Savannah 31406, tel. 912/352–7100 or 800/465–4329, fax 912/235–6408. 174 rooms. Facilities: restaurant, outdoor pool. AE, D, DC, MC, V. $*

Days Inn–Savannah Historic Riverfront. At this imposing seven-story redbrick hotel between the Savannah River and City Market, kids 12 and under eat free. No-smoking rooms are available. The ballpark is 10 minutes north. *201 West Bay St., Savannah 31401, tel. 912/236–4440 or 800/325–2525, fax 912/232–2725. 196 rooms. Facilities: restaurant, outdoor pool, parking (free). AE, D, DC, MC, V. $$*

The Mulberry–Holiday Inn Hotel. This hotel began in 1846 as a livery stable, became a cotton warehouse, and, in the 1960s, a Coca Cola bottling plant. It's been completely renovated, with a formal Georgian exterior and three floors of spacious rooms. It stands on Washington Square in the Historic District, overlooking Emmitt Park. *601 E. Bay St., Savannah 31401, tel. 912/238–1200 or 800/465–4329, fax 912/236–2184. 120 rooms. Facilities: 2 restaurants, outdoor pool, hot tub, parking (fee). AE, D, DC, MC, V. $$*

Where to Eat

Crystal Beer Parlor. This family-friendly place dispenses more root beer floats than alcohol. It's been serving outstanding oyster sandwiches, crab stew, seafood gumbo, and Brunswick stew since 1933. The milk shakes and homemade potato chips are winners, too. Padded wooden booths stand against walls decorated with old photos of the city. It's three blocks south of the Civic Center. *301 W. Jones St., Savannah, tel. 912/232–1153. AE, D, MC, V. $*

Morrison's Cafeteria. This nicely furnished downtown restaurant is another of the South's exemplary cafeterias. The choice of vegetables and salads is extensive, and there is a less expensive children's menu. It's on Johnson Square in the Historic District. *15 Bull St., Savannah, tel. 912/232–5264. AE, D, MC, V. $*

Mrs. Wilkes Boarding House. You'll wait in line for at least 20 minutes before you're grouped with others at tables for a genuine Southern feed. The all-you-can-eat lunches are a groaning board of fried chicken, cornbread, cobblers, grits, and red rice. Only a tiny sign on the wall of this residential neighborhood indicates the restaurant—you'll see the line first. *107 W. Jones St., Savannah, tel. 912/232–5997. No credit cards. Closed weekends. $*

The Pirate's House. This gigantic restaurant in the Historic District has 23 dining rooms, including the original Pirate's House, dating from the 1700s, and a house once owned by city founder James Oglethorpe that's the oldest residence in Georgia. It's a popular tourist stop, despite the pricey menu. The service is speedy for a restaurant this size, and the seafood, pasta, steaks, and chicken dishes are pleasing. Jambalaya, pecan-fried chicken, and praline sundae pie are standouts. There is a children's menu. *20 E. Broad St. at Bay St., Savannah, tel. 912/233–5757. AE, D, DC, MC, V. $$*

The Seashell House. This casual family seafood house arranges its tables sensibly—with a hole in the middle over a trash container, for all the crab shells, shrimp tails, claws, and corn cobs. Crabs and ribs are the mainstays here, and oysters, crawfish, clams, and conch are also served. There is a children's menu. *3111 Skidaway Rd., Savannah, tel. 912/352–8116. AE, MC, V. $*

Entertainments

City Market. There are four blocks of shops, restaurants, and art galleries in this restored city market. Low Country basket weavers work and sell their wares in open-air sheds, sharing space with produce sellers. *Jefferson and W. Saint Julian*

Sts., Savannah, tel. 912/232–4903. Open mid-Mar.–Sept., Mon.–Sat. 10–9, Sun. noon–5; Oct.–early Mar., Mon.–Sat. 10–6, Sun. noon–5.

Juliette Gordon Lowe Girl Scout National Center. Any Brownie or Girl Scout in your family gets a $1 discount when visiting the home of the girl-scouting movement. Lowe's home includes memorabilia on the origins of scouting and its links to Europe's "girl guides." There is a child-oriented gift shop. *142 Bull St., Savannah, tel. 912/233–4501. Admission: $6 adults, $5 ages 6–8. Open Mon.–Tues. and Thurs.–Sat. 10–4, Sun. 12:30–4:30.*

Sights to See

This city is memorable. The oaks, covered with Spanish moss, make its distinctive squares beautiful and mysterious. There is street after street of Federal and Regency homes, wrought iron, and sweeping porches—the entire downtown (2.2 mi) is a National Historic Landmark District.

It was the women of the city who saved it from bulldozers and modernization in the 1950s. Ask children to pick their favorite among the 21 squares originally laid out by city founder General James Oglethorpe.

Carriage tours. Twelve tour companies operate in the city, including a haunted-history trolley, a black heritage trail, riverboat cruises, and a ghost walk. There's much to be said for seeing the city by horse-drawn open carriage. Pick-up sites are at the Hyatt Hotel in Bay Street, Jefferson Street in the City Market, and at the visitor center. Those with reservations are seated first. The tours last 50 minutes and leave on the hour. *Carriage Tours of Savannah, Savannah, tel. 912/236–6756. Admission: $17 adults, $8 ages 4–11. Open daily 9–3 and 6–9.*

Historic Savannah Shuttle-Bus Tours. The cheapest way to see the sights is on the county's free CAT shuttle buses. They depart from the visitor center every 20 minutes Monday through Saturday from 7 to 6, and every 40 minutes Monday through Saturday from 6 to 10 and Sunday from 9:30 to 5. The buses are accessible to people in wheelchairs. *Savannah Visitor Center, 301 Martin Luther King, Jr. Blvd., Savannah, tel. 912/233–5767.*

King-Tisdell Cottage and Tours. The city's black history museum conducts a tour of African-American historic sights arranged by the Association for the Study of Afro-American Life and History. One day's advance registration is required. The tour departs from the Savannah Visitor Center (see Historic Savannah Shuttle-Bus Tours, *above*) at 1 and 3. The compact museum itself is filled with mementos of the achievements and history of local residents. *514 E. Huntington St., Savannah, tel. 912/234–8000. Admission to tours: $15 adults, $7 children under 12 and senior citizens;* *with guide for own vehicle, $10 adults, $7 children and senior citizens. Admission to museum: $2.50. Open Tues.–Sat. noon–5.*

Tybee Island Lighthouse. This beach resort of barrier islands is 18 mi east of Savannah on U.S. 80 (Victory Dr.). You can climb the 128 steps to the lighthouse's top and investigate its small museum. There is great swimming on Tybee's beautiful beaches. *Meddin Dr., Tybee, tel. 912/786–4077. Admission: $4 adults, $3 ages 6–15, senior citizens, active military. Open Wed.–Mon. 9–6.*

GRAPEFRUIT LEAGUE SPRING TRAINING
ORLANDO/DISNEY, VERO BEACH, LAKELAND, TAMPA, ST. PETERSBURG

8

The home of major-league baseball's Grapefruit League spring training, Florida is synonymous with the game. There are dozens of parks on the ocean coast, in interior Florida, and on the Gulf shores, allowing snowbirds to get a jump on their hometown team's new rosters each spring. Many of those same fields are home to minor-league teams after the majors head north.

For one trip, try starting at Disney's new sports complex in Kissimmee, the spring-training ground of the Atlanta Braves. Right next door you'll find Disney World, Disney's Animal Kingdom, Universal Studios, MGM Grand, and Epcot, among other attractions. There are true lodging bargains in this overbuilt area.

Drive I–528 east to I–95, then south to Vero Beach, home of Dodgertown. This is spring training as it was in the 1950's, with a small stadium that's unspoiled by commercialism. Drive northwest to Kissimmee to connect to Interstate 4, and go west to Lakeland, a trip of 100 mi; its Tigertown is the spring home of the Detroit Tigers and the summer home of the Lakeland Tigers. The renovated stadium is laden with character.

Another 30 mi west on Interstate 4 is Tampa, with its sparkling, state-of-the-art ballpark for the New York Yankees in spring and the Tampa Yankees in summer. Yankees legends are recalled here, in banners and columns. Tampa has one of the nation's best zoos, with just the right scale for children. The city's $84-million, three-level aquarium is a marvel. The Ybor City is a must for authentic Cuban food and a look at the city's colorful past.

Continuing on Interstate 4 west to U.S. 19 South brings you to St. Petersburg, where during spring training you can enjoy sea breezes in Al Lang Stadium. This intimate downtown park is right on Tampa Bay. The sand and water at nearby St. Petersburg Beach are a lovely respite.

ATLANTA BRAVES SPRING TRAINING

League: National League • **Class:** Major League Spring Training • **Stadium:** Disney Baseball Stadium • **Opened:** 1997 • **Capacity:** 9,100 • **Dimensions:** LF: 335, CF: 400, RF: 330 • **Surface:** grass • **Season:** March Spring Training

STADIUM LOCATION: 710 S. Victory Way, Kissimmee, FL 34747.

GETTING THERE: From I–4, take 192 West at Exit 25. Turn right onto Victory Way to the Disney Wide World of Sports complex.

PARKING: Ample free parking.

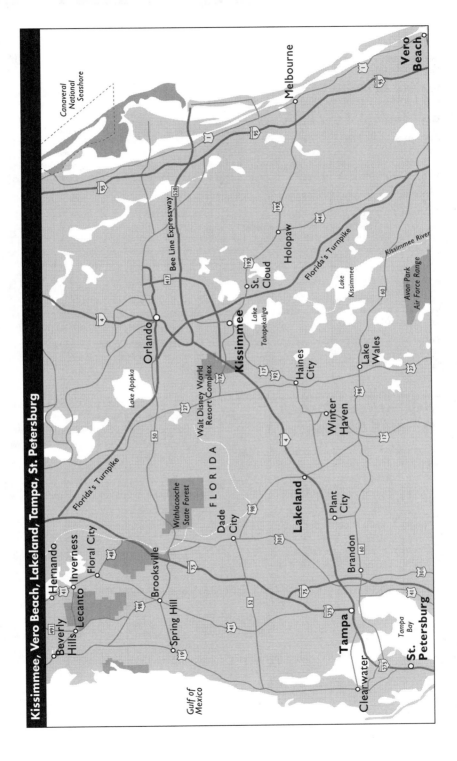

Canaveral
National
Seashore

Vero
Beach

Melbourne

11

95

95

Bee Line Expressway

528

417

95

192

Holopaw

441

St.
Cloud

192

Florida's Turnpike

Kissimmee River

60

Avon Park
Air Force Range

Lake
Kissimmee

Orlando

4

Lake
Tohopekaliga

Kissimmee

Lake
Apopka

17

92

Haines
City

Lake
Wales

27

Walt Disney World
Resort Complex

192

98

27

50

Florida's Turnpike

4

Winter
Haven

17

F L O R I D A

Withlacoochee
State Forest

98

Dade
City

Lakeland

Plant
City

Hernando

41

Inverness

Floral City

48

Brooksville

75

300

Brandon

60

Lecanto

Beverly
Hills

491

98

52

275

Tampa

301

41

Spring Hill

41

19

Tampa
Bay

St.
Petersburg

Clearwater

275

Gulf of
Mexico

TICKET INFORMATION: Box 10,000, Lake Buena Vista, FL 32830, tel. 407/939–1500, fax 407/939–8620. For rookie team games, tel. 941/966–6407.

PRICE RANGE: Tickets go on sale in early Jan. Lower deck reserved $15.50; upper deck reserved and right field reserved bleachers $13.50; lawn seating and general admission $10.50.

GAME TIME: 1:05 and 7:05 PM. Gates are open for the Braves' early morning workouts.

TIPS ON SEATING: There are 7,500 actual seats, but the lawn holds 1,400 more fans along the third-base line and beyond the left-field fence. The lawn seats beyond the left-field fence give you a great view of the grandstand, but you can't see the scoreboard. The sun for afternoon games is in the eyes of fans on the third-base side. There are obstructed-view seats behind the light poles in the back rows of the upper deck.

SEATING PEOPLE WITH DISABILITIES: Throughout the park.

STADIUM FOOD: The food is mediocre and expensive. There are hot dogs, pizza, and other standard fare. The best bets are a tossed salad and grilled chicken sandwich. The fountain drinks are overpriced. There are soft drink machines all along the upper-deck concourse, with slightly cheaper bottles for $3. The **All-Star Cafe,** with its large portions, large prices, sports memorabilia, and loud music, is outside the gates.

SMOKING POLICY: Smoking is not allowed in the stadium. There are designated smoking areas outside the stadium.

VISITING TEAM HOTEL: Coronado Springs Resort (1000 W. Buena Vista Dr., Lake Buena Vista, FL 32830, tel. 407/939–1000).

TOURISM INFORMATION: Orlando/Orange County Official Visitor Center (8445 International Dr., Orlando, 32819, tel. 407/363–5871, fax 407/354–0874). Or call Kissimmee–St. Cloud Visitors Center, tel. 800/526–5466.

Kissimmee: Disney Baseball Stadium

Disney has hit a home run by taking the best ideas from the successful new ballparks of the 1990s and putting them together in the spring sunshine of Florida. This is the best of baseball's new spring training parks.

In typical Disney style, it wasn't enough to build a grand ballpark. The Big Mouse built a big facility—a $100-million, 200-acre Disney's Wide World of Sport complex just 10 minutes south of the Magic Kingdom. Everything here shouts Florida, from the palm trees to the architecture. The 7,500-seat yellow-stucco and dark-green mission-style stadium is graced with stately arches throughout. It holds in excess of 9,000 with lawn seating and is surrounded by spectacular landscaping, manicured Bermuda grass fields, and an attractive, architecturally compatible fieldhouse where the Harlem Globetrotters train each December.

Eighty percent of the seats are in the double-decked grandstand running between first and third base. The grandstand is framed with twin 100-ft-tall towers at each end capped by khaki-green tile roofs. The upper deck seats are partially shaded, and those along first base hang close to the field and offer a great view. There are reserved bleacher seats running from first base to the right-field foul pole. The Atlanta bullpen is beyond the right-field fence. Lawn seating runs from third base all the way behind the fence in left field. The large, hand-operated dark-green scoreboard in left center is topped with flags and four large gold ball finials. There is a video board in right center. The companion fieldhouse runs along the first-base side of the building with baseball practice fields visible beyond center field. The All Star Cafe is located just outside the ballpark entrance.

With all the knowledge of the successful ballparks of the 1990s, Disney and architect David Schwartz (who designed the Ballpark in Arlington) have built a fan-friendly place with roomy seats, plenty of legroom, and a wide concourse of concession stands. There are food stands on the inside concourse behind the lower-deck seating, so fans can get served without missing a pitch. The souvenir shop is located at the ball-park entrance.

The disappointments are not enough to spoil a nearly perfect spring baseball experience. Besides the mediocre food, there isn't a mascot to entertain the kids (Mickey, Goofy, somebody come over to the ballyard and get in the game!).

In 1998, the Atlanta Braves had their inaugural spring training season here, and have agreed to play here for 20 spring-training seasons. The Orlando Rays, the Double A affiliate of the Tampa Bay Devil Rays in the Southern League, play in the stadium during the regular season. We can only imagine what an eye-popping experience it must be for a kid just out of high school to claim this beauty as home for a summer.

The Wide World of Sports includes four practice fields, four international-size soccer fields, a track and field complex, four softball fields, two youth baseball fields, and eleven clay tennis courts. The NFL Experience, an interactive playground, is a football fan's dream complete with a screaming coach urging you to run faster. The fieldhouse has four hardwood basketball courts, as well as a modest memorabilia collection from a courageous young man named Scott Carter, who collected autographed items from athletes like Ben Hogan and Michael Jordan before dying of cancer in 1993. Admission to the complex is $8 adults, $6.75 ages 3–9. If you visit on a game day, a Braves ticket admits you to the complex. There are 45-minute tours daily at 11, 2, and 4.

Where to Stay

You'll find terrific bargains on lodging, as this area competes for customers. Ask the Orlando Visitor Center to send you its Magic Card, which offer some decent discounts. You save a bundle by staying outside Walt Disney World, but you sacrifice some convenience.

Howard Johnson's Fountain Park Plaza Hotel. A pretty lake and picnic area are the backdrop for this highway hotel with resort features. There's a free Continental breakfast. Efficiencies are available. This 10-story hotel is 3½ mi west of Walt Disney World. *U.S. 192, Orlando 34746, tel. 407/396–1111 or 800/654–2000, fax 407/*

248–0266. 400 rooms. Facilities: restaurant, ice-cream parlor, outdoor pool, kiddie wading pool, sauna, hot tub, 2 tennis courts, game room. AE, D, DC, MC, V. $

Ramada Inn Orlando Westgate. This two-story motel shuttles you the 6 mi to Walt Disney World, Epcot, and MGM parks for free. Kids eat free at the restaurant. *9200 W. Irlo Bronson Hwy., U.S. 192, Orlando 34742, tel. 941/424–2621 or 800/228–2828, fax 941/424–4360. 200 rooms. Facilities: restaurant, outdoor pool, playground, game room, coin laundry. AE, D, DC, MC, V. $*

Stadium Inn and Suites. This stand-alone apartment motel composed of three two-story buildings has kitchens in half of the rooms. Some rooms have Murphy beds, a treat for children. *2039 E. Irlo Bronson Hwy., U.S. 192. 14 mi east of Walt Disney World, at Rte. 441, Kissimmee 34741, tel. 407/846–7814 or 800/221–2222, fax 407/846–1863. 114 rooms. Facilities: outdoor pool, hot tub. AE, D, DC, MC, V. $*

Wynfield Inn–Main Gate. This sprawling motel is built around the large swimming pool. Four miles east from Walt Disney World, the motel has a free shuttle to it, Epcot, and MGM Studios. Children 17 and under stay free, and the two adjacent restaurants give a 10% discount to guests. *5335 W. Irlo Bronson Hwy., U.S. 192, 4 mi east of Walt Disney World, Kissimmee 43745, tel. 407/396–2121 or 800/346–1551, fax 407/396–1142. 216 rooms. Facilities: snack bar, outdoor pool, kiddie wading pool, coin laundry. AE, D, DC, MC, V. $*

More Baseball

Ted Williams Museum and Hitters Hall of Fame. Ted Williams's museum in Hernando is arranged like a baseball diamond, with memorabilia, television tapes on his career in baseball and the Marines, and a bat collection—including one from Shoeless Joe Jackson—lining the walls. One wing includes a 20-member Hitters Hall of Fame, as chosen by Williams. *2455 N. Citrus Hills Blvd.; Exit 66 (Wildwood/Inverness) from I–75 N; left on Hwy. 44 for 15 mi, then right on Hwy. 41; in Hernando, left on Hwy. 486 to museum a few mi ahead on left; Hernando, tel. 352/527–6566. Admission: $5 adults, $1 children under 13. Open Tues.–Sun. 10–4.*

Where to Eat

Morrison's Cafeteria. This large, nicely decorated cafeteria has a children's menu and good renditions of American favorites. It is in the Osceola Square Mall. *3831 W. Vine St., Kissimmee, tel. 407/846–6011. AE, D, MC, V. $*

Lilia's Grilled Delights. Children like this inexpensive Polynesian/American restaurant, with umbrellas in fruit drinks, and various sweet chicken dishes. Pulled-pork sandwiches for kids are just 99¢. It is 3 mi south of City Hall. *3150 S. Orange Ave., Orlando, tel. 407/851–9087. AE, D, DC, MC, V. No breakfast. $*

Entertainments

For all the huge Orlando-area attractions for kids, some precautions make the days more fun. Use sunscreen, bring drink boxes, get a stroller for any child six or under, and don't feel you have to get your money's worth by seeing it all.

Animal Kingdom. You ride in safari trucks and boats in this 500-acre re-creation of the world's animal habitats, with 1,000 animals and 4 million trees and plants. There are five theme sections, the animatronic Dinoland USA with its thrilling Countdown to Extinction ride, Asia and its Discovery Riverboats, Camp Minnie-Mickey for young visitors, Africa with authentic Zulu huts, and Safari Village with a 150-ft-wide fake tree, carved with the likeness of more than 320 animals.

Disney–MGM Studios. This is an imaginative, flashy park. Some attractions ("Tower of Terror," "Star Tours") may be too intense for younger children. The Indiana Jones stunt special is unique. Try to visit the "Honey, I Shrunk the Kids" playland before dusk, as it closes early for insurance reasons. There are many clever theme restaurants on the grounds. The park is 2 mi north of U.S. 192.

There are one-day, one-park tickets (to Magic Kingdom, Epcot, Animal Kingdom, or Disney-MGM Studios) listed below, or multiday passes. Separate admissions are charged for water parks Typhoon Lagoon, River Country, and Blizzard Beach, as well as the Discovery Island zoo and Pleasure Island and its theme nightclubs.

Parking is $6 at any of the Walt Disney World properties. *U.S. 192 and I–4, Lake Buena Vista, tel. 407/824–4321. Admission: $44 adults, $35 ages 3–9. Open 9–9, with some variation in closing times. AE, MC, V.*

Epcot Center. Epcot is 3 mi south of the Magic and Animal Kingdoms. There are long waits, and adults may chafe at the commercialization of exhibits. Children may find "Wonders of Life–Body Wars" too intense. The *Circle of Life* film is a winner, and so is the 3-D *Honey I Shrunk the Audience.* You may want to skip the beautiful indoor restaurants in favor of the less expensive ones outside.

Gatorland. It may seem odd to eat fried alligator, but watching a man wrestle a gator is a permanent memory. You'll see dozens of gators, snakes, and tropical birds and learn about their behavior. This attraction works hard at education, with a zoo that puts you very close to poisonous snakes. There's a water park and aviary. *14501 S. Orange Blossom Terr., 3½ mi north of Kissimmee on U.S. 17; Exit 28 east from I–4, then south 5 mi on Rte. 17; Orlando, tel. 407/855–5496. Admission: $16.93 adults, $7.48 ages 3–12. Open Apr.–Sept., daily 9–7; Oct.–Apr., daily 8–5:45.*

Sea World of Florida. Children love the various touch pools; the whale and waterskiing shows are exciting. Sharks, sea lions, dolphins, and manatees get huge exhibits. The "Penguin Encounter" lets you view hundreds of king and Adélie penguins. You'll wait in line for the exciting water coaster, Journey to Atlantis. Parking is $5. Discount tickets to Busch Gardens and Cypress Gardens are available here. *7007 Sea Harbor Dr., Bee Line exit (S.R. 528) from I–4, then exit for Sea World/International Dr., Orlando, tel. 407/351–0021. Admission: $42 adults, $36 ages 3–9. Open 9–7. AE, D, MC, V.*

Universal Studios–Nickelodeon. View back lots, fly on a bicycle through the "E.T. Adventure" (too scary for many five-year-olds), and have a 30-ft gorilla shake your cable car in "Kongfrontation." Experience a tornado in "Twister," including flying cows. An informative tram tour takes you through this movie-making palace. If your kids want to be part of a Nickelodeon show audience, call the production hot line (tel. 407/363–8586) one week early and find out what shows are filming. Audiences are filled on a first-come, first-served basis. Parking is $6; $7 for an RV. *1000 Universal Studios Plaza, Exit 30B from I–4 onto S.R. 435, Orlando, tel. 407/363–8000 or 800/232–7827. Admission: $42 adults, $34 ages 3–9. Open 9–7.*

Walt Disney World. It is good to follow a system, rather than just wandering. The basic Walt Disney World plan: Pre-purchase multiday passes at an AAA office to get the best discounted rate; make reservations for lunch and dinner at Disney restaurants; write down where you parked; arrive a half hour before the gates open, see the most popular rides first, eat lunch early, at 11 AM; force yourself to leave the park from 1 to 4 when the crush is heaviest—go back to your hotel for a swim and a nap; return to the park and stay until closing, eating dinner late on the front patio of a restaurant along the parade route. For our money, "Pirates of the Caribbean" is the top ride and Fantasyland the best area in Walt Disney World. Older children flock to the Blizzard Beach water park.

LOS ANGELES DODGERS SPRING TRAINING

League: National League • **Class:** Major League • **Stadium:** Holman Stadium • **Opened:** 1953 • **Capacity:** 6,500 • **Dimensions:** LF: 340, CF: 400, RF: 340 • **Surface:** grass • **Season:** March Spring Training

STADIUM LOCATION: 4101 26th St., Vero Beach, FL 32960.

GETTING THERE: From I–95, take exit 68 at 43rd Ave. and drive east 5½ mi to 26th St.

PARKING: $2 parking in and around Dodgertown complex.

TICKET INFORMATION: Box 2887, Vero Beach, FL 32961, tel. 561/569–6858.

PRICE RANGE: Box office opens in late Jan. for spring training tickets; box seats $10; standing room $5.

GAME TIME: Spring training games at 1:15 PM. Gates open at 11 AM. Player workouts start before 10 AM around the complex.

TIPS ON SEATING: Players sit on aluminum benches just feet from the front rows of sections 9 & 10 (visitors) and 18 & 19 (Dodgers). There is virtually no escape from the sun, which shines in fans' eyes on the first-base visitors side during day games. There's seating on the grass berms beyond the outfield.

SEATING PEOPLE WITH DISABILITIES: Available on the upper concourse immediately behind the last row of seats in section 13 and 15.

STADIUM FOOD: There are Dodger dogs, which are decent, as well as undistinguished hot dogs, good lemonade, and soft-serve ice cream.

SMOKING POLICY: Prohibited in the seating area and enclosed concession areas. Allowed on the upper concourse.

VISITING TEAM HOTEL: Vero Beach Inn (700 North A1A, Vero Beach, FL 32963, tel. 561/231–1600).

TOURISM INFORMATION: Indian River County Chamber of Commerce (1216 21st St., Vero Beach, FL 32960, tel. 561/567–3491).

Vero Beach: Holman Stadium

This is baseball 1950s style. Branch Rickey brought Brooklyn Dodgers spring training here more than 50 years ago. In the very first inning of the very first exhibition game on March 31, 1948, Jackie Robinson hit a home run. Ironically, Robinson blasted his shot directly into a group of blacks standing in what was called the "Negro section" out past left field.

During World War II, the U.S. Navy used the airport at Vero Beach to train combat pilots. After the war, businessman Bud Holman regained his airport lease and had to figure out what to do with a huge amount of land and a military barracks. Major-league baseball teams training in the Caribbean were considering moving their spring training operations to Florida, and Branch Rickey wanted to build a "baseball college." Holman recruited and signed up the Dodgers. In 1952 the Dodgers signed a 21-year lease with a 21-year option and, in 1953, built a permanent ballpark. They named the stadium for Holman.

In the last 50 years, a great deal has changed at Dodgertown: the Dodgers now own in excess of 400 acres in a complex that includes modern training facilities, a golf course, and a conference center. A fan visiting for a spring-training game would hardly notice, though. What you see is a modest 1950s boomerang-shaped grandstand that extends almost to the foul poles down first and third. The mix of blue and orange seats go only 18 rows high. The simple two-story tan and dark-brown press box behind home plate has a concession stand. Goofy, oversized baseball lights sit on top of lampposts throughout the complex. The outfield wall is a short chain-link fence, completely free of commercial advertising. An attractive grass berm beyond the fence is topped with palm trees, and orange trees nicely frame a three-flag display past center field. Small planes fly by and appear to land just past center field all through the game.

This is as close as most fans will get to a major-league player. Only the short chain-link fence separates you from your heroes. Get to the ballpark an hour early and you may come home with some prized autographs. During the game, you can feel like you are right next to the players, who sit in two rows of aluminum benches just feet from the front row of the grandstand. No dugouts, no kidding.

With 50 years of baseball history and incredible access to major-league stars, this is the pinnacle baseball spring-training experience. Before the game, you can walk along Jackie Robinson Avenue and meet your friends at Robinson and Sandy Koufax Lane. Streets are named after all the Dodgers in the National Baseball Hall of Fame. The future is here as well, with minor-leaguers training in fields all around Holman Stadium.

The Dodgers' Florida State League Single A team, the Vero Beach Dodgers, has played here since 1980, from April to early September (tel. 561/569–4900, ext. 305, for information).

Where to Stay

Visiting Team Hotel: Vero Beach Inn. This four-story, family-owned independent hotel is clean, comfortable, and well landscaped. It has standard rooms. *700 North A1A, Vero Beach, FL 32963, tel. 561/231–1600 or 800/227–8615, fax 561/231–9547. 212 rooms. Facilities: restaurant, pool. AE, D, DC, MC, V. $$*

Where to Eat

Lobster Shanty. This popular seafood restaurant has fresh fish in a multitude of combinations, with many low-cal dishes. There are children's portions and good salads. Service is brisk and the nautical theme includes fountains and highly polished tables. *1 Royal Palm Blvd., Vero Beach, tel. 561/562–1941. AE, D. MC, V. $$*

LAKELAND TIGERS/DETROIT TIGERS SPRING TRAINING

League: Florida State League • **Major League Affiliation:** Detroit Tigers • **Class:** A • **Stadium:** Joker Marchant • **Opened:** 1967 • **Capacity:** 7,100 • **Dimensions:** LF: 340, CF: 420, RF: 340 • **Surface:** grass • **Season:** Apr.–Labor Day

STADIUM LOCATION: 2301 Lakeland Hills Blvd., Lakeland, FL 33805.

TEAM WEB SITE: www.lakeland-tigers.com

GETTING THERE: From I–4 Exit 19 to Lakeland Hills Blvd., turn left, go 1½ mi; stadium is on left.

PARKING: Ample free parking.

TICKET INFORMATION: Box 90187, Lakeland, FL 33804, tel. 941/688–7911, fax 941/688–9589.

PRICE RANGE: Box seats $10; reserved seats $8; general admission $5.

GAME TIME: Mon.–Sat. 7 PM, Sun. 1 PM (Apr.–Aug.); gates open 1 hr before game.

TIPS ON SEATING: Best view of Lake Parker and palm trees beyond right-center-field fence is from high up in general admission bleachers on third-base side. Minor-league team closes bleachers except on Fourth of July.

SEATING FOR PEOPLE WITH DISABILITIES: Near box seats on third-base side.

STADIUM FOOD: The best bargain is the whole pizza ($7). Ask the help to cut them in more than four pieces. There are burgers, hot dogs, and fries, but they are ordinary. The kielbasa is a better bet, but may be too spicy for children. Avoid the watery sodas and choose bottled fruit juices. The Italian ices on a push-up stick ($2) are refreshing.

SMOKING POLICY: Smoking prohibited in seating area.

VISITING TEAM HOTEL: Wellesley Inn (3520 Hwy. 98N, Lakeland, FL 33805, tel. 941/859–3399 or 800/444–8888).

TOURISM INFORMATION: Central Florida Convention & Visitors Bureau (Box 1839, Bartow, FL 33831, tel. 813/534–4372).

Lakeland: Joker Marchant Stadium

One morning we were driving from Orlando to St. Petersburg on I–4 and stopped at Tigertown, the spring home of the Detroit Tigers. We loved the atmosphere and looked for an open gate. Once inside, we saw a white-haired man hitting golf balls from the bullpen near right field into left field. Emily grabbed a Florida State League ball lying near the dugout and got an autograph from Sparky Anderson, the first manager to win world championships with both American and National League teams.

Who is Joker Marchant, we wondered? It turns out he was the longtime city recreation director who pressed to have the stadium built. Why Joker? His name was Marcus Thigpen Marchant; we understood. The Tigers have been in Lakeland since 1933 and had outgrown the 3,500-capacity Henley Field long before the 7,000-capacity, $500,000 Marchant Stadium was opened for the 1967 spring-training season.

They call it Tigertown; the stadium is on Al Kaline Drive, named for Mr. Tiger, the Gold Glove home-run-hitting Hall of Famer. The structure of the stadium is quite like that of the ordinary Florida State League stadiums in Kissimmee, Clearwater, and elsewhere. But the feel is different. The city and the Tigers did a wonderful $600,000 renovation in 1994 that gives this stadium real character. Tiger flags and huge pictures of Tiger stars fly among the umbrellas and picnic tables, creating a warm and friendly atmosphere at minimal cost. The concession stands are lit in neon. Southpaw the Tiger is a fan-friendly mascot who takes part in the contests.

From high up in the general admission bleacher seats on the third-base side, you get the best view of Lake Parker beyond the right-center-field fence and a brightly lighted power plant in the distance. Unfortunately, the minor-league team allows seating in the bleachers only on the Fourth of July. We were struck by the absence of advertising signs on the walls. There was something soothing and dignified about the uncluttered navy-blue walls with palm trees and water behind. Paul Dash, the former groundskeeper for 19 years, explained: "Joker said the signs looked tacky."

Where to Stay

Visiting Team Hotel: Wellesley Inn. This modern six-story peach stucco motel is on the edge of the Lakeland Square Mall. Rooms are bright and nicely decorated. Guests receive a free Continental breakfast. It's 10 minutes from the stadium. *3520 Hwy. 98 N, Exit 18 off I–4, Lakeland 33805, tel. 941/859–3399 or 800/444–8888, fax 941/859–3483. 106 rooms. Facilities: outdoor pool. AE, D, DC, MC, V. $*

Best Western Diplomat Inn. This courtyard has pretty landscaping throughout the grounds. Many rooms have sofas and desks. There is a

free Continental breakfast. It is one exit from the ballpark. *3311 U.S. 98 N, Exit 18 from I–4, Lakeland 33805, tel. 941/688–7972 or 800/528–1234, fax 941/688–8377. 120 rooms. Facilities: restaurant, outdoor pool, exercise room, game room. AE, D, DC, MC, V. $$*

Where to Eat

Landmark Restaurant. Housed in a former dry-goods building in the Munn Park Historic District, this is an endearing mix of mismatched tables, cheery "found" art, and great breakfasts. Don't miss the strawberry pancakes, cheese grits, and French toast. There are salads and fish for lunch. *228 E. Pine St., Lakeland, tel. 941/682–7691. Closed Sun. No dinner. D, DC, MC, V. $*

Sights to See

Frank Lloyd Wright Buildings. The largest collection of architect Frank Lloyd Wright's work outside of Oak Park, Illinois, is at Florida Southern College. The 12 Wright buildings are made of cypress, copper, and coquina shells. Self-guided tour maps are available in the administration building, where you may also join the docent tour at 11 on Thursday for $5. *Ingraham Ave. and McDonald St., Lakeland, tel. 941/680–4111. Administration building open weekdays 8–5.*

Munn Park Historic District. Bookstores, more than 60 antiques shops, and renovated storefronts are clustered along Kentucky Avenue and Pine Street in downtown Lakeland. Self-guided tours are available through the Lakeland Chamber of Commerce (35 Lake Morton Dr., Lakeland, tel. 941/688–8551).

TAMPA YANKEES/NEW YORK YANKEES SPRING TRAINING

League: Florida State League • **Major League Affiliation:** New York Yankees • **Class:** A • **Stadium:** Legends Field • **Opened:** 1996 • **Capacity:** 10,387 • **Dimensions:** LF: 318, CF: 408, RF: 314 • **Surface:** grass • **Season:** Apr.–Labor Day

STADIUM LOCATION: 3802 W. Martin Luther King Blvd., Tampa, FL 33614.

GETTING THERE: From I–275S or N, take N. Dale Mabry (Exit 23) north 3 mi; Legends Field is on left. From airport, take exit to Spruce St.; in approximately 2 mi, turn left onto N. Dale Mabry for 1 mi; Legends Field is on left.

PARKING: Free for Florida State League games; for spring training, all parking near ballpark is reserved. Ample parking ($5) at Tampa Stadium, across N. Dale Mabry from Legends Field and accessible by footbridge over highway.

TICKET INFORMATION: 3802 W. Martin Luther King Blvd., Tampa, FL 33614, tel. 813/879–2244, fax 813/673–3186.

PRICE RANGE: For Florida State League games, all seats reserved: lower box $5; upper box, adult $3, child $1. Yankees spring training tickets: $14, $12, $10, and $8.

GAME TIME: Mon.–Sat. 7 PM, Sun. 1 PM; gates open 1 hr before game. Most Yankees spring training games 1:05 PM and gates open 2 hrs before game.

TIPS ON SEATING: All seats are excellent. Sit on third-base side for a view of Tampa Stadium (view beyond left field is a car dealership). Third-base side is in the sun during day games. Section 200 seats are not at second level.

SEATING FOR PEOPLE WITH DISABILITIES: 240 seats; companion rest rooms on both third- and first-base sides. 80 reserved parking spaces with access to seating area by elevator.

STADIUM FOOD: The food choices are more varied and much better at the spring training games. Both have 12-inch pizzas for $11 on the first-base side. The Clipper Italian Sausage is $3.50. There are microbrews and imported beers for $4.

SMOKING POLICY: Smoking prohibited in seating areas.

VISITING TEAM HOTEL: Holiday Inn Express (4732 N. Dale Mabry Hwy., Tampa, FL 33614, tel. 813/872–6061 or 800/465–4329).

TOURISM INFORMATION: Tampa/Hillsborough Convention & Visitors Center (111 Madison St., Suite 1010, Tampa, FL 33602, tel. 813/223–1111 or 800/448–2672).

Tampa: Legends Field

George Steinbrenner, the man baseball fans love to hate, has produced a winner in his hometown of Tampa. After three decades in Ft. Lauderdale, the New York Yankees have returned to Tampa Bay, where they trained from the 1920s until the early 1960s, moving into a splendid new Tampa ballpark for spring training 1996. The Tampa Yankees of the Class A Florida State League play here, too.

The $17.5-million Legends Field was designed by Lescher and Mahoney of Tampa to evoke Yankees tradition. Part of an exquisitely landscaped $30-million, 31-acre spring-training complex that includes two other baseball fields, Legends Field is owned and operated by the Tampa Sports Authority. The Yankees have a 30-year lease. The football Tampa Bay Buccaneers play in Tampa Stadium, directly across Dale Mabry Highway from right field. There are 10,387 very comfortable and attractive Yankee-blue seats, each with an excellent view of the action.

Huge blue-and-white banners spell out YANKEES and help give the impression that this is a two-level major-league ballpark. The replica of the classic Yankee Stadium facade along the grandstand roof was a great idea executed less successfully than it might have been. The outfield dimensions are identical to those in Yankee Stadium.

Three of the four columns in front of the gift shop honor past Yankees greats—Babe Ruth, Lou Gehrig, and Miller Huggins, the manager of the 1927 world champions. The fourth column is being saved for the next Yankees legend. Fans walk up steps to the main entrance. The six main entryways to the seating area each highlight a legendary Yankees team with a team photo and banners of the stars—from the "Murderers' Row" team of 1927 to the Reggie Jackson–Thurman Munson champions of 1977.

Legends Field is high-tech, with a great sound system and a first-class scoreboard-videoboard in left-center field. The landscaped plaza, the practice field, and the community field are behind the stadium and hidden from view from the stands. The view from inside the ballpark looking to left and center fields is of a highway and a commercial strip. Tampa Stadium dominates the view past right field. The concessions and rest rooms are on a wide, handsome, and convenient concourse.

Where to Stay

Visiting Team Hotel: Holiday Inn Express–Stadium. This pretty hotel is only two blocks from the ballpark. Its two floors overlook the adjoining small man-made Lake Holiday, where ducks swim. The rooms are standard doubles, and there is a free Continental breakfast bar for guests. *4732 N. Dale Mabry Hwy., exit 23A off I–275, Tampa 33614, tel. 813/877–6061 or 800/465–4329, fax 813/876–1531. 200 rooms. Facilities: outdoor pool, fitness center, game room, coin laundry. AE, D, DC, MC, V. $$*

Where to Eat

Columbia Restaurant. It's hard to tear yourself from the terrific Cuban bread, wrapped in paper for each diner, at this venerable Ybor City restaurant, decorated in Spanish tile and greenery. There is an open courtyard in its center, with a balcony, plus three huge dining rooms, two with stages for the nightly flamenco shows. The all-male wait staff is formal, but the dining for lunch is casual. Its signature 1905 salad, with olives, ham, and cheese, is special, as are all fish dishes and its black bean soup. *2117 E. 7th Ave., Tampa, tel. 813/248–4961. AE, D, DC, MC, V. $$*

Bern's Steak House. This well-known meat palace is frequented by tourists eager to see just how good the steaks are. They're excellent, expensive, and accompanied by superb vegetables grown on the restaurant's farm. After your dinner, you can tour the restaurant and wine room before you go upstairs to a room devoted entirely to desserts. Customers sit at booths in this room, decorated with wine vats, and choose from among 80 sweets. Bern's plain warehouse facade does not look appealing from the outside, and the overdone red velvet interior downstairs is a bit much, but the food is excellent. *1208 S. Howard Ave., Tampa, tel. 813/251–2421. No lunch. AE, DC, D, MC, V. $$*

Entertainments

Busch Gardens and Adventure Island. An extensive zoo with endangered species is the add-on in this 336-acre theme park, which has Moroccan and African-style buildings and souk markets. There are the Serengeti Plain, Myombe Reserve for primates, and a skyride and monorail. The international flavor extends to the food, which includes tame versions of many foreign cuisines. Kids are chiefly interested in the thrill rides, such as Montu, the world's largest inverted roller coaster. You literally ride in cars underneath the tracks, which go underground after some big drops. Adventure Island waterpark has separate admission. *Busch Blvd., at McKinley Ave., Tampa, tel. 813/987–5082. Busch Gardens admission: $43.70 adults, $34.70 ages 3–9; parking $4. Open daily 9:30–6 PM. Adventure Island admission: $23.95 adults, $21.95 ages 3–9. Open daily 9–7.*

Florida Aquarium. This impressive $84-million three-level aquarium has Florida's water resources as its theme, from coral reefs to limestone caves and wetlands. Overlooking the Port of Tampa, visitors walk under a huge glass dome resembling a seashell. The emphasis is on habitats; visitors are given audio wands that provide descriptions. The facility is home to more than 4,300 animals and plants. *701 Channelside Dr., Tampa, tel. 813/273–4000. Admission: $11.95 adults, $10.95 senior citizens, $6.95 ages 3–12; parking $3. Open daily 9:30–5.*

Lowry Park Zoo. One of our favorite small zoos in the country, this shaded, peaceful park keeps animals at children's-eye level and keeps the walking times manageable. Its 29 acres are packed with animals in their own habitats, from primates to birds. A new Aquatic Center has a manatee hospital; you can see the tanks where the recovering manatees are living. There is a petting zoo and aviary with tropical birds. *North Blvd. and Sligh Ave., Tampa, tel. 813/935–8552. Admission: $8.50 adults, $7.50 senior citizens; $4.95 children 3–11. Open daily 9:30–5.*

Museum of Science and Industry. This multipurpose science center contains a planetarium, nature trails, an IMAX dome theater, and hundreds of hands-on exhibits, including many space shuttle displays. Visitors wearing goggles and earplugs can sit through a two-minute hurricane in a special room where 75-mph wind velocity and noise are duplicated. The museum is light-filled, with the open-air design popular in the early 1980s that exposed service pipes—painted in bright colors—overhead. *4801 E. Fowler Ave., Tampa, tel. 813/987–6300. Admission: $13 adults, $11 senior citizens, $9 ages 2–13. Open Sun.–Thurs. 9–7, Fri.–Sat. 9–7.*

Ybor City. This National Landmark District contains former and current cigar-making factories, old Latin restaurants, wrought-iron balconies on storefronts, cafés, bakeries, and an interesting State Museum (1818 Ninth Ave., tel. 813/247–6323). The museum catalogues the enterprises and residents of the area, which is named for Don Vicente Martinez Ybor, a cigar maker and Cuban exile, who arrived here in 1885. Ybor City, which has been called Tampa's Latin Quarter, has many shops, vintage clothing stores, and art galleries. Free guided walking tours are available through the Historic District from the Ybor City Chamber of Commerce (1800 E. 9th Ave., Tampa, tel. 813/248–3712). For a daily schedule of other free walking tours, contact the State Museum. *Bounded by 6th Ave., 12th Ave., 23rd Ave., and Nick Nuccio Pkwy., Tampa.*

ST. PETERSBURG DEVIL RAYS/TAMPA BAY DEVIL RAYS SPRING TRAINING

League: Florida State League • **Major League Affiliation:** Tampa Bay Devil Rays • **Class:** A • **Stadium:** Al Lang Field/Florida Power Park • **Opened:** 1947 • **Capacity:** 7,004 • **Dimensions:** LF: 330, CF: 410, RF: 330 • **Surface:** grass • **Season:** Apr.–Labor Day

STADIUM LOCATION: 180 2nd Ave. SE, St. Petersburg, FL 33701.

TEAM WEB SITE: www.stpetedevilrays.com

GETTING THERE: From I–275, Exit 9 (First St.); First St. south 2 blocks to stadium.

PARKING: Parking near stadium operated by City of St. Petersburg; $2 fee.

TICKET INFORMATION: Box 12557, St. Petersburg, FL 33733, tel. 727/822–3384, fax 727/895–1556; for spring training tickets, call 727/898–7297

PRICE RANGE: Field boxes $5; loge box $3; grandstand $3.

GAME TIME: Mon.–Sat. 7:05 PM, Sun. 5 PM; gates open 75 min before game.

TIPS ON SEATING: For best view of Tampa Bay beyond left-field wall, sit on first-base side high up in the stands; small roof shades some of upper grandstand seats.

SEATING FOR PEOPLE DISABILITIES: Behind field box sections 6 and 7.

STADIUM FOOD: Florida ballparks may have ordinary menus, but at least there's usually good brown mustard—a legacy from the senior-citizen fans who grew up with good mustard in Philadelphia and New York. Use it here on a jumbo dog ($3.50) or a warm pretzel ($3). A grill on the outer concourse on the first-base side serves burgers and chicken sandwiches. Avoid the bad lemonade and go right to dessert. You have a choice of Italian ices, Haägen-Dazs ice cream, or yogurt.

SMOKING POLICY: Smoking not allowed in the seating bowl, but permitted on the concourse.

VISITING TEAM HOTEL: Best Western Mirage (5005 34th St. N, St. Petersburg, FL 33714, tel. 727/525–1181 or 800/528–1234).

TOURISM INFORMATION: St. Petersburg, Clearwater, and Dunedin Convention & Visitors Bureau (Tropicana Field, 1 Stadium Dr., Suite A, St. Petersburg, FL 33705, tel. 727/464–7200 or 800/345–6710).

St. Petersburg: Al Lang Field/Florida Power Park

In 1911, Al Lang got sick. As a result, baseball changed forever. Stadium historian Michael Benson tells the story this way: Albert Fielding Lang, the 41-year-old owner of a successful Pittsburgh laundry business, fell ill and was told he had six months to live. He moved to St. Petersburg, Florida, and recovered. When he heard about the long stretch of bad weather that major-league teams were having in their spring training in Arkansas, Lang invited the St. Louis Browns to train in St. Petersburg in 1914 at Coffee Pot Park near the Coffee Pot Bayou. Many other teams followed. As Florida's ambassador to big-time baseball, Lang was the genius who helped bring spring training to the state. Lang's recovery was pretty solid. He lived to be 89.

The Boston Braves trained at Waterfront Park from 1921 to 1937. The St. Louis Cardinals have been training in St. Petersburg since 1938. In 1947, the city built a new $300,000 ballpark at the foot of First Avenue on the waterfront just south of Waterfront Park. The new field was dedicated in Lang's honor to express appreciation for his extraordinary devotion to baseball.

Al Lang Field is set comfortably at the base of the downtown. The cold, gray-concrete exterior belies the warm, intimate interior. The field was shaped like the Polo Grounds until it was rebuilt in 1977 in a more conventional and symmetrical shape. Tall office buildings rise behind home plate, and a major hotel stretches down the right-field line. Palm trees blow in the breeze beyond the right-field wall. You can see Tampa Bay over the left-field wall. There's a real organist performing the "Star Spangled Banner" and there are lots of on-field contests.

In order to attract a major-league team, the community built the $138-million Florida Sun Coast Dome in 1990 and spent an extra $30 million to make it baseball-ready. It is now the home of the Tampa Bay Devil Rays, a National League expansion team. The Devil Rays train,

however, at Al Lang Field, and their Single A Florida State League farm club, the St. Petersburg Devil Rays, plays here from April through Labor Day. The St. Louis Cardinals used Al Lang Field for one last spring training in 1997.

The Dome, now called Tropicana Field (1 Stadium Dr., St. Petersburg, FL 33705; Tampa Bay Devil Rays information, tel. 727/825–3137), is as hideous a piece of sports architecture as you can imagine. From the outside, it looks like a gigantic municipal water tank, a scar across an otherwise delightful city landscape. Inside, no amount of tinkering could add charm to this monstrosity, which is carpeted with artificial turf. The Tampa Bay Walk of Fame, in front of Tropicana Field, recognizes Tampa Bay sports figures from Al Lang to Wade Boggs.

More St. Petersburg Baseball

Old-Timers Softball Game. St. Pete is famous for its Kids 'n Kubs senior-citizen league. You must be at least 75 years old to play, and the cheerleaders are the same age. The free games are played in a city park with bleachers at the foot of 8th Avenue Northeast. *Northshore Park, St. Petersburg, tel. 727/893–7108. Games played end Oct.–mid-Apr., Tues., Thurs., and Sat. at 1.*

Where to Stay

St. Petersburg Hilton Downtown. You can see into the ballpark from the top levels of this 15-floor high-rise hotel. Built next to the marina, it is convenient to all downtown attractions. *333 1st St. S, St. Petersburg 33701, tel. 727/894–5000 or 800/445–8667, fax 727/823–4797. 333 rooms. Facilities: 2 restaurants, outdoor pool, hot tub, exercise room. AE, D, DC, MC, V. $$*

Beach Park Motor Inn. This small, reasonably priced bay-front motel is across the street from the Museum of Fine Arts. Several of its rooms have kitchens. *300 Beach Dr. NE, St. Petersburg 33701, tel. 727/898–6325. 26 rooms. AE, D, MC, V. $*

Heritage Holiday Inn. This three-floor historic downtown hotel, built in the golden era of the 1920s, offers a free Continental breakfast on weekends. The medium-size rooms have high ceilings. *234 3rd Ave. N, St. Petersburg 33701, tel.*

727/822–4814 or 800/283–7829, fax 727/ 823–1644. 75 rooms. Facilities: restaurant, outdoor pool, hot tub. AE, D, DC, MC, V. $$

Inn on the Beach. The two-story wooden inn is worth the 20-minute drive from downtown to the gulf resort of Passe-a-Grille in St. Pete Beach. There are 12 homelike suites with kitchens. Ten of the rooms are doubles; two can sleep four. No two rooms are alike. Most have ceiling fans and window air conditioners. The inn is in a residential neighborhood and just steps from a swimming beach. 1401 Gulf Way, St. Pete Beach 33706, tel. 727/360–8844. 12 rooms. AE, D, DC, MC, V. $$.

Where to Eat

Piccadilly Cafeteria. Fans come for the red velvet cake, but there are dozens of other desserts to consider. The salads may even tempt your children. The children's menu includes several meat-and-two-vegetable combinations. The cafeteria is on U.S. 19S in the Sun Coast Shopping Center, 4 mi from Al Lang Stadium. 1900 34th St. N, St. Petersburg, tel. 727/328–1501. AE, DC, MC, V. $

Skyway Jack's. Early risers can choose from among four dozen different breakfasts, all of them bargains. The restaurant takes its name from the Sunshine Skyway Bridge, which is nearby. 6701 34th St. S, Exit 3 from I–275, St. Petersburg, tel. 727/866–3217. MC, V. No dinner. $

Ted Peters Famous Smoked Fish. All varieties of expertly smoked fish, especially the local favorite, mullet, are sold here. You may eat inside this small restaurant or at an outdoor picnic table. There also are burgers and a great homemade potato salad for people who don't eat fish. 1350 Pasadena Ave. S, St. Petersburg, tel. 727/381–7931. No credit cards. $

Uncle Andy's at Don CeSar Beach Resort. It's too costly for most to stay here, but you can spring for an ice-cream cone in Uncle Andy's ice-cream parlor to see this gorgeous pink rococo landmark. Built on the beach in 1928, it was home to the vacationing Babe Ruth and Lou Gehrig. 3400 Gulf Blvd., St. Pete Beach, tel. 727/360–1881. AE, D, MC, V. $

Entertainments

Great Explorations. There are six pavilions of a hands-on museum in the renovated five-story city pier. Younger children may not like the "Touch Tunnel," a dark maze. "Explore Galore" is a special section aimed at patrons under seven. The pier also contains an aquarium, miniature golf, restaurants, fishing, and shops. 1120 4th St. S, St. Petersburg, tel. 727/821–8885. Admission: $4 ages 4–adult. Open Mon.–Sat. 10–8, Sun. 11–6.

HISTORIC VIRGINIA
NORFOLK, RICHMOND

Two Virginia cities—Norfolk and Richmond—give you very different, but outstanding, baseball experiences. Norfolk's Harbor Park has an exciting backdrop of commercial boat traffic in the Elizabeth River. A facility on the harbor, Nauticus, teaches children about oceans, boats, and marine animals. Williamsburg and the Jamestown Settlement are 25 mi northwest on Route 64, alongside the enticing Busch Gardens amusement park.

Another 30 mi west of Williamsburg on Route 64 brings you to The Diamond in Richmond, a 12,500-seat stadium in the same Triple A International League as Norfolk. The stadium was completely rebuilt in 1984 and radiates serious baseball, with no crazy contests or mascots. This is one of the few state capitols that you can view from a raft, as the James River runs through downtown.

NORFOLK TIDES

League: International League • **Major League Affiliation:** New York Mets • **Class:** AAA • **Stadium:** Harbor Park • **Opened:** 1993 • **Capacity:** 12,057 • **Dimensions:** LF: 333, CF: 410, RF: 338 • **Surface:** grass • **Season:** Apr.–Labor Day

STADIUM LOCATION: 150 Park Ave., Norfolk, VA 23510.

WEB SITE: www.norfolktides.com

GETTING THERE: From I–264, Exit 9 (Waterside Dr.), adjacent to Elizabeth River. At first traffic light, left onto Water St., which leads you to the ballpark.

PARKING: Ample parking available for $2.

TICKET INFORMATION: 150 Park Ave., Norfolk, VA 23510, tel. 757/622–2222, fax 757/624–9090.

PRICE RANGE: Box seats $8; lower and upper reserved seats $6.50 adults, $5.50 children, senior citizens, and active military personnel.

GAME TIME: Mon.–Sat. 7:15 PM, Sun. 1:15 (Apr.–June) and 6:15 (July–Aug.); gates open 75 min before game.

TIPS ON SEATING: All seats reserved. Best harbor view is from third-base side. First few rows of upper reserved seats provide great view of water.

SEATING FOR PEOPLE WITH DISABILITIES: Available throughout park; stadium has elevators.

STADIUM FOOD: In the concourse, try the smoky cheddar sausage ($3, sauerkraut 25¢ extra). It's from the grills on each side of the stadium. The chicken sandwiches, Italian and Polish sausages, and BBQ pork aren't special. There are Vinnie's hot pretzels from a grill, pan pizzas for $4, and fresh lemonade for $2.50. A picnic area is on the far wall behind second base. The three-tier restaurant, Hits at the Park, is past first base and open 2 hrs before game time, but you must have a game ticket to eat there. The crab cakes dinner is excellent but pricey at $15.95. You can feed the kids from its four-item children's menu for less than the ballpark concessions.

SMOKING POLICY: Smoking prohibited throughout stadium with limited exceptions.

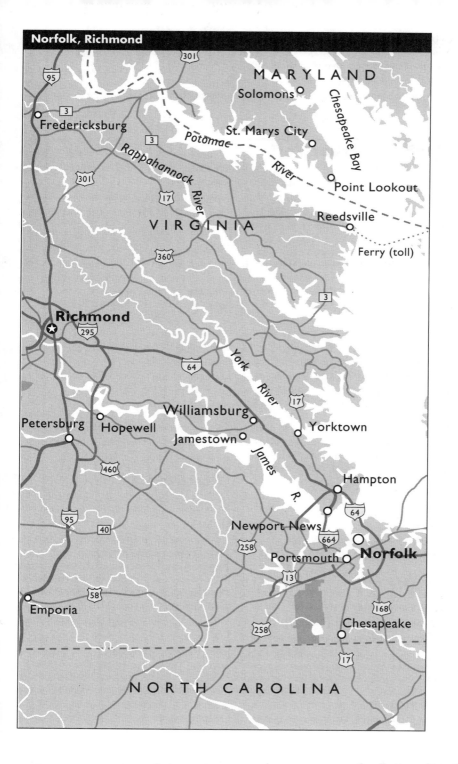

Norfolk, Richmond

MARYLAND

Solomons

Chesapeake Bay

St. Marys City

Potomac River

301

95

3

Fredericksburg

3

Rappahannock River

301

17

VIRGINIA

Point Lookout

Reedsville

Ferry (toll)

360

3

Richmond

295

64

York River

17

Williamsburg

Yorktown

Petersburg

Hopewell

Jamestown

James R.

Hampton

64

460

Newport News

95

40

664

258

Portsmouth

Norfolk

13

Emporia

58

168

258

Chesapeake

17

NORTH CAROLINA

Visiting Team Hotel: Sheraton Waterside (777 Waterside Dr., Norfolk, VA 23510, tel. 757/622–6664 or 800/325–3535).

Tourism Information: Norfolk Convention & Visitors Bureau (236 E. Plume St., Norfolk, VA 23510, tel. 757/441–1852 or 800/368–3097).

Norfolk: Harbor Park

What a difference a decade makes. The baseball in Richmond is first-rate. In Norfolk, the baseball *and* the stadium are first-rate. Richmond's Diamond is built in the classic, imposing 1980s style that people expect at the Triple A level, where many of the players are on the road to the Show. It's a fine place to play and watch a game. Norfolk's new Harbor Park, however, is a notch above—a spectacular 1990s ballpark, ranked among the best of minor-league ballparks by *Baseball America*. You can see trains, boats, and planes from your seat in the ballpark.

Designed by HOK and built for $15 million, the 12,057-seat Harbor Park sits on the bank of the Elizabeth River in Norfolk's revitalized downtown. Metropolitan Park, a 1970 stadium 6 mi from the downtown out near the airport, was showing its age when rival Virginia Beach began to make noises about building a stadium. Norfolk wasn't about to lose baseball to Virginia Beach. The Tidewater Tides, who had played in Met Park in Norfolk, became the Norfolk Tides, and Harbor Park opened in 1993.

The attractive brick entrance is colored in shades of beige. In Richmond most of the seats are in the upper deck. In Norfolk the majority of seats are on the first level. The best aspect of this beautiful new, fan-friendly stadium is the open concourse. You can go to the concession stands, buy what you need, and not miss a pitch. There are scoreboards in left and right, and you can get the scores of other International League games, a minor-league rarity.

The best view of the water is from the second deck on the third-base side in this waterfront park. Mostly what you see is industrial. Freight trains run behind left field. You cannot see the harbor well from many of the lower-level box seats. The Hits at Harbor Park restaurant out the first-base line is built on three levels, with lots of good views. There is an attractive multi-tier grass picnic area just beyond the left-field fence where kids can race around. It is reserved for private groups until 9 PM, when it opens to the public.

Arrive early and listen to the Tide Strolling Brass Band play for the hour before the game. Beware—the sound system is loud here and not friendly to the Tides' opponents. Rip Tide, the mascot, is giant, blue, fuzzy, lively, and friendly. You can get your child's face painted, and there is an excellent souvenir shop at the entrance. There are more contests and on-field antics than in most Triple A stadiums.

Norfolk baseball goes back almost 100 years, and it is worth the time to look at the Tidewater Baseball Shrine plaques along the concourse wall. Future Hall of Famer Pie Traynor, a Portsmouth star before being signed to play third base for the Pittsburgh Pirates, is here. Fastballer Bob Feller pitched for the Navy in Norfolk before going back to the Cleveland Indians. Philosopher and future Yankees great Yogi Berra drove in 23 runs in two games as a 17-year-old Norfolk Tar.

Where to Stay

Visiting Team Hotel: Sheraton Waterside. This impressive 10-story hotel is on the Elizabeth River, next to the Waterside Festival marketplace and less than a half mile from the ballpark. Half the rooms have a harbor view. All rooms are large and decorated in shades of purple. Guests may use a fitness center next door for $6 a day. *777 Waterside Dr., Norfolk 23510, tel. 757/622–6664 or 800/325–3535, fax 757/625–8271. 446 rooms. Facilities: restaurant, outdoor pool. AE, D, DC, MC, V. $$*

Best Western–Center Inn. This quiet, attractive inn is in the southeast part of town, near the Military Circle shopping mall. The two-story inn, set back from the road in a country-club-style setting, is 10 minutes east of the ballpark. *235 N. Military Hwy., Norfolk 23502, tel. 757/461–6600* *or 800/528–1234, fax 757/466–9093. 152 rooms. Facilities: restaurant, indoor and outdoor pools, hot tub, sauna, exercise room, coin laundry. AE, D, DC, MC, V. $$*

Where to Eat

Doumar's Drive-In. This casual restaurant was founded by Abe Doumar, the creator of the ice-cream cone at the 1904 St. Louis Exposition. Now run by his nephew, Albert Doumar, this is the place for fresh limeades, burgers, and sweet, freshly made ice-cream cones. The cone press is within view, batter drippings and all. You can still get car service here. But with ice cream, you're likely to do better inside at the Formica booths. *19th and Monticello Sts., Norfolk, tel. 757/627–4163. No credit cards. $*

Joe's Crab Shack. Its Waterside Festival marketplace location makes it a convenient stop before the ball game. This is a large seafood restaurant with dancing waiters and an indoor playground. Crab cakes, chowders, and Key Lime pie are special. Teddy bears, boats, and fake sharks hang from the ceiling. *333 Waterside Dr. (lower level), Norfolk, tel. 757/625–0655. AE, DC, D, MC, V. $$*

Entertainments

Busch Gardens. This amusement park is based on four European countries during the 17th century—Germany, Italy, England, and France. Adults like this park for the superior food, and kids are delighted by the number and intensity of its rides. The "Escape from Pompeii" water ride is scary, and several other rides—"Loch Ness Monster" and "Drachen Fire" roller coasters, "Big Bad Wolf" free-fall—are best for teenagers. Beer is given out at the hospitality center. Discount coupons for the park and for Water Country are available through the Norfolk Convention Center (tel. 800/368–3097). Parking is $4. *1 Busch Gardens Blvd. (U.S. 60), Exit 242A from I-64, Williamsburg, tel. 757/253–3350. Admission: $35 adults, $28 ages 3–6. Open mid-May–Labor Day, daily 10–7; Apr., weekends 10—7; early Sept.–end Oct., Fri.–Tues. 10–7.*

***Carrie B. Norfolk* Harbor Tour.** This reproduction Mississippi paddle wheeler takes visitors past the Norfolk waterfront, the Navy submarines, dry dock, and aircraft carriers. The noon tour is 90 minutes, the later tour 2½ hours. There also are sunset cruises from June through Labor Day. Phillips Waterside seafood restaurant offers lunch and dinner packages with the cruises. *The Waterside, Norfolk, tel. 757/393–4735. Admission (90-min tour): $11.95 adults, $5.95 ages under 12. Open Apr.–Oct. 2 and 6 PM. AE, MC, V.*

Children's Museum of Virginia. From Norfolk you can take the five-minute ferry across the river and walk to this hands-on museum. Children use a working crane to haul (foam) I-beams in a construction exhibit. They also can climb walls, cover themselves in bubbles, learn about kaleidoscopes, and see constellations in the 64-seat planetarium. *221 High St., Portsmouth, tel. 757/393–8393 or 800/767–8782. Admission: $4. Open Mon.–Sat. 10–5, Sun. 1–5.*

Elizabeth River Ferry. If you don't have time or money for a cruise, this 5-minute paddlewheel trip takes you across the harbor and back. It departs from the Waterside every 30 minutes on the quarter hour. *The Waterside, Norfolk, tel. 757/640–6300. Admission: 75¢ adults, 50¢ children.*

Nauticus–National Maritime Center. This terrific learning museum is part science, part aquarium, and part amusement park. You can learn about the world's major shipwrecks in a fascinating audiovisual display. Visitors can ride in a submarine in Virtual Adventures and try out a naval-battle simulator. There's a kid-friendly touch pool with (baby) sharks and starfish and squid in eye-level tanks. At an adjoining deep-water pier, working ships are docked. Its theater has a big-screen *Living Sea* film for $2 extra. You can park in city lots two blocks south. This attraction is less than a mile from Harbor Park baseball. *1 Waterside Dr., Norfolk, tel. 757/664–1000 or 800/664–1080. Admission: $7.50 adults, $5 ages 4–17, under 3 free with paying companion. Open daily 10–5. MC, V.*

Virginia Zoological Park. This small zoo, on the Lafayette River, has a superb tiger exhibit. The park is easily navigated by small children and is inexpensive. There also are elephants, monkeys, and snakes, among its 300 animals. *3500 Granby St., Norfolk, tel. 757/441–5227. Admission: $2 adults, $1 children; free Sun. and Mon. Open daily 10–5.*

Water Country USA. This 40-acre water park has 30 rides, including "Rambling Water," a calming, lazy river ride. The park is decorated in a '60s surfing theme and is 3 mi from Busch Gardens, which owns it. A 3-day combo pass for the two parks is $55 per person and can be used over a 14-day period. *176 Water Country Pkwy., Williamsburg, tel. 757/229–9300. Admission: $27 adults, $19.50 ages 3–6. Open late May–Labor Day, daily 10–7; early Sept.–mid-Sept., weekends 10–dusk.*

Sights to See

College of William & Mary. This beautiful college is the nation's second-oldest. U.S. Presidents Thomas Jefferson, James Monroe, and John Tyler were graduates. Children may cringe at the hard chairs and severe atmosphere of the Wren Building, where classes have been held since 1695. Students act as tour guides. *Duke of Gloucester St., Williamsburg, tel. 757/221–3278. Open Sept.–May, Mon.–Sat. 9–5.*

Jamestown Settlement. The remains of the first permanent English settlement lie just west of Williamsburg. It is outdoor living history of the 1640s, with the original church tower, house foundations, three reconstructed ships, and a replica of a Powhatan Indian village. You can try on armor at a fort and play early versions of bowling and ring toss. A combination pass with the Yorktown Victory Center is available for $14 adults, $6.75 ages 6–12. *Rte. 31 S and Colonial Pkwy., Williamsburg, tel. 757/229–1607. Admission: $10.25 adults, $5 ages 6–12. Open daily 9–5.*

Walking Tours of Historic Norfolk. A downtown walking tour should include the newly restored Wells Theatre (108 E. Tazewell St., tel. 757/627–6988) and the nearly intact 1890s-to-1930s commercial district. You can get a free brochure and map from the Norfolk Convention and Visitors Bureau. *236 E. Plume St., Norfolk, tel. 800/368–3097.*

Williamsburg. More than 500 buildings make up this living-history museum. Williamsburg was the state capital from 1699 to 1780, and this restoration returns you to those years, public stockades and all. In an old American tradition, the capitol building was surrounded by excellent taverns that still serve memorable meals. All the contradictions are shown—an 18th-century economy based on tobacco and slavery that produced some of the greatest leaders civilization has known. If your children don't have the patience to view historic interiors, you do not need to buy passes if you only walk the streets, browse the shops, or eat in the unique taverns. There is short-term parking in the Williamsburg shops area adjacent to the Historic District. *Rte. 132 and Francis St., Williamsburg, tel. 800/447–8679. Admission: $25 adults, $15 ages 6–12. Open daily 9–5.*

Yorktown National Battlefield and Victory Center. The Revolutionary War comes alive here, at the site of the war's last major battle. You can explore Washington's headquarters site, Surrender Field, and the house where General Cornwallis discussed his surrender. It also is a good place to picnic. At the center, you can see a Colonial-era farm and an army camp. The battlefield is free and open daily 8:30–5. Maps are available for a self-guided tour of the battlefield. *Old Rte. 238, Yorktown, tel. 757/253–4838. Admission: $7.25 adults, $3.50 ages 6–12. Open daily 9–5.*

RICHMOND BRAVES

League: International League • **Major League Affiliation:** Atlanta Braves • **Class:** AAA • **Stadium:** The Diamond • **Opened:** 1954/85 • **Capacity:** 12,146 • **Dimensions:** LF: 330, CF: 402, RF: 330 • **Surface:** grass • **Season:** Apr.–Labor Day

STADIUM LOCATION: 3001 N. Blvd. Richmond, VA 23230

WEB SITE: www.rbraves.com

GETTING THERE: From I–95, take exit 78 (Blvd. exit) 2 blocks south to Stadium. Traveling east or west, I–65 will merge with I–95.

PARKING: $2 at stadium and across street next to bus station.

TICKET INFORMATION: Box 6667, Richmond, VA 23230, tel. 804/359–4444, fax 804/359–0731.

PRICE RANGE: Box seats $8; press box–level seats $6; general admission $5 adults, $3 ages 3–12 and senior citizens, under 3 free.

GAME TIME: Mon.–Sat. 7 PM, Sun. 2 PM; gates open 1 hr before game time.

TIPS ON SEATING: Reserved seats in second deck are close to action, as there is little foul territory here. Roof provides shade on sunny Sunday afternoons.

SEATING FOR PEOPLE WITH DISABILITIES: On main concourse behind home plate with access by elevator; special parking is available on third-base side of stadium.

STADIUM FOOD: The **Diamond Room** restaurant, on the main concourse on the first-base side behind sections 101–104, is open to all fans starting 75 min before the game. There are children's prices—$6.95 for the turkey dinner that costs adults $12.95. Reserve one week to one month ahead for window seats. There's a no-smoking section. The concourse offerings are standard, but the hot dogs and corn dogs are not good. Fruit juices are available by the terraces, as are club sandwiches. There's grilled Italian sausage on the third-base side by the entrance.

SMOKING POLICY: Smoking permitted on the concourse but not in the seating area.

VISITING TEAM HOTEL: Holiday Inn I–64 (6531 W. Broad St., Richmond, VA 23230, tel. 804/285–9951 or 800/465–4329).

TOURISM INFORMATION: Metro Richmond Convention & Visitors Bureau (550 E. Marshall St., Richmond, VA 23219, tel. 804/782–2777 or 800/365—7272).

Richmond:
The Diamond

The Diamond in Richmond got its name because of a letter from an anonymous fan, "a fan on the third-base side." The stadium could have been named for Dr. William H. Parker, the great supporter of amateur athletics in Richmond for whom the predecessor stadium had been named. Or it could have been named for former Richmond Brave Tommie Aaron, the younger brother of Hank Aaron who had died of leukemia in 1983. But the November 1984 letter won the day: "Richmond could use a healthy dose of hope and togetherness and the Diamond can be a special mix of our combined efforts in building the park along with the magic attraction of the game."

The catchy campaign slogan to replace the shabby Parker Field with a state-of-the-art stadium was "Diamonds Aren't Forever." The community rallied to the call with funds supplied by the city, and the suburbs matched by private contributions. "The Diamond" struck a chord with many as the perfect representation of that community partnership. The letter is reprinted on the Richmond Wall of Fame on the stadium's first-base side.

The Diamond sits just off I–95 not far outside town. A field was first built here on the Boulevard in 1934. The high-school football stadium was converted into a baseball stadium in 1954 and named Parker Field for Triple A International League baseball. After the 1984 season, the field was completely rebuilt in 226 days at a cost of $8 million. Amazingly, the double-decked, roofed stadium was ready for the 1985 season. Seven thousand of the 12,500 seats are in the upper deck. Foul territory is limited, and the steep-sloped upper-deck seats are surprisingly close to the action.

You are greeted on the concourse level by Chief Connecticut, a 10- by 20-ft fiberglass Native American acquired from a suburban

Maryland shopping center. Next you will be struck by the wonderful smells from the grill at the third-base side of the entrance. The best food, however, is across the street at Bill's Barbecue. Stop there first.

The truth is that the view from the seats beyond the advertising signs on the stadium wall is uninspiring. Trucks and cars whiz by on I–95 beyond parking lots, hotels, factories, and an aging arena. But the Diamond isn't about beautiful views or on-the-field contests for fans. The Diamond is about baseball. And this is quality Triple A baseball. The Diamond is full of serious, well-informed fans. The crowd is in the game, egged on by the scoreboard flashing "Noise. Noise. Noise."

When the Braves moved south to Atlanta from Milwaukee, their Triple A Atlanta Crackers moved to Richmond. This three-decade affiliation has brought top talent to Richmond, from the brothers Niekro to David Justice and Tommy Glavine. Ted Turner, who owns both Braves teams, umpired a May 10, 1978, exhibition game between his two clubs here.

Where to Stay

If you don't have to plan ahead, you can save money and stay in one of the city's elegant hotels by using one of four visitor centers (1710 Robin Hood Rd., by the ballpark, Exit 78 from I–95 and I–64, Richmond, tel. 804/358–5511; 6th St. Marketplace, 2nd floor, 550 E. Marshall St., Richmond, tel. 804/782–2777; State Capitol grounds, bell tower, Capitol Sq., Richmond, tel. 804/648–3146; Richmond International Airport, Exit 197 from I–64, Richmond, tel. 804/236–3260) to make same-day bookings. The centers offer walk-in customers the lowest prices at the elegant Berkeley Hotel, Linden Row Inn, and Jefferson Hotel, as well as moderately priced lodgings.

Visiting Team Hotel: Holiday Inn I–64. This hotel has a seven-story tower and a main five-story section. The ballpark is 3 mi away. The rooms are standard size, and kids eat free. *6531 W. Broad St., Exit 183 from I–64, Richmond 23230, tel. 804/ 285–9951 or 800/465–4329, fax 804/282– 5642. 280 rooms. Facilities: restaurant, indoor pool, hot tub, exercise room. AE, D, DC, MC, V. $$*

The Jefferson Hotel. This gloriously renovated 1895 hotel has a majestic center stairway, an immense lobby, and high-ceiling rooms with tasteful reproduction antiques. The downtown landmark is on the National Register of Historic Places. Self-parking is $9.50 daily. Swimming is available free to guests across the street at the YMCA's indoor pool. *Franklin and Adams Sts., Richmond 23220, tel. 804/788– 8000 or 800/424–8014, fax 804/225–0334. 275 rooms. Facilities: restaurants, health club. AE, D, DC, MC, V. $$*

Omni Richmond Hotel. This downtown highrise has 19 floors, with good views of the city. Rooms are slightly larger than usual. Underground parking is $9 per day. *100 S. 12th St., Richmond 23219, tel. 804/344–7000 or 800/ 843–6664, fax 804/648–6704. 361 rooms. Facilities: 2 restaurants, indoor pool. AE, D, DC, MC, V. $$*

Where to Eat

Bill's Barbecue. This has been a Richmond institution since 1930 and now has seven locations, including this one across from the ballpark. It serves wonderful fresh limeades, including one version with grape juice added. The chopped pork sandwich is topped with dry coleslaw and wrapped in gray paper with a toothpick. There also are good onion rings and several varieties of pies, like lemon chess and pecan. Its motto rings true: "A trial makes a customer at Bill's Barbecue." *3100 N. Boulevard, Richmond, tel. 804/358–8634. No credit cards. $*

Joe's Inn. This is the kind of warm, neighborhood place that Hollywood romanticizes. Service can be harried, because this wooden-booth spaghetti and pizza place is popular with families, students, and neighbors. There is a kid's menu. It is in the Victorian-era Fan District between Hanover and Grove streets. *205 N. Shields Ave., Richmond, tel. 804/355–2282. AE, MC, V. $*

John and Norman's. This casual spot near the Fan District is known for its breakfasts. There are jukeboxes on the tables and regulars in the chairs. *2525 Hanover Ave., Richmond, tel. 804/ 358–9731. D, MC, V. $*

Entertainments

Raft rides on the James River. You've probably never floated through a major city before. The Richmond Raft Co. will take you through downtown via class 3 and 4 white water for those 12 and older. Or the whole family can take the slower, flat-water run on Sunday at 2 and 4. Buy your tickets and embark at the foot of the former Tredegar Iron Works. *Tredegar St., Richmond, tel. 804/222–7238. Cost: $22–$45 per person. Times vary according to river conditions.*

Science Museum of Virginia. This hands-on museum with more than 250 exhibits and demonstrations is in the city's former Broad Street Railroad Station. An adjoining planetarium and space theater have planet and constellation shows and laser shows. The IMAX movie is $4 extra. *2500 W. Broad St., Richmond, tel. 804/367–0000 or 800/659–1727. Admission: $5 adults, $4 ages 4–12, $4.50 senior citizens. Open Mon.–Thurs. 9:30–5, Fri.–Sat. 9:30–7, Sun. 11:30–5.*

Sights to See

"Bojangles" Statue. Don't miss the monument to Bill "Bojangles" Robinson, the film star and tap dancer, at Leigh and Chamberlayne Parkway near his birthplace. The statue is where Robinson donated a stoplight to protect neighborhood children who followed the same route to school that he took as a child.

Canal Walk. A pleasant walk borders the river from between 10th and Bank streets to the James River Plaza. The Kanawha Canal locks are at 12th and Byrd streets.

Executive Mansion. On an attractive park stands the 1813 Executive Mansion, the oldest governor's residence in the country. Nearby is an elegant equestrian statue of George Washington. *Governor's St., Richmond, tel. 804/371–2642. Open Tues. 2–4, Fri. 10–noon.*

Historic Richmond Tour. Guided walking tours of history, architecture, and specific Richmond sights, like the Hollywood Cemetery, are held each Sunday. The departure site varies depending on the topic. Bus tours leave daily from downtown hotels and the Richmond Visitor's Center. Reservations should be made a day in advance. *Historic Richmond Foundation, tel. 804/780–0107. Admission: $5–$16 adults, $5–$13 ages 6–18. Open Apr.–Oct., Sun. 2–4.*

Maggie L. Walker Home. In Jackson Ward, Richmond's historic black district, called "the birthplace of black capitalism," is the home of Maggie L. Walker, founder of the St. Luke Penny Savings Bank, the first bank founded by a woman. *110½ E. Leigh St., Richmond, tel. 804/780–1380. Open Wed.–Sun. 9–5.*

Monument Avenue. It is worth a drive down this broad 1887-era boulevard. Civil War monuments and a statue of tennis star Arthur Ashe (at Roseneath St.) dot the wide median while mansions and churches line its sides.

Richmond National Battlefield Park. View several Civil War forts and battle sites here. Start at the Chimborazo Visitor Center, once the site of a major Civil War hospital. There's a movie, exhibits, and several self-guided tours. *3215 E. Broad St., Richmond, tel. 804/226–1981. Open daily 9–5.*

Shockoe Slip. Cobblestone streets, tobacco warehouses, new shops, and the elegant Berkeley Hotel mark this area. One of the city's three microbreweries, Richbrau, runs a pub here. *E. Cary St., between 12th and 15th Sts.*

Softball Hall of Fame Museum. There are four memento-crammed rooms, an eight-minute movie, and photos of some of the 100,000 teams in the U.S. Slo-Pitch Softball Association in this museum, 30 minutes south of Richmond. The industrial, church, Hispanic, men's, women's, mixed, and youth leagues cover every state. *3935 S. Crater Rd., Petersburg, VA, tel. 804/733–1005. Admission: $1.50 adults, $1 ages 12–18 and senior citizens, under 12 free. Open weekdays 9–4, Sat. 10–4, Sun. noon–4.*

State Capitol. Richmond, as the capital of the South in the Civil War, is heaven for history buffs. The Thomas Jefferson–inspired Capitol houses the oldest continuous English-speaking lawmaking body in the Western Hemisphere. Jefferson selected the Maison Carrée, a Roman temple built in France, as the model and handpicked the architect to assist him. The Classic Revival–style Capitol with Ionic columns has been in use since 1788 and was completed in

1800. It served as the Capitol of the Confederacy from 1861 to 1865. Side wings were added in 1904–1906 to house the two legislative chambers. The Capitol Rotunda is adorned with one of America's most important pieces of sculpture—a life-size marble statue of George Washington executed from life by the French artist Jean-Antoine Houdon. *Capitol Sq., Richmond, tel. 804/786–4344. Open Apr.–Nov., daily 9–5; Dec.–Mar., Mon.–Sat. 9–5, Sun. 1–5.*

St. John's Church. This is the site where Patrick Henry gave his "Give me liberty or give me death" speech to the Second Virginia Convention in March 1775. Tours of the church and yard are given. *2401 E. Broad St., Richmond, tel. 804/648–5015. Open Mon.–Sat. 10–3:30, Sun. 1–3:30.*

White House of the Confederacy. As the president of the Confederacy, Jefferson Davis lived from 1861 to 1865 in the neoclassical John Brockenbrough House. The mansion contains an extraordinary number of original items, including a cast-iron cannon in the children's room that is capable of firing and the rosewood table where Jackson, Lee, and Davis worked out war strategy. The 35-minute tour may be too much for younger children. *1201 E. Clay St., Richmond, tel. 804/649–1861. Admission: $9 adults, $8.50 senior citizens, $5 students. Open Mon.–Sat. 10–5, Sun. noon–5.*

STAR-SPANGLED BANNER WEEKEND
BALTIMORE, FREDERICK, HAGERSTOWN, DELMARVA

10

Maryland baseball is as varied as the state's topography, which is akin to a mini-America, containing mountains, ocean, plains, and cities. Visionary management is making it possible to see future Baltimore Orioles players at all levels of the minor leagues within Maryland. Start in Baltimore, where Camden Yards, our favorite new major-league ballpark, is the epicenter. This dark-green steel-and-brick classic ballpark has a restored Baltimore & Ohio warehouse running from right field to center. A city street was made part of the park, and it's become an outdoor concourse for some of the best food in baseball. Babe Ruth's birthplace and museum are two blocks northwest of the ballpark and just seven blocks from the city's Harborplace, a waterside mall that set the standard for downtown retail renovations. The National Aquarium is on the harbor, as are the Maryland Science Center and Davis Planetarium.

Ninety minutes west of Baltimore on Interstate 70 is Frederick, the home of the Keys, a Single A Carolina League team. The stadium has been a model for new, small minor-league parks, with a playground for kids, a carousel, and grass berms for restless young viewers. The Antietam National Battlefield is 25 mi west.

North 28 mi is Hagerstown, the home of the Single A Suns in the South Atlantic League. The blue-collar city's 1931 stadium has been renovated, keeping the charm of its covered grandstand but adding a new bullpen, a clubhouse, and picnic and play areas. This city has a spectacular small city park, with a vintage bandshell, ducks on its 50-acre lake, ball fields, and a fine small art museum.

Another Single A South Atlantic League team is in Salisbury, on Maryland's eastern shore. The Delmarva Shorebirds play two hours south of Baltimore, off Route 50. The brand-new stadium has a kids' playground, a carousel, and a grassy berms for overflow crowds. This chicken-producing city has a fine museum of Wildfowl Art, along with a well-kept free-admission zoo.

BALTIMORE ORIOLES

League: American League • **Class:** Major League • **Stadium:** Oriole Park at Camden Yards • **Opened:** 1992 • **Capacity:** 48,262 • **Dimensions:** LF: 335, CF: 400, RF: 318 • **Surface:** grass • **Season:** Apr.–early Oct.

STADIUM LOCATION: 333 West Camden St., Baltimore, MD 21201.

WEB SITE: www.TheOrioles.com

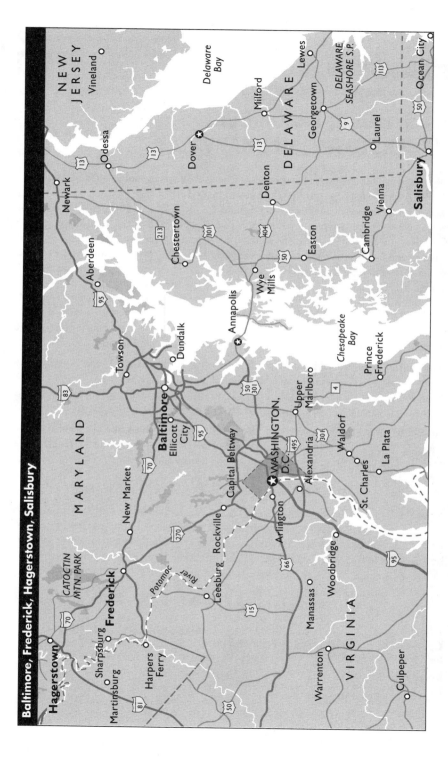

Baltimore, Frederick, Hagerstown, Salisbury

GETTING THERE: From the south, take I–95 Exit 52 or 53. From the north, take I–83 and follow St. Paul St. south to ballpark. From the west, take I–70 to I–695 and U.S. 40. From the east, take U.S. 40 or Eastern Ave. For information about bus, light rail, and park-and-ride routes, call MTA (tel. 410/539–5000). Light rail trains run every 17 minutes.

PARKING: Parking at ballpark is mostly limited to season ticket holders. Many garages nearby in business district.

TICKET INFORMATION: 333 West Camden St., Baltimore, MD 21201, tel. 410/685–9800, fax 410/547–6272.

PRICE RANGE: Club box seats $35; field box seats $16–$30; reserved lower box seats $22; upper and lower reserve seats $11–$13; bleachers $9; and standing room $7.

GAME TIME: Weekdays 7:35 PM, Sat. 7:05 PM, Sun. 1:35 PM; gates open weekdays 90 min before game time and weekends 2 hr before.

TIPS ON SEATING: Buy seats well in advance. Camden Yards is one of toughest tickets to get in baseball. We like seats on first-base side with view of historic Bromo Seltzer Tower. When a game is sold out in advance, 275 standing-room-only tickets go on sale for $7 two hours before game. Fans with SRO tickets may stand behind scoreboard wall in right field or bullpens in left field.

SEATING FOR PEOPLE WITH DISABILITIES: More than 400 seats throughout ballpark are available. Call 410/685–9800 for information about special services. In lot A and lot B/C are 100 parking spaces for vehicles with permits.

STADIUM FOOD: You'll smell **Boog's Bar-b-que** on the Eutaw St. walk before you see its lines. Go pre-game for good ribs, a great pit beef/pork/turkey platter ($7), and maybe Boog Powell's autograph. Don't miss **Uncle Teddy's** freshly made pretzels, doused in butter and cinnamon ($3). Good crab soup ($2.75) is sold in May, Sept., and Oct. at **Pastimes Cafe,** a cafeteria in the warehouse. It sells milk, yogurt, and salads and is quiet after the 2nd inning. Go to the third-base side for crab cakes; good, but they're $6.50 with a bad roll. Turkey-breast sandwiches ($5) and tropical fruit shakes ($2) are sold widely. Grilled chicken sandwiches ($5) and good coleslaw (75¢) are at **Bambino's Ribs** on Eutaw St.

SMOKING POLICY: Smoking prohibited in seating bowl, but allowed on lower and upper level concourses and in other designated areas.

TOURISM INFORMATION: Baltimore Area Convention & Visitors Center (300 W. Pratt St., Baltimore, MD 21201, tel. 410/837–4636 or 800/282–6632).

Baltimore: Camden Yards

For a quarter of a century, America's cities built an unbroken string of horrid, sterile, concrete monstrosities for baseball's boys of summer. And there were those awful fields of plastic grass. All this changed dramatically in 1992 with the opening of Baltimore's Oriole Park at Camden Yards. Finally, somebody got it right—a fan-friendly baseball park right downtown.

Many in Baltimore feared that the Orioles might follow Baltimoreans' beloved NFL Colts, who were just about literally stolen in the middle of the night in 1984. The thought of it was too much for the strong-willed mayor of Baltimore, William Donald Schaefer. When the mayor became governor, he devoted his considerable political skills to insisting that the state legislature approve a new stadium for Baltimore's downtown. Then came a new owner, this time a New York leveraged-buyout king named Eli Jacobs. The new owner, who had a long-standing interest in architecture, insisted on a ballpark, not a stadium. Together, Schaefer and Jacobs set off a rush of superb downtown ballparks, with Camden Yards as their model.

Red brick. Dark-green steel. Real grass. This $105-million, 48,262-seat stadium has a classic ballpark look. HOK's baseball-only design and steel construction provide an intimacy never experienced in the monstrosities of the 1960s and '70s. The asymmetrical field is reminiscent of the old-time parks that were squeezed into neighborhoods. They brought home plate and the right-field foul pole from Memorial Stadium.

Truth be told, without the warehouse, this is merely a fine stadium. It is the redbrick eight-story B & O warehouse that makes Camden Yards the very best of the 1990s stadiums. The warehouse, the longest building on America's east coast, is 1,016 ft long, running from right field to beyond the huge scoreboard in straight-away center. The right-field lights hang from the warehouse roof, making the warehouse, 426 ft from home plate in right field, an integral part of the stadium. The dramatic Cal Ripken, Jr. streak countdown in 1995 took place here with 10-ft-high numbers being unfurled on the side of the warehouse night after night until the magic 2,131 was reached. The 1905 classic railroad warehouse might well have been bulldozed to open a vista toward Baltimore's Inner Harbor but for Eric Moss, a Syracuse University architecture student whose 1987 model featured the warehouse. Baseball fans everywhere owe Eric Moss our thanks.

Take a walk before the game and see if you don't agree that Eutaw Street is one of America's great urban spaces. First visit the 9-ft, 800-pound bronze Babe Ruth statue at the entrance near the north end of the warehouse. Look closely and you will see that the left-handed Ruth has a right-handed glove. Near the historic Camden Station and in front of the ticket windows are 4-ft-high aluminum figures honoring the retired Orioles uniform numbers—Jim Palmer (No. 22), Brooks Robinson (No. 5), Frank Robinson (No. 20), Earl Weaver (No. 4), and Eddie Murray (No. 33).

Once you've passed through the gates, look at the Orioles Hall of Fame plaques at the base of the scoreboard beyond center field. Stop in at the Orioles Baseball Store. Look for baseball-size markers embedded in the walkway that indicate where some of the longest homers hit in Camden Yards have landed. Buy a barbecue sandwich and get an autograph from big Boog Powell, a Baltimore favorite whose booming home runs won him an American League MVP Award in 1970. Cal Ripken, Jr. fans will want to

visit the left-field bleachers. The orange seat in section 86 marks the spot where Cal's 278th home run—the highest number ever by a major-league shortstop—landed on July 15, 1993. The orange seat in the right center field bleachers is where Eddie Murray's 500th major-league home run landed Sept. 6, 1996. The O's Hall of Fame is under the centerfield video board on Eutaw Avenue. Adjacent to Camden Yards is the stadium for the Ravens football team, built in 1997.

To visit the Orioles dugout, press box, scoreboard control room, and club-level suites, join a Camden Yards tour. These 90-minute tours are highly informative. Unfortunately, they don't take you into the locker rooms. *333 W. Camden St., Baltimore, tel. 410/547–6234. Admission: $5 adults, $4 senior citizens and children. Tours daily (except on days of afternoon games) Mar.–Nov., weekdays at 11 and 2, Sat. 10:30–2 (every 30 min), Sun. 12:30–2 (every 30 min).*

Before or after the game, visit Gallery E in section E of the Warehouse, just outside Gates A and C. The gallery features a large collection of good baseball art. *349 W. Camden St., Baltimore, tel. 410/547–6220.*

More Baltimore Baseball

Memorial Stadium. Ironically, Baltimore's Memorial Stadium, the predecessor of Camden Yards, was a pretty fine stadium. When Oriole Park burned to the ground on July 4, 1944, the International League Orioles moved into Municipal Stadium on East 33rd Street. A new ballpark named Memorial Stadium was erected in its place beginning in 1950. Work was completed on the double-decked horseshoe in time for the St. Louis Browns' move to Baltimore in 1954. The Orioles won the World Championship once in each of the next three decades—1966, 1970, and 1983. Cal Ripken, Jr.'s incredible streak began here on May 30, 1982. Memorial Stadium was scheduled for demolition sometime in 2000. From the downtown, drive 3 mi north on Charles Street and turn right on 33rd Street. The stadium is 1 mi farther on your left. Note the wonderful Art Deco lettering at Memorial Stadium's entrance. *1000 E. 33rd St., Baltimore, tel. 410/396–7113.*

The Babe Ruth Birthplace. When they were building the Camden Yards ballpark, they found some bricks and broken bottles in short center field. These were the remains of the George Herman Ruth Saloon. Midway along Eutaw Street, there is a plaque to memorialize the Ruth family saloon. Just blocks away, on February 6, 1895, the Babe was born. Young George's mother had gone to her father's house to escape the noise and distractions of her life over the family saloon. This Baltimore brick row house is now the centerpiece of the Babe Ruth Birthplace, Baltimore Orioles Museum, and Maryland Baseball Hall of Fame.

On Friday, June 13, 1902, young George was dispatched to St. Mary's Industrial School for Boys of the City of Baltimore. At the birthplace museum, they explain his admission to the school by describing the seven-year-old Ruth as "too tough for his parents, too absent for the school system, and too incorrigible for everybody else."

Jack Dunn, the owner of the minor-league Baltimore Orioles, signed Ruth for $600 and at the same time signed papers making him the legal guardian of the 19-year-old. The Oriole veterans called Ruth Dunn's Babe, and the name stuck. Later, with the minor-league Orioles struggling to compete at the box office with the Baltimore Terrapins of the Federal League, Dunn had to sell off his best players to stay in business. The Boston Red Sox picked up the Babe, Ernie Shore, and Ben Egan for $25,000 in 1914.

216 Emory St., off 600 W. Pratt St., Baltimore, tel. 410/727–1539. Admission: $6 adults, $4 senior citizens, $3 ages 5–16. Open Apr.–Oct., daily 10–5 (until 7 when Orioles play at home); Nov.–Mar., daily 10–4.

Babe Ruth Baseball Center at Camden Station. Camden Station, the elegant building just beyond center field in Camden Yards, is being converted into the Babe Ruth Baseball Center, scheduled to open in 2001. A Baltimore Baseball Walk of Fame will connect Camden Station with the Birthplace Museum.

St. Mary's Industrial School. For a special treat, drive 2½ mi southwest from the birthplace museum to the site of the old St. Mary's Indus-

trial School. The building is now occupied by Cardinal Gibbons School, a Catholic boys' school. The field where the Babe learned to play baseball is still here, in a valley behind the main school building. You can walk out to deep center field—Ruth's home plate—and imagine the left-handed Babe aiming at the gray stone school building. After a 1919 fire destroyed the main building, Babe Ruth and Cardinal Gibbons raised the money to rebuild it. Both the birthplace and the school can be seen from the third-base side of the upper deck of Camden Yards. *3225 Wilkens Ave., corner of Caton and Wilkens Aves., Baltimore, tel. 410/644–1770.*

Ripken Museum. This small but high-quality tribute to the Ripken baseball family opened in 1997 in Cal Jr.'s hometown of Aberdeen, Maryland. *8 Ripken Plaza, at Bel Air Ave. (MD.132) and U.S. 40, Aberdeen, tel. 410/273–2525. Admission: $3 adults, $1 ages 6–18, under 6 free. Open Fri.–Sat. and Mon. 11–3, Sun. noon–3.*

Where to Stay

With the exception of the Baltimore Clarion Hotel, all of the following are within walking distance of the ballpark:

Holiday Inn–Inner Harbor. You see this 11-story hotel from the ballpark. The rooms are standard size with new marble vanities and tubs. Those on the sixth floor and above have views of Camden Yards. *301 W. Lombard St., Baltimore 21201, tel. 410/685–3500 or 800/465–4329, fax 410/727–6169. 375 rooms. Facilities: restaurant, indoor pool, parking (fee). AE, D, DC, MC, V. $$*

Baltimore Clarion Hotel. This elegant, 13-story hotel at Mt. Vernon Square is an older property that has been renovated with antiques and fresh flowers. A courtesy shuttle takes you the eight blocks to the Inner Harbor. *612 Cathedral St., Baltimore 21201, tel. 410/727–7101 or 800/252–7466, fax 410/789–3312. 104 rooms. Facilities: restaurant, parking (fee). AE, D, DC, MC, V. $$*

Days Inn Baltimore Inner Harbor. This nine-story hotel is three blocks from the ballpark. The rooms are small but nicely furnished. *100 Hopkins Pl., Baltimore 21201, tel. 410/576–1000 or 800/325–2525, fax 410/576–9437. 250 rooms. Facilities: restaurant, outdoor pool, coin laundry, parking (fee). AE, D, DC, MC, V. $$*

Paramount Inner Harbor Hotel. This seven-story brick hotel has been renovated recently. It is three blocks from the ballpark. *8 N. Howard St., Baltimore 21201, tel. 410/539–1188, fax 410/539–6411. 90 rooms. Facilities: restaurant, parking (fee). AE, D, DC, MC, V. $$*

Radisson Plaza Lord Baltimore. This older, refurbished downtown hotel is 23 stories high, with good views of the city and ironing boards in each room. Guests may use an adjoining indoor pool for $5 per person. *20 W. Baltimore St., Baltimore 21201, tel. 410/539–8400 or 800/333–3333, fax 410/625–1060. 420 rooms. Facilities: 2 restaurants, health club, parking (fee). AE, D, DC, MC, V. $$*

Where to Eat

Nates and Leons. Pick your choice of sandwiches at this modern 100-seat deli across the street from the ballpark. An $8 Bird Feeder Bag includes a sandwich, coleslaw, pickle, brownie, and chips. The recipe for its formidable strawberry shortcake dates from the 1930s, when the family started in the deli business. *300 West Pratt St., at Howard St., Baltimore, tel. 410/234–8100. AE, MC, V. $*

Lexington Market. The venerable John W. Faidley Seafood raw bar is also crab-cake heaven. Patrons eat the city's freshest fish at rough tables next to employees shucking oysters. You can amble a few stalls over to the **A.D. Konstant & Son Confectionery** (tel. 410/685–4422), and try the nut taffies and peanut brittle that Baltimoreans have been eating for a century. *Paca and Lexington Sts., Baltimore, tel. 410/727–4898. AE, D, MC, V. $.*

Maison Marconi's. Writer H. L. Mencken frequented this legendary small town-house restaurant. It offers a mix of Italian food with spectacular hot fudge sundaes for dessert. There is no children's menu, but half-orders of pasta dishes can be requested. *106 W. Saratoga St., Baltimore, tel. 410/727–9522. Reservations essential. MC, V. $$*

Sabatino's. In Little Italy, close to the park, this venerable family favorite is casual and cool and dim inside. There are eight dining rooms, including one shining with mirrors. Its Bookmaker salad, with shrimp, provolone, salami, and orange zest is original and good. It has a children's menu and great pasta dishes. *901 Fawn St., Baltimore, tel. 410/727–2667. AE, D, DC, MC, V. $$*

Women's Industrial Exchange Restaurant. This longtime Baltimore institution serves comfort food from the 1930s and '40s—chicken croquettes, crab cakes, meringue pies, and real turkey sandwiches. Many of its waitresses are past 80 years old. There are knitted and sewn goods for sale, along with jars of preserves. This is tearoom eating. *333 N. Charles St., Baltimore, tel. 410/685–4388. No dinner. MC, V. $*

Entertainments

Two new attractions are scheduled to open in 2001 in Baltimore's Harbor area—a $32-million interactive Children's Museum, at Market Place, and a $15-million Maryland African-American History Museum.

The B&O Railroad Museum. In 1825, Baltimore was the fourth-largest city and fourth-ranking port on the east coast. One hundred miles closer to the rivers and markets of the West than its rivals, Baltimore was the birthplace of the American railroad industry. As others built canals, Baltimore bet its economic future on the railroad. Much of America's early movement of people and goods westward was through Baltimore. The B&O Railroad Museum, just blocks from Babe Ruth's birthplace, captures this important contribution to America's history on a 37-acre site that includes five historic buildings and more than 120 full-size railroad locomotives, cars, and pieces of special-purpose equipment. The centerpiece is an 1884 roundhouse designed by Ephraim Francis Baldwin.

The 1851 Mt. Clare Station serves as the entrance to the displays of railroading memorabilia. America's first passenger trains headed west from this location in 1830. Here Peter Cooper operated the *Tom Thumb*, the first steam engine made in America. The shops that surrounded the station were the country's oldest and the birthplace of many of railroading's most important technologies. In 1844, Samuel F. B. Morse sent his famous "What hath God wrought?" telegraph from Washington, D.C., along the B&O right-of-way to Mt. Clare. *901 W. Pratt St., Baltimore 21223, tel. 410/752–2490. Admission: $6.50 adults, $5.50 senior citizens, $4 ages 5–12; free parking. Open daily 10–5.*

Great Blacks in Wax Museum. This is the country's only wax museum dedicated to African-Americans. It portrays more than 150 leaders, musicians, writers, inventors, athletes, and other pioneering individuals. The museum uses animation, sound effects, and scenes from history. *1601 E. North Ave., 2 mi northeast of Camden Yards, Baltimore, tel. 410/563–3404. Admission: $5.75 adults, $3.75 ages 12–17, $3.25 ages 2–11. Open mid-Jan.–mid-Oct., Tues.–Sat. 10–6, Sun. noon–6; mid-Oct.–mid-Jan., Tues.–Sat. 10–5, Sun. noon–5.*

Maryland Science Center and Davis Planetarium. The fate of the Chesapeake Bay is a focus of this hands-on museum, located at the edge of the Inner Harbor, within walking distance of the ballpark. You can take a water taxi to get here, too. A five-screen IMAX theater can make some people feel queasy, as you are "on" a roller coaster and other adventures. Children 3–13 must have a parent in the theater. *601 Light St., at Key Hwy., Baltimore, tel. 410/685–5225. Admission: $10 adults, $8 senior citizens, military personnel, and ages 13–17, $7 ages 4–12. Open mid-May–Labor Day, Mon.–Thurs. 10–6, Fri.–Sun. 10–8; Sept.–mid-May, weekdays 10–5, weekends 10–6.*

National Aquarium. This is a huge, multipresentation aquarium with a Marine Mammal Pavilion, an Atlantic Coral Reef, an Open Ocean (sharks), and a South American rain forest. A large dolphin oceanarium has daily shows. There's a touch tank and other hands-on experiences in the Children's Cove. On summer weekend days, tickets to this hugely popular attraction can sell out. Try to go late in the day or call Ticketmaster ahead of time for tickets. *501 E. Pratt St., Baltimore, tel. 410/576–3800. Admission: $14 adults, $10.50 senior citizens, $7.50 ages 3–11. Open July–Aug., Sat.–Thurs. 10–5, Fri. 10–8; Sept.–June,* *Sun.–Thurs. 9–6, Fri.–Sat. 9–8.*

U.S. Frigate Constellation. You can climb throughout the nation's oldest warship continuously afloat, which is moored at Constellation Dock in the Inner Harbor within walking distance of Camden Yards. This 1797 frigate carried soldiers to the shores of Tripoli and saw action in the Revolutionary and Civil wars and both world wars. *Pier 1, Pratt and Light Sts., Baltimore, tel. 410/539–1797. Admission: $6 adults, $4.75 senior citizens, $3.50 ages 6—14. Open daily 10–6.*

Sights to See

Fort McHenry National Monument and Historic Shrine. If you have ever wondered why "The Star-Spangled Banner" is such a difficult song to sing, consider that it was hastily written by a Washington lawyer who had just spent a long, anxious night. Francis Scott Key, who had gone to Baltimore to secure the freedom of a friend who had been seized by the British, watched the 25-hour British bombardment of Fort McHenry from a ship on the Patapsco River. The British had burned Washington. This battle for Baltimore was critical to the nation's future. At dawn on September 14, 1814, Key saw the large 42- by 30-ft American flag made by Mary Pickersgill still flying over the fort and was inspired to take the notes for the song that became the national anthem.

Fort McHenry has been restored to its pre–Civil War state. A 15-minute film is shown at the visitor center on the hour and the half hour. Regular tours are led by informative guides. A shuttle-boat service leaves Baltimore's Inner Harbor from Finger Pier opposite the Harbour Court Hotel every half hour daily from Memorial Day to Labor Day between 11 and 5:30. *Fort McHenry, Key Highway/Fort McHenry exit (Exit 55) from I–95, follow signs, Baltimore, tel. 410/962–4299. Admission: $5 adults, senior citizens and under 16 free. Open early June–Labor Day, daily 8–8; Labor Day–early June, daily 8–5.*

FREDERICK KEYS

League: Carolina League • **Major League Affiliation:** Baltimore Orioles • **Class:** A • **Stadium:** Harry Grove Stadium • **Opened:** 1990 • **Capacity:** 5,400 • **Dimensions:** LF: 325, CF: 400, RF: 325 • **Surface:** grass • **Season:** Apr.–Labor Day

STADIUM LOCATION: 6201 New Design Rd., Frederick, MD 21701.

WEB SITE: www.frederickkeys.com

GETTING THERE: From I–270, Market St./MD Rte. 355 exit, No. 31A. Pass I–70 exits, left at traffic light. From I–70, exit Market St., left at traffic light. Left on New Design Rd.

PARKING: Ample free parking adjacent to stadium.

TICKET INFORMATION: Box 3169, Frederick, MD 21705, tel. 301/662–0013, fax 301/662–0018.

PRICE RANGE: Field box seats $10; box seats $8; general admission $6 adults, $4 ages 6–12, senior citizens, and military personnel, under 5 free; 12 and under free in little league shirt; gates open 1 hr before game.

GAME TIME: Mon.–Sat. 7:05 PM, Sun. 2:05 (Apr.–June) or 4:05 (July–Aug.).

TIPS ON SEATING: Smoking and alcohol prohibited in family-section general admission seats on third-base side; these seats have no cover and can get hot on a sunny day. Berms in left and right field foul areas are great for kids to run around on as they try to snag foul balls.

SEATING FOR PEOPLE WITH DISABILITIES: Behind bleacher seats along concourse.

STADIUM FOOD: A kids-only stand for children under 15 sells candy, ice cream, and cookies, for 75¢–$1. The best of regular concourse offerings is a $4.50 roast beef sandwich in the **O'Keys Corral** past third base. Grills are on both third- and first-base sides. Good french fries are boardwalk style, in $2.50 and $4 cups. There are onion rings ($2.75), chicken fingers ($3.50), personal pizzas ($3.75), and real roasted peanuts ($2 per bag). Reservations are required at the **Keys Cafe** on the second-level terrace overlooking home plate. A good six-item buffet dinner is $24. Sandwiches are sold at the **Hit and Run Deli** on the first-base side.

SMOKING POLICY: No smoking in seating bowl; smoking allowed in concourse.

VISITING TEAM INFORMATION: Comfort Inn (420 Prospect Blvd., Frederick, MD 21701, tel. 301/ 695–6200 or 800/424–6423).

TOURISM INFORMATION: Tourism Council of Frederick County (19 E. Church St., Frederick, MD 21701, tel. 301/663–8687 or 800/999–3613).

Frederick: Harry Grove Stadium

Peter Kirk is one of the handful of visionaries who have helped make minor-league baseball the great comeback success story it has been for the last decade. In the mid-1980s, Kirk bought into the Hagerstown Suns. In 1988, Kirk's Maryland Baseball Limited Partnership bought a Double A Eastern League team and brought it to Hagerstown. They took the Single A Carolina League team just 28 mi south to

Frederick, where Mayor Ron Young was eager to have baseball. Governor Schaefer and Mayor Young promised Kirk a new stadium.

One night after a game in the early 1990s, Kirk had two visions—first, "What if we could bring all the future Baltimore Orioles to play in Maryland near the parent team?" Piece by piece the dream is becoming reality.

Kirk's other vision was of fan-friendly stadiums. We were amazed when we first visited Frederick's $5.5-million Harry Grove Stadium. It has plenty of free parking right near the stadium.

The food in the concession stands is good and much less expensive than in the big leagues. You can buy a soda and a hot dog on the concourse and not miss a pitch. There are large grass hillsides beyond the seats on both first base and third for overflow crowds, restless kids, and even middle-aged parents trying to snag a foul ball. There is nonstop entertainment on and off the field, including a chance to jingle your car keys and sing along to "We're the Frederick Keys." Keyote, a 7-ft-tall coyote, is a kid favorite. This is family entertainment at its best.

In planning the stadium, Kirk wanted to make sure fans could walk down from the parking lot and entrance rather than hike up stairs to their seats. He wanted the concessions to be open so that parents could watch their kids without having to miss the game.

Frederick became the standard of comfort, efficiency, and family pleasure for Single A baseball. The construction was simple—1,800 box seats, aluminum-bench general admission seats on concrete, an uncovered grandstand with an open concourse above the seats. The grass berms solve the problem of how many seats to build at minor-league parks. There are 5,400 actual seats at Grove Stadium, but 10,000 can pack in for fireworks.

Some of the easiest autographs in all of professional baseball are acquired here. The seats stop at the outfield grass, and the players have to walk up a hill from the field along the seats to their locker rooms. You can get them going back to their lockers after batting practice or after the game. The Keys' locker room is on the first-base side, and we have filled balls with autographs in as little as 30 minutes here. When we first saw Harry Grove Stadium in 1990, we couldn't imagine anyone doing it any better than this.

We were wrong, of course. Peter Kirk himself has done it bigger and fancier for his Double A Eastern League team in Bowie. If you have an extra day in the Baltimore-Washington area, visit Prince George's Stadium (tel. 301/805–6000) to see the Bowie Baysox—it's Chesapeake Bay country—for a first-class baseball experience.

To our amazement, the modern, efficient stadiums of the late 1980s and early 1990s, of which Frederick is among the very best, have been far surpassed by such Single A beauties as Tampa, Florida, and Lake Elsinore and Rancho Cucamonga, California. Peter Kirk intends to try to keep up with the competition. He added a full-size carousel and playground at Bowie and at Frederick.

A name-the-team contest honored Francis Scott Key, the author of the national anthem, who is buried in the cemetery directly across the street from the stadium. Harry Grove was an official of Frederick's first professional team in the Class D Blue Ridge League in 1915. The stadium was named in Grove's honor when his son helped finance it as a way of bringing professional baseball back to Frederick after a 59-year absence.

Where to Stay

Visiting Team Motel: Comfort Inn. This two-story hotel is in a quiet residential neighborhood 10 minutes from the ballpark. There is a free Continental breakfast. *4200 Prospect Blvd., Frederick 21701, tel. 301/695–6200 or 800/424–6423, fax 301/695–7895. 118 rooms. Facilities: outdoor pool, exercise room, playground. AE, D, DC, MC, V. $$*

Red Horse Motor Inn. This family-owned economy motel has a red horse statue out front. The 2-story section is the original portion—a 4-story addition houses meeting rooms. The rooms are small, clean, and quiet. *998 W. Patrick St. (U.S. 40 W), Frederick 21703, tel. 301/662–0281, or 800–245–6701. 72 rooms. Facilities: restaurant. AE, D, DC, MC, V. $*

Where to Eat

Barbara Fritchie Candystick Restaurant. Eating here is a walk back in time, from the dated but delectable menu items to the pink decor. You can choose meaty turkey potpie with pepper slaw, a bargain oyster sandwich, hefty chipped beef on toast, or delicious apple dumplings. Other desserts include a homemade black walnut pound cake, caramel cake, and pies. The large counter has 56 stools, or you can have table or booth service. Decorative peppermint sticks adorn the facade, installed by the same family that's been running the place since 1920.

1513 W. Patrick St. (Rte. 40 W), Frederick, tel. 301/662–2500. No credit cards. $

The Comus Inn. This pretty inn has an extraordinary view of Sugarloaf Mountain; you can call ahead to find out when the sun sets for the best view. Kids eat free, and baby-sitters are available on Tuesday nights. The extensive menu is supplemented by a large salad bar. There's a special brunch on Sunday. *23900 Old Hundred Rd. (Rte. 109 and Comus Rd.), 12 mi south of Frederick, Comus, tel. 301/349–5100. AE, MC, V. $$*

Dan-Dee Country Inn. Maryland fried chicken is the standout at this casual family restaurant that has long attracted the after-church crowd. Food is served family-style, except for the meat entrées. The children's menu is for those 10 and under. The restaurant, which has nicely landscaped grounds, is at the entrance to Gambrill State Park. *7817 Baltimore Pike (U.S. 40 W), Frederick, tel. 301/473–8282. AE, D, MC, V. $*

Entertainments

Rose Hill Manor and Children's Museum. Children can play with vintage toys and use historic kitchen utensils in this home of former Maryland governor Thomas Johnson. Look at the old ice house, the carriage museum, and the blacksmith shop. *1611 N. Market St. (Rte. 355), Frederick, tel. 301/694–1648. Admission: $3 adults, $2 senior citizens, $1 ages 16 and under. Open Mon.–Sat. 10–4, Sun. 1–4.*

Sights to See

Barbara Fritchie House and Museum. Do you remember this heroine from Whittier's poem, "Shoot If You Must This Old Gray Head, but Spare Your Country's Flag"? This period home and small museum can help illuminate the moment in 1862 when Fritchie waved the Union flag as Confederate troops marched through Frederick. She is buried in the Mt. Olivet Cemetery across the street from the ballpark. *154 W. Patrick St., Frederick, tel. 301/ 698–0630. Admission: $2 adults, $1.50 ages 2– 12 and senior citizens. Open Apr.–Nov., Mon. and Thurs.–Sat. 10–4, Sun. 1–4.*

Frederick historic district. A six-block walking tour departs on the weekends from Frederick Visitor Center, led by experts in the history and architecture of the city. *19 E. Church St., Frederick, tel. 301/663–8687. Admission: $4.50 ages 12 and older. Open Apr.–Dec., weekends 1:30.*

Sugarloaf Mountain. Just 12 mi south of Frederick is a good challenge for young children not yet ready for a major mountain climb. Privately owned, this lovely conservation and recreation area provides the opportunity for hiking, picnicking, and nature study. At an elevation of 1,282 ft, the rugged cliffs on the summit stand 800 ft above the surrounding farmland. Drive 1½ mi up the mountain, park in the east-view lot, and take the orange trail up a steep slope for ¼ mi to the summit. The green trail down the west side of the mountain is aided by stone steps. It is then a short walk back to the east-view parking lot. *7901 Comus Rd. (Exit 22—Rte. 109—from I-270 south from Frederick, south 3 mi to Comus Rd., right on Comus Rd. 2½ mi), Dickerson, tel. 301/874–2024.*

HAGERSTOWN SUNS

League: South Atlantic League • **Major League Affiliation:** Toronto Blue Jays • **Class:** A • **Stadium:** Municipal Stadium • **Opened:** 1931 • **Capacity:** 4,600 • **Dimensions:** LF: 335, CF: 400, RF: 330 • **Surface:** grass • **Season:** Apr.–Labor Day

STADIUM LOCATION: 274 E. Memorial Blvd., Hagerstown, MD 21740.

WEB SITE: www.hagerstownsuns.com

GETTING THERE: From I-70W, Exit 32B (US 40 W) 2 mi, left on Eastern Blvd. From I-81S, Exit 6A through downtown for 3 mi, right on Cleveland Ave. From I-81N, Exit 3E (I-70); follow it to Exit 29N (MD 65), right at Memorial Blvd.

PARKING: Get here early. Only about 500 spaces near ballpark. If you see empty spaces near entrance, there's a reason. Locals know you can get a foul ball through your windshield there.

TICKET INFORMATION: Box 230, Hagerstown, MD 21741, tel. 301/791–6266, fax 301/791–6066.

PRICE RANGE: Box seats $7; general admission $5 adults, $3 students, senior citizens, and military personnel.

GAME TIME: Mon. 6:05 PM, Tues.–Sat. 7:05 PM, Sun. 2:05 PM (Apr.–late June), 5:05 PM (late June–Labor Day); gates open 1 hr before game.

TIPS ON SEATING: General admission seats are right in action. Third-base side is best but sun sets on this side. Don't sit in first row of bleacher seats on first-base side or your view will be blocked by line of fans slowed by bottleneck.

SEATING FOR PEOPLE WITH DISABILITIES: About 50 places accessible by ramps: behind home plate, third-base side, and near right field.

STADIUM FOOD: The place to eat is at the **Sunset Grille** on the third-base side of the ballpark. The first-rate barbecue chicken sandwich is $3. Its Super Dog ($2.75) is superior to most ballpark dogs, as is the Italian sausage ($2.75). Its Hot and Spicy hot dog will be too strong for most kids. A good hamburger is $2.75. There's a children's playground on a cushion of wood chips by the **Nellie Fox** picnic area.

SMOKING POLICY: 400 no-smoking, no-alcohol seats in section 5 behind screen on third-base side.

VISITING TEAM HOTEL: Ramada Inn Convention Center (901 Dual Hwy., Hagerstown, MD 21740, tel. 301/733–5100 or 800/228–2828).

TOURISM INFORMATION: Washington County Convention & Visitors Bureau (1826-C Dual Hwy., Hagerstown, MD 21740, tel. 301/791–3130 or 800/228–7829).

Hagerstown: Municipal Stadium

Hagerstown is one of those towns that almost got left behind in baseball's effort to upgrade minor-league stadiums. Built in 1931 for a team that did not last a full season in the Depression-era economy, Municipal Stadium hosted amateur teams for the next decade. In 1988, baseball owner Peter Kirk and his investors bought a Double A Eastern League team and moved it to Hagerstown, replacing a Single A team. Because the economically depressed western Maryland city could not afford the stadium improvements required to maintain Double A baseball, Kirk's Eastern League team moved out in 1993.

Happily for Maryland baseball fans and connoisseurs of vintage ballparks, Hagerstown didn't miss a season. Owner Winston Blenckstone moved a failing Single A South Atlantic League team here in 1993 from Myrtle Beach, South Carolina. The standards for Single A baseball

required $500,000 in improvements. With support from the city and state, Blenckstone installed a new bullpen, a new clubhouse and offices, and new rest rooms. Hundreds of old bleacher seats down the left-field line were replaced with an attractive fan-oriented picnic, grill, and play area. Despite the improvements, the owner and local fan club are currently pushing for a new, modern park adjacent to I-81.

Improvements have made Hagerstown baseball a more enjoyable experience for fans and players alike, without destroying the feel of the 1931 Municipal Stadium. The fancy box seats come complete with cup holders, but there are only 550 of them. A $5 general admission ticket still gets you a seat right near the action. The old-style covered grandstand is welcome on a sunny Sunday afternoon or when a late summer thundershower passes by.

Playing left field here still requires the skills of an acrobat. A large deposit of limestone causes a distinct grade in left center field up toward the left-field wall. The charitable way to describe this is that the players in left field have a unique warning track so they don't run into the outfield wall. The reality is that they have to run up the side of a ledge, a challenge major-league owners don't want for their high-priced future superstars.

Playing left field isn't the only challenge here. Getting to the game late, you might be tempted by some empty parking spaces near the entrance. Don't take them. Municipal Stadium is one of those ballparks where the foul balls fly out of the field throughout the night. According to the owner, "It's a neighborhood park. That's baseball-speak for 'It's best to get here early. We don't have enough parking spaces.' "

Hagerstown's Municipal Stadium oozes old-time baseball. Babe Ruth's sister lived in Hagerstown, and the new owners in 1993 commissioned a huge 12-by-16-ft mural of the Babe down the right-field line. In 1995, they added a huge hot dog.

Not everyone is nostalgic about Hagerstown baseball. Willie Mays played his first game here on June 24, 1950, after breaking through baseball's color line to play for the Trenton Giants. In his biography, Mays blasted Hagerstown, where he wasn't allowed to stay in the same hotel with his new teammates. For those who think of Maryland as a northern state, remember that the Mason-Dixon line is just north of Hagerstown.

Where to Stay

Visiting Team Motel: Ramada Inn Convention Center. This sprawling hotel has a two-story main building and a five-story tower. The newer and brighter tower rooms are no-smoking. The hotel is along the main highway, about 2 mi from the ballpark. *901 Dual Hwy. (Rte. 40), Hagerstown 21740, tel. 301/733–5100 or 800/228–2828, fax 301/733–9192. 212 rooms. Facilities: restaurant, indoor pool, health club, track, coin laundry. AE, D, DC, MC, V. $*

Days Inn. This is an ordinary two-story highway motel about 2 mi from the ballpark. There's a free breakfast for guests. *900 Dual Hwy. (Rte. 40), Hagerstown 21740, tel. 301/739–9050 or 800/329–7466, fax 301/739–8347. 140 rooms.*

Facilities: restaurant, outdoor pool, playground, coin laundry. AE, D, DC, MC, V. $

Where to Eat

Chic's Seafood. Look for the 400-pound red crab on the roof across from the city park. Rolls of mill paper cover the wood tables for serious steamed crab eaters. The restaurant also serves mussels, great oysters, and clams. The apple crisp is homemade. *300 Summit Ave., Hagerstown, tel. 301/739–8220. MC, V. $$*

Hagerstown City Market. Gather breakfast and eat inside Maryland's oldest continuous farmer's market. Many Amish farmstands are among the 56 stalls here. You'll find superb fruits, vegetables, baked goods, meats, crafts, and flowers. Locals have been shopping here since 1875. *11 West Church St., Hagerstown, tel. 301/790–3200, ext. 112. Open year-round Sat. 5–11; June–Dec., Wed. 11–4 also. No credit cards. $*

Krumpe's Donuts. In an alley between Spruce and Maryland avenues, follow your nose for fresh-baked doughnuts. The Krumpes have been baking for 44 years, and their glazed, twisted, powdered, apple, chocolate, and cake doughnuts are heaven, especially warm. *912 Maryland Ave., Hagerstown, tel. 301/733–6103. No credit cards. $*

Richardson's Family Restaurant. This casual highway restaurant is filled with mementos of the years since its opening in 1948. There is fine frozen custard, real milk shakes, and a larger-than-usual kid's menu. The buffet for kids under five is priced at 75¢ per year of their age. Adults can enjoy the crab cakes, clams, and Maryland oysters. *710 Dual Hwy. (Rte. 40), Hagerstown, tel. 301/733–3660. D, MC, V. $*

Schmankerl Stube Bavarian Restaurant. The name means "cozy room," and this pretty, check-curtained restaurant is that. Don't miss the potato soup, the fried tomatoes, and the apple streusel. All meals come with a hearty German sunflower-seed rye bread. The waitresses and waiters wear Bavarian costumes. The back patio is cheerful, and the wood-floor dining rooms are hyperclean and attractive. *58 S. Potomac St., Hagerstown, tel. 301/797–3354. AE, MC, V. $*

Entertainments

Hagerstown Park. This is one of America's best small-city parks. It has a historic bandshell, steam engines and cabooses for climbing, playgrounds, ball fields, and a multitude of swans and ducks on its 50-acre lake. In summer, there are Wednesday-night gospel concerts and Sunday-evening municipal band concerts. Its concession stand serves snow cones, hot dogs, and burgers, plus 35¢ duck and goose feed. The city's excellent and compact art and history museums are also on the grounds. *501 Virginia Ave., Hagerstown, tel. 301/797–3088. Admission free. Open Mon.–Sat. 10–8, Sun. 10–9.*

Sights to See

Antietam National Battlefield. This 950-acre park, 10 mi south of Hagerstown, is the site of the bloodiest day of the Civil War. On Sept. 17, 1862, more than 23,000 soldiers died when General George McClellan's Army met General Robert E. Lee's. After Lee's withdrawal, Lincoln issued the Emancipation Proclamation. Tour the small museum at the visitor center, view the 26-minute film, and walk the fields. *MD. 34 and 65, Sharpsburg, tel. 301/432–5124. Admission: $2 ages 17 and up; $4 family. Roads open daily dawn–dusk; visitor's center open daily 8:30–6.*

Downtown walking tour. The 18 stops on the self-guided tour are marked by the town's Prussian soldier mascot, Little Heiskell. It covers the area where Jonathan Hager, the German-born founder, laid out the town in 1762. Obtain a map from the Washington County Tourism Bureau (1826 Dual Hwy., U.S. 40, tel. 301/791–3130 or 800/228–7829) or at City Hall (Potomac and Franklin Sts., tel. 301/790–3200).

Maryland Theatre. A fire wall saved this 80-year-old theater in 1974. Restored, the rococo theater offers a peek into America's theatrical past. Its facade is unimpressive, but the interior, with its 1,400 seats, is exquisite. *21 S. Potomac St., Hagerstown, tel. 301/790–2000 or 800/347–4697.*

DELMARVA SHOREBIRDS

League: South Atlantic • **Major League Affiliation:** Baltimore Orioles • **Class:** A • **Stadium:** Arthur W. Perdue Stadium • **Opened:** 1996 • **Capacity:** 5,200 • **Dimensions:** LF: 309, CF: 402, RF: 309 • **Surface:** grass • **Season:** Apr.–Labor Day

STADIUM LOCATION: Just off Rte. 50 and Rte. 13 Bypass.

WEB SITE: www.theshorebirds.com

GETTING THERE: From Salisbury on US 50E, pass Rte. 13 Bypass, exit to right onto Hobbs Rd. From US 50W, exit to left onto Hobbs Rd.

PARKING: Ample free parking.

TICKET INFORMATION: Box 1557, Salisbury, MD 21802, tel. 410/219–3112, fax 410/219–9164.

PRICE RANGE: Field level $11; box seats $9; general admission $6.50 adults, $3 ages 6–12, senior citizens, and active military; free for children in Little League uniforms and under 6.

GAME TIME: Mon.–Sat. 7 PM, Sun. 2 PM; gates open 90 min before game.

TIPS ON SEATING: First rows of general admission are very close to action, but get here early. Even last rows of general admission are closer to action than best seats in many major-league parks. General admission seats are aluminum benches with backs. There are 274 club-level second-deck seats. Alcohol prohibited in designated family areas (sections 119 and 209).

SEATING FOR PEOPLE WITH DISABILITIES: Seating for 90 people spread throughout stadium. Club level accessible by stadium elevator.

STADIUM FOOD: Chicken, not surprisingly, is the main attraction, with grilled chicken breast sandwiches and shredded chicken BBQ sandwiches for $4.50 each. One of the concession stands is called **The Hen House,** and nuggets and fried chicken are served here. A **Kid's Stand,** for those 12 and under, has fruit yogurt, hot dogs, and candy. All items are $1. A pre-game buffet, which includes luxury-level seats, is $17.

SMOKING POLICY: Smoking prohibited except in designated area on concourse on right-field side.

VISITING TEAM HOTEL: Ramada Inn and Convention Center (300 S. Salisbury Blvd. Salisbury, MD 21801, tel. 410/546–4400 or 800/228–2828).

TOURISM INFORMATION: Wicomico County Convention & Visitors Bureau (Box 2333, Salisbury, MD 21802, tel. 410/548–4914 or 800/332–8687).

Delmarva: Arthur W. Perdue Stadium

Arthur W. Perdue founded an egg business in 1920. For most of the next three decades, baseball was big in Perdue's native region until the Eastern Shore League folded in 1949. Baseball returned in 1996 thanks in significant part to the success of Arthur Perdue's chicken company. The Perdue family donated the land and several million dollars for the construction of Arthur W. Perdue Stadium.

Where until recently were chicken houses and tenant farmers, there now sits a small jewel of a stadium. The exterior is red and beige cinderblock with the look of brick set off by a handsome dark green roof. Designed by the Design Exchange of Delaware, Perdue Stadium has seating for 5,200 and a state-of-the-art sound system. Trees and large outfield scoreboards frame the field beyond the fences.

The $10 million stadium has an attractive second deck with six skyboxes and 274 club-level seats. This unusual minor-league second level allows a compact design providing fans in all 5,200 seats extraordinary proximity to the baseball action. There are only nine rows of the dark-green field and box seats, allowing for some of the best general admission seating in all of baseball.

Peter Kirk's trademark design—with the concession stands on a concourse immediately behind the seats—is a fan favorite, as you can follow the action while you stand in line for food. The grassy berms down each foul line allow for overflow crowds on big nights without destroying the intimacy that is the hallmark of minor-league-stadium design. Another Kirk winner is the carousel for kids. The 20-horse carousel, adding cheery music and lights, is on the third-base side.

On the first-base side of the stadium is the Eastern Shore Hall of Fame Museum. Highlighting the history of the Class D Eastern Shore League from 1922 to 1949, it includes the careers of such native sons as Hall of Famer Frank "Home Run" Baker. The Eastern Shore League drew teams from Delaware, Maryland, and Virginia, the three states that make up the DEL-MAR-VA region that is the home of the current team. The team's nickname—Shorebirds—reflects the wide variety of waterfowl in the Delmarva area.

The team plays in the South Atlantic League, the level above the rookie leagues. It's affiliated with the Baltimore Orioles franchise, allowing the fans to follow favorite players as they mature from A-level ball into full-fledged Birds in Baltimore.

Where to Stay

Sheraton Salisbury. This five-story downtown hotel overlooks a tributary of the Wicomico River. The restaurant has a view of the short Riverwalk. Ask for the sales department at extension 117 to get the $85 double-room Shorebirds promotion, which includes two adult general admission tickets. *300 S. Salisbury Blvd., Salisbury, MD 21801, tel. 410/546–4400 or 800/ 325–2525, fax 410/546–2528. 156 rooms. Facilities: restaurant, pool, free airport shuttle. AE, D, DC, MC, V. $$*

Super 8 Motel. North of town by the bypass, this no-frills motel is in a commercial strip next to a small field. The rooms are standard size and utilitarian. There's free toast, juice, and coffee in the mornings. *2615 N. Salisbury Blvd., Salisbury, MD 21801, tel. 410/749–5131 or 800/800–8000. 48 rooms. Facilities: free cribs. AE, D, DC, MC, V. $$*

Where to Eat

English's Family Restaurant. This venerable chain has two locations, both serving its signature sweet-potato biscuits, Maryland fried chicken, Eastern-shore oysters, and apple dumplings with vanilla cinnamon sauce. There is an extensive kid's menu, and children six and under eat free with a paying adult. The restaurants are built around old diners. *2525 N. Salisbury Blvd., Salisbury, tel. 410/742–8133; 735 S. Salisbury Blvd., Salisbury, tel. 410/742–8182. D, MC, V. $*

Old Mill Crab House. This casual, get-messy restaurant serves hard-shell crabs on brown paper. Make sure children don't rub their eyes with fingers filled with crab spice! The children's menu includes fried shrimp, crab, chicken, and pizza. *Rte. 54 and Waller Rd., 8 mi northeast of Salisbury, Delmar, DE, tel. 302/846–2808. AE, MC, V. $*

Zia's Pastaria. The Bubas family uses no microwave ovens in this casual Italian pasta house. Its homemade pesto sauce includes nuts and fresh basil. The children's menu includes ravioli, spaghetti, fettuccine, and chicken. *2408 N. Salisbury Blvd., Salisbury, tel. 410/543–9118. D, MC, V. $*

Entertainments

Salisbury Zoo. This 12-acre, beautifully landscaped free zoo is the perfect scale for smaller children. More than 400 animals live here, including long-eared rabbits, spider monkeys, two jaguars, a sloth, and a toucan. You can take as little as half an hour to walk the zoo or spend an afternoon at the playground at the west entrance. The adjacent city park has a lake and paddleboats. *755 South Park Dr., Salisbury, tel. 410/548–3188. Admission: donations. Open Memorial Day–Labor Day, daily 8–7:30; Labor Day–Memorial Day, daily 8–4:30.*

Ward Museum of Wildfowl Art. A gem of a museum, it is devoted to decoy carving and bird art. Its realistic re-creation of a duck blind gives the flavor of the Eastern Shore. Children like to see the workshop of Lem and Steve Ward, brothers who elevated decoys into art. The work of winning child carvers is featured. *900 S. Schumaker Dr., Salisbury, tel. 410/742-4988. Admission: $4 adults, $3 senior citizens, $2 kindergarten–12th grade. Open Mon.–Sat. 10–5, Sun. noon–5.*

PENNSYLVANIA DUTCH AND 🎫 LITTLE LEAGUE WORLD SERIES
HARRISBURG, READING, WILLIAMSPORT, SCRANTON/WILKES-BARRE

Pennsylvania is filled with historic baseball stadiums, unique family-run amusement parks, and picturesque farms. In Harrisburg baseball is played in City Island Park, in the middle of the Susquehanna River, just a short walk across a bridge from downtown. The Riverside Rascal is the mascot of this Double A Eastern League team.

By driving south of the city on Interstate 83 and picking up Route 422 east, you can go first to Hershey, with its chocolate museum and all-day amusement park, and through Pennsylvania Dutch country on your way to Reading, 35 mi east of Harrisburg. Reading's Memorial Municipal Stadium is a lesson in how to update a 1950 ballpark. The Double A Reading Phillies park, in the Eastern League, has a landscaped plaza and real seats, no benches, for everyone. The city is best known for its acres of outlet malls, but there are also many antiques and collectibles markets and stores concentrating on Pennsylvania potato chips, pretzels, and chocolate. You'll also find one-of-a-kind roadside structures, like a pagoda overlooking Reading and the miniature villages in Roadside America in Shartlesville, 25 mi northwest of Reading.

Driving north 65 mi on Route 61 to Route 81 north brings you to Scranton/Wilkes-Barre and its Lackawanna County Stadium. Even the AstroTurf surface cannot mar the beautiful mountain setting for these Triple A International League games. This is coal country; there's an anthracite mine to explore in the same cars miners used for more than 100 years. Railroads also built this area, and the train industry is shown in films, displays, and artifacts at the Steamtown National Historic Site in Scranton.

Heading south on Interstate 81, then west on the Pennsylvania Turnpike to Interstate 180 North, you'll reach Williamsport, one of America's baseball meccas, 70 mi from Scranton. Every young baseball fan holds central Pennsylvania in special regard, because Williamsport is where the Little League's World Series is played. The city also has its own 1926 minor-league stadium in the municipal park, where the New York–Penn League Crosscutters play short-season A ball. About 35 mi southeast of Williamsport is one of America's most delightful vintage amusement parks, Knoebels Amusement Resort, in the midst of a cool pine forest. If you're traveling in mid-August and have time for a detour, head 170 mi southwest to Point Stadium in Johnstown for the championship of the All-American Amateur Baseball Association, starring 20-year-olds and under from summer leagues across the eastern United States.

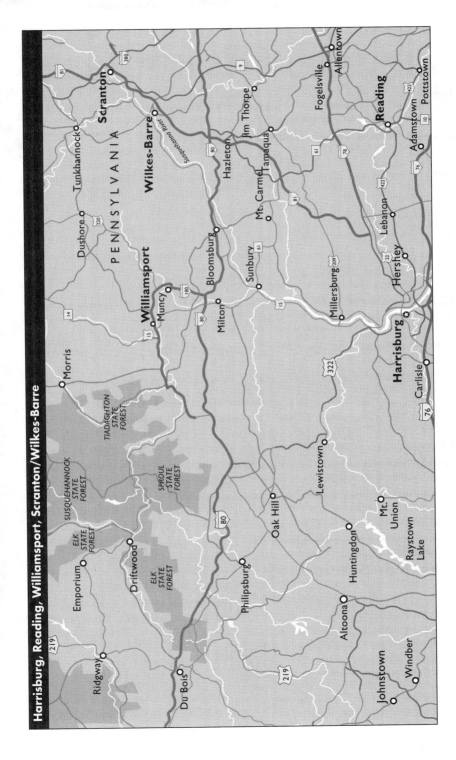

HARRISBURG SENATORS

League: Eastern League • **Major League Affiliation:** Montreal Expos • **Class:** AA • **Stadium:** RiverSide Stadium • **Opened:** 1987 • **Capacity:** 6,300 • **Dimensions:** LF: 335, CF: 400, RF: 335 • **Surface:** grass • **Season:** Apr.–Labor Day

STADIUM LOCATION: City Island, Harrisburg, PA 17101

TEAM WEBSITE: www.senatorsbaseball.com

GETTING THERE: From I–83, 2nd St. exit (Exit 23) to Market St.; Market St. Bridge to City Island. Replica trolley buses go from downtown to City Island. Walking across bridge from downtown to City Island is recommended.

PARKING: Parking at lot on island, $1.

TICKET INFORMATION: Box 15757, Harrisburg, PA 17105, tel. 717/231–4444, fax 717/231–4445.

PRICE RANGE: Box seats, $8; reserved grandstand, $6; general admission $5 adults, $3 ages under 13 and over 59.

GAME TIME: Mon.–Sat. 7:05 PM, Sun. 1:05 PM; gates open 90 min before game.

TIPS ON SEATING: General admission seats are on third-base side. Aluminum benches do not have backs and setting sun shines in your eyes in early innings. Reserved grandstand seats on first-base side have backs; some sections no-smoking.

SEATING FOR PEOPLE WITH DISABILITIES: On first-base side behind box seats with protective plastic screen.

STADIUM FOOD: The food on City Island (ribs and chicken) just outside the park is better than the stadium food, but it cannot be brought in. On the bright side, food in the park is inexpensive—small fries, hot dogs, popcorn, and drinks are all $1. At the grill under the grandstand on the first-base sides, are sausages, burgers, BBQ chicken, and chicken fingers. Funnel cakes, pretzels, and pizza also are sold. There are microbrewed beers.

SMOKING POLICY: Smoking is not permitted in the seating areas, but is allowed in the back concourse.

VISITING TEAM HOTEL: Hilton Hotel and Towers (1 N. 2nd St., Harrisburg, PA 17101, tel. 717/233–6000 or 800/445–8667).

TOURISM INFORMATION: Capital Region Chamber of Commerce (114 Walnut St., Harrisburg, PA 17108, tel. 717/232–4121).

Harrisburg: RiverSide Stadium

Harrisburg's RiverSide Stadium is one of those places where the setting is so fine that it takes your mind off the fact that the ballpark is mediocre. RiverSide Stadium is the centerpiece of City Island Park, a 62-acre recreation complex on an island in the middle of the Susquehanna River. Here you can ride a miniature train around the island, take a boat ride on the river, play miniature golf, go for a swim, play volleyball, watch a soccer game, have a meal, or play at a children's playground. The view of the State Capitol and the Harrisburg skyline across the river is first-rate. It is hard to imagine a more delightful package of activities.

They have played professional baseball in Harrisburg since 1883. Minor-league and Negro League teams played on this site for most of the first half of the 20th century. In 1952, the Harrisburg Senators signed a 26-year-old stenographer named Eleanor Engle to play shortstop. Engle suited up for four games, but the professional baseball establishment voided her contract before she could get into the action.

Because of flooding on the island, no professional baseball was played there or anywhere else in Harrisburg from 1953 until 1987, when RiverSide Stadium was built for a new Double A Eastern League franchise. The city built the stadium using the same field layout of the wooden-bleachered Island Park, this time investing heavily in flood protection.

This stadium has been a work in progress. It opened in 1987 with a simple covered grandstand and wooden bleachers seating 4,000 at a cost of $1.9 million. In 1988, they added 808 box seats. Reserved aluminum bleachers with backs were built behind each dugout in 1990. In 1993, when Charlie Sheen and Tom Berenger were making the movie Major League II at Baltimore's Camden Yards, producers needed a nearby site for the early spring-training scenes. Harrisburg was the place. They filled the area down the first-base line with potted palm trees and put up ads for Florida companies on the outfield wall—an instant Florida in Pennsylvania. For the 1994 season, a new, no-smoking reserved section and picnic area went in where the moviemakers had had their palm trees. With general admission bleachers down the third-base line, the stadium now seats 6,300.

Harrisburg has a new mascot, the blue Riverside Rascal, a red-nosed river monster. The nickname Senators does not come from the legislature across the river but from a long-ago association with the Washington Senators.

The stands overlook the island's attractive grove of trees. Flags fly in left field, and a simple scoreboard fills right center. Unfortunately, you can't see the river or the Capitol from the stadium seats, but it is worth a walk to the top of the grandstand at midgame to view this wonderful setting. The bridge from downtown to the island and all the major City Island attractions are lit up with strings of small lights.

They are serious about their baseball here in Harrisburg. In 1995, new owners announced they were going to move the team to Massachusetts. The city leadership went ballistic, minor-league baseball stalled the move, and the city eventually purchased the team. This unusual arrangement should guarantee Senators baseball on City Island for a long time to come.

Where to Stay

Visiting Team Hotel: Hilton Hotel and Towers. This downtown high-rise hotel is within walking distance of the ballpark. The upper floors of the modern, 15-story hotel have great views of the city and the river. It has "Bounceback Weekend" rates of $109 per room, with kids free and free Continental breakfast for every guest. 1 N. 2nd St., Harrisburg 17101, tel. 717/233–6000 or 800/445–8667, fax 717/233–6271. 340 rooms. Facilities: restaurant, indoor pool. AE, D, DC, MC, V. $$

Holiday Inn Express. This two-story motel at the edge of the Susquehanna River is in walking distance from the ballpark. There's a free breakfast bar. 525 S. Front St., Harrisburg 17104, tel. and fax 717/233–1611 or tel. 800/465–4329. 117 rooms. Facilities: health club. AE, D, DC, MC, V. $$

Super 8 Motel–North. The surroundings are a traffic interchange, but this two-story motel is a direct 5 mi from the ballpark, right down Front Street along the Susquehanna River. 4125 N. Front St., Exit 22 from I–81, Harrisburg 17110, tel. and fax 717/233–5891 or tel. 800/848–8888. 57 rooms. Facilities: outdoor pool. AE, D, DC, MC, V. $

Where to Eat

Broad Street Market. At this vintage farmer's market vendors sell prepared foods as well as produce. There is cluster seating throughout the two buildings, the Brick Market and Stone Market. Beiler's Poultry sells barbecue chicken, ribs, and cooked yams. There's Vietnamese noodle soup at Golden Gate, Jamaican jerk chicken at Auckland's Place, and Jamaican fish sandwiches at T. Oliver's. Jimmy's is a sit-down breakfast and lunch counter. There's also International Foods & Deli (Lebanese), Fisher's Deli (subs and pizza), and Yong's Kitchen (Chinese). Bradford's Bread has superb grab-and-go baked goods. Philadelphia-style pretzels are sold at Auntie Anne's Hot Pretzels. 1233 N. 3rd St., 3 blocks from Front St., Harrisburg, tel. 717/236–7923. $

Gingerbread Man. You can watch the small marinas on the Susquehanna River from the glassed-in porch at this casual restaurant just across the Market Street Bridge, south of Harrisburg. The sandwiches and desserts are gigantic. The portions on the children's menu are the right size. *313 S. Front St., Wormleysburg, tel. 717/737–1313. AE, D, DC, MC, V. $*

Entertainments

Hershey's Chocolate World. You ride in an amusement park–style car while viewing equipment and vats of display chocolate. Up to 30-minute waits are common for this popular 10-minute tour. Everyone receives a free candy-bar souvenir before being discharged into a huge company store with several casual restaurants. *800 Park Blvd., Hershey, tel. 717/534–4900. Admission free. Open mid-June–Labor Day, daily 9–6:45; Labor Day–mid-Nov., daily 9–4:45; mid-Nov.–Dec., call for hrs; Jan.–Mar., Mon.–Sat. 9–4:45, Sun. noon–4:45; Apr.–mid-June, daily 9–4:45.*

HersheyPark. This well-planned amusement park has 60 rides, seven roller coasters, 20 kiddie rides, and a walk-through zoo. Its wooden roller coaster, the Wildcat, stretches over 2 acres. A pro soccer team, also known as the Wildcats, plays in HersheyPark Stadium. A new county fair tent on a midway has animals, quilts, and Pennsylvania Dutch foods. Nearly all Harrisburg and Hershey hotels offer money-saving HersheyPark discount packages or coupons. *300 Park Blvd., Hershey, tel. 717/534–3090 or 800/437–7439. Admission: $30.95 ages 9–54, $16.95 ages 3–8 and senior citizens; $14.95 after 5 PM. Open June–Aug., daily 10–10; mid-May and Sept., daily 10–8; closing times may vary.*

Pride of the Susquehanna. This 40-minute ride is relaxing, but you view the least interesting parts of City Island and Harrisburg. There's an on-board snack bar. *City Island Marina, Harrisburg, tel. 717/234–6500. Admission: $4.95 adults, $3 ages 2–12. Open June–Aug., Tues.–Fri. noon–4, weekends noon–8.*

Whitaker Center for Science and Arts. This new three-story building in downtown has performances in dance and a good science center with more than 200 exhibits. There are marvelous experiments with light, temperature, sound, and static electricity. There are also hands-on experiments and a good gift shop. *222 Market St., Harrisburg, tel. 717/214–2787.*

Admission: $9.75 adults, $5 ages 3–17. Open Mon.–Sat. 10–6, Sun. noon–6.

Sights to See

You can call for a copy of the excellent "Citywide Sights" brochure from the Office of the Mayor (Harrisburg, tel. 717/255–3040). It offers a detailed listing of the architecture, history, neighborhoods, and parking downtown.

Peace Garden. The two blocks from Emerald Street to Maclay Street in the city's 5-mi **Riverfront Park** are dedicated to the pursuit of peace. The beautiful walk is adorned with inspiring quotes from world leaders. *Emerald and Maclay Sts., Harrisburg, tel. 717/255–3020.*

State Capitol and Museum. Pennsylvania has one of the most impressive of our nation's capitol buildings. "Commonwealth"—a gold-leaf statue nicknamed "Miss Penn"—stands atop the enormous Capitol dome that dominates the skyline of Harrisburg. The 52-million-pound dome, modeled after that of St. Peter's Basilica in Rome, rises 272 ft from the ground. There are two notable groups of statuary at the front of the Capitol done by Pennsylvania sculptor George Grey Barnard. Inside the Italian Renaissance building, the marble staircase is modeled on the grand stairway of the Opera House in Paris. Paintings by Pennsylvania artists Edwin Austin Abbey and Violet Oakley decorate the lobby and the other major chambers of the building. The beautifully restored and ornate Senate Chamber is most striking, dark rich green and gold with marble and mahogany and French gold drapes. The Pennsylvania General Assembly provides excellent free guided tours of the Capitol building. The rotunda is always open. For information, write the Pennsylvania General Assembly. *State Capitol, Harrisburg 17108, tel. 717/787–6810. Tours weekdays on the ½ hr, weekends on the hr except noon.*

State Museum of Pennsylvania. The 65-acre Capitol complex includes a free museum with exhibits that portray the commonwealth's cultural and natural heritage. The emphasis is on geology and industry rather than history and politics. There are rocks, cars, carriages, furniture, and a Conestoga wagon. The Curiosity Corner is a hands-on learning center for children. At the planetarium you can attend star shows. *3rd and North Sts., Box 1026, Harrisburg 17108-1026, tel. 717/787–4978. Admission: Curiosity Corner $2; planetarium $2 adults, $1.50 ages under 13 and senior citizens. Open museum, Tues.–Sat. 9–5, Sun. noon–5; Curiosity Corner, Tues., Thurs., and weekends 1–4; planetarium, weekends at 1 and 2:30.*

READING PHILLIES

League: Eastern League • **Major League Affiliation:** Philadelphia Phillies • **Class:** AA • **Stadium:** Memorial Municipal • **Opened:** 1950 • **Capacity:** 8,500 • **Dimensions:** LF: 330, CF: 400, RF: 330 • **Surface:** grass • **Season:** Apr.–Labor Day

STADIUM LOCATION: Rte. 61S. Centre Ave., Reading, PA 19605.

TEAM WEBSITE: www.readingphillies.com

GETTING THERE: From Pennsylvania Turnpike, Rte. 222N to Rte. 422W to Rte. 61S. From I–78, Rte. 61S.

PARKING: Ample free parking.

TICKET INFORMATION: Box 15050, Reading, PA 19612, tel. 610/478–8491, fax 610/373–5868.

PRICE RANGE: Box seats, $8; reserved seats, $6; general admission $5 adult, $3 ages 5–14 and over 63.

GAME TIME: Mon.–Sat. 7:05 PM, Sun. 1:05 PM; gates usually open 90 min before game.

TIPS ON SEATING: Sit along the first-base side for easy access to the attractive patio area by the grill.

SEATING FOR PEOPLE WITH DISABILITIES: In right- and left-field grandstands.

STADIUM FOOD: The food is inexpensive and good. The best bet is the excellent pizza—cheese or pepperoni—for $1.50 a slice. Hot dogs are a bargain at $1.50 and have old-fashioned square-style buns. The **Food Grove** behind the right-field bleachers does a good job on sandwiches—grilled chicken and sausage ($2.50), burgers ($2–$2.25). There are homemade pretzels and funnel cakes ($2) and heavy meatball sandwiches ($2.50). Wash down the BBQ peanuts ($2) with lemonade or spring water ($1). Other bargains are the hot fudge and butterscotch sundaes for $2.25. **The Deck,** a multitier bar with limited food selections behind the left-field wall, is open to all fans after the game begins. It features the local Yuengling beer.

SMOKING POLICY: Smoking prohibited in seating areas, but allowed in upper concourse directly behind general admission seats, in concourse, and in right-field food court.

VISITING TEAM HOTEL: Wellesley Inn (910 Woodland Ave., Reading, PA 19610, tel. 610/374–1500 or 800/444–8888).

TOURISM INFORMATION: Reading-Berks Visitors Information Association (801 Hill Rd., VF Outlet Village, Wyomissing, PA 19610, tel. 610/375–4085 or 800/443–6610).

Reading: Memorial Municipal Stadium

Memorial Municipal Stadium in Reading, Pennsylvania, is a model of what can be done with an ordinary ballpark. Veteran Reading Phillies fans say the changes made in the last decade have dramatically improved this stadium. Before these renovations, box seats were folding chairs, the bleachers were wooden, and the grand-stand had no roof. Today's stadium bears little resemblance to the ballpark built in 1950.

Owner Craig Stein bought the team in 1986 and immediately established a partnership with the city and the Reading Municipal Memorial Stadium Commission that has produced substantial improvements virtually every year. Investments of more than $2.5 million have transformed the ballpark into a minor-league success story.

At the entrance, a landscaped plaza and new brick arches signal a commitment to excellence that continues inside. Just inside the entrance is a display case full of Reading baseball memorabilia. The concourse is red, white, and blue, wide and comfortable; a Reading-baseball Hall of Fame extends along the first-base side. The third-base-side concourse has a large, colorful mural of kids playing baseball.

The folding chairs and wooden bleachers have all been replaced by real seats—8,500 blue, green, yellow, and red plastic seats. This is an extraordinary commitment to the comfort of fans for a minor-league stadium. Flags fly from the grandstand roof. Ironically, the one we looked for wasn't there. Just weeks after Mike Schmidt—the only player whose number has been retired by the Reading Phillies—was inducted into the Hall of Fame, the flag that flies from the grandstand roof with his number, 24, was shredded in a windstorm. Several replacement flags also tattered in the wind at that flag site. So Schmidt, who played for Reading in 1971, is honored in displays within the stadium.

We were especially impressed with the attractive picnic area behind the first-base bleachers. In many stadiums, this area under and behind aluminum bleachers looks like a trash dump. Here it is a beautifully treed patio-like area with small concession stands nearby. On the third-base side just past the grandstand, there is a picnic area for parties.

One distinctive feature from the original stadium remains—an attractive brick wall that surrounds the entire field. Wooden outfield fences stand inside it. The view beyond the wall is as eclectic as we saw anywhere: a mix of industrial plants and churches backed by mountains. The fire tower beyond right field on Mt. Penn is the most distinctive local landmark. Railroad tracks run close to the stadium, and planes from the nearby airport fly right over the grandstand roof.

The Phillies have an unusual mascot, Screwball—a red, white, and blue baseball on legs—and plenty of promotions. We attended one of the five fireworks nights in the season, even though there wasn't a holiday anywhere in sight. We particularly enjoyed Reading's practice of thrilling up to 10 birthday kids by inviting them to throw out a first ball.

Where to Stay

Visiting Team Hotel: Wellesley Inn. This four-story motel is 3 mi south of the ballpark. Guests are given Continental breakfast. The rooms are standard in size and furnishings. Ironing boards are provided. *910 Woodland Ave., Paper Mill Rd. exit off Rte. 422, Reading 19610, tel. 610/374–1500 or 800/444–8888, fax 610/374–2554. 105 rooms. AE, D, DC, MC, V. $$*

Days Inn–Reading. Guests receive a free Continental breakfast at this well-kept motel, which is 8 mi north of the ballpark. Its rooms are freshly decorated. *15 Lancaster Pike, Exit 21, Hwy. 22 N, from Pennsylvania Turnpike, Reading 19607, tel. 610/777–7888 or 800/325–2525, fax 610/777–5138. 142 rooms. Facilities: outdoor pool, exercise room, game room. AE, D, DC, MC, V. $$*

Red Caboose Inn. It's an hour south of the ballpark, but here's your chance to sleep in a caboose in the middle of Amish country. Each of the 36 cabooses sleeps six (one double bed and four bunks); one has video games. You'll need to reserve the cabooses four weeks in advance in summer. There are also seven rooms in an adjoining farmhouse. Meals are served in a dining car, and there's free country music in a barn on Wednesday and weekend nights in summer. *Rte. 741, Strasburg 17579, tel. 717/687–5000 or 888/687–5005, fax 717/687–5000. 43 rooms. Facilities: dining car, playground. D, MC, V. $$*

Where to Eat

Arner's Family Restaurants. Children have many choices at this sunny, fast-service restaurant, including their own menu, half orders of any adult entrée, and a reduced price at the extensive salad bar. Arner's is known for its broiled crab cakes and its wide variety of vegetables. This site is eight blocks from the ballpark, the closest of its four Reading locations. There is a garden room in the rear. *9th and*

Exeter Sts., Reading, tel. 610/929–9795. AE, D, DC, MC, V. $

The Crab Barn. Kids eat free from the children's menu here on Sunday with a paying adult. King crabs, blue crabs, softshells, and Dungeness are available, along with shrimp, chicken, and fish sticks for children. The dining room is on the second floor, and four tables are housed in a third-floor loft. There are crayons and special place mats for kids. The restaurant is just a couple of miles from the ballpark. *2613 Hampden Blvd., Reading, tel. 610/921–8922. AE, MC, V. $$*

The Peanut Bar and Restaurant. There are a multitude of sandwich choices at this noisy, popular restaurant, which encourages you to throw peanut shells on the floor. The children's menu includes spaghetti, grilled cheese sandwiches, and chicken tenders. Its signature dessert is frozen, chocolate-covered pretzel pie. *332 Penn St., Reading, tel. 610/376–8500 or 800/515–8500. AE, D, MC, V. $*

Entertainments

Roadside America. This one-of-a-kind attraction is 25 mi northwest of Reading and worth the drive. Picture a gigantic miniature village spanning history, with moving trains, trolleys, airplanes, animals, cars, and coal-mine equipment. This Cadillac of roadside tourist attractions was the life work of hobbyist Laurence Gieringer. You'll view the huge scene in light and "nighttime" darkness during the patriotic Evening Pageant. An employee told us it takes six years to dust the entire exhibit. *Rte. 22, Exit 8 from I–78, Shartlesville, tel. 610/488–6241. Admission: $4 adults, $1.50 ages 6–11. Open July–Labor Day, weekdays 9–6:30, weekends 9–7; Labor Day–June, weekdays 10–5, weekends 10–6.*

Strasburg Railroad. America's oldest short-line railroad takes you on a 45-minute ride through Amish farmland. As it's popular for school trips, advance reservations are a good idea. *Rte. 741,*

Strasburg, tel. 717/687–7522. Cost: $7.75 adults, $4 ages 3–11, under 3 free.

Dorney Park. Pennsylvania has several amusement-park treasures and this is one, just 30 minutes from Reading. Open since the 1860s, it is both modern and vintage. A large water park, Wildwater Kingdom, adjoins it. There are bumper boats, two wooden coasters, a 90-ft Ferris wheel, a 1921 Dentzel carousel, a Care Bears show, miniature golf, and the sit-down Memories restaurant. Admission includes both parks. Parking is $5. *3830 Dorney Park Rd., Rte. 222 (Pennsylvania Turnpike Exit 16) east from Hwy. 309, Allentown, tel. 610/395–3724. Admission: mid-Apr.–June, $28 adults and children over 48", $5.95 children under 48", under 3 free, $10 discount after 5 PM. Open mid-Apr.–Labor Day, daily 10–10.*

Sights to See

The Pagoda. This 72-ft-high Japanese structure overlooks the city and Schuylkill Valley. It was built in 1908 as a luxury resort hotel on Mt. Penn, but when it was denied a liquor license, it never opened. Visitors can walk into the pagoda, which was restored in 1992 and is now used for offices; the view is worth the drive up the mountain. *Skyline Dr., Mt. Penn, Reading. Open daily 11–5.*

Unusual Shopping

Wilbur Chocolate Factory Outlet. The home of the original chocolate chip, the Wilbur Bud, is 35 mi southwest of Reading. Chocolate has been made in this factory since 1884. Its Ideal Dutch Process Cocoa is used in Amish cakes. You can visit its free Candy Americana Museum, too. It is next to the city park and town square. *46 Broad St., Lititz, tel. 717/626–3249.*

Tom Sturgis Pretzel Outlet. You can buy big plastic bags of some of the region's best pretzels at bargain prices here. It's near the Shillington farmer's market. *325 Lancaster Pike W (Rte. 222), Shillington, tel. 610/775–0335.*

WILLIAMSPORT CROSSCUTTERS

League: New York–Penn League • **Major League Affiliation:** Pittsburgh Pirates • **Class:** Short Season A • **Stadium:** Bowman Field • **Opened:** 1926 • **Capacity:** 4,200 • **Dimensions:** LF: 345, CF: 405, RF: 350 • **Surface:** grass • **Season:** mid-June–Labor Day

STADIUM LOCATION: 1700 W. 4th St., Williamsport, PA 17701.

TEAM WEBSITE: www.crosscutters.com

GETTING THERE: From the south, Rte. 15 to Maynard St., right on Maynard, left on 4th St., 1 mi to stadium. From the north, Rte. 15 to 4th St., left on 4th St., ballpark on left.

PARKING: Ample free parking at stadium.

TICKET INFORMATION: Box 3173, Williamsport, PA 17701, tel. 570/326–3389, fax 570/326–3494.

PRICE RANGE: Reserved box seats, $5; general admission $3.75 adult, $3 under 12 and senior citizens.

GAME TIME: 7:05 PM; gates open 1 hr before game.

TIPS ON SEATING: General admission seats are fine. Only 900 blue box seats, so you're close to action. Except for bleacher seats beyond first base, general admission seats are aluminum benches with backs under a roof. Remember, this is a 1920s stadium; make sure you don't sit behind one of 8 poles that hold up grandstand roof.

SEATING FOR PEOPLE WITH DISABILITIES: On both first- and third-base sides.

STADIUM FOOD: There is one large concession area under the stands offering normal and inexpensive baseball fare and a small stand past the grandstand on the third-base side. The best items are the Italian sausage with onions and peppers, for $2.50, and the pan pizzas at $3. The hot dogs are made by the Hatfield Company in Philadelphia and are quite mild. Many eaters go for the chili topping, for an extra 25¢. An unusual dessert is the pie-shaped wedge of chocolate chip cookies, sold for $2 and decorated with frosting. Cracker Jack is a reasonable $1, and frozen lemonade is $1.50. The soft pretzels ($1.25) are kept warm and are chewy. Ice-cream sundaes come in four varieties for $2.

SMOKING POLICY: No alcohol/no smoking section in bleachers directly behind home plate.

VISITING TEAM HOTEL: Holiday Inn (1840 E. 3rd St., Williamsport, PA 17701, tel. 570/326–1981 or 800/465–4329).

TOURISM INFORMATION: Lycoming County Tourist Promotion Agency (454 Pine St., Williamsport, PA 17701, tel. 570/326–1971 or 800/358–9900).

Williamsport: Bowman Field

There's baseball to see in Williamsport even if you can't get here for the Little League World Series in late August. The Williamsport Cutters play in Bowman Field. Built in 1926, it is one of the oldest minor-league parks still in use. A plain and simple New York–Penn League stadium, Bowman Field seats 4,200 with a partially covered grandstand. In 1929, they renamed the ballpark after businessman J. Walton Bowman, who had led the 1925 campaign to raise the $75,000 needed for construction. Lights were added in 1932. In 1934, the outfield walls were brought in (45 ft in center field), as only 10 home runs had been hit in the first eight seasons.

The field had deteriorated so much by the 1950s that Little League Baseball declined to take the ballpark from the city, saying that renovation costs to prepare it for the Little League World Series would be too great. From 1964 to 1987, Bowman Field was illuminated by lights originally used in New York's Polo Grounds. The ballpark was substantially upgraded in 1987. The wooden box seats were replaced and new lights installed without losing the stadium's old-time feel. The bleachers in left field were supplanted by a picnic area in 1988, reducing the capacity to 4,200. Further improvements were made in 1994. Renovations for the 2000 season include a new entrance and improved rest rooms and concession stands.

The view from the grandstand is one of the most idyllic in all of baseball, with houses and a tree-covered hillside beyond the outfield walls. There are nonstop contests and lucky numbers as well as good music in the intervals between baseball action. Kid Cub is the friendly bear mascot.

They have played professional baseball in Williamsport since 1907, starting with the Class B Tri-State League. In 1923 Williamsport joined the New York–Penn League, which became today's Class AA Eastern League in 1938. For the next 50-plus years, Williamsport was in and out of the Eastern League. The city returned to the New York–Penn League, now a short-season Class A league, in 1994.

To honor the region's logging past, the team adopted the nickname Crosscutters in 1999, when they became a farm team of the Pittsburgh Pirates.

Two of minor-league baseball's most bizarre moments took place at Bowman Field. In 1955, a young Reading outfielder named Roger Maris looked back over his shoulder while chasing a long fly ball and ran right through the outfield fence.

On August 31, 1987, with a Reading player on third base, Williamsport catcher Dave Bresnahan took a peeled round potato and threw it over the third baseman's head and into left field. When the runner tried to score from third, Bresnahan tagged him with the real ball. Bresnahan's professional playing career ended that night. But a year later, 4,000 fans showed up when Williamsport held Dave Bresnahan Day and retired his number 59. Admission that day was one dollar and one potato. Look on the concourse near the souvenir shop for the Bresnahan number 59 and pay tribute to a .149 hitter with a sense of humor.

Williamsport: Lamade Field

"Oh, my gosh!" exclaimed our young son Hugh as he left the Little League Museum and turned the corner at the top of the hill overlooking Lamade Field. The Saturday in August when they play for the World Championship of Little League is an "Oh, my gosh!" experience. Down at the bottom of this hill sits a most beautiful green diamond, expertly manicured and ready for a big game. But it's different. It's smaller. It's not like the big-guy stadiums we had been in. It's the kind of stadium a little kid could imagine playing in. To a five-year-old, it's simply perfect.

On World Series Saturday, this 10,000-seat grandstand fills up early. And the families were filling the huge grassy hill beyond the outfield wall with blankets and beach towels. The festivities began two hours before game time.

It was like a carnival inside the stadium and out. Groups of people stood just behind the stadium frantically trading pins from their towns and teams, as these were the last hours of a busy week of meeting people from across the country and around the world. Little League Baseball began in Williamsport in 1939, and the first World Series was played in 1947. The final game, always played on a Saturday, marks the end of tournament play for 7,400 chartered Little League programs around the world. Three million children from 102 countries now participate in the Little League Baseball program. Tournament play begins in mid-July. One month later, eight regional champions come to Williamsport, representing four United States regions and four international regions. Starting in 2001, the World Series will expand from 8 teams to 16 and a second stadium will be built behind Lamade Field to accommodate the extra games.

The 44-acre complex includes the offices of Little League Baseball, a museum, the stadium, and other facilities. A huge American flag waves in right center field behind a very short, dark-green fence with Dugout, the Little League mascot, painted on it. The offices and museum sit atop the hill. The view over the buildings is of more hills and trees behind. An open-air box full of television cameras hangs from the roof covering the grandstand.

Unless you are one of the lucky few in the VIP seating section directly behind home plate, you are sitting on a hard bench without a back. Bring a pillow, a blanket, or a seat cushion. The stadium was built in 1959 by Little League Baseball with a contribution from *Grit*, the national weekly newspaper published in Williamsport. The field was named for Howard J. Lamade, a *Grit* official and member of the Little League Board of Directors.

The sound system is spectacular, and the music—"Put Me In, Coach; I'm Ready to Play" seemed particularly appropriate—keeps the crowd energized before the game and during the too-long television commercial breaks between innings. The on-the-field entertainment includes a military marching band, a Mummers band, and the Phillie Phanatic, the mascot for the Philadelphia Phillies. It's a great show. The Little League Pledge is recited in four languages. Dignitaries are introduced and "The Star-Spangled Banner" sung before we even realized two hours had gone by. The wait until 3:50 PM to accommodate national TV wasn't painful at all. But beware: despite the fact this is a youth event, there are lots of smokers here.

The series is plenty professional for kids, and it might seem like too much pressure for a 12-year-old. But don't worry—this isn't exactly the big leagues. In one game we saw, the United States manager made a pitching change. The pitcher went to left field. The catcher became the pitcher. The third baseman became the catcher. The left fielder went to first base, and the first baseman to third. What would Abbott and Costello have done with material like this?

When you are in Williamsport for the World Series, always have a pen ready for an autograph. There's no telling who you might run into. We saw Hall of Famer Stan Musial, and as we walked out of the stadium, there was New York Yankees pitching great Tommy John, whose young son had sung "The Star-Spangled Banner."

Consider going to Thursday championship games. These tend to be more competitive than the Saturday games, which have been domi-

nated by the international teams for the last two decades.

More Williamsport Baseball

Carl E. Stotz Field. Don't go to Williamsport and fail to visit the Original Field; this was the site of the first dozen Little League World Series championships, beginning in 1947 until the move to the much larger Lamade Field in 1959. The Original Field has been lovingly restored and maintained by a volunteer group. The clubhouse has been turned into a small museum, open by appointment, which celebrates youth sports. It contains the personal collection of Carl Stotz, the founder of Little League baseball. It displays uniforms from the first year and the world's very first remote-controlled scoreboard. There are Little League games at 6 PM most weekdays from May through July. *100 West 4th St, Williamsport, tel. 570/323–4160. Donations welcome. Museum open by appointment.*

Memorial Park. This is where the very first Little League baseball game was played on June 6, 1939. Lundy Lumber defeated Lycoming Dairy 23–8. A statue of Carl Stotz with young ballplayers honors this spot. It sits beyond the right-field wall of Bowman Field on the other side of the community pool. *100 W. 4th St., Williamsport.*

Peter J. McGovern Little League Baseball Museum. Opened in 1982 and named in honor of Peter J. McGovern, the first president of Little League baseball, this museum pays tribute to Little League baseball from the first game to the last pitch of the most recent World Series. In addition to housing extensive historic videos and memorabilia, it is a fun place for kids. The lobby is a reduced-size re-creation of Lamade Stadium, with a huge 110-ft-wide, 15-ft-high photograph from the 1982 World Series showing the fans in the stands. At the Play Ball Room on the lower level kids can bat and pitch and then watch themselves on an instant-feedback monitor. There are educational opportunities here as well: The Play It Safe Room on the lower level displays safety equipment and makes a strong antidrug pitch; the nutrition exhibit gives future stars the opportunity to choose between excellent and poor meals; displays show how gloves and balls are made; and the decision to allow girls to compete in 1974 and the establishment of a Challenger Division for youngsters with disabilities in 1989 are highlighted. The museum is on a hill just above Lamade stadium. *Rte. 15, Box 3485, Williamsport 17701, tel. 570/326–3607. Admission: $5 adults, $3 senior citizens, $1.50 ages 5–13, $13 family. Open Memorial Day–Labor Day, Mon.–Sat. 9–7, Sun. noon–7; Labor Day–Memorial Day, Mon.–Sat. 9–5, Sun. noon–5.*

Where to Stay

Lodging is at a premium and prices are significantly higher during the Little League World Series; book a year in advance, if possible. Some of the more distant hotels on East Third Street, the so-called Golden Strip commercial area, may still have vacancies until January, seven months before the Series.

Visiting Team Hotel: Econo Lodge. This two-story hotel is a 15-minute drive from the Little League ballpark and has been fully renovated. The rooms have cherry veneer furniture, comfort chairs, and new 25-inch televisions. It's in a commercial strip of restaurants and movie theaters, near both the Giant and Loyal shopping plazas, 5 mi from downtown. *2401 E. 3rd St., Faxon St. exit from I-80, Williamsport 17701, tel. 570/326–1501 or 800/424–6423, fax 570/326–9776. 98 rooms. Facilities: restaurant. AE, D, DC, MC, V. $*

Genetti Hotel and Convention Center. This classic, 10-story downtown hotel was recently renovated. The older rooms have high ceilings; the newer ones don't. *200 W. 4th St., Williamsport 17701, tel. 570/326–6600, fax 570/326–5006. 166 rooms. Facilities: restaurant, outdoor pool, coin laundry. AE, D, DC, MC, V. $*

Holiday Inn. This two-story hotel is a 15-minute drive from the Little League ballpark. It's in the commercial strip of restaurants and movie theaters, 5 mi from downtown. *1840 E. 3rd St., Faxon St. exit from I-80, Williamsport 17701, tel. 570/326–1981 or 800/465–4329, fax 570/323–9590. 160 rooms. Facilities: restaurant, outdoor pool. AE, D, DC, MC, V. $$*

King's Inn. This '60s-era hotel, remodeled in 1993, is directly opposite the Little League Stadium. It consists of two one-story structures built into a hill. *Rte. 15, South Williamsport 17701,* *tel. 570/322–4707, fax 570/322–0946. 48 rooms. Facilities: restaurant. AE, D, DC, MC, V. $*

Sheraton Inn. This downtown inn overlooks the Susquehanna River and is a boarding point for the downtown trolley. You can ask for either a city- or river-view room in this 5-story brick box-style hotel that's surrounded by a parking lot. The rooms and halls are spacious and have modern furnishings. *100 Pine St., Williamsport 17701, tel. 570/327–8231 or 800/325–3535, fax 570/322–2957. 148 rooms. Facilities: restaurant, indoor pool. AE, D, DC, MC, V. $$*

Where to Eat

Bev's Kozy Korner Kafe. Generous, inexpensive meals are served at this large downtown Williamsport restaurant. Homemade banana- and chocolate-cream pies are special. Little League week brings a bargain dinner buffet for those 10 and under. There is counter and table service. *357 Pine Street, Williamsport, tel. 570/327–1077. No credit cards. $*

Charlie's Caboose. You can eat in a caboose, two railcars, or a freight-station house at this downtown restaurant on rails. It's a tablecloth-dinner-only restaurant, with everything from chicken sandwiches to roast duck. The children's menu offers spaghetti, burgers, and chicken fingers. The vegetable platter, seafood, and pasta are good. If you want to sit in the two-table caboose, reserve ahead. *500 Pine St., Williamsport, tel. 570/327–9128. AE, MC, V. $$*

Triangle Tavern. Diners have been enjoying memorable family-style Italian meals here for four decades. The signature spaghetti sauce and homemade Italian salad dressing are the big draws. There are also pizzas and individual deep-dish apple, cherry, and blueberry pies, as well as children-size portions of spaghetti and chicken fingers. It's 12 minutes north of the Little League ballpark. *308 Shiffler Ave., Williamsport, tel. 570/322–9945. MC, V. $*

Entertainments

Clyde Peeling's Reptiland. Kids love holding and touching the nonpoisonous snakes, lizards, and tortoises. The many poisonous snakes are safely behind glass. The educational talks are geared to kids, with a wealth of living props and interesting audiovisual shows. This walk-through attraction 12 mi south of Williamsport contains a Subway restaurant. Picnic facilities are available. *Rte. 15, Allenwood, tel. 570/538–1869. Admission: $7 adults, $5 ages 4–11. Open May–Sept., daily 9–7; Oct.–Apr., daily 10–5.*

Herdic Trolley. Trolley passengers can see Memorial Park, where the first Little League baseball game was played. This trolley takes a one-hour trip through downtown Williamsport and Millionaire's Row. The motorized car is named for Peter Herdic, who started the Williamsport Passenger Railway Company. The regular trolley tour expands for Little League World Series Week. The Historic Little League Tour (Williamsport City Bus, tel. 717/326–2500) starts at the Little League Museum and Lamade Stadium. The tour makes special stops at Point Park and Original Field. On Tuesday and Thursday, visitors can add a one-hour cruise on the *Hiawatha* paddle wheeler on the Susquehanna River (tel. 717/321–1205 or 800/358–9900). *Trolley Gazebo, Sheraton Inn, Pine and Court Sts., Williamsport, tel. 570/326–2500 or 800/248–9287 in PA. Admission: $2. Open May–Sept., Tues. and Thurs. 10:45–3:15, Sat. 9–11.*

Knoebels Amusement Resort. This is one of the most delightful noncommercial amusement parks in America. About 35 minutes southeast of Williamsport, it's nestled in a stream-crossed pine forest. The family-run park is cool on the hottest days. Step back in time with several handcrafted rides, free admission, and free park-

ing. Its new thrill rides delight older kids, and the boat, helicopter, and rocketship rides for younger children are better than the usual too-tame kiddie rides. All ages will scream on the wooden Phoenix roller coaster, resurrected from ruin in San Antonio. This park has great food—Cesari's pizza, pierogis, and addictive french fries. Its sit-down Alamo Restaurant specializes in coal-country food, including waffles with chicken sauce. The huge Crystal Pool has slides, a wading pool, and tube rides. The park takes pride in its brass-ring 1913 carousel and carousel museum. A mining museum, pioneer steam train, and two covered bridges are also on the grounds. Many families stay at the adjacent campground. *Rte. 487, Rte. 15 S from Williamsport to Rte. 61 E to Rte. 487 N, Elysburg, tel. 570/672–2572 or 800/487–4386. Rides 50¢–$2; all-ride pass, weekdays, $19.50 adults, $14 under 48"; pass including roller coaster, $5 extra adults, $3.50 extra children; $7.50 discount on basic pass after 5 PM; pool admission weekends $4 adults, $3 children under 12, weekdays $4 adults, $2.50 children; extra fee for slides. Open mid-June–early Sept., daily 11–10; Apr.–May, weekends noon–6 or 8.*

Memorial Pool. This large, clean city pool, with a wading pool for children 5 and under, is just yards from Memorial Park. After a long day of driving, you can cool off before the game. *Memorial Park, 1700 W. 4th St., Williamsport, tel. 570/322–4637. Admission: $2.50 adults, $2.25 ages 7–17, $1.50 ages 6 and under. Open Mon., Wed., Sat., Sun. 1–8, Tues., Thurs., Fri. 1–6.*

SCRANTON/WILKES-BARRE RED BARONS

League: International League • **Major League Affiliation:** Philadelphia Phillies • **Class:** AAA • **Stadium:** Lackawanna County Stadium • **Opened:** 1989 • **Capacity:** 10,832 • **Dimensions:** LF: 330, CF: 408, RF: 330 • **Surface:** artificial turf • **Season:** Apr.–Labor Day

STADIUM LOCATION: 235 Montage Mountain Rd., Moosic, PA 18507.

TEAM WEBSITE: www.redbarons.com

GETTING THERE: Stadium is just off I–81 between Scranton and Wilkes-Barre. From I–81, Montage Mountain Rd. exit (Exit 51), stadium on east side of I–81.

PARKING: Plenty of parking at stadium, $1.

TICKET INFORMATION: Box 3449, Scranton, PA 18505, tel. 570/969–2255, fax 570/963–6564.

PRICE RANGE: Lower box seats $7; upper boxes $5.50; upper reserved $5; bleachers $4.50.

GAME TIME: Mon.–Sat. 7:30 PM, Sun. 6 PM; gates open 90 min before game time.

TIPS ON SEATING: Bleacher seats, at field level down first- and third-base lines, are a good buy. Upper grandstand reserved seats are as high above playing field as upper-deck seats in major-league stadiums. View beyond outfield walls is better from seats on third-base (visitors) side.

SEATING FOR PEOPLE WITH DISABILITIES: Behind box seats behind home plate.

STADIUM FOOD: There is good regional food here—cheese steaks, potato pierogis, and thick-crust pizza. The deli on the ground floor, first-base side has hoagies. Adjacent is one of two grills with excellent steak-and-cheese hoagies. Across the aisle is a "kidcessions" stand. Its $2.75 Grumpy meal (named after the mascot) includes a hamburger, cheeseburger, or a good hot dog, with chips, fries, and a drink. Fresh-baked cookies are 3 for $1.50. Vendors sell juices for $1.75. Avoid the nonfresh peanuts. The pizza is baked on site. A glass-fronted **Stadium Club,** behind first base, is open to all ticket holders (and to the public weekdays 11–2); it has good chicken wings and fajitas. Its salad, sandwich, and kid's menus are extensive.

SMOKING POLICY: Smoking is allowed only in designated areas in the concourse under the stands.

VISITING TEAM HOTEL: Radisson Lackawanna Station Hotel (700 Lackawanna Ave., Scranton, PA 18503, tel. 570/342–8300 or 800/333–3333).

TOURISM INFORMATION: Northeast Territory Visitors Bureau (Airport Aviation Center, 201 Hangar Rd., Suite 203, Avoca, PA 18641, tel. 570/457–1320 or 800/245–7711).

Scranton/Wilkes-Barre: Lackawanna County Stadium

The Philadelphia Phillies play in one of the very worst of all the major-league baseball stadiums. In 1989, when a new stadium was built for its Triple A International League franchise, it was designed to match the Phillies' horrid Veterans Stadium. To prepare future Phillies for their step into the big leagues, they duplicated the height of the outfield wall, the dimensions to the outfield fence, and, unfortunately, the fake grass.

Surprise—even the plastic that covers the field cannot ruin the experience at Lackawanna County Stadium. Set in a valley, the stadium has one of the finest natural settings in all of baseball. From inside the park, the view of the surrounding tree-covered cliffs is one of the best of any East Coast ballpark we visited.

The baseball rivalry between Wilkes-Barre (pronounced "barry") and Scranton dates back to the 19th century, with both cities often fielding teams in the same minor leagues. In 1951, the Wilkes-Barre Barons folded, soon followed by the Scranton Red Sox in 1953.

To bring baseball back to this coal-mining region, Scranton and Wilkes-Barre combined forces, stitching together the nicknames of the former rivals into the Scranton/Wilkes-Barre Red Barons. (The nickname didn't come from the World War I flying ace.) Four seats from the old Scranton field are sitting now in the administrative office of the team just off the main concourse.

The 10,832-capacity Lackawanna County Stadium was built right at the base of Montage Mountain between the two cities. The nicely landscaped entrance is attractive, with tan blocks and a green roof with flags flying above. The double-decked grandstand presents a big-league feel and gives fans throughout the stadium an excellent view of the action. There are 20 skyboxes, with two available for group rental on a game-by-game basis. The outfield wall is blue with a modest amount of orange lettering and numbers. The only ads are on billboards beyond the outfield fence. There are scoreboards in left-center and right-center of the batter's eye. The bullpens are tucked neatly behind the fences near the left and right field foul poles. There is a picnic deck above the bullpen in right field.

The Phillie Phanatic visited the night we were there. The local mascot, The Grump, is also a hairy green thing. This one has a great big red mouth and a red gum ball–like nose. The Grump, according to local legend, was hatched when a prehistoric egg was found during stadium excavation. Grump is lovable and the food and the music are good.

From November through March, the right field area is converted to an NHL-size ice skating rink. The rink sits just under the stadium restaurant and is very popular with the locals.

Fans of the wonderful movie *Field of Dreams* will want to know that the young ballplayer who only played in a single major league game and later became a doctor—Archibald "Moonlight" Graham—won the New York State League batting title hitting .336 for Scranton in 1906.

Where to Stay

Visiting Team Hotel: Radisson Lackawanna Station Hotel. This majestic six-story French Renaissance hotel was the station for the Delaware, Lackawanna and Western railroad. Its lobby ceiling is Tiffany stained glass, the floor is terrazo tiles, and imposing marble columns are set off by tile panels of scenes along the rail route. Despite the elegance, the hotel and its restaurant, Carmen's, are affordable ($89 double) and child-friendly. The rooms have lovely antique reproduction furniture, expensive draperies, and modern baths. *700 Lackawanna Ave., Scranton 18503, tel. 570/342–8300 or 800/ 333–3333, fax 570/342–0380. 146 rooms. Facilities: restaurant, hot tub, exercise room, game room. AE, D, DC, MC, V. $$*

Hampton Inn. Within one mile of the ballpark, this four-story motel is on a hill, with a view of Montage Mountain. The rooms are attractive and basic. Guests receive a free Continental breakfast. *22 Montage Mountain Rd., Scranton 18507, tel. 570/342–7002 or 800/426–7866, fax 570/342–7012. 129 rooms. Facilities: restaurant, indoor pool, hot tub, exercise room. AE, D, DC, MC, V. $$*

Marriott Courtyard. This three-story hotel is adjacent to the ballpark complex and has a fine view of Montage Mountain. It is surrounded by a parking lot and built around an interior court-

yard. Rooms are modern, spacious, and have two double beds. *16 Glenmaura National Blvd., Scranton 18507, tel. 570/969–2100 or 800/ 228–9290, fax 570/969–2110. 120 rooms. Facilities: indoor pool. AE, D, DC, MC, V. $$*

Where to Eat

Smith's Family Restaurant. The cottage-style white-frame restaurant has been part of this residential and warehouse neighborhood since 1934. This is plain, inexpensive food and the clientele are families and older neighbors. A counter and booth section gets heavy use at breakfast, and the two dining rooms, with their captain's chairs and wood paneling, are decorated with parish notables and the daily specials. There is a large offering of lighter menu items and sandwiches. Chicken and ribs are for heavier appetites. It's 3 mi northeast of the ballpark at Cherry Street, following Route 11 (Main Street), which turns into Cedar Avenue. *1402 Cedar Ave., Scranton, tel. 570/961–9192. Open weekdays 5:30–10, Sat. 5:30–8. No credit cards. $*

Cooper's Seafood House. You can't help but notice the larger-than-life octopus and pirates hanging on the roof of this ship-shaped restaurant. Inside is a cornucopia of marine artifacts, photos of historic Scranton and of Babe Ruth, and several whimsical and inviting dining rooms. Walking through the hallways, you can view the entire 20th century in frames. There's a vintage children's toy exhibit at the entry and a 40-ft whale is the ceiling ornament in the no-smoking room. Children's meals are served in paper ships and desserts include the classic coconut ice-cream ball in chocolate sauce. The fish soups and seafood dishes are nicely prepared, and unusual items, like alligator, mako shark, and blue marlin, are served. *701 N. Washington Ave., Scranton, tel. 570/346–6883. Open Mon.–Thurs. 11–midnight, Fri.–Sat. 11 AM–1 AM, Sun. 1–9. D, MC, V. $$*

Coney Island Lunch. This storefront restaurant is larger and newer than its competitor, The Original Coney Island, and serves a few more items, like bean soup, a good coconut cream pie, and homemade rice pudding. But the basic menu is the identical-tasting Texas wieners and Texas hamburgers, at the same bargain price of

$1.30 each. There are photos of a young Babe Ruth and Shoeless Joe Jackson on the walls. The Karampilas family began the Coney Island tradition in Scranton and eaters are lucky to have two restaurants to indulge their passion for these spicy, satisfying sandwiches. *515 Lackawanna Ave., Scranton, tel. 570/961–9004. Open Mon.–Sat. 10–7, Sun. noon–7. No credit cards.* $

The Original Coney Island. Look for the yellow-and-white checkerboard exterior near the downtown railroad bridge. You are stepping back in time at this establishment, opened in 1923. The Texas wieners are split, grilled, and topped with your choice of mustard, onions, and chili sauce. The hamburgers and wieners are served in a soft, all-purpose bun that's several cuts above the usual cottonlike bun. Both sandwiches are very good, but children might want them without the spicy chili. Other than french fries, drinks, chips, and gum, there's nothing else sold. Most of the locale is below street level. It has a 10-stool counter and six vintage wooden booths, with mirrors and glass globe lights. *100 Cedar Ave., Scranton, tel. 570/961-8288. Open Mon.–Sat. 10–8. No credit cards.* $

Entertainments

Lackawanna Coal Mine. Wear jackets to this fascinating attraction, as you will descend 300 ft via a mine cable car into the damp darkness of a huge anthracite mine. (There are jackets available if you forget yours.) This mine was first opened in 1860 and its underground world of child laborers, physical dangers, and miners who worked for 18¢ an hour—breathing coal dust for 12 hours, six days a week—is a scary and awesome spectacle. The guides are excellent, as they are all former miners. The last tour leaves at 4:30 and the adjoining anthracite museum closes at 5. There is a gift shop with many small coal-related items and mood rings that are attractive to children. The restored mine, which closed in 1966, is in a park containing a swimming pool and children's fishing ponds. It is reached from I-81, Exit 51 west to Davis Street, continuing on North Keyser Avenue for 5 mi. *N. Keyser Ave., McDade Park, Scranton, tel. 570/963–6463 or 800/238–7245. Admission: $6 adults, $4 ages 3–12. Open Apr.–Nov. daily 10–4:30.*

Steamtown National Historic Site and Trolley Museum. You'll learn all about steam railroading from films, displays, and artifacts and by exploring a huge 1902 working roundhouse and repair yard at the Scranton yard of the Delaware, Lackawanna & Western railroad. You can climb on several rail cars and watch "Steel and Steam," an excellent 18-minute film created for the National Park Service, which runs this visitors center and museum complex. You can see how difficult railroad work is by viewing the repair troughs where mechanics work. An excursion train, powered by a steam locomotive, takes passengers to Moscow, Pennsylvania, and back, a scenic tour through northeast Pennsylvania. A trolley museum adjoins Steamtown and shows the city's past, when it was known as "Electric City," for its many electric-powered trolleys. Trolley rides are offered on the former Laurel Line to the Lackawanna Visitors Center at Montage Mountain. There is an extra fee for the train and trolley excursions. *150 S. Washington Ave., entrance at Bridge St., at Lackawanna Ave., Scranton, tel. 570/340–5200. Admission: $7 adults, $6 senior citizens, $2 ages 5–15. Open daily 9–5.*

Johnstown: Point Stadium

The Johnstown Johnnies of the independent Frontier League play at this 1926 ballpark, but we plan our visit in mid-August for the championship of the All-American Amateur Baseball Association (AAABA). Playing in the championship are college stars 20 and under from summer leagues across the eastern half of the country.

Point Stadium reminds you of Fenway Park. Forced to fit into the geography of a long-established city, the ballpark's most noticeable feature is its 70-ft netting in left field. A towering pop-up to left that scales this fence lands in a city street or the car dealership beyond. A foul ball over the stands on the first-base side lands in the river. Babe Ruth and Lou Gehrig played here in 1927, and Satchel Paige pitched here in 1945. The ballpark hosted one of the first night games when lights were installed in 1930. The Pittsburgh Crawfords and the Homestead Grays played Negro National League games here in the 1930s. Now a single-level ballpark, it once had an upper deck.

The founder of Johnstown identified this ground for recreation in 1800, as it is the scenic spot where the Little Conemaugh and Stonycreek rivers join to form the Conemaugh River. The Johnstown Flood of 1889 crashed into the hill just across the river from the site of the current stadium. The story of how the flood killed 2,209 people and wiped out the town in just minutes is told in the nearby Johnstown Flood Museum (304 Washington St., Johnstown, tel. 888/222–1889). Walk by City Hall at Market and Main to see the water-level markers from the famous floods of 1889, 1936, and 1977. The Johnstown Flood National Memorial is 10 mi northeast of Johnstown at the site of the infamous South Fork Dam (tel. 814/495–4643).

For a great view of the ballpark and the entire Conemaugh Valley, take the world's steepest vehicular incline or a 30-minute hike up the side of Yoder Hill (tel. 814/536–1816). There is an ice-cream shop and a restaurant at the top of the incline. For travel information, contact the Cambria County Visitor's Bureau (tel. 800/237–8590). *Point Stadium, 345 Main St., Johnstown, tel. 814/536–8326.*

BIG APPLE BASEBALL
TRENTON, NEW YORK, NEW HAVEN

12

Treats for baseball fans traveling in the New York City area include Trenton's waterfront stadium, the venerable Yankee Stadium, and the classic Greek-style Yale Field in New Haven.

Begin in Trenton, which had been without professional baseball for 44 years until this handsome park on the Delaware River opened in 1994 for Double A Eastern League ball. You can eat New Jersey diner food a few blocks from the ballpark, or in one of the Italian family establishments in the Chambersburg restaurant district, less than a mile from the park. The state capitol complex includes a free museum. Princeton University is 14 mi northeast, with its ivy-covered stone buildings. Two worthwhile amusement parks, Sesame Place and Six Flags Great Adventure, are each less than 20 mi from Trenton.

From Trenton, drive north on Interstate 95, crossing the Hudson River into the Bronx and onto the Major Deegan Expressway. Yankee Stadium is at Exit 6, about an hour from Trenton. For many fans, the New York Yankees epitomize baseball, as the most prestigious ball club with the most memorable players in the history of the sport.

Taking the subway to Yankee Stadium is the preferred route; go early to explore Monument Park in center field. The subway is your ticket to most of Manhattan's attractions, as well as the must-see Botanic Gardens in Brooklyn, which makes you forget you are in a city. The gardens are just two blocks from the site of the now-demolished but long-remembered Ebbets Field, home of the Brooklyn Dodgers. Be a tourist and go to the top of the Empire State Building, to the Statue of Liberty, and the petting zoo in Central Park. It's a long subway ride to Shea Stadium in Queens, but it's worth it to see the Panorama of New York, the world's largest architectural model, that is in the nearby Queens Museum of Art.

Taking the Cross-Bronx Expressway to Interstate 95 north, you'll reach New Haven in 65 mi. Here you'll find Double A Eastern League ball in the 1927 stadium where George Bush played baseball for Yale. It was elegantly renovated in 1994, but its huge hand-operated scoreboard remains, along with a modern one. Yale University has spawned a number of quirky, superlative eateries. In nearby East Haven, there is a captivating trolley museum. Forty miles east is an all-day excursion site at Mystic Seaport.

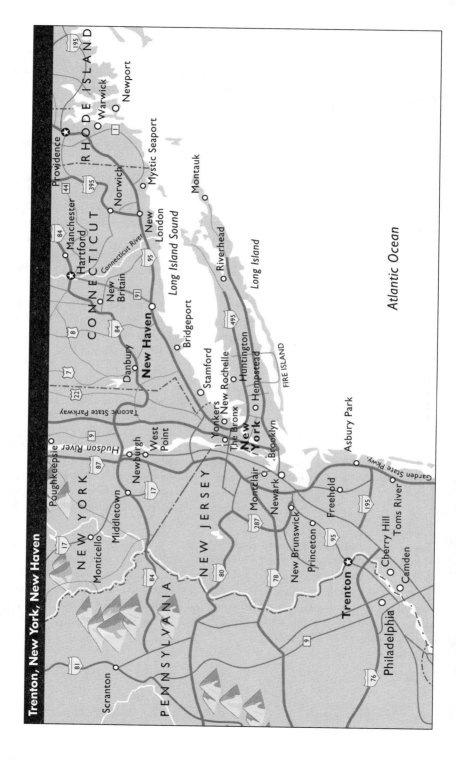

TRENTON THUNDER

League: Eastern League • **Major League Affiliation:** Boston Red Sox • **Class:** AA • **Stadium:** Mercer County Waterfront Stadium • **Opened:** 1994 • **Capacity:** 6,606 • **Dimensions:** LF: 330, CF: 407, RF: 330 • **Surface:** grass • **Season:** Apr.–Labor Day

STADIUM LOCATION: 1 Thunder Rd., Trenton, NJ 08611

WEB SITE: www.trentonthunder.com

GETTING THERE: From New Jersey Turnpike, Exit 7A to Rte. 195 W. Take Exit 2 at S. Broad St. This will merge with US 206. Continue on S. Broad St./US 206 for 2 mi. Left at Lalor St. to Rte. 29 and right at Delaware River.

PARKING: $1; on-street parking available.

TICKET INFORMATION: 1 Thunder Rd., Trenton, NJ 08611, tel. 609/394–3300, fax 609/394–9666.

PRICE RANGE: Pavilion seats $8; terrace $5 adults, $3 ages 5–14 and senior citizens, under 5 free; standing room $4 adults, $3 senior citizens and ages 5–14.

GAME TIME: Mon.–Sat. 7:05 PM (May–Labor Day), Sat. (Apr.) and Sun. 1:35 PM; gates open 90 min before game.

TIPS ON SEATING: View of the Delaware River over right-field wall from seats on third-base side; it is windy off the river, so jackets are often needed.

SEATING FOR PEOPLE WITH DISABILITIES: Along concourse level, above pavilion and terrace seats, and behind club seats.

STADIUM FOOD: Indulge in a great New Jersey pork-roll hero sandwich, with red sweet peppers, cheese, onions, and a fabulous chewy roll ($5). There are daily hero specials and big, crunchy Thunder (hot) Dogs for $3. French's bold and spicy mustard is the only kind in the park. A kid's meal of hot dog, chips, and baseball cards is $2.75. Healthier than the ice-cream cones or chocolate-covered ice-cream bars (both $3) are the Italian ices, hand-scooped in cups ($2). The hot french fries are better than ordinary, and a stand sells chicken nuggets. Giant chocolate chip cookies are $1.95. The glassed-in **Stadium Club Restaurant** offers a full buffet meal and a view from the top of the park.

SMOKING POLICY: Smoking prohibited throughout ballpark; permitted in designated area outside park down right-field line.

VISITING TEAM HOTEL: MacIntosh Inn (3270 Brunswick Pike, Lawrenceville, NJ 08648, tel. 609/896–3700, or 800/444—2775).

TOURISM INFORMATION: Trenton Convention & Visitors Bureau (Lafayette at Barrack St., Trenton, NJ 08608, tel. 609/777–1770).

Trenton, New Jersey: Mercer County Waterfront Stadium

In 1994, when Trenton opened its new Waterfront Stadium, New Jersey's capital city had not had a professional baseball team since 19-year-old Willie Mays hit .353 for the Trenton Giants in 1950. The Giants fell victim to television and the other amusement opportunities that made minor-league baseball's postwar boom short-lived.

The arched redbrick entranceway to the new Mercer County Waterfront Stadium is especially handsome. Unfortunately, the rest of the building is faced in concrete. The Delaware River flows along the right-field side of the stadium. Over the center-field walls you'll see the Champale factory, a reminder of Trenton's manufacturing days. Our favorite Trenton monument is the huge lettered sign on a bridge as you enter the city: TRENTON MAKES—THE WORLD TAKES.

Although the concourse is covered, the seating area is not. The scoreboard is colorful in green and navy, and the seats are dark green, but, surprisingly, most of the rest of the interior lacks the elegance of the stadium entrance. If you hike up the steep steps to the main concourse, high above the stands, you can visit the concession stands and still see the action. The concessions, the bathrooms, and the souvenir stand, like everything else here, are clean, efficient, and functional.

Home runs over the right-field fence go into the river. You can walk down the concourse on the first-base side and watch the boaters on the Delaware River. Be sure to look for Boomer, the 6-ft, 4-inch blue Thunderbird mascot.

Where to Stay

Visiting Team Motel: MacIntosh Inn. On busy Route 1, 10 minutes north of the ballpark, is this four-story economy motel. Double rooms are standard size. There is a free Continental breakfast. *3270 Brunswick Pike, Lawrenceville 06848, tel. 609/896–3700, or 800/444–2775, fax 609/896–2544. 116 rooms. Facilities: exercise room. AE, D, DC, MC, V. $$*

Nassau Inn. Campus visitors favor this nicely furnished five-story inn two blocks from Princeton University's Nassau Hall. *10 Palmer Sq., Princeton 08540, tel. 609/921–7500 or 800/862–7728, fax 609/921–9385. 215 rooms. Facilities: 3 restaurants. AE, DC, MC, V. $$$*

Palmer Inn–Best Western. This busy two-story motel is set back from the highway. The rooms are comfortable, its lobby small, and guests are given a free, limited-menu breakfast. The hotel is 15 minutes from the park and 3 mi from Princeton University. Children stay free. *3499 Rte. 1 S, Princeton 08540, tel. 609/452–2500 or 800/688–0500, fax 609/452–1371. 105 rooms. Facilities: restaurant, pool, sauna, exercise room. AE, D, DC, MC, V. $$*

Where to Eat

Ballpark Deli. Chewy hoagies are the ticket at this small corner restaurant, one block from the

ballpark. The restaurant is filled with baseball memorabilia. It sells a variety of overstuffed sandwiches, as well as fruit juices and hot dogs. *Lamberton and Cass Sts., Trenton, tel. 609/695–9400. No credit cards. No dinner except game nights. $*

Maneta's Diner. This well-worn diner dispenses comfort food of creamed chipped beef, crab cakes, beef goulash, and, to drink, brown cows. It offers an unusual kids' menu, with shrimp, veal cutlet, and roast sirloin. There are 22 flavors of ice cream and several fountain desserts. The diner is 3 mi from the ballpark. *2654 S. Broad St. (Rte. 206), Trenton, tel. 609/888–0208. AE, MC, V. $*

Trionfetti's. Here you can eat a real tomato pie, which resembles pizza, but with the cheese layered underneath the tomato. There is pasta of many types, chicken dishes, mussels, and, for children, buffalo wings and spaghetti. Less than a mile from the ballpark, it's in the Chambersburg restaurant district. *598 Chestnut St., Trenton, tel. 609/777–9400. No credit cards. $*

Entertainments

Sesame Place. Bert, Ernie, and the gang roam this water-theme park run by Anheuser-Busch. Guests walk the grounds in their bathing suits, as street wear is not permitted on most attractions. You can leave purses and clothes in pay lockers as you enter. There are imaginative sand playgrounds, a lazy-river raft ride, stage revues, and special computers that kids play with tokens. A new roller coaster, Vapor Trail, is for older children. Very crowded on hot weekends, the park is much nicer during the week. The theme park is 9 mi from the Trenton ballpark. *U.S. 1, Langhorne, PA, tel. 215/752–7070. Admission: $29.95, $26.95 senior citizens, children under 2 free; after 4 PM $19.95; parking $6. Open mid-May–May 24, 10–5; May 25–June 21, weekdays 10–5, weekends 10–7; June 22–Aug. 25, daily 9–8; Aug. 26–Sept. 1, daily 10–7; Sept. 2–Oct. 12, weekends 10–5.*

Six Flags Great Adventure. This is an all-day destination, beginning with the drive-through animal safari on the edge of the New Jersey Pine Barrens, where some 1,500 animals live. The grounds also include a large theme amusement park with a boardwalk, Movietown, and

100 rides, as well as a water park and a young children's park. The $4 AAA ticket discount is tripled on Wednesday. *Rte. 537, Jackson, NJ, tel. 908/928–1821. Admission to both parks: $45.75 adults, $22.90 those under 48″, $26.60 senior citizens, children 3 and under free; $15.90 safari only; parking $6. Open mid-May–Labor Day, daily 10–10; Sept.–May, Sat. 10–10, Sun. 10–8.*

Sights to See

New Jersey State House. First constructed as a modest building in 1790, the State House was rebuilt in 1885 after a fire destroyed the front wing. The result is a French Academic Classical Revival–style building faced with a double portico supported by Corinthian columns. A 1991 restoration refreshed the building. Take a tour to get the full feeling of the place. *W. State St., Trenton, tel. 609/633–2709. Open weekdays 7–6; free tours by reservation (tel. 609/292–4661). Tues.–Wed. and Fri. 9–4.*

New Jersey State Museum. Adjacent to the State House you'll find four stories of interesting exhibit space and a 150-seat planetarium. The museum preserves the cultural, historic, artistic, and scientific resources of the state. There is a huge dinosaur model to examine. The planetarium's regular and laser shows are limited to those age six and older. *205 W. State St., Trenton, NJ, tel. 609/292–6308. Open Tues.–Sat. 9–4:45; Sun. noon–5. Closed state holidays.*

Trenton City Museum. A mansion named Ellarslie in the city's Cadwalader Park holds lively interactive exhibits. The Italianate villa was built in 1848 for summer use; the city bought it in 1888. Landscape designer Frederick Law Olmstead, the designer of New York's Central Park, was hired by the city to design the 100-acre Cadwalader Park around the building. *W. State St. and Parkside Ave., Trenton, NJ, tel. 609/989–3632. Admission: donations. Open Tues.–Sat. 11–3, Sun. 2–4.*

Washington Crossing State Park. At this park, you can see where George Washington crossed the Delaware River before the Battle of Trenton. Historic markers show where the Continental Army marched on Christmas Day, 1776. Its visitor center (open Wed.–Sun. 9–4:30) has descriptive exhibits. *355 Pennington Rd., Titusville, NJ, tel. 609/737–0623. Parking $3 weekends. Open Memorial Day–Labor Day, daily 8–8; Labor Day–Memorial Day, daily 8–sundown.*

Princeton University. The fourth college established in North America, it was chartered in 1746 as the College of New Jersey. Ten years later, the college moved from its original site in Elizabeth to Princeton; Nassau Hall, then one of the largest buildings in the colonies, was built to house the school and served as home of the Continental Congress in 1783. The main campus of the university is one of the nation's most beautiful, with a broad range of architectural styles anchored by predominantly Gothic dormitories. The Orange Key Guide Service provides one-hour campus tours year-round (Mon.–Sat. 10, 11, 1:30, and 3:30; Sun. 1:30 and 3:30). *Maclean House, 73 Nassau St., Princeton, NJ, tel. 609/258–3603.*

NEW YORK YANKEES

League: American League • **Class:** Major League • **Stadium:** Yankee Stadium • **Opened:** 1923 • **Capacity:** 57,545 • **Dimensions:** LF: 318, CF: 408, RF: 314 • **Surface:** grass • **Season:** Apr.–Sept.

STADIUM LOCATION: 161st St. and River Ave., Bronx, NY 10451.

WEBSITE: www.yankees.com

GETTING THERE: Take Subway 4, C, or D to 161st St. station. For additional transit information, call 718/330–1234. By car from Manhattan, take FDR Dr. north to Harlem River Dr. N. Continue to W. 155th St. Go east over Macombs Dam Bridge to Jerome Ave. From north, take I-87 south across Tappan Zee Bridge. Stadium is at Exit 6 from I-87. You can take a New York Waterway ferry to the stadium from Pier 17 at South Street Seaport (6:10 PM), or from East 34th St. at 6:30 PM, or East 90th St. at 6:50 PM. For information, call 800/533–3779.

PARKING: Come by subway. If you must drive, arrive early. Stadium lots within walking distance charge $8–$15.

TICKET INFORMATION: 161st St. and River Ave., Bronx, NY 10451, tel. 718/293–6000, fax 718/293–4331.

PRICE RANGE: Club seats, field, and loge $35 (season only); main and loge box seats $29; tier box $18.50; main reserved $16; tier reserved $13.50; bleachers (day of game only) $8; senior citizens (day of game) $4.

GAME TIME: 7:35 PM; weekday day games, 1:05 PM; weekend day games, 1:35 PM; gates open 90 min before weekday games, 2 hrs before weekend and holiday games.

TIPS ON SEATING: Except on Opening Day and Old Timers Day, plenty of seats available. Bleachers available on day-of-game basis, but pretty rowdy and not recommended for families. Main box seats just behind walking concourse and field box seats are excellent and reasonably priced. Main reserved seats just behind main box seats. You can often get much closer to home plate by buying main reserved rather than main box seats.

SEATING FOR PEOPLE WITH DISABILITIES: Five sections specifically designated: Sections 2, 7, 8, 10, Loge Section 8. Elevators at Sections 15, 22.

STADIUM FOOD: This park has basic ballpark fare, but at a higher quality and price than most. For all items except pasta and bakery sweets, it's wise to head first for the **Sidewalk Cafe,** on the field level at Section 15. It serves the park's notable sweet sausages with a great chewy roll. There are also good chicken fingers (real white meat, not pressed composite), crunchy french fries, and a real steak sandwich; it's the only place to get a kid's meal, which includes juice, Cracker Jack, and a hot dog for $4.50. Three dozen picnic tables under umbrellas fill its pleasant patio. A **Sbarro Express** sells baked ziti for $7 and personal pizzas for $6.50. There's also **TCBY** yogurt and a bakery with good cakes and so-so cookies and brownies.

SMOKING POLICY: Smoking prohibited throughout stadium except in limited designated smoking areas. Prohibition appears widely ignored outside seating bowl. There are two alcohol-free family sections.

VISITING TEAM HOTEL: No designated hotel for visiting team.

TOURISM INFORMATION: New York Convention and Visitors Bureau (2 Columbus Circle, New York, NY 10019, tel. 212/397–8222).

New York City: Yankee Stadium

In 1913 the New York Giants invited the New York Yankees to share the Polo Grounds in upper Manhattan. The Giants handily outdrew the upstart Yankees until the Yankees acquired Babe Ruth for the 1920 season. Ruth hit 54 and 59 home runs in 1920 and 1921, respectively. Fans started to flock to Yankees games, and Giants owner John McGraw served an eviction notice on the Yankees.

"The House That Ruth Built"—Yankee Stadium—became the most famous baseball park ever built. Babe Ruth reinvented baseball here as a power game. In the Bronx, across the

Harlem River from the Polo Grounds, Yankees owners Ruppert and Huston found a 10-acre plot that was served by the Lexington Avenue subway. More than 30 World Series—not games, series—have been played here, with the Yankees winning 25 world championships.

In the 1923 opening game, John Philip Sousa and the Seventh Regiment Band played, and Babe Ruth hit the game-winning home run. Ruth hit his 60th home run of the season here in 1927. Roger Maris broke Ruth's record with blast number 61 here in 1961. Baseball fans remember Yogi Berra jumping into Don Larsen's arms after Larsen pitched a perfect game in the 1956 World Series, and Reggie Jackson hitting home runs on three straight pitches to win the final game of the 1977 World

Series. This is where Babe Ruth and Lou Gehrig stood at home plate to say their good-byes. Joe DiMaggio, Yogi Berra, and Mickey Mantle each won three Most Valuable Player awards while playing here.

When you get off the subway, don't rush right into the stadium. The area is well lighted and well policed. Take in the sounds and sights and smells of the pre-game stadium neighborhood. Walk along River Avenue and peek into a few of the souvenir shops outside the stadium. Follow the majestic, coliseumlike concrete exterior walls to the Gate 4 entrance to see a humongous Louisville Slugger baseball bat. Softball, basketball, and handball games are played at fields and courts all around the stadium.

The place to start inside Yankee Stadium is Monument Park. In this well-landscaped area, the legends of the game are honored. When first built, the area in center field, 490 ft from home plate, became known as Death Valley, as many mighty blasts became long fly-outs. In 1932, a stone monument honoring Miller Huggins, manager of the 1927 Yankees, arguably the greatest baseball team in history, was erected in Death Valley. Gehrig and Ruth monuments were added in 1941 and 1949, respectively. These monuments were actually in fair territory at the time. Yankees manager Casey Stengel, frustrated with a center fielder who was having a hard time picking up a ball among the monuments, once yelled: "Ruth, Gehrig, Huggins, someone throw that darned ball in here NOW!" When Yankee Stadium was rebuilt in 1974–75, the monuments and the memorials were moved behind the center-field fence. A monument to Mickey Mantle was added in 1996; one for Joe DiMaggio in 1999. To get a jump on the crowd and avoid a long wait in line, enter the stadium at Gate 2 and head for the staircase at the end of the aisles between the field- and main-level seats in Section 36. Monument Park closes 45 minutes prior to the start of the game.

On the inside, Yankee Stadium is every bit as formal and elegant as it seems from the outside: the sea of dark blue seats, the monuments, the classic white facade above the scoreboards beyond the outfield wall, the huge white Yankees insignia

in the larger-than-normal area between home plate and the screen. This is impressive. The original triple-decked Yankee Stadium was built in 1923 at a cost of $2 million. The most striking feature was a copper Art Deco frieze facade that encircled the roof. Since the 1974–75 reconstruction of the stadium, this elegant feature remains on top of the outfield bleachers only. Death Valley was eliminated as left and center fields were brought in considerably.

Two gift shops are on the field level beyond left and right fields (Sections 21 and 24). Get a replica baseball card of yourself in the pinstripes from the booth on the main level, Section 4.

You may have decided you prefer the small, family-oriented ballparks of the minor leagues to the large stadiums of the major leagues. You may have decided New York is not for you. But make plans to go to Yankee Stadium. There is more baseball history per square foot here than you will see in a lifetime anywhere else. One day, it may be too late. The Bronx Bombers should stay in Yankee Stadium in the Bronx, but they may not. The lease on Yankee Stadium expires in 2002, and if you wait, you might be watching the Yankees playing in the New Jersey Meadowlands or on the West Side of Manhattan.

More New York Baseball

Ebbets Field. When Ebbets Field was built in 1913 by Dodgers owner Charles Ebbets, the stands were squeezed close to the field, creating an extraordinary intimacy between fans and players. It was here on opening day 1947 that the great Jackie Robinson began to break through baseball's greatest injustice, becoming the first African-American to play in the major leagues. And here was one of baseball's greatest signs—haberdasher Abe Stark's 3-by-30-ft HIT SIGN WIN SUIT ad on the right-field wall under the scoreboard. The pain and pleasure shared in rooting for the Dodgers brought Brooklyn's many ethnic groups together in a single community that would never have been possible without the ties of baseball. In 1958 the Dodgers moved to Los Angeles. Ebbets Field was demolished in 1960, ending one of baseball's most extraordinary eras.

From the Brooklyn Museum at the corner of Eastern Parkway and Washington Avenue, walk down Washington one block to the entrance of the Brooklyn Botanic Garden and three more blocks along the garden. Take a left on Montgomery Street and go two blocks. The huge 20-story-plus apartment complex, once called Jackie Robinson Apartments and now called Ebbets Field Apartments, stands where Ebbets Field once was. Ironically, there is a large sign on the McKeever Place entrance: PLEASE NO BALL PLAYING. Across McKeever is an urban playground devoted mostly to basketball and a large mural of Jackie Robinson's life on the wall of the middle school named in his honor. A 1962 cornerstone on the apartments at 1720 Bedford Avenue states simply: "This is the former site of Ebbets Field."

Polo Grounds. Perhaps the most famous offensive and defensive plays in baseball history took place in the Polo Grounds, across the Harlem River from Yankee Stadium. History does not record that anyone played polo here, but the land, a gift of the King of England, had been a 17th-century farm. In 1890, James J. Coogan built a ballpark here in a rectangular area between Coogan's Bluff and an adjacent ball field known as Manhattan Field. When the New York Giants moved here in 1891, it was named Polo Grounds after the Giants' field on 110th Street where baseball had been played since 1880 on an actual polo grounds. A horseshoe-shape steel and concrete stadium was built after a 1911 fire destroyed the ballpark.

The "Shot Heard Round the World" was fired at 4:11 PM on October 3, 1951. The Giants had surged in the last six weeks of the season to tie the Dodgers atop the National League. In the bottom of the ninth of the playoff game, with the Giants trailing 4–2 and two men on base, Bobby Thomson hit a game-winning three-run home run. Just three years later, on September 29, 1954, Willie Mays made a sensational over-the-shoulder catch of Vic Wertz's 450-ft blast, spun, and threw a strike to second base to help the Giants beat the Cleveland Indians in the World Series. After the 1957 season, the Giants moved to San Francisco. The New York Mets played here in 1962 and 1963 while they waited

for Shea Stadium to be completed. In 1964, the old stadium was leveled.

The Polo Ground Towers, four huge 30-story apartment buildings, now sit where Willie Mays once roamed. There is a bronze plaque on the building at 2999 8th Avenue (Frederick Douglass Boulevard) indicating the approximate location of home plate and noting that the New York Giants had been world champions six times when they played here from 1891 to 1957. The site is near the West 155th Street Station served by the "D" Line. It is across the river from Yankee Stadium via the Macombs Dam Bridge.

Shea Stadium. Shea Stadium is no Ebbets Field or Polo Grounds. William A. Shea was the man former mayor Robert Wagner put in charge of bringing National League baseball back to New York City after the stinging departure of New York's two National League teams, the Giants and the Dodgers. The stadium named after Shea opened in 1964 right next door to the New York World's Fair in Queens. Best known for the 1969 World Series victory of the "Miracle Mets," Shea Stadium hosted the New York Yankees in 1974 and '75 while Yankee Stadium was being rebuilt. To reach Shea Stadium by subway, take the No. 7 Flushing line to the Willets Point–Shea Stadium station. By car, take the Grand Central Parkway and exit at Shea Stadium.

Yogi Berra Museum. A $2 million museum devoted to this Yankee Hall of Fame catcher adjoins Yogi Berra Stadium on the campus of Montclair State University in Montclair, New Jersey. Yogi's mitt from Don Larsen's perfect game, his most valuable player rings, uniforms, and other memorabilia are on display. *8 Quarry Rd., Montclair, NJ, tel. 973/655–2377. Admission: $4 adults and senior citizens, $2 children and students. Open Wed.–Sun. noon–5.*

Where to Stay

Several services, including the Hotel Reservations Network (tel. 800/964–6835), offer discounted rates. Weekend rates at most hotels are dramatically less than those on weekdays.

Excelsior Hotel. This quiet hotel, located behind the Museum of Natural History, offers bargain rates and large rooms. The two-room suites include kitchenettes. The standard double room has a living room with a pullout couch. All have dated Scandinavian-style furniture. *45 W. 81st St., New York 10024, tel. 212/362–9200 or 800/368–4575, fax 212/721–2994. 160 rooms, 103 suites. Facilities: coffee shop. AE, D, MC, V. $$*

Clarion Hotel Fifth Avenue. This convenient high-rise hotel is around the corner from the New York Public Library and Lord & Taylor. It draws guests with location and a $160 price on weekends. Rooms are small but serviceable. Coffee and muffins are served to guests in the small lobby on weekend mornings. Most views are of the backside of neighboring buildings. Parking is $25 daily at a garage two blocks away. Guests can swim and exercise at the nearby Vertical Club (335 Madison Ave.) for $15 daily. *3 E. 40th St., between 5th and Madison Aves., New York 10016, tel. 212/447–1500 or 800/ 668–4200, fax 212/685–5214. 189 rooms. Facilities: restaurant. AE, D, DC, MC, V. $$$*

Gramercy Park Hotel. This 75-year-old hotel gives guests keys to Gramercy Park, which it overlooks, during their stay. Some rooms have kitchenettes, and single rooms have either double beds or a queen-size bed. The 18-story hotel is utilitarian, clean, and affordable. A nearby garage charges guests $21 daily. *2 Lexington Ave., between Gramercy Park N and 22nd St., New York 10010, tel. 212/475–4320 or 800/ 221–4083, fax 212/505–0535. 500 rooms. Facilities: restaurant, beauty salon. AE, D, DC, MC, V. $$$*

Travel Inn. This tourist motel is in the rapidly improving West 42nd Street area and offers the bonus of free indoor parking. The seven-story motel looks as if it belongs at a freeway exchange, with balconies and pool deck chairs, but it works for families traveling to Manhattan. The rooms are large and utilitarian. *515 W. 42nd St., between 10th and 11th Aves., New York 10036, tel. 212/695–7171 or 800/869–4630, fax 212/967–5025. 160 rooms. Facilities: restaurant, outdoor pool, health club. AE, D, DC, MC, V. $$*

Wyndham Hotel. This lovely small hotel is well priced for New York and has a great location. News of its value has spread, and advance reservations are a must. The garage next door

charges $37 daily, but there is one at 58th Street between Broadway and 8th Avenue at $22 daily. The hotel is not part of the Wyndham chain. The $160 double rate does not drop on weekends. *42 W. 58th St., between 5th and 6th Aves., New York 10019, tel. 212/753–3500 or 800/ 257–1111, fax 212/754–5638. 150 rooms, 54 suites. Facilities: restaurant (winter only). AE, D, DC, MC, V. $$$*

Where to Eat

Jimmy's Bronx Cafe. This large, casual seafood and Caribbean restaurant is favored by Latino baseball players and baseball fans before and after the games. Its owner knows many ballplayers, and their photos line the walls. The restaurant holds a 250-seat main dining room, a 400-seat patio, a downstairs party room, and a sports bar. There is a children's menu. Paella and flan are the standouts here. *281 W. Fordham Rd., off the Major Deegan Expressway, Bronx, tel. 718/ 329–2000. AE, D, DC, MC, V. $$*

All-Star Cafe. There is so much visual excitement at this sports-theme restaurant that you'll find it hard to concentrate on eating. The celebrity owners have identified their menu favorites, like Andre Agassi's spaghetti pomodoro and Ken Griffey, Jr.'s chicken-fried steak and mashed potatoes. Other investors are Shaquille O'Neal, Wayne Gretzky, and Joe Montana. Four satellite dishes on the roof of this Times Square building feed into 17 big screens arranged in a circle, displaying all manner of sports events and celebrity interviews. The seats are oversize baseball gloves, with the tables resembling baseballs. Memorabilia from famous players are in glass cases throughout the two-story restaurant. You may be called upon to participate in a free-throw contest on the restaurant's basketball court. A big-league scoreboard hangs from the rafters. *1540 Broadway, New York, tel. 212/840–8326. D, MC, V.$$*

Mickey Mantle's Restaurant and Sports Bar. This is not a boozy, smoky sports bar but a light, cheerful restaurant down Central Park South from the Plaza Hotel. There's a room for kids' birthday parties, and $7–$8 children's meals are offered from a Little League menu. The adult portions are generous, with pasta, seafood, and even several low-calorie items. The $13 chicken potpie is exceptional. Mickey Mantle signed two photos over our table: "This is the 1927 Yankees the greatest team of all time. Except for the 1961 Yankees" and beneath it "The 1961 Yankees—The greatest team of all time." The restaurant is full of prints, photos, and other memorabilia of the players and great stadiums, much of it for sale. Some classic uniforms— including Satchel Paige's 1951 St. Louis Browns and Joe DiMaggio's 1948 Yankees jerseys—are definitely not for sale. Souvenir hats, T-shirts, and postcards are sold at the front. *42 Central Park S, New York, tel. 212/688–7777. AE, D, DC, MC, V. $$*

Grand Central Oyster Bar. The huge, domed tile ceiling gives you the illusion of eating inside a very large tunnel. Sit at the counter and watch the toque-hatted chefs custom-prepare your oyster stew and pan roasts; more than 90 different seafood dishes are offered. This is a treat for children, who can be counted on to like the chowders at least. *Grand Central Terminal, lower level, 42nd St. and Lexington Ave., New York, tel. 212/490–6650. AE, D, DC, MC, V. Closed Sun. No breakfast and no lunch Sat. $$*

Gray's Papaya. Hot dogs washed down with papaya drinks may be New York City's most ubiquitous regional food. You can find papaya drink stands in storefronts and mobile trucks throughout the city. This combination is the ultimate, inexpensive fast food, but these hot dogs are several cuts above the usual ballpark fare, and papaya juice is refreshing and healthful. Gray's is open 24 hours daily. *402 Avenue of the Americas, New York, tel. 212/260–3532. No credit cards.$*

Stage Deli. Since 1937, this midtown deli has been turning out egg creams, smoked fish, baked apples, potato pancakes, and cheesecake. Yes, it's tourist heaven, but the corned beef sandwiches can't be beaten. They are so stuffed that a half is sufficient for most children. Here is where Joe DiMaggio sipped chicken soup before games, and other celebrities' photos line the wall. Sandwiches are named for New York notables; every table has good brown mustard and a bowl of huge pickles. *834 7th Ave., New York, tel. 212/245–7850. AE, D, MC, V. $$*

Tutta Pasta Ristorante. This inexpensive pasta restaurant, south of Washington Square Park, is part of a small chain of authentic Italian restaurants with charm and terrific pasta. There are grilled pizzas for $10 and 25 varieties of pasta from $8–$15. Half-orders are available for children. The wooden tables are pressed close to your neighbor's, making the atmosphere convivial and communal. There is another outlet in Little Italy (26 Carmine St., tel. 212/463–9653). *504 LaGuardia Pl., between Houston and Bleecker Sts., New York, tel. 212/420–0652. AE, DC, MC, V. $$*

Entertainments

American Museum of Natural History. At the world's largest museum of its type, you see one jaw-dropping dinosaur reconstruction after another. The five-story-tall Barosaurus in the entry of the main hall and the immense blue whale suspended overhead in the Hall of Ocean Life are hard to forget. Don't try to zip through this in an hour. Its Hall of Human Biology uses holograms and animation to teach anatomy and evolution. The new Hall of Planet Earth has an ecological theme. Admission for the shows in its Hayden Planetarium, including several for young children, and for the IMAX theater is extra; combination tickets are sold. *Central Park W and 79th St., New York, tel. 212/769–5100. Suggested admission: $9.50 adults, $7.50 senior citizens and students with ID, $6 children. Open Sun.–Thurs., 10–5:45, Fri.–Sat., 10–8:45.*

Brooklyn Botanic Garden. Who could have guessed that one of the most peaceful and relaxing afternoons of our entire tour of America would have come in New York City? The Brooklyn Botanic Garden is an urban jewel, just two blocks from the site of the former Ebbets Field. Founded in 1910 on a reclaimed waste dump, it is 52 acres of shaded beauty, with a sunny Japanese koi and turtle pond; a children's garden; a garden of the herbs, trees, and flowers mentioned in Shakespeare's works; a fragrance garden; and other specialized plots. There is a pleasant open-air restaurant on the grounds. In the basement of its Steinhardt Conservatory is a small children's museum devoted to the plants found in cities with interactive displays. In summer, the admission fees often include entry to the adjacent Brooklyn Museum (tel. 718/638–5000), which has an impressive mummy collection on the third floor. *1000 Washington Ave., Brooklyn, tel. 718/623–7200. Admission: $3 adults, $1.50 senior citizens, students, and ages 6–16; free on Tues. and Sat. 10 AM–noon. Open Apr.–Sept., Tues.–Fri. 8–6, weekends 10–6; Oct.–Mar., Tues.–Fri. 8–4:30, weekends 10–4:30.*

Central Park. The 840 acres of this urban forest, designed in 1858 by Frederick Law Olmstead, are filled with diversions. There are baseball diamonds, playgrounds, boat ponds, a lake, and the Lehman children's petting zoo (admission: 10¢; open daily 10–5). There's also the Wildlife Conservation Center (5th Ave. and 64th St., tel. 212/360–3456; admission: $3 adults, $1.50 senior citizens, 50¢ ages 3–12; open weekdays 10–5, weekends 10:30–5:30), a zoo with 450 animals, including red pandas and lions, spread out on 5½ acres. Near 5th Avenue and 76th Street are characters from *Alice in Wonderland* crafted in bronze to climb on. The park's hand-carved carousel (90¢ per ride) is at the 65th Street transverse. Strawberry Fields is a 2½-acre garden and green memorializing John Lennon of the Beatles, who lived across the street on Central Park West at 72nd Street. *5th Ave. to Central Park West, from 59th to 110th Sts., New York, tel. 212/427–4040.*

Empire State Building Observatory. Avoid the shills selling you tickets to travel movies as you wait in line for tickets to the observatory. The real show is just looking out over the city. You buy your tickets and take escalators and two high-speed elevators up to the 86th- and 102nd-floor observatories. Signs at the ticket booth tell you how many miles of visibility there are; on clear days, 25-mi views are possible. Take a map to pick out landmarks. Take jackets as well, as it's nearly always windy. The last tickets are sold at 11:25 PM. *5th Ave. at 34th St., New York, tel. 212/736–3100. Admission: $6 adults, $3 children under 12 and senior citizens. Open daily 9:30 AM–midnight.*

Manhattan Walking Trails. In 1995, Heritage Trails New York unveiled four walking trails connecting 50 historic sights in downtown Manhattan by a series of 2,376 colored dots on the

city's sidewalks. Information and a colorful, informative $5 brochure are available by calling or visiting the Heritage Trails Hub & Visitor Information Center. *26 Wall St., at Broad St., New York, tel. 212/767–0637. Open daily 9–5.*

Panorama at the Queens Museum of Art. Flushing Meadows–Corona Park in the New York City Borough of Queens was the site of the 1964–65 World's Fair. Robert Moses, the master builder of New York, had Lester Associates build the world's largest architectural model. The almost 10,000-square-ft $700,000 model of New York City now contains 895,000 individual structures at a scale of 1 inch to 100 ft. The Empire State Building is 15 inches tall, and Yankee Stadium is 2 inches tall.

By subway, take the No. 7 Flushing line to the Willets Point–Shea Stadium station. The museum is next to the Unisphere, the enormous steel globe from the World's Fair, about a 10-minute walk through the park from the station. By car, take the Grand Central Parkway, exit at Shea Stadium, and follow the signs to the museum. Parking is free. *Flushing Meadows–Corona Park, Queens, tel. 718/592–9700. Admission (suggested donation): $4 adults, $2 children and senior citizens. Open Wed.–Fri. 10–5, weekends noon–5.*

Staten Island Ferry. This is a free and shorter alternative to the three-hour Circle Line (tel. 212/563–3200) boat tour of Manhattan. You join the commuters for the half-hour ferry ride from Battery Park to Staten Island, but be warned that the park is littered and the ferry terminal isn't in great shape either. Nevertheless, the views of the Statue of Liberty and lower Manhattan are worth it. Try to visit after peak rush-hour times. The ferries leave every 20 minutes to half hour; call ahead for the exact schedule. *South Ferry, Battery Park at Whitehall St., New York, tel. 718/390–5253. Admission: free. Open all the time.*

Statue of Liberty National Monument & Ellis Island. If you feel up to it, climb the 151-ft statue's 300 steps for a great view. Younger children may not be happy devoting the time necessary to see Ellis Island immigration museum (tel. 212/363–8340), but older children are likely to be drawn into the gripping visual history depicted in its cavernous great hall, where 12 million immigrants were processed into America. Tickets can be bought in advance for the ferry, which makes a loop to both sites, at the Castle Clinton National Monument in Battery Park, starting at 8:30 AM daily. Ferries leave Manhattan every 30 minutes, and return trips leave the statue every 90 minutes. Because of large crowds, the first two sailings are permitted to climb to the top of the crown on weekends and holidays only. *Liberty Island, Ellis Island, upper New York Bay, New York, ferry tel. 212/269–5755. Monument and museum admissions: free. Ferry admission: $7 adults, $6 senior citizens, $3 ages 3–17. Open daily 9–3:30.*

NEW HAVEN RAVENS

League: Eastern League • **Major League Affiliation:** Seattle Mariners • **Class:** AA • **Stadium:** Yale Field • **Opened:** 1927 • **Capacity:** 6,200 • **Dimensions:** LF 340, CF: 405, RF: 315 • **Surface:** grass • **Season:** Apr.–Labor Day

STADIUM LOCATION: 252 Derby Ave., West Haven, CT 06516.

TEAM WEBSITE: www.ravens.com

GETTING THERE: From I–95, Exit 44 E or Exit 45 W to Rte. 10, follow Yale Bowl signs. From I–91, Exit 1 (downtown), follow Rte. 34 to ballpark. From Merritt and Wilbur Cross Pkwys., Exit 57 (Rte. 34 east) 4 mi to ballpark or Exit 59 (Whalley Ave.), and follow Yale Bowl signs. From downtown, north on Chapel St., left on Derby Ave. to ballpark.

PARKING: Available in Lot 2, at Marginal Dr. on Rte. 34, for $2. Other parking is available inside the Yale Bowl, on Yale Ave., for $1.

TICKET INFORMATION: 63 Grove St., New Haven, CT 06510, tel. 203/782–3140 or 800/728–3671, fax 203/782–3150.

PRICE RANGE: Luxury box seat $15; box seat $8; reserved seat $6; general admission $4 adults, $2 ages 5–12 and over 66, under 4 free.

GAME TIME: Mon.–Sat. 7:05 PM, Sun. 2:05 PM; gates open 1 hr before game.

TIPS ON SEATING: General admission seats in bleachers on third-base side are quite a bargain, especially for senior citizens and children. Best views outside stadium are from top rows of reserved seats in grandstand looking across to Yale Bowl football and track stadium.

SEATING FOR PEOPLE WITH DISABILITIES: Space on upper ring of reserved section accessed by ramp on right-field side of ballpark. Handicapped-accessible parking is available in Lot 1, adjacent to the ballpark, for $1.

STADIUM FOOD: The food stands, a bit dim and claustrophobic under the seats, offer good local food to sample. Hummel hot dogs (only $2), are made locally and are better than average. The New Haven Brewing Company developed a private label beer for the team, Black Bird Premium Ale, sold only at Yale Field. Prepackaged Italian ices are $1.50, and warm Otis Spelunker cookies are 50¢. Pizza is also available. A picnic area stretches down the right-field line and behind the right-field wall.

SMOKING POLICY: Smoking prohibited in seating area.

VISITING TEAM HOTEL: Days Inn Hotel (490 Saw Mill Rd., West Haven, CT 06516, tel. 203/933–0344 or 800/325–2525).

TOURISM INFORMATION: Greater New Haven Convention & Visitors Bureau (1 Long Wharf Dr., New Haven, CT 06511, tel. 203/777–8550 or 800/332–7829).

New Haven, Connecticut: Yale Field

You've seen the photograph—an aging Babe Ruth handing a manuscript of his autobiography for the university library to a lean, young captain of the Yale University baseball team. It happened here at Yale Field, and the young player became president of the United States. George Bush is not the only president to leave a mark at Yale Field. Former president and Yale law professor William Howard Taft had a special double seat installed directly behind home plate to accommodate his extraordinary size. The seat remained for 65 years.

A president of Yale, who later got a *really* impressive job as Commissioner of Baseball, A. Bartlett Giamatti, watched many college games here. He once wrote of the game he loved: "None of us can go to a ballgame without in some way being reminded of your best hopes, of your earlier times, some memory of your best memory. It's always nostalgic, even when it's most vital and present.... It's not paradise, but it's as close as you're going to get to it in America."

Yale defeated Wesleyan 39–13 on this spot in 1865. In 1927, a brand-new ballpark designed to resemble Yankee Stadium was constructed, complete with steel poles, concrete arches, and a covered grandstand. After World War II, steel from the war ships was used to build the monster 25-ft-high wall in center field, 405 ft from home plate.

Although the Yale team continued to play here, professional baseball left in 1932, not to return until a major stadium renovation for the 1994 season. Bart Giamatti would have loved this elegant restoration of his Yale Field. The $3.3 million renovation retained the character of the historic field while adding modern comforts, new bleachers, and party picnic areas down the foul lines. The huge hand-operated scoreboard in the outfield is still used alongside a modern, high-tech scoreboard.

As Giamatti warned, it's not quite paradise. To retain the character of the field, considerable compromises on comfort and efficiency had to be made. The bathrooms and concession stands are stuffed under the grandstand seating area without the space and openness of the concourses in modern stadiums. Although these compromises are noticeable, the wonderful restoration was full justification.

The classic 1920s stadium is not, however, used to justify a stodgy approach to the fans. The ownership of the New Haven Ravens puts on a great show full of on-field contests. Rally the Raven, who was hatched out of a 7-ft egg at a nearby shopping mall in February 1994, delights the fans at Yale Field. This place really explodes when the Ravens give the fans cause to stomp on the old-style metal floor.

Where to Stay

Visiting Team Motel: Days Inn Hotel. This seven-story motel has hot tubs in some rooms. Ask for the "Rock Bottom Rate," a program through Connecticut Days Inns. Guests who can book 29 days in advance are eligible for even lower "Super Saver" rates. *490 Saw Mill Rd., at Exit 42 from I–95, West Haven 06516, tel. 203/ 933–0344 or 800/325–2525, fax 203/937– 1678. 102 rooms. Facilities: restaurant, indoor pool. AE, D, DC, MC, V. $$*

Super 8. This is an ordinary interchange motel behind a Taco Bell restaurant. Cribs are free here. It's 8 mi from Mystic Seaport (see *below*). *173 Rte. 12, at Exit 86 from I–95, Groton 06340, tel. 203/448–2818 or 800/848–8888, fax 203/ 446–0162. 99 rooms. AE, D, MC, V. $*

The Whaler's Inn. Three old, renovated inns have been joined as one property in downtown Mystic, adjacent to the drawbridge. The rooms are homey, with reproduction antiques and decorative touches. Guests can walk to the seaport museum and through the town's quaint shops and marina area. *20 E. Main St., Mystic 06355, tel. 203/536–1506 or 800/243–2588, fax 203/ 572–1250. 41 rooms. Facilities: restaurant. AE, MC, V. $$*

Where to Eat

Louis Lunch. There's room for about 30 customers in this dark wooden cottage, which is believed to be the birthplace of the hamburger. Various traditions reign—the bathroom is marked Room 363, some waiters refuse tips, and the limited menu has weird misspellings. Don't ask for ketchup or mustard—Louis doesn't do these condiments. You can get cheese, onion, or tomato slices. The incomparable burgers, which come on white toast, are cooked in ancient vertical cast-iron broilers. You usually can get root beer and Boston cream pie. While you sit in the high-backed booths, you can examine the table carvings of long-ago Yale undergraduates. *261 Crown St., New Haven, tel. 203/562–5507. No credit cards. Closed Sun. $*

Bee Bee Dairy Restaurant. This cheery downtown restaurant is a local stop for breakfast, fast lunches, and ice cream. Its short-stack pancakes ($1.75) and half waffles are the right size for children. There is an extensive selection of ice cream, frozen yogurt, and sherbet, plus sinful hot fudge sundaes. *33 W. Main St., Mystic, tel. 203/536–4577. MC, V. $*

Frank Pepe's Pizzeria. Believed by many to be the original home of pizza in the United States, this is one of several superlative pizza shops on Wooster Street. The 150-seat shop is known for its wood-oven pizza covered with Rhode Island little-neck clams. You can watch the bakers work in the open kitchen. Also try its 50-seat annex restaurant, the Spot–Frank Pepe's (163 Wooster St., tel. 203/865–7602). *157 Wooster St., New Haven, tel. 203/865–5762. No credit cards. Closed Tues. $*

Sea Swirl. The great clams at this roadside drive-in are not cheap. An order is $5 for strips and $7 for the meatier bellies. There is also good corn chowder. You have your choice of broth or milk in the clam chowder, and, for dessert, there's hard or soft-serve ice cream. You can eat in your car or at the adjacent picnic tables. *Rtes. 1 and 27, Mystic, tel. 203/536–3452. MC, V. $*

Yankee Doodle Sandwich Shop. In this tiny restaurant your children can see what the original fast-food shops looked like. The counterman and waitress work in a fast blur to satisfy the crowds at the counter's 12 stools. You can have a satisfying scrambled egg breakfast for $1.30. Breakfast ends at 11:30. *260 Elm St., New Haven, tel. 203/865–1074. No credit cards. $*

Entertainments

Mystic Seaport Museum. Plan to spend a full day exploring the whaling ships and the restored 19th-century village in Mystic. You can climb through the tall ships, sign up for the crew via computer, and learn about geography and sea life through interactive displays. The exhibits are unusual—an oyster-sorting shop and a barrel factory have workers in costume who explain their jobs. The children's museum has many good hands-on activities. For additional fees you can ride on several of the ships. The grounds have several pleasant sit-down restaurants. Look for admission discount coupons in area stores. The museum admission ticket is good for two days. *Rte. 27, Mystic, tel. 860/572–0711. Admission: $16 adults, $8 ages 6–12, ages 5 and under, free. Grounds open daily 9–6, exhibits daily 9–5.*

Shore Line Trolley Museum. You can take unlimited rides in vintage trolleys at this special museum. There are more than 100 trolleys on the grounds, with dedicated volunteers eager to tell you their history. Children like switching the rattan seats to the opposite direction at the end of each short trip. The small gift shop has trolley-related toys. *17 River St., East Haven, tel. 203/467–6927. Admission: $5 adults, $4 senior citizens, $2 ages 11 and under. Open Memorial Day–Labor Day, daily 11–5; May, Sept., and Oct., weekends 11–5; Apr. and Nov., Sun. 11–5.*

Sights to See

Yale University. Hear the carillon in Harkness Tower and marvel at the Gothic look of this university, established in 1701. The Sterling Memorial Library (120 High St., tel. 203/432–1775) looks like a monastery. One-hour campus tours of the country's third-oldest university are available 10–4 from the Yale Information Office at Phelps Gateway, at the Green, the central square (among nine) in New Haven. The office also has maps for self-guided tours. Children may want to see the Brontosaurus skeleton in the Peabody Museum (170 Whitney Ave., tel. 203/436–0850; free weekdays 3–5; other times $3 adults, $1 ages 3–15; open Mon.–Sat. 10–5, Sun. noon–5). *Yale Information Office, 341 College St., New Haven, tel. 203/432–2302.*

THE URBAN RENEWAL LEAGUE
BRIDGEPORT, NEWARK, ATLANTIC CITY

13

New downtown baseball stadiums are turning aged Northeast cities into places where families actually can vacation. Welcome to the urban renewal league.

In the late 1990s, we heard a number of troubled East Coast cities had come up with the idea of joining together, forming an independent, professional baseball league, and building first-class minor-league ballparks as a part of their economic development plans. Independent baseball seemed precarious enough—where, we wondered, would these cash-strapped cities find the resources to build the stadiums? Looking to Lansing and Akron on the minor-league level and Baltimore and Cleveland on the major-league level, the cities were betting their economic futures on baseball.

Somehow, against the odds, it seems to be working. The ballparks are up, and they are packed with happy fans willing to spend. Best of all, the national stereotypes are wrong: these urban centers are on the rebound, and are now fun and safe places to visit.

Start first in the port city of Bridgeport, where the city's transportation industry is reflected all around the ballpark. Initially a whaling center, the city was overtaken by railroads. Watching a night game in its attractive new stadium, with the harbor activity in the distance, makes this a special New England baseball experience.

West 150 mi on I–95 lies Newark, with another new waterfront park that is true to Newark's industrial heritage. The city's nearby Ironbound district, bordered by rail lines, contains compact blocks of Portuguese restaurants and bakeries. Newark's unusual city museum contains a zoo and an art gallery and was remodeled by famed architect Michael Graves.

Heading south 2½ hours on the Garden State Parkway brings you to Atlantic City, whose wide beaches and boardwalk have been revived. The city's peach-and-turquoise new stadium evokes the ocean, and its entryway displays two of the most impressive baseball murals in the country.

BRIDGEPORT BLUEFISH

League: Atlantic League • **Affiliation:** Independent • **Class:** NA • **Stadium:** The Ballpark at Harbor Yard • **Opened:**1998 • **Capacity:** 5,300 • **Dimensions**: LF: 325, CF: 400, RF: 325 • **Surface:** grass • **Season:** late May–early Sept.

STADIUM LOCATION: 500 Main St., Bridgeport, CT 06604.

TEAM WEB SITE: www.bridgeportbluefish.com

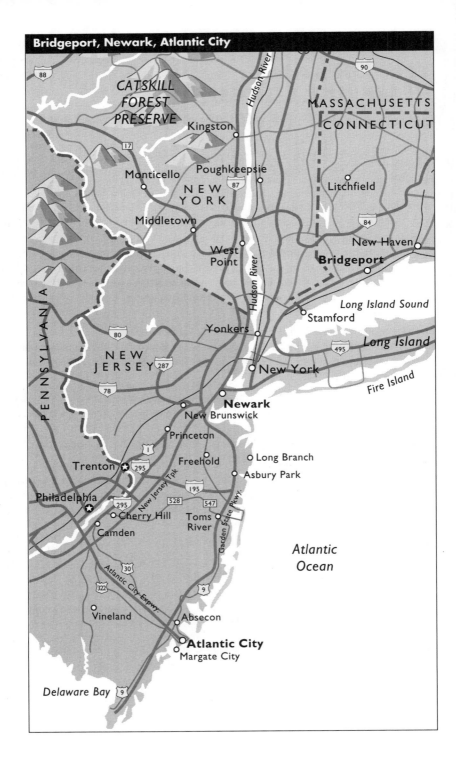

88

90

CATSKILL
FOREST
PRESERVE

MASSACHUSETTS

CONNECTICUT

Kingston

17

Monticello

Poughkeepsie

N E W
Y O R K

87

Litchfield

Middletown

New Haven

West
Point

Bridgeport

Hudson River

Long Island Sound

Stamford

Yonkers

80

495

Long Island

N E W
J E R S E Y

287

New York

Fire Island

78

Newark

New Brunswick

P E N N S Y L V A N I A

Princeton

1

Long Branch

Trenton

295

Freehold

Asbury Park

195

Philadelphia

New Jersey Tpk

295

528

547

Garden State Pkwy.

Cherry Hill

Toms
River

Camden

Atlantic City Expwy.

30

Atlantic
Ocean

322

9

Vineland

Absecon

Atlantic City

Margate City

Delaware Bay

9

GETTING THERE: The ballpark is downtown at Exit 27 off I–95. From Rte. 8 southbound, take Exit 1 and turn left on Prospect St. Turn right at Lafayette Blvd. and left on Frontage Rd., which runs into Main St. The Port Jefferson Ferry Port offers ferry service to Long Island. For New Haven rail schedules, call 800/638–7646. For bus services, call 800/346–3753.

PARKING: There is ample parking for $2.

TICKET INFORMATION: 500 Main St., Bridgeport, CT 06604, tel. 203/345–4800, fax 203/345–4830.

PRICE RANGE: Premium box seats $10; box seats $8; loge box seats $6; reserved seats $4 adults, $2 senior citizens and ages 12 and under.

GAME TIME: June–Sept., Mon.–Sat. 7:05 PM, Sun. 1:05 PM. In May, games are Mon.–Sat. at 6:35 PM.

TIPS ON SEATING: The $6 loge box seats are a good buy. The view past the ballpark from the first-base side is of cars on I–95 and downtown. The view from the third-base side is of a huge power plant and of trains passing. The sun sets on the third-base side.

SEATING FOR PEOPLE WITH DISABILITIES: There is special seating throughout the seating bowl. Go to Home Plate Plaza between gates B & C for entrance to the ballpark. Elevators are located at sections 11 & 12.

STADIUM FOOD: A local barbecue caterer, **High on the Hog,** sells good beef and pork sandwiches for $4.25. The ballpark grill also sells a decent sausage with peppers and Philly cheese steaks. Try the hand-scooped **Timothy's ice cream,** especially Harbor Yard's own flavor, pecan maple crunch. There are also very good hand-scooped Italian ices for $1.50.

SMOKING POLICY: Smoking is not permitted in any part of the ballpark.

VISITING TEAM HOTEL: Bridgeport Holiday Inn (1070 Main St., Bridgeport, 06604, tel. 203/334–1234 or 800/465–4329).

TOURISM INFORMATION: Coastal Fairfield County Convention & Visitors Bureau (297 West Ave., Norwalk, CT 06850, tel. 800/866–7925).

Bridgeport: The Ballpark at Harbor Yard

Boats, trains, trucks, automobiles, and a ferry—Bridgeport's ballpark has them all. The action beyond the outfield wall is nearly as interesting as the game on the field. Fifty miles north of New York City, cars and trucks speed high above and beyond the left-field wall on an elevated stretch of I–95. A grand ferryboat sits just past center field ready to take its passengers across Long Island Sound. And trains pass just beyond the outfield fence and in front of the huge United Illuminating Company plant that dominates the skyline past right field.

The ownership team was led by a husband and wife team, Mary-Jane Foster and Jack McGregor, committed to redeveloping the city's waterfront area. The city spent $15 million and built a late-1990s Single A–quality minor-league ballpark.

This once-successful industrial city is now fighting its way back from bankruptcy. The name Harbor Yard was selected to highlight Bridgeport's harbor and evoke images of Baltimore's famed Camden Yards. The eight-acre site lies near the scene of the most extraordinary event in Bridgeport history: on November 20, 1887, P. T. Barnum's winter circus quarters burst into flames. Lions, elephants, and zebras ran loose through the city.

Professional baseball got its start in Bridgeport just two years before, in 1885 at Barnum Park. James H. "Orator" O'Rourke, born in Bridgeport in 1852, played 19 years in the major leagues, and returned to manage a local professional team. O'Rourke was inducted into the National Baseball Hall of Fame in 1945.

Fans enter the ballpark from the parking lot down the third-base line and walk up stairs past a lively picnic area to a walking concourse that runs across the top of the seating bowl. Twenty skyboxes form a roof over the concourse, and concession stands stretch from first to third bases. The Kids Cove play area, featuring speed pitch and other games for kids, is out beyond the right-field foul pole.

B. B. the Bluefish mascot—part of the spring spawn of 1997 according to the local legend—was born off the coast of Cape Hatteras and swam toward Long Island Sound in time for the 1998 season. B. B. is said to love the Blues Brothers and pitcher Vida Blue.

Where to Stay

Bridgeport Holiday Inn. This bustling, nine-story downtown hotel has several rooms with good views of the city. The rooms are small, clean, and recently remodeled. *1070 Main St., Bridgeport 06604, tel. 203/334-1234 or 800/465-4329, fax 203/367-1985. 184 rooms. Facilities: restaurant, indoor and outdoor pools. AE, D, DC, MC, V. $$*

Where to Eat

White's Diner. This 1940s treasure serves some of the city's best breakfasts and lunches. The homemade muffins are delightful, especially the lemon poppy variety. Hearty breakfast specials include some unusual omelets. The diner is open daily until 3 pm. *280 Boston Ave., Bridgeport, tel. 203/366-7486. No credit cards. $*

American Steak House. This cafeteria-style restaurant with a large salad bar has inexpen-

sive steak lunches and dinners. Ribs, chicken, and baked and fried fish are also served, as well as a multitude of pies for dessert. There are smaller portions for children and senior citizens. *210 Boston Ave., Bridgeport, tel. 203/576-9989. MC, V. $*

Entertainments

The Barnum House. Circus lovers will appreciate the vast collection of showman P. T. Barnum's memorabilia. Old posters, photographs, and costumes illustrate the efforts and reach of the traveling circus throughout the 1900s. *820 Main St., Bridgeport, tel. 203/331-9881. Admission: $5 adults, $4 senior citizens and students, $3 ages 4-18. Open Tues-Sat. 10-4:30, Sun. noon-4:30.*

Beardsley Park Zoo. This small zoo has fewer than 200 animals, but contains a charming children's zoo within its 35 acres. An indoor rain forest features South American creatures. *Beardsley Park, 1875 Noble Ave., Bridgeport, tel. 203/394-6565. Admission: $5 adults, $3 senior citizens and ages 3-11. Open daily 9-4.*

The Discovery Museum. This perky science center uses art to illustrate scientific principles throughout its colorful displays. On weekends there are science shows and access to a planetarium. Space discovery is covered in the Challenger Learning Center. *4450 Park Ave., Bridgeport, tel. 203/372-3521. Admission: $6 adults, $4 senior citizens and ages 3-17. Open Mon.-Sat. 10-5, Sun. noon-5.*

NEWARK BEARS

League: Atlantic League • **Affiliation:** Independent • **Class:** NA • **Stadium:** Riverfront Park • **Opened:** 1999 • **Capacity:** 6,000 • **Dimensions:** LF: 329, CF: 394, RF: 323 • **Surface:** grass • **Season:** May–mid-Sept.

STADIUM LOCATION: 10 Bridge St., Newark, NJ 07102.

TEAM WEB SITE: www.newarkbears.com

GETTING THERE: The stadium is in downtown Newark at the junction of I-280 and Route 21, just north of the New Jersey Performing Arts Center. From I-280, take Exit 15 at Downtown Newark-Ironbound and turn right on Route 21 south (McCarter Highway). Go one block to Bridge Street. The stadium is on the right. From Newark Airport, take Route 78 east. Stay right and follow Routes 1 & 9 to Route 21 north into downtown. Stay left, turn right on Miller St., and then right on Broad Street. Take a right on Bridge Street. The stadium is on the left. The park is two blocks from New Jersey Transit's Broad Street Station. A $1 downtown shuttle bus from the Amtrak station stops at the Broad Street Station.

PARKING: There is plenty of parking nearby in private lots for $3 and $4.

TICKET INFORMATION: 10 Bridge St., Newark, NJ 07102, tel. 973/483–6900, fax 973/483–6975.

PRICE RANGE: Box seats $8; reserved seats $6. Senior citizens, military, and ages 4–12 get $1 discount on all seats.

GAME TIME: Weekdays 7:05 PM, Sat. 6:05 PM, Sun. 1:05 PM; gates open 1 hr before game.

TIPS ON SEATING: The reserved seats are aluminum benches with backs. They are an excellent buy, as there are only 10 rows in front of them. They're beyond the dugouts on both sides. The view from the first-base side is of cars on I–280 and trains going over the Passaic River on an imposing, high black bridge. From the third-base seats, you get a view of the Newark skyline. Planes flying into Newark Airport zoom beyond the outfield fence all through the game. The home team dugout is on the first-base side. The sun sets behind home plate.

SEATING FOR PEOPLE WITH DISABILITIES: Along the concourse at the top of the seating bowl.

STADIUM FOOD: The concessions are ordinary, with a small chicken sandwich for $4.50. The large Italian sausages ($4.25), with peppers, onion, and a good sesame bun, are the best bet, although there's only bright yellow mustard to go with them. Large Cracker Jack bags are $2.50. Newark is known for good pizza, but nothing good has shown up in the park yet.

SMOKING POLICY: Smoking prohibited in the stadium. Smoking allowed in designated areas outside gates C & E.

VISITING TEAM HOTEL: Hilton Gateway Hotel (Raymond Plaza West, Newark 07102, tel. 973/ 622–5000 or 800/445–8667).

TOURISM INFORMATION: Metro Newark Chamber of Commerce (1 Newark Center, 22nd Fl., Newark, NJ 07102, tel. 973/242–6237).

Newark: Riverfront Park

Baseball deserted Newark in 1950, and it's been pretty much downhill there ever since. Until recently. The city is on the rebound, and baseball is providing part of the bounce.

The Newark Bears are back after a 50-year absence. The original Bears, the Yankees' top farm club, were one of the all-time great minor-league teams. They won the Triple A International League pennant by an astonishing 25½ games in 1937. The Newark Eagles won the 1946 Negro League World Series. Both teams played in fabled Ruppert Stadium, named after the boss of the Yankees, Col. Jacob Ruppert. The Bears skipped town in 1949, and the Eagles left in 1950. Ruppert Stadium was demolished in 1967. You can go down by the Wilson Avenue exit of the Pulaski Skyway and you won't find a trace, not even a small memorial. Baseball was dead in Newark.

Enter native son Rick Cerone, the former Yankees catcher. Cerone was absolutely committed to bringing baseball back to his home town. And in 1999, with the support of the city and county governments, the House That Rick Built—he calls it "The Den"— went up and baseball was back.

A crucial part of the city's revitalization, Riverfront Park sits on the river in the industrial sector of Newark's downtown, just north of the New Jersey Performing Arts Center. The stadium itself cost $19 million to build and was finished in a remarkable seven months, in time for the start of the second season of the fledgling, independent Atlantic League. The Bears played their first season in 1998 in the new Bridgeport stadium.

The 6,000-seat stadium has the classic, fan-friendly late-1990s minor-league design, with a food and facilities concourse up above the seating bowl. Curiously, the concession area and skyboxes are bland gray and mud brown. But the atmosphere here is otherwise festive and fun, with a full complement of on-field contests, music between innings, and a large video scoreboard high above the right-field fence. Rip 'N Ruppert is a big friendly bear mascot named after the long-gone ballpark.

On a clear day, you can see the magnificent Manhattan skyline—the Empire State Building, the Twin Towers, and all—over the centerfield fence.

Where to Stay

Visiting Team Motel: Hilton Newark Gateway. Just steps from the imposing Newark Penn train station, this convenient hotel is a good base for exploring Newark. Travelers use it for New York City stays, as it's under $100 and just a 15-minute New Jersey Transit ride to the city. You can also take a #308 bus to Six Flags Great Adventure theme park and receive discounted admission. The hotel's rooms are long and narrow, with padded floral window treatments and small baths. There's a large rooftop outdoor pool with a good 10-story view. A free hot breakfast is included. On weekdays, an adjoining mall offers shopping and quick lunches. The train station also includes several restaurants, a bakery, bookstore, florist, etc. *Raymond Boulevard, Newark, 07102, tel. 973/622–5000 or 800/445–8667, fax 973/824–2188. 253 rooms. Facilities: 4 restaurants, outdoor pool, exercise room, airport shuttle, parking (fee). AE, D, DC, MC, V. $$*

Robert Treat Hotel. This 12-story downtown hotel is near the New Jersey Performing Arts Center and a half-mile from the ballpark. The 35-year-old building has been renovated; it has modern, good-sized rooms and a large business center. *50 Park Pl., Newark 07102, tel. 973/622–1000, fax 973/622–6410. 169 rooms. Facilities: restaurant, exercise room, parking (fee). AE, D, DC, MC, V. $$*

Where to Eat

Roque & Rebelo. Directly behind the Newark Penn train station is the Ironbound district, bordered by four railroad lines. It is filled with Portuguese restaurants, bakeries, jewelry stores, and streets adorned with decorative flags. This family tablecloth restaurant serves heaping portions of authentic Portuguese and Spanish dishes, like paella, codfish stew, and broiled sardines. Kids like the homemade potato chips. The flan and roast pork sandwich are exceptional. The dining room is narrow, with paneled walls and landscape prints. A bar is in a separate room. *90 Ferry St., at Congress St., Newark, tel. 973/589–6588. AE, MC, V. $*

Iberia Peninsula. This pleasant brick restaurant is popular with families looking for genuine Portuguese seafood. There is a brisk take-out business, with patrons hauling out large serving tins of family-size dishes. Choose a round wooden table at a distance from the active bar. Good broiled fish, a ten-meat barbecue, and pork dishes are on the menu. A free parking lot is across the street, and the city's $1 purple loop buses stop there, too. *67 Ferry St., at Prospect St, Newark, tel. 973/344–1657. AE, D, DC, MC, V. $$*

Sights to See

New Jersey Historical Society. An interactive children's center, KIDS, is part of this complex of Georgian town houses. Younger visitors also will like the Life in Early New Jersey exhibits. The remainder of the collections focus on furniture, decorative arts, and a research library. *230 Broadway, Newark, tel. 973/483–3939. Admission: $3, $2 senior citizens. Open Wed.–Fri. and 1st and 3rd Sat. each month 10–4.*

Newark Museum. A minizoo, an art and history museum, and an excellent gift shop await you in this handsome 1909 downtown complex, renovated by famed architect Michael Graves in 1989. Four buildings, including a brick Federal home, make up the museum, which includes a small planetarium, the Newark Fire Museum, and collections of coins, Oriental art, sculpture, and art of Africa, American Indians, and the Pacific rim. Children like getting close to the hissing cockroaches, turtles, tamarins, and snakes. *49 Washington St., Newark, tel. 973/596–6550. Admission: free (donations welcome). Open Wed.–Sun. noon–5.*

ATLANTIC CITY SURF

League: Atlantic League • **Affiliation:** Independent • **Class:** NA • **Stadium:** Sandcastle Ball Park • **Opened:** 1998 • **Capacity:** 5,836 • **Dimensions:** LF: 309, CF: 400, RF: 309 • **Surface:** grass • **Season:** May–mid-Sept.

STADIUM LOCATION: 545 N. Albany Ave., Atlantic City, NJ 08401.

TEAM WEB SITE: www.acsurf.com

GETTING THERE: The ballpark is just west of downtown. From the Atlantic City Expressway going east, take Exit 2 (Route 40/332/Black Horse Pike). Take Route 40/322 east for 1½ mi to the park. From the west, take Route 40 east to Hamilton Township (Mall) where it joins with Route 322. Follow Route 40/322 for 11 mi to the ballpark. Or, take Route 30 east to Route 9. Go south on Route 9 for 4 mi to Route 40/322. Take Route 40/322 east for 4 mi to the ballpark.

PARKING: Ample free parking at the stadium.

TICKET INFORMATION: 545 N. Albany Ave., Atlantic City, NJ 08401, tel. 609/344–8873, fax 609/344–7010.

PRICE RANGE: Club seats $12; premium box seats $9; lower box seats $8; upper box seats $7; reserved, $6 adults, $4 senior citizens, $3 children 3–12.

GAME TIME: Mon.–Sat. 7:05 PM, Sun. 2:05 or 4:05 PM; gates open 1 hr before game.

TIPS ON SEATING: The reserved seats here are a bargain, as they're real seats just past the dugouts. The view from the third-base side over the right-field fence is of the Atlantic City skyline. The Oriental Avenue reserved section, just past first base, is a no-alcohol family section. The home team dugout is on the third-base side. The sun sets behind home plate.

SEATING FOR PEOPLE WITH DISABILITIES: Throughout the stadium. There are steep stairways into the park, but there is an elevator to the main concourse at the stadium entrance.

STADIUM FOOD: Cheese steaks, funnel cakes, and BBQ sandwiches are good here. The large servings of chicken tenders and fries are a bargain at $4. There are push-up Italian ices, soft pretzels, and pan pizza. In the 7th inning, the team's owner sells freshly baked chocolate chip cookies, 2 for $1. By buying a fun pack, families can get 4 hot dogs, 4 sodas, 4 reserved seats, and 4 Surf T-shirts for $50, a $26 savings.

SMOKING POLICY: Smoking in the seating bowl is prohibited. There are designated smoking areas on the main concourse.

VISITING TEAM HOTEL: Comfort Inn North (539 Absecon Blvd., Rte 30, Absecon, NJ 08201, tel. 609/641–7272 or 800/228–5150).

TOURISM INFORMATION: The Greater Atlantic City Convention & Visitors Bureau (314 Pacific Ave., Atlantic City, NJ 08401, tel. 609/348–7100).

Atlantic City: Sandcastle Ball Park

This park, built for the inaugural 1998 season of the Atlantic League, makes its strongest architectural statement at the entrance. Fans enter the ballpark by walking up a large stairway, flanked on each side by twin towers of sandstone and salmon blocks. Also on both sides are marvelous large and colorful collages of baseball history, including an oversized glove and bat, along with paintings of Aaron, Cobb, DiMaggio, Feller, Lloyd, and Ruth.

Surprisingly, Atlantic City never had its own professional minor-league team. Professional baseball's history here is limited to a Negro League team, the Atlantic City Bacharachs. In 1999 *Out From the Shadows: Negro League Baseball in*

America, a bronze sculpture paying tribute to the black baseball experience, was dedicated just outside the stadium entrance.

Fans enter at the top of the stairway, onto the main concourse where concessions and souvenirs are sold, and then head back down into the seating bowl. Inside the ballpark, one is first struck by the sea of lively teal-colored seats all along the field level. This is Atlantic City and they are trying hard to make the connection to the nearby ocean. The ever-present mascot Splash is a large green, full-bellied sea serpent. Here, he's called a "surfent." The public address announcer just can't help but announce at the start of each Surf at bat: "Surf's Up!"

The ocean isn't the only game in town. Monopoly was invented here and taking a tour of The Sandcastle is like a trip around the game board. The seating sections have familiar names, such as Baltic Avenue and Marvin Gardens.

Fans can view the Atlantic City skyline and see the names of famous hotels and casinos in bright neon high above the right-field wall. Unfortunately, the obligatory three stories of ads on the outfield wall obscure the full impact of the skyline, especially from the field-level lower box seats.

You never can tell who you might see in these independent leagues. When we visited Atlantic City, we saw three-time American League All-Star Ruben Sierra drive in a key run and score another in an exciting one-run Surf win.

More Atlantic City Baseball

Pop Lloyd Stadium. The restoration of this fine park is an even better tribute to Negro League baseball than the wonderful sculpture at the entrance to the Sandcastle. John Henry "Pop" Lloyd was elected to the Hall of Fame in 1977 on the strength of his 26-year career in black baseball, from 1905–31, including a stint with the Atlantic City Bacharachs in the 1920s. The great shortstop was called "the black Honus Wagner." The brick ballpark with covered grandstand was used by the Negro leagues and has been nicely restored and landscaped. Now a softball field, Pop Lloyd Stadium is about a dozen blocks west of the convention center

near Route 30. It is on Huron Avenue between Indiana and Martin Luther King avenues.

Where to Stay

Visiting Team Motel: Comfort Inn North. This new roadside motel is close to the ballpark, on the marsh approach to Atlantic City. Ask for an upper room in this 7-story facility, as they have a view of the Atlantic City skyline. The rooms are clean and freshly painted, with traditional furnishings. *539 Absecon Blvd., Absecon, NJ 08201, tel. 609/641–7272 or 800/228–5150, fax 609/646–3286. 205 rooms. Facilities: exercise room. AE, D, DC, MC, V. $$*

Days Inn. This convenient five-story hotel on the Boardwalk has free parking and free stays for children under 16. The rooms are sizable and well maintained. Oceanfront rooms cost more, as do weekend stays. *Boardwalk, at Morris Ave., Atlantic City 08401, tel. 609/344–6101 or 800/329–7466, fax 609/348–5335. 105 rooms. Facilities: restaurant, outdoor pool, free parking. AE, D, MC, V. $$*

Where to Eat

Country Kitchen. You're on the Boardwalk, with a view of the dunes, at this cheery breakfast haven. There are good pancakes, waffles, fruit platters, and omelets. The large dining room has lace curtains, flagstone floors, reproduction antique tables, ceiling fans, and fox hunting prints. Kids' breakfasts are $3.29–$3.99. The restaurant is on the ground floor of the Days Inn. *Boardwalk, at Morris Ave., tel. 609/344–6101. AE, D, MC, V. $*

Dock's Oyster House. This 1897 formal dinner restaurant, the city's oldest, has children's meals and a friendly atmosphere, prompted by patron sing-alongs with the pianist. The founding Dougherty family still runs the restaurant. The oyster stew, crab, and lobster dishes are standouts, as are the Jersey tomato salads and desserts. There are 30 candlelit tables and free adjoining parking. *2405 Atlantic Ave., Atlantic City, tel. 609/345–0092. AE, DC, MC, V. $$$*

White House Sub Shop. The orange-and-blue neon sign draws you into this city culinary landmark. There's usually a short wait to get seated in one of the 8 booths, and there's always a line of carry-out patrons, too. The reason? The subs here are terrific, on chewy rolls, with your choice of cheese steak, deli meats, etc. Try a half-sub first—it's a lot of sandwich. The assembly line at the stainless steel counter keeps up with the demand; more than 22 million have been sold since the shop opened in 1946. Celebrities' photos line the wall. There's only one choice for dessert—Tastykakes, very good packaged cakes from Philadelphia. *Mississippi and Arctic Aves., Atlantic City, tel. 609/345–1564. MC, V. $*

Entertainments

The Boardwalk. The famed rolling chairs are back in force on this busy wooden walkway between the bathing beach and the casinos, hotels, and amusement and shopping centers. You may bicycle on the Boardwalk in the mornings and there are several rental shops. Swimming is good on this well-patrolled beach. There are a few public bathrooms, changing booths, and several vendors renting beach chairs and umbrellas. Don't miss the wonderful macaroons at longtime bakeries **Fralinger's** (1325 Boardwalk at Tennessee Avenue and at Ocean One Mall) and **A. H. Roth's** (2627 Boardwalk, between California and Texas Streets). The chocolate-dipped taffy paddles at Fralinger's are another seaside must. Several franchised attractions, like the All-Star and Hard Rock cafés, Ripley's Believe it or Not, and a Warner Brothers store are found amidst the casinos. There's an expensive 20-ride amusement park and video games arcade on the Steel Pier at Virginia Ave. *Boardwalk, Atlantic City. Admission: free. Open daily 24 hrs.*

Ocean Life Center and Historic Gardner's Boat Basin. This eight-acre aquatic complex has an aquarium, eco tours of beaches and salt marshes, parasailing rentals, Atlantic City cruises, deep-sea fishing, whale and dolphin watches, and summertime movies under the stars. *800 New Hampshire Ave., Atlantic City, tel. 609/348–2880. Admission to Ocean Life Center/Aquarium: $6 adults, $5 senior citizens, $4 ages 3–12. Beach and marsh tours: $5. Open daily 9–6.*

Sights to See

Absecon Lighthouse. New Jersey's largest lighthouse, first lit in 1857, has been renovated and is open for visitors to climb its 228 steps. It is the third-tallest lighthouse in the country. *Pacific and Vermont Aves., Atlantic City, tel. 609/441–9272. Admission: $4 adult; one child free with each adult, $1 per additional child. Open Thurs.–Mon. 11–4.*

Atlantic City Art Center and Historical Museum. This lively museum has a fascinating and funny film, several showcases of entertainment and Miss America memorabilia, and an extensive photo collection. Take a picture with Mr. Peanut, in full regalia, as he strolls here. All visitors get a green Heinz pickle pin. The art center and the museum are in two separate buildings on Garden Pier, at the north end of the Boardwalk. The art center has rotating exhibits. *Boardwalk, at New Jersey Ave., Atlantic City, tel. 609/347–5837. Admission: free (donations welcome). Open daily 10–4.*

Lucy the Margate Elephant. As you drive out of Atlantic City into neighboring Margate, urge the children to watch for the larger-than-life wooden elephant. This 1881 structure, now a National Historic Landmark, was once a hotel. You can climb the stairs inside the elephant's legs and see the upper rooms. Lucy is six stories high and weighs 90 tons. Citizens saved her from demolition in the 1970s and she is in beautiful shape today, a visual link to the Victorian era. A gift shop contains a large variety of elephant items, plus old player pianos and a mandolin orchestra machine that can be played for 25¢. *9200 Atlantic Ave., Margate, tel. 609/823–6473. Tour admission: $3 adults, $1 ages 12 and under. Open daily 10–8.*

SEAFOOD, SHIPS, AND FENWAY

14

PAWTUCKET, BOSTON, CAPE COD LEAGUE, LOWELL, PORTLAND

A four-to-five-day trip can cover a lot of baseball in the compact Northeast, even spanning the distance from Rhode Island to Cape Cod and Portland, Maine.

Pawtucket, Rhode Island, is the home of McCoy Stadium, an International League park. It's a 1942 Works Progress Administration stadium with winding staircases, no mascot, and no on-field hijinks. Here they play serious baseball like your parents used to watch. Diner fans will be in heaven in Pawtucket and nearby Providence, where dozens of originals still exist.

Boston, 50 mi north of Pawtucket, on Interstate 95, is the home of Fenway Park, one of baseball's cathedrals. The carnival atmosphere surrounding the park entrances is produced by fried clam vendors, souvenir stands, and cap sellers all vying for your attention. This is a big-league park that's intimate, idiosyncratic, and beautiful. Park your car, buy a visitor's transport passport, and ride the T to the city's many attractions for children, including its computer museum, swan boats, aquarium, science museum, and children's museum.

Driving south on Route 3 after a night game, you'll reach Plymouth, home of the Rock, in an hour. Explore the waterfront in the morning, and then drive another hour southeast on Route 6A to Cape Cod to watch the premier college summer-league games. There are hundreds of beachfront motels throughout the Cape, and each village has its own clambakes, lobster suppers, and community band concerts. A restored railroad takes you through cranberry bogs and the Great Salt Marsh.

Thirty-five miles northwest of Boston is Lowell, a reviving mill city built by water and power looms. Its baseball team, the Spinners, is named for its 19th-century heritage. At the friendly first-class park along the Merrimack River you can watch the baby Boston Red Sox.

Portland, Maine, is 110 mi north of Boston on Interstate 95. Pro ball returned in 1994 after a 45-year absence. A Double A Eastern League team plays in an attractive downtown park that sits behind a 1915 redbrick arena, a brick police-horse barn, and a football field. The city is beautifully situated on Casco Bay, where you can choose from dozens of boat excursions daily. The historic downtown area is fun to walk, and there's a classic, worn amusement park on a white-sand beach 25 minutes south of Portland at Old Orchard Beach.

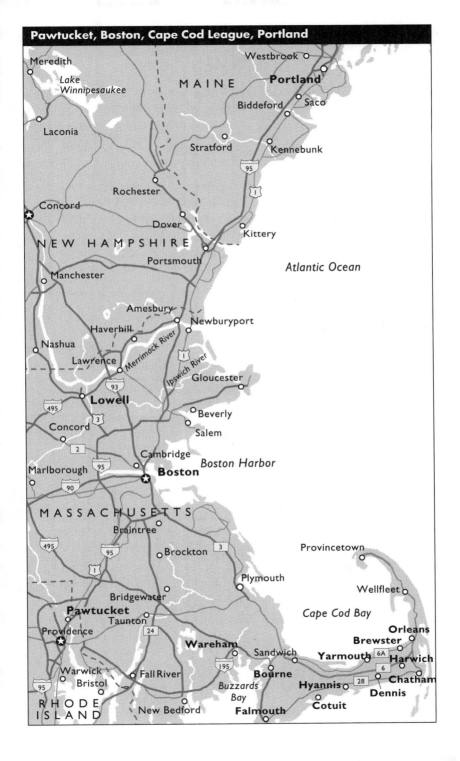

Meredith

Lake
Winnipesaukee

MAINE

Westbrook

Portland

Biddeford   Saco

Laconia

Stratford

Kennebunk

95

Rochester

I

Concord

Dover

Kittery

NEW HAMPSHIRE

Portsmouth

Atlantic Ocean

Manchester

Amesbury

Newburyport

Haverhill

Merrimack River

Nashua

Lawrence

Ipswich River

I

Gloucester

93

Lowell

495

Beverly

3

Concord

Salem

2

Cambridge

Boston Harbor

Marlborough

95

Boston

90

MASSACHUSETTS

Braintree

Provincetown

495

95

Brockton

3

I

Plymouth

Wellfleet

Bridgewater

Cape Cod Bay

Pawtucket

Taunton

Orleans

Providence

24

Brewster

Wareham

Sandwich

Yarmouth **6A** **Harwich**

Warwick

Fall River

6

195

Bourne

Chatham

Bristol

Hyannis **28**

95

*Buzzards
Bay*

Dennis

RHODE
ISLAND

New Bedford

Falmouth

Cotuit

PAWTUCKET RED SOX

League: International League • **Major League Affiliation:** Boston Red Sox • **Class:** AAA • **Stadium:** McCoy Stadium • **Opened:** 1942/99 • **Capacity:** 10,031 • **Dimensions:** LF: 325, CF: 379, RF: 325 • **Surface:** grass • **Season:** Apr.–Labor Day

STADIUM LOCATION: 1 Columbus Ave., Pawtucket, RI 02860.

TEAM WEBSITE: www.pawsox.com

GETTING THERE: From I–95N, Exit 28, School St. Bear right off exit, 2 blocks on School St. Left on Pond St. to Columbus Ave. Right on Columbus to stadium parking lot. From I–95S, Exit 2A, Newport Ave. Follow Newport Ave. 2 mi to Columbus Ave. Turn right, 1 mi on Columbus.

PARKING: Parking limited; 650 free spaces at stadium, spill-over parking on streets and at school beyond outfield wall.

TICKET INFORMATION: Box 2365, Pawtucket, RI 02861, tel. 401/724–7300, fax 401/724–2140.

PRICE RANGE: Box seats $7; general admission $5 adults, $4 under 13 and senior citizens.

GAME TIME: Apr.–mid-May, weeknights 6, Sat. 7 PM, Sun. 1 PM; mid-May–Labor Day, Mon.–Sat. 7 PM, Sun. 1 PM; gates open 2 hrs before game.

TIPS ON SEATING: Call to order tickets in advance. PawSox sell out a number of games each year. Box seats are recommended.

SEATING FOR PEOPLE WITH DISABILITIES: Some of stadium's very few field-level seats reserved; vans may drive in on first-base side for direct access to seating area next to visitor's dugout.

STADIUM FOOD: Think Portuguese and Italian here. The PawSox even have an official coffee syrup—Silmo Milk Mate. The indulgence purchase is fried dough for $2.50; they are huge ovals that are cooked as you watch and are covered with cinnamon and confectioner's sugar. Italian sweet sausage is charbroiled with peppers and onions for $2.75, but may be too spicy for children. A $2.50 grilled hamburger is a bargain. The frozen lemonade ($2) helps in the heat, as does the Brigham's ice cream.

SMOKING POLICY: Smoking prohibited in seating areas and allowed in concourse.

VISITING TEAM HOTEL: Comfort Inn (2 George St., Pawtucket, RI 02860, tel. 401/723–6700 or 800/424–6423).

TOURISM INFORMATION: Greater Providence Convention & Visitors Bureau (30 Exchange Terrace, Providence, RI 02903, tel. 401/274–1636 or 800/233–1636).

Pawtucket, Rhode Island: McCoy Stadium

Real baseball fans appreciate McCoy Stadium in Pawtucket, Rhode Island. Just 5 mi north of Providence, this is a gritty, blue-collar town with a gritty, no-nonsense stadium. Don't come here looking for fuzzy mascots or on-the-field contests. Somebody tried to start a wave the afternoon we were there, and it didn't last a minute. This is Triple A baseball in the International League. The players are headed for the big leagues, and everyone takes baseball seriously.

The longest game in the history of professional baseball started at McCoy Stadium on April 18 and finished on June 23, 1981. Pawtucket beat Rochester 3–2 in 33 innings. In this early test of his Ironman legend, Cal Ripken, Jr. went 2 for 13. Wade Boggs was 4 for 12. A large collection of memorabilia from the longest game is on display just inside the main gate entrance. The perfect gift for baseball insomniacs—a cassette tape of the entire radio play-by-play—is on sale at the concession stand.

We love the winding staircases with 34 larger-than-life paintings of Pawtucket's baseball stars.

The team has been a Red Sox franchise since 1973. As you work your way up the stairs to your seats, you see images of such Red Sox stars as Wade Boggs, Roger Clemens, and Jim Rice.

This is a 1942 WPA stadium named for Paw-tucket mayor Thomas P. McCoy. Virtually all of the seating is under roof and far above the play-ing field. President Franklin Delano Roosevelt spoke here, and Louis Armstrong, Ella Fitzger-ald, and Yogi Berra performed here. Substantial renovations were made for a 50th-anniversary rededication on July 4 weekend, 1992. A 1999 renovation expanded the seating capacity and modernized bathrooms.

It's a hitter's park, with the shortest center field in all of Triple A baseball—380 ft. The dugouts are built under the stands. Parking is limited here, so come early and watch the scene at the PawSox dugout. Just before a game, the dugout looks like a well-stocked fishing pond. The local kids bring large plastic containers with a side cut out. They put balls and pens into the container and fish from the top of the dugout for PawSox autographs below. It is quite a sight.

The locals like this baseball-purist experience and the chance to see the future stars of the neighboring Boston Red Sox. The park fre-quently sells out, so this is one minor-league game where you may want to call ahead for tickets.

Where to Stay

Visiting Team Motel: Comfort Inn. This five-floor brick hotel is nicely decorated and clean. Its standard doubles are roomy but face the adjacent highway. Deluxe doubles are larger and away from traffic noise. Guests receive a free Continental breakfast. *2 George St., Exit 27 from I-95, Pawtucket 02860, tel. 401/723-6700 or 800/424-6423, fax 401/726-6380. 135 rooms. Facilities: restaurant, outdoor pool. AE, D, DC, MC, V. $$*

Where to Eat

Modern Diner. Half of the delight of eating here is visual, as this is one of the nation's most remarkable diners. It's a vintage maroon-and-buff Sterling streamliner diner with a bow end,

set in the middle of a parking lot, looking nearly untouched since it was built in 1940. It's now on the National Register of Historic Places. Inside are wooden booths with large mirror panels. Try to visit on a Friday for the excellent clam chowder. You can order beyond-the-norm items such as fried-egg sandwiches and frappes, a drink that also goes by the regional moniker "cabinets." Unusual, good pancakes—blueberry, plum, pumpkin, cranberry, apple, and banana—are on the breakfast menu, which is available all day. It's five minutes west of the ballpark. *364 East Ave., Pawtucket, tel. 401/726-8390. No credit cards. No dinner Sat.-Wed. $*

Angelo's Civita Farnese. There are six commu-nity tables where guests are mixed and matched, if they wish, at the center of this inex-pensive and cozy family restaurant on Federal Hill. Eight booths along the perimeter are for those who prefer not to mingle. Prices are low and no reservations are taken, but waits rarely exceed 15 minutes at dinner. The signature dish is stewed veal and sweet peppers, which is also sold as a sandwich. Half-orders of homemade macaroni and other pasta are available. Spaghetti accompanies nearly every dish, and a full plate of pasta costs as little as $3.10. *141 Atwells Ave., Providence, tel. 401/621-8171. No credit cards. $*

Gregg's. This 180-seat restaurant, one of four in the state, is known for its rich chocolate layer cake, Reuben sandwiches, and real turkey sand-wiches and dinners. Children can have half-orders of pasta, fish-and-chips, and 4-ounce hamburgers. The homemade apple pie, made with 5 pounds of apples, and the meat loaf are toothsome. It's in a residential-commercial area 6 mi south of the ballpark. *1940 Pawtucket Ave., East Providence, tel. 401/438-5700. AE, D, DC, MC, V. $*

Providence Cheese and Tavola Calda. The square pizza and focaccia are standouts at this premier take-out delicatessen on Federal Hill. Anything from the deli's cases would make a memorable pre-game picnic. You can sit at one of the tables in the side courtyard in good weather. *178 Atwells Ave., Providence, tel. 401/421-5653. AE, MC, V. $*

Diners began in Providence when horse-drawn canteens, devised by entrepreneur Walter Scott in 1892, served pies and coffee to mill workers. It's a point of civic pride that this city has kept its vintage diners. Consider these survivors: At **Silver Top Diner** (13 Harris Ave., tel. 401/331–8247) don't miss the blueberry pancakes in a preserved Kullman diner, built in 1941. Try also the 1946 **Krystal's** (581 Atwells Ave., tel. 401/751–1650), the 1950s **Seaplane Diner** (307 Allens Ave., tel. 401/941–9547), the 1930s **Wampanaug Diner** (2800 Pawtucket Ave., East Providence, tel. 401/434–9880), and the upscale, '50s-furnished **Downcity Diner** (151 Weybosset St., tel. 401/331–9217).

Entertainments

Basketball Hall of Fame. This Cooperstown for basketball fans is 90 minutes west of Pawtucket in Springfield. You can walk through a tunnel decorated with the shoes of famous players, test your shooting ability at 15 baskets in the Spalding Shoot-Out, and play a one-on-one virtual game with Bill Walton. Check your hang time and jumping ability at the Wilson Imagymnation Theater. Watch past and present clips from famous games. Women players, wheelchair athletes, and the Olympic Games receive special notice. An Honors Court memorializes 207 great players. *1150 W. Columbus Ave., Springfield, MA, tel. 413/781–6500. Admission: $8 adults, $5 ages 7–15 and senior citizens. Open daily 9:30–5:30.*

Children's Museum of Rhode Island. This interactive museum is in a renovated factory in the Providence jewelry district. Look for the 11-ft dragon on its roof. Kids can climb down a manhole, crawl in a sewer maze, and learn about 250 years of immigration to Rhode Island by four ethnic groups. A pets and people exhibit, one of seven permanent sites, is cosponsored by the Humane Society. *100 South St., Providence, tel. 401/723–5437. Admission: $4.50; free 1st Sun. of month. Open Tues.–Sun. 9:30–5; June–Aug., Mon. 9:30–5.*

Roger Williams Park and Zoo. This excellent city zoo has a good African-animals exhibit and a monkey house. You can see the polar bears underwater. *1000 Elmwood Ave., Providence, tel. 401/785–9450. Admission: $6 adults, $3.50 ages 3–12 and senior citizens. Open Nov.–Apr., daily 9–5; May–Oct., weekdays 9–5, weekends and holidays 9–6.*

Sights to See

Brown University. It is worth seeing University Hall, on the main campus of this popular Ivy League school founded in 1764. The four-story brick building was copied from Princeton's Nassau Hall. A bust of John Jay, first chief justice of the U.S. Supreme Court, in the John Hay Library is supposed to bring students good luck if they rub its now-shiny nose. Tours of the campus begin at the admissions office in Corliss-Broekett House (45 Prospect St., at Angell St.). The university is on the city's east side. *College Hill, Providence, tel. 401/863–1000.*

State Capitol. The Rhode Island State Capitol is a massive white Georgian marble structure sitting high on Smith Hill. It overlooks but is physically removed from the city life of Providence. Begun in 1895 and completed in 1904, it was built according to a design by the New York firm McKim, Mead & White, inspired by the U.S. Capitol, St. Paul's Cathedral in London, and New York's City Hall. The Capitol is 235 ft high from the terrace to the top of the statue on the marble dome, George Brewster's gilded "Independent Man." It is the second-largest unsupported marble dome in the world (the largest is atop St. Peter's Basilica in Rome). Gilbert Stuart's portrait of George Washington hangs in the State Room. *82 Smith St., bordered by Smith, Gaspee, and Francis Sts., Providence, tel. 401/277–2357. Open weekdays 8:30–4:30; free tours by appointment only (tel. 401/277–2357), weekdays at 10 and 11.*

BOSTON RED SOX

League: American League • **Class:** Major League • **Stadium:** Fenway Park • **Opened:** 1912 • **Capacity:** 33,871 • **Dimensions:** LF: 310, CF: 390, RF: 302 • **Surface:** grass • **Season:** Apr.–Oct.

STADIUM LOCATION: 4 Yawkey Way, Boston, MA 02215.

TEAM WEBSITE: www.redsox.com

GETTING THERE: Take Green Line on T to Kenmore Square, 3 blocks north of Fenway. For transit information, call 617/722–3200 or 800/392–6100. By car from south, take Exit 20A/Rte. 9 east from I–95. Go east on Rte. 9 about 10 mi. Turn left on Brookline Ave., right on Boylston St., and left on Yawkey Way. From north, take Rte. 93 south. Take Storrow Drive to Kenmore/Kenmore Square exit and bear right on Boylston St. Take right on Ipswich St. and right on Yawkey.

TICKET INFORMATION: 4 Yawkey Way, Boston, MA 02215, tel. 617/267–1700 or 617/482–4769 (24 hrs), fax 617/236–6640.

PRICE RANGE: Field box $35; infield roof box $32; right field roof box $26; grandstand $24; outfield grandstand $18; lower bleachers $14; upper bleachers and standing room $12.

GAME TIME: 7:05 PM; day game times vary. Gates open 90 min before game.

PARKING: Expect to pay $15 for a lot that doesn't block your car. Prudential Center Garage ($8 if you show a Sox ticket stub) on Boylston St. between Dartmouth and Exeter offers easy access to Mass. Turnpike.

TIPS ON SEATING: Watch out for poles, which can obstruct views. Sections 32 and 33 near Green Monster prohibit alcohol. Bleachers can get rowdy and do not provide access to rest of ballpark.

SEATING FOR PEOPLE WITH DISABILITIES: In locations throughout ballpark. Listening devices for people with hearing impairments are available at Customer Service Booths.

STADIUM FOOD: The quality of food inside the park is uneven, but **Legal Seafoods** sells its terrific clam chowder here ($4.50), and you can bring in any food except items in cans. There are good take-out stands surrounding the park. The Fenway Frank is bland, but there's good barbecue from local restaurant **Bob the Chef's.** There's average Chinese food at a ground-floor stand, and pizza from Papa Gino's. The best bet is the chowder, plus real lemonade, which is sold in a large souvenir cup for $3.25. Boston's own Hood ice-cream treats and Richie's Italian slushes are sold. A $3.25 kid's meal has a hot dog, soda, and goldfish crackers.

SMOKING POLICY: Seating area smoke-free; billboards announce, "Fenway Park should have a place in your heart. Not in your lungs."

TOURISM INFORMATION: Greater Boston Convention & Visitors Bureau (Prudential Plaza, Box 490, Boston, MA 02199, tel. 617/536–4100 or 800/888–5515).

Boston: Fenway Park

"Ladies and gentlemen...boys and girls...welcome to Fenway Park" is the formal and familiar greeting of the public address announcer in one of baseball's classic ballparks.

The anticipation builds as you walk to the park. The streets are full of people darting in and out of the pubs and shops and around the food carts and souvenir tables that surround Fenway. You enter this small, redbrick arched building just as fans have before you for more than 85 years. You walk through a dark, dank area beneath the grandstand and then through a portal. There it is. It is truly breathtaking. Only here and at Chicago's Wrigley Field is there a feeling so pure and wonderful for the baseball fan.

As marvelous as Fenway Park is, baseball history has not been kind to the Fenway faithful. The whole story seems to be told on the roof above the right-field bleachers. Just below the sign for the Jimmy Fund—which has helped raise millions of dollars for the Dana–Farber Cancer Institute—are the numbers 9 4 1 8. These are the retired numbers of four great Red Sox players—Ted Williams, Joe Cronin, Bobby Doerr, and Carl Yastrzemski. They represent the numerical symbol of "the Curse of the Bambino." September 4, 1918 (9/4/18), was the eve of the World Series. Babe Ruth pitched and won the game the very next day, and the Red Sox won the World Series. Financially strapped Red Sox owner Harry Frazee sold Ruth to the Yankees for $100,000 cash and a $300,000 loan with a mortgage on Fenway Park. The Red Sox have not won a World Series since. In 1998 the stadium was repainted and the numbers were put back in numerical order.

Fenway Park got its name when Red Sox owner General John I. Taylor decided to switch from Huntington Grounds in 1911 to a plot of marshy land nearby that was owned by the Fenway Realty Company. General Taylor was a major stockholder in the real estate company. The Fens was an area planned by Frederick Law Olmstead as part of a proposed ring of parks for the Boston area.

When the Red Sox were planning their new stadium, the era of the wooden ballpark was coming to a close. Pittsburgh and Philadelphia had built new concrete-and-steel ballparks, and Boston was not to be outdone. Osborne Engineering of Cleveland designed Fenway, and it was built in 1912 for $650,000 without public funds. The front was modeled on Philadelphia's 1909 Shibe Park; it was built without an upper deck. There's a lot of history here. President John F. Kennedy's grandfather, Boston mayor John F. "Honey Fitz" Fitzgerald, tossed out the first ball at the 1912 opener; the game was subsequently knocked off the front pages by the sinking of the Titanic. President Franklin Delano Roosevelt gave the last campaign speech of his life here on November 4, 1944. Six months later he was dead.

The Green Monster, the huge green fence in left field, was not part of the 1912 ballpark. Lansdowne in left field was only 325 ft from home plate, and there was a railroad track just across the street. To remedy this, they built a wall in left field with an embankment just in front of it. This became known as Duffy's Cliff after Red Sox left fielder Duffy Lewis, who was the first to learn how to play it. In 1934, Duffy's Cliff was flattened and a 37-ft-high metal fence was installed. But even then it was not as we see it today. In the late 1930s and '40s, the wall was mostly covered with large advertisements. They were painted over in 1947 in Fenway green. In 1978, Yankee Bucky Dent popped a ball to left, and it somehow ended up in the net over the Monster for one of the shortest and most important home runs ever hit. Dent's pop-up enabled the Yankees to beat the Red Sox in a one-game playoff for the American League crown. Fenway's Green Monster and Wrigley's ivy are the two most distinctive features in any of America's ballparks.

We like to get to games early and watch batting practice, always hoping to snag a ball in the process. Nowhere is this experience as special as it is at Fenway. Stand as close to the field as you dare on the third-base side at the foot of the Green Monster, and watch the visiting-team batters slam the ball into and over the wall and right by your ear.

Your eyes can't miss the animated neon CITGO sign just over the Green Monster that mimics the triangular shape of the bleacher seats in center field. Before the fans fill the bleachers, look for the red seat in a sea of blue deep in the triangle. This is where a Ted Williams home run landed, 502 ft from home plate. They added bullpens in front of the bleachers in right and right center field in 1940. Contrary to what you might think, these bullpens weren't for the convenience of pitchers. The area is known as Williamsburg, as it was built to increase the output of the left-hand-hitter Ted Williams, who had hit .327 with 31 homers in his rookie season of 1939. The bullpens reduced the right-field home-run distance by 23 ft. Appropriately, Williams hit a home run in his very last at bat in the major leagues, September 28, 1960, into the right-field Red Sox bullpen. Not much else has changed in the 50-plus years since Ted Williams began playing here. A large scoreboard was constructed in 1976 and upgraded in 1988. In 1989, the enclosed "600 Club" seats behind home plate were added.

Okay, we won't kid you—there's not much legroom here. Someone is bound to spill some beer on you in such close quarters. Balls bounce wildly off the crazy angles in the outfield, and no lead is safe with the Green Monster so close to home. The concession area is dark. The food is mostly bad. You paid too much to park, and your car is blocked on every side. But believe us, you will love every minute of this.

Unfortunately, time is running out on this hopelessly and wonderfully outdated relic. The Red Sox are finding it difficult to compete financially for top players with the teams in Baltimore and Cleveland having fancy new stadiums that seem to be printing money. With all our hearts we say, "Save Fenway!" But the reality is that plans for a new stadium, adjoining the current park, are well underway. Because this is heresy to some fans (we've seen "Save Fenway" bumper stickers across the country), management is working hard to meld the old Fenway into the new. The park's Green monster, unique field dimensions, and manual scoreboard will be saved and the current infield used as a public park. There will be 10,000 more seats in the new park and none will be obstructed.

The carnival atmosphere outside Fenway includes the souvenir shops, sports pubs, and take-out food stands all vying for your business. The adjacent restaurants, such as Pizzeria Uno (645 Beacon St., at Brookline Ave., tel. 617/536–2337) and the Boston Beer Works (61 Brookline Ave., tel. 617/262–4911) often are too crowded for comfort, but there are dozens of other choices in the Kenmore Square area. The Sausage Connection (Brookline Ave. and Lansdowne St.) has much better Italian sausage, onions, and peppers ($4) than the ballpark grill. If you show your ticket at RFA Amusements (under Fenway, 82 Lansdowne St., tel. 617/247–9252), you get a free game on one of its 20 candlepin bowling lanes. This is a worthy choice to make, a post-afternoon game to give the parking lots and crowded T trains a chance to empty.

There is a large souvenir shop, the Lansdowne Shop, inside Fenway on the left-field side; it can also be entered from Brookline Avenue. Twins Enterprises (19 Yawkey Way, Boston, tel. 617/421–8686 or 800/336–9299 for retail catalog), a souvenir store across from Fenway's main entrance, bills itself as "the Supermarket of Sports Souvenirs" and appears to live up to its claim.

Tours of Fenway Park (Red Sox Service Gate D, corner of Yawkey Way and Van Ness St., tel. 617/236–6666. Admission: $5 adults, $4 senior citizens, $3 ages under 16) are conducted weekdays at 10, 11, noon, and 1; on nongame days, there's also a tour at 2. Call in advance for a reservation.

More Boston Baseball

Braves Field. The Boston University football team plays at Nickerson Field, on the site where the Boston Braves played baseball from 1915 to 1952. Three World Series and the 1936 All-Star Game were played here. The Red Sox won the World Series here in 1915 and 1916 (played here because at the time Braves Field held more seats than Fenway), while the Braves lost to Cleveland in 1948. Babe Ruth pitched 13 straight innings of shut-out ball to help the Red Sox beat the Brooklyn Dodgers in the 1916 series. The Braves moved to Milwaukee in 1953 and Atlanta in 1966. In 1970, Boston University laid out its football carpet from the first-base dugout to right center field. The stands down the first-base line remain, along with much of the concrete outer wall in right field. The handsome, arched ticket office is now used as the Boston University Police Station. A 1988 plaque in a courtyard on the Commonwealth Avenue side of the ticket office pays tribute to Braves Field. *Nickerson Field, 1 block off Commonwealth Ave. at Harry Agganis Way.*

Huntington Avenue American League Baseball Grounds. A 1956 plaque on Northeastern University's Godfrey Lowell Cabot Physical Education Center (365 Huntington Ave.) explains that four games of the 1903 World Series were held on this site, with the Boston Americans defeating the Pittsburgh Nationals five games to three. The center houses a modest display of World

Series memorabilia. The real treat is a small park behind the building. Go a half block down Forsyth Street and turn left at World Series Way to find a statue of the great Cy Young looking in toward home plate for a signal from the catcher. The home-plate-shape plaque, 60 ft away, explains that the games played here in 1903 were the first modern World Series. Let the kids pretend to catch and bat with the man who pitched the first perfect game of the 20th century here on May 5, 1904. The Boston Pilgrims (called the Americans for the World Series) played here from 1901 to 1911 before moving to Fenway Park as the Red Sox in 1912. Huntington Avenue was left field. The centerfield fence was 530 ft from home in 1903 and moved back to 635 ft in 1908.

Where to Stay

Howard Johnson Lodge–Fenway. Parking is free at this two-story hotel, which backs up to Fenway Park. Guests receive a free cassette walking tour if they ask for the "AAA Freedom Trail Package," which lowers rates to $115 per night. The rooms are standard lodgings. *1271 Boylston St., Boston 02215, tel. 617/267–8300 or 800/446–4656, fax 617/267–2763. 94 rooms. Facilities: restaurant, outdoor pool. AE, D, DC, MC, V. $$*

Hotel Buckminster. Built as a hotel in 1903, this impressive stone-front building saw use as a dorm for Boston University before being completely renovated in 1991 and reopened as a European-style hotel. Many of its spacious units are suites, and several have kitchens and dishwashers. The rooms are furnished in Chippendale reproductions, with forest-green draperies. The two-bedroom suites, joined by a hallway and including a wet bar, cost between $100 and $140 per night. It is one block from Fenway Park and the Kenmore Square T station. It has no parking garage; you can use street meters or a private adjoining garage, which charges $20 daily. *645 Beacon St., Boston 02215, tel. 617/236–7050 or 800/727–2825, fax 617/262–0068. 100 units. Facilities: restaurant. AE, D, DC, MC, V. $$$*

Howard Johnson Hotel–Kenmore. This well-used seven-story concrete hotel, built in the 1960s, overlooks the T tracks coming into Kenmore Square. It's a two-block walk from Fen-

way Park. Most rooms are small, with contemporary furnishings. The "AAA Freedom Trail Package" lowers rates to $125 per night. *575 Commonwealth Ave., Boston 02215, tel. 617/267–3100 or 800/446–4656, fax 617/424–1045. 179 rooms. Facilities: restaurant, indoor pool. AE, D, DC, MC, V. $$*

Tremont House Hotel. This 15-floor hotel is in the theater district, two blocks from the Boston Common, and is one of the few nice downtown hotels where rooms are under $100. Built in 1924, the hotel has been fully renovated. All rooms have free cable movies. The rooms and baths are small, but the bedrooms are nicely furnished in reproduction antiques. It is a half block from the Medical Center stop on the Orange Line of the T. A neighborhood pocket park with children's climbing equipment is next door. *275 Tremont St., Boston 02116, tel. 617/426–1400 or 800/331–9998, fax 617/482–6730. 288 rooms. Facilities: restaurant. AE, D, DC, MC. $$*

Where to Eat

Jacob Wirth Company Restaurant. You creak on wooden floors in this charming restaurant with round mahogany tables. It's the oldest German eatery in America. Since it was founded in 1868, the dark-wood decor of the famous alehouse hasn't changed much. It serves exemplary clam chowder, red cabbage, Wiener schnitzel, scrod, and inexpensive sandwiches. Eight baseball Hall of Famers, including Cy Young and Tris Speaker, all of whom ate and drank here, have reproductions of their Baseball Hall of Fame plaques on a wall. A photo of Babe Ruth hangs over the bar. The children's meals are served with carrot and celery sticks; the selection includes turkey and mashed potatoes, grilled cheese, hamburgers, peanut butter and jelly sandwiches, and a salad. It's a 7-minute T ride from Fenway or a 20-minute walk. The restaurant validates an hour's parking in the next-door lot. *37–39 Stuart St., at Tremont St., Boston, tel. 617/338–8586. AE, D, MC, V. $$*

Durgin Park. You must experience the crusty waitresses, the noise, and the feeding-hall atmosphere because the food is exceptional in this second-floor restaurant. Regional specialties like Indian pudding, baked beans, and lobster are unequaled. A specialty is prime rib, but kids can opt for chicken fingers or fish off their own menu. Open for lunch and dinner, the restaurant has an oyster bar and long communal tables. *340 Faneuil Hall Marketplace, Boston, tel. 617/227–2038. AE, D, DC, MC, V. $$*

Emack & Bolio's. Indulge in calorie-laden refreshment at this local ice-cream shop, which has several outlets in the area. Its cones are handmade and the ice-cream flavors are imaginative. It's worth the 10-minute walk from the Swan Boats in the Public Garden (*see below*) for these cones, instead of settling for a frozen dessert from a concession truck. *290 Newbury St., at Gloucester St., Boston, tel. 617/247–8772. No credit cards. $*

Entertainments

Buy a Visitor's Passport, which gives you unlimited transport on all subway and bus lines for $5 per day. They are sold at the Boston Common Information Offices (Tremont St. in the Common) and at the Prudential Center (near Copley T station). These offices also give out pamphlets with valuable attraction coupons and restaurant discounts. A CityPass is good for nine days and covers admission to the Gardner Museum, JFK Library, John Hancock Observatory, Museum of Fine Arts, the Museum of Science, and the New England Aquarium. It is sold at the entrance of each attraction, at $26.50 adults; $20.50 senior citizens, $13.50 ages 12 to 17.

Boston Tea Ship and Museum. It's corny and touristy, but our kids loved learning history by throwing canvas chests of "tea" over the rails of this reproduction of a Revolution-era ship. The costumed guides aim their history lessons at kids, and it works. A small museum, explaining the ship and the Revolution's origins, is below deck. There are photo ops with colonist cutouts. The closest T stop is South Station on the Red Line. The ship is anchored on the bridge approaching the Children's Museum and there are history dramas every 30 minutes. *Congress St. Bridge, Boston, tel. 617/338–1773. Admission: $8 adults, $4 ages 4–12, $7 senior citizens and high school and college students. No credit cards.*

Children's Museum of Boston. Here you'll find four floors of controlled mayhem, as children

race from trying on costumes to flipping life-size photographs of children from other races and cultures. A big crowd-pleaser is the see-through toilet. A 40-ft wooden Hood Dairy milk bottle in front of the museum dispenses carry-out sandwiches, salads, and drinks. There is also a McDonald's outlet on the museum's first floor. *300 Congress St., Museum Wharf, Boston, tel. 617/426–8855. Admission: $7 adults, $6 ages 2–15 and senior citizens, $2 children age 1; $1 Fri. 5–9. Open Mon.–Thurs., Sat. 10–5, Fri. 10–9.*

Freedom Trail. A faded red stripe marks 3 mi of sidewalk passing in front of the city's historic landmarks, including the Old North Church and Bunker Hill Monument. Maps are available from the National Park Service Visitor's Center (15 State St.) or the Boston Common Information Office (Tremont St.). The trail is too long to accomplish with young kids, but there's a shorter version for children 6 to 12 called "Boston by Little Feet," which covers several of the trail's highlights. This abbreviated tour leaves from the statue of Samuel Adams in Faneuil Hall Square. *Faneuil Hall Sq., Boston, tel. 617/367–2345. Admission: $6 ages 6–adults. Tours May–Oct., Sat. at 10, Sun. at 2.*

Museum of Science. Learn about nature, medicine, and astronomy in this museum with more than 600 hands-on exhibits. Creative displays explain the laws of physics in an interesting fashion. The city's computer museum, with several interactive exhibits, has moved here. There are separate fees to view the museum's four-story Omni theater, its laser shows, and the Charles Hayden planetarium. The T stop is Science Park on the Green Line. *Science Park, Boston, tel. 617/723–2500. Admission: $10 adults, $7 children and senior citizens, under 4 free. Open Sat.–Thurs. 9–5, Fri. 9–9. AE, MC, V.*

New England Aquarium. From woodland pools to oceans, this extensive aquarium presents all manner of fish and amphibians in various environments. Its centerpiece is a 190,000-gallon three-story cylindrical transparent tank containing a coral reef. Visitors walk a ramp around the tank, getting close to sea turtles and sharks. A penguin colony lives at its base, in a salt-water basin. Sea-lion shows are held every 90 minutes daily, beginning at 10:30, at Discovery, a floating auditorium. Nature films are shown throughout the day in the theater. There is an Aquarium stop on the Blue Line of the subway. *Center Wharf, Atlantic Ave. exit off Rte. 3 N, Boston, tel. 617/973–5200. Admission: $12 adults, $10 senior citizens, $6 ages 3–11. Open weekdays 9–5, weekends 9–6.*

Swan Boats. Fans of Robert McClosky's classic book *Make Way for Ducklings* will remember the Swan Boats. You wait in line to board these graceful antique boats on a sweep around the lagoon in the Public Garden. Athletic teens power the boats by pedaling, the same energy used when the boats debuted in 1877. Children will be amused by the antics of the ducks that fill the lagoon. After debarking, walk to the park gates at Beacon and Charles streets and find the statues of the book's Mrs. Mallard and her duck family. The Park Street stop on the Red Line is closest. *Boston Public Garden Lagoon, near Charleston and Boylston Sts., Boston. Admission: $1.95 adults, 95¢ ages under 13. Open Apr. 19–June 20, daily 10–4; June 21–Labor Day, daily 10–5.*

Sights to See

John Fitzgerald Kennedy Presidential Library and Museum. This impressive museum has an excellent 17-minute documentary film, memorabilia, and videotapes. Kennedy's Oval Office desk is here, along with details of such groundbreaking initiatives of his as community mental-health centers. The Red Line T stop is JFK–University of Massachusetts. The library operates a free shuttle bus every 20 minutes to and from the T stop. *Morrissey Blvd., Exit 14 from I–93/Rte. 3, Boston, tel. 617/929–4523. Admission: $8 adults, $4 ages 13–17, $6 senior citizens; 12 and under, free. Open daily 9–5.*

State House. The children's self-tour of this gold-domed building points out oddities like the sacred codfish that's on display in the Senate chambers. Charles Bulfinch designed the building's brick front, and the first African-American regiment to serve in the Civil War is memorialized by Augustus Saint-Gaudens in a bas-relief statue in front of the capitol. The T stop is Park Street. *Beacon St., at Park St., Boston, tel. 617/727–3676. Free tours weekdays 10–4. Open weekdays 10–5.*

Cape Cod Baseball League

If you are a college freshman, sophomore, or junior baseball superstar, the Cape Cod Baseball League is where you want to spend your summer. Along with the Shenandoah Valley League and other NCAA-sanctioned summer leagues, the Cape Cod Baseball League attracts the most talented young college players. Major-league baseball makes a financial contribution to help support these summer leagues, and major-league scouts are ever present. The league is run by volunteers, who keep baseball going on the Cape for the sheer love of the game.

The league motto is "Where the stars of tomorrow shine tonight," and it is no exaggeration. Among former Cape Cod League stars, 144 are now in the major leagues, including 1995 American League MVP Mo Vaughn, and Frank Thomas.

Organized baseball has been played on the Cape since 1885. It began as a semi-pro league, with such stars as Hall of Famers Pie Traynor and Mickey Cochrane. The NCAA has sanctioned the league since the late 1960s. Since 1985, players have been using wooden bats, adding to the glamour for college players used to that annoying ping of aluminum bats. The chance to watch future superstars swinging wooden bats has attracted many scouts, and the presence of so many scouts has attracted top-caliber players.

The longest trip in the 10-team league is 46 mi from Wareham on the west to Chatham on the east. Many of the "road trips" are less than 10 mi. Games start the second week in June, and the season ends in early August. Admission is free to all games. Most teams sell 50–50 tickets (raffle tickets whose proceeds are split between the club and the winning ticket holder) and pass the hat to keep the club financially sound.

The East Division teams include **Brewster Whitecaps** (Cape Cod Regional Technical High School, on Rte. 124 just north of Exit 10 off Rte. 6), **Chatham Athletics** (Veterans Field, just off Rte. 28 in Chatham Center), **Harwich Mariners** (Whitehouse Field, behind Harwich High

School on Oak St.), **Orleans Cardinals** (Eldredge Park, on Rte. 28 near Exit 12 from Rte. 6), and the **Yarmouth-Dennis Red Sox** (Merrill "Red" Wilson Field at Dennis-Yarmouth High School, Station Ave., South Yarmouth).

The West Division teams are **Bourne Braves** (Coady School Field, across Trowbridge Rd. from Bourne High School in Bourne Village), **Cotuit Kettleers** (Elizabeth Lowell Park, 2 mi south of Rte. 28, Cotuit; turn right on Main St. and right again on Lowell Ave.), **Falmouth Commodores** (Guv Fuller Field, behind Gus Canty Community Center, 790 E. Main St., Falmouth), **Hyannis Mets** (McKeon Field, High School Rd., 2 blocks south of Main St. behind Barnstable Grade Five Building), and **Wareham Gatemen** (Clem Spillane Field, Wareham High School, 1 mi west of Wareham Center, Rte. 6). Most games start at 7 PM. The games in Bourne, Brewster, Cotuit, and Yarmouth-Dennis start at 5 because the ballparks do not have lights. The Hyannis home games also start at 5 PM.

The Chatham Athletics play at Veterans Field, where the fog rolled in and out the night we were there faster than at San Francisco's Candlestick Park. The U-shape wooden grandstand—five rows high—fits snugly into a hillside behind home plate. There are trees out left field. Fans bring blankets and picnic on the hillside beyond center and right field. There is a fabulous children's playground on the right-field side and an elegant train station on the hill beyond the playground. The Chatham coaches and players give clinics during the summer on the Little League ball field on the first-base side. Fans get a certificate for free ice cream for returning foul balls and are encouraged to volunteer to make sandwiches for the players.

When the Hyannis Mets play at McKeon Field, the school playing field behind home plate is full of kids racing around, playing catch, and stopping only to chase down a foul ball. There are small wooden bleachers on each side of the screen behind home plate. As with most other Cape Cod League parks, a two-story all-purpose cinderblock building houses the public address announcer on the second floor behind home plate. The one in Hyannis is dark baseball green and doubles as the concession stand at the back, where they sell homemade clam chowder. A larger, five-row wooden bleacher sits oddly on a scruffy hillside behind the third-base dugout. Small trees stand behind the outfield fence, and a hotel is well beyond the fence and scoreboard in right. Look on top of the light pole in right-center field to see if the osprey is still there. Ferries come into the town port every hour; you'll probably hear their horns.

The Chatham and Hyannis parks have the kind of raw, rustic charm that gives the Cape Cod League its authentic character. We visited several of the other fields and were especially charmed by Orleans's Eldredge Park and Cotuit's Elizabeth Lowell Park. The Orleans Cardinals play in an attractive ballpark with a four-tier grass grandstand cut out of a hill on the first-base side. Bring your own lawn chairs. Wooden steps help you maneuver the grass grandstand. The Cotuit Kettleers play in a gorgeous setting completely surrounded by trees. Wooden bleachers rise behind each dugout, but there are no lights. The "Kettleer Kitchen" building on the third-base side offers food and souvenirs.

For schedules, contact the Cape Cod League, tel. 508/996–5004, www.capecodbaseball.com.

LOWELL SPINNERS

League: New York–Penn League • **Major League Affiliation:** Boston Red Sox • **Class:** Short Season A • **Stadium:** Edward A. LeLacheur Park • **Opened:** 1998 • **Capacity:** 4,863 • **Dimensions:** LF: 337, CF: 400, RF: 301 • **Surface:** grass • **Season:** Mid-June–Labor Day

STADIUM LOCATION: 450 Aiken St., Lowell, MA 01854.

TEAM WEBSITE: www.lowellspinners.com

GETTING THERE: The ballpark is on the Merrimack River on the edge of downtown. From Rtes. 495 and 3, take the Lowell Connector (exit 35C) to Thorndike St. (Exit 5B) onto Dutton St. Go past City Hall, take a left onto Father Morissette Boulevard, and a right on Aiken Street. Parking is on the right and the ballpark to the left.

PARKING: Parking across the street for $2.

TICKET INFORMATION: 450 Aiken St., Lowell, MA 01854, tel. 987/459–2255, fax 978/459–1674.

PRICE RANGE: Box seats $6.50; reserved seats $5.50; general admission $3.50.

GAME TIME: Mon.–Sat. 7 PM, Sun. 5 PM; gates open one hour before game time.

TIPS ON SEATING: Despite the fact that the sun sets over third base, the best seats are the box and reserved seats behind the home team dugout on the first-base side. From there, you have a view of the Merrimack River and the scoreboard. The general admission seats are aluminum benches with backs down the third-base line starting at the end of the visiting team's dugout.

SEATING FOR PEOPLE WITH DISABILITIES: Along the main concourse. There is an elevator at the entrance and another behind home plate on the third-base side. For special arrangements call 987/459–1702.

STADIUM FOOD: Lines can be slow for jumbo dogs and sausages at the park's two grills. There are muffins, biscotti, black and white cookies, and granita slushes at an espresso cart on the concourse. Prices are reasonable, with $1.50 hotdogs, $1.25 popcorn, and puffy fried dough for $2.

SMOKING POLICY: Smoking is prohibited at the ballpark.

VISITING TEAM HOTEL: Doubletree Inn (50 Warren St., Lowell 01852, tel. 978/452–1200, or 800/222–8733).

TOURISM INFORMATION: Greater Merrimack Valley Convention & Visitors Bureau (22 Shattuck St., Lowell, 01852, tel. 978/459–6150).

Lowell: Edward A. LeLacheur Park

In his campaign for the presidency, Paul Tsongas made much of his role in the revival of his beloved Lowell, Massachusetts. The town that boomed in the 19th century by being in the forefront of the new textile industry failed to keep up with technology and crashed in the early 20th century. In the last two decades, Lowell has made a remarkable comeback through a strategic combination of historic preservation and new technology.

Unfortunately, Senator Tsongas lost his battle with cancer one year too soon to see his dream of a professional baseball team in a brand-new Lowell stadium come true. In 1998, the Lowell Spinners opened Edward A. LeLacheur Park, named after the state representative instrumental in the construction of the ballpark. The

hockey arena that is part of the same city revitalization plan is named for Tsongas.

The $13-million, 5,000-seat ballpark is a state-of-the-art Single A facility. The brick-and-steel structure sits on the edge of the downtown at the bend of the Merrimack River. The view over the left-field wall is of the river, while the view beyond the wall in right center is of the handsomely restored Aiken Street Bridge. With breezes off the river, this is not a home run hitter's park, and it can get cool even on a summer night.

Originally, the field was to be dug out so that fans could enter at the top and walk down to their seats. However, this plan fell through when large amounts of silt were found, delaying the intended 1997 opening. The famed HOK architects from Kansas City then redesigned the ballpark so that fans enter down the first-base line and go up one level to a concourse, complete with brick concession stands and press box.

From there, fans walk down into the seating bowl.

The team moved here after the 1995 season from Elmira, New York, as part of the transition of the short-season New York–Penn League from older, scruffy parks to newer, more modern ballparks. The Spinners, nicknamed appropriately to honor the industry that made Lowell famous, are an affiliate of the Boston Red Sox, giving Sox fans a chance to see future stars early in their careers. The huge green-and-purple Canaligator mascot is just plain fun.

Where to Stay

Visiting Team Hotel: Doubletree Hotel. Tucked behind a downtown street, this nine-story hotel has odd-numbered rooms with a view of a canal, lock, and dam. The lobby and rooms are spacious and well-kept, with large windows. An adjacent parking garage is free to guests. *50 Warren St., Lowell 01852, tel. 978/452–1200 or 800/222–8733, fax 978/453–4764. 249 rooms. Facilities: restaurant, indoor pool, wading pool, sauna, exercise rooms. AE, D, DC, MC. $$*

Where to Eat

Center City Marketplace. Cobblestone streets bring you to this city market, just steps from the Visitor's Center. Several stalls sell homemade pizza, fast-serve pastas, ice cream, sandwiches, and Chinese and Mexican food. There are a handful of chairs inside the market and several park benches on the street. *45 Palmer St., Lowell, tel. 978/452–7571. No credit cards. $*

Arthur's Diner. This small wooden wagon-style diner, circa 1932, is the place for speedy breakfasts and lunches. It's built over a mill canal, across the street from Kerouac Park, and has four wooden booths and 13 red stools. The $2 Boott Mill sandwich, fried egg, meat, and home-

fries on a bulky roll, is a popular take-out item. There are $1.65 BLTs, 50¢ sodas, and $1.50 burgers. *112 Bridge St., Lowell, tel. 978/452–8647. No credit cards. $*

La Boniche. This pleasant, casual restaurant occupies the ground floor of the handsome Bon Marché building in downtown Lowell. Simple French food is served on wooden tables in a room decorated with lace curtains and flowers. *143 Merrimack St., Lowell, tel. 978/458–9473. No breakfast. MC, V. $*

Entertainments

Lowell National Historical Park. Visit a noisy 1920s cotton mill, ride on canal boats, and tour worker housing in this classy adaptation of the city's industrial history. At the National Park Service Visitor Center in Market Mills, you watch a fine video show, "Lowell: The Industrial Revolution." A free trolley transports you to two mills and other exhibits. Combination tickets with a canal tour are available. *67 Kirk St., Lowell, tel. 978/970–5000. Admission: $4 adults, $2 ages 6–16 and students. Open daily 9:30–5:30.*

Sports Museum of New England. In Lowell's historic district, this small museum has an eclectic collection, including uniforms and photos of two Massachusetts residents who played in the women's professional baseball league, an enormous pair of red boxing gloves more than six ft tall, and a folk art–style painting of Fenway Park. There are soccer and hockey memorabilia and, of course, Ted Williams and Larry Bird photos and uniforms. The museum has a model of Braves Field and a piece of the famous parquet floor from the Boston Garden. *25 Shattuck Street, Lowell, tel. 978/452–6775, www.sportsmuseum.org. Admission: $3 adults, $2 children and senior citizens. Open Tues.–Sat. 10–5, Sun. noon–5.*

PORTLAND SEA DOGS

League: Eastern League • **Major League Affiliation:** Florida Marlins • **Class:** AA • **Stadium:** Hadlock Field • **Opened:** 1994 • **Capacity:** 6,500 • **Dimensions:** LF: 315, CF: 400, RF: 330 • **Surface:** grass • **Season:** Apr.–Labor Day

STADIUM LOCATION: 271 Park Ave., Portland, ME 04102.

TEAM WEBSITE: www.portlandseadogs.com

GETTING THERE: From south, I–295 to Congress St. E (Exit 5), merge onto Congress St., left at St. John St., merge right onto Park Ave. (N. I). From north, I–295 to Exit 6A (Forest Ave. S), right on Park Ave.; ballpark is just past Exposition Building on right.

PARKING: Limited free parking near stadium; private lots nearby cost $4–$5. Free lot at University of Southern Maine is 10-minute walk. Shuttle buses (tel. 207/774–0351; $1) to stadium from downtown parking lots start 1 hr before game time.

TICKET INFORMATION: Box 636, Portland, ME 04104, tel. 207/874–9300, fax 207/780–0317.

PRICE RANGE: Box seats (sold out) $6 adults, $5 under 17 and over 62; reserved $5 adults, $4 children and senior citizens; general admission $4 adults, $2 children and senior citizens.

GAME TIME: 7 PM; some Sat. 1 PM, some Sun. 1 or 4 PM; gates open 90 min before game time.

TIPS ON SEATING: Call ahead for tickets; some games each year are sold out in advance. General admission seats are fine if you get to stadium early enough to get good ones. Seats beyond third base are less than 20 rows from field and do not face late-afternoon sun.

SEATING FOR PEOPLE WITH DISABILITIES: In last row of box seats; special free parking at stadium.

STADIUM FOOD: Among unusual and inexpensive offerings here are the greasy but good fried pollack sandwich ($2) and the sweet Sea Dog ice-cream biscuit ($1.50), two chocolate-chip cookies pressed onto a circle of vanilla ice cream. There is also broccoli-and-cheese stuffed bread ($2) and an average ice-cream brownie. The grill on the first-base side serves good barbecue chicken, grilled sausage and peppers, and passable steak-and-cheese sandwiches, for $3.75 each. A sub shop in the concourse has minestrone, chicken noodle soup, chili, and three varieties of subs. Grape and apple juice are sold, and there's a milk and cookies stand.

SMOKING POLICY: Smoking prohibited except in designated area behind left-field stands.

VISITING TEAM HOTEL: Radisson Eastland Plaza (157 High St., Portland, ME 04101, tel. 207/775–5411 or 800/333–3333).

TOURISM INFORMATION: Convention & Visitors Bureau of Greater Portland (305 Commercial St., Portland, ME 04101, tel. 207/772–5800).

Portland, Maine: Hadlock Field

It was a long time coming, and the fans in Portland, Maine, responded. Professional baseball had not been played in Portland since 1949. So when Daniel Burke, a retired television executive, brought baseball back to Portland in 1994, the fans poured in, setting a new Eastern League annual attendance record of 375,187.

Hadlock Field seats 6,500 and you'd better call in advance to reserve a seat, as several games each year are sold out before the day of the game. This beautiful stadium was built by the city for the Class AA Eastern League franchise of the expansion Florida Marlins. Part of the Portland Sports Complex, the ballpark was built on the site of the high school field already named in

honor of Edson Hadlock, the man who coached baseball at Portland High School from 1950 to 1978.

On the southern edge of Portland's downtown, just below the Maine Medical Center, Hadlock Field has that just-right combination of old and new that has made Baltimore's Camden Yards so popular. The field sits just behind the handsome redbrick Portland Exposition Building, a 1915 classic arena. The Exposition Building, Portland's answer to the warehouse at Camden Yards, eliminates much of the seating that could be on the first-base side. The grandstand appears to be shaped like a fisherman's hook, with the long end down the third-base line. On the hillside beyond first base and behind the arena are a hockey rink, a brick police-horse barn, and a football field.

In an Iowa-meets-Maine moment, general manager Charlie Eschbach built a cornfield in the park one night, and players walked through the stalks. This "Field of Dreams" stunt was so popular that the team vows to repeat it each season.

The front of the stadium is particularly attractive, with a significant part of the facade in brick and an oversize Sea Dog guarding the entrance. Flags fly above the skyboxes, but the main seating area has no roof. There is very little foul territory, as the seats are close to the field. The inside of the dugouts and a strip of wall down the third-base side are brick.

The fans in the general admission seats make quite a racket banging their feet on the aluminum grandstand floor to cheer on the home team. You'll want to hope a Sea Dog hits a home run or the Sea Dogs win the game so that you can see how inventive a retired television mogul can be with modern technology. A lighthouse pops up above the fence in center field, issuing a deep, loud whistle, shooting off fireworks, and spinning a bright light on top. The festive scoreboard in left-center-field sports flying flags and a clock on top.

Slugger the Sea Dog, a seal with a dog's head, quickly became a fan favorite. He's already gone flipper-to-hand with the likes of Barbara Bush, Frank Gifford, and Stephen King. In real life, he's not nearly so menacing as he looks in the team's logo. No one has figured out how to write with a flipper, so Slugger doesn't sign autographs. But each night a Sea Dog player does sign in the concourse about 45 minutes before the game. There is a photo display of "Mainers in the Majors" on the third-base concourse. Trash collectors dressed as orange and blue fish monsters encourage fans to fill their pouches to keep the stadium clean.

Where to Stay

Because Portland is a walking city, we recommend that you pay a little more and stay in a downtown hotel.

Visiting Team Hotel: Radisson Eastland Hotel Portland. This imposing redbrick city landmark has harbor views from many of its rooms. The large, formal lobby has marble floors, Oriental carpets, and chandeliers. The rooms are pleasant, with wing-back chairs and flowered drapes. You can walk to the Old Port area and to the ballpark shuttle. *157 High St., Portland 04101, tel. 207/775–5411 or 800/333–3333, fax 207/ 775–2872. 204 rooms. Facilities: 2 restaurants, lounge, exercise room, sauna, parking (fee). AE, D, DC, MC, V. $$*

Holiday Inn By the Bay. This convenient downtown hotel is not on the water, but many of its rooms have sweeping views of the harbor. The rooms and hallways have been tastefully remodeled, and the standard rooms are ample and light-filled. It is a two-block walk from the Children's Museum and the Old Port area. *88 Spring St., Portland 04101, tel. 207/775–2311 or 800/ 465–4329, fax 207/761–8224. 239 rooms. Facilities: restaurant, indoor pool, saunas, health club, parking (free). AE, D, DC, MC, V. $$*

Oak Leaf Inn. This bargain hotel in the city's Arts District has a sweeping entry arch, high-ceiling rooms, and European character. It is not air-conditioned and has tubs, not showers; its '50s-era furnishings are slowly being upgraded from the residence hotel it once was. In part of the Old Port area, it is convenient to the waterfront and to ballpark shuttles. Its lobby is on the second floor. There is no extra charge for cots. Less expensive rooms have shared baths. A city parking lot (fee) is a block away. *51A Oak St., Portland 04101, tel. 207/773–7882, fax 207/ 781–5459. 42 rooms. AE, D, MC, V. $$*

Regency. This hotel, near the waterfront, is in an 1895 redbrick armory building, elegantly converted into comfortable rooms and a small, flower-filled lobby. Some of the rooms have fireplaces, and all have reproduction antiques, elegant linens and drapes, and period wallpaper. It is on the National Register of Historic Places. *20 Milk St., Portland 04101, tel. 207/774–4200 or 800/727–3436, fax 207/775–2150. 95 rooms. Facilities: restaurant, hot tub, saunas, steam rooms, health club, parking (fee). AE, D, DC, MC, V. $$$*

Where to Eat

Benny's Famous Fried Clams. This roadside shack along Commercial Street adorned with fishing floats has 12 tables and umbrellas for outside eating. Many patrons take out their delicious, hand-cut french fries, fried clams, clam cakes, and clam burgers. The Maine potatoes really make a difference with these creamy french fries. The platter prices are low—$5.50 for two crab cakes, coleslaw, fries, and garlic rolls. Crisp clam cakes are $1 each. It's less than 2 mi from the ballpark, but you can't bring food into the stadium. *199 W. Commercial St., Portland, tel. 207/774–2084. No credit cards. $*

DiMillo's. The harbor views are spectacular from the side and, especially, the upper deck of this floating restaurant. You walk a gangplank to get aboard the former car ferry, which is festooned with such nautical artifacts as a diving suit and ship models. The huge wood reception desk has a live lobster tank. It may be too windy some days to sit up top, but make sure you look around and view the whale wall, a 450-ft-long waterfront mural on the Maine State Pier, by artist Robert Wyland. The seafood is excellent; its overfilled lobster roll is one of the best and most generous we've seen. There is a children's menu. Parking on Long Wharf is paid for by the restaurant. *25 Long Wharf, Portland, tel. 207/772–2216. AE, D, DC, MC, V. $$*

Keaney's Pancake Shoppe. This downtown storefront breakfast and lunch counter has cheery apple stencils and red-and-white oil-cloth-covered tables throughout. The no-smoking room is separate. Silver-dollar pancakes in varieties as diverse as pineapple and banana are offered, along with creamed chipped beef on toast. A $2 breakfast special is served from 6 to 10:30 AM, and there is a children's menu. *617 Congress St., tel. 207/773–2785. No dinner. No credit cards. $*

Port Bake House. Across the street from the docks, this is a good stopping place on your walking tour for morning muffins or light lunches of sandwiches and salads. Two varieties of homemade soup and 11 types of substantial bread are cooked daily. There is limited outdoor seating. *205 Commercial St., Portland, tel. 207/773–2217. MC, V. $*

Entertainments

Casco Bay Harbor Cruises. More than 50 boat excursions from the docks of Portland set out daily. Three major boat companies offer a range

of times and activities, including whale watches, deep-sea fishing, dinner cruises, harbor sea-lion cruises, and trips to Nova Scotia. They include **Olde Port Mariner Fleet** (Long Wharf, 170 Commercial St., Portland, tel. 207/775–0727 or 800/437–3270 outside Maine); **Casco Bay Lines** (Casco Bay Ferry Terminal, Commercial and Franklin Sts., Portland, tel. 207/774–7871), the mail, school, and supply lines for Maine islands; and **Bay View Cruises** (Fisherman's Wharf, 184 Commercial St., Portland, tel. 207/761–0496).

Children's Museum of Maine. This clever, two-story museum has a computer room, space-shuttle cockpits that children can operate, a play firehouse with pole and rescue equipment, a bank, and many hands-on exhibits involving insects and the environment. There is a café on its lower level. *142 Free St., Portland, tel. 207/828–1234. Admission: $5 ages 1 and up. Open June–Aug., Mon.–Sat. 10–5, Sun. noon–5; Sept.–May, Wed.–Sat. 10–5, Sun. noon–5.*

Palace Playland at Old Orchard Beach. This vintage amusement park is on a 7-mi-long white-sand swimming beach 25 minutes south of Portland. Its Galaxy roller coaster is tame enough for preteens, and its large, vintage Dodgem cars are in good condition. There's an 11-ride kiddieland, a 56-ft-high triple water slide, a 1910 Philadelphia Toboggan carousel with a calliope, and a 75-ft Sunwheel Ferris wheel. *1 Old Orchard St., Exit 5 off Maine Turnpike, Old Orchard Beach, tel. 207/934–2001. Admission: free; rides $1–$2 each; all-day pass $18, $12 kids' rides only. Open weekdays noon–10, weekends 11–10. MC, V.*

Sights to See

Portland was first established by the British as a fishing and trading settlement in 1632. The city has preserved much of its 19th-century Victorian feel from when it was completely rebuilt after the Great Fire of 1866.

Portland's Downtown District. The Greater Portland Convention and Visitors Bureau (305 Commercial St., tel. 207/772–6828) has an excellent visitor's guide, map, and suggestions for "a wandering tour" focused on the Old Port area. You can walk along **Congress Street,** the commercial and transportation spine of Portland, and see the boyhood home of poet **Henry Wadsworth Longfellow** (485 Congress St., tel. 207/772–1807), who dubbed Portland a "Jewel by the Sea." Turn down Exchange Street, now a lively shopping area, to see some of the best examples of the buildings constructed after the city's 1866 fire. Continue walking to the wharfs along **Commercial Street** and watch the catch come in at the Portland Fish Pier. The visitor center is well stocked with maps and brochures that will enhance your walking tours, including informative guides to Congress Street and Old Port Exchange, prepared by Greater Portland Landmarks (tel. 207/774–5561).

Unusual Shopping

L.L. Bean. The Freeport home of this famed Maine sporting-goods and clothing retailer is 20 minutes from Portland. Mr. Bean developed a simple scoring system for baseball that never caught on, but he remained a lifelong fan. Babe Ruth was a grateful customer of his, using Bean's outdoor gear on hunting trips. *Depot St., Freeport, tel. 207/865–4761.*

BASEBALL ACROSS THE BORDER

15

BURLINGTON, OTTAWA, QUEBEC CITY

Baseball in Canada and the northern New England states has a pastoral quality—small stadiums in public parks. The stadiums are generally old, and
summer nights in Canadian and Vermont parks recall past decades, with
more sport and less commercialism to them. Burlington's Centennial Field—an
old-fashioned university stadium with a covered roof grandstand—is one of the
oldest parks in the minor leagues. Vermont's largest city, Burlington, is on the eastern shore of Lake Champlain. The "Queen City" is the perfect launching point for
nautical adventures—with cruises to the Green Mountains and the Adiron-
dacks—as well as hiking, crafts, and tasting tours of the nearby Ben & Jerry's ice-
cream factory. Don't miss Burlington's 1930 Art Deco theater.

From Burlington, you can cross Lake Champlain by ferry and drive north on Rte.
87. Ottawa is 335 mi northwest across the border. You should stop halfway to
see Montreal, a beautiful, architecturally sophisticated city with a sparse baseball
tradition. From Montreal, Route 40 West takes you to Ottawa, Canada's impressive capital city. The Rideau Canal flows through the heart of the city, surrounded
by parks and imposing federal buildings. You can watch the Changing of the
Guard before enjoying a Triple A baseball game in the first-rate JetForm Park.

The "Gibralter of America," Quebec City, is 460 km (285 mi) northeast of
Ottawa, on Route 40 East. Situated on a rocky escarpment high above the St.
Lawrence River, this walled city has charming brick streets, Victorian greystones,
a bustling working port, and impressive parks and vistas. A horse-drawn carriage
ride will cost you about a dollar a minute, but it's worth it for a beautiful night-
time view of this French city's spectacular historic spots. Its colorful baseball stadium is in the city center and features a Quebec skyline view.

VERMONT EXPOS

League: New York–Penn League • **Major League Affiliation:** Montreal Expos • **Class:** Short Season Class A • **Stadium:** Centennial Field • **Opened:** 1922 • **Capacity:** 4,000 • **Dimensions:** LF:
330, CF: 405, RF: 323 • **Surface:** grass • **Season:** mid-June–Labor Day

STADIUM LOCATION: University Rd. and Colchester Ave., Burlington, VT 05401.

TEAM WEB SITE: www.vermontexpos.com

GETTING THERE: The ballpark is located on the University of Vermont campus east of downtown
Burlington. Take I–89 north or south to Exit 14W. Bear right onto East Avenue for one mile. Take a right
at the light onto Colchester Avenue.

PARKING: Parking at the field is $2, but is quite limited. Get there early to take a free shuttle from the uni-
versity on East Avenue. Otherwise park at Trinity College at the end of East Avenue and walk two blocks
to the park.

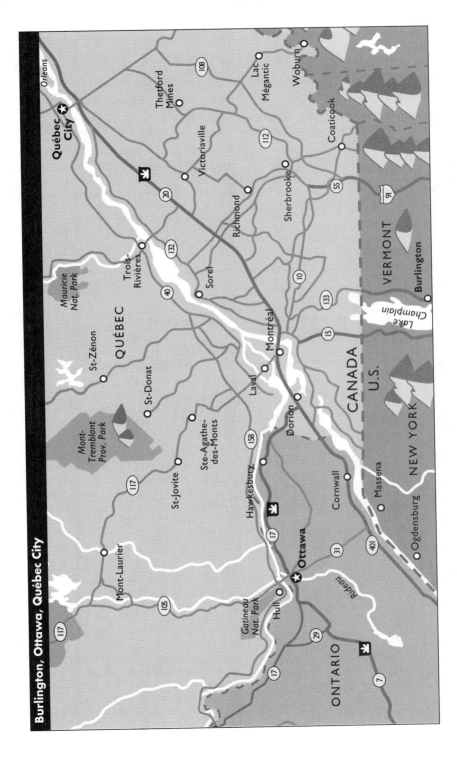

Burlington, Ottawa, Québec City

TICKET INFORMATION: Box 4, Winooski, VT 05404, tel. 802/655–4200, fax 802/655–5660.

PRICE RANGE: Reserved $6; general admission $4 adults, $3 senior citizen, $1 ages 12 and under.

GAME TIME: Mon.–Sat. 7:05 PM, Sun. 2:05 PM. Gates open 90 minutes before game.

TIPS ON SEATING: You can't beat the price of general admission, but bring a seat cushion; your seat is a concrete slab. The reserved seats are wooden and they're under a roof and behind a screen. The sun sets behind third base.

SEATING FOR PEOPLE WITH DISABILITIES: There's a tented area for people with disabilities on the third-base side next to the general admission bleachers.

STADIUM FOOD: The grill is under a tent past the grandstand, down the third-base line. It has top-class food—$3 cheeseburgers, chicken gyros, a fair BBQ sandwich, and an Italian sausage ($3.25). Craft breweries are plentiful in Vermont and several varieties of these specialty beers are sold here. A concession truck sells $2.50 hot fudge sundaes, $2 ice-cream sodas and $2 onion rings. The soft pretzels with cinnamon are very good and a special treat are the $2 chessters, chocolate cookies filled with frozen custard.

SMOKING POLICY: Smoking prohibited in seating areas and in the walkways under the stands.

VISITING TEAM HOTEL: Best Western Inn (1076 Williston Rd., South Burlington, VT 05404, tel. 802/863–1125 or 800/528–1234).

TOURISM INFORMATION: Lake Champlain Regional Chamber of Commerce (60 Main St., Suite 100, Burlington, VT 05401, tel. 802/863–3489).

Burlington: Centennial Field

The University of Vermont has been playing baseball at Centennial Field since 1906. The current park dates from 1922, making it one of baseball's oldest ballparks still in use by professional baseball.

As the fabled New York–Penn League, a short-season Class Single A league, has recently sprouted fancy new ballparks in the Hudson Valley, Lowell, and elsewhere, it is great to see others update classic venues and preserve an important element of baseball history. Centennial Field is a fine example of the traditional covered-roof grandstand with a section of wooden chairs behind home plate and under the roof. There are large sections of concrete-slab general admission seating down each baseline. Bring your seat cushion and get ready to scrunch in tight as games often approach the ballpark's 4,000 capacity. An old-style ticket building sits at the entrance separate from the grandstand and does double duty as a concession stand.

High above the left-field fence sit two rows of advertising and a large scoreboard. They hang on the back of an ancient grandstand for what was originally the University of Vermont's football field. The university dropped football in the 1970s and now plays soccer there.

Professional baseball has been an on-again, off-again proposition in Burlington since 1902. Ken Griffey, Jr. played here during his meteoric rise through the minor leagues when the Seattle Mariners had an Eastern League Double A franchise here in the 1980s. The Vermont Expos began play in the New York–Penn League in 1994.

Champ, a lime-green sea monster with a long tail and huge blue sneakers, is one reason why they are packing them into Centennial Field. Samuel de Champlain saw a huge sea monster during his 1609 voyage along what is now Lake Champlain. Champ arrives from center field on a four-wheeler before each game and whoops the crowd into a pre-game frenzy. They sell a poster here of a dejected-looking player sitting in the dugout with the caption: "I've spent my entire life preparing for this and these people are here to see a big green fuzzy mascot."

You'll want to wear long pants and bring blankets for the cool evening games. Also pack insect repellent as the mosquitoes are formidable.

Where to Stay

Visiting Team Motel: Best Western Inn. This modern four-story hotel resembles clusters of condominiums spaced around a pool. Although it's off a busy commercial street, the rooms are set back and quiet. The grounds include 52 treed acres with a nature trail and fishing pond. They have a free Continental breakfast and 24-hour shuttle service to the airport. Rooms are modern and standard-size. *1076 Williston Rd., South Burlington, VT 05404, tel. 802/863–1125 or 800/528–1234, fax 802/658–1296. 173 rooms. Facilities: restaurant, indoor and outdoor pools, hot tub, game room, exercise room, fishing pond, coin laundry. AE, D, DC, MC, V. $$*

Anchorage Inn. One mile from the ballpark, in a busy commercial area, this is a modern three-story hotel. Guests are given a free Continental breakfast. It has a faint ski-lodge look, even though it's across the street from a shopping mall. *108 Dorset St., South Burlington, VT, tel. 802/863–7000 or 800/336–1869, fax 802/658–3351. 89 rooms. Facilities: indoor pool, sauna, hot tub. AE, D, DC, MC, V. $$*

Where to Eat

Anything's Pastable. Watch fresh pasta being made, as chefs roll out more than 100 flavors of spaghetti, linguine, and ravioli. This downtown Italian deli, located next to City Hall Park, also has homemade soups, sandwiches, and bread. Many Vermont regional food specialties are for sale. There are only 8 tables and they fill up fast. *173 College St., Burlington, tel. 802/860–7144. AE, MC, V. $*

Church Street Marketplace. A European-style commercial center has been created in downtown Burlington, with 22 restaurants, most of which operate sidewalk cafés during the summer. There are street musicians, entertainers, produce stalls, craft carts, and a general buzz of walkers enjoying the mood. One hundred and sixty local and national specialty shops are packed into the area, including wood, textile, and glass art by Vermont craftspeople. The

market encompasses six streets. *Church St., bounded by Pearl and Main Sts., Burlington, tel. 802/863–1648.*

Perry's Fish House. Fishnets hang over your head and marine artifacts fill the walls at this quality seafood restaurant. The broiled bluefish and crab dishes are special. There's also a children's menu. *1080 Shelburne Rd. (Rte. 7), South Burlington, tel. 802/862–1300. AE, D, DC, MC, V. $$*

Entertainments

Ben & Jerry's Ice Cream Factory Tour. This ice-cream plant has become a huge tourist attraction, with steady crowds paying to take thirty-minute tours to see how Chunky Monkey is made. There are free samples plus a scoop shop and funky gift shop. It's a carnival atmosphere outside the factory, with jugglers, musicians, spin art, a calliope, food stands selling baked potatoes, and picnic tables, all enveloped by the sweet smell of cones baking. There's a hilltop kids' playground. *Route 100, Waterbury, VT, tel. 802/244–8687. Admission: $2 adults, $1.75 senior citizens, ages 12 and under free. Open June, daily 9–5; July–Aug., daily 9–8; Sept.–Oct., daily 9–6; Nov.—May, daily 10–5.*

Lake Champlain Ferries and History Cruises. There are ferries between Burlington and Port Kent, New York, a one-hour trip that gives passengers a scenic look at Lake Champlain. The trips also are popular during fall foliage season. History cruises take place at 11, 1, and 3 throughout the summer and fall, and passengers are given details of Lake Champlain battles and shipwrecks. Longer cruises on the *Spirit of Ethan Allen II* depart from the Burlington Boathouse, College Street, Burlington, tel. 802/862–8300. *King Street Dock, Burlington, tel. 802/864–9804. Round-trip ferries: $5.75 adults, $2.25 ages 6–12. History cruises: $7 adults, $3.50 children. Open late May–mid-Oct., daily.*

Lake Champlain Science Center. A free downtown shuttle brings you to the Burlington waterfront, home to this science center and an 8-mi hiker/biker trail. A shipwreck room is underwater and marsh creatures, turtle tanks, and sea creatures are featured. There's also a touch tank and interactive exhibits in this one-floor center. *1 College St., Burlington, tel. 802/*

864–1848. Admission: $3 adults, $2 children, under 2 free. Open June–early Sept., daily 11–5, mid-Sept.–May, weekends 12:30–4:30.

Sights to See

Flynn Theatre. This Art Deco showplace began restoration in 1981, reviving fabulous floral designs along the side-wall pilasters. Bright geometric stencils on the lobby walls were first created in 1930. The 1,453-seat theater is now used as a performing arts center. It's located at the base of the Church Street Marketplace. Free tours by appointment. *153 Main St., Burlington, tel. 802/652–4500.*

Shelburne Museum. New England's heritage is vividly illustrated by 37 historic structures on this 45-acre complex known for its fine collection of folk and decorative art. There's also fun for children with a 500-ft model circus parade, a steam locomotive, a jail, and a round barn. The U.S.S. *Ticonderoga*, a side-wheeler, is berthed here and you can walk across a three-lane covered bridge. There are daily craft demonstrations and beautiful grounds to walk. *U.S. Route 7, Shelburne, VT, tel. 802/985–3346. Summer/fall admission: $17.50 adults, $10.50 students, $7 ages 6–14. Winter/spring tour admission: $7 adults, $3 ages 6–14. Open late May–mid-Oct., daily 10–5; mid-Oct–late May, daily 1 PM for guided tours. D, MC, V.*

OTTAWA LYNX

League: International League • **Major League Affiliation:** Montreal Expos • **Class:** AAA • **Stadium:** JetForm Park • **Opened:** 1993 • **Capacity:** 10,332 • **Dimensions:** LF: 325, CF: 404, RF: 325 • **Surface:** grass • **Season:** Apr.–Labor Day

STADIUM LOCATION: 300 Coventry Rd., Ottawa, Ontario K1K 4P5.

TEAM WEB SITE: www.ottawalynx.com

GETTING THERE: The stadium is just east of downtown. From Highway 417 (Queensway), exit at St. Laurent Boulevard South. Turn right onto Tremblay Road, right on Belfast Road, and left on Coventry Road to the stadium.

PARKING: There is plenty of parking at the stadium for C$5.50.

TICKET INFORMATION: 300 Coventry Rd., Ottawa, Ontario K1K 4P5, tel. 613/747–5969, fax 613/747–0003.

PRICE RANGE: First-level infield seats C$8.50, first-level outfield seats and upper-level seats C$6.50.

GAME TIME: May–June, weekdays 7:05 PM, weekends 2:05 PM; June–Sept., daily 7:05 PM. Gates open 90 mins. before game time.

TIPS ON SEATING: There are no aluminum bleachers here; all 10,000 seats are the real thing. The view beyond the stadium is undistinguished in every direction. The sun sets behind home plate on the third-base side and the home team dugout is also on the third-base side. There are family sections in all three seating categories where alcohol is prohibited.

SEATING FOR PEOPLE WITH DISABILITIES: There is seating on the main concourse level. Access is through Gate 2.

STADIUM FOOD: You can get a stir-fry dinner here, vegetarian, chicken, or shrimp, for C$10.95–C$12.95. There is good soup, salads, and exceptional ribs and onion rings. Another unusual food for a ballpark is the banana split for C$4.95. Sugar-coated, deep-fried beaver tails (dough) come in six varieties, including raspberry and garlic butter. These sinful delights are C$3.25. A sit-down sports restaurant, **Tufts** (tel. 613/746–7579), on the stadium's third floor, is open three hours before games.

SMOKING POLICY: Smoking is prohibited in the seating areas.

Visiting Team Hotel: Chimo Hotel (1199 Joseph Cyr St., Ottawa, Ontario K1J 7T4, tel. 613/744–1060 or 800/387–9779).

Tourism Information: Ottawa Tourism and Convention Authority (130 Albert St., Suite 1800, Ottawa, Ontario K1P 5G4, tel. 613/237-5150).

Ottawa: Jetform Park

Everything comes in twos here. For the price of a single ticket, you get two national anthems, and all the announcements come in English and French as well. They even have two signs proudly proclaiming the Ottawa Lynx as the 1995 champions of the Triple A International League—English to the left-field side of the batter's eye and French to the right-field side. There are pairs of lynx paw prints on the outfield wall giving distances from home plate, one in feet and the other in meters.

This is quality Triple A baseball and JetForm Park is a first-rate ballpark. A large metal statue of a batter greets fans in front of the sleek-looking two-story stadium entrance. All 10,000 seats are good. There are 32 suites, a restaurant, and a press box at the top of the grandstand. A souvenir shop and many concession stands are on the concourse underneath the seating area. With the exception of an ordinary Single A–style scoreboard in right center field, everything is state-of-the-art.

The man responsible for all this is Howard Darwin, a longtime business and sports entrepreneur in Ottawa. After its four-decade absence, Darwin was determined to bring professional baseball back to Ottawa. The Ottawa Senators had played in the International League in the early 1950s when Darwin was a young businessman. Darwin got an expansion franchise in 1992, and the city built a C$17-million stadium for the inaugural season. The stadium, built on a former snow dump area outside the downtown, was designed by local architect Brian Dickie in consultation with the Kansas City–based ballpark architects Ellerbe Becket. A high-technology firm, JetForm Corporation, bought the naming rights for 10 years for C$1.5 million.

Lenny is a gray lynx mascot in a baseball uniform, and the Lynx have their share of on field contests and lively music. There is a large picnic and kids' play area at the end of the grandstand down the left-field line, elevated above the field level. Stop by the Beaver Tails pastry cart on the concourse level on the third-base side for deep-fried dough in the shape of a beaver tail. We loved the apple and cinnamon and the raspberry, leaving the garlic butter and cheese tails for others. But as with most Triple A parks, the emphasis here is on the baseball.

More Canada Baseball

Montreal baseball. Midway on the drive from Ottawa to Quebec lies one of the world's great cities. Unfortunately, Montreal isn't a world-class baseball town. The one shining moment came in April, 1946, when 15,745 fans watched Jackie Robinson make his first start in what had been a white man's game. The Dodgers sent Robinson to Montreal where racial tensions were less pronounced than in the United States. The Montreal Royals played in the Triple A International League from 1928 to 1960. Their stadium, Delorimier Downs, was torn down in 1971. A middle school and running track stand there now. A small brick-and-concrete memorial in the shape of a baseball diamond is at 2101 Ontario Street, at avenue du Lorimier. The Montreal Expos played at Parc Jarry from 1969 to 76, before moving to Stade Olympique, a horrid domed stadium with plastic grass. Parc Jarry has been converted into a championship tennis stadium, Stade du Maurier, at rue Jarry and rue Faillon. There is a statue of Jackie Robinson just outside the main gate to Stade Olympique.

Where to Stay

Visiting Team Motel: Chimo Hotel. Parking is free in this 10-story modern hotel in Glouchester, less than a half mile from the ballpark. A large atrium pool is glassed in and sky-lit. The rooms are bright and freshly furnished. It's east of downtown—a 5-minute drive from Parliament Hill. *1199 Joseph Cyr St. at St. Laurent Blvd.*

and the Queensway, Ottawa, Ontario K1J 7I4, tel. 613/744–1060 or 800/387–9779, fax 613/744–7845. 257 rooms. Facilities: two restaurants, indoor pool, sauna, hot tub, fitness center. AE, D, DC, MC, V. $$

Best Western Hotel Jacques Cartier. Save money by staying in a park setting just outside the city. Get a top floor in this 9-story modern hotel that overlooks Ottawa from the west. It's located at the Hull Marina on the Ottawa River, across from Jacques Cartier Park and the Canadian Museum of Civilization. 131 rue Laurier, Hull, tel. 819/770–8550 or 800/528–1234, fax 819/770–9705. 129 rooms. Facilities: indoor pool. AE, D, DC, MC, V. $$

Lord Elgin. This imposing structure is on a busy street but has a majestic interior and frequent bargain packages. Built in the 1940s, the rooms have high ceilings, oversized furniture, and elegant drapes and fixtures. It's across the street from Confederation Park. Many of the upper rooms in the 11-story landmark have great park and city views. 100 Elgin St., at Laurier Ave., Ottawa, Ontario K1P 5K8, tel. 613/235–3333 or 800/267–4298, fax 613/235–3223. 312 rooms. Facilities: restaurant. AE, D, DC, MC, V. $$$

Where to Eat

Nate's. Enjoy hot chocolate with bananas at this longtime bargain deli where the breakfast special is a mere C$1.75. The blintzes are special and the bagels and Rideau rye bread are authentic. Bright lighting and green vinyl upholstery make the place more clinical than homey, but the food is good. Notices of specials, such as fish-and-chips, smoked meat sandwiches, and corned-beef hash, hang from ceiling signs. 316 Rideau St., Ottawa, tel. 613/789–9191. AE, D, MC, V. $

Wringer's Restaurant and Laundrymat. The perfect combination for travelers, this casual café lets you eat while your wash is whirling. An automated light board lets you know when your load's done. Breakfasts feature oatmeal, eggs, and muffins. Lunch and dinner includes soups, sandwiches, and rice dishes. 151 Second Ave., Ottawa, tel. 613/234–9700. AE, MC, V. $

Zak's Diner. The Byward Market encompasses produce stalls, theme restaurants, elegant shops, and blocks of interesting walking. This '50s diner

serves breakfast all day, and offers meatloaf specials, juicy burgers, and a full soda fountain. There are tabletop jukeboxes and a basic children's menu. 16 Byward Market, Ottawa, tel. 613/241–2401. AE, DC, MC, V. $

Entertainments

Canal and River Tours. Short scenic cruises of the Rideau Canal and Ottawa River are a good way to see the city's sights. The 90-minute tours depart from the Ottawa Locks. Paul's Boat Lines, Ottawa Locks, Ottawa, tel. 613/225–6781. Fares: C$12 adults, C$10 senior citizens and students, C$6 ages 4–12. Open mid-May–mid-Oct., daily 10–8:30.

Dow's Lake Pavilion. You can rent canoes, boats, and paddleboats to ride on the Rideau Canal, as well as inline skates to travel alongside it. The Boathouse Restaurant allows you to eat at the waterfront, which hums with small watercraft. Dow's Lake, Ottawa, tel. 613/232–1001.

Sights to See

Canadian Museum of Civilization. An impressive modern structure houses the Canadian Children's Museum, Canadian Postal Museum, IMAX theaters, and the Museum of Civilization. Admission fee drops by $3 from mid-October through April. Film admission is extra. 100 rue Laurier, tel. 819/776–7000 or 800/555–5621. Admission: C$8 adults, C$7 senior citizens, C$6 ages 13–17, C$3 ages 2–12. Free Sun. 9–noon. Open July–mid-Oct., daily 9–6; late Oct.–June, Tues.–Sun 9–5. AE, D, MC, V.

Changing of the Guard. The ceremonial Changing of the Guard, a visual symbol of Canada's link to Great Britain, takes place at 10 AM daily from late June to late August, weather permitting, on the east lawn of the Parliament Buildings. Band members and guards are resplendent in their tall bearskin hats and bright red coats. The commanding officer inspects uniforms and weapons. After the band plays O, Canada, the commander of the retiring guards hands over the key to the guardhouse to the incoming commander. Arrive at 9:45 AM to hear an explanation of the ceremony. Parliament Hill, Ottawa, tel. 613/993–1811. Open late June–late Aug., daily 10 AM.

Parliament Buildings. The House of Commons is in the Center Block of the Parliament Buildings, sitting high on Parliament Hill overlooking the Ottawa River. This stunning Gothic building with its green copper roof was originally built between 1859 and 1866 and rebuilt after a fire in 1916. After your tour, take the elevators to the observation deck just under the clock of the 300-ft **Peace Tower,** the glorious monument to Canada's World War I dead. Great views of the city are offered from the tower. A carillon artist plays daily from 2 to 2:10 PM. Pick up tour tickets at the Info-Tent just west of the buildings. *Parliament Hill, Ottawa, tel. 613/996–0896. Open mid-May–Labor Day, weekdays 9–8:30 PM, weekends and holidays 9–5:30; Labor Day–mid-May, daily 9–4:30.*

Rideau Hall. If you miss the Changing of the Guard, the sentries are relieved on the hour daily 10 to 6 in July and August at Rideau Hall. This is the residence of the governor-general of Canada, the Canadian citizen who represents the Queen. Free tours of the residence are offered. *1 Sussex Dr., at Rockcliffe Park entrance, Ottawa, tel. 613/998–7113 or 800/465–6890. Open daily 10–6.*

Reflections of Canada. This free 30-minute symphony of sound and light tells Canada's history and is projected magnificently on the Center Block of the Parliament Buildings. There are English and French versions after dark. *Parliament Hill, Ottawa, tel. 613/239–5000. Open mid-May–Labor Day, daily.*

QUEBEC CAPITALES

League: Northern League • **Affiliation:** Independent • **Class:** NA • **Stadium:** Stade de Quebec • **Opened:** 1939 • **Capacity:** 4,567 • **Dimensions:** LF: 315, CF: 380, RF: 315 • **Surface:** grass • **Season:** June–August

STADIUM LOCATION: 100 rue de Cardinal Maurice-Roy, Quebec, PQ GIK 8Z1.

TEAM WEB SITE: www.capitalesdequebec.com

GETTING THERE: The ballpark is in Victoria Park just minutes from the Old City. Take Autoroute 40 from downtown, then 440 (Charest) into Basse Ville. Turn left on Couronne (Hwy. 173), drive ½ mi and the ballpark is on your left.

PARKING: There is free parking at the stadium and in nearby lots.

TICKET INFORMATION: 100 rue du Cardinal Maurice-Roy, Quebec PQ GIK 8Z1, tel. 418/521–2255, fax 418/521–2266.

PRICE RANGE: Box C$12, reserved C$8, general admission C$5. Students and senior citizens receive a C$2 discount on all tickets.

GAME TIME: Mon.–Sat. 7:05 PM, Sun. 2:05 PM.

TIPS ON SEATING: Sit on the first-base side as there's a nice stock of trees just over the left-field fence with the Quebec skyline beyond. The sun sets behind first base and is in the eyes of fans on the third-base side. The salmon-colored high-back benches in general admission are covered by the grandstand roof.

SEATING FOR PEOPLE WITH DISABILITIES: There is limited seating behind home plate.

STADIUM FOOD: The stadium basics are here—hot dogs and sausages, pizza, nachos, soda, and beer. There's good nonalcoholic cider, hot chocolate, and doughnuts.

SMOKING POLICY: This is Quebec: Nearly everyone smokes; there are no non-smoking areas.

VISITING TEAM HOTEL: Confortel Hotel (6500 Blvd. Wilfrid Hamel, L'Ancienne-Lorette, tel. 418/877–4777).

TOURISM INFORMATION: City Region Tourism and Convention Bureau (835 Avenue Wilfrid-Laurier, Quebec City, PQ GR1 2L3, tel. 418/649–2608).

Quebec City: Stade de Quebec

To help fight the Depression in the late 1930s, the Province of Quebec built several ballparks under a program similar to the WPA in the United States. Today, with a fresh coat of paint and leadership from one of minor-league baseball's most successful entrepreneurs, Miles Wolff, Quebec's 1938 municipal stadium has come alive again.

The golden years of baseball in Quebec came after World War II. The Quebec Braves of the Canadian-American League packed fans into Stade de Quebec from 1946 to 1955. From 1971 to 1977, when it folded, the Montreal Expos Double A Eastern League team, the Quebec Carnavals, played here with stars like Gary Carter.

In the mid-1990s, with the building unoccupied for 20 years, there was talk of demolishing the ballpark. Jeff Cote, a youth-league and college coach, had tried hard for years to bring professional baseball back to Quebec without success. Reading *Baseball America* one day in the mid-1990s, Cote called the newspaper's owner about his dream. Miles Wolff had plenty of experience turning baseball dreams into reality, first with the Durham Bulls and later with the independent Northern League.

Wolff moved his family to Quebec in 1998 and with Cote launched the Capitales de Quebec. Recognizing the weather realities, Wolff opted for a team in the 86-game, short-season Northern League that he had already established.

Located just one mile north of the Old City in Victoria Park, Stade de Quebec underwent a more than $1-million face-lift in anticipation of the return of pro ball. The brightly painted yellow exterior of the grandstand is striking. Equally eye-catching are the two floors of windows across the back of the entire grandstand. The design was to give the ballpark the appearance of a high school. The salmon-colored high-back benches in the general admission section look like church pews and are completely covered by the grandstand roof. The Quebec skyline rises above the outfield fence in left field.

History panels along the internal concourse tell the colorful story of baseball in Quebec, and the new souvenir shop has a section of memorabilia. Capi, a big friendly lion, is the mascot of the Capitales. Remember, this is the heart of French Canada, and the public address announcer speaks only French.

Where to Stay

Visiting Team Hotel: Confortel Hotel. This modern, two-story hotel is 15 minutes east of the ballpark. The rooms are large, with contemporary furnishings. There is no restaurant on-site, but a free Continental breakfast is included in a sunny lobby room. *6500 Blvd. Wilfrid Hamel, L'Ancienne-Lorette, Quebec, G2E 2J1, tel. 418/877-4777 or 800/363-7440, fax 418/877-0013. 140 rooms. AE, D, DC, V. $$*

Hotel Chateau Bellevue. This Victorian greystone, built in 1848, fronts the Parc des Gouverneurs and has views of the St. Lawrence River and the Chateau Frontenac. The rooms are small and the hallways narrow, but there is free parking and a congenial staff. *16 rue de la Porte, at Ave. Ste. Genevieve, Vieux Quebec G1R 4M9, tel. 418/692-2573 or 800/463-2617, fax 418/692-4876. 58 rooms. AE, D, DC, V. $$*

Hotel Marie-Rollet. The rooms are small but charming in this convenient Victorian manse hotel. There are four stories and a rooftop terrace. The building was constructed for Ursuline nuns and is now a less expensive alternative to pricey Old Quebec lodgings. *81 rue Sainte-Anne, at Avenue Chauveau, Vieux Quebec, G1R 3X4, tel. 418/694-9271 or 800/275-0338. 10 rooms. MC, V. $$*

Where to Eat

Buffet L'Antiquaire. You can eat on the sidewalk, inside, or at eight upstairs tables in this busy bistro one block from the city port. Located on a street filled with interesting antiques shops, this casual restaurant serves fish normande (breaded fish in lemon sauce), chicken stews, and a very good C$4 burger, fries, and salad. There is fresh lemonade for C$1.95, a good French onion soup, and tourtiere, a hearty meat pie. *97 St. Paul, Vieux Quebec, tel. 418/694-0896. AE, MC, V. $$*

Chez Temporal. You will feel like you're in France in this quiet, backstreet bistro that serves light breakfasts, lunch, and dinner plates. Its ten wooden tables face two stained-glass windows. Homemade soups, salads, and sweets are favorites. Hot chocolate and coffee are served in immense white bowls. They often have French Canadian sugar pies—flaky dough covered with butter and brown sugar. *25 rue Couillard, off rue St. Jean, Vieux Quebec, tel. 418/694–1813. V. $*

La Creperie Le Petit Chateau. There are stone walls, floral vinyl tablecloths, and a pretty outdoor patio at this informal crepe restaurant. A kid's menu, for those 10 and under, includes soup or juice, a sausage crepe or spaghetti, ice cream, and milk. For adults, there are flamed crepes, beef dishes, and the city standby, croque-monsieur, an open-faced ham and melted cheese sandwich. *5 rue Saint Louis, Vieux Quebec, tel. 418/694–1616. MC, V. $$*

Entertainments

Quebec City Cruises. A concise history of the city is given, along with impressive scenery of the harbor, during 90-minute cruises three times daily. There are evening cruises during summer. *Quai Chouinard, 10 rue Dalhousie, Vieux Quebec, tel. 418/692–1150. Admission: C$19.95 adults, C$17.95 senior citizens, C$9.95 ages 6–12. Open daily 11:30, 2, 4. AE, MC, V.*

Sights to See

Chateau Frontenac. It's too expensive to stay here, but you can tour the massive 1893 baroque hotel. Winston Churchill and Franklin D. Roosevelt strategized here twice during World War II. The hotel is one of the city's best-known landmarks, with its turrets and massive copper roof, and commands the best views of the St. Lawrence River. *1 rue des Carrieres, Vieux Quebec, tel. 418/691–2166. Admission: C$6 adults, C$5 senior citizens, C$3.50 ages 6–16. Open May–mid-Oct., daily 10–6; mid-Oct.–Apr., weekends 12:30–5.*

Musée de la Civilisation. Ever-changing exhibits in this modern complex along the waterfront feature French history, folk art, sports, and several areas for children. The displays are among the most clever you've seen in museums, using light, space, and music to create separate worlds in this three-level building. The museum also is responsible for eight historic attractions along rue Dalhousie, including the Batterie Royale, a Living Heritage Workshop (42 rue Notre-Dame), Notre Dame Church, two parks, and the former trading post of Place-Royale, now an urban market and meeting place. *85 rue Dalhousie, Vieux Quebec, tel. 418/643–2158. Admission: C$7 adults, C$6 senior citizens, C$4 students, C$2 ages 12–16, under 12 free. Open mid-June–mid-Sept., daily 10–7; mid-Sept.–mid-June, Tues.–Sun. 10–5.*

Parliament Building. Quebec City is the capital of the Province of Quebec. The single-chamber Parliament Building, the scene of much fiery successionist rhetoric in recent decades, is an impressive Second Empire–style building not far from the Saint-Louis gate of the Old City. The front of the building is decorated with 22 bronze statues of Quebec's most famous citizens. You may not tour the building without a guide. *Grande Allee, Quebec, tel. 418/643–7239. Open weekdays 9–4:30, weekends 10–4:30.*

COOPERSTOWN AND THE HUDSON VALLEY
FISHKILL, ONEONTA, COOPERSTOWN

16

Every baseball fan should make a pilgrimage to Cooperstown, New York, home of the Baseball Hall of Fame. While you're here, plan on attending several New York–Penn League games, too. This league is one of our favorites because of its history-steeped cities and stadiums.

Start with the Hudson Valley Renegades. They play in Fishkill, New York, in a stadium just 18 mi south of Hyde Park. Visit Franklin and Eleanor Roosevelt's separate homes and the "other" CIA, the Culinary Institute of America, which trains many of the country's best chefs. The Renegades play Single A ball in this small park where the bouncy spirit and funny mascots mean frequent sellouts. The U.S. Military Academy at West Point is 20 mi southwest; the views of the Hudson River there are lovely.

From Fishkill, drive west on Interstate 84 and pick up the New York Thruway, Interstate 87, north to Albany. From here you head west on Route 20 and south on two-lane Route 166 into Cooperstown. It's a 135-mi trip. You can spend a full day in the picture-perfect town of Cooperstown, at minimum. Reserve a hotel room as far in advance as possible. The town's Main Street is filled with baseball memorabilia shops. A few blocks from the Hall of Fame, you can go boating and swimming in the crystal-clear Otsego Lake. At the Cooperstown Bat Company, 2 mi north of town, you can watch baseball bats being made.

From Cooperstown, continue south on Route 166, then south on Route 28 to reach Oneonta, 23 mi away. Damaschke Field is in the same Single A league, but this endearing, primitive park has none of the flash and hoopla of new parks. The grandstand looks as it did in 1939, when it was built. The National Soccer Hall of Fame and Museum is in Oneonta.

HUDSON VALLEY RENEGADES

League: New York–Penn League • **Major League Affiliation:** Tampa Bay • **Class:** Short Season A • **Stadium:** Dutchess Stadium • **Opened:** 1994 • **Capacity:** 4,320 • **Dimensions:** LF: 325, CF: 400, RF: 325 • **Surface:** grass • **Season:** mid-June–early Sept.

STADIUM LOCATION: 1090 Rte. 9D, Wappingers Falls, NY 12590.

TEAM WEB SITE: www.hvrenegades.com

GETTING THERE: From north or south on New York State Throughway, Exit 17 in Newburgh to I–84 E, across Newburgh-Beacon Bridge to Exit 11 immediately after tollbooth, Rte. 9D north 1 mi to stadium, on right. From east or west, I–84 to Exit 11, Rte. 9D north 1 mi to stadium, on right.

PARKING: Limited to first 1,200 cars at $3. Shuttle bus service from parking lot ¼ mi from stadium.

TICKET INFORMATION: Box 661, Fishkill, NY 12524, tel. 914/838–0094, fax 914/838–0014.

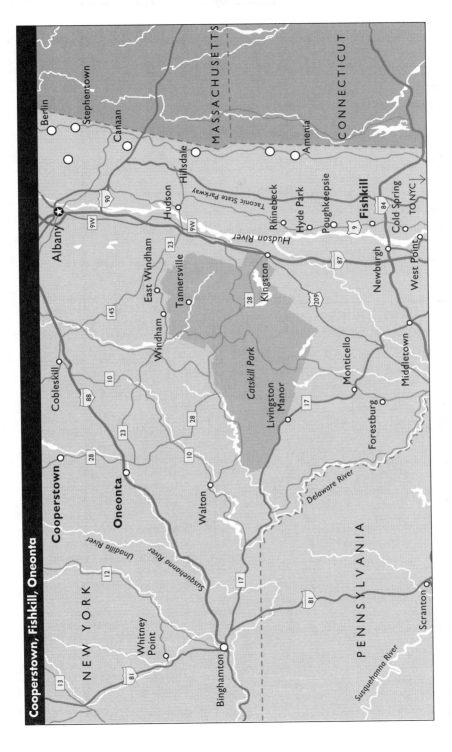

PRICE RANGE: Box seats $8; reserved seats $7; reserved bleacher $5; general admission $4.50.

GAME TIME: Mon.–Sat. 7:15 PM, Sun. 5:15 PM; gates open 75 min before night games and 1 hr before day games.

TIPS ON SEATING: Call ahead and buy reserved or box seats early. Many games sold out in advance, especially in Aug.

SEATING FOR PEOPLE WITH DISABILITIES: On internal concourse just behind box seats in Sections 101, 105, 106, 107, and 111.

STADIUM FOOD: Food is not a highlight. The best treat is the frozen orangeade and lemonade, which you scrape out of cups ($2.50). Quite ordinary grilled sausages, hamburgers, and chicken are available from grills near the tents down each foul line. The park also offers soft-serve ice cream.

SMOKING POLICY: Smoking prohibited in seating area but allowed in outer concourse.

VISITING TEAM HOTEL: Ramada Inn–West Point (1055 Union Ave., Newburgh, NY 12550, tel. 914/564–4500 or 800/228–2828).

TOURISM INFORMATION: Greater Southern Dutchess Chamber of Commerce (300 Westage Business Center, Suite 100, Fishkill, NY 12524, tel. 914/897–2067).

Hudson Valley: Dutchess Stadium

The 4,320-capacity Dutchess Stadium in Fishkill was built in what must be a record time of 71 days. Construction began on April 8, 1994, and they were still painting it on opening night, June 18. Dutchess County, New York State, and private funders shared in the $5.2-million cost. A quick walk through the park reveals Dutchess Stadium as a model of architectural simplicity. The uncovered grandstand is small, with 1,462 dark-green box seats, 812 purple reserved seats above the internal concourse, and 8 skyboxes and a press box under a green roof. There are aluminum bleachers without backs past the dugouts and behind box seats on each side. Small picnic areas with grills extend down each baseline.

Dutchess Stadium gives you an attractive view of trees beyond the outfield fence. The view past the right-field foul line includes a highway, a mountain, and an elegant redbrick building that, surprisingly, is a jail. The animated scoreboard in left center is far above the New York–Penn League norm. The entranceway is an outline of a baseball diamond in green, gray, and beige concrete. Parking is limited and on an unfinished

surface. There are plans to improve the parking and landscape. But no amount of landscaping will make up for the inadequate access to and egress from the stadium. If you have to get out of the parking lot and on the road in a hurry, leave early.

Whatever the limitations of this stadium, they are more than overcome by the fan-friendly atmosphere provided by the Renegades. The team bonded with its community almost instantly, with sellouts more often than not in its inaugural year of 1994. The team colors—dark green and purple—are attractively reflected in the box and reserved seats. There are two mascots: Rookie, a 6-ft, 7-inch raccoon, does a great job of entertaining the fans when he is not flirting with his girlfriend, Renée.

The music and sound effects join with the animated scoreboard and energetic public address announcer to make for a loud and lively time at the ballpark. When fans want the Renegade pitcher to blaze a fastball past an opposing batter, the scoreboard flashes "Renegade Express," while the public address system blares the sounds of a roaring train, and the fans in the aluminum bleacher seats stamp their feet. A local kid leads the crowd in singing "Take Me Out to the Ball Game" at the seventh-inning stretch each game.

Where to Stay

Fishkill Holiday Inn. This three-story hotel is part of a hotel row on Route 9. The rooms are standard, with modern furnishings, dark floral spreads, and good desks. The hotel is five minutes east of the ballpark. *511 Rte. 9, Exit 13 from I–84, Fishkill 12525, tel. 914/896–6281 or 800/465–4329, fax 914/896–5410. 156 rooms. Facilities: restaurant, outdoor pool, health club. AE, D, DC, MC, V. $$*

Holiday Inn Express. This modern four-floor hotel has inside corridors and a Continental breakfast. It is 6 mi south of Hyde Park. *341 South Rd. (Rte. 9), Poughkeepsie 12601, tel. 914/473–1151 or 800/465–4329, fax 914/473–8127. 123 rooms. Facilities: outdoor pool, coin laundry. AE, D, DC, MC, V. $$*

Super 8 Motel. The two-story Tudor-style motel offers a free Continental breakfast. Children 12 and under stay free. It costs $5 to rent a crib. *528 Albany Post Rd. (Rte. 9), Hyde Park, 12538, tel. 914/229–0088 or 800/848–8888, fax 914/229–8088. 61 rooms. AE, D, MC, V. $*

Where to Eat

Hudson's Ribs & Fish. This quaint, Cape Cod–style seafood and steak restaurant specializes in live lobsters and hot popovers with strawberry butter. Children have their own menu. It's 10 mi east of the ballpark. *Rte. 9, 3 mi north of I–84, Fishkill, tel. 914/297–5002. AE, MC, V. $$*

The American Bounty and **St. Andrew's Café— Culinary Institute of America.** These fine restaurants are on the campus of America's "other CIA," the country's premier cooking college. Students prepare and serve your meals under the guidance of their professors. The café gives the nutrition rankings of all its foods. There are two even more formal restaurants, Caterina di Medici (Italian) and the Escoffier (French). All four have formally set tables with cloths and china. Children's appetites will be best served at the casual St. Andrew's Café, a contemporary restaurant with wood-oven pizzas, grilled specialties, and an outdoor terrace. The American Bounty focuses on regional food, particularly Hudson Valley produce and American wines. *433 Albany Post Rd., Hyde Park, tel. 914/471–6608. Reservations essential. AE, DC, MC, V. Closed 3 wks in July. $$*

Brass Anchor. Diners can watch the water at this rustic seafood restaurant on the Hudson River. There are plastic patio chairs outside and wooden, nautical-theme tables inside. Lobster and shrimp are the standouts here; the children's menu includes fried shrimp, chicken, and hamburgers. *31 River Point Rd., Poughkeepsie, tel. 914/452–3232. AE, D, DC, MC, V. Closed Nov.– Feb. $*

Entertainments

Splash Down. There are raining mushrooms, water cannons, and a pirate ship named *Shipwreck Island* to climb on at this small water park, which also has a miniature golf course and an activity pool with balls. Toddlers and crawlers can use a cushioned pollywog pond. *2200 Rte. 9 N, 2 mi north of Exit 13 from I–84, Fishkill, tel. 914/896–6606. Admission: $17 adults and children 46" and taller, $13 children 34–42", $10 children under 34"; $4, 3–7 PM. Open daily 10–7. AE, MC, V.*

Sights to See

Eleanor Roosevelt National Historic Site. Val-Kill was Eleanor Roosevelt's home. Known as the First Lady of the World, Mrs. Roosevelt pressed her husband to face the plight of the disadvantaged and played a leading role in comforting Americans wounded in World War II. As chair of the United Nations Human Rights Commission years after FDR's death, Eleanor Roosevelt was the catalyst for the adoption of the Declaration of Human Rights. She used Val-Kill as a retreat for decades and moved here after FDR's death. The home was almost lost to bulldozers in 1984 and now is run by the National Park Service. There is a 19-minute video and a 15-minute tour of the cottage. You can take a 2½-mi walking trail from FDR's Springwood to Eleanor's Val-Kill. *Rte. 9G, ½ mi north of St. Andrews Rd., Hyde Park, tel. 914/229–9115 (National Park Service). Admission: $5, under 17 free. Open May–Oct., daily 9–5; Mar.– Apr. and Nov.–Dec., weekends.*

Franklin Roosevelt Birthplace and Library. Franklin Delano Roosevelt was born in Hyde Park on January 30, 1882. Children are given an informative brochure on FDR's childhood at the house they called Springwood. In "The Snuggery" next door to the family room, there is a television—the 34th RCA console television made, a gift to the president in 1939 from David Sarnoff. Fala, Roosevelt's most famous dog, is buried in the rose garden near FDR and Eleanor between the house and the museum. There is much for children to explore on the grounds, including stables and an ice house.

A June 17, 1935, letter from Harry Hopkins, director of the Works Progress Administration, spelled out the concept behind the WPA program that was responsible for the construction of many baseball stadiums in communities across America: "The real objective is to take three and a half million unemployed from the relief rolls and put them to work on useful projects." A wing of the museum is devoted to the contributions of FDR's much-admired wife, Eleanor. Admission to the library includes entry to the home. *519 Albany Post Rd. (Rte. 9), Hyde Park, tel. 800/337–8474. Admission: $10, under 17 free. Home open daily 9–5; museum daily 9–6.*

United States Military Academy. Twenty miles southwest of Fishkill is the Army's famed college. You can drive or walk through sections of the grounds, and guided tours are given through the visitor center in Building 2107, outside South Post's Thayer Gate. The chapels are impressive, especially Cadet Chapel with its huge pipe organ. A free museum, in Olmstead Hall at Pershing Center, will only interest older children. Standard tours last 55 minutes. *Rte. 9 W, West Point, NY, tel. 914/938–2638. Tour admission: $4 adults, $2 ages under 13. Grounds open daily 9–4:45; tours Mon.–Sat. 10–3:30, Sun. 11–3:30.*

Vanderbilt Mansion. Two miles up the road from the FDR home is a riverfront product of the gilded age. This three-story Italian Renaissance–style mansion was designed for Frederick W. Vanderbilt by McKim, Mead & White. Finished in 1898 at a cost of $660,000, it looks more like a grand city library than a country home. Vanderbilt died in 1938, and FDR himself talked Vanderbilt's niece into donating the mansion to the federal government as a historic property. *Rte. 9, Hyde Park, tel. 914/229–9115. Admission: $8, under 17 free. Open May–Oct. and Christmas wk, daily 9–5; Nov.–Apr., Thurs.–Mon. 9–5.*

ONEONTA TIGERS

League: New York–Penn League • **Major League Affiliation:** Detroit Tigers • **Class:** Short Season A • **Stadium:** Damaschke Field • **Opened:** 1905 / 39 • **Capacity:** 4,200 • **Dimensions:** LF: 333, CF: 401, RF: 335 • **Surface:** grass • **Season:** mid-June–Aug.

STADIUM LOCATION: 95 River St., Oneonta, NY 13820.

TEAM WEB SITE: *www.minorleaguebaseball.com/teams/nyp-onephp3*

GETTING THERE: From I–88, Exit 15 toward town on NY 23W ½ mi, left as NY 23W becomes Main St., take immediate left on Grand St., which winds around and becomes Prospect St., left on Market St., and immediate left on Gas Ave. to stadium. From Cooperstown, take NY 28 south 17 mi to I–88. Take I–88 mi 5 more mi to Exit 15.

PARKING: Ample free parking.

TICKET INFORMATION: 95 River St., Oneonta, NY 13820, tel. 607/432–6326, fax 607/432–1965.

PRICE RANGE: $3.50 adults, $2.50 under 16, free under 6.

GAME TIME: Mon.–Sat. 7:15 PM, Sun. 6 PM; gates open 75 min before game except Sun., when they open 1 hr early.

TIPS ON SEATING: Everything is general admission. Sit in bleachers down left-field line, and you can talk with players in visiting team bullpen.

SEATING FOR PEOPLE WITH DISABILITIES: At field level on each side of grandstand.

STADIUM FOOD: The food is a bargain. A good grilled sausage with peppers is $2.50. Ice-cream bars and sodas are $1. Alcohol is not sold or allowed in the stadium.

SMOKING POLICY: No restrictions.

VISITING TEAM HOTEL: Town House Motor Inn (318 Main St., Oneonta, NY 13820, tel. 607/432–1313).

TOURISM INFORMATION: Otsego County Chamber of Commerce (12 Carbon St., Oneonta, NY 13820, tel. 607/432–4500).

Oneonta: Damaschke Field

Damaschke Field is about baseball, not hoopla. This is baseball the way Sam Nader likes it. No mascot. No beer. No fancy logo or trendy nickname. Just baseball. "This is family entertainment. A pleasant night, as inexpensive as possible. I don't want to change the atmosphere. I don't need any skyboxes. It's not fair to the taxpayers," explains Nader, a former two-term mayor of Oneonta who brought professional baseball to town and has kept it here for 30 years.

You won't have to spend five minutes with a clerk, a computer, and a seating chart to figure out if you want a field box seat or a club-level seat or a reserved grandstand seat or a whatever. Just go up to the blue-and-white cinderblock ticket office, pay your $3.50, and walk through the chain-link-fence gate.

But watch out that you don't get run over by a player. The main concourse is crawling with them as the game approaches. Your kids want autographs of future major leaguers? No problem. Our children sat on the bench at the locker-room door, just yards from the front gate on the first-base side. They filled two New York–Penn League balls with signatures in about 15 minutes. These are players fresh out of college and some talented teenagers, all just starting their professional careers. Most won't make the big leagues, but there are future stars among them. Don Mattingly began his career here, hitting .349 in 1979 as an 18-year-old. Football star John Elway hit .318 in 1982 while debating between a career in football and one in baseball.

They have played baseball on this field since 1905. And, yes, Babe Ruth played here, too. In October of 1920, just two weeks after eight Chicago White Sox players were indicted for throwing the 1919 World Series, the mighty Babe and his All-Stars barnstormed through town. The local newspaper called on the Merchants Association and school authorities to end business early so everyone could see Ruth smack a home run. Three thousand people showed up, and Ruth knocked one over the left-center-field fence, which was about 30 ft farther back than it is today.

The small, covered blue-and-white grandstand seating 750 fans was built in 1939 and has hardly changed a bit. The fans sit on blue wooden benches without backs. A rickety navy-blue wooden press box perches on the roof. A huge net protects people on the small concourse behind the grandstand. The bleachers down the first-base line are wooden benches, while the third-base bleachers are aluminum. There are tiny box-seat areas divided by metal poles down each line. Each has a sign with the owner's name—Sam Nader's is the second box on the first-base side; drop by and say "hi"—and the box holders sit on blue metal folding chairs.

The ballpark lies in the middle of a city park, where the view is first rate, with the foothills of the Catskills beyond the outfield wall. The scoreboard in center field, donated in 1977, is blessedly free of ads. It is wonderfully simple: green with just the basics, not even an inning-by-inning recap. Nader—he makes all the decisions here—had the field renamed in 1968 to honor Ernest C. "Dutch" Damaschke, who served as chairman of the city's Parks and Recreation Commission for 35 years.

No beer is sold or allowed in the park. To Sam Nader, beer is inconsistent with a pleasant family night at the ballpark. Smoking, unfortunately, is allowed everywhere.

A tiny, old stadium like Damaschke Field provides the best opportunities to talk with the players. In addition to the benches near the locker rooms before the game, the best place is by the visiting-team bullpen, down the third-base line.

Where to Stay

Visiting Team Motel: Town House Motor Inn. You will have no problem walking the five minutes to the ballpark from this two-story motel. Oneonta is a college town (State University of New York at Oneonta); its Main Street is safe and filled with pedestrians through early evening. This frame hotel offers a free Continental breakfast and standard double rooms. *318 Main St., Oneonta 13822, tel. 607/432–1313, fax 607/432–3887. 40 rooms. AE, D, MC, V. $$*

Super 8 Motel. From this two-story frame motel beside the Susquehanna River you can see the ballpark a little over a mile in the distance. The motel is behind the Southside Shopping Mall. The rooms are clean and conventional. Guests receive free doughnuts and beverages in the morning, and children 12 and under stay free. *Rte. 23, Southside (Oneonta) 13820, tel. 607/432–9505 or 800/848–8888, fax 607/432–9505. 60 rooms. Facilities: coin laundry. AE, D, DC, MC, V. $$*

Where to Eat

Scorchy's Metropolitan Diner. You can get breakfast anytime at this hangout on the corner of Main Street. You may sit at its 14-stool counter or in one of the well-used booths. The meat loaf is everything a blue-plate special should be. There are also fish-and-chips, homemade slaw, burgers, and kids' meals. *139 Main St., Oneonta, tel. 607/432–2154. No credit cards. $*

Brooks House of Bar-B-Q. Meat lovers drive out of their way for Brooks's pit-barbecue chicken, beef, and pork, especially its ribs. There is a children's menu, and you can eat outside or inside this casual restaurant. *Rte. 7, ¼ mi west of*

Exit 16 from I–88, Oneonta, tel. 607/432–1782. MC, V. $

Neptune Diner. This restaurant offers everything from pancakes to surf and turf, with an emphasis on exceptional Greek food, including gyros, souvlakia, and rice and bread puddings. It stands across the street from the Southside Mall, a mile southwest of the ballpark. *Rte. 23, Southside (Oneonta), tel. 607/432–8820. AE, MC, V. $*

Sights to See

National Soccer Hall of Fame and Museum. Just minutes from Damaschke Field, you'll find America's oldest soccer ball, a relic from an 1863 game on Boston Common, plus uniforms, trophies, and a video room. The ultimate plan is to build a 61-acre soccer campus complete with a major stadium. The museum will become part of that complex. *5–11 Ford Ave., Oneonta, tel. 607/432–3351. Admission: $8 adults, $4 ages 6–11. Open Wed.–Mon. 10–5.*

Cooperstown

Baseball Hall of Fame–Cooperstown. Baseball's mecca is 23 mi from Oneonta. It's a charming village to visit, made more so by the magnetic attraction of baseball. In 1907, the Mills Commission concluded: "The first scheme for playing baseball, according to the best evidence obtainable to date, was devised by Abner Doubleday at Cooperstown, New York, in 1839." It's a great story, but it is not accurate. Doubleday, later a distinguished Civil War soldier, was at West Point that summer, not Cooperstown. Nonetheless, the National Baseball Library and Museum was established in Cooperstown and the first greats of baseball were enshrined in the Hall of Fame on August 27, 1939. Cooperstown is a wonderful place to be with your kids and your memories as the summer ends and the baseball season comes to a close.

The **Hall of Fame Museum**'s strength is its depth of material—the "General History of Baseball" walks you right through from the earliest game of town ball to modern times. Many of the items that are part of baseball's lore are here—the bat Babe Ruth used to hit his 60th home run in 1927, Ty Cobb's 1926 glove, Walter Johnson's locker, Jackie Robinson's warm-up jacket, Hank Aaron's uniform the night he hit his 715th career home run in 1974, and on and on.

There are plenty of treats in the specialty exhibits as well, but none of these exhibits live up to their potential. We were pleased to see a special display called "Women in Baseball" and a Rockford Peaches uniform but disappointed in the exhibit's lack of depth. "It's so small," complained our then-eight-year-old daughter, Emily. The display on "Black Baseball" is equally disappointing.

On the third floor, the section on baseball cards has the most prized of all baseball cards—the 1909 Honus Wagner tobacco-company card. It is so rare because it was recalled when Wagner objected to being associated with a tobacco product.

In the library wing sits famed sports writer Grantland Rice's typewriter, with a date and a simple byline, typed on an otherwise empty page, from the day he retired. "Baseball at the Movies" is also in the library wing. Here you can see Geena Davis's Rockford Peaches uniform from *A League of Their Own* and Robert Redford's New York Knights uniform from *The Natural*, as well as clips from a number of other baseball movies.

The Hall of Fame gallery isn't flashy, but it is impressive. There are two rows of bronze plaques, in order of induction date, hung on the natural wood-paneled walls of a rectangular room with alcoves marked by marble pillars. A glass-roofed rotunda is at one end, with nine alcoves that will begin to be filled by 2001. Visitors are quiet as they read the career capsules of the players, umpires, managers, and baseball executives who have been voted into the hall since 1936. There is a discreet note that the facts described on the plaques are as they were known at the time the plaques were made, so you may find some exaggerations as you walk along these hallowed walls.

If your schedule permits, start your visit after dinner. If you buy your ticket after 7 PM, it is good for the next day as well. Watch the movie, find your favorite players' plaques, and begin the tour of the general history exhibit. Return the next day for the specialty exhibits.

Before arriving, you might want to join the Friends of the Hall of Fame for $25 and receive an individual season pass to the museum, a T-shirt, a yearbook, and a quarterly newsletter. You can also buy combination tickets with the nearby Farmer's and Fenimore House museums. *25 Main St., Box 590, Cooperstown 13326, tel. 607/547–7200. Admission: $9.50 adults, $8 senior citizens, $4 ages 7–12. Open early May–late Sept., daily 9–9; Oct.–Apr., daily 9–5. AE, D, MC, V.*

Doubleday Field. Before you become immersed in the memorabilia shops that line both sides of Cooperstown's Main Street, visit Doubleday Field, just down the street from the Hall of Fame. Legend has it that this is where the mythical Doubleday game was played. The ballpark was rebuilt for the 100th anniversary in 1939 with funds from WPA. The entrance is picture-perfect, with a redbrick facade and white wooden trim, a fine setting for the obligatory family-vacation photo. The capacity of the old brick-and-wood grandstand has been expanded with aluminum bleachers down each base-line to accommodate the annual July Hall of Fame game between two major-league teams. Major leaguers must not enjoy pitching here, as left field is only 296 ft from home. *Village of Cooperstown, 22 Main St., Box 346, Cooperstown, tel. 607/547–2411.*

Where to Stay

Try to make your reservations in February or March for your summer visit. The motels in this small town (2,200 people) can fit you in with two to three weeks' notice in summer, but you'll pay top price. Motels are expensive during the summer—$100 and up for a double—and the rates drop dramatically in the off-seasons. The Hall of Fame Weekend (end of July–beginning of August) boosts rates even higher. To save money, call the county Chamber of Commerce (tel. 607/432–4500) early, get its travel guide, and book one of the many guest houses.

Tunnicliffe Inn. A half block from the Hall of Fame is this three-story brick, Federal-style building, which allows children to use sleeping bags in their parents' room. Parking is limited to seven vehicles in the rear, so nearby overflow lots are used. *34–36 Pioneer St., Cooperstown*

13326, tel. 607/547–9611. 17 rooms. Facilities: 2 restaurants. AE, D, MC, V. $$

The Cooper Inn. The original part of a two-story brick Georgian mansion, built in 1812, has four guest rooms and three sitting parlors; a wing built in 1936 contains five two-bedroom suites. There is a manicured, shaded lawn. The inn is two blocks from the Hall of Fame. Guests have access to the golf, tennis, and swimming pool at the affiliated Hotel Otsego. Continental breakfast is served in the breakfast room of the main house. Main and Chestnut Sts., Cooperstown 13326, tel. 607/547–2567 or 800/348–6222, fax 607/547–1271. 15 rooms. Facilities: breakfast room. AE, MC, V. $$$

Cooperstown Best Western Inn. Behind a McDonald's and overlooking a field and hills, this hotel offers guests a free Continental breakfast and clean, well-lit rooms. It is 3 mi southwest of town. Ask for a room facing east, overlooking the pretty farmland. The clerks wear baseball jerseys and sell discount combination passes to the Hall of Fame, the Farmer's Museum, and the Fenimore House. Rte. 28, Cooperstown 13326, tel. 607/547–9439 or 800/528–1234, fax 607/ 547–7082. 62 rooms. Facilities: indoor pool, game room, coin laundry. AE, D, DC, MC, V. $$

Hotel Otsego. Built in 1909, this five-story hotel is the grande dame of the lake, with a sweeping view from its veranda. It looks like a small college, with an imposing, white-columned entry. Half of the rooms, which are decorated handsomely, have a lake view. A full breakfast and dinner are included. Parking is free. 60 Lake St., Cooperstown 13326, tel. 607/547–9931 or 800/ 348–6222, fax 607/547–9675. 137 rooms. Facilities: restaurant, outdoor pool. AE, MC, V. $$$

The Lake Front Motel. This late-1950s-era motel is on the waterfront, with some rooms overlooking Otsego Lake. The two-story motel is 1½ blocks from the Hall of Fame and offers free parking. There is lake swimming at the adjacent public beach. 10 Fair St., Cooperstown 13326, tel. 607/547–9511. 44 rooms. Facilities: restaurant. MC, V. $$

Where to Eat

TJ's Place. The service is speedy, but your children may be distracted by the sports videos

being screened while you eat. This is a combination restaurant and baseball memorabilia and merchandise store. It offers a wide selection of baseball-motif sandwiches, plus Italian entrées, salads, and soups. The portions and drinks are huge. 124 Main St., Cooperstown, tel. 607/547–4040. AE, D, DC, MC, V. $

Doubleday Cafe. At this upscale diner on Main Street the specials are posted on a chalkboard. Its basics are hamburgers, sandwiches, and chicken, plus Mexican food on the weekends. The breakfast muffins are particularly good. 93 Main St., Cooperstown, tel. 607/547–5468. D, MC, V. $

Tunnicliffe Tap Room. Patrons are allowed to carve their names into the wooden tables of this vintage restaurant; you can even find Mickey Mantle's. It serves sandwiches, burgers, steaks, and pasta dishes in a casual setting downstairs. Children under 10 eat for $4.95, including a beverage. More formal dining is offered upstairs. 34 Pioneer St., Cooperstown, tel. 607/547–9611. AE, D, MC, V. $

Entertainments

Classic Boat Tours. You can tour the crystal-clear Otsego Lake on a classic mahogany launch. The one-hour trip is a good way to learn about James Fenimore Cooper and this amazing lake. The boats have an 8-passenger minimum. Fair St. Dock, Cooperstown, tel. 607/547–5295. Admission: $8.50 adults, $5 ages 3–12. Runs mid-May–mid-Oct., daily at 10, 11, 1, 2, 3, 4, 6. MC, V.

The Farmer's Museum and Town Ball. You can time-travel in this living-history museum, with its restored buildings where craftspeople blow glass, shoe horses, and weave baskets. A combination ticket is available with the Baseball Hall of Fame and Fenimore House Museum. The town trolley stops here. If your schedule permits, time your visit to the Farmer's Museum to allow you to take in a game of Town Ball, demonstrated by the Leatherstocking Base Ball Club in conjunction with the museum. They play an early 1800s game by rules with a distinctly sandlot feel. Play is with a soft leather ball and the players do not have gloves. Lake Rd., Cooperstown, tel. 607/ 547–1400. Admission: $9 adults, $4 ages 7–12. Combo ticket with Baseball Hall of Fame: $15 *adults, $6.50 children. Open June–Labor Day, daily 9–5; May and Labor Day–Oct., daily 10–4; Apr. and Nov., Tues.–Sun. 10–4; Dec., weekends 10–4.*

Unusual Shopping

Cooperstown's Main Street. Browse through the excellent store in the Hall of Fame Museum and a few other stores before you buy. Our impression is that the baseball stores here are growing rapidly and improving their products.

If your time is limited, try a few of the following, recognizing that this is not a definitive list of quality stores. Our favorite is **Gallery 53 Artworks** (118 Main St., Cooperstown, 13326, tel. 607/547–5655), dedicated to original baseball art. We particularly like **National Pastime** (81 Main St., tel. 607/547–2524 or 800/462–9391) and **Mickey's Place** (74 Main St., tel. 607/547–5775 or 800/528–5775). **Cooperstown Bat Company** (66

Main St., tel. 607/547–1090) sells bats with gorgeous color decals, many autographed by Hall of Famers. If you have time, visit its Fly Creek factory (2½ mi north on Rte. 28, tel. 607/547–2415). For cards, we like **Pioneer Sports Cards** (106 Main St., tel. 607/547–2323) and **Baseball Nostalgia** (Doubleday Plaza, next to Doubleday Field, tel. 607/547–6051). The **Doubleday Batting Range** (Doubleday Court, tel. 607/547–5168) also adjoins the Field. Take a few swings in the batting cage, then send home a phony newspaper for $5 telling how you were a big hit in Cooperstown. The **American Baseball Archives** (99 Main St., tel. 607/547–1273) features a baseball wax museum and a superb collection of Mickey Mantle memorabilia. The virtual-reality exhibit lets you feel the impact of a Roger Clemens fastball. *Admission: $5.95 adults, $2.95 ages under 13, $3.95 senior citizens. Open Memorial Day–Labor Day, daily 9–9. AE, D, MC, V.*

BUFFALO WINGS, RED WINGS, [17] AND BLUE JAYS
BUFFALO, ROCHESTER, TORONTO

Watching baseball by the Great Lakes puts you in three exciting ballparks—the nation's premier minor-league park in Buffalo, the stunning new park in downtown Rochester, and the massive dome in Toronto, one of the world's great international cities.

In Buffalo, you go directly downtown to see its imposing minor-league park. In hopes of getting a major-league team, Buffalo built a serious stadium with a view of the city skyline. The city didn't get a major-league team, but fans enjoy big-time amenities, including some of the best food in baseball. The Bisons, a Triple A team and part of the American Association, are affiliated with the Cleveland Indians. The city has a venerable zoo and a children's science center.

Driving 86 mi northeast to Rochester, you'll again be in the heart of downtown watching baseball. Frontier Park is a handsome redbrick and dark-green structure holding some of the sport's most enthusiastic fans. The city's famed red hots and white hots are grilled at the park and there's a live organist plus a Walk of Fame detailing city sports heroes. The nation's fourth-oldest amusement park is right on Lake Ontario and a lively children's museum, carousel, and new retro diner are all within walking distance of the park.

You may want to stop at Niagara Falls on your way to Toronto, which is four hours from Rochester. You'll see Toronto's famed CN Tower before you see its SkyDome. As domes go, it isn't bad. The city, with its park system, impressive architecture, nearby islands, and multitude of inexpensive ethnic restaurants, has something for most tastes. Public transport is convenient and plentiful, from streetcars to subways to ferries. The Blue Jays share the SkyDome with the Toronto Argonauts, but the most beloved sport in Toronto is hockey, as its extensive Hall of Fame demonstrates.

BUFFALO BISONS

League: International League • **Major League Affiliation:** Cleveland Indians • **Class:** AAA • **Stadium:** Dunn Tire Park • **Opened:** 1988 • **Capacity:** 20,900 • **Dimensions:** LF: 325, CF: 404, RF: 325 • **Surface:** grass • **Season:** Apr.–Labor Day

STADIUM LOCATION: 275 Washington St., Buffalo, NY 14203.

TEAM WEB SITE: www.bisons.com

GETTING THERE: From I–190, Elm St. exit, left on Swan St. For information about public transit, call Niagara Frontier Transportation Authority (tel. 716/855–7300).

PARKING: Ample parking in private downtown lots, $4.

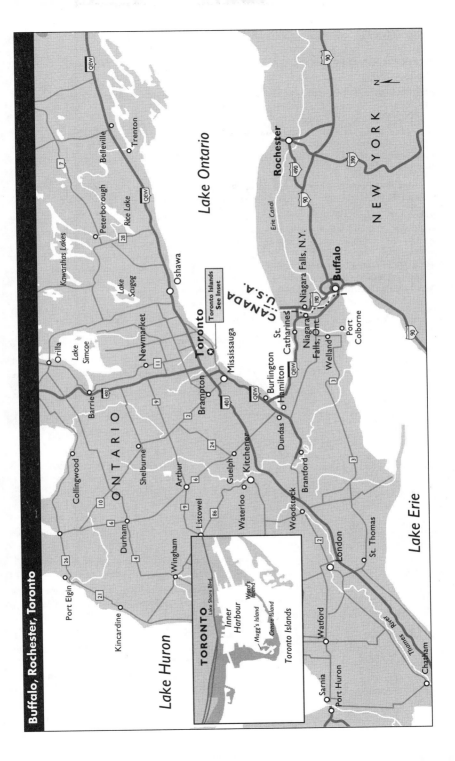

Buffalo, Rochester, Toronto

TICKET INFORMATION: Box 450, Buffalo, NY 14205-0450, tel. 716/846–2000 or 800/283–0114, fax 716/852–6530.

PRICE RANGE: Field- and club-level special reserved seats $9; field- and club-level reserved seats $7.50; bleacher seats $5 adults, $4 under 15 and senior citizens.

GAME TIME: Mon.–Sat. 7:05 PM, Sun. 2:05 PM; gates open 1 hr before game.

TIPS ON SEATING: Best seats taken by season ticket holders. Call well in advance and order reserved seats. Top rows of last two sections down left-field line—sections 123 and 125—are no-alcohol family sections.

SEATING FOR PEOPLE WITH DISABILITIES: On walking concourse level just above special reserved seating area in Sections 100–114, 123, and 125; parking spaces in Exchange St. parking lot.

STADIUM FOOD: The food is outstanding. The star: roast beef on weck, fragrant meat on a chewy salt-topped roll ($4.25). Try Buffalo chicken wings, plus celery (or carrots) and bleu cheese. The veggies are great for kids. There are bins of fresh-roasted peanuts, good coleslaw at the **Sub Shop,** and tossed salads. Kids may like the (fried) onion chips, but avoid the greasy fried bologna sandwich. The **Kid's Corner** at the Oak Street exit serves loganberry juice, milk, and popcorn for $1. Kid's pizza, hot dogs, grilled cheese, and pb&j sandwiches are $1.25 each. Italian ices are $1.50; a good custard cone is $2. Upstairs, **Pettibone's Restaurant** has toasted ravioli ($4.75), a kid's menu, and 40 no-smoking seats by the windows. It's open weekdays from 11:30 to 3 and reopens at 4 on game days.

SMOKING POLICY: Smoking prohibited in seating areas.

VISITING TEAM HOTEL: Buffalo Downtown Holiday Inn (620 Delaware Ave., Buffalo, NY 14202, tel. 716/886–2121 or 800/465–4329).

TOURISM INFORMATION: Greater Buffalo Convention and Visitors Bureau (107 Delaware Ave., Buffalo, NY 14202, tel. 716/852–0511 or 800/283–3256).

Buffalo: Dunn Tire Park

Buffalo's ballpark—built with major-league ambitions—is the nation's premier minor-league stadium. The city longed for major-league baseball and, to overcome its cold spring climate, made major investments. The city hired the premier baseball-stadium architects—HOK Sport of Kansas City—and spent nearly $42 million. Buffalo built the bottom half of a modern major-league stadium—a street level complete with 17 concession booths, souvenir shops, and modern facilities with a club level above. Had Buffalo been successful in getting a major-league team, an upper deck would have been added where the bluish green roof is today. As it is, the club-level seats give the Buffalo ballpark a second level that is rare in minor-league baseball. Buffalo has a major-league 40-by-50-ft scoreboard in straightaway center field. The outfield fence was reconfigured for the 1996 season to resemble the parent club Cleveland's Jacobs Field and to produce more home runs.

Best of all, the city built the stadium right downtown, a daring move in the late 1980s. The feel from the street level is major league all the way. Past the attractive street-level arches at the Swan Street entrance, inside the stadium you can see some of the city's skyline, including the top of the historic Post Office building over third base.

Beyond the right-field fence, there is an ordinary parking garage. Beyond left field is a huge net to stop balls from hitting cars on the ramp to the interstate highway. The seats in right field are benches without backs.

Unfortunately, the name of this fine stadium is for sale. Whatever happened to the dignified practice of naming a stadium after a leading citizen, a baseball person, or as a war memorial? After a period in 1995 as the Downtown Ballpark in Buffalo, it was renamed North AmeriCare Park, then Dunn Tire Park.

Bison is an obvious nickname for a city named Buffalo. The baseball-green outfield walls have the outfield dimensions outlined with a white bison. The Bisons have one of baseball's best mascots—Buster T. Bison. Buster has a little cousin named Chip. And these aren't the only strange creatures that inhabit this stadium. We saw the Earl of Bud dancing on the dugout in the fourth inning. Other vendors here are dressed as Conehead and Zorro.

A Buffalo-baseball Hall of Fame stands on the first-base side of the concourse. Two players sign autographs near it for about 20 minutes starting an hour before every game. There are fireworks every Friday night. Every Sunday at the park is Kid's Day. Below the right-field bleachers a children's playground and picnic area provide a field-level view of the game.

More Buffalo Baseball

War Memorial Stadium. Buffalo's War Memorial Stadium—built for football and track and field in 1936–37 with Works Progress Administration (WPA) funds—was the site of that spectacular closing scene when the clinching home run explodes off the lights in *The Natural*, Robert Redford's 1984 bouquet to baseball. The stadium was not used for baseball until 1961. Nicknamed the Rockpile, the stadium deteriorated along with the neighborhood in the 1960s. Summer riots in 1967 led to a curfew that forced the Bisons to play night games in Niagara Falls. A gang invaded the clubhouse during batting practice in 1969. Buffalo lost its Triple A franchise in 1970. The American Football League Buffalo Bills played here from 1960 to 1972. Baseball returned in 1979 and gained popularity after the team was purchased by Rich Products in 1983.

The site looks like a modern-day Stonehenge, as the Buffalo Urban Renewal Agency saved two massive concrete corner structures in its redevelopment of the stadium complex into a community center. At the top of the structures, two sculpted bison face off. Today, the complex includes a small baseball field, a football field, and other community facilities. To see the remains of War Memorial Stadium, go north on Main Street from downtown. Take a right on

Best Street to Jefferson Street. Home plate was near Dodge Street, with right field at Best Street. The monument at Best and Jefferson was behind center field.

Where to Stay

Downtown Buffalo has very few hotels; this is a city where you'll need reservations. If you don't have them, you'll stay out by the airport, a 30-minute drive from the ballpark.

Visiting Team Motel: Buffalo Holiday Inn–Downtown. This busy eight-story hotel is only five minutes from the park and offers guests a free full breakfast. The rooms are on the small side, but the upper floors have a nice view of the city. It is recessed from the busy street it faces and is next door to a drugstore. *620 Delaware Ave., Buffalo 14202, tel. 716/886–2121 or 800/465-4329, fax 716/886-7942. 168 rooms. Facilities: restaurant, outdoor pool, coin laundry. AE, D, DC, MC, V. $$*

Others to consider downtown: The **Radisson Suite Hotel** (601 Main St., Buffalo 14203, tel. 716/854-5500, $$$); **Buffalo Hilton** (120 Church St., Buffalo 14202, tel. 716/845-5100, $$); **Best Western Inn–Downtown** (510 Delaware Ave., Buffalo 14202, tel. 716/886–8333, $$).

Where to Eat

Parkside Candy. This faded beauty is a dimly lit Art Deco relic, with unforgettable sundaes (known here as frappés) and homemade chocolates. The molasses paddles (75¢), sponge candy, and bittersweet hot fudge are stars. Desserts are the attraction, but there are also sandwiches. The interior has secluded wooden booths around the perimeter, stained glass, and torch lamps that add up to the genuine atmosphere of a 1930s-era soda parlor. *3208 Main St., Buffalo, tel. 716/833-7540. MC, V. $*

Eckl's Beef and Weck. Near Rich Stadium, home of the Buffalo Bills football team, it is an authentic place to eat Buffalo's best sandwich, made of fragrant sliced beef piled on a chewy salt roll. There are 27 tables plus bar seating. *4936 Ellicott Rd., Orchard Park (southeast Buffalo), tel. 716/662-2262. No credit cards. $*

Ted's Red Hots. Children may find Ted's hot sauce too sharp, but they'll be happy with the charcoal-grilled hot dogs and crisp onion rings. Red hots (thin, red-colored hot dogs with a very thin casing) are a regional specialty, and they're served here with another Buffalo standby, loganberry juice. There are seven Ted's locations in the area; this site has indoor booths and outdoor seating in good weather. *2312 Sheridan Dr., Tonawanda (north Buffalo), tel. 716/ 836–8986. No credit cards. $*

Entertainments

Buffalo Museum of Science. This towering turn-of-the-century building has several sections that appeal to children, featuring a climbing wall and an inventive Pretend Play area with a beaver lodge, two boats, nature puppets, and a dinosaur nest. There are more traditional exhibits behind glass, including an impressive collection of stuffed animals, including several who once lived in the Buffalo Zoo. *1020 Humboldt Pkwy., Buffalo, tel. 716/896–5200. Admission: $5.25 adults, $3.25 ages 2–18 and senior citizens, $12.50 family (except during special exhibits). Open Tues.–Sun. 10–5, Fri. until 10 PM.*

Buffalo Zoo. This zoo is aging, but the various animal compounds are compact, which makes it easy to walk. Kids and adults can get a thrill from the white tiger, the gorilla rain forest, and the children's zoo. There are carousel, train, and camel rides for $2 each. The Zootique gift shop has terrific and cheap animal masks. Free, very professional magic shows are given indoors from July to Labor Day at 1 and 3. A restaurant is on the grounds, and strollers can be rented for $2. Parking is $3. *300 Parkside Ave., Buffalo, tel. 716/837–3900. Admission: $7 adults, $3.50 ages 4–16, $3 senior citizens. Open daily 10–4.*

Sights to See

Buffalo and Erie County Historical Society. It's the only remaining building from the 1901 Pan-American Exposition. It was then the New York State Building. Now a statue of Lincoln sits behind the building overlooking a small lake in Delaware Park. Its exhibits tell the economic and social history of the Buffalo region. *25 Nottingham Ct., Buffalo, tel. 716/873–9644. Admission: $3.68 adults, $1.58 ages 7–15, under 7 free. Free admission Sat. 10–noon. Open Tues.–Sat. 10–5, Sun. noon–5.*

McKinley Assassination Site. The 1901 Exposition is remembered as the site of the shooting on September 6, 1901, of President William McKinley, who had come to speak at the Exposition. The exact site where McKinley was assassinated—the Exposition's Temple of Music—is marked only with a small plaque set into a rock in a median strip in a residential neighborhood. *Fordham Dr., not far from Lincoln Pkwy., 3 blocks north of Historical Society, Buffalo.*

Niagara Square. A more appropriate memorial to President McKinley—a large obelisk—stands in Niagara Square in the downtown just blocks from the new ballpark. The magnificent Art Deco City Hall dominates one side of the square, flanked by statues of the two Buffalo residents who became president—Millard Fillmore and Grover Cleveland. *Bordered by Jeroe, Perkins, Nasara, and Court Sts., Buffalo.*

Theodore Roosevelt Inaugural National Historic Site. If you're staying at the hotel used by the visiting baseball teams, you'll notice the handsome Greek Revival mansion across the street. The longtime home of a prominent Buffalo family, the Wilcox Mansion was saved from bulldozers because Theodore Roosevelt took the oath of office here. He became the 26th president of the United States on September 14, 1901, just hours after President McKinley died. *641 Delaware Ave., Buffalo, tel. 716/884–0095. Admission: $3 adults, $2 senior citizens, $1 ages 6–13, $6.50 family. Open weekdays 9–5, weekends noon–5.*

ROCHESTER RED WINGS

League: International League • **Major League Affiliation:** Baltimore Orioles • **Class:** AAA • **Stadium:** Frontier Field • **Opened:** 1997 • **Capacity:** 10,840 • **Dimensions:** LF: 335, CF: 402, RF: 325 • **Surface:** grass • **Season:** Apr.–early Sept.

STADIUM LOCATION: One Morrie Silver Way, Rochester, NY 14608.

TEAM WEB SITE: www.redwingsbaseball.com

GETTING THERE: The stadium is just west of the High Falls district in downtown Rochester. From I–490 East, take Exit 12 (Allen Street). Cross Broad Street and follow the signs to the stadium. From I–490 West, take Exit 14 and go two intersections to Main Street. Turn on Plymouth Avenue and follow the signs.

PARKING: There is plenty of parking available at stadium lot D on Morrie Silver Way for $4.

TICKET INFORMATION: One Morrie Silver Way, Rochester, NY 14608, tel. 716/454–1001, fax 716/454–1056.

PRICE RANGE: Premium box $9; upper box (rows A–O) $7.50; reserved (rows P–U and sections 201 & 227) $5. Reserved seats for senior citizens and ages 14 and under, $4.50. Standing room $4.

GAME TIME: Mon.–Sat. 7:15 PM, Sun. 2:15 PM. Gates open 75 minutes before game time.

TIPS ON SEATING: Sit on the first-base side for a great view of the downtown skyline. The home team dugout is also on the first-base side. The sun sets on the third-base side, so fans down the right-field line might have sun in their eyes in evening games. Section 224 is the family, no-alcohol section.

SEATING FOR PEOPLE WITH DISABILITIES: There are more than 100 seats throughout the stadium for people with disabilities.

STADIUM FOOD: You can get Rochester's famed red hots and white hots here. These two varieties of hot dogs are sold throughout the city; reds have spicier beef and pork and whites have veal, ham, beef, and milk powder in them. Both are lower-fat than standard "tube steaks." The grill also features a home plate—a cheeseburger with home fries and macaroni salad. There also are very good pulled pork sandwiches, Philly cheese steaks, Italian sausage, burritos, and flowering onions. Frank's Italian ice is hand-scooped.

SMOKING POLICY: Smoking is prohibited except in designated areas beyond the grandstand on both sides of the park.

VISITING TEAM HOTEL: Crowne Plaza (70 State St., Rochester, NY 14614, tel. 716/546–3450 or 800/227–6963).

TOURISM INFORMATION: Greater Rochester Visitors Association (126 Andrews St., Rochester, NY 14504, tel. 716/546–3070 or 800/677–7282).

Rochester: Frontier Field

The roots of the International League go back to 1884, giving it the longest history of continuous play of any minor league. Rochester, New York, has had a team in the league since 1885. Stadiums like Rochester's Silver Stadium were classic International League venues with the emphasis on excellent Triple A baseball and few frills. Opened in 1929 as Red Wing Stadium, this old ballpark saw seven decades of Hall of Fame–caliber players, including Stan Musial (the Cardinals farm team played here from 1929 through 1961) and Jim Palmer (Rochester's relationship with the Orioles since 1961 is the longest at the Triple A level). And, yes, when Cal Ripken, Jr., played here in 1981, he played in every game.

The International League isn't what it used to be. The American Association disbanded following the 1997 season, and the Buffalo Bisons, Indianapolis Indians, and Louisville Riverbats joined the International League. Durham's famous Single A Bulls jumped to Triple A as part of the expansion of major-league baseball. Buffalo, Durham, Indianapolis, and Norfolk all have outstanding new ballparks. Pawtucket completed a $16-million renovation for the 1999 season, and Louisville opens a new ballpark in 2000. Rochester joined the ranks with a new beauty in 1998.

Silver Stadium has been demolished and the Rochester Red Wings play at Frontier Field in the shadow of the landmark Eastman Kodak tower. This is the formula adopted by the parent club in Baltimore—build a great new ballpark in the downtown and watch the fans flood to your doorstep. In 1998, *Baseball America* ranked Rochester's fans as minor-league baseball's best. Rochester Community Baseball, Inc., was established in 1957 to save professional baseball in Rochester and 8,022 people bought stock in the club.

Tradition did not stop Rochester from building a thoroughly modern facility. The redbrick and dark-green steel structure cost $35.3 million and was designed by Ellerbe Becket, the architects for Atlanta's Turner Field and the Bank One Ballpark in Phoenix. It is surrounded by parking lots and topped by 36 skyboxes and a press box. There's an excellent souvenir shop and a large wide concourse full of concessions. There are two video scoreboards, a real organ, and a large red-winged bird mascot named Spikes.

Unfortunately, advertisements stacked four high beyond the outfield fence block some of the cityscape beyond. The back of the ads almost make up for this flaw as they are huge Kodak photos of seven Rochester legends that can be viewed from the parking lot. The Frontier Field Walk of Fame within the stadium near the Plymouth Avenue entrance on the left-field side features the stars of Rochester sports history.

Where to Stay

Visiting Team Hotel: Crowne Plaza. Seven blocks from the ballpark, in downtown, you'll find this large convention hotel. Guests have views of the river from most of the seven floors. The rooms are modern and large, if a little bland. *70 State St., Rochester 14614, tel. 716/546–3450 or 800/227–6963, fax 716/546–8712. 362 rooms. Facilities: restaurant, outdoor pool, fitness center. AE, D, DC, MC, V. $$*

Four Points Sheraton. Large modern rooms, many of them overlooking the Genesee River, fill this convenient downtown hotel. The 14-story high-rise is connected to the adjacent Convention Center by an enclosed skyway. There's underground parking for a fee. *120 E. Main St., Rochester 14604, tel. 716/546–6400 or 888/596–6400, fax 716/546–1341. 466 rooms. Facilities: restaurant, indoor pool. AE, D, DC, MC, V. $$*

Where to Eat

Bill Gray's. Huge grilled hamburgers followed by a chocolate almond ice-cream cone are a Rochester tradition. The combination is so popular, there are eight Bill Gray's restaurants in the city and six sister operations called Tom Wahl's. For the full summer experience, visit the Bill Gray's next to Seabreeze Amusement Park, right on Lake Ontario. There are lines of fans for the burgers, onion rings, fries, and separate counters for those just seeking ice cream. Happy eaters sit at Formica tables, watching the grill men work. Another outlet (100 Midtown Plaza, at E. Main St. and Clinton Ave., tel. 716/232–4760) is eight blocks from the ballpark and closes at 5 PM. *4870 Culver Rd., Rochester, tel. 716/266–7820. MC, V. $*

Highland Park Diner. This 1948 diner, built by the Orleans company and completely restored in 1986, is the best of old and new. You get comfort food in comfortable seats. Its apple pie is a standout, and there's real turkey and mashed potatoes. *960 S. Clinton Ave., at S. Goodman, Rochester, tel. 716/461–5040. AE, D, MC, V. $*

Rochester Public Market. This year-round market, 2 mi northeast of the ballpark, has stalls selling fragrant breads, overstuffed sandwiches, sausages, ethnic specialties, and crafts. Walk the rows and collect breakfast or lunch. *N. Union St., at Railroad Ave., Rochester, tel. 716/428–6907. Open Tues., Thurs. 5 AM –1 PM, Sat. 5 AM–3 PM. $*

Skyliner Diner. A full-service new diner has been installed outside of the Strong Children's Museum in downtown Rochester. It's a stainless-steel and Formica heaven, with hearty blue-plate specials. There are kid's menus for breakfast and lunch that include turkey sandwiches, spaghetti, burgers, and fresh vegetables, plus tiny sundaes. *One Manhattan Sq., Rochester, tel. 719/263–2703. AE, MC, V. $*

Entertainments

Seabreeze Amusement Park/Raging Rivers Waterpark. Many of the 75 rides in this park, the fourth-oldest in the country, give you spectacular views of Lake Ontario. There are four varied roller coasters, a hand-carved carousel in a Victorian-style building, a skyride, and a water park. The whole place is beautifully maintained and family-owned. *4600 Culver Rd., Rochester, tel. 716/323–1900. Admission (ride and slide) $14.95 adults, $9.95 persons under 48"; after 5 PM $8.50. Open May–Labor Day, daily noon–10.*

Strong Museum. The original Sesame Street set and a large collection of baby boomer toys are found in this kicky children's museum. Children may try on costumes and play house in a turn-of-the-century parlor and kitchen. There are many interactive history exhibits, including a wooden sailing ship. A 1918 Herschell carousel can be ridden. *One Manhattan Sq., at Chestnut St. and Woodbury Blvd., Rochester, tel. 716/263–2700. Admission: $6 adults, $5 senior citizens and students, $4 ages 3–17. Open Mon.–Thurs. 10–5, Fri. 10–8, Sat. 10–5, Sun. noon–5.*

Sights to See

High Falls. Just blocks from the ballpark is the Brown's Race Historic District, adjacent to the Genesee River. This former flour-milling area features a natural waterfall, a restored water-wheel, 19th-century industrial buildings, and exhibits on city history in the Center at High Falls Museum. There are laser and fireworks shows on many summer nights. *60 Browns Race, Rochester, tel. 716/325–2030. Open Tues.–Sat. 10–4, Sun. noon–4.*

George Eastman House. Photographers will enjoy the exhibits on film, photography, and Kodak founder George Eastman. The works of more than 8,000 photographers, hundreds of Hollywood movies, and the personal collections of Cecil B. DeMille and Martin Scorsese are housed in the International Museum of Photography and Film. There is a one-hour guided tour of the 52-room Colonial Revival mansion and gardens. There are film programs Wednesday–Sunday at 8 PM for an extra fee. *900 East Ave., Rochester, tel. 716/271–3361. Admission: $6.50 adults, $5 senior citizens and students, $2.50 ages 5–12. Film programs: $5. Open daily 10–4:30.*

Susan B. Anthony House. See the house where Susan B. Anthony was arrested for the crime of voting in 1872. Leaders of the suffrage movement met in this Victorian home, where Anthony lived for 40 years. She met here with Frederick Douglass and Elizabeth Cady Stanton. It is now a National Historic Landmark filled with suffrage photos. *17 Madison St., Rochester, tel. 716/235–6124. Admission: $6 adults, $4.50 senior citizens, $3 students, $2 under 13. Open Thurs.–Sun. 1–4. D, MC, V.*

TORONTO BLUE JAYS

League: American League • **Class:** Major League • **Stadium:** SkyDome • **Opened:** 1989 • **Capacity:** 50,516 • **Dimensions:** LF: 328, CF: 400, RF: 328 • **Surface:** artificial turf • **Season:** Apr.–Sept.

STADIUM LOCATION: One Blue Jays Way, Toronto, Ontario M5V 1J1.

GETTING THERE: SkyDome is in the downtown just west of the CN Tower. From the west, take QEW/Gardiner Expressway east and exit at Spadina Avenue. Go north on Spadina one block, right on Blue Jays Way. From the east, take Gardiner Expressway west and exit at Spadina Avenue. Go north on Spadina one block, right on Blue Jays Way. Toronto has an excellent transit system. Union Station on the Yonge/University subway is near the stadium. For transit information, tel. 416/869–3200.

PARKING: Public parking is not available at the SkyDome for Blue Jays games. There are many private and public lots within walking distance.

TICKET INFORMATION: One Blue Jays Way, Suite 3200, Toronto, Ontario M5V 1J1, tel. 416/341–1000, fax 416/341–1245.

PRICE RANGE: SkyClub baseline C$36; field-level bases C$32; field-level baselines C$29.50; SkyClub outfield C$29.50; 100-level outfield C$22; SkyDeck infield C$22; SkyDeck bases C$15; SkyDeck baselines C$6.

GAME TIME: Weekdays 7:05 PM, Sat. 1:05 or 4:05 PM, Sun. 1:05 PM. Gates open 90 min before game.

TIPS ON SEATING: The 200-level seats are excellent. The first three or four rows at the 100-level past the outfield wall are a good buy, but your view of the jumbotron may be obstructed. When the dome is open, the setting sun shines on the upper level (500) on the first-base side. The home dugout is on the third-base side.

SEATING FOR PEOPLE WITH DISABILITIES: Seats are designated throughout the park. Guest Relations, tel. 416/341–3034 will make special arrangements if necessary. To reserve a parking space, tel. 416/341–3004. Gate 7 is the entrance for fans with disabilities.

STADIUM FOOD: Foot-long hot dogs are a novelty here, but the honey garlic sausages and Kretschmer dogs taste better. Stacked roast beef and corned beef on rye sandwiches at Biltner's International Deli stands are good, even if the only mustard is bright yellow. The best, and most addictive, food in the park are Maddison's hot cinnamon-sugar mini-doughnuts. A bag is $3.50. A close second are the Bavarian-style beer nuts. A Tex-Mex grill serves decent fajitas, but we'd stick with the sausages and beef sandwiches. There's a McDonalds and a Hard Rock Cafe in the park.

SMOKING POLICY: Smoking is not allowed in the seating or concourse areas. Smoking is permitted in the Puffer's Lounges behind aisles 136, 215, 233, and 511.

TOURISM INFORMATION: Tourism Toronto (207 Queen's Quay W, Suite 509, Toronto, ON, Canada M5J 1A7, tel. 416/203–2500 or 800/363–1990).

Toronto: SkyDome

We don't like domes, and we don't like plastic grass. And now there are better domes with real grass in Phoenix and Seattle. So why visit here? Because Toronto is one of the great cities of the world and, frankly, SkyDome isn't all that bad. The last time we visited, the roof was rolled back, and it seemed almost like real baseball. At least until someone got one of those horrid artificial turf hits.

When the Blue Jays came to town in 1977, they played in Exhibition Stadium in the middle of the Canadian National Exhibition site. This place was built for track and field meets and parades. In the 1970s, it worked better for rock concerts than baseball. So even with its limitations, Sky-Dome was an improvement when it opened in 1989. The place was alive with excitement in the early 1990s when the Jays won the World Series two years in a row. The 1992 and 1993

World Series banners hang between the Canadian and American flags at the top of the dome in straightaway center field.

Setting baseball aside, this is an impressive building, as it should be for its $500-million price tag. The roof weighs 11,000 tons and covers 8 acres. It comes in four sections. It takes about 20 minutes to open, as three of the sections slide inside the fourth. With the dome closed, you could still fit a 31-story building in here. The huge video scoreboard is 33 ft by 115 ft and cost $17 million.

The Toronto Argonauts of the Canadian Football League play in the SkyDome from June through November (tel. 416/341–5151). In America, we have seen how multi-use stadiums necessarily lack the intimacy and quirkiness that we love in baseball-only ballparks. Here's the bad news—Canadian Football League fields are 30 yards longer than fields used in the National Football League. So we are talking about a lot of foul territory, and not many seats very close to the baseball action.

There's no telling what you might see in the hotel suites in centerfield. We saw a bride and groom standing behind a "Just Married" sign. From the third-base side when the dome is open, you can see the Big Needle. There is a bright yellow Playland for young kids under four ft tall on the level-one concourse behind first base at section 117. A 45-minute walking tour of the SkyDome, plus a 15-minute film, is held daily, usually 10–4. Entrance to the tour, tel. 416/341–2770, is between gates 1 and 2. Admission is C$10.50 adults, C$8 senior citizens and youths, C$6.50 children.

Where to Stay

Best Western Primrose Hotel. Its convenient downtown location near Yonge Street and Maple Leaf Gardens allows you to keep the car garaged and use the nearby subway and streetcar. The rooms are big enough and the price reasonable for the city. The 23-story hotel allows two children under 12 to share rooms free with parents. *111 Carlton St., Toronto, Ontario M5B 2G3, tel. 416/977–8000 or 800/268–8082, fax 416/977–6323. 337 rooms. Facilities: 2 restaurants, outdoor pool, exercise room, parking (fee). AE, D, DC, V. $$*

Delta Chelsea Inn. There are frequent weekend deals at this huge downtown hotel that caters to families with a supervised playroom. Parents pay for two and a half hours of playtime per child and are given a pager. There's also a teen center with video games. The rooms are standard size, and newly redone in pastels; many have balconies. *33 Gerrard St. W, Toronto, Ontario M5G 1Z4, tel. 416/595–1975 or 800/243–5732, fax 416/585–4302. 1,591 rooms. Facilities: 5 restaurants, indoor pool, fitness center, parking (fee). AE, D, DC, V. $$$*

Executive Motor Hotel. The rooms are small, but the price is right at this modest three-story downtown hotel that caters to business travelers during the week. Free parking is a bonus, and there are free donuts and beverages for breakfast. Kids 16 and under stay free. *621 King St., Toronto, Ontario M5V 1M5, tel. 416/504–7441, fax 416/504—4722. 85 rooms. AE, D, DC, MC, V. $$*

Where to Eat

Lee Garden. Toronto has three Chinatowns, and the stretch along Spadina Avenue is the busiest. The specialty here is seafood—soft-shell crabs, a myriad of shrimp dishes, and oysters and black bean sauce. You'll sit family-style with others at tables. You may wait in line to get in, but the service is speedy and the food is light. No gummy sweet and sour pork here. *331 Spadina Ave., Toronto, tel. 416/593–9524. AE, MC, V. $$*

Mr. Greek. The service is fast and families are welcome at this Greektown standby. Inexpensive shish kabobs, salads, gyros, and souvlaki are featured, along with Greek music. The "L.L.B.O." sign on the door means it's licensed to sell alcohol. *568 Danforth Ave., Toronto, tel. 416/461–5470. MC, V. $*

Shopsy's Deli. Jewish comfort food has been dispensed here since the 1920's. Cheese blintzes are extraordinary—no need to smother them in sour cream or cherries. Corned beef on rye, matzo-ball soup, melt-in-your-mouth brisket—it's all here in this busy family restaurant that seats 300. There are two newer outlets, at 284A King St. W., tel. 416/599–5464, and 1535 Yonge St., tel. 416/967–5252. *33 Yonge St., Toronto, tel. 416/365–3333. MC, V. $*

Entertainments

Centreville Amusement Park. Every 15 minutes, ferries at the foot of Bay Street and at Queen's Quay at Harbourfront take day passengers to the Toronto Islands, visible from the city. Entry is free to this 600-acre playland, and there are a minifarm, lagoons, miniature golf, and boat rentals for those who don't want to spend the day on thrill rides. There's a large kiddie ride section, with a train and a Western village. *Centre Island, Centreville, tel. 416/203–0405. Admission (all-day ride tickets): C$17.95 adults, C$12.80 under 49", C$58 family rate. Open June–Labor Day, daily 10:30–8; May and Sept., weekends 10–6. MC, V.*

Ontario Place. This 96-acre family entertainment park is on Lake Ontario, west of downtown and across Lakeshore Boulevard from the Canadian National Exhibition (CNE) grounds.

Come prepared to get wet in the water attractions. The Bumper Boats and Wilderness Adventure Ride are fun. Cool Hoops has two dozen basketball hoops with odd-shaped backboards and weird angles. Children's Village, for ages 12 and under, has many slides and moon bounces. There is a parking fee and IMAX admission is extra. A water taxi (tel. 416/869–1372 round-trip C$10) leaves from downtown's York Street Pier to Ontario Place every 90 minutes. *955 Lakeshore Blvd. W, Toronto, tel. 416/314–9900. Admission: C$22 ages 6–54, C$11 ages 4–5 and senior citizens, family fee for four, C$35. Prices increase during the CNE and include admission to the fair. Open mid-June–Labor Day, daily 10 AM–midnight; mid-May–mid-June and Sept., daily 10–6. MC, V.*

Sights to See

Bata Shoe Museum. The limestone building housing four floors of shoes is shaped like a shoebox. Inside is a collection of 10,000 shoes, from styles worn by Elton John to Indian moccasins. Elvis's shoes are here and so are Winston Churchill's. *327 Bloor St. W, Toronto, tel. 416/979–7799. Admission: C$6 adults, C$4 senior citizens, C$2 ages 5–14, C$12 family pass. Free first Tues. of the month. Open Tues.–Sat. 10–5, Sun. noon–5.*

Canadian National Exhibition. The Exhibition, held from mid-August through Labor Day each year, is like a grand state fair complete with Ferris wheel, crafts, horse shows, and Pee Wee baseball. For decades Exhibition Stadium, home of the Blue Jays from 1977 to 1988, was the heart of the CNE complex. Baseball was first played on this site in 1885. The grandstands used by the Blue Jays were constructed in 1948 and 1959 and demolished in 1999. There are shuttle buses to the subway. *Exhibition Place, Toronto, tel. 416/393–6300.*

Canada's Sports Hall of Fame. If you are at the Exhibition, drop by this tribute to Canadian athletes, even though there is virtually nothing on baseball. The hall will be expanding greatly and moving to Ottawa in July 2002. *Exhibition Place, Toronto, tel. 416/260–6789. Open weekdays 10–4:30.*

CN Tower. The 1,815-ft tower, believed to be the world's tallest free-standing structure, is right next door to the SkyDome. It is a special treat to see when the dome is open. There are two observation decks, at 1,465 and 1,120 ft. On clear days, you can see Niagara Falls. A revolving restaurant is 1,150 ft up and patrons get free admission to decks. *301 Front St. W, Toronto, tel. 416/360–8500. Admission to lower deck: C$15 adults, C$13 senior citizens, C$11 ages 4–12. Fee for highest desk, C$3.74 extra. Open daily 8 AM–11 PM. AE, MC, V.*

Hockey Hall of Fame. Hockey enthusiasts will want to visit Great Bell Hall to see Lord Stanley's Cup and take a few shots on goal in the interactive exhibits. There is a full-scale replica of the Montreal Canadiens' dressing room, a collection of goalie masks, plus films and history exhibits on the sport. *Yonge and Front Sts., Toronto, tel. 416/360–7765. Admission: C$10 adults, C$6 senior citizens and ages 3–13. Open Mon.–Sat. 9:30–6, Sun. 10–6. AE, MC, V.*

Ontario Parliament Buildings. Toronto is the seat of government for the 9 million residents of the Province of Ontario. The Romanesque-style sandstone Legislative Building was completed in 1893. Visit the elegant Legislative Chamber at the top of the grand staircase and the displays from local historical societies and museums. Consider walking the lovely Queen's Park grounds. *Queen's Park, Toronto, tel. 416/325–7500. Guided tours late May–Labor Day, daily 9–4; Labor Day–late May, weekdays 9–4.*

BUCKEYE BASEBALL
CLEVELAND, AKRON, TOLEDO

18

Baseball is big in northern Ohio. It helped revive downtown Cleveland and Akron, and it put Toledo on the nation's sports map with the clever Mud Hens logo. In addition to Cleveland's glorious Jacobs Field stadium, there is the world-famous Rock and Roll Hall of Fame and its lakefront neighbor, the Great Lakes Science Center. A short walk up the lakefront brings you to Cleveland Browns Stadium, on the site of former Municipal Stadium, once home of the Indians. The flats area along the Cuyahoga River has been revitalized with dozens of restaurants, a light rail stop, and an outdoor amphitheater. If you can't get a ticket to a sold-out Indians game, take a guided tour through the stadium's stunning modern architecture.

Akron, the rubber city, is 45 mi south of Cleveland. Its team, the Aeros, is named for the city's aerospace industry. The classic boomerang-shaped grandstand, adjacent to the Ohio & Erie Canal, has brought the city new restaurants, a science center, sports bars, and a spirit of fun and possibility.

West of Cleveland 115 mi, along the Ohio Turnpike, is Toledo, a glass-making center with a comfortable ballpark on what was once a horse track. Children will beg to stop at Cedar Point, an amusement park on Sandusky Bay, halfway between Cleveland and Toledo. It's worth it, and your entry fee includes the use of its clean beach. Toledo is a city with surprises, including the finest small zoo in the country. It is imaginative, with beautiful restoration of its clever Depression-era animal houses. The ballpark has a Triple A team. You can swim before the game at one of the adjacent city pools.

CLEVELAND INDIANS

League: American League • **Class:** Major League • **Stadium:** Jacobs Field • **Opened:** 1994 • **Capacity:** 42,800 • **Dimensions:** LF: 325, CF: 405, RF: 325 • **Surface:** grass • **Season:** Apr.–Sept.

STADIUM LOCATION: 2401 Ontario St., Cleveland, OH 44115.

TEAM WEB SITE: www.indians.com

GETTING THERE: Jacobs Field is a 10-minute walk from Tower City Center, where all RTA trains go. For additional transit information, call Regional Transit Authority (tel. 216/621–9500). By car from south, take I–77 north to E. 9th St. exit to Ontario St. From east, take I–90/Rte. 2 west to downtown. Stay on Rte. 2 to E. 9th St. Turn left to stadium.

PARKING: Plenty of parking downtown within walking distance of Jacobs Field; $10 at stadium, less farther away.

TICKET INFORMATION: 2401 Ontario St., Cleveland, OH 44115, tel. 216/420–4200, fax 216/420–4396.

PRICE RANGE: Field box, view box, and club seats, season tickets only; lower box $22; lower reserved, mezzanine, and upper box $18; upper reserved $10; bleachers $14; reserved general admission, standing room $6.

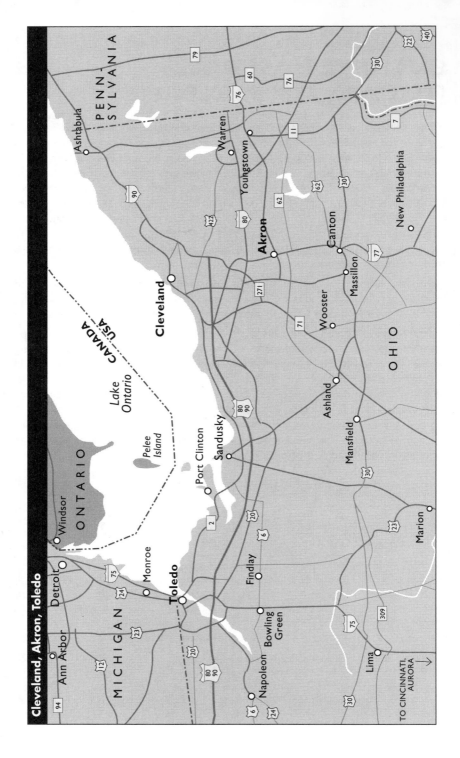

Cleveland, Akron, Toledo

GAME TIME: 7:05 PM, day games 1:05 PM; gates open 90 min before game.

TIPS ON SEATING: Don't be picky here. If you can get a ticket for an Indians game at Jacobs Field, be happy.

SEATING FOR PEOPLE WITH DISABILITIES: Throughout stadium. Parking spaces available in on-site garage directly beyond left field. Call 216/420–4200 for brochure for Indians fans with disabilities.

STADIUM FOOD: Egg rolls, ribs, chili bowls, salads, fajitas, pizza, and cheesecake make up the diverse menu here. The bakery at Section 129 is a good first stop for a fruit cup or a cinnamon roll. The delis have good chicken Caesar salads, fresh turkey breast sandwiches, and so-so corned beef sandwiches. The best bargain is the $2.50 soft taco with sour cream at Section 154. Five pierogis are $3 and come loaded with buttery onions. Cleveland's excellent Pierre's ice cream gives you two large scoops for $2.50. Bertman's spicy brown Ballpark Mustard, another great Cleveland item, is the only mustard served. **KidsLand,** at Section 116, has lower prices than other concession stands for everything but red licorice (50¢ more) and sells milk and peanut butter and jelly sandwiches. There's a picnic area in KidsLand, plus picnic plazas throughout the stadium, with the largest in center field. The fancy, glass-fronted multilevel **Terrace Restaurant,** past the club-level seating down the third-base line, is open to season ticket holders only.

SMOKING POLICY: No-smoking facility with designated smoking areas. Not allowed in seating bowl.

TOURISM INFORMATION: Cleveland Convention & Visitors Bureau (Terminal Tower, Suite 3100, 50 Public Sq., Cleveland, OH 44113, tel. 216/621–4110 or 800/321–1004).

Cleveland: Jacobs Field

A decade ago, you could walk up to the ticket booth in Cleveland and buy tickets right behind the Indians dugout. It was one of the weirdest sights we have ever seen in sports—2,000 people in a stadium built to hold 80,000. It was Municipal Stadium, a Depression-era ball field right by Lake Erie.

The faded, usually almost empty Municipal Stadium was a perfect symbol of Cleveland's down-and-out era of the 1960s and '70s, when the city was known as "the Mistake by the Lake." In the 1970s, Cleveland went into bankruptcy, and the Cuyahoga River actually caught fire in 1969.

It's different in Cleveland now. They have a beautiful ballpark and a winning team. Sports fans in Cleveland have rediscovered baseball. If you are planning a trip to Jacobs Field, plan ahead. In recent years, every ticket to every game was sold before the first pitch was thrown on opening day.

They did it right in Cleveland this time—no concrete doughnut in a sea of asphalt here. Following the lead of Baltimore and using the same architects, HOK Sport of Kansas City, they fit a huge sports complex neatly into the fabric of the city. With a landscape team led by Sasaki Associates, the Gateway Sports Complex has been a key element of the astonishing revitalization of downtown Cleveland.

The 28-acre Gateway Sports Complex includes, in addition to Jacobs Field, Gund Arena, the home of the Cleveland Cavaliers of the NBA. Built on the edge of downtown on the site of a decaying market, the complex has considerable tree-lined public space and a million dollars' worth of public art.

At the main entrance on East 9th Street (Gate C) stands a statue of Cleveland's great Hall of Fame pitcher Bob Feller, about to deliver one of his awe-inspiring fastballs. Nearby, a set of granite benches, the work of artist Nancy Dwyer, spells out WHO'S ON FIRST? Another set of Dwyer benches spells out MEET ME HERE in front of the adjacent Gund Arena, at Ontario and Huron streets. Inside the park are several large baseball paintings and scores of banners celebrating Indians stars and great moments in Cleveland baseball history.

Opened in 1994 and called the Jake by the locals, the field is named after the Jacobs family, who bought the Indians in 1986. The ballpark's playing field is 18 ft below street level, helping to keep the 42,400-capacity stadium on a reasonable downtown scale. In 1920s slang, "It's jake" meant everything was fine. This park is jake with us.

In contrast to the traditional redbrick exterior of Baltimore's Camden Yards, Cleveland opted for a sleek, modern look. With its white exterior, exposed steel beams, and vertical light towers, Jacobs Field is making a strong architectural statement—you are in steeltown.

Walk up to the upper deck on the third-base side to see the boats on the Cuyahoga River's Collision Bend. From the first-base side at the upper level, you can see the skyscrapers of downtown and the elegant stone-gated Erie Street Cemetery and Church on East 9th Street below.

A huge American flag flutters in the lake breezes in center field. A 19-ft-high mini–Green Monster stands in left field, complete with the scores of all major-league games being played that day. A gigantic three-screen, 120-by-220-ft scoreboard, unfortunately littered with too much advertising, hangs above the bleachers. From behind home plate, you can see Cleveland's downtown office buildings over the standing-room-only porch above the left-field mini-Monster and past the flag in center. Three decks of seats rise beyond right field.

The Indians Team Shop, on the third-base side, is well worth a visit even if you have to wait in line. The shop includes an excellent display of Cleveland baseball memorabilia, along with replica Cleveland uniforms and hats back to 1908. It also has a display of photos of the members of the Indians Hall of Fame.

KidsLand, on the lower level down the right-field line, has a kid-oriented souvenir shop, a food stand, a picnic area, and a playground with a dozen (made-in-Ohio) Little Tike houses, slides, and cars for young children. We ran into Slider, the Indians' colorful purple-and-yellow mascot, here. Kids especially like Homer Zone, an interactive video game behind home plate near Gate D, where batters can experience what it feels like to hit one into the bleachers at Jacobs Field (eight pitches for $2).

With Jacobs Field sold out before the season starts, your best bet for a visit might be to take the official tour. Tours leave from the Indians

Team Shop on Ontario Street and last about 45 minutes. Proceeds from the tours benefit Cleveland Indians Charities. *Tickets, tel. 216/ 241–8888 at least 11 days in advance; information, tel. 216/420–4400. Admission: $5 adults, $2.50 ages under 15 and over 59. Tours May– Sept, Mon.–Sat. every ½ hr 10–2, excluding day games, special events, and holidays.*

Gund Arena is down the left-field line across Ontario Street from Gate A. Hour-long public tours leave from the Arcade entrance. *Huron Ave. at E. 6th St., tel. 216/420–2010. Admission: $5 adults, $3 ages under 13 and senior citizens. Tours Fri. at 1 PM.*

More Cleveland Baseball

League Park. The legendary League Park at East 66th Street and Lexington Avenue opened in 1891 and closed for good in 1947. This was a wonderfully quirky ballpark of another era, with an oddly shaped outfield configuration and no lights. The right-field fence was only 290 ft from home plate, and in 1929 Babe Ruth hit his 500th home run over the 40-ft-high chicken-wire fence there. The field where Hall of Famers Tris Speaker and Bob Feller played is now a neighborhood recreation center. Most of the ballpark was demolished in 1951, but the field has been preserved, and Cleveland Indians home-run slugger Larry Doby's RBI Program (Reviving Baseball in Inner Cities) plays its games here. Now called League Park Center, the two-story ticket booth built in 1909 still stands, along with the redbrick exterior wall along East 66th Street, a portion of the grandstand, and the remains of what appears to have been a dugout on the first-base side. A historical marker notes that Cy Young pitched the very first game played here, on May 1, 1891, for the Cleveland Spiders, and that the Cleveland Buckeyes won the 1945 Negro World Series here. The site has been on the National Register of Historic Places since 1979. To get here, drive east from downtown on Lake Superior for approximately 3 mi. Take a right on 66th Street. In six blocks, you will find League Park between Lexington and Linwood avenues.

Municipal Stadium. Completed in 1931 at a cost of nearly $3 million, Municipal Stadium was the first city-owned major-league baseball stadium in the United States. It was also the largest baseball stadium ever built, as Cleveland was bidding to host the 1932 Olympics, an honor that went instead to Los Angeles. Originally, the outfield wall in center field was 470 ft from home plate, with the power alleys 463 ft. Babe Ruth said, "You'd have to have a horse to play outfield there." In 1947, after more than a decade when the Indians played here only on Sunday and holidays, new owner Bill Veeck moved the Indians to Municipal Stadium full-time. An inner fence was built with center field 410 ft from home. Veeck hired Larry Doby, the first African-American in the American League, and won the World Series in 1948. When you visit the Rock & Roll Hall of Fame and the Great Lakes Science Center, take a look left down the lake at the site where monumental Municipal Stadium stood. It was demolished in late 1996 and was reborn in 1999 as the once-again home of the Cleveland Browns football team.

Where to Stay

Sheraton Cleveland City Centre. Half of the rooms in this 22-story hotel have views of the lake and the Rock & Roll Hall of Fame; the others face the city. All rooms have contemporary furnishings and contain irons, ironing boards, and hair dryers. Guests can pay $8 daily for access to the nearby Athletic Club (1326 E. 9th St.), which has an indoor pool, a sauna, a hot tub, indoor and outdoor tracks, and racquetball courts. The hotel is across from the convention center and a four-block walk from Jacobs Field. *777 St. Clair Ave., at E. 6th St., Cleveland 44114, tel. 216/771–7600 or 800/321–1090, fax 216/566–0736. 470 rooms. Facilities: restaurant, hair salon, health center, parking (fee). AE, D, DC, MC, V. $$*

Embassy Suites. Near Playhouse Square and within walking distance of all downtown attractions, this modern hotel has 11 floors of nicely decorated two-room suites. Guests receive a full breakfast and an afternoon reception. Each room has an iron and ironing board. *1701 E. 12th St., Cleveland 44114, tel. 216/523–8000 or 800/362–2779, fax 216/523–1698. 288 suites. Facilities: restaurant, indoor pool, parking (fee). AE, D, DC, MC, V. $$*

Holiday Inn Lakeside City Center. If you get a room facing the lake in this convenient, 18-story hotel, you can watch the ships and pleasure boats on Lake Erie and the small-plane traffic at adjacent Burke Lakefront Airport. This 23-year-old hotel is well used; the rooms are standard in size and decor. But you are only two blocks from the Rock & Roll Hall of Fame and nine blocks from the ballpark. It's wise to leave the car here and walk to the park. *1111 Lakeside Ave., Cleveland 44114, tel. 216/241–5100 or 800/465–4329, fax 216/241–7437. 370 rooms. Facilities: restaurant, indoor pool, sauna, exercise machines, coin laundry, parking (fee). AE, D, DC, MC, V. $$*

Where to Eat

New York Spaghetti House. An unassuming Tudor cottage across the street from the ballpark houses the city's oldest downtown restaurant. Its bustling, veteran waiters are characters, and its delicious, thick spaghetti sauce is legendary. Downstairs, candles, table lights, carnations, red-checked tablecloths, and warm-toned murals give the main dining room a dim, cozy feel for families and a romantic look for others. Lunch is a bargain—one spaghetti special is $4.99. You can order a half-portion of spaghetti for children, as the servings are generous. Patricia Brigotti, a granddaughter of the founders, operates a gallery of local and regional artists in the upstairs dining rooms. *2173 E. 9th St., Cleveland, tel. 216/696–6624. AE, D, MC, V. No lunch Sun. $$*

Ninth Street Grill. This bright, modern restaurant is on the second floor of a block-long enclosed shopping mall just two blocks from the Rock & Roll Hall of Fame and nine blocks from the ballpark. It serves upscale versions of pizza, chicken sandwiches, various pastas, and salads. Through the glass back wall you have a good view of the city's 70,000-pound Claes Oldenburg FREE red rubber-stamp sculpture. On the mall's first floor is a food court with nine even more casual restaurants. The **French Bakery & Bistro** sells cookies resembling baseballs. While you wait for your food, your kids can run across the mall to the **Cleveland Indians Company Team Shop,** packed with great Indians memorabilia. *Galleria, E. 9th St. and Sinclair Ave., Cleveland, tel. 216/579–9919. AE, D, MC, V. $$*

Entertainments

Crawford Auto-Aviation Museum. Operated by the Western Reserve Historical Society, this museum contains early bicycles, an 1897 gasoline-powered car, vintage cars from the turn of the century, a Sears catalog car, and a street of old-time shops. Cleveland once led the country in car making, and this collection has touring and racing cars. Admission also gives you entry to the two mansions that make up the society's History Museum. *10825 East Blvd., Cleveland, tel. 216/721–5722. Admission: $6.50 adults, $4.50 ages 6–12, $5.50 senior citizens. Open Tues.–Sat. 10–5, Sun. noon–5.*

The Flats. Restaurants line each side of the Cuyahoga River in this former industrial section, which now offers tour boats, Jet Ski rentals, a bandshell, and a power plant that's been renovated into more restaurants and a comedy club. The river still is used by working tugboats and barges. As you sit at waterside, you are surrounded by some of the city's 50 impressive bridges, a busy rail line, and the skyline of the city. (The Cleveland Children's Museum, tel. 216/791–7114, will send you a copy of its "Bridge Hunt" if you want to track the bridges that connect the city's east and west sides.) A shuttle to Indians games leaves from Nautica Boat Lines, and a water taxi takes you from the east to the west bank of the flats. There is a light-rail stop on the east side of the flats. *Foot of Saint Clair and Superior Aves., Cleveland, tel. 216/566–1046.*

Great Lakes Science Center. Next door to the Rock & Roll Hall (see below) is the lakefront's latest attraction, an impressive science center with more than 350 displays and hands-on exhibits. The bountiful and shipwreck-filled Great Lakes are the emphasis here. An IMAX theater has a separate admission at the same rate as that of the museum. *601 Erieside Ave., Cleveland, tel. 216/694–2000. Admission: $7.75 adults, $5.25 ages 3–17; combination ticket $10.95 adults, $7.75 children. Open daily 9:30–5:30.*

The Rock & Roll Hall of Fame and Museum. The '70s outrage acts like Alice Cooper's seem to get the biggest play in this unusual I. M. Pei building with huge open spaces and walls of flashy graphics. The steel-and-glass triangle has seven floors and a guitar-shaped wing. You begin touring on the ground floor, with two excellent short films, which can take 15 minutes of waiting time to get into on busy weekend days. Stars' costumes, instruments, hand-written songs, and other fine memorabilia are well displayed. The film on the fourth floor is not suitable for younger children. Wonderful displays throughout allow you to wear headsets and choose songs you'd like to hear. There's a good memorial to Cleveland's Alan Freed, radio's tireless promoter of rock and roll, with vintage radio sets tuned to influential music broadcasters, arranged by decade and city. The cafeteria-style café inside the Hall has rich desserts, some sandwiches, and photos of stars eating. *One Key Plaza, at E. 9th St. and Erieside Ave., Cleveland, tel. 216/781–7625. Admission: $14.95 adults, $11.50 ages 9–11 and senior citizens, ages 8 and under free. Open Memorial Day–Labor Day, Sun.–Tues. 10–5:30, Wed.–Sat. 10–9; Labor Day–Memorial Day, Thurs.–Tues. 10–5:30, Wed. 10–9. AE, MC, V.*

Sights to See

The Arcade. This 1890s structure on the National Register of Historic Places once hosted the Republican National Convention. Shops and restaurants fill many of its floors. Inside, beautiful brass balconies and a soaring atrium make this a one-of-a-kind urban shopping mall from the last century. *401 Euclid Ave., Cleveland, tel. 216/621–8500. Open weekdays 7–7, Sat. 7–6.*

Playhouse Square. Cleveland has renovated three grand movie palaces, all within steps of each other on Euclid Avenue. Free guided tours of the theaters for kids are given one weekend each month. There is also a children's and a Broadway theater series for children ages three and up. *Playhouse Square Center, 1501 Euclid Ave., Cleveland, tel. 216/771–4444.*

Terminal Tower Observation Deck. See the city's skyline, the Lake Erie shoreline, steel mills, Cleveland's bridges, and the Cuyahoga River from the top of what was for decades the city's tallest building, the 52-story Terminal Tower. Erected on Public Square, the Gothic tower took 11 years to build before it opened in 1930. Across Public Square is the Old Stone Church, a stopping place on the Underground Railroad. The Soldiers and Sailors Monument in the square is topped with a Statue of Liberty. Ticket sales stop 30 minutes before the enclosed deck closes. *50 Public Sq., Cleveland, tel. 216/621–7981. Admission: $2 adults, $1 ages 6–16. Open Memorial Day–Labor Day, daily 11–5; Labor Day–Memorial Day, daily 11–4.*

Unusual Shopping

West Side Market. Food mavens have long done their shopping at this fresh-food heaven. There are more than 180 stalls of fresh fruit, vegetables, baked goods, live poultry, and ethnic meats, spices, and prepared foods from a host of European and Asian countries. The low prices and high quality will make you cry over your supermarket's offerings. Come early in the day with a large carry-all bag. *W. 25th St., at Lorain Ave., Cleveland, tel. 216/664–3386. Open Mon. and Wed. 7–4, Fri. and Sat. 7–6. Closed Sun., Tues., and Thurs.*

AKRON AEROS

League: Eastern League • **Major League Affiliation:** Cleveland Indians • **Class:** AA • **Stadium:** Canal Park • **Opened:** 1997 • **Capacity:** 9,277 • **Dimensions:** LF: 331, CF: 400, RF: 337 • **Surface:** grass • **Season:** Apr.–early Sept.

STADIUM LOCATION: 300 S. Main St., Akron, OH 44308.

TEAM WEB SITE: www.akronaeros.com

GETTING THERE: Canal Park is in Akron's downtown. From I–76 or I–77 South, exit onto Route 59 East, exit at Exchange Center and turn right on Center Street, then left on Main Street. From I–76 West or I–77 North, exit at Main Street/Downtown. Follow exit onto Broadway, left on Exchange Street, right on Main Street.

PARKING: There are 12,000 spaces within a ten-minute walk.

TICKET INFORMATION: 300 S. Main St., Akron, OH 44308, tel. 330/253–5151, fax 330/253–3300.

PRICE RANGE: Reserved seats $8 adults, $6 ages 12 and under, senior citizens; bleachers $7 adults, $5 children and senior citizens.

GAME TIME: Mon.–Sat. 7:05 PM, Sun. 2:05 PM; gates open 1 hr before game.

TIPS ON SEATING: All 7,536 reserved seats are close to the action. There is a bleacher area seating almost 900 on aluminum benches just beyond the right-field wall. The sun sets over the left-field wall, so sit on the third-base side. The home team dugout is on the third-base side. Section 123 is the Family Section, where no alcohol is allowed.

SEATING FOR PEOPLE WITH DISABILITIES: There is seating for people with disabilities and their companions throughout the ballpark.

STADIUM FOOD: There is standard ballpark fare at various stands with flight-oriented names. The Galaxy Grill has good chicken sandwiches and the bullpen barbecue has fair pork sandwiches. The buffet restaurant behind right-field bleachers is by reservation only. As you walk to the game, stop at the **Peanut Shoppe** (176 S. Main St., tel. 330/376-7020) for great nuts from two vintage roasters.

SMOKING POLICY: Smoking is prohibited except in the Diamond Boardwalk, accessible behind sections 100 & 114.

VISITING TEAM HOTEL: Radisson Hotel Akron City Centre (20 West Mill St., Akron, OH 44308, tel. 330/384–1500 or 800/333–3333).

TOURISM INFORMATION: Akron/Summit Convention & Visitors Bureau (77 E. Mill St., Akron 44308, tel. 330/374–7560 or 800/245–2454).

Akron: Canal Park

In Akron, the Aeros have been a launching pad for new baseball talent. Canal Park, the $31-million Aeros stadium designed by HOK Sports of Kansas City, opened April 10, 1997. The winning pitcher that night was a 21-year-old fireballer named Jaret Wright. Within six months, Wright had jumped from Class AA, the middle rung of the minor leagues, to become a World Series starter for the Cleveland Indians.

Canal Park represents all that is best about minor-league baseball, providing a full night of modestly priced family fun: nonstop music, on-field contests between innings, and a fuzzy red-white-and-blue mascot named Orbit, outfitted with rocket boosters, who launches T-shirts into the stands with a giant slingshot. The majority of the 9,097 seats in this fan-friendly stadium are blue armchairs complete with cup holders and plenty of leg room.

The park runs only 20 rows deep, almost all the way from the left-to-right-field poles. There's a wide concourse of food, drink, and souvenirs at the street entrance level above the seating bowl. Downtown office buildings sit beyond the state-of-the-art video scoreboard in right center field. Trees and a green hillside lie just beyond the left-field wall and above the canal.

The Aeros drew an Eastern League record-setting 473,272 fans in their first year and 521,122 in their second, so call ahead to order seats.

More Akron Baseball

Firestone Stadium. Just south of Canal Park in the heart of Akron's former rubber-making district, we discovered a real baseball jewel. Firestone Stadium is one of a half-dozen small ballparks built in the 1920s to host industrial-league baseball teams representing the city's rubber companies. This 1,500-capacity grandstand was taken over by the city in 1988 and now hosts softball games virtually every summer weeknight and all day on weekends. You'll see young and old, men and women, fast and slow pitch. This yellow-brick beauty shows its age, but is a living tribute to the Midwest's manufac-turing heritage. A ground-floor room holds Akron's amateur softball hall of fame. *S. Main St. between Wilbeth Rd. and Firestone Pkwy., tel. 330/375–2804.*

Where to Stay

Visiting Team Hotel: Radisson Hotel Akron City Centre. This 20-story hotel is four blocks from the ballpark. Rooms are decorated with reproduction antiques. Double rooms are larger than standard size. *20 W. Mill St., Akron 44308, tel. 330/384–1500 or 800/333–3333, fax 330/434–9365. 274 rooms. Facilities: 2 restaurants, indoor pool, hot tubs, exercise room. AE, D, DC, MC, V. $$*

The Hilton at Quaker Square. Guests sleep in former Quaker Oats silos in this renovated factory that's on the National Register of Historic Places. The rooms are round and spacious and have thick concrete walls. A former Capitol Limited train is parked in the adjoining Quaker Square complex of shops and railroad diners. *135 S. Broadway, Akron 44308, tel. 330/253–5970 or 800/445–8667, fax 330/253–2574. 173 rooms. Facilities: 3 restaurants, indoor and outdoor pools. AE, D, DC, MC, V. $$*

Where to Eat

Mary Coyle's. Look for the vintage pink-and-green neon sign that marks this 1937 ice-cream parlor. There were once five Mary Coyle's in Akron. This one remains and now has Italian pasta dinners, plus a chocolatier who wraps your choices in beautiful boxes and ribbons. Try a tin roof, sherbet freeze, or strawberry phosphate. *780 West Market, Akron, tel. 330/253–1511. MC, V. $*

Lou and Hy's. This cluttered deli is locked in the 1950's. A wall of felt sports pennants faces the requisite wall of celebrity photos. The corned beef and pickles are New York quality, and the strudel and chicken paprika pass any Hungarian cook's test. *1949 West Market, Akron, tel. 330/836–9159. D, MC, V. $*

West Point Market. This gourmet grocery and café has been one of America's most innovative stores since 1936. Think of a gourmand running your local supermarket, with a gardening department, wine store, restaurant, bakery, and kitchen store thrown in. The market brews its own root beer, often has strolling musicians, and is filled with so many tasting stations that you can eat lunch just browsing. *1711 West Market, Akron, tel. 330/864–2151. AE, MC, V.* $

Entertainments

The Akron Zoological Park. This zoo is perfect for young children: small, easy to walk, doable in 90 minutes. There's a Tiger Valley that's Noah's Ark–like in scale: two tigers, two lions, and two bears. Really, how many more do you need? Parking is $1 and there is a nice picnic pavilion. *500 Edgewood Ave., Akron, tel. 330/375–2250. Admission: $5 adults, $4 ages 2–14 and senior citizens. Open Mon.–Sat. 10–5, Sun. 10–6.*

Geauga Lake Amusement Park. This long-standing amusement park, a half hour east of Akron, has been expanded and renovated for a full day of fun. There are more than 100 rides spread over 240 acres, including two wooden coasters, and a water park with slides, a wave pool, and a beach area for children. *SR 43, Aurora, tel. 330/562–7131. Admission: $21.99 people over 48″, $12.99 senior citizens, $8.99 people under 48″; parking $5. Open weekdays 11–10, weekends noon–10. AE, D, MC, V.*

Goodyear World of Rubber. If you're here at the Goodyear headquarters on a weekday, there's a free tour of rubber trees and an animated replica of Charles Goodyear discovering vulcanization. A film and self-guided tour are also available. *1201 E. Market St., Akron, tel. 330/796–7117. Admission: free. Open weekdays 8–4:30.*

National Inventors Hall of Fame and Inventure Place. This is one of the nation's best hands-on science museums. You don't just complete preconceived experiments here—you create your own. There's a wood shop with real saws, a fiber optics play area, and a huge water experiment station. It's like a wild dorm party at MIT—we saw kids throwing balls from a five-story balcony and measuring the results. *221 S. Broadway, Akron, tel. 800/968–4332. Admission: $7.50 adults, $6 ages 3–13 and senior citizens. Open Wed.–Sat. 9–5, Sun. noon–5. AE, D, MC, V.*

Pro Football Hall of Fame. It's no Cooperstown, but this sister city to Akron attracts many current and former players to sign memorabilia at this hall. There are films, induction ceremonies in July, and an appointment-only research library. *2121 George Halas Dr. NW, Exit 107A, at I–77 and U.S. 62, Canton, tel. 330/456–8207. Admission: $9 adults, $6 senior citizens, $4 ages 6–14, family rate $22. Open: daily 9–8.*

Sea World. This Sea World site, next to the Geauga Lake Amusement Park, has 90 acres of marine life. Aquatic shows, a penguin encounter, shark exhibits, Shamu the whale, and an interactive bottlenose dolphin habitat are on the grounds. *SR 43, Aurora, tel. 216/562–8101. Admission: $28.95 adults, $20.95 ages 3–11. Open daily 10–6. MC, V.*

TOLEDO MUD HENS

League: International League • **Major League Affiliation:** Detroit Tigers • **Class:** AAA • **Stadium:** Ned Skeldon Stadium • **Opened:** 1965 • **Capacity:** 10,025 • **Dimensions:** LF: 325, CF: 410, RF: 325 • **Surface:** grass • **Season:** Apr.–Labor Day

STADIUM LOCATION: 2901 Key St., Maumee, OH 43537.

TEAM WEB SITE: www.mudhens.com

GETTING THERE: From Ohio Turnpike, Exit 4 north to Toledo onto Reynolds Rd., right onto Heatherdowns, and right onto Key St. From Detroit, I–75S to Exit 201A (Rte. 25), right on Key St. From Dayton, I–75 via Rte. 475 to Maumee exit (Rte. 24), left on Key St.

PARKING: Plenty of free parking at stadium.

TICKET INFORMATION: Box 6212, Toledo, OH 43614, tel. 419/893–9483, fax 419/893–5847.

PRICE RANGE: Box seats $6.50; reserved seats $5; general admission $4.

GAME TIME: Mon.–Sat. 7 PM, Sun. 2 PM; gates open 1 hr before game.

TIPS ON SEATING: It's worth it to buy box seats here. Kids and senior citizens get $1 off even on box seats. In sections K and L, right near home plate, smoking and alcohol are prohibited. If you buy reserved seats, ask for first-base side, where there are real seats. On third-base side (visitors' dugout), there are benches with backs. General admission seats are aluminum benches without backs and beyond bases.

SEATING FOR PEOPLE WITH DISABILITIES: In front of box seats on first-base side on home plate side of dugout.

STADIUM FOOD: The pizza, bratwurst, deli sandwiches, and salads are the best bets here. The pizza is baked on-site and has a thick crust and less grease than most. **The Grillery** behind home plate has exceptional bratwurst and natural-casing hot dogs ($1.50). Kiddie drinks are $1.50, and you and your children can sit in booths inside the cavernous concession-stand area to eat. You can get garden salads, Caesar salads, fruit cups, and just-sliced corned beef, ham, or turkey sandwiches at the deli. Homemade, frosted brownies are $1.25 at the deli. There are also burgers, grilled chicken sandwiches, and good french fries available. The hand-scooped ice cream is Pierre's, a fine regional brand.

SMOKING POLICY: No smoking/no alcohol in sections K and L near home plate on first-base side.

VISITING TEAM HOTEL: Ramada Inn (2429 S. Reynolds Rd., Toledo, OH 43614, tel. 419/381–8765 or 800/272–6232).

TOURISM INFORMATION: Greater Toledo Convention and Visitors Bureau (401 Jefferson Ave., Toledo, OH 43604, tel. 419/321–6404 or 800/243–4667).

Toledo: Ned Skeldon Stadium

In Toledo, the baseball team is called the Mud Hens, and you are probably thinking that this clever nickname is a product of the minor-league logo-and-name-changing mania of the '90s. Correct, but it was the 1890s. A mud hen is a bird with short wings and long legs that inhabits swamps or marshes. In 1896, the Toledo baseball team played at Bay View Park and there were plenty of mud hens in the marshland outside the ballpark. Team mascot Muddy the Mud Hen, a large, pinstriped yellow bird, carries on the tradition today.

Teams have been playing professional baseball in Toledo since 1883, and for almost all of that time they have been called the Mud Hens. Ned Skeldon Stadium is the 11th ballpark of Toledo's professional teams. Swayne Field, built in 1909 and considered the best minor-league park of its era, was torn down and replaced by a shopping center in 1955 when the team moved to Wichita. In 1965, baseball returned to Toledo thanks largely to the efforts of Lucas County Commissioner Ned Skeldon, who led the charge to establish the community nonprofit

group that owns the team. A former Thoroughbred racetrack was converted into a 10,025-capacity baseball park when Toledo was awarded its Class AAA International League franchise. The Lucas County Recreation Center baseball stadium was renamed for Skeldon in 1988. The ballpark sits in a sports complex that includes softball fields, three swimming pools, and the county fairgrounds.

The large roof on both sides of the park, covering much of the seating area and extending well past first and third bases, is a remnant of the horse-racing track; the stretch to the finish line was in front of the third-base grandstand. General admission seating is on aluminum benches not covered by the roof. The old-style concourse under the grandstand is brightly spruced up with colorful concessions signs for the deli and the Dog Hut.

This is typical, gritty 1960s Triple A International League stadium, but with contests and antics on and off the field more like what you find in Single A baseball. The Mud Hens have a fan-friendly booth at the gate to sign up for contests. A new ballpark is scheduled to be built in the downtown warehouse district for the 2002 season.

Many celebrities have played in Toledo, but the most interesting person to have played ball here is perhaps the least known. In Toledo, they will tell you that Jackie Robinson was not the first African-American to play baseball in the major leagues. Sixty-three years before, Moses Fleetwood Walker, the son of an Ohio clergyman, played for the 1884 Toledo Blue Stockings in the American Association, then considered a major league. Walker immediately ran into a wall of bigotry. Toledo pitcher Tony Mullane ignored catcher Walker's signals, saying he would not take orders from a black man.

Native American Jim Thorpe, the hero of the 1912 Olympics, hit three home runs in one game for the Hens in 1921. Casey Stengel managed at Toledo from 1926 to 1931, winning the Junior World Series in 1927 before going on to a Hall of Fame career as the skipper of the New York Yankees. Pete Gray, the great one-armed outfielder, played here. Jamie Farr, the actor who brought the Mud Hens national attention as Corporal Klinger's favorite team on M*A*S*H, has made many special appearances at the ballpark.

Where to Stay

Visiting Team Hotel: Ramada Inn. Between a Bob Evans restaurant and a Toys R Us on a busy commercial street, this hotel has a free shuttle to the ballpark. The rooms in the eight-floor tower cost $10 more than the main-floor and wing rooms because of the countryside views and distance from road noise. The center of the hotel is an indoor pool with brightly colored banners overhead. *2429 S. Reynolds Rd., Toledo 43614, tel. 419/381–8765 or 800/272–6232, fax 419/381–0129. 264 rooms. Facilities: restaurant, indoor pool, coin laundry. AE, D, DC, MC, V. $$*

Cross Country Inn. This well-kept budget hotel, part of a regional chain, is 2 mi from the ballpark, at the edge of Toledo and suburban Maumee. It adjoins a field next to a freeway exit. The long, rectangular rooms are modern and plain. Patrons check in at a drive-through window resembling one at a suburban bank. *1704 Tollgate Dr., Exit 4 from Ohio Turnpike, Maumee 43537, tel. 419/891–0880 or 800/621–1429, fax 419/891–1017. Facilities: outdoor pool. AE, D, DC, MC, V. $*

Holiday Inn West. The ballpark is a five-minute drive from this newer 11-story hotel, which is on a busy commercial strip adjacent to Southwyck Mall, 7 mi from downtown. The rooms are larger than ordinary, with contemporary furnishings. *2340 S. Reynolds Rd., Exit 4 from Ohio Turnpike, Toledo 43614, tel. 419/865–1361 or 800/465–4329, fax 419/865–6177. 217 rooms. Facilities: restaurant, indoor pool, beauty salon, exercise room, coin laundry. AE, D, DC, MC, V. $$*

Where to Eat

Tony Packo's Cafe. This may be the only restaurant decorated with celebrity-signed hot dog buns, shellacked and mounted on walls. There are signatures from Esther Williams, Nancy Reagan, Charlton Heston, Patti LaBelle, Ray Charles, and Burt Reynolds. Customers order from a counter and sit at tables with red-checked vinyl cloths. The eatery serves extraordinary hot dill pickles and sells an entire line of condiments, such as spoonable ketchup and chunky hot peppers. Its sausages, macaroni and cheese, mashed potatoes, strudels, and fruit dumplings are exemplary. On Saturday and Sunday afternoons, a magician entertains, and on Friday and Saturday nights, a Dixieland jazz band prompts crowds to dance around the restaurant to "When the Saints Go Marchin' In." *1902 Front St., at Consaul St., Toledo, tel. 419/691–6054. AE, D, MC, V. $*

Maumee Bay Brewing Company. This impressive brewery and wood-fired brick-oven pizza restaurant is housed in what was Toledo's premier hotel, circa 1859. Beautifully renovated, this Greek Revival palace is listed on the National Register of Historic Places. It has light ash floors, exposed-brick walls, views of the Maumee River, and huge copper kettles and serving tanks behind glass. The spacious restaurant, with a pub section downstairs, has excellent sandwiches, pizzas, pastas, and salads. An entire dining room is no-smoking. Its steak soup and cheddar beer soup are appealing and unusual. The Mud Hen pie consists of coffee ice cream with a cookie-crumb crust. For adults, there are varieties of ales, lagers, and specialty brews. *27 Broadway, off Summit St. at Oliver St., Toledo, tel. 419/243–1302. AE, MC, V. $$*

Entertainments

Cedar Point. This all-day amusement park, perched on Lake Erie's Sandusky Bay since 1870, has a nice beach and picnic areas for patrons. It's roller-coaster heaven, with five coasters, including Magnum XL-200 and the inverted Raptor, two of the most thrilling in the country. Both are too frightening for preteens, as is the 15-story plunge ride, the RipCord. The Wildcat is a good roller coaster–like ride for children ages 6–12. Several vintage rides were rescued from Cleveland's late, lamented Euclid Beach Park, including Cedar Downs (a racing carousel), and the wooden Blue Streak coaster. In Berenstain Bears Bear Country, a clever indoor science center–playground leads to an outdoor funland of swings, sandboxes, a train, and tree houses. Children also love driving the Turnpike Cars and going on the sports-car rides. At Aunt Em's restaurant, you can get pepperoni rolls, a regional favorite. There are two hotels and a campground on the Cedar Point grounds. The park is an hour west of Cleveland and 45 minutes east of Toledo. *U.S. 6, Sandusky, 10 mi north of Ohio Turnpike Exit 7, tel. 419/626–0830. Admission: $29.95 people over 48″, $6.95 children 48″–age 3, $16.95 senior citizens; $18.95 after 5 PM; parking $5.*

Toledo Firefighters Museum. This free museum is housed in Fire House 18, built in 1920 and replaced in 1975. It shows how the city's fire protection evolved from volunteer bucket brigades to the computer-directed system of today. The city's first fire pumper, an 1837 hand-pulled tanker, is on display. In the model child's bedroom on the second floor, kids can act out fire emergencies and plan escape routes. *918 Sylvania Ave., Toledo, tel. 419/478–3473. Open June–Aug., Sat. noon–4; Sept.–May, weekends noon–4.*

Toledo Zoo. This is our favorite small zoo in the country, and it has plenty of good competition. First built in the depression, by WPA artists, its gorgeous and fanciful vintage buildings have been beautifully renovated. The high-ceilinged former carnivore house is a riot of blue, purple, and mauve inside, with two cafeterias. You can eat in the former lion cages at bright blue tables behind bright blue iron bars. The aquarium has dozens of windows looking in to sharks, stingrays, and snapping turtles. The zoo's two Nile hippos can be viewed from an underwater tank, and there's a good petting zoo. For $1, you can ride a carousel; a ride in a bright red train is $1.25. A playground is imaginatively done, as are all the graphics in this zoo. There's a South African rain forest, with sloths and iguanas, plus giraffes, cougars, and monkeys. Polar-bear and African-predators exhibits are part of its 9-acre expansion. The zoo belongs to the 100-member American Zoological Association, which gives free entry to members of other zoos. It's 3 mi south of Toledo. *2700 Broadway; Exit 201A off I-75, follow Collinwood Ave. (Rte. 25) south; Toledo, tel. 419/385–4040. Admission: $5 adults, $2.50 ages 2–11 and senior citizens; parking $2. Open Apr.–Sept., daily 10–5; Oct.–Mar., daily 10–4.*

Unusual Shopping

Libbey Factory Outlet. Toledo is a glass-producing city; the already low prices of this outlet and its bargain room really drop for the items in its tent sale, held each June through August. These are first-quality glasses, canisters, platters, dinnerware, mugs, candleholders, and gift sets. *1205 Buckeye St., near I-75 and I-280, North Toledo, tel. 419/727–2374.*

Mud Hens Souvenir Store. This is the main store of eight Mud Hens stores in the area, a testament to the popularity of its terrific logo. Located under the third-base stands, it contains many items under $1 for young fans, as well as former uniforms for $250. *2901 Key St., Maumee, tel. 419/891–9520 or 800/736–9520.*

LUGNUTS AND THE MOTOR CITY
LANSING, DETROIT

19

Baseball tradition runs strong in the motor cities of Michigan. They played professional baseball on the same corner in Detroit for 100 years. But in the late 1990s Lansing and Detroit both bowed to the inevitability of progress and built fan-friendly, eye-popping new ballparks in their downtowns.

Lansing led the way in 1996 with a shiny new park and a clever nickname, the Lugnuts, that caught on in the capital city. Lansing is known for government and cars. It was here that R.E. Olds first began turning buggies into motor cars. The downtown is walkable, with a pleasing array of hiking trails along the river and a state history museum that is one of the best of its type.

Drive east for 88 mi on I–96 to Detroit. After years of debate about whether or not to save historic Tiger Stadium, Detroit finally opted for a new baseball palace for the new millennium. Comerica Park opened in 2000. Good downtown transport allows you to leave your car parked while you visit the stadium and other tourist spots via a light rail system and antique trolleys. The city has an island park, several ethnic enclaves with exceptional restaurants, and a world-class zoo in neighboring Royal Oak.

LANSING LUGNUTS

League: Midwest • **Major League Affiliation:** Chicago Cubs • **Class:** A • **Stadium:** Oldsmobile Park • **Opened:** 1996 • **Capacity:** 11,000 • **Dimensions:** LF: 305, CF: 412, RF: 305 • **Surface:** grass • **Season:** Apr.–Labor Day

STADIUM LOCATION: 505 E. Michigan Ave., Lansing, MI 48912.

WEB SITE: www.lansinglugnuts.com

GETTING THERE: Take I–96 to U.S. 496. Exit at Larch Street. The stadium is just blocks from downtown on the corner of Larch and Michigan.

PARKING: Parking is available on the street and in paid lots around the ballpark.

TICKET INFORMATION: 505 E. Michigan Ave., Lansing, MI 48912, tel. 517/485–4500, fax 517/485–4518.

PRICE RANGE: Box seat $6, reserved seat $5.50, general admission (lawn) $4.50.

GAME TIME: Apr., Mon.–Sat. 6:05 PM, Sun. 2:05 PM. May–Aug., Mon.–Sat. 7:05 PM, Sun. 2:05 PM. Aug.–Sept., Mon.–Sat. 7:05 PM, Sun. 6:05 PM. Gates open 75 minutes before game.

TIPS ON SEATING: Box seats are a good buy here, as they're just 50¢ more than reserved seats. The tip of the elegant state capitol dome is visible, barely, from seats far down the right-field line. The sun sets over third base and shines into fans' eyes on the home team, first-base side. S and T are no-alcohol sections just beyond the bullpen on the third-base side. General admission seating is on grass berms in front of picnic areas beyond the fence in the power alleys of left and right center field.

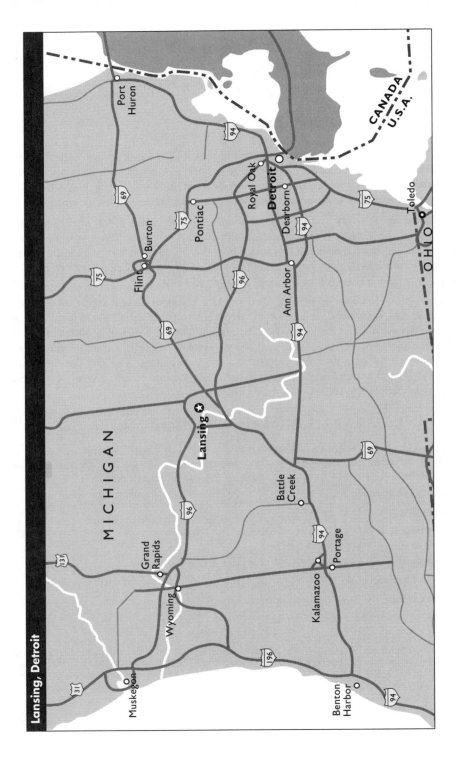

SEATING FOR PEOPLE WITH DISABILITIES: Seating is available along the concourse at the top of the seating bowl.

STADIUM FOOD: The Turkey Man, down the left-field line, has real smoked turkey from a grill for $5.25. He also sells grilled corn on the cob. **The Dashboard Diner,** beyond the left center-field wall, serves good hot dogs, nachos, and soda. There are picnic tables above the grass berms beyond left- and center-field walls. **The Pit Stop,** on the first-base side, serves specialty beers.

SMOKING POLICY: Smoking is prohibited throughout the ballpark.

VISITING TEAM HOTEL: Holiday Inn South (6820 S. Cedar St., Lansing, MI 48911, tel. 517/694–8123 or 800/465–4329).

TOURISM INFORMATION: Greater Lansing Convention & Visitors Bureau (119 Pere Marquette, Box 15066, Lansing, MI 48901, tel. 517/487–6800 or 800/648–6630).

Lansing: Oldsmobile Park

With a nickname like "Lugnuts," how could they miss? With seating for 11,000, Oldsmobile Park is one of the largest of the new Single A ballparks. The Lansing Lugnuts have been packing them in right from the start, drawing an amazing 538,326 in the inaugural 1996 season.

The $12.7-million ballpark was designed by the firm of HNTB of East Lansing. The inside is terrific, but the entrance is even better. There's a grand fountain along with benches and landscaping, all topped off with two wonderful sculptures. *Hometown Hero,* by Richard Hallier, is a bronze of a player signing a ball for a boy with two friends waiting on a nearby bench. *The Natural,* by Gary Price, is a young boy in uniform standing with a ball and glove. On the wackier side, Lugnuts supporters raised $34,000 to mount a 5,000-pound stainless steel nut on top of the brick smokestack on Cedar Street across from the stadium.

The Olds Motor Vehicle Company was incorporated in Lansing in 1897, and they drive the automobile connection pretty hard. The public address announcer urges the fans to "Go nuts!" The concession stands have names like Pit Stop, Filling Station, and Chrome Plated Grill. Big Lug, the mascot, is a large purple dinosaur in a baseball uniform and yellow tie who has large tusks and lugnuts for nostrils.

The park is a short 305 ft at each foul pole with high walls, but it quickly juts out to decent lengths and shorter walls. There's a chrome rounded roof over 26 skyboxes that hang over the stadium's walking concourse. The seats are dug out below street level. Unfortunately, the stands sit up above the field enough to reduce the sense of intimacy you find in most Single A ballparks. This greatly reduces the chances for autographs that are so much a part of the minor-league experience. To get that souvenir ball signed you need to line up near the right-field foul pole before the game.

Where to Stay

Visiting Team Motel: Holiday Inn South. Rooms are predictable but large at this five-story businessmen's hotel. Families will be enticed by the free cribs and children stay for nothing. The pool is in the basement, but has good light from upper windows. It's only 10 minutes south of the ballpark. *6820 S. Cedar St., Lansing, 48911, tel. 517/694–8123 or 800/465–4329, fax 517/699–3753. 300 rooms. Facilities: restaurant, indoor pool, fitness center, sauna, game room. AE, D, DC, MC, V. $$*

Hampton Inn. This efficient, three-story motel has balconies in many rooms and a free Continental breakfast. Rooms have been recently remodeled and the lobby areas are cheery. It's about 15 minutes west of the ballpark. *525 N. Canal Rd., at I–96, Exit 93, Lansing 48917, tel. 517/627–8381 or 800/426–7866, fax 517/627–5502. 103 rooms. Facilities: fitness center. AE, D, DC, MC, V. $$*

Radisson. The only hotel in downtown Lansing is just blocks from the ballpark, capitol, and science center. Parking is free and there's complimentary transport to the airport, bus, and train. Rooms are large and nearly all have good city views in this 11-story hotel. *111 N. Grand Ave., Lansing 48933, tel. 517/482–0188 or 800/333–3333, fax 517/487–6646. 260 rooms. Facilities: restaurant, indoor pool, sauna, hot tub. AE, D, DC, MC, V. $$*

Where to Eat

Clara's. The city's grand train depot has been renovated into an antiques-filled restaurant, with elevated booths and patio dining. The menu is a small book, with dozens of pasta dishes, salads, unusual drinks, and desserts. The children's menu has several vegetables and non-fried foods, a rarity. *637 E. Michigan Ave., Lansing, tel. 517/372–7120. AE, D, DC, MC, V. $$*

Parthenon. Families and government employees have been patronizing this downtown restaurant for decades. Authentic Greek dishes, including souvlaki and moussaka, are excellent, and children may order half-portions. It's a casual tablecloth type of place, with the front windows giving views of a pedestrian mall. *277 S. Washington Sq., Lansing, tel. 517/484–0573. AE, D, DC, MC, V. $$*

Entertainments

Potter Park and Zoo. This small zoo combines the best features of a park and zoo, with picnic facilities, canoe rentals, and a variety of birds, animals, and reptiles. Pony and camel rides are a kid favorite. Parking is $1.50. *1301 S. Pennsylvania Ave., Lansing, tel. 517/483–4222. Admission: $2.50 adults, $1 ages 3–15. Open Memorial Day–Labor Day, daily 9–7; rest of year, daily 9–5.*

Sights to See

Impression 5 Science Center. Housed in a 100-year-old former factory, this imaginative museum is for all ages, with hands-on projects outside and computer and chemistry experiments inside. A wooden fort and maze is full of balance and motion exhibits. *200 Museum Dr., Lansing, tel. 517/485–8116. Admission: $4.50 adults, $3 ages 3–17 and senior citizens. Open Mon.–Sat. 10–5, Sun. noon–5.*

Michigan Library and Historical Center. Located just three blocks southwest of the capitol, the Center includes the Michigan Historical Museum, the Library of Michigan, and the State Archives. The Historical Museum presents Michigan history from prehistoric times through the end of the 20th century. There are 26 permanent galleries on four levels, including a walk-through Upper Peninsula copper mine, an S&H Green Stamp Redemption Center, and a mock-up of the 1957 Detroit Auto Show. An Al Kaline home run is one of the clips shown in the post–World War II kitchen and TV room. *717 W. Allegan St., Lansing, tel. 517/373–3559. Open weekdays 9–4:30, Sat. 10–4, Sun. 1–5.*

Riverfront Park. You can walk for 8 mi on a scenic trail by the Grand River to the North Lansing Dam and fish ladder, through Potter Park, and on to East Lansing. Several impressive sculptures are along the trail, which also takes you past the science and nature centers. *Downtown entry between Cedar St. and Grand Ave., Lansing, tel. 517/483–4277.*

State Capitol. The Michigan capitol, completed in 1879, took as its model the newly enlarged capitol in Washington, D.C. The large, symmetrical building with a tall central dome is a Renaissance Revival design. Blocks of thick glass on the first floor reflect the dome above. A 1992 restoration brought the capitol building back to its 1879 elegance. Free tours are held every 30 minutes and last 45 minutes. There are also detailed walking tour pamphlets for both the capitol building and the Capitol Square grounds. *Capitol and Michigan Aves., Lansing, tel. 517/373–2353. Tours weekdays 9–4, Sat. 10–3.*

DETROIT TIGERS

League: American League • **Class:** Major League • **Stadium:** Comerica Park • **Opened:** 2000 •
Capacity: 42,000 • **Dimensions:** LF: 346, CF: 422, RF: 330 • **Surface:** grass • **Season:** Apr.–Sept.

STADIUM LOCATION: Brush, Montcalm, Witherell and Adams Sts., Detroit, MI.

WEB SITE: www.detroittigers.com

GETTING THERE: From I–75, take the Grand River exit. The ballpark is in downtown Detroit, east of Woodward Avenue and across the street from the Fox Theater. The Washington Boulevard Trolley Car, tel. 313/933–1300, stops at the ballpark, downtown hotels, and the Renaissance Center.

PARKING: There is paid parking at the stadium and in commercial lots throughout downtown.

TICKET INFORMATION: 2121 Trumbull Ave., Detroit, MI 48216, tel. 313/962–4000, fax 313/965–2138.

PRICE RANGE: Infield box seats $30, lower outfield box $25, upper box $20, mezzanine $15, pavilion $14, upper reserved $12, fan stands $8.

GAME TIME: 7:05 PM, day games 1:05 PM, select Sat. 5:05 PM. Gates open 90 min before game.

TIPS ON SEATING: The entire outfield is open, giving fans a view of the Detroit skyline. The setting sun for a night game will be in the eyes of fans on the third-base side. The home team dugout is on the third-base side. The $8 fan stands tickets are bleachers with backs in the right-field lower deck.

SEATING FOR PEOPLE WITH DISABILITIES: Seating is available on both the lower and upper deck.

STADIUM FOOD: Baseball's best mustard, a brown cream-style hot mustard made by the local **Red Pelican Mustard Company,** makes the dogs here special. The pizza served is by **Little Caesar's,** and there are stands selling deli sandwiches, Italian sausages, lemon ice, and hot pretzels.

SMOKING POLICY: Smoking is prohibited in all seating areas, but is allowed in designated smoking areas.

TOURISM INFORMATION: Metropolitan Detroit Convention & Visitors Bureau (100 Renaissance Center, 19th fl., Detroit 48243, tel. 800/338–7647.)

Detroit: Comerica Park

The Detroit Tigers played major league baseball at the corner of Michigan and Trumbull avenues for 100 years. Bennett Park opened in 1900 with a seating capacity of 8,500. Ty Cobb began his Hall of Fame career there in 1905. In 1911, home plate was moved to where left field had been and this 1912 version of the park opened the same day as Boston's Fenway. After the 1937 season, they completely rebuilt it and renamed it Tiger Stadium.

The front rows of the upper deck at Tiger Stadium were a great place to watch a game. They hung out over the field-level seats, stunningly close to the action. When the Tiger faithful were cheering their boys on, the upper deck shook. As much fun as we had here, it was time to retire the historic stadium at 2120 Trumbull Avenue. This funky, hulking old battleship of a park just had too many problems, too many obstructed seats, and too few modern comforts for major-league baseball fans. Great it was. Fenway and Wrigley, it was not.

The Tigers begin the new millennium with a brand-new ballpark. After years of controversy,

including legal action to protect the historic status of Tiger Stadium, the voters approved a new park in 1996. Located 1 mi east of Tiger Stadium, Comerica Park is part of the renewal of downtown Detroit. A football stadium will be built just east of the baseball stadium to allow the NFL Lions to return from a several-decade sojourn in the suburbs.

Comerica Park is named after one of Detroit's most established banks. Sixty percent of the $290 million it cost to build the Tigers' new lair came from the private sector. The state, county, and city picked up the rest of the tab. The classic brick and steel exterior building was designed by Smith, Hinchman, and Grylls of Detroit along with HOK of Kansas City and the Rockwell Group. The entire outfield is open, providing a striking view of Detroit's skyline.

A colorful, giant tiger statue greets you at the main entrance and Paws, a large, friendly tiger, is the mascot. A 100-ft circular food court complete with carousel is behind the seats on the first-base side. There is a Ferris wheel in the beer garden behind the seats on the third-base side. The field sits 26 ft below street level. A wide concourse, in stark contrast to the narrow aisles and concourses of Tiger Stadium, is open to the playing field. Not all of history is lost. The flagpole from the 1912 stadium has been installed at Comerica Park.

Where to Stay

The Atheneum Suite Hotel. Located in Greektown, about five blocks southeast of the ballpark, this 10-story hotel is a better value than most downtown. The suites are large and decorated in plush, traditional fabrics. *1000 Bush Ave., Detroit 48226, tel. 313/962–2323 or 800/772–2323, fax 313/962–2424. 13 rooms, 160 two-bedroom suites. Facilities: restaurant. AE, D, DC, MC, V. $$$*

Hotel St. Regis. Prices here are lower than suggested by the rooms' deluxe furnishings. This seven-story hotel is near the renovated Fisher Theatre, 3 mi north of the ballpark. *3071 W. Grand Blvd., Detroit 48202, tel. 313/873–3000 or 800/848–4810, fax 313/873–2574. 221 rooms. Facilities: restaurant. AE, DC, MC, V. $$*

Shorecrest Motor Inn. Conveniently located two blocks from the Renaissance Center, about 1½ mi from the ballpark, this small budget motel has been recently renovated. Rooms are standard size and pleasantly decorated. *1316 E. Jefferson Ave., Detroit 48207, tel. 313/568–3000 or 800/992–9616, fax 313/568–3002. 54 rooms. Facilities: restaurant. AE, DC, MC, V. $*

Where to Eat

Cyprus Taverna. This Greektown favorite has bargain lemon rice soup and eggplant dishes. The setting in this storefront fixture is very much casual. Children can order half-portions. *579 Monroe St., Detroit, tel. 313/961–1550. AE, D, DC, MC, V. $$*

Mexican Village Restaurant. Huge meals are standard in this whitewashed, casual eatery. Players from visiting and local baseball and hockey teams often visit for some of the city's most authentic Mexican food. All the chefs are natives of Mexico. Guests may ask for toned-down versions of spicy favorites. *2600 Bagley St., Detroit, tel. 313/237–0333. AE, D, MC, V. $*

Traffic Jam and Snag. Affordable meals built around homemade breads, pies, and an on-site dairy make this a popular Wayne State University hangout. Antiques create something of a rustic atmosphere. They serve lunch and dinner only, with a menu that changes almost daily. There's also a children's menu. *5111 W. Canfield St., at 2nd St., Detroit, tel. 313/831–9470. D, MC, V. $$*

Entertainments

Belle Isle. Not many cities have a 1,000 acre island park, but Detroit has a 9-hole golf course, a nature conservatory, aquarium, small zoo, and a Great Lakes Museum, tel. 313/852–4051, on this preserve. The island is 3 mi from downtown. The zoo, tel. 313/852–4083, has a 3-mi walkway through the animal exhibits. *E. Jefferson Ave. and E. Grand Blvd., at MacArthur Bridge, Detroit, tel. 313/842–4078. Zoo admission: $3 adults, $2 senior citizens, $1 ages 2–12. Open daily 10–5. Great Lakes Museum admission: $2 adults, $1 senior citizens and ages 12–18; free on Wed. Open Wed.–Sun. 10–5.*

Detroit Zoo. Natural habitats have been re-created for more than 1,200 animals at this exceptional zoo, north of Detroit. It was the first U.S. zoo to adopt exhibits surrounded by moats, rather than cages. Standouts include the Chimps of Harambee great ape habitat, free-flight aviary, and the penguinarium with underwater viewing. There's a free miniature railroad and excellent reptile museum. This is a big, 125-acre zoo, so you might want to take the free train to the far end (African Train Station) and walk back. *8450 Ten Mile Rd., at Woodward Ave., Royal Oak, tel. 313/398–0903. Admission: $7.50 adults, $5.50 senior citizens and ages 13–18; $4.50 ages 2–12. Open May–Oct., daily 10–5; Nov.–Apr., Wed.–Sun. 10–4.*

Sights to See

Eastern Market. Produce, meats, flowers, and ethnic foods are in abundant supply at this 11-acre, Saturday-only city market. Browse the market, have a walking lunch, and marvel at the huge array of flower stalls, believed to be the largest of any American market. *2934 Russell, at Gratiot Ave., Detroit, tel. 313/853–1560. Open Sat. 6–4.*

Motown Museum. The studio and control room where Diana Ross, the Jackson Five, and

Smokey Robinson and the Miracles first recorded are preserved here, along with records, costumes, and history of Motown Records and artists. The brick building was the headquarters of Berry Gordy, Jr., founder of Motown Records. *2648 W. Grand Blvd., Detroit, tel. 313/875–2264. Admission: $6 adults, $3 ages 12 and under. Open Tues.–Sat. 10–5, Sun.–Mon. noon–5.*

Museum of African-American History. A replica of the Birmingham jail door that held Martin Luther King, Jr. is a prize exhibit along with historic memorabilia from other famous African-American achievers. A reference library and permanent archives are part of the museum. *University Cultural Center, 315 E. Warren Rd., Detroit, tel. 313/823–9800. Admission: $5 adults, $3 ages 3–12. Open Tues.–Sun. 9:30–5.*

STABLES AND THE SPEEDWAY 20
LOUISVILLE, INDIANAPOLIS

A baseball trip covering Louisville and Indianapolis can be as short as two days or as long as a week, depending on how many other appealing diversions, from the Louisville Slugger factory to the Indianapolis Speedway, you want to add. The new downtown Louisville stadium is just eight blocks from the Slugger factory, instantly recognizable with its 120-ft bat as exterior art, in a historic waterfront warehouse district. You can stay at the glorious Seelbach Hotel, affordable on weekends, walk the downtown area with its restored movie palaces, and see the exciting Kentucky Derby Museum at Churchill Downs.

North 98 mi, on Interstate 65, is Indianapolis, with its $18 million ballpark, which has a picnic berm and seating bowls above the recessed field. The team, the Indianapolis Indians, is in the Triple A International League. The stadium is a recent addition to an impressive renovation of downtown Indianapolis. The city has the world's largest children's museum, a spectacular cageless zoo, and the RCA Dome. You can be driven around the actual track of the Indianapolis Speedway and have your picture taken in a racecar at its Hall of Fame museum.

LOUISVILLE RIVERBATS

League: International League • **Major League Affiliation:** Cincinnati Reds • **Class:** AAA • **Stadium:** Slugger Stadium • **Opened:** 2000 • **Capacity:** 13,800 • **Dimensions:** LF: 320, CF: 401, RF: 340 • **Surface:** Grass • **Season:** Apr.–Labor Day

STADIUM LOCATION: Preston and Main streets, Louisville, KY 40202.

TEAM WEB SITE: www.batsbaseball.com

GETTING THERE: From I–65 south, exit on Jefferson Street. Drive two blocks to Preston St. and turn right.

PARKING: Parking for $3 at city-run lots within a 5-block radius of Preston and Main streets.

TICKET INFORMATION: 401 W. Main St., Louisville, KY 40202, tel. 502/367–9121, fax 502/368–5120

PRICE RANGE: Upper deck reserved $8; field reserved $7; outfield reserved $5; outfield berm $4; right field bleachers $3.

GAME TIME: Weekdays 7:15 PM, Sat. 6:15, Sun. 1:15 PM; gates open 90 min before games.

TIPS ON SEATING: Seats on the third-base side face the sun.

SEATING FOR PEOPLE WITH DISABILITIES: Seating available throughout the park.

STADIUM FOOD: The new park has kept many of the beloved concessions, including Ehrler's, a local dairy that sells inexpensive family-sized banana splits, huge hand-dipped cones, and made-to-order milk shakes. There are brats and mettwurst, BBQ pork platters, a BBQ sandwich, and grilled chicken breast sandwiches. The barbecue is Owensboro-style, with lots of meat in a tomato-based sauce. Tortilla chips are made in Louisville, and they're served hot and fresh here.

SMOKING POLICY: No smoking in the seating sections.

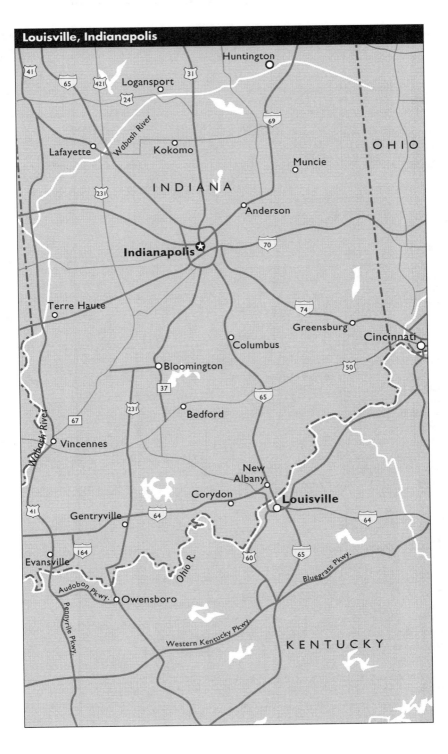

Louisville, Indianapolis

Visiting Team Hotel: Executive Inn (978 Phillips La., Louisville, KY 40209, tel. 502/367–6161 or 800/626–2706).

Tourism Information: Louisville & Jefferson County Visitors Bureau (400 S. 1st St., Louisville, KY 40202, tel. 502/584–2121 or 800/626–5646).

Louisville: Slugger Stadium

The new, $33-million ballpark is a great improvement over its predecessor, Cardinal Stadium, which had the largest seating capacity in minor-league baseball, at 33,500. The new park, built by HTNB, seats one-third the people, making it a more intimate baseball setting. It is part of the city, adjoining the Ohio River downtown, and capitalizes on the excitement of downtown baseball. Best of all, there's real grass. Who would have imagined they played baseball on green plastic in the bluegrass state?

Professional baseball was born in Louisville in 1876 when the key meetings to form the National League were held in a Louisville saloon. Louisville was a charter member of the league. In 1902, Louisville joined the American Association and stayed there for 61 years. After a stint in the International League, Louisville returned to the American Association as the St. Louis Cardinals Triple A franchise. The team was known as the Redbirds and it became the first minor-league team to draw more than 1 million fans. The team is now back in the International League and a franchise of the Cincinnati Reds. Its name, RiverBats, reflects its new riverfront location.

More Louisville Baseball

Cardinal Stadium. Come to the state fairgrounds to see where past Louisville sluggers have played. The huge grandstand at Cardinal Stadium is completely covered by a roof and the grandstand seats are an array of colors—red, yellow, blue, and green. The festive red concourse area under the seats is lit up like a carnival midway.

The concourse wall has a history of baseball in Louisville back to 1876 from a dozen excellently designed display panels. *Phillips Lane and Freedom Way, Louisville 40213.*

Louisville Slugger Factory. For 20 years the famous Louisville Slugger bats were made across the Ohio River in southern Indiana. No more. Hillerich & Bradsby moved its corporate headquarters, museum, factory, and warehouse back to Louisville in 1996. A 120-ft metal Louisville Slugger bat rises above the Main Street entrance. The redbrick facilities are at Eighth Street, just two blocks up from the river and a half block from the Louisville Science Center on the nicely revitalized Main Street. H&B turns out PowerBilt golf clubs and more than a million wooden baseball bats a year.

It all began in 1884, when Pete Browning broke a bat at a Louisville game attended by John Andrew Hillerich. Hillerich took Browning back to his father's woodworking shop and turned a bat for the ballplayer. Browning got three hits with it the next day. The Hillerichs decided there was money in making baseball bats. On September 1, 1905, Honus Wagner became the first ballplayer to have his signature on a Louisville Slugger bat. Today, a majority of major leaguers have bat contracts with the company. The H&B museum has a collection of bats from many of the most famous players who ever played the game. After you tour the plant and museum, drop by the souvenir store to order a personalized 34-inch white-ash bat for $43 to memorialize your baseball trip to Louisville. *800 W. Main St., Louisville 40202, tel. 502/585–5226. Admission: $5 adults, $4.50 senior citizens, $3 children ages 6–12, children under 6 free. Open mid-July–June, Mon.–Sat. 9–5; tours every 30 min.*

Where to Stay

Visiting Team Hotel: Executive Inn Hotel. Guests can walk to Cardinal Stadium from this dark-wood, English Tudor–style hotel, which is across the street from the fairgrounds. Bargain packages that include free Kentucky Kingdom admission are available. *978 Phillips La., Watterson Expressway at fairgrounds, Louisville 40209, tel. 502/367–6161 or 800/626–2706, fax 502/*

363–1880. 478 rooms. Facilities: 2 restaurants, indoor and outdoor pools, health club. AE, D, DC, MC, V. $$

Days Inn–Central Louisville. This three-story hotel is in an older residential section, two mi from Slugger Stadium, Churchill Downs, and the airport. It is popular with families visiting University of Louisville students. *1620 Arthur St, Louisville 40208, tel. 502/636–3781 or 800/329–7466, fax 502/634–9544. 143 rooms. Facilities: outdoor pool. AE, D, DC, MC, V.*

Seelbach Hotel. This glorious 1905 hotel has an unusual lobby of fine woods, marble, and brown-hued murals. Charles Dickens, Ernest Hemingway, and F. Scott Fitzgerald slept here. Even the modest rooms have lovely antique beds, armoires, and high ceilings. *500 4th St, Louisville 40202, tel. 502/585–3200 or 800/333–3399, fax 502/585–3200. 321 rooms. Facilities: 2 restaurants, parking (fee). AE, D, DC, MC, V. $$*

Where to Eat

Lynn's Paradise Cafe. It's impossible to resist the huge, unusual meals served in this kitsch-filled room of imagination. The decor includes cowboy items, old toys, kitchen appliances, and lava lamps. None of the tables match, and the waitresses wear vintage 1950s aprons. The chefs in this former Laundromat turn out terrific French toast, fresh juices, and waffles for breakfast and new American classics for dinner. Children are given crayons, toys, and their own menu. Plastic kitties often adorn each plate as a take-home prize. *984 Barrett Ave., Louisville, tel. 502/583–3447. AE, MC, V. $$*

Paul Clark's BBQ. Eaters can get Owensboro-style barbecue here, with its distinctive tangy vinegar taste. This casual restaurant, which is five minutes from the ballpark, also serves a good vegetable casserole, homemade coleslaw, and southern green beans. *2912 Crittenden Dr., Louisville, tel. 502/637–9532. No credit cards. $*

Entertainments

Belle of Louisville. Listen to a calliope on a paddle-wheel ride on the Ohio River aboard the oldest operating Mississippi-style stern-wheel steamboat. This 1914 beauty, a National His-

toric Landmark, makes several two-hour cruises. A second boat, the *Spirit of Jefferson*, leaves from the Greenwood Road pier on Friday and Saturday only, 1:30–3:30 and 7–9. Belle: *Wharf at 4th Ave. and River Rd., Louisville, tel. 502/574–2355. Fares: $10 adults, $7 senior citizens, $6 ages 3–12. Open Memorial Day–Labor Day, Tues.–Sun. 1–2 boarding for a 2–4 cruise, 6–7 boarding for a 7–9 sunset cruise. MC, V. Spirit: Greenwood Rd. pier. Fares: same as for Belle. Open Memorial Day–Labor Day, Fri.–Sat. 1:30–3:30 and 7–9.*

Kentucky Derby Museum at Churchill Downs. A 360-degree screen shows an exciting film of Derby day every half hour, with vibrant color and sound. You can climb onto a full-size horse figure in a paddock, view the famous racetrack, and pet a live former champion horse. The Derby Cafe is open 11–3 weekdays. *704 Central Ave., Louisville, tel. 502/637–7097. Admission: $6 adults, $5 senior citizens, $2 ages 5–12. Open daily 9–5. MC, V.*

Kentucky Kingdom Amusement Park. More than 60 rides and the huge Hurricane Bay wave pool fill this park, which is at the fairgrounds. Avoid the wooden roller coaster—the violent head-jerking causes discomfort for adults and children. There are dozens of other, calmer ride choices, but watch your beginning swimmers carefully in the wave pool, which can be too rough for the inexperienced. Inner tubes are included in the park admission. Teenagers like the free-fall ride, Hellavator, and the Top Eliminators dragster race, which has an extra fee. *Kentucky State Fairgrounds, Crittenden Dr. exit from I–264 or I–65. Louisville, tel. 502/366–2231. Admission: $29.99 adults and children 48" and taller, $15 children ages 3–48" and senior citizens; $17.99 after 5 PM. Open Sun.–Thurs. 11–9, Fri.–Sat. 11–11; Hurricane Bay closes weekdays at 6, weekends at 7. D, MC, V.*

Sights to See

Louisville Walking Tour. The Main Street Association (tel. 502/562–0723) has an elegant brochure describing Louisville's nine-block "Time Machine" walk. You can follow Fourth Street, which was the dominant commercial and social avenue of the city in the early 1900s. Presidents Teddy Roosevelt and Franklin Roosevelt both paraded here. It's car-free for several blocks. The Galleria shopping mall (Fourth Avenue between Muhammad Ali Blvd. and Liberty St.) has 80 stores and a dozen restaurants. Don't miss three beautiful old theaters on Fourth Avenue, especially the **Palace,** a John Eberson–designed Atmospheric Theatre, which creates the impression of being outdoors, with stars on the ceiling, alfresco statues, and marble staircases. Only 23 of his Atmospheric Theatres exist, and this is one of the largest. Adjoining are the vintage **Ohio** and **Kentucky** theaters. Tours of the Palace are offered. *Palace Theatre, 625 4th Ave., Louisville, tel. 502/583–4555. Admission: $2 adults, children under 6 free.*

INDIANAPOLIS INDIANS

League: International League • **Major League Affiliation:** Milwaukee Brewers • **Class:** AAA • **Stadium:** Victory Field • **Opened:** 1996 • **Capacity:** 13,000 • **Dimensions:** LF: 320, CF: 402, RF: 320 • **Surface:** grass • **Season:** Apr.–Labor Day

STADIUM LOCATION: Maryland and West Sts., Indianapolis, IN 46225.

TEAM WEB SITE: www.indyindians.com

GETTING THERE: From I–70, Exit 79A (West St.), follow it north for 3 min to ballpark, across street from RCA Dome. From I–65N, Exit 114 to Martin Luther King Blvd., follow it south to ballpark.

PARKING: $2 on-site parking; parking garage across street also charges $2.

TICKET INFORMATION: 1501 W. 16th St., Indianapolis, IN 46202, tel. 317/269–3545, fax 317/269–3541.

PRICE RANGE: Box $10 adults, $9 children (under 15); reserved $8 adults, $7 children; grandstand $6 adults, $5 children; bleachers and lawn $6 adults, $5 children.

GAME TIME: Mon.–Sat. 7 PM, Sun. 2 PM; gates open 5:30 PM regular games, 5 PM double-headers, 12:30 PM Sun.

TIPS ON SEATING: General admission lawn berm seats have good views of city and action.

SEATING FOR PEOPLE WITH DISABILITIES: 131 seats distributed in every price level; stadium has elevators.

STADIUM FOOD: The specialty here is Tribe fries—spicy wedges of potatoes. The rest of the menu includes Italian sausages, hamburgers, hot dogs, pizza, popcorn, slush puppies, and popcorn. You can continue to watch the games from the concession concourse level.

SMOKING POLICY: Smoking prohibited throughout stadium.

VISITING TEAM HOTEL: Ramada Inn East (7701 E. 42nd St., Indianapolis, IN 46226, tel. 317/897–4000 or 800/272–6232).

TOURISM INFORMATION: Indianapolis City Center (Pan American Plaza, 201 S. Capitol Ave., Indianapolis, IN 46225-1022, tel. 317/237–5206 or 800/323–4639).

Indianapolis: Victory Field

Our strong preference is almost always to try to preserve the old ballparks. Nevertheless, after watching a game at 64-year-old Bush Stadium in Indianapolis, it was hard to second-guess the city's decision to build a new stadium downtown. When built in 1931 by then-Indians owner Norman A. Perry, the 13,000-seat, roofed, single-deck Bush Stadium was state-of-the-art concrete and steel. Its distinctive ivy-covered redbrick walls remind fans of Chicago's Wrigley Field. In fact the stadium is a virtual clone of Wrigley Field before Wrigley's upper deck was built in 1928. For that reason, Bush Stadium was used in the filming of *Eight Men*

Out, the 1988 film about the 1919 baseball scandal that rocked the nation.

Once a decision is made to build a new stadium, the extensive maintenance needed to preserve these classic ballparks stops, and they can go downhill fast. That is what had happened at Bush Stadium by the time we visited. It is, however, still well worth a visit for fans of historic stadiums. Much baseball history has been made at this ballpark. Indianapolis won 12 championships here while hosting teams in three Triple A leagues—the American Association, the International League, and the Pacific Coast League. Hank Aaron played for the Indianapolis Clowns. In 1954, 20-year-old Herb Score struck out 330 on the way to winning 22 games. In 1956, Roger Maris drove in 75 runs with 17 home runs for the Indians.

The city bought the stadium in 1967 and renamed it in 1968 in honor of the Indians' president, Owen J. Bush, a Detroit Tiger teammate of Ty Cobb. There are 15 wonderful life-size color paintings of some of the greats who have played here on the inner concourse wall, making a trip to the old stadium well worth the effort. Beyond the fence in right center field is a tepee, apparently the home of an Indian mascot. Bush Stadium is just 10 minutes from downtown Indianapolis. From the Circle in the downtown, go north on Meridian Street and take a left on 16th Street to 1501 West 16th Street. The old ballpark is now a car racetrack.

The $18 million, 13,000-seat downtown ballpark was designed by HOK, the premier baseball-stadium architects, to maintain the intimate feel of Bush Stadium. The city and the Indians split the cost of the new stadium, which opened July 11, 1996. It takes its name from Victory Gardens, the former name of Bush Stadium. The playing field is 20 ft below street level and has lower and upper seating bowls. The main entrance is behind center field, and fans travel around a walkway to their seats. The exterior is blond and sandy-brown brick, and the seats are forest green. An electronic scoreboard set in the right-field wall is protected by a plastic shroud. Fans can sit on a picnic berm beyond the outfield wall, where they can see a set of train tracks and smoke stacks from a power plant south of the ballpark.

Where to Stay

Visiting Team Motel: Ramada Inn East. This two-story motel is in a field off an interstate exchange, 10 minutes northeast of the ballpark. There are standard rooms and business-class rooms, which have desks and refrigerators. The hotel has a pleasant atrium and indoor pool. *7701 E. 42nd St., at I–465, Pendleton Pike exit, Indianapolis 46226, tel. 317/897–4000 or 800/272–6232, fax 317/897–8100. 192 rooms. Facilities: restaurant, indoor and outdoor pools, exercise room, game room. AE, D, DC, MC, V. $*

Courtyard by Marriott Downtown. Guests can watch the game from the upper floors of this eight-story 1966 hotel, which is across the street from the new stadium. Half the rooms are doubles; the rest have king-size beds. The furnishings are contemporary. *501 W. Washington St., Indianapolis 46204, tel. 317/635–4443 or 800/321–2211, fax 317/687–0029. 233 rooms. Facilities: restaurant, outdoor pool, playground, coin laundry. AE, D, DC, MC, V. $$*

Crowne Plaza Union Station. Imagine building a hotel around 13 Pullman train cars. The cars, which have been gutted and fitted with two double beds and private baths, are on the second floor of this three-story downtown hotel, which is adjacent to the city's convention center and six blocks from the ballpark. This is a splurge hotel. *123 W. Louisiana St., Indianapolis 46225, tel. 317/631–2221 or 800/227–6963, fax 317/236–7474. 276 rooms. Facilities: restaurant, indoor pool, exercise room. AE, D, DC, MC, V. $$$*

Where to Eat

Shapiro's. This traditional Jewish deli has great corned beef, puddings, and home-canned peaches. Patrons walk through a cafeteria line and try not to get too much. You may order half-sandwiches, which are more than enough for children. The Formica tables are seat-yourself, and there's a take-out section. *808 S. Meridian St., Indianapolis, tel. 317/631–4041. No credit cards. $*

Dodd's Town House. You'll need reservations for special dinners at this family favorite. Its panfried steaks and chicken compete with the pies, particularly the buttermilk pie, for fans. *5694 N. Meridian St., Indianapolis, tel. 317/257–1872. AE, D, DC, MC, V. No lunch Mon. and Sat. $$*

Hollyhock Hill. The decor has stayed loyal to the 1928 hollyhock theme, and, luckily, the fried chicken has maintained its quality, too. Lazy Susans serve hearty meals family-style. Brownies and peppermint ice cream are the customary desserts. *8110 N. College Ave., Indianapolis, tel. 317/251–2294. MC, V. $*

Entertainments

Children's Museum. You'll need several hours to cover the five floors of the largest children's museum in the world. There's a planetarium (shows, $2), an extensive computer area, and a hands-on center for younger children. Kids can explore an Indiana limestone cave, view a life-size *Tyrannosaurus rex*, and check out a mummy. A carousel offers rides (50¢). The large-screen Cinedome Theater ($4.50 adults, $3.50 ages 2–17) shows two films. The museum, just north of downtown, houses a restaurant. *3000 N. Meridian St., Indianapolis, tel. 317/924–5431. Admission: $8 adults, $7 senior citizens, $3.50 ages 2–17; free 1st Thurs. of month 5–8 PM. Open daily 10–5; 1st Thurs. of month, 10–8. MC, V.*

Indianapolis Motor Speedway and Speedway Hall of Fame. It's thrilling to be able to drive around this track, even though you're going 35 mph in a 15-minute bus tour, not the 230 mph that racecars reach. The track is nicknamed the Brickyard because initially the 2½-mile oval was paved with 3 million bricks. Just a yard of bricks remains at the start-finish line. The museum holds ornate Art Deco trophies, laughable early safety helmets made of leather, and other racing memorabilia, plus a film. The bus tour, given about every 90 minutes, is an extra $3 adults, $1 children. *4790 W. 16th St., Indianapolis, tel. 317/481–8500. Admission: $3 adults, $1 ages 6–15. Open daily 9–5.*

Indianapolis Zoo. This downtown, cageless zoo has several habitats and several daily demonstrations of animal behavior. A good place to cool off is at the large aquarium, which has a water-show extravaganza with whales and dolphins at 11, 1,

and 3 PM. Be prepared for many extra-admission items, like rides on camels, elephants, ponies, and a 1920 Parker carousel. There is a Subway restaurant on the premises, along with several outdoor cafés. The zoo is 1 mi west of downtown, 600 yards past the White River Bridge. The grounds stay open an hour after the admission office closes at 5. *1200 W. Washington St., Indianapolis, tel. 317/630–2001. Admission: $9.75 adults, $6 ages 3–12, $7 senior citizens; $3 parking. Open daily 9–5. D, MC, V.*

Sights to See

Indianapolis City Center. This excellent one-stop resource center is near the Indiana Convention Center and the RCA Dome. You'll find a three-dimensional scale model of the city to orient you and a multimedia slide show. *Pan American Plaza, 201 S. Capitol Ave., Indianapolis, tel. 317/237–5206 or 800/323–4639. Open weekdays 10–5:30, Sat. 10–4.*

Indiana State Capitol Building. Completed in 1878, this Renaissance–style capitol building was constructed mostly with Indiana limestone, granite, and marble. The capitol is topped by a 234-ft copper-covered stone dome. There are self-guided tours of the building, which is in the center of downtown. Free guided sessions are by appointment. *Capitol Ave. and Washington St., Indianapolis, tel. 317/233–5293. Open weekdays 9–3.*

National Art Museum of Sport. This museum is a good way to introduce sports-fiends to art. On the campus of Purdue–Indiana University–Indianapolis, it shows paintings and sculptures chiefly of male athletes. *University Place Hotel Conference Center, 850 W. Michigan St., Indianapolis, tel. 317/274–2700. Donations appreciated. Open weekdays 8–5.*

RCA Dome. Formerly known as the Hoosier Dome, this air-supported domed stadium has a self-cleaning roof. Tours last 45 minutes and leave from the Indianapolis City Center. Visitors also see a movie about the myriad sports and entertainment activities in this 60,500-seat stadium. *100 S. Capitol Ave., Indianapolis, tel. 317/237–5200. Admission: $5 adults, $4 ages 5–17 and senior citizens. Tours Mon.–Sat. at 11 and 1, Sun. at 1 only.*

CHICAGOLAND
CHICAGO, GENEVA, KANE COUNTY

Illinois has a strong baseball tradition. America only has two cities, New York and Chicago, that have two major-league teams. And Chicago's manic fan tradition is spreading: nearby Geneva's relatively new team is enjoying sellout crowds.

Chicago has the classical splendor of Wrigley Field, as pure a baseball experience as it gets. From the ivy on its brick back wall to the hand-recorded scoreboard for all major-league games, there is tradition at every corner. The children's attractions in this city add up to an illuminating summer vacation, with the Field Museum of Natural History, the Shedd Aquarium, the Chicago Children's Museum, and the free Lincoln Park Zoo. The Navy Pier's 150-ft Ferris wheel and the Sears Tower Skydeck offer superb views of the sparkling city.

Forty miles west of Chicago, off Interstate 90, is Geneva, home of the Kane County Cougars, one of baseball's biggest suburban success stories. Opened in 1991, the stadium continues to have sellout after sellout despite its proximity to Chicago's two major-league teams. Antiques stores cluster downtown, and you can cycle and roller blade along the Fox River.

CHICAGO CUBS

League: National League • **Class:** Major League • **Stadium:** Wrigley Field • **Opened:** 1914 • **Capacity:** 38,710 • **Dimensions:** LF: 355, CF: 400, RF: 353 • **Surface:** grass • **Season:** Apr.–early Oct.

STADIUM LOCATION: 1060 West Addison St., Chicago, IL 60613.

TEAM WEB SITE: www.cubs.com

GETTING THERE: Wrigley Field, on north side of Chicago, is bounded east and west by Sheffield Ave. and Clark St. and north and south by Waveland Ave. and Addison St. From I–90/I–94, take Addison St. exit east 5 mi to stadium. Call 312/836–7000 for information about rail and shuttle bus information.

PARKING: Parking is limited and expensive ($15–$18). Call to order parking passes for Cubs lot (1126 West Grace St., tel. 800/347–2827; $15).

TICKET INFORMATION: 1060 West Addison St., Chicago, IL 60613, tel. 773/404–2827 or 800/347–2827, fax 773/404–4014.

PRICE RANGE: Prices lower on nonsummer weekdays. Field box seats $20–$25; family section $20; terrace reserved $16; bleacher seats $15; upper deck reserved, adult $10, ages 13 and under $6.

GAME TIME: 1:20 PM except Fri., 2:20 and 18 games 7:05 PM; gates open 2 hrs before game.

TIPS ON SEATING: Seats on lower level farther back under upper deck have obstructed views. Upper deck seats are better than obstructed-view seats. Small section in left-field bleachers reserved for families.

SEATING FOR PEOPLE WITH DISABILITIES: Arrange for seating and parking for people with disabilities in advance: call 773/404–4107.

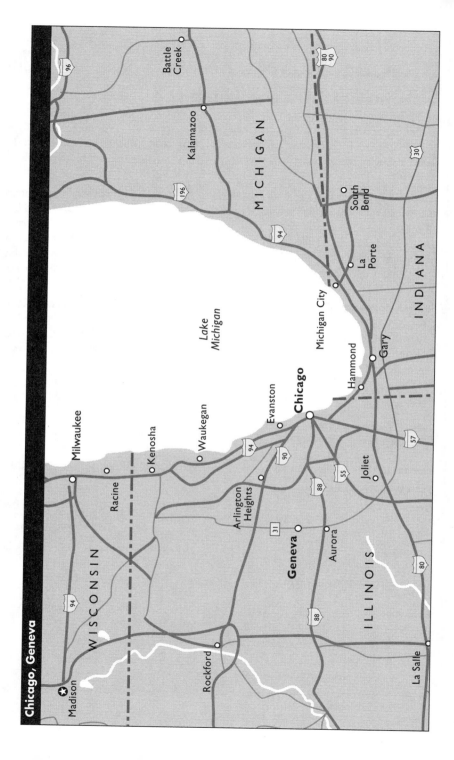

STADIUM FOOD: There's is a 25% early bird discount on food and nonalcoholic beverages for the first hour after the gate opens. On the main concourse are the **Italian Market, Bullpen Barbecue,** and **Chili Peppers Mexican Fair,** along with standard hot dog booths. Avoid Diamond's Grill, where mushrooms and ketchup are added to the grilled pork chop sandwich, and the walleye pike and BBQ chicken sandwiches contain cheese. Warning to parents: most of the "Tropical Delights" frozen drinks have alcohol. The fruit bar popsicle is good ($1.75).

SMOKING POLICY: Smoking prohibited in seating areas.

TOURISM INFORMATION: Chicago Office of Tourism (78 E. Washington St. Chicago, IL 60602, tel. 312/744–2400 or 800/822–0292, IL Office of Tourism–Sears Tower).

Chicago: Wrigley Field

Former baseball commissioner A. Bartlett Giamatti has written of the thrill of walking into a ballpark and first seeing the field: "... after we ascend the ramp or go through the tunnel and enter the inner core of the little city, we often are struck, at least I am, by the suddenness and fullness of the vision there presented: a green expanse, complete and coherent, shimmering, carefully tended, a garden." To our minds, there is no place closer to this ideal of the garden in the city than Chicago's Wrigley Field. For a pure baseball fan, it simply doesn't get any better than a sunny afternoon at Wrigley.

Wrigley Field was built right into the fabric of a city neighborhood. Enter from the main gate at North Clark Street. The swarm of people standing in front of the red "Welcome to Wrigley Field" sign lets you know you are about to enter a very special place. Most approaches to Wrigley have all the charm of the back side of an aging resort hotel. It's what's inside that counts.

Unlike the megamillion-dollar parks of today, this baseball jewel evolved over decades. Designed by Zachary Taylor Davis and built for $250,000 in four weeks in 1914, the single-decked ballpark, then called Weeghman Park, was the home of the Chicago ChiFeds of the Federal League.

When the Federal League, an upstart association that had attempted to be a third major league, folded after two years, Charles Weeghman and his associates bought the National League Cubs and moved them from their West Side Grounds to the Addison Street site, renaming it Cubs Park. Joa, a live bear cub, lived in a cage outside the ballpark during the 1916 season. In 1916, Weeghman first allowed fans to keep balls that went into the stands. This would not become a common practice until a judge in 1923 ruled that keeping baseballs was not stealing.

In 1921, chewing-gum executive William Wrigley bought the team. The ballpark was renamed Wrigley Field in 1927, the year the upper deck was added to double capacity to 40,000. Wrigley was the site of Babe Ruth's famous "called shot" home run off Cubs pitcher Charlie Root in game three of the 1932 World Series. Legend has it that in the fifth inning of a tie game, the great Bambino let two strikes go by, pointed to right-center field, and hit a massive home run exactly where he had pointed. "I'd play for half my salary if I could bat in this dump all the time," Ruth commented after the series.

The bleachers as we know them today—the home of Chicago's "Bleacher Bums" and undoubtedly the most famous bleachers in all of baseball—were added in 1937. Architects Holabird & Root carefully designed the new bleachers so that houses on Waveland and Sheffield avenues beyond the outfield walls could continue to watch the games for free from their rooftops as they still do today. At first, the bleachers were solid across the outfield. After complaints by batters who lost pitches against the background of white shirts, a section of seats was blocked off to give the hitters a solid background against which to hit—the batter's eye you see in all ballparks today.

A young Cub executive and future Hall of Famer named Bill Veeck had a huge 27-ft-high, 75-ft-wide green-and-white scoreboard built on the top of the center-field bleachers. Here the scores of all major-league baseball games are recorded by hand. After games, a flag is flown from a center-field pole—a blue flag with a white W indicates a Cubs win; a white flag with a blue L indicates a loss. The only ball ever to hit the scoreboard was hit by Sam Snead in 1951, and it was a golf ball. Roberto Clemente once barely missed it. Veeck is also responsible for planting the ivy on Wrigley's brick outfield walls, perhaps the most distinctive and charming aspect of this wonderful ballpark. Balls that disappear into the ivy are ground-rule doubles.

Philip K. Wrigley bought lights for Wrigley Field in the winter of 1941 but donated them to a shipyard to help with the World War II effort the day after the attack on Pearl Harbor. After a decades-long controversy, lights were installed 47 years later in August of 1988. Eighteen night games are now played at Wrigley Field each year. Much to the relief of many, the lights have not destroyed Wrigley's greatness. In the 1950s, the grandstand seats in right field were rebuilt to improve visibility. During the late 1960s and early 1970s, the upper deck was rebuilt in sections. An attractive brick wall circles the playing field.

The breezes from Lake Michigan can change the nature of the game at Wrigley. With its short power alleys and the wind blowing out, Wrigley can be a home-run hitter's dream, as home-run king Sammy Sosa has shown. But with a cool wind blowing off the lake into the batters' faces, home runs become scarce. Number 14 flies on a flag on the left-field foul pole to honor Ernie Banks, the shortstop Hall of Famer they call "Mr. Cub." Number 26 flies on a flag in right in honor of Hall of Famer Billy Williams. From the picnic deck behind home plate at the upper level, there is a wonderful view of the city and of the neighborhood bars and souvenir shops that surround Wrigley Field.

The top of the visitors dugout on the first-base side says "Welcome to the Friendly Confines of Wrigley Field." And it is friendly, warm, and intimate. The seats are right near the field, unlike those at many of the concrete doughnut monstrosities built in the 1960s with their huge foul territories. The atmosphere is as much that of a party as of a baseball game. No crowd anywhere in baseball gets into the seventh-inning stretch like a Wrigley crowd. No hyped-up exploding video scoreboard is needed to get fans into the game here. The crowd sings a boisterous rendition of "Take Me Out to the Ball Game," a tradition made famous by the late Hall of Fame announcer Harry Caray. The rowdiest of all Cubs fans—the shirtless "Bleacher Bums"—sit in the bleachers in right-center field. A home-run ball into any bleachers by an opposing player is certain to be rejected by the fans and tossed back onto the field.

For information on 90-minute tours of Wrigley Field that are held several Saturdays each summer, call 312/831–2827. A $12 donation to a Cubs charity is the price of admission. There is a Cubs Walk of Fame with stars in the sidewalk in front of the ticket windows.

Where to Stay

Comfort Inn of Lincoln Park. This four-story motel is 1 mi from Wrigley Field and offers a free Continental breakfast. This is the original Comfort Inn in the United States, with a Victorian decor that underscores its heritage. *601 W. Diversey Pkwy., Chicago 60614, tel. 773/348–2810 or 800/424–6423, fax 773/348–1912. 74 rooms. Facilities: outdoor whirlpool, indoor hot tub, parking (fee). AE, D, DC, MC, V. $$*

Best Western River North. This redbrick highrise was built pre–World War II but was completely remodeled inside and out in 1994. The seven-floor hotel is convenient—the Hard Rock Cafe and Michael Jordan's Restaurant are one block away, and the Miracle Mile is a four-block walk. You get free coffee and a paper in the morning. *125 W. Ohio St., Chicago 60610, tel. 312/467–0800 or 800/528–1234, fax 312/467–1665. 148 rooms. Facilities: restaurant, indoor pool, health club. AE, D, DC, MC, V. $$*

City Suites Hotel. The rooms have European styling in a Deco theme here. The hotel was built in the 1920s and once served the vaudeville and gangster set. It is five blocks from Wrigley. There is a free Continental breakfast. *933 W. Belmont Ave., Chicago 60657, tel. 312/404–3400 or 800/248–9108, fax 312/404–3405. 45 rooms. Facilities: coin laundry, parking (fee). AE, D, DC, MC, V. $$*

Days Inn–Gold Coast. This property is known here as the former Hotel Lincoln. Across the street from the Chicago Zoo, it is 2 mi south of Wrigley. Most rooms have twin or queen beds, and only suites have two double beds. It offers guests a free Continental breakfast. *1816 N. Clark St., Chicago 60614, tel. 312/664–3040 or 800/325–2525, fax 312/664–3045. 243 rooms. Facilities: restaurant, parking (fee weekends). AE, D, DC, MC, V. $$*

Ohio House. This popular, small 1950s-era motel is in the bustling River North area, with Michael Jordan's Restaurant one block away. The rooms are freshly painted and standard size, and the price is right. There's an all-night drugstore and an all-night McDonald's within walking distance. It's a 15-minute elevated train (El) ride to Wrigley from here. *600 N. La Salle St., Chicago 60610, tel. 312/943–6000, fax 312/ 943–6063. 50 rooms. Facilities: coffee shop. AE, D, DC, MC, V. $$*

Park Brompton. English country is the decorating theme in this small hotel, which is across from the lakefront and from Lincoln Park. It's a 10-minute drive from Wrigley Field. Guests receive a free Continental breakfast. *528 W. Brompton Ave., Chicago 60657, tel. 312/404– 3499 or 800/727–5108, fax 312/404–3495. 52 rooms. Facilities: coin laundry. AE, D, DC, MC, V. $$*

The Surf. The rooms in this small hotel are done in French country style. It's close to the Lincoln Park Zoo, in a quiet residential neighborhood that's 10 blocks from Wrigley Field. There is a free Continental breakfast. *555 W. Surf St., Chicago 60657, tel. 312/528–8400 or 800/787–3108, fax 312/528–8483. 55 rooms. Facilities: coin laundry, parking (fee). AE, D, DC, MC, V. $$*

Where to Eat

The Busy Bee. This busy Polish restaurant offers good, inexpensive food, including a hearty meat loaf, sandwiches, and steaks, served either at the counter or at tables. It is a traditional hand-shaking stop for decades of politicians. In a Wicker Park neighborhood of art galleries and bookstores, it is close to the El, at the Damen Street stop. *1540 N. Damen St., at North Ave., Chicago, tel. 312/772–4433. MC, V. $*

The Berghoff. This dim, clubby restaurant serves great German food and root beer floats. It's old-style Chicago, with murals of the city's origins surrounding the dining rooms on each of its two levels. It's in the downtown Loop and has been "on Adams and State since 1898." *17 W. Adams St., tel. 312/427–3170. AE, MC, V. Closed Sun. $$*

Ed Debevic's. This is the granddaddy of the new '50s diners, with lots of neon reflecting on real mashed potatoes, chicken pot pie, burgers, sodas, and pies. The waitresses have their wisecracks down pat. *640 N. Wells St., Chicago, tel. 312/664–1707. AE, D, DC, MC, V. $*

Lou Mitchell's. Women are handed a tiny box of Milk Duds or a doughnut hole as they walk in, setting the tone here. There are awe-inspiring pecan rolls, fresh orange juice, malt waffles, stewed fruits, and omelets of every type. *560 W. Jackson St., Chicago, tel. 312/939–3111. No credit cards. $*

Manny's Coffee Shop. You can pick up blintzes, fragrant corned beef, chopped liver, chicken pot pies, and great potato pancakes at this quintessential Jewish deli. It is cafeteria-style. *1141 S. Jefferson St., Chicago, tel. 312/939–2855. No credit cards. $*

Pizzeria Uno and Due. The cornmeal crust is outstanding in this pair of restaurants. Diners get a history of pizza with their meal. The two restaurants are within steps of each other and are far superior to any of their nationwide chain extensions. Due is larger and has a terrace. Uno, the original creator of deep-dish pizza, has been baking it since 1943. *Uno: 29 E. Ohio St., Chicago, tel. 312/321–1000. Due: 619 N. Wabash, Chicago, tel. 312/943–2400. AE, D, DC, MC, V. $*

Giordano's Pizza (730 N. Rush St., tel. 312/ 951–0747) and **Gino's** (930 N. Rush St., tel. 312/337–7726) are other good pizza sources.

Sammy Sosa's Restaurant. Your kids will drag you here. It's crowded, with a sports-bar atmosphere, but the food isn't bad. It shares a neighborhood with a musical-themed McDonald's, a Hard Rock Cafe, and Planet Hollywood, so it's tourist heaven. There are $9 hamburgers, $10 calamari and Caesar salads, plus ribs, pasta, and, yes, Gatorade. *500 N. La Salle, St. at Illinois St., Chicago, tel. 312/644–3865. AE, D, MC, V. $$*

Entertainments

Chicago Children's Museum. At the entrance to the Navy Pier stands this new, three-floor museum. Children love crawling through its landfill exhibit, "The Stinking Truth About Garbage." They can also create rubbish art and Lego masterpieces. There's a "Touchy Business" sensory exhibit for kids under six, with a machine to manipulate that's part airplane, part boat, and part tractor. A special lab lets older children be inventors. *700 E. Grand Ave., Chicago, tel. 312/527–1000. Admission: $6.50. Open Tues.–Sun. 10–5; free Thurs. 5–8 PM.*

Field Museum of Natural History. The world's largest reconstructed dinosaur, a four-story Brachiosaurus, is at the door of this museum. The newest dinosaur, Sue, is the largest T-Rex reconstruction in the world. You can learn about Egypt by viewing 23 mummies and by participating in hands-on stone building and Nile River navigation. There's too much to see in one visit, so pick a few sections and avoid overload. *1400 S. Lake Shore Dr., at Roosevelt Rd., Chicago, tel. 312/922–9410. Admission: $7 adults, $4 ages 3–17, senior citizens, students; free Wed. Open daily 9–5.*

Lincoln Park Zoo. This world-class zoo contains a 5-acre farm, a children's zoo and nursery, a great ape house, and a penguin and seabird house. There are giant Clydesdales, trees full of koalas, and a large collection of big mammals. Children's-zoo demonstrations are weekdays 10–2, weekends 10–4. There is pay parking in summer and a restaurant on the premises. *2200 N. Cannon Dr., Chicago, tel. 312/742–2000. Admission free. Open daily 9–5.*

Museum of Science and Industry. Ride a train through a coal-mine shaft, see a captured German U-boat, and walk through a 16-ft pulsating heart. If you want to avoid lines, be aware that the coal mine is busiest midday. The Omnimax theater is extra. *57th St. and Lake Shore Dr., Chicago, tel. 773/684–1414. Admission: $7 adults, $6 senior citizens, $3.50 ages 3–11; free Thurs. Open weekdays 9:30–4; weekends 9:30–5.*

Navy Pier. Fun is the sole activity on this 50-acre complex on Lake Michigan. You can rent in-line skates or ride a carousel. Riding its 150-ft Ferris wheel gives you a great view of the city. There are arcades and shops, including a store called Oh Yes Chicago, which sells city street signs and other memorabilia. You can also ride the free trolley or take a 15-minute water taxi ride to the Aquarium. Parking is costly ($8 for two hours and up), so consider a bus. (Bus 29 Northbound State Street is among those stopping at the pier.) *600 E. Grand Ave., between Illinois St. and Grand Ave., Chicago, tel. 800/595–7437.*

Shedd Aquarium and Oceanarium. You can see two Beluga whales, electric eels, penguins, and sharks in this huge facility, which is adjacent to the Field Museum. It's wise to bring a sweater for the Oceanarium. You can buy passes to just the aquarium and its coral-reef exhibit. There's a good 15-minute show at the coral reef. A new Amazon exhibit takes you into flooding forests. A restaurant and snack bar are in the building. *1200 S. Lake Shore Dr., Chicago, tel. 312/939–2426. Admission: $11 adults, $9 ages 3–11 and senior citizens; aquarium only, $5 adults, $4 children; Oceanarium Mon., $6 adults, $5 children. Open daily 9–6.*

Sights to See

Sears Tower Skydeck. A speedy elevator takes you up 103 floors to marvel at the view. You can see Comiskey and Wrigley fields, the orange Calder "Universe" mobile, Adler Planetarium, and other landmarks. Mornings are less crowded here than nights. The entrance is on Jackson Place. *233 S. Wacker Dr., Chicago, tel. 312/875–9696. Admission: $8.50 adults, $5.50 ages 5–12, $6.50 senior citizens, $21 family. Open Mar.–Sept., daily 9 AM–11 PM; Oct.–Feb., daily 9–10.*

Thomas Hughes Children's Library. On the second floor of the stunning, metal-trimmed Harold Washington Library Center is the world's largest children's library space. There's a Story Stairs area, where parents can read to preschoolers; a Learning Center, with Macintosh computers; and a huge selection of books and audiovisual materials. *400 S. State St., Chicago, tel. 312/747–4300. Open Mon., Wed., and Fri.–Sat. 9–5; Tues. and Thurs. 11–7; Sun. 1–5.*

KANE COUNTY COUGARS

League: Midwest League • **Major League Affiliation:** Florida Marlins • **Class:** A • **Stadium:** Philip B. Elfstrom Stadium • **Opened:** 1991 • **Capacity:** 5,900 • **Dimensions:** LF: 335, CF: 400, RF: 335 • **Surface:** grass • **Season:** early Apr.–Labor Day

STADIUM LOCATION: 34W002 Cherry Ln., Geneva, IL 60134.

TEAM WEB SITE: www.kccougars.com

GETTING THERE: From I–88, take the Farnsworth Rd. North exit (which becomes Kirk Rd). Travel north on Kirk for 5½ mi to Cherry Ln. (½ mi north of Fabyan Pkwy.). From I–90 take Rte. 59 south to Rte. 64 (North Ave.). Take Rte. 64 west to Kirk Rd. Travel south on Kirk Rd. 3 mi to Cherry Ln. (first stoplight south of Rte. 38). Go right on Cherry Ln. to the stadium.

PARKING: Parking at the stadium is free. The main lot is unpaved, and there is only one exit.

TICKET INFORMATION: 34W002 Cherry Ln., Geneva, IL 60134, tel. 630/232–8811, fax 630/232–8815.

PRICE RANGE: Box seat $8; reserved seat $7; bleacher seat $6; lawn seat $5.

GAME TIME: Weekdays 7 PM, Sat. 6 PM (Apr.–May) or 5 PM (June–Aug.), Sun. 2 PM. Gates open 2 hours before games.

TIPS ON SEATING: There are only seven rows of box seats, so the reserved seats are quite close. The box seats are real seats, and the reserved seats are aluminum benches with backs. The lawn seating begins just past the dugouts, but the hills are quite steep and were in bad shape when we visited. The bleacher seats beyond right center field are a family fun section. For $100, you can take seven of your friends to watch the game from a hot tub on the right-field deck; the fee includes soda, beer, and service by a waiter.

SEATING FOR PEOPLE WITH DISABILITIES: There is seating for people with disabilities on the concourse and behind screen on the first- and third-base sides. Parking is free for people with disabilities along the first-base (south) side of the stadium.

STADIUM FOOD: The pork chop sandwich ($4.75) is the specialty here and is quite good. The brats ($3) also are excellent. There is variety here with fajitas ($3.50) and tacos ($2.75), which are sold at the end of the concourse on the first-base side. The grills are located in both the first- and third-base sides just beyond the concourse. Try the funnel cakes ($3) at the ice cream stand on the third-base side beyond the concourse.

SMOKING POLICY: Smoking is prohibited in the seating area but allowed on the concourse.

VISITING TEAM HOTEL: Travelodge Naperville (Naperville Rd. at East-West Tollway, Naperville, IL 60563, tel. 630/505–0200 or 800/578–7878).

TOURISM INFORMATION: Geneva Chamber of Commerce (8 S. 3rd St., Geneva, IL 60135, tel. 630/232–6060).

Geneva: Philip B. Elfstrom Stadium

The Kane County Cougars were the right team in the right place at the right time. They weren't the first team to locate in a fast-growing suburb of a major metropolis. They didn't build the finest stadium. They weren't the only team to feature nonstop family entertainment with contest after contest between the baseball innings. But the Cougars put it all together as well as anyone.

The Kane County Cougars came into existence when a Baltimore Orioles franchise moved here from Wausau, Wisconsin, for the 1991 inaugural season and drew an astonishing 240,290 fans. The conventional wisdom was that a minor-league team couldn't make it just 40 mi from not one but two major-league teams. The conventional wisdom underestimated the number of young families in the emerging suburbs thirsting for affordable family entertainment.

Philip B. Elfstrom Stadium was built in 1991 by the Kane County Forest Preserve District and named for one of its longtime leaders. Geneva, Illinois, 40 mi west of Chicago, is a 19th-century Victorian town now largely populated by Chicago commuters and antiques shops. The Cougars quickly became the area's number-one family entertainment stop.

The main grandstand is fairly standard for a 1990s Single A stadium. The field is below the concourse so fans can watch the action from all concession stands. There is lawn seating on grassy hills down both the third- and first-base lines. The capacity has been expanded by adding seating down the first-base line and bleachers beyond the right-field wall, an unusual touch for Single A baseball. In most ballparks, the bleachers are for rowdy, boozy guys and families are wise to avoid them. Not here in family-friendly Kane County, where the bleachers are the designated family fun section. Another face-lift on the third-base side added more seats and a deck called Louie's Left Field Corner for the 2000 season. There is a large scoreboard beyond the left-field fence. From the grandstand, fans see a well-treed area beyond the outfield fence.

Ozzie T. Cougar, a huge friendly brown cougar with a long tail and a baseball jersey and hat, quickly established himself as one of minor-league baseball's most popular mascots. The Cougars have been pioneers in the minor-league efforts to entertain fans between the innings. They do it all here—from the dizzy bat contests and mascot races to the Goose Is Loose Race and a human bowling ball competition.

This is a park with plenty of attractions. Jake the Diamond Dog is a real golden retriever who lives in a dog-house right near the ball boy on the first-base side. Jake takes a basket with water bottles to the umpires between innings. The Million Dollar Mitt is an enormous inflatable

mitt beyond the outfield wall in right center field. If a Kane County player hits a home run in the advertiser's sign in the mitt, the player gets $100,000, a fan gets $450,000, and a charity gets $450,000. On Sunday, kids are allowed on the field to chase player autographs 30 minutes before the game. On Saturday and Sunday, you can run the bases after the game, and there are fireworks every Saturday night.

There isn't much baseball history here. The Orioles farm team left after two seasons and were replaced by future Florida Marlins stars. There were occasionally teams in the Kane County/Fox Valley area back as far as the 1890s, but the best story of the limited pre-Cougar era involves a league that folded at mid-season in 1910. The Kankakee team in the Class C Northern Association owed 19-year-old center fielder Casey Stengel $67 in back pay when it withdrew from the league in July. The ever-inventive Stengel, a wily future Hall of Fame manager, confiscated the team's uniforms as his payment. In 1911, Stengel hit .352 for Aurora to lead the Class C Wisconsin-Illinois League in batting.

Where to Stay

Visiting Team Hotel: Travelodge Naperville. This hotel stands in a commercial strip of fast-food and family restaurants. Guests receive a free Continental breakfast. The utilitarian rooms' only extra is a loveseat. It's a 15-minute drive east from the ballpark. *1617 Naperville Rd. at I–88, the East–West Tollway, Naperville, IL 60563, tel. 630/505–0200 or 800/255–3050, fax 630/505–0501. 103 rooms. Facilities: coin laundry. AE, D, MC, V. $*

The Herrington Inn. Geneva's Rock Springs Creamery has been restored into this elegant riverfront inn. In the late 19th century on the home site of the town's first permanent settler, James Herrington, the Creamery began processing butter and milk for the fast-growing community. The attractive limestone building on the river's edge now houses 40 guest rooms and a restaurant. Guests receive a Continental breakfast, and each room has a minibar, a whirlpool, a fireplace, and a balcony. Chilled milk and warm cookies are part of its turndown service. *15 S. River Lane, on the west side of Fox River*

Bridge, Geneva, IL 60134, tel. 630/208–7433 or 800/216–2466, fax 630/208–8930. 40 rooms. Facilities: restaurant, whirlpool, spa. AE, D, DC, MC, V. $$$

Super 8. This small hotel is just 3½ mi south of the ball field. The nine-year-old three-story motel has the beige and dark brown Tudoresque exterior that is standard in this chain. The rooms are clean and plain, with double and single bed combinations. There is a Continental breakfast bar. Rollaways are $6. 1520 E. Main St., St. Charles, IL 60174, tel. 630/377–8388 or 800/ 800–8000, fax 630/377–1340. 66 rooms, 2 suites. AE, D, MC, V. $

Where to Eat

The Country Inn at Mill Race Inn. This complex, on the Fox River at the entrance to Herrington Island Park, houses five distinctive restaurants. The Country Inn includes part of a stone blacksmith shop built in 1842 on the east side of the Fox River. In 1933, Ann and Marjorie Forsythe opened the former blacksmith shop as a tea room for people shopping at the local antiques shops. It's grown into the inn complex. The menu is classic American and Swedish cuisine. The Swedish meatballs are served on black-pepper fettucine with lingonberries and a sour cream sauce. There's also prime rib and good salmon. 4 E. State St., east side of Fox River Bridge, Geneva, tel. 630/232–2030. AE, MC, V. $$

Entertainments

Fabyan Forest Preserve. One mile south of Geneva is this forest preserve, a public park with no entrance fee that preserves several buildings from a magnificent turn-of-the-century estate. These include the Fabyan Villa, a giant shingled windmill at the gate on the Route 25 side, and a lighthouse on an island that is accessible by a bridge. A villa, designed in 1907 by Frank Lloyd Wright and now a museum, is on the west side of the river, along Route 31. Rte. 31, Geneva, tel. 630/232–4811. Villa open mid-May–mid-Oct., Wed. 1–4, weekends 1–4:30.

Mill Race Cyclery. You can pick up a trail guide and rent bicycles or Rollerblades here to take on the Fox River Trail. After passing under a bridge, you're in the glorious Herrington Island Park in the Fox River. 11 E. State St., at Water St. at the Geneva Dam, Geneva, tel. 630/232–2833. Bike rentals: $7/hr, $27 daily. Rollerblade rentals: $7/hr with protective gear. Open weekdays 10–8, Sat. 10–5, Sun. 11–5.

WILD AND OUTSIDE
ST. PAUL, DULUTH

Minneapolis–St. Paul has both major- and minor-league teams, but the choice is clear. Bigger is not better. Head for St. Paul, in the independent Northern League, for the most fun you can have in a ballpark. The stadium is scruffy and located by the rail yards. There are wacky on-field contests, the announcing is hilarious, and the fan-first philosophy shows. St. Paul has a lovely city park, Como Park, with a free-admission kiddie amusement land and a small zoo. It also has an outstanding children's museum and science center. More commercial amusements are found at Camp Snoopy at the Mall of America, in Bloomington, 12 mi southwest of St. Paul, where 375 stores compete for your wallet, or Valleyfair, a huge amusement park and waterpark in Shakopee, 31 mi southwest of St. Paul.

North 100 mi on I–35 is Duluth, the largest freshwater port in the world. The warehouses along the wharf have been born again as hotels and restaurants and there's a lively boardwalk. The old depot is home to four museums including a children's museum. Watch ships from 65 countries go by the Aerial Lift Bridge or from the Ore Docks Observation Platform. The baseball fans here are enthusiastic and you'll encounter the same Northern League focus on fun.

ST. PAUL SAINTS

League: Northern League • **Affiliation:** Independent • **Class:** Independent/Short Season • **Stadium:** Midway Stadium • **Opened:** 1982 • **Capacity:** 6,311 • **Dimensions:** LF: 320, CF: 400, RF: 320 • **Surface:** grass • **Season:** June–Labor Day

STADIUM LOCATION: 1771 Energy Park, St. Paul, MN 55108.

WEB SITE: www.spsaints.com

GETTING THERE: From west, I–94 to Hwy. 280 to Kasota/Energy Park Dr. exit. East on Energy Park Dr. 1 mi to stadium. From east, I–94 to Snelling Ave. N to Energy Park Dr. exit. West ¼ mi on Energy Park Dr.

PARKING: Lot opens 3 hrs before game for tailgate parties. Parking $3.

TICKET INFORMATION: 1771 Energy Park, St. Paul, MN 55108, tel. 651/644–6659, fax 651/644–1627.

PRICE RANGE: Reserved $6 adult, $5 youth/senior citizens; general admission $4 adult, $3 children and senior citizens.

GAME TIME: Mon.–Sat. 7:05 PM, Sun. 2:05 PM; stadium opens 1 hr before game.

TIPS ON SEATING: Most games sell out. 200 general admission seats go on sale 2 hrs before game. Best seat in house is in barber's chair behind home plate. Haircuts are $10. A 20-minute massage in the stands is $7.

SEATING FOR PEOPLE WITH DISABILITIES: 50 seats on main aisle.

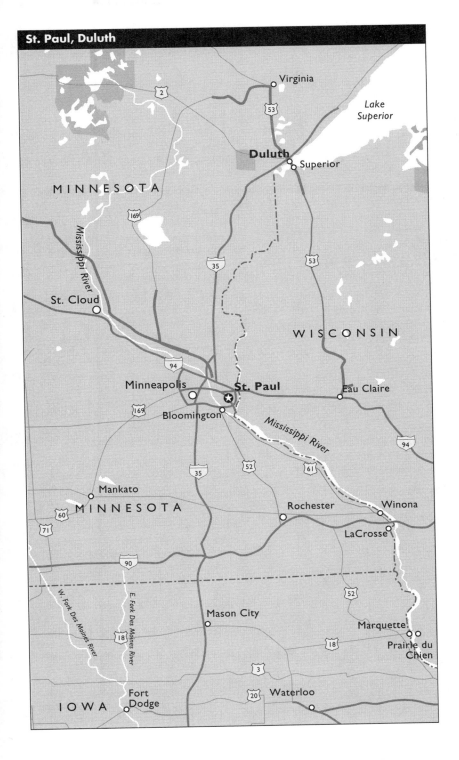

STADIUM FOOD: Hot and addictive minidonuts are sold from a truck outside the park. Once inside, make a beeline for one of the two field-level concession stands and order the fantastic Walleye sandwich for $4.50. They sell out before game time. Good brats are $4. The Kool Jerk Calypso Chicken, sold from a stand beyond the third-base bleachers, is worth the $4.25. The official beer, Pig's Eye, is dispensed by vendors with backpacks. Iced mocha is $3. As you leave the park, vendors often sell smoked fish, like Northern goldeneye, at give-away prices.

SMOKING POLICY: Smoke- and alcohol-free seats in bleachers along right-field fence.

VISITING TEAM HOTEL: Holiday Inn Express (1010 Bandana Blvd. W., St. Paul, MN 55108, tel. 651/647–8711 or 800/465–4329).

TOURISM INFORMATION: St. Paul Convention and Visitors Bureau (102 Norwest Center, 55 E. 5th St., St. Paul, MN 55101, tel. 651/297–6985 or 800/627–6101).

St. Paul:
Midway Stadium

"Fun is good," says Mike Veeck, the president of the St. Paul Saints. And we had more fun in St. Paul than in any of the other cities we visited. Veeck can't help himself. It's in his genes. His father was Bill Veeck, the zaniest, most fan-conscious owner in the history of baseball. Veeck Senior got into the Hall of Fame despite a career as a baseball iconoclast. He was the owner of the Cleveland Indians, the Chicago White Sox, and the St. Louis Browns. Veeck Senior is the guy who planted the ivy at Wrigley Field. He's the one who sent 3-ft, 7-inch Eddie Gaedel to bat against the Detroit Tigers on August 19, 1951. In a crouch, Gaedel's strike zone was about 1½ inches. He walked on four pitches.

If you want to understand why major-league baseball is losing fans while minor-league baseball is gaining them, visit the Twin Cities of Minneapolis–St. Paul. These twins have long had a sibling rivalry over everything from baseball to economic development. For six decades, they were opponents in the American Association. Then St. Paul lost its minor-league team in 1961 when the Washington Senators moved to Minneapolis. Minor-league baseball returned to St. Paul in 1993 with the start-up of the audacious Northern League, a renegade group of investors and baseball people fed up with the arrogance and greed of today's major-league baseball.

Nowhere is the minors' supremacy over the majors more apparent than in the Twin Cities. The Minnesota Twins play on plastic grass under

a roof in the sterile and ugly Metrodome. The fans—and there aren't many anymore—seem somnolent. In Minneapolis baseball, there's a sense of complacency. In St. Paul, there's excitement, community, and a waiting list for season tickets.

For "REAL GRASS AND REAL BEER," as the sign in center field in Midway Stadium says, go across the river from the Metrodome. The St. Paul Saints are playing to sellouts in the funky, geranium-filled ballpark, where fans can get haircuts and massages during games and a pot-bellied pig delivers new balls to the umpire. Saint, the "prince of pork, the sultan of swine, the Buddha of bacon," is a real live pig who rests under the grandstand between assignments.

In St. Paul, they play in a scruffy concrete and aluminum municipal stadium that seats only 6,311 people. In 1957, St. Paul built $2 million, 10,000-seat Midway Stadium for its longtime Triple A American Association team. But after just four seasons, the team was history when a major-league team moved in across the river and the stadium was leveled. The new Midway Stadium, built in 1982, sits in an industrial park with a train track just feet from the left-field wall and a six-story fire-department practice building beyond right field. Veeck calls Midway "the ugliest ballpark in the country." But it has a sense of fun and community that's absolutely irresistible.

The fans come first with the Saints owners, who help run the turnstiles and roam the park for fan-friendly ideas. In contrast to the pretentiousness of the major-league owners, the owners here watch the game on folding chairs behind a chain-link fence right next to where the pig rests. "The corporate money sucked the life out of baseball," laments Saints president Veeck. "Our club offers the fan hope, in our players and in their world." Veeck now shares his time and philosophy of fan-driven baseball with the Charleston RiverDogs as well.

If you think the snail should be the mascot of major-league baseball, you'll find the pace a lot faster in the Northern League. There's a 20-second clock in center field, and a horn goes off when pitchers exceed the time per pitch that the major leagues require but never enforce.

The Saints' endearing off-field nuttiness with contests, imaginative music, and comedic announcing is joined by exciting action on the field. The night we were at Midway Stadium, the hometown Saints blew a lead in the top of the eighth and regained it in the bottom of the inning. With two outs in the top of the ninth and the Saints' 6,311 fans on their feet and screaming for the final out, a train passed and blew its whistle. The fans turned and waved and screamed to the train. The flustered umpire called time-out. Play resumed for the final pitch and the final out. Then Veeck blew up the night's profits with a spectacular fireworks show that kept the sellout crowd entranced and cheering late into the night. Really. That's the way it is here in St. Paul, where they work hard to live up to the team's motto, "Wild and Outside."

Where to Stay

Make sure you get the coupon book from the St. Paul Convention & Visitors Bureau (tel. 651/ 297–6985). It offers genuine savings for lodgings, restaurants, museums, and shopping.

Visiting Team Hotel: Holiday Inn Express. This unusual hotel in a renovated train repair shop is a half-mile from the ballpark. The comfortably furnished rooms are built around a spacious courtyard that holds a pool, a sauna, and a breakfast area. There are a free Continental breakfast and evening snacks. The walls contain photos of the structure in its earlier life as a repair and paint yard. *1010 Bandana Blvd. W, St. Paul 55108, tel. 651/647–1637 or 800/ 465–4329, fax 651/647–0244. 109 rooms. Facilities: indoor pool, wading pool, sauna. AE, D, DC, MC, V. $$*

Days Inn Civic Center. This newly remodeled, eight-story hotel has good views of the Cathedral of St. Paul. It is downtown and convenient to the museums. Guests receive a free Continental breakfast. *175 W. 7th St., St. Paul 55102, tel. 651/292–8929 or 800/325–2525, fax 651/ 292–1749. 203 rooms. Facilities: restaurant, free parking. AE, D, DC, MC, V. $$*

Embassy Suites St. Paul. This downtown, all-suite hotel is near the museums. Each suite has two rooms, including a living room with a couch that folds out to a double bed. Guests can choose a king bed or two double beds in the bedroom. All guests receive a free breakfast. *175 E. 10th St., St. Paul 55101, tel. 651/224– 5400 or 800/362–2779, fax 651/224–0957. 210 suites. Facilities: restaurant, indoor pool, hot tub, sauna, coin laundry, free parking. AE, D, DC, MC, V. $$*

Where to Eat

Cafe Latté. This great soup, salad, and sandwich place is in the midst of a row of small, attractive shops a mile west of downtown. Its fresh American food is served cafeteria-style. Its high quality and low prices fill this 150-seat restaurant with customers all day long. *850 Grand Ave., St. Paul, tel. 651/224–5687. AE, DC, MC, V. $*

Downtowner Cafe. You can get inexpensive breakfasts at this storefront restaurant two blocks west of the Civic Center. Cajun eggs and sausage are a specialty. The tables are Formica and the cooking is short-order. *253 W. 7th St., St. Paul, tel. 651/228–1221. No credit cards. No dinner. $*

Rain Forest Cafe. This wildly popular special-effects restaurant is on the first floor of the Mall of America, next to Bloomingdale's. The sound of thunder, flashes of lightning, and large aquariums give you the feel of eating in a jungle. There are oversize drinks and huge portions of food. You can expect at least a 90-minute wait on weekends. There are no reservations, so check in early and see the mall while you wait. The restaurant is smoke-free. *Mall of America, Bloomington, tel. 612/854–7500. AE, D, DC, MC, V. $$*

Twin City Grill. You can get old-fashioned favorites in this check-tablecloth restaurant, which resembles a 1940s diner. Especially good are the meat loaf, Northern Lakes fish, and several varieties of rich milk shakes. There is a children's menu. *Mall of America, North Garden Entrance, Bloomington, tel. 612/854–0200. AE, D, DC, MC, V. $$*

Entertainments

Capital City Trolley. Old-fashioned rubber-wheeled trolleys run throughout the city and pick up passengers at red and green stop signs. *55 E. 5th St., St. Paul, tel. 651/223–5600. Fare: 25¢; children under 6 free; Sun., children under 13 free with paying adult. Capital route, every 15 mins., Mon.–Sat. 11–5; After Hours route, every 10 mins, Mon.–Sat. 5–11; Lunch Express route (links Space Center area with downtown, World Trade Center, Town Square, and Lowertown areas), every 13 mins, weekdays 11–2.*

Como Park. The entry is free to this charming kiddie-land amusement park, which contains 15 rides, a small zoo, and a beautiful greenhouse. You can feed the seals for 50¢. Sparky the sea lion performs while you sit in a concrete amphitheater. The gorillas and the pelicans usually draw crowds. The conservatory, a glass Victorian beauty, is filled with flowers and runs an admirable Summer Garden Program in which youth volunteers design, plant, and maintain plantings in the park. *Lexington Ave. and Kaufman Dr., St. Paul, tel. 651/487–8200. Open Apr.–Sept., daily 8–8; Oct.–Mar., daily 8–5. Conservatory: 50¢ adults, 25¢ children; open Apr.–Sept., daily 10–6; Oct.—Mar., daily 10–4.*

Minnesota Children's Museum. The museum's downtown installation has dozens of hands-on exhibits in six galleries. Children can work with tools, cranes, and an indoor waterworks and explore an anthill maze and a re-creation of a Twin Cities ethnic neighborhood. Toddlers and infants have a special exhibit, Minnesota Habitat, scaled to their sizes and interests. *10 W. 7th St., St. Paul, tel. 651/225–6000. Admission: $5.95 adults and children over 3, $3.95 children under 3 and senior citizens. Open Mon.–Wed. and Fri.–Sun. 9–5, Thurs. 9–8.*

Minnesota History Center. This museum has family-focused shows and several interactive exhibits. Visitors can examine a 24-ton boxcar and a voyageur canoe and climb on a 24-ft

mock-up of a grain elevator. There is an on-site cafeteria and pay parking. *345 Kellogg Blvd. W, St. Paul, tel. 651/296–6126. Admission free. Open Tues.–Wed. and Fri.–Sat. 10–5, Thurs. 10–9, Sun. noon–5.*

Padelford Packet Riverboats. Five paddleboats tour the Mississippi River from Harriet Island, offering exciting views of the Twin Cities. These stern-wheel cruises have historic narration that younger children may not follow closely. *Harriet Island, St. Paul, tel. 651/227–1100. Admission: $10 adults, $7.50 ages under 13. Open Memorial Day–Labor Day, departures daily at noon and 2; Labor Day–Memorial Day, departures weekends at 2.*

Valleyfair. This huge amusement park is 30 mi southwest of downtown and includes an adjacent waterpark, White Water Country, in its admission. The amusement park has a well-preserved 1915 Philadelphia Toboggan Company carousel. IMAX films are shown on a six-story screen. The booming sound may be too intense for younger children. There are good river-raft rides and six heart-stopping roller coasters. The water park has slides, a splash station for younger children, and a lazy river ride. Parking is $6. *1 Valleyfair Dr., Rte. 101, 9 mi west of I–335 and Rte. 13, Shakopee, tel. 612/445–7600. Admission: $27.95 persons over 48", $7.95 children age 4–48" and senior citizens. Open late May–Labor Day, daily 10–10 or midnight on occasion. D, MC, V.*

Sights to See

Take a look at the streamlined Mickey's Diner (36 W. 7th St., tel. 651/222–5633), a vintage hash house that's on the National Register of Historic Places. Its appeal is visual. Inside, it's cramped and the food isn't worth the second-hand smoke.

Fitzgerald Theater. Formerly known as the World Theater, this is the elegant playhouse from which Garrison Keillor now broadcasts "A Prairie Home Companion" on Saturday-afternoon live shows, starting at 4:45 when he's in Minnesota. This 916-seat theater also hosts local and traveling shows. *10 E. Exchange St., at Wabasha St., St. Paul, tel. 651/290–1221. Admission: $17.50–$23; tickets to all attractions available through Ticketmaster (Dayton's Department*

Store, downtown, tel. 651/989–5151); box office open on "Prairie Home Companion" broadcast days, Sat. 10–6:15. AE, D, MC, V.

State Capitol. Local architect Cass Gilbert, who did the Woolworth Building in New York, created this U.S. Capitol look-alike in 1905. The House and Senate chambers have been restored. Free 45-minute tours are given regularly, and special tours focusing on women in government, art, and architecture can be arranged. *Aurora Ave., between Cedar and Park Sts., St. Paul, tel. 651/296–2881. Open weekdays 8:30–5, Sat. 10–4, Sun. 1–4; tours weekdays 9–5, Sat. 10–3, Sun. 1–3.*

Unusual Shopping

Dome Souvenirs Plus. If you do go near the Dome in Minneapolis, there is a sports mavens' emporium across the street from gate A. It's as funky as the Dome is stiff. There's a free baseball museum, souvenirs for sale, and a modest food counter with ballpark comestibles at lower prices than the Dome's. The walls are full of old uniforms, bats, and autographed photos of the owner with some of baseball's greats. *406 Chicago Ave. S, Minneapolis, tel. 612/375–9707.*

Mall of America. Near the entrance to the "Mystery Mine Ride" in the Camp Snoopy amusement park here is a home plate; the mall is on the former site of Metropolitan Stadium. Built in 1955 to attract a major-league team, it finally got one in 1961. In 1965, the All-Star Game and the World Series were both played here. The Twins moved to the Metrodome in 1982. The biggest hit in Metropolitan Stadium history was a 520-ft home run by Hall of Famer Harmon Killebrew in 1961. Stand at home plate and look all the way across Camp Snoopy for the red-chair replica hanging on the wall above the Log Chute. That's where Killebrew's blast landed. *Cedar Ave. and Killebrew Dr., Bloomington, tel. 612/883–8800.*

DULUTH-SUPERIOR DUKES

League: Northern League • **Affiliation:** Independent • **Class:** N.A. • **Stadium:** Wade Stadium • **Opened:** 1941 • **Capacity:** 4,100 • **Dimensions:** LF: 340, CF: 380, RF: 340 • **Surface:** grass • **Season:** late May–Sept. 1

STADIUM LOCATION: 101 N. 35th Ave. W, Duluth, MN 55807.

TEAM WEB SITE: www.dsdukes.com

GETTING THERE: The ballpark is 3 mi south of downtown. Take I-35 to 40th Ave. West exit. Take 40th to Grand Ave. Go right on Grand for six blocks to 34th Avenue West, then take a right on 34th and go two blocks. The stadium and parking lot are on the right.

PARKING: Free parking at stadium.

TICKET INFORMATION: 207 W. Superior St., No. 206, Duluth, MN 55802, tel. 218/727–4525, fax 218/727–4533.

PRICE RANGE: Box seats $8; grandstand general admission $6; bleacher general admission $5. Fifty cents off for youth and senior citizens in the grandstand and bleachers except Fri. and Sat.

GAME TIME: Mon.–Sat. 7:05 PM, Sun. 2:05 PM; gates open 1 hour before game.

TIPS ON SEATING: The home team dugout is on the first-base side. The setting sun causes problems for those along third base.

SEATING FOR PEOPLE WITH DISABILITIES: Seating is located in front of the bleachers, with a good view.

STADIUM FOOD: Brats are the bargain here at $2.50. All the prices are reasonable, with hotdogs $2.25, cheeseburgers $2.50, and soda $1.50.

SMOKING POLICY: Smoking permitted in top six rows of the grandstand and in the bleachers; smoking not allowed on the concourse.

Duluth: Wade Stadium

Duluth and Superior were rivals associated with the Northern League since 1903. In 1956 they merged and were renamed the Dukes (a nickname used by the Duluth team in the 1930s). In the 1940s and 1950s the team drew as many as 100,000 fans a season. As with much of minor-league baseball, attendance plummeted in the 1960s; the Dukes had the best record in the Northern League in 1970 but drew only 22,747 fans. They didn't field a team in 1971 and the league went out of business a year later.

When baseball entrepreneur Miles Wolff was considering bringing back the Northern League in the early 1990s, he discovered what he considered a jewel of an old ballpark in Duluth. Wade Stadium was built in 1941 as part of President Roosevelt's Works Progress Administration (WPA) to spur economic recovery. Wolff fell in love with the city and the historic stadium and gave the twin port cities of Duluth-Superior a franchise in the reconstituted Northern League in its inaugural year of 1992.

This is not a flashy new ballpark, it's a solid old WPA stadium. The partially covered grandstand and the wall enclosing the stadium were built with 381,000 paving bricks taken from Grand Avenue when it was torn up and paved in 1940. The stadium had gotten a bit shabby after the original Northern League team folded in the early 1970s; it was used by high-school and college teams for two decades. The city and the "Save the Wade Foundation" restored the stadium for the 1992 Northern League season and have been making improvements every year. This throwback ballpark is a perfect setting for the zany antics and first-rate baseball for which the Northern League has become famous.

The teams affiliated with major-league teams have as a priority developing players and getting them ready for the big show. But in the independent leagues the object is to win. In Duluth,

this kind of baseball has built a strong base of fans who are intensely into the games. None more so than Homer D. Hound, the lovable Dukes' mascot.

Words to the wise: always bring a jacket, as even warm afternoons turn cold once the winds blow in from Lake Superior.

Where to Stay

Visiting Team Hotel: Black Bear Casino & Hotel. This three-story modern hotel is adjacent to I-35. The standard rooms are large, with contemporary furnishings; some rooms have hot tub baths. *1789 Hwy. 210, Carlton, MN 55718, tel. 218/878–2327, fax 218/878–7466. 157 rooms. Facilities: restaurant, cafeteria, indoor pool, kiddie pool, sauna. AE, D, DC, MC, V. $$*

Fitger's Inn. This splurge lodging offers elegant rooms, some with balconies and/or views of Lake Superior. Most also have fireplaces. It's located in a renovated downtown brewery. *600 E. Superior St., Duluth, 55802, tel. 218/722–8826 or 888/ 348–4377, fax 218/722–8826. 60 rooms. Facilities: restaurant, hot tubs. AE, D, DC, MC, V. $$$*

Holiday Inn Hotel & Suites. Attached to Canal Park by a skywalk, this 15-story downtown hotel is part of a giant shopping complex. Most rooms overlook Lake Superior and are spacious. Its restaurant, Porter's, is famous for its Caesar salad. *200 W. First St., Duluth, MN 55802, tel. 218/722–1202 or 800/465–4329, fax 218/ 722–0233. 296 rooms, 56 suites. Facilities: restaurant, 2 indoor pools, hot tubs, sauna. AE, D, DC, MC, V. $$*

Where to Eat

Pickwick Restaurant. This family-run restaurant is nearly a century old and features hearty, European ethnic fare, along with steaks and seafood. Heavy wooden tables are set with linen for dinner and less formally for lunch. It's downtown and there's a children's menu. *508 E.*

Superior St., Duluth, tel. 218/727–6746. AE, D, DC, MC, V. $$

Grandma's Miller Hill. Despite its publike atmosphere, Grandma's is a perfect spot to take the kids. Spaghetti, cheese sticks, and chicken strips are among the finger foods aimed at the younger eater. The main menu features American cuisine. It's 5 mi from downtown, near the Miller Hill mall. *2202 Maple Grove Rd., Duluth, tel. 218/722–9313. AE, D, MC, V. $$*

Hacienda del Sol. This inexpensive restaurant is filled with artifacts from Mexico and serves up abundant platters of Southwestern cuisine. Kids can choose from cheese tortillas and miniature tacos, among other items. *319 E. Superior St., Duluth, tel. 218/722–7296. AE, MC, V. $*

Entertainments

Grand Slam Adventure World. This indoor amusement arcade is alongside a boardwalk and shops at Canal Park. There's miniature golf, batting cages, basketball courts, bumper cars, and video games. There are separate fees for each activity. *395 S. Lake Ave., Duluth, tel. 218/722–5667. Open May–Labor Day, daily 9–8.*

North Shore Scenic Railroad. Two-hour excursion trains along Lake Superior and through nearby woods depart from the city's renovated depot. Guides provide lively narration. *The Depot, 506 W. Michigan St., Duluth, tel. 218/722–1273. Admission: $9 adults, $5 ages 3–13. Runs Memorial Day–Labor Day, daily 12:30 and 3, Fri and Sat. 10 AM also; Labor Day–mid-Oct., weekends 12:30 and 3.*

The Vista Fleet. Narrated cruise boats travel the Duluth-Superior Harbor, taking you close to ore freighters and foreign-flagged vessels. The boats, the *Vista King* and *Vista Star*, go through the Aerial Lift Bridge in order to sail into Lake Superior. *DECC Dock, 323 Harbor Dr.,*

Duluth, tel. 218/722–6218. Admission: $9 adults, $4 ages 3–11. Open May–mid-Oct., daily 9:30 AM–7:30 PM.

Sights to See

The Depot. A renovated railroad depot holds the city's children's museum, historical society, art museum, and the Lake Superior Museum of Transportation. Admission includes entry to all four museums and a trolley ride. There's a recreation of 1910 Duluth in Depot Square, a living-history museum with 22 stores, an operating street car, and an immigration waiting room. The children's museum includes interactive exhibits and a two-story tree detailing environmental habitats. *506 W. Michigan St., Duluth, tel. 218/727–8025. Admission: $8 adults, $5 ages 3–11, $20 family pass. Open May–mid-Oct., daily 10–6; mid-Oct.—Apr., Mon.–Sat. 10–5, Sun. 1–5.*

Lake Superior Maritime Visitor Center. The visitor center is adjacent to the Aerial Lift Bridge in Canal Park and includes replicas of ship cabins and displays explaining maritime engineering. The boat traffic is so extensive in Duluth there's even a Boatwatcher's Hotline, tel. 218/722–6489. *Canal Park Dr., Duluth, tel. 218/727–2497. Open Memorial Day–Labor Day, daily 10–9; Apr.–Memorial Day and Labor Day–mid-Dec., Sun.–Thurs. 10–4:30, Fri.–Sat. 10–6; mid-Dec.—Mar., Fri.–Sun. 10–4:30.*

Lake Superior Zoo. This compact year-round zoo is ideal for small children and is free to those three and under. Bird and small-animal cages are constructed to allow visitors to get very close. A special dark building houses nocturnal animals. A separate children's zoo has animals to pet. *72nd Ave. W and Grand Ave., Duluth, tel. 218/733–3777. Admission: $5 adults, $2 ages 4–11. Open mid-Apr.–mid-Oct., daily 9–6; mid-Oct.–Apr., daily 10–4.*

FIELD OF DREAMS 23
CEDAR RAPIDS, DES MOINES, DAVENPORT

Iowa baseball includes a magical site, the Dyersville farm where the movie *A Field of Dreams* was set. Visitors have been playing on the field, for free, every day in good weather since the movie crew built a ball diamond in the cornfield.

Start your Iowa vacation in Davenport to watch the Quad Cities River Bandits play in John O'Donnell Stadium beside the Mississippi River. Paddleboats meander behind the stadium and the beautiful 1939 Centennial Bridge hangs at roof level along the first-base side. This 66-year-old stadium has been modernized and survived a flood; its scoreboard explodes after runs and victories. Cross the river to watch the barges float through Lock and Dam 15 and continue on to Moline's excellent children's museum. Lunch should be at Lagomarcino's, a vintage candy store and ice cream parlor.

Herbert Hoover's birthplace and presidential museum is 50 mi west of Davenport on Interstate 80, in West Branch. After passing Iowa City, head north on Route 380, first turning west and stopping for a farm-style meal at the Amana Colonies. A half-hour northeast is Cedar Rapids, home of Quaker Oats. Watching a game in the city's Veterans Memorial Stadium is like traveling back in time. The design, prices, and food all are reminiscent of 1949, when the park was built. The Kernels are a Single A, Midwest League team.

You'll find baseball magic 60 mi northwest of Cedar Rapids, where 70,000 visitors a year play pick-up games on the *Field of Dreams* cornfield diamond. The town is also home to the Ertl Toy Company, where you can take a free factory tour and visit an outlet shop for miniature tractors and farm toys. Continue west on Route 20 until you reach Interstate 35, the major north–south route that will speed you to Des Moines, which is 155 mi from Dyersville. Sec Taylor Stadium is a 10,500-seat gem at the junction of the Des Moines and Racoon rivers, with a great view of the golden state capitol dome. There is an engaging Living History Farm just north of town, in Urbandale, and a family-oriented theme park, Adventureland, on the city's east side. Big leaguer Bob Feller rates his own museum in his hometown of Van Meter, 12 mi west of Des Moines.

CEDAR RAPIDS KERNELS

League: Midwest League • **Major League Affiliation:** Anaheim Angels • **Class:** A • **Stadium:** Veterans Memorial Stadium • **Opened:** 1949 • **Capacity:** 6,000 • **Dimensions:** LF: 325, CF: 385, RF: 325 • **Surface:** grass • **Season:** Apr.–Labor Day

STADIUM LOCATION: 900 Rockford Rd. SW, Cedar Rapids, IA 52404.

TEAM WEB SITE: www.kernels.com

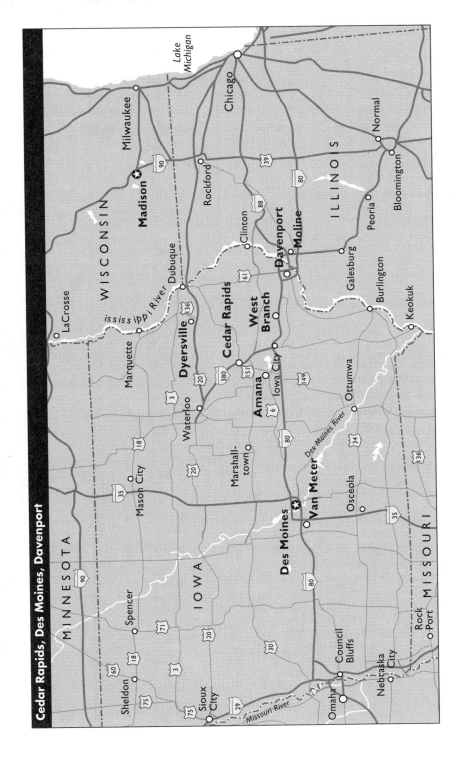

GETTING THERE: From I–380, Wilson Ave. exit (Exit 18), west 1½ mi to Rockford Rd. Right on Rockford, I mi to stadium, corner of 8th Ave. and 15th St. SW.

PARKING: Ample free parking.

TICKET INFORMATION: Box 2001, Cedar Rapids, IA 52406, tel. 319/363–3887, fax 319/363–5631.

PRICE RANGE: Box seats $6; general admission $4 adults, $3 children and senior citizens.

GAME TIME: Mon.–Sat. 7 PM, Sun. and other afternoon games 2 PM; gates open I hr before game.

TIPS ON SEATING: Only 4 rows of box seats; general admission seats under grandstand excellent. Grandstand is a designated no-smoking area.

SEATING FOR PEOPLE WITH DISABILITIES: Just beyond dugout on first-base side between grandstand and right-field bleachers.

STADIUM FOOD: Don't miss the pork chop sandwich for $3.50 from the grill on the first-base side behind the bleacher seats. Another bargain is the creamy hand-dipped ice cream in the concourse on the third-base side. It's $1.25 a scoop and the scoops are huge. The large candy stand has 50 varieties of candy. A picnic area with six green-and-white striped umbrellas is by the grill. Hot dogs and chili dogs are served behind the grandstand on the third-base side. The big condiment table includes great mustard, sauerkraut in a crock pot, jalapeños, relish, and onions.

SMOKING POLICY: Smoking prohibited in box seats and in any seats under grandstand.

VISITING TEAM HOTEL: Best Western Village Inn (100 F Ave. NW, Cedar Rapids, IA 52405, tel. 319/366–5323 or 800/858–5511).

TOURISM INFORMATION: Cedar Rapids Area Convention & Visitors Bureau (119 1st Ave. SE, Cedar Rapids, IA 52406-5339, tel. 319/398–5009)

Cedar Rapids: Veterans Memorial Stadium

Watching a ball game from the packed grandstand of Veterans Memorial Stadium in Cedar Rapids, Iowa, on a steamy summer night is about as close as you'll ever get to going back in time. With a ballplayer at the plate showing a lot of sock like the players did way back when, it was an eerie experience. It felt like 1949, the year this fine old stadium was built.

As the stadium sits up on a hill, fans have a bit of a climb to their seats. The elevated location provides a fine view of the Cedar Rapids skyline beyond center field. Veterans Memorial Park, dedicated in 1992, includes an Air Force plane that can be seen beyond the center-field wall from the grandstand, as well as two tanks and an anchor. Out beyond right field are several of the grain-processing plants that are the backbone of the Cedar Rapids economy. Kingston Stadium, a 13,000-seat high-school football stadium, is near the ballpark on the third-base side.

The stadium design is simple. There are four rows of box seats, only 500 in all. The general admission seats are just behind the box seats and are covered by a roof. But you have to watch where you sit, as the 10 dark-green poles holding up the grandstand roof can obstruct your view. Remember, this is the 1940s. There are aluminum bleachers down each baseline, with a picnic area beyond the bleachers on the third-base side.

As much as we enjoyed this almost 50-year-old stadium, it has one serious design flaw. The concourse area under the grandstand is too small and crowded. It does not allow the fans to get from the first-base side to the third-base side without climbing the ramp and walking through the grandstand seating area. On nights with large crowds, pedestrian traffic jams block the first few rows of the general admission seating in the grandstand. The two team locker rooms are below the center of the grandstand, breaking the concourse into two halves.

They have been playing professional baseball in Cedar Rapids since 1891. The Kernels wear replica uniforms of the 1938 Cedar Rapids Raiders for periodic "Turn Back the Clock" Days and hope to include a museum tribute to Cedar Rapids baseball history in their next renovation. There are plans for a new stadium, but no ground-breaking date has been set.

Where to Stay

Visiting Team Hotel: Best Western Village Inn. This utilitarian four-story hotel is on an isolated and quiet downtown block, overlooking the Cedar River. The rooms are small and clean, with contemporary furniture. *100 F Ave. NW, Cedar Rapids 52405, tel. 319/366–5323 or 800/ 585–5511, fax 319/366–5323. 86 rooms. Facilities: restaurant. AE, D, MC, V. $*

Crowne Plaza Five Seasons Hotel. This is Cedar Rapids' downtown convention hotel, and its 16 stories look out over the city. The rooms are spacious and traditionally furnished. The 20-year-old hotel was refurbished in 1999. *350 1st Ave. NE, Cedar Rapids 52401, tel. 319/363–8161 or 800/996–3426, fax 319/363–3935. 275 rooms. Facilities: restaurant, indoor pool, sauna, exercise room. AE, D, DC, MC, V. $$*

Where to Eat

Skyora Bakery. Visitors to Czech Village can stop for incomparable breakfast kolaches and huge cinnamon rolls here. There are six tables in front of the counter, next to shelves selling gooseberries, cherries, sauerkraut, popcorn, and bread. The bakery is down the street from the **Czech Museum** (10 16th Ave. SW, tel. 319/ 362–8500). *73 16th Ave. SW, Cedar Rapids, tel. 319/364–5271. No credit cards. Closed Sun. $*

Country Junction. This ordinary country-style family restaurant has three dining rooms, plus a coffee shop. The local-dairy ice cream is very good, and its sandwiches and dinners are fine but nothing special. It is convenient to the Ertl toy factory and Field of Dreams. *Hwys. 136 and 20, Dyersville, tel. 319/875–7055. AE, D, MC, V. $*

Metro Grill. Neon and funky artwork fill the walls of this casual family restaurant that specializes in wood-oven pizzas, pastas, and grilled meats. There are healthy menu choices, sandwiches, and a children's menu available. The restaurant, which has booth and table service, is

15 minutes northeast of the ballpark. *4407 1st Ave. SE, Cedar Rapids, tel. 319/393–9727. AE, D, DC, MC, V. $*

Sports Page Family Restaurant. The owner, Jim Googler, cooks the steaks, and the seafood is fresh, a rarity in Iowa. This Formica-booth restaurant is very casual, with a sports theme and memorabilia on the walls. The children's menu offers spaghetti and burgers. The restaurant is about 8 mi northeast of the ballpark. *38th St. and 1st Ave., Cedar Rapids, tel. 319/362– 3350. MC, V. $*

Entertainments

Dyersville National Farm Toy Museum. A half-hour drive north of Cedar Rapids brings you to the home of Ertl Toys, the world's largest producer of farm toys. Display cases show metal toys through the ages. The museum includes a film and a huge miniature circus made with meticulous detail. *1110 16th Ave. SE, at Hwys. 20 and 136, Dyersville, tel. 319/875–2727. Admission: $4, $1 ages 6–11, children under 6 free. Open daily 8–7.*

Ertl Toy Company. This toy maker offers a serious 45-minute factory tour that is open to children. Everyone wears goggles and sees the spray painting, the metal manufacturing, and the decal sticking that go into the production of miniature trucks, tractors, and toy banks. The tour is too long for some preschoolers. Reservations are necessary, particularly in summer. *Dyersville, tel. 319/875–2000. Tours May–Sept., weekdays at 10, 11, 1, and 2; Oct.–Apr., weekdays at 10 and 1.*

Sights to See

Amana Colonies. The colonies are settlements that specialize in farming, crafts, and food. The original settlers were members of the Community of True Inspiration, who were persecuted heavily in Germany. They first moved to Buffalo in the 1840s, outgrew their land, and then found 26,000 acres along the Iowa River. The church society continues, but in 1932 the residents voted to end the communal meals and other aspects of their successful socialist experiment. Visitors may tour a furniture shop, a wool mill, and several wineries for free and are asked to pay small admission fees to view a barn museum, a communal kitchen, and a history museum. A self-guided tour map is available at the colonies' Visitors Bureau (Rtes. 151 and 220, tel. 319/622–7622 or 800/245–5465).

Bill Zuber's Homestead Restaurant. Children's games were allowed in the Amana villages, but such organized games as baseball were forbidden by the church elders. Nonetheless, word of an exceptional young athlete spread. One day in 1930, C. C. (Cy) Slapnicka, a scout for the Cleveland Indians, came to the villages and found 17-year-old Bill Zuber doing his assigned chore helping with the onion harvest in the community-kitchen gardens. The scout found a baseball-size onion and asked young Zuber if he could hit a faraway barn. The kid threw the onion over the barn roof and 10 years later was pitching in Yankee Stadium. Zuber was noted more for his speed than his control, once putting Red Sox star Ted Williams in the hospital. His greatest thrill was a 1–0 victory over a Yankee lineup that included Joe DiMaggio. After a 10-year career was cut short by an arm injury, Zuber and his wife, Connie, bought a two-story brick hotel built in 1862 in the Amana village of Homestead. Zuber died in 1982, but his baseball legacy lives on here. Inside is a display of baseball memorabilia, including signed balls and a Babe Ruth–autographed photo. The dining-room walls are covered with photos of sports stars and other celebrities. There's a hearty, German-American menu served family-style. All meats are Amana-raised, and pork is never as good outside this state. *V St., Homestead, tel. 319/622–3911. AE, D, MC, V. $*

Field of Dreams. Dyersville, Iowa, where they filmed the 1989 baseball classic *Field of Dreams*, is 60 mi northeast of Cedar Rapids. Don't miss this. This is every bit as fabulous as it looked on the big screen. We all know that the sites of many movies are substantially enhanced by the moviemakers. Not here. The field and farmhouse are as they were in the movie. More than 70,000 visitors come each year. There were at least 50 people playing pickup baseball on the field and sitting in the bleachers the entire time we were there. Bring your glove, take your turn in the outfield, and stand in line to take a few cuts at the ball. If you want to be here when the corn is high, come some time after mid-June. The Field of Dreams Ghost Players appear from the corn field, as in the movie, from June through September on the second to last Sunday of each month. The two families that own the land covering the movie site are feuding, and there are plans to charge admission to a corn maze by one owner. *Hwys. 20 and 136, 25 mi west of Dubuque and 95 mi northwest of Davenport. Admission free.*

Unusual Shopping

Ertl Toy Outlet Store. A quarter of a mile north of the factory, you may buy the closeouts and specials on farm sets, cars, trucks, dolls, and sports-hero replicas. *Hwy. 136, Dyersville, tel. 319/875–5613.*

Two farms were used in filming *Field of Dreams* and, you guessed it, there are two souvenir stands.

The Field of Dreams Movie Site. This shop, to the side of the farmhouse, has the widest choice of souvenirs. *28963 Lansing Rd., Dyersville, tel. 888/875–8404.*

Left & Center Field of Dreams. This stand has souvenirs plus snacks. As part of the generous spirit that surrounds this site, if you don't have baseball equipment, you can use its balls, bats, and gloves for free. *29227 Lansing Rd., Dyersville, tel. 800/443–8981.*

IOWA CUBS

League: Pacific Coast League • **Major League Affiliation:** Chicago Cubs • **Class:** AAA • **Stadium:** Sec Taylor Stadium • **Opened:** 1947/92 • **Capacity:** 10,500 • **Dimensions:** LF: 335, CF: 400, RF: 335 • **Surface:** grass • **Season:** Apr.–Labor Day

STADIUM LOCATION: 350 SW 1st St., Des Moines, IA 50309.

TEAM WEB SITE: www.iowacubs.com

GETTING THERE: From I–235, 3rd St. exit; follow 3rd St. south through downtown to Court Ave. Left on Court and right on 2nd Ave. From south side of Des Moines, 7th or 9th St. to Cherry St., right on Cherry to 5th St., take 5th St. to Elm St., turn left then right on 2nd Ave.

PARKING: Stadium parking $3; limited, as ballpark is on edge of downtown. Parking on street and in private lots within walking range of stadium.

TICKET INFORMATION: 350 SW 1st St., Des Moines, IA 50309, tel. 515/243–6111, fax 515/243–5152.

PRICE RANGE: Club box seats $9; field box seats $7; reserved grandstand $7 adults, $5 under 14; general admission $5 adult, $3.50 under 14, under 4 free in lap.

GAME TIME: Mon.–Sat. 7:15 PM, Sun. 2:05 (Apr.–May) or 6:05 (June–Sept.); gates open 90 mins before game.

TIPS ON SEATING: Club box seats sold to season ticket holders. Reserved grandstand seats behind home plate provide great view of capitol beyond center field. Section X down first-base line is only no-smoking, no-alcohol section, but setting sun shines in your eyes in early innings of night games.

SEATING FOR PEOPLE WITH DISABILITIES: Available throughout stadium; parking adjacent to stadium in west lot.

STADIUM FOOD: There is a wonderful variety of food. The grilled Iowa Chop, which can be found behind the seats out the first-base line, is heaven for $5. Split one for two children. Add fresh-squeezed orangeade or lemonade for $2.50. Meaty ribs ($3) are smoked in the concourse, along with potato spuds ($2.50). Good brats and tasty boneless rib sandwiches are $3 and are available from the grills on the first- and third-base sides. Healthy fare includes chef salads, veggie and turkey breast sandwiches. A hot sliced caramel apple is $2. There are both good ice cream and frozen yogurt. There are picnic areas down the left-field line and on the mezzanine level behind home plate. Both are open to all fans after pre-game parties are over.

SMOKING POLICY: Smoking is prohibited in the seating areas.

VISITING TEAM HOTEL: Des Moines Marriott (700 Grand Ave., Des Moines, IA 50309, tel. 515/245–5500 or 800/228–9290).

TOURISM INFORMATION: Division of Tourism, Iowa Department of Economic Development (200 E. Grand Ave., Des Moines, IA 50309, tel. 515/242–4705 or 800/345–4692).

Des Moines:
Sec Taylor Stadium

Sometimes it's best to start over. Sec Taylor Stadium in Des Moines, Iowa, was built in 1947 and was clearly below the standard expected for Triple A baseball in the 1990s. With the potential of losing the top franchise of the Chicago Cubs, the city leveled the entire stadium. It built a $12 million, high-tech 10,500-capacity minor-league stadium for the 1992 season.

Wisely, city officials built it on the exact site of the old stadium. It would be hard to find a finer place. Named since 1959 for Garner W. ("Sec") Taylor, for 50 years the sports editor of the *Des*

Moines Register and Tribune, the stadium sits at the junction of the Raccoon River, which runs behind the stadium on the first-base side, and the Des Moines River, which flows behind the outfield wall. Unfortunately, you can see only the Raccoon River and that only from the picnic area on the mezzanine level looking behind home plate. There is, however, a spectacular view of the impressive gold-domed state capitol building beyond the flag flying in center field.

The entranceway is attractively landscaped, and the wide concourse has a full supply of concession stands, an excellent souvenir store, and plenty of bathrooms. Designed by HOK with a mezzanine level of skyboxes and press box, the stadium provides cover to only a few rows of the otherwise open grandstand. Everything about this stadium is modern and first-rate; all but 1,000 of the seats are individual stadium chairs.

The wall in left field also serves as the Cub Club, a members-only restaurant overlooking the field. Balls that hit the restaurant wall are in play. Players must hit the ball over the wall to get a home run. In 1995, a dozen skyboxes were built in left field with a sports ticker scoreboard 4½ ft tall and 39 ft long along the roof line of the skyboxes.

The team recently changed hands, but remains in local control. It was purchased by a group headed by a Pulitzer Prize–winning editor—appropriate for the journalistic heritage behind the stadium name.

Perhaps Des Moines's greatest claim to baseball fame came before the first Sec Taylor Stadium was built. The city hosted the first minor-league game under permanent lights in 1930.

Where to Stay

Visiting Team Hotel: Marriott Hotel. This 33-story downtown hotel has excellent views of the city. The rooms are large and comfortable. There's a lot of busy convention business here, but at least the hotel is part of Des Moines' skywalk system. *700 Grand Ave., Des Moines, 50309, tel. 515/245–5500 or 800/228–9290, fax 515/245–5567. 415 rooms. Facilities: 2 restaurants, indoor pool, exercise room. AE, D, MC, V. $$*

Hotel Savery. This venerable downtown hotel, built in 1919, has an 11-story redbrick exterior and a remodeled interior. The lobby has historic charm and a stenciled ceiling, but other areas are more contemporary. Room sizes vary. The hotel is within walking distance of the ballpark and is connected to the city's network of skywalks. *401 Locust St., Des Moines 50309, tel. 515/244–2151 or 800/798–2151, fax 515/244–1408. 221 rooms. Facilities: 3 restaurants, hot tubs, health club (fee), indoor pool, sauna, indoor track. AE, D, DC, MC, V. $$*

Kirkwood Civic Center Hotel. Built in 1929, this 12-story downtown hotel is an Art Deco treasure. Room furnishings are an eclectic mixture of old and new, and public spaces are enlivened by hand-painted murals of old Des Moines. The hotel is in the city's Court Avenue district, with several restaurants and a coffeehouse nearby. The ballpark is a quarter-mile walk. *400 Walnut St., Des Moines 50309, tel. 515/244–9191 or 800/798–9191, fax 515/282–7004. 160 rooms. Facilities: 3 restaurants. AE, D, DC, MC, V. $$*

Where to Eat

Spaghetti Works. This antiques-filled, exposed-brick former warehouse is a safe bet for children. Pasta of all descriptions is on the menu, and the service is generally speedy. There are good salads and a children's menu for small eaters. The high-backed wood booths fill up first. *310 Court Ave., Des Moines, tel. 515/243–2195. AE, D, MC, V. $*

Drake Diner. There are two diners in this local chain: This one is adjacent to the Drake University campus, and the North End Diner (5055 Merle Hay Rd., Johnston, tel. 515/276–5151) is just north of I–80 at the Merle Hay exit. Both have sleek chrome-and-neon exteriors and a classy, updated 1950s look inside. You can sit at the counter, in booths, or at tables. They serve an exceptional meat loaf, real mashed potatoes, and large salads. The ample menu also has healthy choices and a wide selection of breakfast items. *1111 25th St., Des Moines, tel. 515/277–1111. AE, D, MC, V. $*

Java Joes. This large popular coffeehouse is near the ballpark. It's smoke-free and has a thoughtful children's play alcove. Late-night offerings include folksingers, classical music, poetry- and play-readings, and jazz. Eaters like its hearty sandwiches, homemade soups, pastries, and coffee drinks. The high-ceilinged space is enlivened with vintage neon signs and billboards, recycled from an old sign company. *214 4th St., Des Moines, tel. 515/288–5282. AE, D, MC, V. $*

King Ying Low. The decor has changed little since this Chinese restaurant, the city's oldest, opened in 1907. In the Court Avenue district, the restaurant has a narrow storefront and is easy to miss. The color scheme is red and green, and the ambience is comfortable and familiar, not elegant. Its moo shu pork is a standout. *233 4th St., Des Moines, tel. 515/243–7049. AE, MC, V. $*

Stella's Blue Sky Diner. For a dose of 1950s nostalgia and great malts, head to the skywalks that crisscross downtown Des Moines. On the skywalk level of the Capitol Square building, which is near the ballpark, Stella's Blue Sky Diner is a hit with youngsters, who delight in having waiters and waitresses pour malts into glasses perched on customers' foreheads. There are jukeboxes on each table, so bring quarters. The decor runs to lava lamps, vintage working televisions, and bowling trophies. The menu is heavy on American blue-plate specials. *400 Locust St., Des Moines, tel. 515/246–1953. AE, MC, V. Closed Sun. $*

The Waterfront. This excellent locally owned seafood restaurant has fresh fish flown in daily from East Coast contract fishing rigs. There are a chowder and oyster bar, a seafood market, and live lobsters in tanks. There is a children's menu, as well as items other than fish, such as chicken fingers. *2900 University Ave., West Des Moines, tel. 515/223–5106. AE, D, MC, V. Closed Sun. $$*

Entertainments

Adventureland. This clean, nicely landscaped theme park is a manageable size for children, with thrill rides, Wild West and magic shows, and two water rides, including a white-water raft ride. There are three large roller coasters and a "slow coaster," "the Underground," which takes visitors down into an Old West mining camp. New in 1999 was the Space Shot, a gravity-defying ride that hurls passengers 200 ft in the sky in less than 2 seconds. Benches and shady spots are available near the rides for parents to perch on. *I–80, Exit 142A, at U.S. 65, Des Moines, tel. 515/266–2121. Admission: $21 adults, $19 ages 4–9, $16.50 senior citizens. Open Memorial Day–late Sept., weekends 10–8. Closing times vary. AE, D, MC, V.*

Blank Park Zoo. This small, accessible zoo is in southwest Des Moines, not far from the airport. The monkey section is tops, and children also are fascinated by the prairie-dog settlement. The only indoor exhibits are in the Discovery Center, where you can see snakes and fish. There are walk-through habitats that show landscapes and wildlife common to Africa and Australia. Train and camel rides are available at an extra fee, as is food to feed the goats and fish. *7401 SW 9th St., Des Moines, tel. 515/285–4722. Admission: $4.25 adults, $3.50 senior citizens, $2.75 ages 2–11. Open May–mid-Oct., daily 10–5.*

Des Moines Botanical Center. This large geodesic dome filled with 1,700 varieties of unusual plants dominates the riverfront near the freeway in downtown Des Moines. Inside, you take an escalator to an African rain-forest environment and see midwestern oddities, such as a producing banana tree. Exotic birds fly inside the dome, giving visitors close-up views when they alight. Exhibits of annual and perennial plants change regularly, and there are frequent lectures and hands-on plant demonstrations. *909 E. River Dr., Des Moines, tel. 515/242–2934. Admission: $1.50 adults, 75¢ senior citizens, 50¢ ages 6–18. Open Mon.–Thurs. 10–6, Fri. 10–9, weekends 10–5.*

Kate Goldman Children's Theatre. This 250-seat theater is in the Des Moines Playhouse, one of the nation's oldest community theaters. It presents a full season of children's and family entertainment throughout the school year, and the Playhouse usually offers a family musical during the summer. *831 42nd St., just north of I–235 at 42nd St. exit, Des Moines, tel. 515/277–6261. Ticket prices vary.*

Living History Farms. This 600-acre outdoor museum of farming shows visitors how agriculture was practiced from Native American times through the present. The farmsteads' buildings, crops, and furnishings are true to their era. These include a Native American settlement from 1700; an 1850 pioneer farm; a replica of an 1875 town with 17 shops, a school, homes, and a turn-of-the-century farm. Employees in authentic costumes demonstrate farming practices and crafts. You should plan to spend at least three hours. There are seasonal special events, such as baseball games with historic costumes and rules, and nostalgic celebrations on the Fourth of July, Labor Day, and Memorial Day. *2600 NW 111th St., Urbandale, tel. 515/278–2400. Admission: $8 adults, $7 senior citizens, $5 ages 4–12. Open May–Oct., Mon.–Sat. 9–5, Sun. 11–6.*

Science Center of Iowa. Heat, light, electricity, and earth and physical sciences are covered in hands-on exhibits at this museum 45 blocks west of downtown in Greenwood Park, which also houses the Des Moines Art Center. The Science Center has a planetarium, which presents laser shows daily for an additional $1.50. There are family laser shows on weekends at 1 and 3. In the evening, it presents laser rock shows, which charge $5.75 admission. The Science Center often has traveling exhibits on topics such as space travel or dinosaurs and has a full schedule of demonstrations. *4500 Grand Ave., Des Moines, tel. 515/274–4138. Admission: $5 adults, $3 ages 3–12 and senior citizens. Open Mon.–Sat. 10–5, Sun. noon–5.*

Sights to See

Bob Feller Hometown Exhibit. Van Meter, Iowa, didn't settle for the obligatory "Home of" sign for its hometown hero. This tiny Iowa town, 12 mi west of Des Moines, has created a wonderful monument to baseball's greatest living right-handed pitcher. We expected a few pieces of memorabilia displayed in the front window of a loyal fan's business office. We were surprised by an attractive new building designed by Feller's architect son on land donated by the local bank. There is a first-rate brick relief sculpture by Jay Tschetter on the parking-lot side of the museum that depicts Feller's Hall of Fame career. The museum, which opened in 1995, includes two well-conceived exhibit rooms full of Feller memorabilia. Our favorite item is the catcher's mitt used by Feller's father, William, to catch for young Bob on their Van Meter farm. Signed photos, balls, and other memorabilia are for sale. *310 Mill St., Van Meter 50261, tel. 515/996–2806. Admission: $2 adults, $1.50 senior citizens, $1 ages 12 and under. Open Mon.–Sat. 10–5, Sun. noon–4.*

State Capitol. The Iowa capitol building, in Des Moines, is among the most ornate in the nation. Begun in 1871 and completed in 1886, this neo-Romanesque building has a large gilded central dome with four smaller, equally ornate domes on its corners. The most striking view is from one flight up the Grand Staircase on the floor containing the House and Senate chambers. From here you can best see the statues and half-moon-shape paintings around the base of the dome. You can't enter the door marked "THIS WAY TO DOME" unless you are on a tour. *E. 9th St. and University Ave., Des Moines, tel. 515/281–5591. Free tours by reservation, weekdays 9–3:30, Sat. 9:30–3.*

State of Iowa Historical Building. Just down the hill from the capitol is this modern museum containing creative displays on early Native American life, settlers' lives, and Iowa geology, history, and transportation. *600 E. Locust St., Des Moines, tel. 515/281–6412. Donations appreciated. Open Tues.–Sat. 9–4:30, Sun. noon–4:30.*

QUAD CITY RIVER BANDITS

League: Midwest League • **Major League Affiliation:** Minnesota Twins • **Class:** A • **Stadium:** John O'Donnell Stadium • **Opened:** 1939 • **Capacity:** 5,200 • **Dimensions:** LF: 340, CF: 390, RF: 340 • **Surface:** grass • **Season:** Apr.–Labor Day

STADIUM LOCATION: 209 S. Gaines St., Davenport, IA 52802.

TEAM WEB SITE: www.riverbandits.com

GETTING THERE: From I–74, State St. exit, to River Dr., right on River Dr., 3 mi to stadium at corner of S. Gaines St. and River Dr. From I–80, Harriston St. exit, to River Dr., right on River Dr., 3 blocks to S. Gaines St.

PARKING: Ample free parking.

TICKET INFORMATION: Box 3496, Davenport, IA 52808, tel. 319/324–2032, fax 319/324–3109.

PRICE RANGE: Box seats $7; general admission $5 adults, $4 ages 5–14 and over 64, under 5 free.

GAME TIME: Apr.–May, Mon. and Wed.–Sat. 6 PM, Sun. 2 PM; June–Sept., Mon. and Wed.–Sat., 7 PM, Sun. 4 PM, Tues. 3 PM; gates open 1 hr before game.

TIPS ON SEATING: Sit on third-base side for best view of riverboats and spectacular Centennial Bridge. Only 8–10 rows of box seats and 3 rows of reserved, so general admission seats in grandstand are fine. But look before you sit, as poles holding up grandstand roof could obstruct your view.

SEATING FOR PEOPLE WITH DISABILITIES: Just past dugout on first-base side between grandstand and bleachers.

STADIUM FOOD: Treat yourself to a great brat or cheddar wurst at the grills on the first- and third-base sides. There's also a good local brown mustard, Boetje's, from Rock Island. The sausages are better than the pork sandwich. Small sodas are a bargain for 75¢. Unusual offerings include caramel apple chips for $2, bandit pie (Frito chips with chili and cheese) for $3, and root beer floats for $3. Corn dog mininuggets are $2.25. A pizza slice is $3.

SMOKING POLICY: Smoking prohibited in section 200 in general admission area under grandstand and directly behind home plate—family section.

VISITING TEAM HOTEL: Blackhawk Hotel (3rd and Perry Sts., Davenport, 52801, tel. 319/328–6000 or 800/553–1173).

TOURISM INFORMATION: Quad Cities Convention & Visitors Bureau (1900 3rd Ave., Rock Island, IL 61204-3097, tel. 309/788–7800 or 800/747–7800).

Davenport/Quad Cities: O'Donnell Stadium

You remember John O'Donnell Stadium. You saw a picture of it in the newspaper. The classic photograph from the extraordinary Midwest floods of the summer of 1993 was of John O'Donnell Stadium under water. It's dry now, and it is a jewel of a park. This is an old-time ballpark like Cedar Rapids', with exactly the right amount of modernization.

Davenport's Levee Improvement Commission decided in 1930 that it was time to turn the garbage dump along the Mississippi River waterfront into a city landmark to honor those who had served in the military. Municipal Stadium was dedicated in 1931 with a 25-piece band playing. The stadium was a modest-size covered grandstand with the curve of the outfield fence in contour with the river.

We found 83-year-old Bill Montgomery, a retired tavern owner, in his seat near the home-team third-base dugout. As an 18-year-old, he attended the first game in 1931 and has been a loyal fan and a community baseball advocate ever since. Montgomery claims to have gotten the very first flat tire on the gorgeous 1939

Centennial Bridge to Rock Island that hangs at roof level along the first-base side. The view at night of this bridge, with its five arches illuminated with large light bulbs, is spectacular. In 1970, the name was changed to John O'Donnell Stadium to honor a longtime sports editor of the *Davenport Times-Democrat*.

One of the community leaders who helped keep professional baseball in Davenport along with Bill Montgomery was George Majerkurth. According to Montgomery, Majerkurth was the umpire when Babe Ruth was alleged to have called his shot in the most famous home run ever hit at Chicago's Wrigley Field, on October 1, 1932. Years later, Majerkurth told Montgomery that Babe was actually gesturing to the pitcher that he had one strike left.

This version was confirmed by Woody English, the Chicago Cubs' captain in the 1932 World Series between the Cubs and the Yankees. English, who was playing third base, said that in the third game, Babe Ruth held two fingers up indicating two strikes. "He never said he called it. When asked, he replied the papers said I did," English recalled indignantly later.

For the 1989 season, the city invested more than $4.5 million in one of the very best restorations of an old ballpark that we have seen. The exterior is an elegant series of brick archways leading to a completely covered grandstand.

The stadium sits in a city park complete with a handsome bandstand. Gambling riverboats cruise by on the Mississippi River. Bleacher seats extend beyond the grandstand on both the first- and third-base sides, and picnic and play areas stretch down each baseline.

Davenport has been a leader in bringing excitement to minor-league baseball. After decades of using the nickname of their major-league affiliate, they became the Quad Cities River Bandits in 1991. The notion of tying the team name to the local community and designing a distinctive logo—in this case a baseball with a red bandanna—helped launch minor-league logo mania across the nation. In 1991, they added an exploding scoreboard that shoots off firecrackers for River Bandit home runs and wins. The design of the exploding scoreboard in left-center field echoes the lighted arches of Centennial Bridge and has the team logo on top.

O'Donnell Stadium continues to evolve. In 1999 plans were put into place for major, multi-million-dollar renovations that should keep this classic ballpark up and running for the foreseeable future.

Where to Stay

Visiting Team Hotel: Blackhawk Hotel. This classic brick 11-story downtown hotel has been renovated into a convention center. The standard rooms are small, with older, small bathrooms, many with the original tile from 1914 suites. The lobby is majestic, with some shops on the ground floor. Guests are repeatedly encouraged to patronize the city's gambling riverboat. The hotel is less than a mile from the ballpark. *3rd and Perry Sts., Davenport, 52801, tel. 319/328–6000 or 800/553–1173, fax 319/322–4778. 152 rooms, 36 suites. Facilities: restaurant, sauna, exercise room, coin laundry. AE, D, DC, MC, V. $$*

Best Western Riverview Inn. There are great views of the Mississippi River from this six-story riverfront hotel within walking distance of the ballpark. The rooms are contemporary and well used. *227 LeClaire St., at River Dr., Davenport 52801, tel. 319/324–1921 or 800/528–1234, fax 319/324–9621. 150 rooms. Facilities: restau-*rant, indoor and outdoor pools, hot tub, sauna, coin laundry. AE, D, DC, MC, V. $$

Where to Eat

Iowa Machine Shed Restaurant. Apple dumplings and roast pork attract families to this rustic, barn-style restaurant. The portions are huge and the atmosphere cheery, with a multitude of farm antiques on the walls and checkered napkins at the table. There is a children's menu as well as a large salad bar here. Breakfasts are hearty. The restaurant is 15 minutes north of the ballpark. *7250 Northwest Blvd., Exit 292 south from I-80, Davenport, tel. 319/391–2427. AE, D, DC, MC, V. $$*

Lagomarcino's. This storefront restaurant is a not-to-be-missed jump back in time in downtown Moline. The candy store–lunch counter has been dispensing its own ice cream, homemade rye bread, and fountain drinks since 1918. Its ceiling is white tin, the booths are mahogany, and the lamps are Tiffany-style. You can order real turkey sandwiches, phosphates (an old-fashioned, fruit-flavored carbonated drink), strawberry shortcake, and memorable hot fudge. *1422 5th Ave., Moline, IL, tel. 309/764–1814. No credit cards. Closed Sun. $*

Sights to See

Herbert Hoover Presidential Library and Birthplace. Herbert Hoover was born in 1874 in West Branch, Iowa, just 50 mi west of Davenport. His parents and grandparents had come to Iowa in covered wagons. The small 14-by-20-ft birthplace cottage is the centerpiece of a National Historic Site managed by the National Park Service. It includes a blacksmith shop similar to the one Hoover's father operated in the 1870s, an 1853 Quaker schoolhouse, an 1857 meetinghouse, and the Hoover gravesite. In the Presidential Library-Museum, a short film and excellent display recount Hoover's five decades of public service, painting him as a great man and a flawed politician. As a former president, Hoover proposed a set of reforms to improve American life, including an end to political ghostwriters and adding a fourth strike to baseball. We're glad that one wasn't adopted, as the games are long enough, thank you, Mr. President. *Herbert Hoover National Historic Site, ½ mi north of Exit 254 from I–80, West Branch, tel. 319/643–2541. Admission: $2 adults, $1 senior citizens, children under 16 free. Open daily 9–5.*

Mississippi River Visitors Center. You can watch barges, tugboats, and sailboats go through

Lock and Dam 15. Park rangers explain the process, and displays illustrate the mechanics. There is a great visual explanation of the Mississippi's stairway of water. *Rodman Ave., Rock Island, IL, tel. 309/794–5338. Open mid-May–Labor Day, daily 9–9; Labor Day–mid-May, daily 9–5.*

HEARTLAND BASEBALL 24
KANSAS CITY, OMAHA AND THE COLLEGE WORLD SERIES, WICHITA

It may surprise nonbaseball initiates to learn that the heartland is a hotbed of the game. And we do mean hot. Players (and fans) learn to tolerate double-headers in 105-degree temperatures.

Start with the region's popular major-league team, the Kansas City Royals, who play at the huge and distinctive Kauffman Stadium in the Truman Sports Complex. The area surrounding the stadium has several moderately priced hotels, and there are good bargains to be found at older downtown hotels, too. In terms of other baseball attractions, Kansas City is the Negro Leagues' Cooperstown: the excellent Negro Leagues Baseball Museum is part of the 18th and Vine Historic District, which also includes the Kansas City Jazz Museum and is just down the road from the famed Arthur Bryant's barbecue. Good eating is a Kansas City pre-occupation, and there are many legendary casual dining establishments to choose from.

Two hundred miles northwest is Omaha, home of baseball's College World Series. For ten days every June, the city is filled with hundreds of the nation's best college players and thousands of fans. They all cram into Johnny Rosenblatt Stadium on the bluffs in southeast Omaha. For the rest of the summer the stadium is home to the Golden Spikes, a AAA team of the Royals.

Wichita is southwest 300 mi, a park-filled river city with a fine zoo. There's a crazy tradition of baseball-round-the-clock played by summer collegiate leagues and amateur baseball teams during a marathon weekend each summer at Lawrence-Dumont Stadium, a ballpark on the Arkansas River that's also used by the Wichita Wranglers of the AA Texas League. If you're interested in one of the best summer college leagues, detour 30 minutes east to El Dorado, Kansas, where the El Dorado Broncos of the Jayhawk League play in McDonald Stadium.

KANSAS CITY ROYALS

League: American League • **Class:** Major League • **Stadium:** Kauffman Stadium • **Opened:** 1973 • **Capacity:** 40,529 • **Dimensions:** LF: 330, CF: 400, RF: 330 • **Surface:** grass • **Season:** Apr.-early Oct.

STADIUM LOCATION: One Royal Way, Kansas City, MO 64129.

TEAM WEB SITE: www.kcroyals.com

GETTING THERE: The Truman Sports Complex is located at the junction of I–435 and I–70 southeast of downtown. From north or south, take I–435 to the stadium exits. From east or west, take I–70. The Metro/Royals Express bus, tel. 816/221–0660, operates on two routes: from downtown/Crown Center and from the Country Club Plaza.

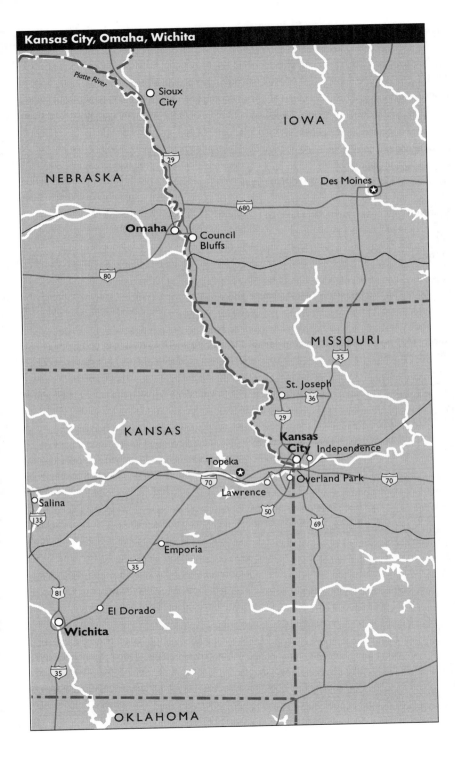

PARKING: Plenty of parking at the stadium for $6.

TICKET INFORMATION: Box 419969, Kansas City, MO 64141, tel. 816/921–8000.

PRICE RANGE: Club box $17; field box $15; plaza reserved $13; view-level box $12; view-level reserved $11; general admission $7 adults, $3.50 children. On Monday and Thursday, view-level reserved seats are half price ($5.50). Eight times during the season special family packages available: four tickets, four drinks, four hot dogs, and a bag of peanuts for $32.

GAME TIME: Mon.–Sat. 7:05 PM; Sun. 1:05 PM; gates open 90 min before game.

TIPS ON SEATING: General admission tickets down the left- and right-field foul lines go on sale 90 minutes prior to each game at gates C and D. The sun sets behind third base, so seats on the first-base side are in the sun.

SEATING FOR PEOPLE WITH DISABILITIES: On the plaza level between sections 103 and 108 and in each of the general admission areas. Elevators are available in the lobby of the Royals offices. There are 200 reserved parking spaces.

STADIUM FOOD: There are gourmet hamburgers here, with brown mustard, onions, and $2 baked beans on the side. Vendors put mustard on your hot dogs in the stands. Happily, one of the city's best barbecue makers, Gates BBQ, sells turkey, ham, pork, and beef sandwiches at the park for $5.50. There are good brats and polish sausages with kraut for $4, and a strawberry drink for $2.50.

SMOKING POLICY: Smoking prohibited in the seating areas and on the concourse. There are designated smoking areas throughout the stadium.

TOURISM INFORMATION: The Convention and Visitors Bureau of Greater Kansas City (City Center Square, 1100 Main, Suite 2550, Kansas City, MO 64105, tel. 816/221–5242 or 800/767–7700).

Kansas City: Kauffman Stadium

When you think of the plains of western Missouri and Kansas, perhaps you think of the pioneers in covered wagons. But when you exit Interstate 70 into the Harry S. Truman Sports Complex, you might think two spaceships have just landed from an alien planet. Side by side, sharing a huge parking lot, are Kauffman Stadium, home of the baseball Royals, and Arrowhead Stadium, home of the football Chiefs. What would Harry, let alone the pioneers, make of this?

The concrete exterior of Kauffman Stadium, with its circular walking ramps that look like a triple-decker Los Angeles freeway, are off-putting in this age of downtown brick ballparks. But get over it. Inside it works. Despite a number of classic 1970s flaws, the stadium is a treat. Best of all, in 1995 they corrected the most egregious flaw when they replaced the artificial turf with real grass.

When the history of the "new-old" ballparks of the 1990s is written, Kauffman Stadium will merit note as a genuine pioneer. For it was here that a simple truth first came to light—you can't build a great baseball park that serves as a football venue, too. Unfortunately, the truth is expensive, forcing cities like Kansas City and Baltimore to shell out tons of money for two pro stadiums. But without the breakthrough in Kansas City, there likely would be no Camden Yards.

The stadium opened in 1973 under the name Royals Stadium and hosted the major league All-Star Game that year. On May 15, 1973, Nolan Ryan threw the first of his seven major league no-hitters here. The stadium was renamed in 1993 to honor corporate leader, philanthropist, and team owner Ewing M. Kauffman.

The stadium's most striking feature is a 12-story-high scoreboard flanked by huge fountains. The scoreboard is shaped like an elongated home plate and topped with a gold crown. Fireworks go off behind it after Royals home runs and victories. The fountains, which might strike some as more appropriate for a horse-racing track, are another of the ballpark's distinctive elements.

The numbers 10, 5, and 20 under the scoreboard represent the retired uniforms of Dick Howser, George Brett, and Frank White. A state-of-the-art JumboTron video board was added beyond the left-field fence in 1990. The flags flying near the video board represent league and division championships and the 1985 world championship. The World Series trophy is displayed in the Royals Hall of Fame behind section 103 on the plaza level.

Concessions are sold on the open plaza behind the field-level seats, allowing fans a limited view of the game while standing in line. Kids will enjoy the Fun Zone at Gate B behind section 116. There are video games, a pitching-speed radar, and a headless cardboard cutout of a Royals player, providing a perfect vacation photo op. Sluggerrr, the Royals' crown-topped lion mascot, roams the seats when he's not dancing on top of the video board.

More Kansas City Baseball

Municipal Stadium site. Kansas City's Municipal Stadium hosted games 5, 6, and 7 of the first Negro Leagues World Series in 1924. Opened in 1923 as Muehlebach Field to house professional baseball both black and white, the ballpark seated 16,000. The city's African-American fans were famous for turning out in their best clothes and hats to watch the world-renowned Monarchs. The Fashion Parade was the highlight of opening day each year. Hall of Famer Satchel Paige pitched here for the Monarchs in the 1930s and '40s, and in 1951 Mickey Mantle played here for the Kansas City Blues, the Triple A farm club of the New York Yankees. The capacity was expanded to 35,020 in 1955 when the major league Athletics moved to Kansas City from Philadelphia. In 1964, the Beatles played Municipal, and in 1965, Paige returned at the age of 59 to pitch three scoreless innings for the Athletics against the Boston Red Sox. The Royals played here from 1969 to 1972 before moving to the new stadium. After that Municipal fell into decay and was eventually razed. The site now holds the Old Ballpark Community Garden. It is six

blocks east of the Negro Leagues Baseball Museum. *Brooklyn Ave., between 21st and 22nd Sts., Kansas City.*

Negro Leagues Baseball Museum. It was six decades after Fleetwood Walker was banned from baseball in 1887 that Jackie Robinson broke the color barrier and brought on the end of segregation in the so-called major leagues. The Negro Leagues Baseball Museum tells the history of black baseball from the 1860s to the 1950s, providing the unvarnished details, good and bad. This is a story not just of baseball but of the transformation of American culture. It is appropriate that this fine museum, a testament to the human spirit, is located in Kansas City, for it was here at the Paseo YMCA on February 13, 1920, that Rube Foster brought together the owners of the major black teams and formed the Negro National League. The highlight of the museum is the Field of Legends, featuring life-size bronze sculptures of a dozen of the most important players in Negro Leagues history, complete with biographical information. Impressively, despite the efforts of the white establishment of their time to deny their greatness, virtually every one of these stars will be recognizable even to a casual baseball fan. The gallery is arranged on a time line of one hundred years of African-American and baseball history. The museum opened an office in 1991, a gallery in 1994, and this full-scale museum in 1997. It is located in the 18th & Vine Historic District, once a hotbed of Kansas City jazz and black culture. *1616 E. 18th St., Kansas City, tel. 888/221–6526. Admission: $6 adults, $2.50 ages 12 and under. Open Tues.– Sat., 9–6, Sun. noon–6.*

Where to Stay

A city-wide hotel service offers low rates on rooms in 70 establishments. Contact Kansas City's Hotel/Motel Reservation Service, tel. 816/453–7280 or 800/877–4386.

Adams Mark. Ask for stadium-side rooms at this hotel that's across the road from the sports complex. There's shuttle service to Worlds of Fun and Oceans of Fun amusement parks, to downtown, and to the Country Club Plaza. Rooms are modern, but uninspiring. Game packages are available. *9103 E. 39th St., I–70 and Truman Sports Complex, Kansas City, MO 64133, tel. 816/737–0200 or 800/444–2326, fax 816/737–4712. 374 rooms. Facilities: 2 restaurants, indoor and outdoor pools, health club, tennis courts. AE, D, DC, MC, V. $$*

Holiday Inn–Sports Complex. Located directly across from the ballpark, this seven-story hotel is for sports fans. There's an outdoor basketball court and bicycles. About half the rooms have stadium views. *4011 Blue Ridge Cutoff, Kansas City, MO 64133, tel. 816/353–5300 or 800/465–4329, fax 816/353–1199. 163 rooms. Facilities: restaurant, indoor pool, sauna, game room, free bicycles. AE, D, DC, MC, V. $$*

Radisson. There are bargains to be found at this Art Deco downtown hotel where you eat your Continental breakfast in the former location of Harry Truman's hat shop. A gilded bronze statue of *Dawn* is featured in the elegant lobby of the 1931 hotel, which is on the National Register of Historic Places. The plumbing is old-fashioned, but many of the rooms have two bedrooms, and crown molding and other 1930s accents are found throughout. Weekend specials are as low as $89 for a double. *106 W. 12th St., Kansas City, MO 54105, tel. 816/221–7000 or 800/333–3333, fax 816/221–3477. 240 rooms. Facilities: restaurant, exercise room. AE, D, DC, MC, V. $$*

Where to Eat

Arthur Bryant's. You've got to like hot to appreciate the vinegary barbecue sauce that has made Arthur Bryant's pork ribs and brisket sandwiches famous. Service is cafeteria-style, the tables unmatched, but no one cares. Servers will give you gallons of sauce to lug home. Try the baked beans and very good french fries. *1727 Brooklyn St., Kansas City, MO, tel. 816/231–1123. AE, MC, V. $*

The City Market. This is the largest open-air farmer's market in the Midwest, with more than 148 stalls selling baked goods, produce, meats, and crafts. It's a good place to get breakfast or lunch, particularly on Saturday, when most of the action occurs. There are tables, as well as a barbecue joint, Winslow's, tel. 816/471–7427. The market is open March–December, week-

days 10–5, weekends 7–4. *20 E. 5th St., Kansas City, MO, tel. 816/842–1271. $*

Savoy Grill. An all-male staff serves some of the city's best food in this 1903 landmark. Mission lamps, green leather banquettes, dark wainscoting, and stained-glass windows decorate this tablecloth restaurant where W. C. Fields and Teddy Roosevelt dined on Yankee pot roast, clam chowder, lobster, and prime rib. So can you. Children can get half portions. *Central at 9th St., Kansas City, MO, tel. 816/842–3890. AE, MC, V. $$*

Stroud's. You might want to avoid the inevitably busy Saturday nights at this home of panfried chicken. Very good cinnamon rolls are another draw at this informal restaurant that has been busy since its founding in 1933. *1015 E. 85th St., Kansas City, MO, tel. 816/333–2132. AE, CB, MC, V. $*

Winstead's. Milk shakes and steakburgers are unforgettable at this vintage lunch counter hangout, which serves breakfast, lunch, and dinner. There are four Winstead's branches; the two listed below are closest to the ballpark, about 10 mi away. Burgers come in singles, doubles, or triples. There are very good fries and onion rings and many blast-from-the-past beverages, including limeades, orangeades, and special malts. *101 Brush Creek Blvd., Kansas City, MO, tel. 816/753–2244. Also at 1200 Main St., Kansas City, MO, tel. 816/221–3339. AE, D, MC, V. $*

Entertainments

Kansas City Zoo. There are more than 400 wild animals living in African-style habitats, including the Okavango Elephant Sanctuary. Domesticated animals such as Scottish highland cows and Sicilian donkeys are featured, along with an Australian outback section. There are a total of 1,500 animals in this sprawling, 200-acre zoo. A $71-million expansion in 1998 added an IMAX theater (fee extra). There are pony and camel rides, a safari boat, and a year-round train ride. Parking is $2. *6700 Zoo Dr. Swope Park, off I–435 and 63rd St., Kansas City, MO, tel. 816/871–5701. Admission: $6 adults, $3 ages 3–11, Tues. $2 admission ages 3 and up. Open May–mid-Oct., daily 9–5; mid-Oct.–Apr., daily 9–4.*

Worlds of Fun and Oceans of Fun. This amusement park and neighboring water park are 20 minutes northeast of downtown. The amusement park has Mamba, a mile-long roller coaster reaching speeds of 75 mph; two towering drop rides, Detonator and RipCord; and Timber Wolf, a wooden coaster. You'll also find a large kiddie land, live musical revues, and a nightly laser show. Parrots perform, as do aquatic divers. At Oceans of Fun, there are seven water slides, a lazy river, a wave pool, and a kiddie complex with spray cannons and a pirate's ship. Parking is $5 and combination tickets for the two parks are available. *I–435 at Exit 54, Kansas City, MO, tel. 816/454–4545. Worlds of Fun admission: $29.95 adults, $14.50 senior citizens, $6.95 ages 3–48", $14.50 after 4 PM, $10 discount with a Barq's root beer can. Oceans of Fun admission: $18.95 adults, $13.50 senior citizens, $5.95 ages 3–48", $13.50 after 4 PM. Parks open Memorial Day–Labor Day, daily 10–closing times vary. Worlds of Fun open mid-Apr.–Memorial Day and Labor Day–mid-Oct, weekends 10–9. D, MC, V.*

Sights to See

The Country Club Plaza. One of the nation's oldest and best-designed shopping centers is south of downtown. Its red Spanish tiles, turrets, and unified yellow brick encompass department stores, hotels, specialty shops, movie theaters, and restaurants. The Plaza is illuminated nightly by thousands of Christmas lights from Thanksgiving to mid-January. *450 Ward Parkway, Kansas City, tel. 816/753–0100.*

Hallmark Visitor's Center. The world's largest card maker offers a free tour with interactive exhibits featuring famed artists, explanations of printing processes, and a chance to watch Hallmark artists at work. There is a 13-minute film. *25th St., off Pershing, Crown Center Plaza, Kansas City, tel. 816/274–5672. Open weekdays 9–5, Sat. 9:30–4:30.*

Harry S. Truman Library and Museum. Here you'll find, among other things, a replica of the Oval Office, including the original "The Buck Stops Here" sign. (Wooden reproductions of the sign are available at the gift shop for $5, along with bargain copies of the Ben Shahn print of Truman at the piano.) An excellent film on Truman by Charles Guggenheim, an Academy Award–winning documentarian, runs regularly. President and Mrs. Truman are buried in a landscaped courtyard. Tours of Bess Truman's Victorian home, where the couple lived after 1919, are available through the Truman Home Ticket and Information Center, 223 N. Main St., Independence, tel. 816/254–9929. Admission: $2, under 17 free. The train depot that was the final destination on Truman's 1948 whistlestop campaign is at Pacific Avenue and Grand Street. *500 West U.S. Highway 24, Independence, MO 64050, tel. 816/254–9929. Admission: $5 adults, $4.50 senior citizens, $3 ages 6–18. Open Mon.–Sat. 9–5, Thurs. 9–9, Sun. noon–5.*

Kansas City Jazz Museum. Neon signs and Art Deco graphics welcome you to this beautifully designed museum, which adjoins the Negro Leagues Museum. Exhibits on the lives of Duke Ellington, Charlie Parker, Dizzy Gillespie, and dozens of other performers fill this innovative, interactive space. Record covers, instruments, and lots of listening posts are found throughout, and live jazz is played nightly at the neighboring Blue Room. The Gem Theater, a 500-seat arts center, is also part of the complex. *1616 E. 18th St., Kansas City, tel. 816/474–8463. Admission: $6 adults, $2.50 ages 11 and under. Combination ticket with Negro Leagues Museum: $8 adults, $4 ages 11 and under. Open Tues.–Sat. 9–6, Sun. noon–6.*

Kansas City Museum. As history museums go, this former mansion trumps others with marble floors and stained-glass windows. Kids care more about the planetarium, working soda fountain, and natural history hall. *3218 Gladstone Blvd., Kansas City, MO, tel. 816/483–8300. Admission: $2.50 adults, $2 ages 3–17 and senior citizens. Planetarium admission: $3.50. Open Tues.–Sat. 9:30–4:30, Sun. noon–4:30.*

OMAHA GOLDEN SPIKES

League: Pacific Coast League • **Major League Affiliation:** Kansas City Royals • **Class:** AAA • **Stadium:** Johnny Rosenblatt Stadium • **Opened:** 1948 • **Capacity:** 22,000 • **Dimensions:** LF: 332, CF: 408, RF: 332 • **Surface:** grass • **Season:** Apr.–Labor Day

STADIUM LOCATION: 1202 Bert Murphy Dr., Omaha 68107.

TEAM WEB SITE: www.goldenspikes.com

GETTING THERE: The stadium is 2½ mi south of downtown. Take 13th Street South; exit off I–80 and drive one block south to the stadium.

PARKING: Ample free parking.

TICKET INFORMATION: 1201 Bert Murphy Dr., Omaha 68107, tel. 402/734–2550. For College World Series tickets, call 402/554-4404.

PRICE RANGE: Field box $7.50; view box $5.50; general admission $3.50. $1 discount ages 6–18 and senior citizens. Free ages 5 and under.

GAME TIME: Mon.–Sat. 7:05 PM, Sun. 1:35 PM; gates open 90 min before game.

TIPS ON SEATING: The yellow reserved view box seats in the front of the internal concourse are excellent. Sit on the third-base side, as the sun sets behind third base. Sections E–M are shaded by a huge skybox and the press box, but avoid seats in these sections blocked by the eight pillars and the first four rows just behind the concourse.

SEATING FOR PEOPLE WITH DISABILITIES: Seating is on the internal concourse behind home plate.

STADIUM FOOD: There is good homemade pizza for $2.75 a slice and honey popcorn for $3. Upgrade the regular hot dog ($2) to a Royal dog for $3.25. Every Sunday at the park, fans get a free hot dog and soft drink if they bring a label from a Dubuque meat product. There are frozen malts, decent bratwursts, and sodas are only $1.50. On hot days, head for the glassed-in, air-conditioned **Stadium View Club** restaurant, behind first base. It has three spacious levels, with tables surrounded by captain's chairs, and it's open to any ticket holder. There's a varied menu—toasted ravioli, Caesar salad, a cod dinner, and very good hot apple pie. There's no smoking allowed in the club restaurant. Just outside the park is **Zesto's Ice Cream** stand, which serves good roast chicken as well as frozen treats. You can bring food into the stadium.

SMOKING POLICY: Smoking is prohibited in the seating area and the concourse. There are designated smoking areas near the front gate and behind sections CC and DD on the first-base side.

VISITING TEAM HOTEL: Ramada Hotel Central (7007 Grover St., Omaha, NE 68106, tel. 402/397–7030 or 800/272–6232).

TOURISM INFORMATION: Omaha Convention & Visitors Bureau (6800 Mercy Rd., Suite 202, Omaha 68106, tel. 402/444–4660).

Omaha: Johnny Rosenblatt Stadium

The city of Omaha has taken one of those aging Triple A behemoths and given it a classy $20-million facelift. Surprisingly, this 22,000-capacity 1948 stadium has a festive, modern, fan-friendly feel. An attractive royal-blue steel structure frames the concrete hilltop stadium entrance. Built in 1996, this huge press box was designed to accommodate the hundreds of reporters who flock to Omaha each June for ten days of the College World Series.

They have been playing professional baseball in Omaha since 1879. By 1885, Omaha had joined the Western League, where it remained, with a Depression-era sabbatical, until 1955. The city built the stadium in 1948 as Memorial Stadium and renamed it in 1964 to honor Omaha mayor Johnny Rosenblatt, who helped bring Triple A baseball to town. In 1969, Omaha began its long association with the Kansas City Royals, becoming a proving ground for such stars as George Brett. The team had been a member of the AAA American Association since 1955, but in 1998 made the switch to the Pacific Coast League as a part of Triple A consolidation.

In 1999, Omaha finally dropped the Royals name and had fans pick a name associated with the city, as so many other minor-league teams had done years before. The fans chose the Golden Spikes, to reflect the famous ceremony when the Central Pacific and the Union Pacific railroads were linked to complete the first transcontinental rail line. Omaha had been a key hub of the Union Pacific.

With a stadium nicknamed the Blatt and a tame lion mascot they call Casey, when you go to a game in Omaha it's Casey at the Blatt. There is a tree-shaded picnic area at the stadium entrance, where a Dixieland band plays most Fridays and weekends. Clowns and face painting are found in the picnic area before Sunday games.

Inside, the stadium is filled with brightly painted red, yellow, and blue seats. The huge royal-blue press box has a pointed roof bearing the stadium name in red. This structure sits atop the grandstand, shading virtually all of the seats between the dugouts. Some of the red wooden general admission seats under the press box are 1948 originals.

Henry Doorly Zoo sits in the trees just beyond the right-field wall. There is an exciting scoreboard high above the left-field wall complete with exploding fireworks and topped by a crown design to reflect the association with the Royals. The organ music is live, allowing for some risky spontaneity. In the early 1990s, the organist got tossed out of the game for playing the Mickey Mouse theme song after a controversial call.

As in many old stadiums, you have to go behind the stands for concessions, and the waits can be long. Happily, there is a wide variety of good food and drinks along with televisions to let you keep track of the game.

College World Series

Rosenblatt Stadium takes on the atmosphere of a college football weekend during the second week of June each year, when it plays home to the College World Series. Of the more than 275 NCAA colleges and universities playing Division I baseball, only eight survive to compete for the championship in Omaha.

They have been playing the College World Series here for five decades and will likely continue to hold it here for the foreseeable future. Complete with tailgate parties in the parking lot, this has become a major social event for the city of Omaha. Over the course of the week, more than 200,000 fans attend the games. There were 700 press credentials issued at a recent World Series here. Virtually all of Roseblatt's 22,000 seats are filled each night. Advance tickets customarily sell out, but a small number of same-day tickets are sold at the stadium. A package of 10 outfield bleacher seats costs $30.

The National Collegiate Athletic Association, tel. 317/917–6222 or www.ncaa.org (championship site), has details on the world series.

Where to Stay

Visiting Team Hotel: Ramada Hotel Central. There's a cluster of bargain freeway motels and fast-food restaurants at this I–80 72nd Street exit. This hotel is clean, with small oblong rooms that all have irons and hair dryers. It's 5 mi to the ballpark. *7007 Grover St., Omaha, NE 68106., tel. 402/397–7030 or 800/272–6232, fax 402/397–8449. 215 rooms. Facilities: Pizza Hut restaurant, indoor pool, health club. AE, D, DC, MC, V. $$*

Ak-Sar-Ben Super 8 Motel. The beds are king-size and there are oversize desks in this well-kept bargain motel. It is south of downtown, about 5 mi west of the ballpark and 1 mi from Omaha's large Furniture Mart. The neighborhood has several hotels and apartment buildings. *7111 Spring St., Omaha, NE 68106, tel. 402/390–0700 or 800/800–8000, fax 402/391–2063. 74 rooms. AE, D, DC, MC, V. $$*

Comfort Inn. Queen-size beds are standard in this new two-story facility, a half-mile north of the ballpark. The setting is near the freeway, in a growing commercial district, but it's convenient. There's a free Continental breakfast. *2920 S. 13th Ct., Omaha, NE 68108, tel. 402/324–8000 or 800/228–5150, fax 402/342–8000. 79 rooms. Facilities: indoor pool, game room. AE, D, MC, V. $$*

Where to Eat

Bohemian Cafe. Big neon signs announce this longtime city landmark, whose menu reflects the immigrant culture that built the city's stockyards. Both Czech and American food is served, but focus on the dumplings, apple strudel, kolaches, and veal dishes. There is a children's menu. It's about one mile to the ballpark. *1406 S. 13th St., Omaha, tel. 402/342–9838. AE, D, MC, V. $$*

Johnny's Cafe. This is a meat-lovers paradise, located just yards from the famed stockyards. It's dim and comfortable inside, despite the neighboring freeway and railroad tracks. Johnny's opened in 1922 as a saloon with a lunch counter, but the third generation of the Kawa family is now serving prime rib, fillet, and pork chops, in name-your-own-size cuts. There is a terrific beefsteak tomato salad with Maytag blue cheese. The leather banquettes, dark paneling, wrought-iron lamps, and paddle fans look elegant, but you'll find few coats and ties here. There is a children's menu. *4702 S. 27th St., U.S. 75–L St. exit, Omaha, tel. 402/731–4774. AE, D, DC, MC, V. $$*

Spaghetti Works. Located in the Old Market, this family restaurant is filled with antiques and serves inexpensive pasta and salads. Just outside the restaurant is a converted railroad car, **Sweet Car Named Desire,** that houses an ice-cream shop with frozen bananas and $2 peach and apricot cones. *502 S. 11th St., Omaha, tel. 402/422–0770. AE, D, MC, V. $*

Ted and Wally's. Phosphates, egg creams, and banana splits are dispensed in this high-ceilinged soda fountain in the Old Market section of town. You'll sit at booths or round parlor tables under the light of many colorful neon signs. There's a multitude of shakes, malts, freezes, sodas, and floats to choose from. *1115 Howard St., Omaha, tel. 402/341–5527. No credit cards. $*

Entertainments

Fun Plex. Half water park, half amusement park, this entertainment complex has well-supervised go-carts for small and large children. You'll also find a kiddie roller coaster, flying swings, a large water slide, a sand "beach" next to a kiddie mushroom shower, and a large wave pool. Parking is free, and there's a nice shaded picnic area. *7003 Q St., at I–80 Exit 449, Omaha, tel. 402/331–8436. Admission: $12.95 rides only, $10.95 water park only. $16.95 combination. Open mid-June–early Sept., Sun.–Thurs. 11–10, Fri.–Sat 11–11.*

Henry Doorly Zoo. An indoor tropical rain forest is a main attraction at this complex located next to the ballpark. Beneath the forest's 80-ft-high ceiling you'll find waterfalls, vampire bats, and pygmy hippos. Other exotic creatures, such as white tigers, snow leopards, white rhinos, and red pandas are also here. You can stay cool walking through the zoo's aquarium, which contains a coral reef tank, and visit the free-flight aviary and the animal nursery. A steam train travels throughout the 110-acre park. An IMAX theater requires an extra fee. *3701 S. 10th St., Omaha, tel. 402/733–8401. Admission: $7.50, $6 senior citizens, $4 ages 5–11. Open daily 9:30–5. MC, V.*

Sights to See

Durham Western Heritage Museum. This museum is located in the city's Union Station, and in it you'll find life-size interactive sculptures telling about early life in the restored Art Deco depot. There are classic train cars and a 90-ft model-train layout of 1930 Omaha. *801 S. 10th St., Omaha, tel. 402/444–5071. Admission: $3, $2.50 senior citizens, $2 ages 5–12. Open Tues.–Sat. 10–5, Sun. 1–4.*

Old Market. This five-block area once housed the city's food manufacturers and is now a National Historic District. The impressive turn-of-the-century warehouses, many with wood overhangs, now hold restaurants, shops, and apartments. Horse-drawn carriages for hire travel the brick-lined streets, and there are bikes for rent. Street musicians, jugglers, and outdoor cafés make the area lively at night. On summer Saturdays, there's a 45-vendor farmers' market. *Farnam, Jones, 10th, and 13th Sts., Omaha.*

WICHITA WRANGLERS

League: Texas League • **Major League Affiliation:** Kansas City Royals • **Class:** AA • **Stadium:** Lawrence-Dumont Stadium • **Opened:** 1934 • **Capacity:** 6,111 • **Dimensions:** LF: 344, CF: 401, RF: 312 • **Surface:** artificial infield • **Season:** Apr.–Labor Day

STADIUM LOCATION: 300 South Sycamore, Wichita, 67213.

TEAM WEB SITE: www.wichitawranglers.com

GETTING THERE: The stadium is located across the Arkansas River from downtown Wichita. Take I-135 to Kellogg Avenue west. Go north on Broadway, then west on Lewis, which turns into Maple, which runs into Sycamore.

PARKING: $1 priority parking close to the stadium. Additional free and on-street parking available.

TICKET INFORMATION: Box 1420, Wichita, KS 67201.

PRICE RANGE: Club $10; box $8; reserved $6; bench reserved $4; $2 discount ages 12 and under and senior citizens on club, box, and reserved seats; $1 discount for bench reserved.

GAME TIME: Mon.–Sat. 7:15 PM, Sun. 2:15 PM (Apr.) and 5:15 PM (May–Aug.), Tues. 6:15 PM (May–Aug.). Gates open 1 hr before game.

TIPS ON SEATING: The $6 reserved tickets are the best buy. You will want to sit on the third-base side so the setting sun will be at your back. For shade, buy reserved seats under the press building in sections 101–109. Beware of the bench seats, as they have no backs and there are 14 poles that may obstruct your view.

SEATING FOR PEOPLE WITH DISABILITIES: At the top of sections 102, 104, and 106 and in the Hard Ball Cafe. There is an elevator just inside the main gate.

STADIUM FOOD: Prices are low: $1.75 for a hot dog, $3 for a BBQ beef sandwich. There are decent deli sandwiches and subs. Frozen lemonade and slush puppies are sold at **Wilbur's Wateringhole** on the concourse. There are funnel cakes ($4). The **Hard Ball Cafe** is down the right-field line and seats 170. It is open to fans once the game starts. There is good charbroiled chicken and sausage there, but be aware that smoking is allowed in the restaurant.

SMOKING POLICY: Smoking prohibited in the seating area. Smoking allowed on the concourse and in the Hard Ball Cafe. Section 102 behind home plate and under the press box is a no-smoking, no-alcohol section.

VISITING TEAM HOTEL: The Broadview (400 W. Douglas Ave., Wichita, 67201, tel. 316/262–5000 or 800/362–2929).

TOURISM INFORMATION: Wichita Convention & Visitors Bureau (100 S. Main, Suite 100, Wichita, KS 67202, tel. 316/265–2800 or 800/288–9424).

Witchita: Lawrence-Dumont Stadium

Raymond (Hap) Dumont was one of those great baseball entrepreneurs we could use more of today. A Wichita sporting goods salesman, Dumont founded the National Baseball Congress (NBC) in 1931 to boost equipment sales.

For three years, he ran Kansas state baseball tournaments at Island Park. When the ballpark was destroyed by fire in 1933, Dumont asked the city to build a new stadium. The city fathers turned him down, arguing a two-week state tournament didn't justify a new ballpark. The persistent, inventive Dumont responded with a proposal for a national tournament to follow the state event. In 1934, the city built a 3,500 seat ballpark across the Arkansas River (pronounced here R-Kansas) and named it Lawrence Stadium after one of Wichita's founders.

Dumont offered the legendary Satchel Paige $1,000 to bring his Bismarck, North Dakota, team to the inaugural NBC World Series. "I didn't even have $1,000 at the time," explained Dumont. But the gamble paid off. Crowds came, Paige's team won, and a national institution was launched. Paige's 60 strikeouts still stand as the tournament record.

To speed up tournament games, Dumont invented a 20-second pitch timer that works like a basketball shot clock. At the NBC World Series, a pitcher must throw within 20 seconds of getting the ball (as required by the rules of baseball) or a buzzer goes off. The umpire calls a ball or strike depending on whether the pitcher or batter caused the delay. The clock sits just above the outfield fence in right center field. Tournament games are played in an average of two hours and fifteen minutes.

Dumont was creative. He employed one of baseball's first female umpires and installed a compressed-air automatic plate duster. In one tournament, Dumont told batters they could run to either first or third base. That rule lasted only one game.

Dumont had the stadium expanded to 6,000 seats to accommodate the growing popularity of the tournament. He died in 1971, and the stadium was renamed Lawrence-Dumont Stadium in 1978. Since 1989, the city has spent more than $6 million to renovate the stadium. As a result, one of the oldest stadiums still in use in professional baseball has most of the conveniences of a modern ballpark. A large ice-sports complex adjoins the park.

Wichita has had minor-league teams off and on since 1905. The Rich family corporation purchased the Triple A Wichita Aeros in 1984 and moved them to Buffalo. A Texas Double A team came to town in 1987, and the Rich family bought it in 1989.

The one-story white-stucco offices built for the minor-league Wichita Wranglers and the NBC sit at the stadium entrance with ten skyboxes and press booths forming a second deck above the grandstand. Both the offices and the second deck are covered with a handsome maroon metal roof. The Hard Ball Cafe restaurant is beyond the grandstand on the first-base side. There is a pool for parties at the Hard Ball Cafe and an OK Corral play area for children just beyond the café. Wilber T. Wrangler, a large horse mascot in a baseball uniform, displays amazing spirit in spite of the wilting Kansas heat.

Beyond the long stem of the J-shaped grandstand on the third-base side is the Wichita Baseball Academy, two batting cages fans can use during the game ($1 for 15 pitches). Sadly, because of the large number of games played at the ballpark in the first two weeks of August for the NBC World Series, the infield is artificial turf. The flying saucer–like object beyond the batter's eye in center field is the downtown convention center across the Arkansas River.

The National Baseball Congress World Series, made up of 32 of the best college summer teams, including those from the prestigious Jayhawk and Alaska Leagues, is played in the first two weeks in August. The ultimate baseball-fan challenge comes at mid-tournament with the "Baseball Round the Clock!" marathon. Upward of 250 hearty fans sit through 17 games in 56 hours. *The NBC World Series, Box 1430, Wichita, KS 67201, tel. 316/267–3372.*

Where to Stay

Visiting Team Motel: The Broadview. A former 1922 railway hotel built in 1922, the Broadview retains much of its grandeur, with a massive lobby and spacious rooms. It is 800 yards from the ballpark, across a bridge over the Arkansas River. Airport transportation and a Continental breakfast are included in the price of the room. *400 W. Douglas Ave., Wichita, KS 67302, tel. 316/262–5000 or 800/362–2929, fax 316/262–6175. 262 rooms. Facilities: 2 restaurants, exercise room, outdoor pool. AE, D, DC, MC, V. $$*

Hyatt Regency. This fancy new high-rise hotel overlooks the Arkansas River and the ballpark. It is connected to the city's performing-arts and convention center. Most rooms have terrific city views. The decor is modern, with large bathrooms. *400 W. Waterman, Wichita 67202, tel. 316/293–1234 or 800/223–1234, fax 316/293–*

1200. 298 rooms. Facilities: 2 restaurants, health club, indoor swimming pool. AE, D, DC, MC, V. $$

Where to Eat

The Beacon. Breakfast is served all day at this cozy blue concrete restaurant next door to the Wichita Eagle newspaper. A multitude of egg dishes, plus homemade soups and pies, are the attractions here. The prices are low and the service is friendly. 909 E. Douglas, Wichita, tel. 316/263–3397. AE, D, MC, V. $

Stroud's Restaurant. This famous chicken restaurant began in Kansas City and is equally popular here. It is located on the outskirts of Wichita and resembles a country roadhouse, with old barn wood on the walls, calico curtains, and vinyl checked tablecloths. A piano player plays show tunes as happy eaters clear plates of crusty fried chicken. Catfish, strip steak, and pork chops also are on the menu. 3661 N. Hillside, Wichita, tel. 316/838–2454. AE, D, MC, V. $

Entertainments

Joyland. This sweet, family-run amusement park has 23 rides, including a dozen for small children. It is a bargain to visit, with a $2 entry fee and pay-as-you-go rides. A 1909 Wurlitzer band organ features a mechanical clown playing circus tunes with drums, cymbals, castinets, and a triangle. Other features include a Ferris wheel, a wooden roller coaster, a haunted house, a carousel, a parachute drop, and a flume ride. A large go-cart track carries an extra fee. Free parking. 2801 S. Hillside, Wichita, tel. 316/684–0179. Admission: $2. One-price wristbands $12.50. Open Apr.–May, Sat. 2–10, Sun. 2–9; June–Aug., Wed.–Fri. 6 PM–10 PM, Sat. 2–10, Sun. 2–9; Sept.–mid-Oct., Sat. 2–10, Sun. 2–9.

Sedgwick County Zoo. All the geographic bases are covered in this small, excellent zoo, from prairie to Asian steppes, African veld, pampas, and Australian outback. A train covers the terrain, but it's a comfortable walk. There are many daily animal demonstrations and "keeper chats," as well as a children's farm, a small rain forest, and rare chimps. 5555 Zoo Blvd., Wichita, tel. 316/942–2212. Admission: $6 adults, $5 senior citizens, $3 ages 5–11. Open June–Aug. 9–5; Sept.–May 10–5. D, MC, V.

Sights to See

Indian Center Museum. This impressive riverside museum celebrates Indian heritage through displays, collections, and demonstrations. The Osage Indians were removed from this area to the south, with Congress selling their lands to settlers for $1.25 an acre. The sculpture Keeper of the Plain, on the museum grounds at the confluence of the Big and Arkansas rivers, is a city landmark. 650 N. Seneca St., Wichita, tel. 316/337–9174. Admission: $2 adults, $1 ages 6–12. Open Mon.–Sat. 10–5, Sun. 1–5. MC, V.

Old Cowtown Museum. Restored buildings create a living history that focuses on Wichita as a cattle town in the years 1865 to 1880. There are replicas of a saloon, farm, general store, school, blacksmith shop, and carpenter shop, plus Wichita's first jail. A five-acre working farm gives kids a chance to see barn animals. 1871 Sim Park Dr., Wichita, tel. 316/264–0671. Admission: $6 adults, $3 ages 5–11. Open Mon.–Sat. 10–5, Sun. noon–5.

Old Town District. A spruced-up warehouse district with brick streets, vintage lights, and boardwalks, this area includes eclectic antique malls, restaurants, and specialty stores. There is free parking, and 19th-century trolleys connect you to the baseball park and downtown hotels. The district is six blocks east of Wichita's downtown. Mosley, Washington, 2nd Sts., Wichita. Trolley service, tel. 316/265–7221.

Unusual Shopping

Coleman Factory Outlet Store and Museum. Campers, outdoorsmen, and soccer parents will want to see the low prices on duffel bags, thermal blankets, folding chairs, cookstoves, canoes, lanterns, and outdoor goods of every description. There also are blenders, juicers, mixers, and of course Coleman coolers. A tiny museum shows artifacts from 50 years of outfitting expeditions. 235 N. St. Francis St., Wichita, tel. 316/264–0836. Open weekdays 9–6, Sat. 9–1.

More Kansas Baseball

McDonald Stadium. If you like your baseball simple and old-fashioned, make a stop at McDonald Stadium in El Dorado, Kansas, 30 minutes east of

Wichita on I–35. The El Dorado Broncos play summer collegiate baseball in the wooden-bat Jayhawk League in June and July. Jayhawk League alumni include Barry Bonds, Roger Clemens, Rafael Palmeiro, and Ozzie Smith.

The Broncos play in a Works Progress Administration (WPA) ballpark built in the 1930s. In 1972, the park was named for James W. "Mac" McDonald, a local teacher and strong supporter of youth baseball. The cozy, covered 750-seat concrete grandstand is showing its age, but it's a great place to spend a summer afternoon or night. A steady breeze blowing consistently to center field makes hot Kansas summers tolerable for fans and great fun for hitters. The county fairgrounds are on the first-base side of the ballpark, and a Little League complex is beyond the right-field fence. Look for the bull's-eye on the top of the metal city maintenance shed 417 ft from home plate beyond the left-field fence. The burgers and Polish sausage grilled under the grandstand are a good buy at $2 each.

Other teams in the Jayhawk League include the Elkhart Dusters, Hays Larks, Liberal Beejays, Nevada (MO) Griffons, and Topeka Capitols. Jayhawk League teams have been very successful in the National Baseball Congress World Series in Wichita. For information on the Jayhawk League, call 316/835–2589. *210 N. Griffith St., El Dorado. Web site www.eldoradobroncos.org.*

BIG SKY BASEBALL
HELENA, BUTTE

H itters like mountain baseball because the thinner air allows the ball to travel farther. We like it for the scenery, which makes even an ordinary game special. Helena and Butte both have breathtaking views. These are unusual rookie-league parks.

Helena has a cozy wooden grandstand, with Mount Helena beyond right center field and the Capitol dome and the spires of St. Helena Cathedral behind the outfield. This is rookie ball for the Milwaukee Brewers in the Pioneer League. The city has many remnants of its gold-mining past. Twenty miles north of Helena you can take an unforgettable flatboat canyon tour of the Missouri River at Gates of the Mountains Recreation Area.

South 55 mi from Helena off Interstate 15 is Butte, home of the Copper Kings rookie-league team and the Berkeley Pit, an immense open-pit copper mine. The baseball stadium, Alumni Coliseum, is rudimentary, but has a spectacular view of the Rocky Mountains. It's an impressive backdrop for this team, affiliated with the Anaheim Angels. The city of Butte is unlike any other in America, with its rough mining edges visible in the former bordellos and mines, and current gambling joints, all on display.

HELENA BREWERS

League: Pioneer League • **Major League Affiliation:** Milwaukee Brewers • **Class:** Rookie/Short Season • **Stadium:** Kindrick Field • **Opened:** 1943 • **Capacity:** 1,800 • **Dimensions:** LF: 328, CF: 390, RF: 315 • **Surface:** grass • **Season:** mid-June–Labor Day

STADIUM LOCATION: Warren and Memorial Sts., Helena, MT 59601.

TEAM WEB SITE: www.helenabrewers.com

GETTING THERE: From I-15, Cedar St. exit west. This turns into Main St. Left at Memorial St. just past city swimming pool and park.

PARKING: Free but limited; overflow parking available at adjacent city pool and park.

TICKET INFORMATION: Box 4606, Helena, MT 59604, tel. 406/449–7616, fax 406/449–6979.

PRICE RANGE: Box seats $6.50; dugout reserved $5.50; general admission $4.75 adults, $3.75 ages under 13 and senior citizens.

GAME TIME: Mon.–Sat. 7:05 PM, Sun. 5:05 PM; gates open 1 hr before games.

TIPS ON SEATING: Best view of mountains, Capitol dome, and St. Helena Cathedral is from top of general admission bleacher seats on first-base side. Setting sun shines in eyes of fans on third-base side.

SEATING FOR PEOPLE WITH DISABILITIES: Box seat area behind home plate accessible by ramps.

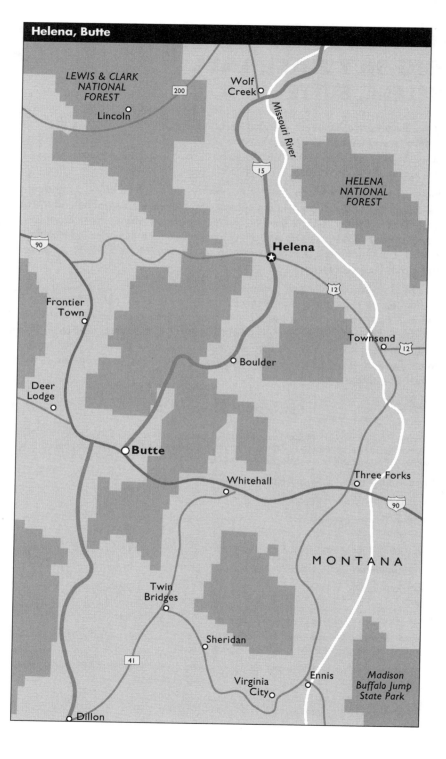

LEWIS & CLARK
NATIONAL
FOREST

Wolf
Creek

200

Lincoln

Missouri River

15

HELENA
NATIONAL
FOREST

90

Helena

12

Frontier
Town

Townsend

12

Deer
Lodge

Boulder

Butte

Three Forks

Whitehall

90

M O N T A N A

Twin
Bridges

Sheridan

41

Ennis

Virginia
City

Madison
Buffalo Jump
State Park

Dillon

STADIUM FOOD: The grill on the first-base side serves burgers, Polish dogs, BBQ roast beef, and broiled chicken sandwiches ($3.50). Iced tea is available, and small soft drinks are $1.50. A generous slice of better-than-average pizza costs $2.25. Special beers and wine coolers are available at the concession stand near the bullpen down the first-base line. Hot dogs are 50¢ on Tuesday, all-you-can-eat pasta is $4 on Wednesday, and Thursday sodas are 50¢.

SMOKING POLICY: Smoking prohibited in seating areas.

VISITING TEAM HOTEL: Super 8 (2201 11th Ave., Helena, MT 59601, tel. 406/443–2450 or 800/800–8000).

TOURISM INFORMATION: Helena Area Chamber of Commerce (225 Cruse Ave., Suite A, Helena, MT 59601, tel. 406/442–4120 or 800/743–5362).

Helena: Kindrick Field

It is hard to imagine a finer place to watch a ball game than atop the right-field bleachers at Kindrick Field in Helena, Montana. Mount Helena is just 2 mi beyond right center field. The Capitol dome and the spires of St. Helena Cathedral are visible just beyond the outfield walls, with the snow-capped Rocky Mountains in the far distance. Stand up between innings, turn around, and try to find the sleeping giant of the mountains. Hint: First look for the nose.

When the stadium was laid out in 1943, the assumption was that all games would be played during the day. Now, night games are the rule and right-handed batters and fans on the third-base side have a tough time seeing the ball because of the setting sun shining in their eyes.

The Montana State League began play in 1892, and Helena had professional teams in several leagues off and on until 1914. The city has been a member of the short-season, rookie-league Pioneer League since pro ball returned here in 1978. Kindrick Field is named for a local businessman who financed the construction of the field in the mid-1940s. The grandstand is wooden and the roof sags. But Helena, unlike Butte, isn't content to coast on its great vistas. In 1995, the city government fronted the money for a $500,000 renovation of the aging park. A new fence and scoreboard as well as almost 2,000 new blue box seats, modern bathrooms, and a clubhouse are key aspects of the upgrading effort. The entranceway was substantially upgraded, with a new ticket booth and a souvenir stand.

There's a lot of on-field fan activity in this park. There's a hot tub, Gilligan's Island, past the right-field line, that can hold up to 10 fans. Kids who sing "Take Me Out to the Ball Game" on the field are rewarded with ice-cream cones, and every season brings a popular Diamond Dig (where fans dig in the field for a diamond ring), the San Diego Chicken, and a beater car giveaway.

We were constantly amazed by the people we would run into on our trip through the minor leagues. The biggest surprise came in Helena. There he was—Calvin Griffith—the man who took major-league baseball from us. Bruce grew up a Washington Senators fan, and we have two seats from the old Griffith Stadium in our living room. Calvin Griffith, whose uncle Clark Griffith played for the 1892 Missoula club before his Hall of Fame career as manager-owner of the Senators, was the man who moved the Washington team to Minnesota. But there were no hard feelings that night. We got a few autographs and reminisced for an hour.

Where to Stay

Visiting Team Hotel: Super 8 Motel. This three-story hotel is in a historic district, 10 blocks from the State Capitol buildings. Its double rooms have two queen beds. Cribs are free. *2200 11th Ave., Helena 59601, tel. 406/443–2450 or 800/848–8888, fax 406/443–2450. 110 rooms. Facilities: free parking. AE, D, MC, V. $$*

Park Plaza. This attractive seven-floor hotel has a small modern lobby and contemporary rooms. It is next to the Gaslight Cinemas in the downtown walking mall. Children 12 and under stay free; the cost for children 13–18 is $8 each per night. *22 N. Last Chance Gulch, Helena 59601, tel. 406/443–2200, 800/332–2290 in Mont., fax 406/442–4030. Facilities: restaurant, free parking. AE, D, DC, MC, V. $$*

The Sanders Bed and Breakfast. The attractive 1875 mansion has its original Queen Anne antiques and furnishings. Each room has a private bath, and guests are given homemade cookies and lemonade at 4. It is three blocks from downtown, eight blocks from the Capitol, and directly down Ewing Street 15 blocks from the ballpark. Children are welcome. *328 N. Ewing St., Helena 59601, tel. 406/442–3309, fax 406/443–2361. 7 rooms. AE, D, MC, V. $$*

Where to Eat

Rialto Bar & Grill. This hole-in-the-wall restaurant is on the city's walking mall, amid several bookstores. It serves great burgers, fries, chicken wings, and barbecue beef sandwiches in Formica booths. Gambling machines are in the back. *52 N. Last Chance Gulch, Helena, tel. 406/442–1890. No credit cards. Closed Sun. $*

Stonehouse Restaurant. The decor is a bygone-mine theme in this upscale seafood and pasta restaurant. It's in Reeder's Alley, now a quaint shopping area but once the living quarters for gold-rush miners. Built as a private home in the 1890s, it now has several dining rooms. *120 Reeder's Alley, Helena, tel. 406/449–2552. AE, D, MC, V. Closed Sun. $$*

Yat Son. This well-loved family restaurant has been in business for a century. In updated quarters just yards away from its original site, it serves a wide variety of Cantonese and American food. You can get shrimp with snow peas or steaks, fried chicken, or burgers. There are several children-size entrées. *2 S. Last Chance Gulch, at Main St. and Broadway, Helena, tel. 406/442–5405. AE, D, MC, V. $*

Entertainments

Gates of the Mountains Recreation Area. Sunscreen is a must for an awe-inspiring boat tour of this spectacular canyon, formed by the Missouri River 20 mi north of Helena. You are likely to see bald eagles and mountain goats, pointed out by knowledgeable guides who also show you the sites of major forest fires. There is one stop for a

brief exploration of a canyon park. *Gates of the Mountains Landing, Helena National Forest, Exit 209 from I–15, tel. 406/458–5241. Admission: $10 adults, $8.50 senior citizens, $6.50 ages 4–17. Tours weekdays at 11, 1, and 3; Sat. at 10, noon, 2, and 4; Sun. and holidays, on the hr 9–5.*

Last Chance Gulch Tour. In 1864, four out-of-luck prospectors declared a gulch in Helena to be their "last chance." They struck gold and the gulch became Helena's Main Street, now largely a pretty walking mall. You can take an interesting one-hour tour through the city in a train of bumpy, open-sided cars. You can learn about the gold collection in the Norwest Banks building on Lawrence Street and see where actress Myrna Loy grew up. The car-train leaves from the side of the State Historical Museum, at 6th and Roberts streets. *Prospect Ave., Helena, tel. 406/442–1023. Fare: $5 adults, $4 senior citizens, $3.50 ages under 13. Departs daily at 9, 10, 11, 1, 2, 3, and 4; June–Sept., also at 6.*

State Historical Museum. The biggest hit for children is trying out the various saddles on three horse replicas in the entry. The museum's stuffed white buffalo is unusual. Several artifacts describe the accomplishments of the state's African-American cowboys and soldiers. *225 N. Roberts St., Helena, tel. 406/444–2694. Donations appreciated. Open weekdays 8–6, weekends 9–5.*

Sights to See

State Capitol. The dome of this neoclassical sandstone capitol is copper. The House of Representatives displays Charles M. Russell's largest painting, *Lewis and Clark Meeting the Flathead Indians at Ross' Hole*, now valued for insurance purposes at $16 million. Look for Russell's trademark buffalo-head signature and note that Russell put the Native Americans, not Lewis and Clark, at the center of his painting. Make sure you visit the statue of Jeannette Rankin behind the grand staircase in the Capitol Rotunda. Rankin, the first woman elected to the Congress of the United States, was one of our country's leaders in the fight for women's right to vote. *6th and Montana Sts., Helena, tel. 406/444–4789. Open daily 8–5; 45-min tours hourly, Mon.–Sat. 9–4, Sun. 9–3.*

BUTTE COPPER KINGS

League: Pioneer League • **Affiliation:** Anaheim Angels • **Class:** Rookie/Short Season • **Stadium:** Alumni Coliseum • **Opened:** 1962 • **Capacity:** 1,750 • **Dimensions:** LF: 345, CF: 475, 360 • **Surface:** grass • **Season:** mid-June–Labor Day

STADIUM LOCATION: Montana Tech Campus, West Park St., Butte, MT.

TEAM WEB SITE: www.copperkings.com

GETTING THERE: From I-90, Montana St. exit north to Park St. West to stadium on Montana Tech campus.

PARKING: Free parking available next to stadium; overflow parking available on campus.

TICKET INFORMATION: Box 186, Butte, MT 59703, tel. 406/723–8206, fax 406/723–3376.

PRICE RANGE: Reserved $5.50; general admission $4.50 adult, $4 children, senior citizens, and military personnel; under 6 free.

GAME TIME: Mon.–Sat. 7 PM, Sun. 6 PM; gates open 1 hr before game.

TIPS ON SEATING: All seats have extraordinary view of Rocky Mountain highlands. Seats in top right corner of general admission grandstand on first-base side have best view of mountains and less sun in your eyes.

SEATING FOR PEOPLE WITH DISABILITIES: Along first- or third-base foul line.

STADIUM FOOD: The offerings are inexpensive and better than you'd expect. A grill on the first-base side serves hamburgers, bratwurst, Polish sausage, and chicken sandwiches. There is also corn-on-the-cob, and the team's own brand of beer, Copper Kings Ale. A picnic pavilion is on the third-base side.

SMOKING POLICY: No-smoking section in general admission area above first-base dugout.

VISITING TEAM HOTEL: War Bonnet Inn (2100 Cornell Ave., Butte, MT 59701, tel. 406/494–7800 or 800/443–1806).

TOURISM INFORMATION: Butte-Silver Bow Chamber of Commerce (2950 Harrison Ave., Butte, MT 59701, tel. 406/494–5595 or 800/735–6814).

Butte:
Alumni Coliseum

For raw physical beauty, it is hard to imagine a finer setting for baseball than Alumni Coliseum in Butte, Montana. From the covered hilltop grandstand, you have an almost unobstructed scenic view of the Rocky Mountains over the center- and right-field fences.

The Berkeley Pit, not far from the stadium, was once the largest truck-operated open-pit copper mine in the United States. As a result, the Butte team is called the Copper Kings.

This stadium is rudimentary. The covered, cinderblock grandstand has fixed reserved seats and general admission seats along the foul lines.

Picnic tables, a speedpitch, and a playground also are at the field. The press box is a small wooden cage in the back row of the grandstand. Because the Copper Kings share this field with the Montana Tech University football team, there are 3,000 seats out beyond left field in the football bleachers.

The play is uneven here in the Pioneer League. In Idaho Falls, we saw three runners score on a Copper King wild pitch. In Butte, we saw a fabulous running catch by Butte's center fielder against the fence in left center.

We had fun in this mountain park. The weather on a July night was almost perfect, and it didn't grow dark until the very last innings of the game. (Bring a jacket because of the westerly winds and high elevation.) The Copper Kings have a full array of contests and give-aways. We nearly won a late-model used car in one on-field contest.

Where to Stay

The Capri Motel. This inexpensive '50s-era motel is next door to the now abandoned Orphan Girl mine in downtown Butte. The rooms have sliding glass doors that overlook the central parking lot. Some of the rooms have a second bedroom with twin beds in an alcove. Free morning doughnuts and coffee are provided. *220 N. Wyoming St., Butte 59701, tel. 406/723–4391 or 800/342–2774, fax 406/723–4391. 64 rooms. Facilities: coin laundry. AE, D, MC, V. $*

Comfort Inn of Butte. This three-story motel is near Butte Plaza Mall, behind a restaurant. A free Continental breakfast is served. *2777 Harrison Ave., at Exit 127 off I–90, Butte 59701, tel. 406/494–8850 or 800/424–6423, fax 406/494–2801. 150 rooms. Facilities: restaurant, hot tub, sauna, coin laundry, casino. AE, D, DC, MC, V. $$*

Finlen Hotel and Motor Inn. Built in 1923, this venerable but inexpensive downtown hotel is a monument to the faded glory of the Copper Kings. Once a grand hotel, it is now a clean and unusual alternative to interstate lodging. The marble-floored lobby is a step backward in time. The rooms have high ceilings and vintage 1960s furnishings. *100 E. Broadway, Butte 59701, tel. 406/723–4121 or 800/729–5461. 50 rooms. AE, D, MC, V. $*

Where to Eat

M & M Cafe. This one-of-a-kind establishment is an 1890s saloon, eatery, and gambling house. There's a bar on one side, a food counter on the other, and Texas hold-em poker games in the back room. A remnant of the mining era, it's a gritty place, with keno machines in plain view of the kids. Jack Kerouac and other devotees of the open road ate here. Its oyster stew is a bargain. *9 N. Main St., Butte, tel. 406/723–7612. No credit cards. $*

Matts's Place. This family-run soda fountain, opened in 1931 and now the oldest drive-in in Montana, has homemade ice cream, terrific burgers and fries, and tons of atmosphere. The

Cokes are served in old-fashioned bottles, at the counter or with table service. You can get a hamburger with egg, a burger spread with nut paste, or a glass of cold buttermilk. It is 1½ mi north of the ballpark. *2339 Placer St., Butte, tel. 406/782–8049. No credit cards. Closed Sun.–Mon. $*

Peking Noodle Parlor. In the Tam family since 1916, this downtown restaurant is famous as a noodle parlor for the immigrant copper workers. The high-backed booths are private, and the atmosphere is old Chinatown. Noodle dishes of every description are served, along with western standbys like steak sandwiches. The prices are reduced for children's portions. *117 Main St., Butte, tel. 406/782–2217. MC, V. Closed Tues. $*

Entertainments

Mining Camp and Museum. This re-creation of an 1899 mining camp includes a Chinese laundry, an herb store, an assay office, a sauerkraut factory, a print shop, a bank, and a dozen other shops. Built around an inactive silver and zinc mine, the original Orphan Girl, this cobblestone history museum allows kids to see what mining life was like. The buildings are spread campus-style, allowing you to stroll throughout and stop at whatever catches your eye. *W. Park and Granite Sts., Butte, tel. 406/723–7211. Admission: donations ages 12 and up. Open mid-June–Labor Day, daily 9–9; Labor Day–late Nov. and Apr.–mid-June, Tues.–Sun. 10–5.*

Old No. 1 Streetcar Ride. You can see the Berkeley Open Pit Mine, immigrants' living quarters, the bordellos, and the Copper King Mansion in this 90-minute tour. Make sure you look at three enormous copper doors to the now closed Central High School. There are sights in this Old West town that are never seen in eastern cities and that are remade each decade. The 1880s town hospital is still standing and is now an apartment building. The gift shop at the Berkeley Pit has many intriguing kid's items fashioned from copper. *2950 Harrison Ave., Butte, tel. 406/494–5595 or 800/735–6814. Admission: $6 adults, $4 ages 4–12. Tours daily at 10:30, 1:30, 3:30, and 7.*

Sights to See

Our Lady of the Rockies. This 90-ft concrete statue of the Virgin Mary was put in place on the edge of the Continental Divide in 1985 by the Nevada Air National Guard, the Montana National Guard, and the U.S. Army Reserve from Butte. It's intended as a tribute to motherhood. Two-hour bus tours depart twice daily from the Butte Plaza Mall. *3100 Harrison Ave., Butte, tel. 406/782–1221 or 800/800–5239. Admission: $10 adults, $9 senior citizens, $5 ages 5–12. Tours June–Oct. at 10 and 2. D, MC, V.*

WILD WEST BASEBALL
IDAHO FALLS, BOISE

26

I daho Falls, along the Snake River, has a colorful history of good rookie-league ball. Its modest concrete stadium offers lots of fan contests and a fancy scoreboard salvaged from another ballpark. The city boasts a lovely greenbelt adjoining its natural and man-made falls. Another popular park complex has a zoo, a kiddie land, a playground, and an indoor ice rink.

Five hours west on I–84 is Boise, the city of trees, with its Memorial Stadium on the Western Idaho Fairgrounds. There's a county fair feeling here, and the fans are extremely passionate. You may need to call ahead for tickets.

The city has a lovely zoo, a lively downtown, and is home to America's only candy bar shaped like a potato, the Idaho Spud. Its well-preserved state penitentiary, last used in 1973, is worth a visit.

IDAHO FALLS PADRES

League: Pioneer League • **Major League Affiliation**: San Diego Padres • **Class**: Rookie/Short Season • **Stadium**: McDermott Field • **Opened**: 1940/76 • **Capacity**: 2,800 • **Dimensions**: LF: 350, CF: 400, RF: 350 • **Surface**: grass • **Season**: mid-June–Labor Day

STADIUM LOCATION: 568 W. Elva, Idaho Falls, ID 83402.

TEAM WEB SITE: www.ifbraves.com

GETTING THERE: From I–15, take Broadway exit. East across Snake River. Immediate left onto Memorial Dr., right on Mound Ave. to stadium.

PARKING: Limited free parking at stadium. This is a small park; try to park as far from entrance as possible to avoid foul balls.

TICKET INFORMATION: Box 2183, Idaho Falls, ID 83403, tel. 208/522–8363, fax 208/522–9858.

PRICE RANGE: Reserved $5.75; general admission $4 adults, $3 ages under 13 and senior citizens.

GAME TIME: Mon.–Sat. 7:15 PM, Sun. 5 PM.

TIPS ON SEATING: General admission seats directly behind home plate are close to action and in a no-smoking section. Two fans are selected to sit in "Horizon Air 1ST CLASS" seats for each game.

SEATING FOR PEOPLE WITH DISABILITIES: Row behind reserved seats on first-base side of home accessible by ramp.

STADIUM FOOD: Grilled cheeseburgers and hot dogs are available from a stand on the third-base side. A picnic area is down the left-field line. Microbrewed regional ales are sold from a stand on the first-base side. The popcorn and nachos with salsa, sold on the first-base side, are good.

SMOKING POLICY: Section directly behind home plate is no-smoking.

VISITING TEAM HOTEL: **Days Inn Stardust** (700 Lindsay Blvd., Idaho Falls, ID 83402, tel. 208/522–2910 or 800/325–2525).

TOURISM INFORMATION: **Greater Idaho Falls Chamber of Commerce** (505 Lindsay Blvd. Idaho Falls, ID 83405, tel. 208/523–1010).

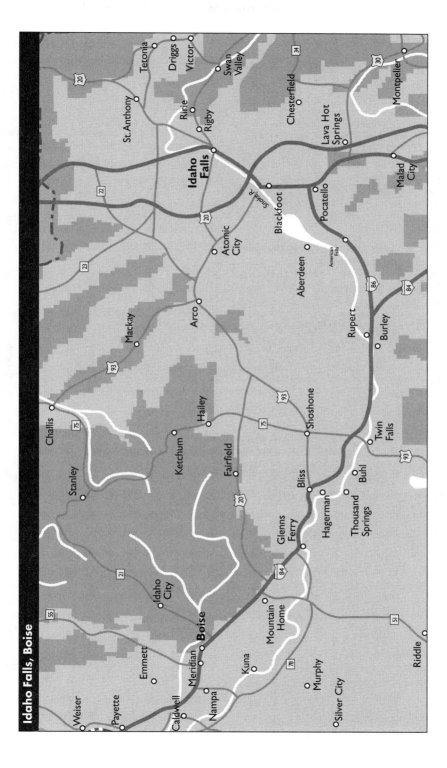

Idaho Falls: McDermott Field

McDermott Field in Idaho Falls, Idaho, is just what Central Casting would order for a movie on rookie-league baseball. The surroundings don't match the physical beauty of Idaho Falls' Pioneer League rivals, but it is a simple, cozy, and unpretentious place. McDermott is a compact neighborhood park where everyone is close to the action and foul balls are constantly flying into the adjacent children's park and stadium parking lot.

They have been playing Pioneer League baseball games in Idaho Falls since 1940, longer than anywhere else. The veteran Idaho Falls baseball fans we sat with bemoaned the loss of the 5,000-seat wooden Highland Park that was on this site until burned down by arsonists in the mid-1970s. Highland Park, built in 1940 by the Works Progress Administration, they told us, was more spacious, with more comfortable seats and a roof. Future New York Yankees player and coach Billy Martin began his professional career at Highland Park in 1946, playing for the Idaho Falls Russets, a team named for Idaho's famous potato.

The insurance money from the fire allowed the city to build a modest concrete stadium without a roof and with seat backs only for the reserved seats. The rebuilt stadium was named for E. F. McDermott, general manager of the *Post Register* of Idaho Falls and known as Mr. Baseball of the Pioneer League. The billboards are only one row high on the outfield wall. Billboards along the dark-green walls behind the seating areas add to the stadium's cozy feel. The surprise here is the large scoreboard beyond the left-field fence, which has up-to-date player stats like those in the more advanced minor leagues. Idaho Falls bought it from a Salt Lake City AAA Pacific Coast League team that was about to scrap it when it tore down an old stadium. Other than the fancy scoreboard, there are few frills here.

Not having much money doesn't stop the Idaho Falls team from providing the 1,000 or so fans who come each night with a good time. There are plenty of contests and an imaginative game

of baseball bingo about once a week. Fans who buy programs get contest coupons.

Remember, this is rookie-league ball. Even some future stars are struggling at this critical early time in their careers. The night we visited, the home team scored three runs on a bases-loaded wild pitch. Even the umpire had to share a laugh with the first-base coach on this one.

Where to Stay

Visiting Team Hotel: Days Inn Stardust. Within sight of the Snake River, this sprawling downtown motor lodge has a free Continental breakfast and spacious rooms. *700 Lindsay Blvd., Idaho Falls, ID 83402, tel. 208/522–2910 or 800/325–2525, fax 208/529–8361. 248 rooms. Facilities: restaurant, outdoor pool, exercise room. AE, D, DC, MC, V. $$*

Best Western Driftwood. Some of the rooms in this two-story, remodeled hotel have views of the falls. The 2.7 mi greenbelt around the falls and the falls themselves are just steps away. *575 River Pkwy., Idaho Falls 83402, tel. 208/523–2242 or 800/528–1234, fax 208/523–0316. 74 rooms. Facilities: outdoor pool, coin laundry. AE, D, DC, MC, V. $$*

Cavanaugh's Hotel. If you want to see the Snake River Falls, ask for a room in the eight-story section. The low-rise section along the riverfront does not have a falls view, but is along the outdoor pool. The rooms are standard size and have a contemporary decor. *475 River Pkwy., Idaho Falls 83402, tel. 208/523–8000 or 800/325–4000, fax 208/529–9610. 141 rooms. Facilities: outdoor pool, hot tub, sauna. AE, D, DC, MC, V. $$*

Where to Eat

Le Baron's Lounge. This 1950s-style coffee shop is popular with many locals because of its low prices. You can get homemade biscuits and a full breakfast for under $2. There's a children's menu for breakfast. Roasted chicken, breaded veal, and liver and onions are dinner favorites. *1700 Yellowstone Ave., Idaho Falls, tel. 208/523–1564. MC, V. $*

Bubba's Bar B Que. This extremely casual restaurant is in a former Bonanza Steakhouse building with pig ornaments throughout. It's known for its ribs, salad bar, and buttermilk pie. There's an all-you-can-eat rib special every Monday night for $9.95. The children's menu includes turkey, kid ribs, pork, and chicken. The restaurant is 10 mi south of the ballpark. *888 E. 17th St., Idaho Falls, tel. 208/523–2822. D, MC, V. $*

Jake's Steak and Fish House. This bright, contemporary fish restaurant has a good salad bar and a varied children's menu. Locally caught trout is a specialty. Both booths and tables are available in the hunter-green and dark-wood dining room. *851 Lindsay Blvd., Idaho Falls, tel. 208/524–5240. AE, D, MC, V. $$*

Entertainments

Tautphaus Park Zoo. This well-maintained park complex has a small zoo, an ice rink, the Funland amusement park, a playground, and several tennis courts. You can rent a stroller for $2.50. Funland has miniature golf, a merry-go-round, a train, a Ferris wheel, little airplane rides, and an octopus ride. The zoo and park are ¾ mi off 17th Street, which is a main road. *South Blvd. and Rogers St., Idaho Falls, tel. 208/529–1470 or 208/525–9814 (Funland). Zoo admission: $3 adults, $1.75 senior citizens, $1.50 ages 13–17, 75¢ ages 4–12. Funland coupon books: 15 tickets for $8; 25 tickets for $14; most rides cost 2–5 tickets. Zoo open daily 9–7:30; Funland open Mon.–Sat. noon–7:30, Sun. 12:30–7:30.*

Sights to See

Idaho Falls. A 2½-mi greenbelt adjoins the falls, half of which are natural and half man-made. In a landscaped picnic area along the Snake River, you can watch ducks, joggers, and walkers. This is a cool retreat on a summer afternoon. *River Pkwy., ½ mi east of I–15, Broadway exit, Idaho Falls.*

BOISE HAWKS

League: Northwest League • **Major League Affiliation**: Anaheim Angels • **Class**: Short Season A • **Stadium**: Memorial Stadium • **Opened**: 1989 • **Capacity**: 4,600 • **Dimensions**: LF: 335, CF: 400, RF: 335 • **Surface**: grass • **Season**: mid-June–Labor Day

STADIUM LOCATION: Western Idaho Fairgrounds, 5600 Glenwood St., Boise, ID 83714.

TEAM WEB SITE: www.diamondsportsworld.com/hawks

GETTING THERE: The stadium is on the Western Idaho Fairgrounds. Take Route 84 to Cole Road and go north 3 mi to the fairgrounds.

PARKING: Plenty of free parking at the south end of stadium.

TICKET INFORMATION: 5600 Glenwood St., Boise, ID 83714, tel. 208/322–5000, fax 208/322–7432.

PRICE RANGE: Box seats $8.25; Hawk's Nest Stadium Club restaurant seating, $8.25; reserved seats $6.25; reserved bench $5.25; reserved bleacher $4.25. Children 5 and under free in the reserved bleachers.

GAME TIME: Mon.–Sat. 7:05 PM, Sun. 6:05 PM; gates open 1 hr before game.

TIPS ON SEATING: The setting sun is in your eyes on the first-base side, so the best seats are behind home plate and on the third-base side. As games often sell out, call in advance for the reserved seats on the third-base side. Or, call ahead and reserve seating in the Hawk's Nest restaurant on the third-base side. There's a two-person minimum, and reservations must be made in advance.

SEATING FOR PEOPLE WITH DISABILITIES: Between the grandstands on both sides of home plate and beyond the first-base grandstand.

STADIUM FOOD: As you might expect, there are excellent baked potatoes here. The **Specialty Food Court** has a good variety of food, including grilled Italian sausages and thick, delicious chicken sandwiches, and the concession stands serve Dip n' Dots ice cream. A covered picnic area sits behind the first-base grandstand.

SMOKING POLICY: Smoking is prohibited in the grandstands. There are designated smoking areas behind the concourse.

VISITING TEAM HOTEL: **Holiday Inn** (3300 Vista Ave., Boise, ID 83705, tel. 208/344–8365 or 800/ 465–4329).

TOURISM INFORMATION: **Boise Convention & Visitors Bureau** (168 North 9th St., Suite 200, Boise, ID 83702, tel. 208/344–7777 or 800/635–5240).

Boise:
Memorial Stadium

Memorial Stadium sits on the Western Idaho Fairgrounds northwest of the State Capitol. When the French-Canadian trappers emerged from the semiarid plain and came across a forest along a river, they named the area Boisé, meaning wooded. There's a stock of trees past the outfield wall in right field that continues along the Boise River. Unfortunately, a recreational vehicle park between the stadium and the river mars the view of the Boise Foothills beyond the trees.

The Boise Hawks played in the Northwest League, a short-season Class A league, for a good part of the 1970s and consecutively since 1985. The Hawks dominated the league in the 1990s. William Pereira, Jr.'s Diamond Sports bought the controlling interest in the team in 1988 and built the $2.2 million Memorial Stadium in 1989, making this one of the few privately owned stadiums in professional sports.

Memorial Stadium is a made-for-the-movies fairgrounds ballpark—somewhat scruffy, with a distinct county fair feel. The park was built just before the 1990s rush of modern minor-league stadiums and Camden Yards clones: the grandstands don't connect and fans have to work their way through a maze of tunnels to the hodgepodge of concession stands and souvenir booths. But the effort is well worth it, as Memorial Stadium offers one of the widest ranges of food anywhere in baseball. It's Idaho—try a baked potato for dinner (sold, inexplicably, at the ice-cream stand on the third-base side).

The grandstand behind home plate is uncovered, with a modest press box on top. The first- and third-base grandstands are close to the field and protected from foul balls by netting. The

symmetrical outfield wall is decorated with the usual minor-league advertising and a special $100,000 Home Run Challenge. If a Boise Hawk hits a ball through a small hole in the Idaho Lottery ad in left center field, the player and a fan split the $100,000.

Call ahead to get the best seats, as first-rate baseball and an extraordinary array of promotions, for a short-season league team, draw huge crowds. Here we saw something we had never seen before—a throw out the first axe on Lumberjack Night. A colorful yellow, red, white, and blue Humphrey the Hawk serves as mascot.

Boise baseball has a proud tradition dating back to the 1880s. Hall of Fame pitcher Walter Johnson pitched here for the nearby town of Weiser in the semipro Idaho State League in 1906 and 1907. He pitched 77 consecutive scoreless innings in 1907 and was signed by the Washington Senators.

Where to Stay

Visiting Team Hotel: Holiday Inn. This two-story airport hotel is built around an indoor fun center with a pool, saunas, and hot tubs. The rooms are large and modern. Kids stay and eat free and there's a free shuttle to the airport. *3300 Vista Ave., Boise 83705, tel. 208/344– 8365 or 800/465–4329, fax 208/344–8156. 265 rooms. Facilities: restaurant, indoor and outdoor pools, hot tubs, saunas, fitness center, airport shuttle. AE, D, DC, MC, V. $$*

Super 8 Lodge. This budget hotel is near the airport and has free shuttle service. All beds are queen-size, and there are free muffins and coffee in the morning. *2773 Elder St., at Vista Ave., tel. 208/344–8871 or 800/800–8000, fax 208/ 344–8871. 110 rooms. Facilities: indoor pool. AE, D, DC, MC, V. $*

Where to Eat

Noodles. A variety of good pasta dishes and brisk service make this downtown restaurant a winner with kids and adults alike. Children's and senior citizens' menus have reduced prices and portions. Parking is discounted with Noodles' stamp. *800 W. Idaho St., Boise, tel. 208/342–9300. AE, MC, V. No breakfast. $$*

Big Bun Drive-In. This vintage, family-owned hamburger restaurant gives a glimpse into our pre-McDonald's past. There are more than 40 different sandwiches, including kiddie budget burgers for 65¢ and hot dogs for 69¢. Fried fish dinners and a variety of ice-cream shakes, spins, floats, and sundaes abound. *5816 Overland, Boise, tel. 208/375–5361. $*

The Rockin Taco. Enjoy corn or flour tortillas filled with meats, cheese, and seafood at this informal taco and wraps restaurant in a scenic, older section of town. Outside garden seating is available, as are indoor tables. Buckets of clams are served as appetizers, and there are huge taco salads. *1512 N. 13th St., Boise, tel. 208/331–1700. MC, V. $*

Entertainments

Discovery Center of Idaho. This colorful science museum has more than 200 exhibits, many of them hands-on. There are experiments with electricity, water, hearing, sight, and smell. Kids particularly like the bubble machines. *111 Myrtle St., Boise, tel. 208/343–9895. Admission: $4, $3 senior citizens and ages 3–18. Open Tues.–Fri. 9–5, Sat. 10–5, Sun. noon–5.*

World Center for Birds of Prey. Dozens of live falcons, hawks, and eagles, which you can observe flying and in captivity, are found here. A large staff of bird experts guides you through displays on ecology, bird behavior, and conservation. *5666 W. Flying Hawk Ln., Boise, tel. 208/362–8687. Admission: $4, $3 senior citizens and ages 4–16. Open Mar.–Oct., daily 9–5; Nov.–Feb., daily 10–4.*

Zoo Boise. This small, well-designed zoo has many standard animal attractions—zebras, lions, bears—but also has native creatures such as bighorn sheep, antelope, and several varieties of deer. The prairie dog exhibit is particularly extensive and interesting. It's a good zoo for small children, as animals are close to you and there are playgrounds and lots of shade. *Julia Davis Park, Capitol Blvd. at Battery St., Boise, tel. 208/384–4260. Admission: $4, $2 senior citizens, $1.75 ages 1–4. Thurs. admission is discounted 75¢–$2. Open daily 10–5.*

Sights to See

Old Idaho Penitentiary. There are walking tours through this prison complex, used from 1870 to 1973, on the National Register of Historic Places. Prisoners quarried the stone for the buildings and tended the extensive rose gardens. Inmate baseball teams first formed in the 1880s. The prison's main team was called the Outlaws from the 1930s until the pen closed. The games were played in the field beyond the south wall—even convicted murderers were allowed to join in. A license-plate factory, dairy barn, and a tattoo exhibit are also on the grounds. *2445 Old Penitentiary Rd., Boise, tel. 208/368–6080. Admission: $4, $3 senior citizens and ages 6–12. Open daily 10–5.*

State Capitol. Idaho's neo-classic State Capitol building was modeled after the United States Capitol. The central section and dome were completed in 1912. A bronze-plated eagle 4 ft high sits atop the dome. Native sandstone, hauled by Idaho Penitentiary convicts from a quarry in nearby Table Rock, is a basic material. The interior has gorgeous marble, while the pillars are a trick, dyed to look like marble. On the first floor, you'll find an ancient symbolic sundial and a grand golden equestrian statue of George Washington carved from a yellow pine. This is the nation's only capitol building heated by a geothermal well. *6th, 8th, Jefferson, and W. State Sts., Boise, tel. 208/334–2844. Admission: Free. Open daily 8–4.*

EVERGREEN BASEBALL
SEATTLE, TACOMA

27

Seattle is one of America's most exciting cities, with innovative architecture, coffeehouses on every corner, a working harbor, and 9-acre city market. It's been a long wait for Seattle's ballplayers to run on real grass, but the city has now built them a glorious new ballpark, Safeco Field. It's everything a covered stadium should be—open, airy, yet not cavernous. And it has adopted one of the best features of minor-league parks, a wide-open concourse that allows fans to walk through the stadium and collect concessions while still watching the game.

Thirty miles south of Seattle, the Tacoma Rainiers play Class AAA Pacific Coast League baseball in Cheney Stadium, a large, partly covered structure. This lumber town is dotted with several public-fishing piers, a rarity in America these days, and has a fine park that includes a zoo and aquarium. The restored Union Station complex, which houses a state historical museum, is brightened by the fabulous glass creations of artist Dale Chihuly, who lives in Tacoma.

SEATTLE MARINERS

League: American League • **Class:** Major League • **Stadium:** Safeco Field • **Opened:** 1999 • **Capacity:** 45,600 • **Dimensions:** LF: 331, CF: 405, RF: 326 • **Surface:** grass • **Season:** Apr.–early Oct.

STADIUM LOCATION: First Avenue South & Atlantic St., Seattle, WA 98134.

TEAM WEB SITE: www.mariners.org

GETTING THERE: Safeco Field is just south of historic downtown. From I–5 going south, take Union Street or James Street exit to 2nd Avenue, which deadends at a large surface parking lot. From I–5 going north, take exit 163 to Spokane Street and turn right at 4th Avenue South to reach the Kingdome and Union Station parking lots. From the west, follow I–90 to 4th Avenue South. Seattle has outstanding, inexpensive public transport. For bus routes and park & ride lots, tel. 206/553–3000.

PARKING: Parking is available at many pay lots around the field. For a brochure listing sites and rates, tel. 206/346–4005.

TICKET INFORMATION: Box 4100, Seattle, WA 98104, tel. 206/346–4000, fax 206/346–4050.

PRICE RANGE: Terrace club $33, lower box $28, field $25, view box and lower outfield reserved $16, view reserved $13, left-field bleachers $7, center-field bleachers $5.

GAME TIME: Mon.–Sat. 7:05 PM, Sun. 1:35 PM; gates open 90 min. before game. Center-field (NE) gate opens 3 hours before game with access to outfield seating.

TIPS ON SEATING: Just be happy to get a seat here. The lower outfield reserved seats are a good buy at $16. Some $5 tickets are available day of game, but they sell out fast. The home team dugout is on the first-base side. There is no-alcohol family seating in sections 103 and 342. There's an inventive children's playground in the center field concourse with benches for waiting parents.

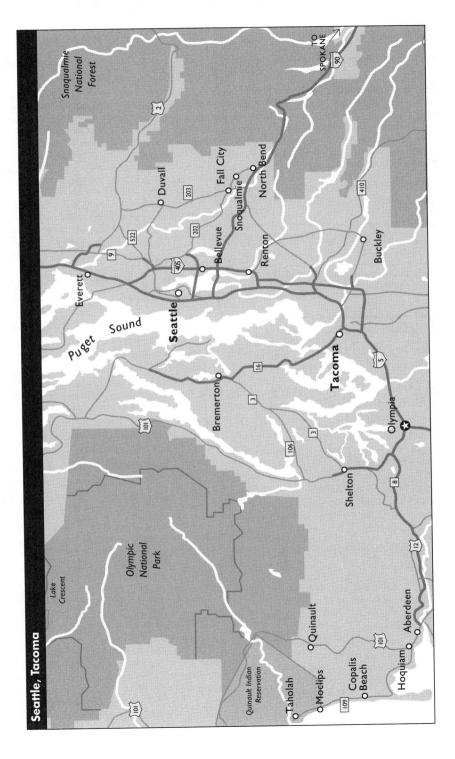

Seattle, Tacoma

SEATING FOR PEOPLE WITH DISABILITIES: Seating is located in all price levels. There are elevators with access to all levels at sections 146 (LF gate), 129 (home plate gate), and 114 (RF gate).

STADIUM FOOD: We applaud the park's effort to include regional and ethnic foods, such as oysters on the half shell, Penn Cove mussels, and Asian specialties, including a sushi bar. Among the features are **Ivar's,** a famed Seattle waterfront restaurant that has set up a raw bar here; **Porter's Holy Smokes** barbecue stand, which has long waits for terrific brisket sandwiches and ribs; the **Caliente Corner,** serving better-than-average tacos, nachos, churros, and Mexican beer; and the **Bullpen Pub,** a nicely appointed bar where patrons can look through peepholes into the bullpen. A kid's concession stand, **Moose's Munchies,** has Popsicles, juice, milk, and peanut-butter-and-jelly sandwiches. (There are benches for parents to rest between the kid's stand and the kid's playground.) Throughout the stadium, most of the popcorn is pre-popped, but cookies ($3) are baked on-site and the peanuts are fresh roasted. The basic hot dog ($2.75) is grilled and served in a yeasty, just-baked bun. It's much better than the usual dog. You can also bring in outside food, and there's a large picnic area, the **Outside Corner,** with many tables and great views of the harbor, the Space Needle, glorious sunsets, and Mount Rainier.

SMOKING POLICY: Safeco Field is a no-smoking facility. Smoking is permitted only on the landings of each ramp on right-field (SE) and left-field (NW) corners of the ballpark.

TOURISM INFORMATION: Seattle/King County Convention & Visitors Bureau (800 Convention Place, Seattle, WA 98101, tel. 206/461–5840)

Seattle: Safeco Field

The grass is back. It was a long wait. Between October 2, 1969, when the Seattle Pilots played their last game at highly regarded Sick's Stadium, and July 15, 1999, when the Mariners made their first appearance at Safeco Field, there were 1,755 games at the horrible Kingdome, under a roof and on plastic.

Safeco Field sits just south of the Kingdome, bordering the historic downtown to the north and the city's industrial area to the south. The stadium, which takes its name from a large financial corporation with headquarters in Seattle, is a marvel of technology and architecture. At a cost of $500 million plus, it should be.

Designed by NBBJ Seattle, Safeco Field has a rolling roof unlike any other in the baseball world. It doesn't completely seal the stadium, but rather is like an umbrella, protecting against rain but not against extreme temperatures. If it's cold or hot outside, it will be cold or hot at Safeco Field, even when the lid is on. The retractable roof is made of rubberized sheet metal, weighing 20 million pounds and covering 8.9 acres. It has three moving sections that travel on steel rails and stack up over the seats beyond right and center field. Opening or closing the roof takes 10 to 20 minutes, depending on the wind and other weather factors.

The immense roof has dictated the large size of the stadium. You lose a little of the intimacy that other new major-league parks have been able to capture, but the trade-off works for a city with Seattle's weather. And there are places in the park with incredible intimacy. In seats by the bullpens, you're practically nose to nose with the warm-up pitcher, separated only by a screen.

There's a sense of freedom at the park that comes from standing-room vantage points found throughout. You don't feel locked into your seat; you are able to roam and watch.

The stadium also works with its industrial neighbors. There's heavy rail traffic right next door—about 50 trains a day. It adds to the excitement and noise when a train rumbles through during a game.

There are 11 scoreboards and display boards throughout Safeco Field, of both the high- and low-tech varieties. The main scoreboard, 190 ft long and 56 ft high with a giant video screen, sits above the cheap seats beyond center field. In left field, there is a Fenway Park look-alike hand-operated scoreboard showing the line score of the game.

The stadium includes baseball-theme installations by nine local artists. The compass rose, the Mariners' symbol, has been created out of shell bits on the floor by the front gate and signed by the players from the team's first year in the stadium. There are great baseball quotes worked into the floor, including our favorite, from Tallulah Bankhead: "There have been only two geniuses in the world—Willie Mays and William Shakespeare."

Artist Tina Hoggatt did large color paintings of baseball greats at each of the game's nine positions, including top players from the Negro Leagues, All American Girls Baseball League, and Japanese Major Leagues. An "outsider art" piece is Ross Palmer Beecher's quilt of metal license plates from baseball cities.

An enormous bronze mitt by artist Gerard Tsutakawa, found outside the park at the northwest (left-field) corner, has already become a meeting spot and a favorite place for photos.

The main entrance to the park resembles a symphony hall, with a green overhang. The red-brick, outside walls are decorated with potted plants. All in all, this is a handsome, exciting park.

Tours of Safeco Field run daily except when home games begin prior to 6 PM. *First Ave. S and Atlantic St., Seattle, tel. 800/696–2746 or 206/622–4487 for times. Admission: $7 adults, $5 senior citizens, $3 ages 12 and under.*

More Seattle Baseball

Everett Memorial Stadium. Just 25 mi north of Safeco Field you'll find a very different baseball experience. The Everett Aquasox play in the Short-Season Single A Northwest League, where the rawest of major-league prospects are found. The trip for these ballplayers from Everett to the parent team in Seattle will cover a lot more than 25 mi. Memorial Stadium, where the Aquasox play, is an Ebbets Field re-creation, built by former owner Bob Bavasi, son of Brooklyn Dodgers general manager Buzzie Bavasi. Aquasox, by the way, are a cross between the Pacific tree frog, the Central American red-eyed tree frog, and legendary third baseman Brooks Robinson. *39th and Broadway, Everett, tel. 425/258–3673 or www.aquasox.com.*

Where to Stay

Pacific Plaza Hotel. This convenient downtown hotel, located less then a mile from the ballpark, keeps its 1928 charm and is a relative bargain for Seattle. The rooms in its eight stories are small but quaintly decorated. Cars can be parked in a nearby public lot. Continental breakfast is included in the room price. *400 Spring St., Seattle 98104, tel. 206/623–3900 or 800/426–1165, fax 206/777–7130. 160 rooms. AE, D, DC, MC, V. $$*

Days Inn Town Center. The exterior isn't appealing, but the price and convenience are fine at this small, four-story hotel. The modest-sized rooms were under renovation at press time. Free parking is a bonus. The hotel is a mile north of the ballpark and about six blocks from the Pike Place Market. *2205 7th Ave., Seattle 98121, tel. 206/448–3434 or 800/325–2525, fax 206/441–6976. 91 rooms. AE, D, DC, MC, V. $$*

Holiday Inn Express. Located near the Space Needle, this six-story hotel is good for longer stays, as it has 55 efficiency rooms. The accommodations are clean and modern, but the neighborhood is a busy commercial area. (A new Holiday Inn is planned to open near the ballpark in 2001.) *226 Aurora Ave. N, Seattle 98109, tel. 206/441–7222 or 800/465–4329, fax 206/441–0786. 195 rooms. Facilities: indoor pool. AE, D, DC, MC, V. $$*

Where to Eat

Ho Ho Seafood Restaurant. The International District, home to one of America's largest Asian communities, is just blocks from the ballpark. It makes sense to eat dinner here, as the parking meters stop at 6 PM. There are numerous casual Hong Kong–style seafood palaces to choose from, with tanks of huge crabs in the windows. Ho Ho's is a good choice—in classic style, lazy Susans sit in the middle of the round Formica tables, the better for families to share. Meaty steamed Pacific oysters make a delicious appetizer, as do the Dungeness crab and clams. Hot pots of noodles with prawns and lobster in bean sauce are beautifully prepared. *653 S. Weller St., tel. 206/382–9671. AE, MC, V. $*

Lowell's. This is a good starting point for tourists with cars who want to take in the crowded Pike Place Market. It has three floors of windows looking out over Puget Sound, and you get an hour of free parking with your meal. It's open for breakfast at 7 AM, serving genuine oatmeal, large muffins, and $2 eggs. For lunch, try the turkey sandwich or the good clam chowder. *1519 Pike Pl., tel. 206/622–2036. AE, D, MC, V. $*

Piroshki, Piroshki. The piroshki is a Russian stuffed egg dumpling that comes in potato, prune, apple, or sausage-and-mushroom varieties. Here you can watch them being made on the premises. They're wonderful walk-around food, but this storefront bakery has small tables and chairs for dining in and watching the passing market parade. *1908 Pike Pl., tel. 206/441–6068. MC, V. $*

Entertainments

A CityPass, valid for nine days, cuts admission to six popular attractions in half. Sold at hotels, visitor centers, and the attractions, the CityPass gives you entry to the Space Needle, Museum of Flight, Pacific Science Center, Seattle Aquarium, Seattle Art Museum, and Woodland Park Zoo. *CityPass, tel. 707/256–0490; $25.75 adults, $22 senior citizens, $14.50 ages 6–13.*

The Space Needle. Ride a $1 monorail from the Westlake Center downtown to the Seattle Center, the site of the 1962 World's Fair, where you'll find the famed Space Needle. The 74-acre center complex also includes the Fun Forest Amusement Park, a science center, and a children's museum. The Needle rises 605 ft into the sky and has an observation deck and two revolving restaurants at the top. Admission is free to those eating at the restaurants, which are fancy. *Broad St. and 5th Ave, Seattle, tel. 206/443–2111 or 800/937–9582. Elevator admission: $9 adults, $8 senior citizens, $4 ages 5–12. AE, DC, D, MC, V.*

Pacific Science Center. The center, adjacent to Space Needle, contains an IMAX theater and a laserium. Experimental technology, using robots and computers, is part of the TechZone. Younger kids love donning plastic aprons and playing in the outdoor Water Works exhibit.

You'll also find a Tropical Butterfly House and an insect zoo. Laser shows are held Tuesday through Sunday nights and require a separate $7 admission. Admission to the Center includes an IMAX film or laser matinee. *Seattle Center, Seattle, tel. 206/443–2001. Admission: $9.50 adults, $7.50 senior citizens and ages 6–13, $5.50 ages 2–5. Open mid-June–Labor Day, daily 10–6; Sept.–mid-June, weekdays 10–5, weekends 10–6.*

Gameworks Seattle. Steven Spielberg, Sega, and Universal Studios financed this video-game theme park. From racing games like Daytona USA to old favorites like Ms. Pac Man and Asteroids, this is 30,000 square ft of noise, lights, and joysticks. There are a few nonvideo games, including foosball and air hockey tables. *7th and Pike St., Meriden Square, Seattle, tel. 206/521–0950 or www.gameworks.com. Admission: $20 for 1 hr unlimited play, $30 for 2 hrs. Open Mon.–Sat. 10 AM–1 AM, Sun. 10 AM–11 PM.*

Sights to See

Pike Place Market. Watch the fishmongers throw huge mackerel and salmon at each other in one of America's oldest working markets. The produce is more varied and beautiful than anything you'll ever find in a supermarket. Pike Place Market is nine acres of stands, crafts stalls, neon signs, and character. A skywalk with elevators and stairs leads you to the harbor. *Pike St. and 1st Ave., Seattle, tel. 206/682–7453. Open Mon.–Sat. 9–6, Sun. 11–6.*

Pioneer Square. This historic district is a walker's and shopper's delight. Pioneer Square was Seattle's first neighborhood, settled in 1852 on the eastern shore of Elliott Bay. Here Chief Sealth, the leader of the native residents, aided the new arrivals and sold them the use of his name. The original totem pole at Pioneer Place was stolen from a Tlingit Indian village in 1890. An arsonist burned the pole in 1938, and the city paid the Tlingits to carve the replacement you see today. The Great Fire of 1889 leveled the wooden-framed downtown. Brick buildings built after the fire make up the heart of today's 20-block historic district, just south of downtown and just north of Safeco Field. The late-19th-century buildings are now full of wonderful restaurants, bookstores, and antiques and crafts shops. *S. Washington and S. Jackson Sts., 2nd and S. Main Sts., Seattle.*

Klondike Gold Rush National Historical Park. This visitor center in the Pioneer Square Historic District tells the story of the gold speculators and of turn-of-the-century Seattle with an exhibit and several videos. On July 17, 1897, a steamer carrying more than two tons of gold from the Yukon River wilderness arrived at Seattle, launching a stampede to northwestern Canada's Klondike area. Seattle became the place gold seekers came to to outfit themselves for the difficult trip north. There are gold panning demonstrations and guided tours of Pioneer Square offered daily mid-June–Labor Day. *117 S. Main St., tel. 206/553–7220. Admission free. Open daily 9–5.*

Maritime Heritage Center. The boat-making craft that has played such a critical role in Seattle's history comes alive at the south end of Lake Union Park, just north of downtown. At the Center for Wooden Boats, you can take a brisk sail in a racing sloop or take the oars of a turn-of-the-century rowboat. Or try a seat in your favorite catboat or peapod. Sixty boats are available for rent by the hour. *1010 Valley St, South Lake Union, Seattle, tel. 206/382–2628. Admission free. Open daily 11–6.*

Northwest Seaport. Watch restoration work in progress and tour the 165-ft-long 1897 sailing schooner *Wawona*. This ship hauled the timber and cod that fueled the economy of the Pacific Northwest. Also visit the 1889 tug *Arthur Foss*, featured in the classic 1933 film *Tugboat Annie. 1002 Valley St, Seattle,. tel. 206/447–9800. Admission free. Open June–Aug., Mon.–Sat. 10–5, Sun. noon–5; Sept.—May, Mon.–Sat. 10–4, Sun. noon–4.*

TACOMA RAINIERS

League: Pacific Coast League • **Class:** AAA • **Stadium:** Cheney Stadium • **Opened:** 1960 • **Capacity:** 9,600 • **Dimensions:** LF: 325, CF: 425, RF: 325 • **Surface:** grass • **Season:** Apr.–Labor Day

STADIUM LOCATION: 2502 S. Tyler, Tacoma, WA 98405.

TEAM WEB SITE: www.rainiers.com

GETTING THERE: From I–5 North or South, take Exit 132 (Hwy. 16 W). Take the 19th Street East exit and take the first right, onto Cheyenne Street. Follow the road around to the stadium parking lot.

PARKING: Stadium parking is $2. It can be slow exiting the stadium lots when there is a large crowd.

TICKET INFORMATION: Box 11087, Tacoma, WA 98411, tel. 253/752–7707 or 800/281–3834, fax 253/752–7135.

PRICE RANGE: Box seats, adults $10, ages 14 and under, senior citizens, and military $8; reserved seats, adults $6, children, senior citizens, and military $4; general admission, adults $5, children, senior citizens, and military $3.

GAME TIME: Mon.–Sat. 7:05 PM, Sun. 1:35 PM. Gates open one hour before game.

TIPS ON SEATING: You can see Mount Rainier from the general admission seats high up on the third-base side. These seats also are preferable for night games as the sun sets behind third base. The sun will be in your eyes for day games, so on Sunday you might want a reserved seat under the stadium roof. Nostalgia buffs often seek out the first rows of reserved seats, which came from famous Seals Stadium in San Francisco. The home team dugout is on the first-base side.

SEATING FOR PEOPLE WITH DISABILITIES: There is seating throughout the park. Fans with valid handicap permits may park near the ticket office.

STADIUM FOOD: The mountain burger with Canadian bacon is very good ($3.50). This is the land of specialty coffees, and the ballpark is no exception. You can drink espresso, cappuccino, and caffe latte.

SMOKING POLICY: Smoking is not allowed in the seating area or at the concession stands. Smoking is allowed only on the outer concourse of the stadium.

VISITING TEAM HOTEL: LaQuinta Inn (1426 E. 27th St., Tacoma, WA 98421, tel. 253/383–0146 or 800/531–5900).

TOURISM INFORMATION: Tacoma-Pierce County Visitor & Convention Bureau (906 Broadway, Tacoma, WA 98401, tel. 206/627–2836 or 800/272–2662).

Tacoma:
Cheney Stadium

The walk from the parking lot to 40-year-old Cheney Stadium should put a baseball fan in just the right mood for a ball game. People are milling through the large, festive concourse on their way to concession stands and souvenir shops. Kids are flinging balls at the speed pitch.

The Tacoma Rainiers play just 30 mi south of Seattle in a fine but fading 1960 stadium with a large covered grandstand. It was built for $1 million in 100 days to be ready for the Triple A affiliate of the San Francisco Giants. The stadium is named after Ben Cheney, a lumberman-philanthropist who was a minority owner of the San Francisco Giants. When the Giants moved from Seals Stadium to Candlestick Park, Cheney had some Seals seats sent to Tacoma, where they're now found in the reserved sections. The erector-set-like light towers also are from Seals. There is a wonderful life-size sculpture of Cheney in a seat behind home plate.

They have been playing baseball in Tacoma since 1874, when an amateur team, the Invincibles, lost its only game, 29–28, and folded. A Tacoma team was part of the Pacific Coast League in 1904 and 1905, and the city rejoined the league in 1960 as an affiliate of the Giants—future Giants greats Willie McCovey and Juan Marichal honed their craft here. Tacoma has had a series of major-league affiliations since, most significantly the Oakland A's of Mark McGwire and Jose Canseco and, currently, their neighbors to the north, the Seattle Mariners. Tacoma is now the longest-running continuous franchise in the Pacific Coast League. On the third-base side on the concourse wall there is a colorful mural of life-size players wearing eight different uniforms of Tacoma professional base-

ball. There is a Tacoma Baseball Hall of Fame on the first-base side.

The Rainiers promise "off-the-wall fun," and they deliver. The mascot is a reindeer named Rhubarb. In the middle of the 4th inning, there is a Run with Rhubarb when kids 14 and under run from the right-field foul pole to near the home team dugout. Then Rhubarb signs autographs in a booth behind the grandstand on the first-base side.

There is a great view of Mount Rainier, which lies 60 mi beyond first base, from the general admission seats high up on the left-field side. There is an excellent minor-league scoreboard in left center. This is a pitcher's ballpark with a 28-ft-high wall in center field 425 ft from home plate. One advantage for hitters is the limited amount of foul territory. The aluminum-bench bleachers in general admission pinch in toward the foul poles, providing excellent sight lines.

More Tacoma Baseball

Olympic Stadium. We didn't think there was anything like Hoquiam's Olympic Stadium left in America. Here in western Washington, 90 mi west of Tacoma and 20 mi from the Pacific Ocean, lies a great huge ocean liner of a ballpark. And it's all wood. From the outside, it looks like a mammoth gray-shingled warehouse. Inside, it has the funky feel of a seashore amusement park. Olympic Stadium is another product of the Works Progress Administration (WPA) that contributed most of the $200,000 it cost to build the ballpark in 1938.

The grandstand is a huge, odd C-shaped wooden structure entirely covered by a roof and held up by more than 50 pillars and poles. The wooden bench seating is 14 rows deep and will hold 7,800 people. The best seats are behind home plate and down the first-base side.

The roof and grandstand continue around the foul pole in right field and all the way to deep center field. These seats are painted the maroon and gray of the local high-school football team, which plays its games on the outfield grass. Hoquiam means "hungry for wood," and the logging industry has always been a major part of the regional economy. Appropriately, the grandstand ends about halfway up the third-base line, allowing a full view of the nearby hillside full of trees. A semipro team, the Rain, plays baseball here, as well as high-school and junior college teams. Call the City of Hoquiam Parks Department, tel. 360/533–3447, to get a schedule. *101 28th St., Hoquiam, WA, tel. 360/532–9313.*

Where to Stay

Visiting Team Hotel: LaQuinta Inn. This budget choice is next to Exit 135 off I–5 in a commercial cluster. Its rooms are spacious, and there is a free Continental breakfast. Ask for an upper floor in this seven-story motel to avoid freeway noise. *1426 E. 27th St., Tacoma 98421, tel. 253/383–0146 or 800/531–5900. 157 rooms. Facilities: restaurant, outdoor pool. AE, D, DC, MC, V. $$*

Shilo Inn. Families and business travelers looking for moderate prices appreciate the microwave, refrigerator, and video player in each room. The rooms of the four-story inn are all standard size. There is a free Continental breakfast. *17414 S. Hosmer, Tacoma, tel. 253/475–4020 or 800/222–2244, tax 253/475–1236. 121 rooms, 11 efficiencies. Facilities: indoor pool, fitness center, coin laundry. AE, DC, MC, V. $$*

Where to Eat

Harbor Lights. Most of the tables at this nicely appointed restaurant have good views of the harbor and Commencement Bay. Northwest oysters are fixed nine ways, including pan stews and omelets, and Dungeness crab comes in cocktails, cracked, and in stews. The clam chowder is very good. Children 10 and under have five reduced-price entrées to choose from, four of them fish. *2761 Ruston Way, Tacoma, tel. 253/752–8600. AE, D, DC, MC, V. $$*

Rock Pasta and Brewery. Brick-oven pizza is a specialty of this casual downtown restaurant.

You can choose from 35 toppings, including sliced almonds, caramelized onions, and roasted pecans. Four types of pasta can be dressed in four sauces, for inexpensive dinners. There also are calzones and salads. *1920 Jefferson St., Tacoma, tel. 253/272–1221. MC, V. $*

Entertainments

Point Defiance Zoo & Aquarium. Puget Sound marine life and Pacific Rim animals are featured here. The layout is optimal for close viewing. There are beluga whales, polar bears, sea otters, and walruses on display. Huge tanks in the Discovery Reef Aquarium contain tropical fish. *5400 N. Pearl St., Tacoma, tel. 253/591–5337. Admission: $7 adults, $6.55 senior citizens, $5.30 ages 4–13. Open Memorial Day–Labor Day, daily 10–7; Labor Day–Memorial Day, daily 10–4. MC, V.*

Port Defiance Park. You can hike, visit a Japanese garden, and take a logging train ride through a replica of a lumber camp here. There's a public fishing pier, where boats and fishing poles are available for rent. Within the park also is the sweet **Never Never Land,** which holds interest only for young children. It features a walk-through woods dotted with tableaux from children's stories. *5400 N. Pearl St., Tacoma, tel. 253/752–0047. Train rides: $2.50 adults, $1.50 senior citizens and ages 3–12. Never Never Land admission: $3 adults, $2.25 senior citizens, $2 ages 3–12. Open daily dawn to dusk.*

Sights to See

Washington State History Museum. Take a video ride down the rushing Columbia River and explore early settlers' housing in this nicely arranged walking tour through Washington history. The waterfront museum is adjacent to the restored 1911 Union Station, which has been filled with glass sculptures by native son Dale Chihuly. *1911 Pacific Ave., Tacoma, tel. 253/272–3500 or 888/238–4373. Admission: $7 adults, $6 senior citizens, $5 ages 13–18 and military, $4 ages 6–12. Open Memorial Day–Labor Day, Mon.–Sat. 10–6, Sun. 11–6; Labor Day–Memorial Day, Mon.–Sat. 10–5, Sun. 11–5. MC, V.*

More Washington Baseball

Yakima County Stadium. The Yakima Bears play in the Northwest League in a fine 3,000-seat ballpark opened in 1993. Fans see mountains out beyond the ballpark and a racetrack just past the right-field fence. Yakima, in south-central Washington, is about 145 mi southeast of Seattle and 165 mi northeast of Portland. *810 W. Nob Hill Blvd., Yakima, WA, tel. 509/457–5151.*

Seafirst Stadium. The Spokane Indians play in a wonderful old ballpark on the Interstate Fairgrounds. It was built in 90 days in 1958 for the Dodgers Triple A team, which was forced out of Los Angeles when the big-league team moved from Brooklyn. The park hosted Pacific Coast League baseball for almost 25 years. The Seafirst Stadium of today seats 7,100 and is the product of major renovations in 1979 and 1986. The Brett brothers—including Hall of Famer George—own the Indians, a member of the Short-Season Single A Northwest League. The stadium has a large, family-friendly entrance with a county fair atmosphere and mountains beyond the outfield wall.

Spokane, about 280 mi east of Seattle on the Idaho border, has a 1950s feel and an excellent Riverfront Park with a 1909 carousel designed by Charles Looff, who built Coney Island's first carousel. A gondola built for the 1974 Expo overlooks the Spokane Falls. Bing Crosby grew up here, and an exhibit of his memorabilia at Gonzaga University includes a photo of Crosby on the university's baseball team. *602 N. Havana, Spokane, tel. 509/535–2922.*

THE EMERALD CITIES
PORTLAND, EUGENE

28

Startling beauty is a constant along the Pacific Coast. A trip combining Portland and Eugene will convince you that cool nights and forests are essential backdrops for the game.

Portland is the city of roses, public art, beautiful bridges over the Willamette River, and a wealth of family activities, from exploring Washington Park to an exceptional science center to the nation's oldest amusement park. The girls' Little League Softball World Series is played here at Alpenrose Stadium. Portland's ballpark, with the largest capacity in Single A or Double A baseball, has the fan-friendly Rocky Raccoon to keep the action going.

To get to the Emerald City, Eugene, take I–95 (not the yellow brick road) south 108 mi. Eugene is a comfortable, progressive university town, filled with fitness enthusiasts. The Emeralds play in a classic Works Progress Administration stadium with wooden bench seats.

PORTLAND ROCKIES

League: Northwest League • **Major League Affiliation:** Colorado Rockies • **Class:** Short Season A • **Stadium:** Civic Stadium • **Opened:** 1926 • **Capacity:** 23,105 • **Dimensions:** LF: 309, CF: 407, RF: 325 • **Surface:** artificial • **Season:** mid-June–Labor Day

STADIUM LOCATION: 1844 Morrison St., Portland, OR 97207.

WEB SITE: www.portlandrockies.com

GETTING THERE: From downtown, take Jefferson St. to N.W. 18th Ave. and turn right to Morrison St. From I–84, take I–5 N, then I–405 across Fremont Bridge; follow I–405 S in right lane to Everett St. exit; turn right on Couch St., left on N.W. 19th Ave., cross Burnside St., go one block to Morrison St., and turn right to N.W. 20th Ave. For public transit, call Tri-Met (tel. 503/238–7433).

PARKING: 4,000 parking spaces on street within 5-block radius of stadium. Nearest public lot is 8 blocks east of stadium at S.W. 10th and Yamhill; walk to Washington St. and take Bus 15 to and from stadium.

TICKET INFORMATION: Box 998, Portland OR 97207, tel. 503/223–2837, fax 503/223–2948.

PRICE RANGE: VIP boxes on season basis only. Reserved $6.50; general admission $5.50 adults, $4.50 children and senior citizens; left-field bleacher seats day of game only, $2.50 adults, $1 ages under 13.

GAME TIME: Mon.–Sat. 7:05 PM, Sun. 2 PM; gates open 1 hr before game.

TIPS ON SEATING: Reserved seats on first-base side behind Rockies dugout are worth the extra dollar or two. Bargain-price tickets ($2.50 adults, $1 ages under 13) are sold for left-field bleachers, known as Rockpile, only on day of game from ticket booth at N.W. 18th Ave. and Morrison St.

SEATING FOR PEOPLE WITH DISABILITIES: Tickets sold at booth at N.W. 20th Ave. and Morrison St. Designated parking spaces for people with disabilities permits on N.W. 18th and 20th avenues at Morrison St. and in 30-minute-and-over zones and metered spaces.

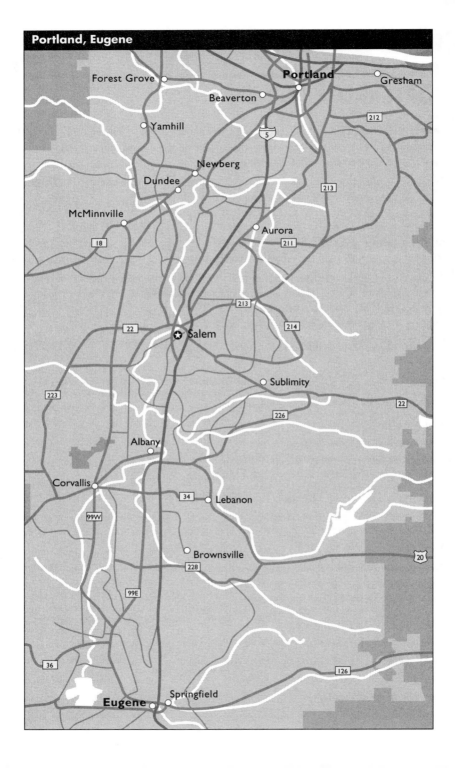

STADIUM FOOD: Vegetarians get a break with gardenburgers, grilled along with hamburgers, hot dogs, and sausages. You can sit in the **Bullpen Barbecue** next to the pitcher's bullpen along the right-field line for $5 per person. A kid's meal includes hot dog, chips, soft drink, baseball cards, and red licorice for $3.50.

SMOKING POLICY: Smoking permitted only in plaza of main stadium and above bleachers in Rockpile; prohibited in all seating areas.

VISITING TEAM HOTEL: Radisson Hotel Portland (1441 S.E. Second Ave., Portland, OR 97232, tel. 503/233–2401 or 800/333-3333).

TOURISM INFORMATION: Portland Oregon Visitors Association (26 S.W. Salmon St., Portland, OR 97204, tel. 503/222–2223 or 800/345–3214).

Portland: Civic Stadium

Why is a team in the short-season Northwest League, just one step up from rookie ball, playing in a 23,105-seat stadium? Opened in 1926 for football, the stadium did not host baseball until 1956 when the Triple A Portland Beavers were forced to move from the wooden 1901 Lucky Beavers Stadium at the fire marshal's strong suggestion.

Portland became a charter member of the prestigious Triple A Pacific Coast League in 1903. The Portland team played in the PCL all but six years until it lost its Triple A franchise to Salt Lake City in 1994. In 1995, the Colorado Rockies moved its Northwest League franchise to Portland's Civic Stadium and immediately shattered the attendance record for the short-season league, averaging 6,571 fans.

Just west of Portland's vital downtown, in a residential neighborhood, the stadium is surrounded by apartments and shops. The Multnomah Athletic Club, which first built a 1,000-seat stadium here in 1885, towers over the stadium beyond right field. The main grandstand used today was built by the club in 1926. In 1967, the Athletic Club sold the stadium to the City of Portland, which was the first owner to install artificial turf for an outdoor baseball and football stadium. The owners, Jack and Mary Cain, are fan-friendly baseball people who provide good times and top entertainment. Rocky Raccoon, the local mascot, is a hit. There is space to roam, with a walkway the full length of the J-shape covered grandstand. The long stem of the J is on the first-base side. The Rockpile bleachers sit above left field and a 25-ft-high wall.

More Portland Baseball

Alpenrose Stadium and Dairy. Home of the Little League Softball World Series, the stadium is one of the nation's sweetest ball fields. Although this girls' championship, held in the middle of August each year, is less famous than the boys' championship played a week later in Williamsport, Pennsylvania, the experience is every bit as exciting. From the flower-bedecked hilltop grandstand, a great view stretches beyond the rose-strewn green scoreboard in center field. The dairy farm also holds a bicycle track, a miniature Western village, a 600-seat opera house, and a museum of musical instruments and dolls. *6149 S.W. Shattuck Rd., Multnomah exit off I–5 S, Portland, tel. 503/244–1133. Admission free (fee for bike track). Grounds open June–Aug., Sun. 1:30–4:30.*

Where to Stay

Visiting Team Motel: Radisson Hotel Portland. This downtown 10-story hotel is close to the Convention Center and Memorial Coliseum. Eighty percent of the rooms have double queen-size beds; the rest have kings. Rollaways are $10. The furnishings are plush and modern. Ask for an upper-floor room for good views of the river and its bridges. *1441 S.E. Second Ave., Portland 97232, tel. 503/233–2401 or 800/333-3333, fax 503/238–7016. 238 rooms. Facilities: restaurant, outdoor pool, fitness center. AE, D, DC, MC, V. $$$*

Imperial Hotel. The rooms are large in this bargain downtown hotel. The 1908 redbrick beauty is 12 blocks from the ballpark. It has a large lobby, European-style rooms, and small bathrooms. *400 S.W. Broadway, Portland 97205, tel. 503/228–7221 or 800/452–2323, fax 503/223–4551. 136 rooms. Facilities: restaurant, free airport shuttle. AE, D, DC, MC, V. $$*

Mallory Hotel. The eight-story, turn-of-the-century hotel is two blocks from the ballpark. Several of the smaller rooms have bargain rates. *729 S.W. 15th St., Portland 97205, tel. 503/223–6311 or 800/228–8657, fax 503/223–0522. 122 rooms, 20 suites. Facilities: restaurant, free parking. AE, D, DC, MC, V. $$*

McMenamins Kennedy School. Your children can't avoid the classroom in the summer if you stay at this renovated school. The large guest rooms are named after the school's former teachers, and have large windows and black-boards with chalk. All beds are queen-size; roll-aways are $15. *5736 N.E. 33rd, Portland, OR 97211, tel. 503/249–3983 or 888/249–3983, fax 503/288–6559. 35 rooms. Facilities: restaurant, outdoor hot tub, cinema. AE, D, MC, V. $$*

Where to Eat

Dan and Louis Oyster Bar. This Portland stand-out since 1907 now resembles a nautical museum that serves lunch and dinner. Young children can eat for as little as $2.99. Adults may want the more costly panfried oysters or shrimp or the crab and oyster stews. *208 S.W. Ankeny St., Portland, tel. 503/227–5906. AE, D, MC, V. $$*

B. Moloch/Heathman Bakery & Pub. A brew pub of Widmer, the state's largest microbrewer, it adjoins the elegant Heathman Hotel. The wood-fired ovens cook pizza and chicken. Children are welcome in the casual, art-filled restaurant, which also serves breakfast. *901 S.W. Salmon St., Portland, tel. 503/227–5700. AE, D, DC, MC, V. $$*

Lorn and Dottie's Luncheonette. This center-city diner serves huge breakfasts and lunches. Sit at the counter for blue-plate cuisine, and don't miss the crisp waffles. *322 S.W. 2nd Ave., Portland, tel. 503/221–2473. MC, V. $*

Sights to See

Portland is ideally located. Pacific Ocean beaches are just over an hour west. Mt. Hood is an hour east and visible from the city. The Columbia and Willamette rivers meet here, and the fertile Willamette Valley is just to the south. Call ahead for a free "City Kids Fun Book" from the Association for Portland Progress (tel. 503/224–8684).

Oaks Amusement Park. This lovely tree-shaded amusement park is the oldest in the United States still in operation. Created in 1905 for the Lewis and Clark Exposition, it has 25 rides, miniature golf, a 1924 carousel, and a year-round roller rink with a Wurlitzer organ. There's a good kiddie section with a minitrain. *S.E. Oaks Pkwy., tel. 503/233–5777. Admission free. Open Memorial–Labor Day, daily 1–10; closed nonholiday Mon.*

Oregon Museum of Science and Industry (OMSI). Six exhibit halls make up this extensive hands-on science center. Visitors "travel" through outer space, make electricity, and view an exceptional astronomy show. A separate IMAX theater and nightly laser shows are in an adjacent planetarium. *1945 S.E. Water Ave., Portland, tel. 503/797–4000. Admission: $6.50 adults, $4.50 senior citizens and ages 4–13. Open Tues.–Wed. and Fri.–Sun. 9:30–5:30, Thurs. 9:30–8.*

Washington Park and Oregon Zoo. Designed by the Olmsted brothers, this 145-acre park sits high above the city's west side. Look for the International Rose Garden's Children's Park. Kids enjoy the zoo's African Rain Forest, Asian elephants, and zoo railway. There are man-made thunderstorms in the Bamba du Jon Swamp. *4001 S.W. Canyon Rd., tel. 503/226–7627. Zoo admission: $5.50 adults, $4 senior citizens, $3.50 ages 3–11; zoo railway fare $2.75. Open Memorial–Labor Day, daily 9:30–6; Labor Day–Memorial Day, 9:30–5.*

Unusual Shopping

Powell's City of Books. One of the largest and best book stores in the United States, it covers two full city blocks and has a funky coffee shop. *1005 W. Burnside St., Portland, tel. 503/228–4651 or 800/878–7323.*

Saturday Market. This outdoor market of 200 food and art vendors opens each weekend under the west end of the Burnside Bridge. *S.W.*

Ankeny at 1st Ave., between Front St. and the MAX tracks, Portland, tel. 503/222–6072.

More Oregon Baseball

Volcanoes Stadium, Salem. Oregon's capital city lies on the I–5 route, directly between Eugene (64 mi to the south) and Portland (51 mi to the north). Salem and its neighbor host a Northwest League team, the Salem-Keizer Volcanoes. The Volcanoes—appropriately named for Oregon's hundreds of volcanoes, seven of which have erupted in the past 300 years—play at the 4,296-seat Volcanoes Stadium. The stadium was built in six months, in time for the 1997 season, to accommodate a San Francisco Giants farm team that relocated from Bellingham, Washington. The ballpark provides the minor league basics, but, unfortunately, at an ordinary site, with the traffic on I–5 over the right-field wall providing a constant distraction. *6700 Field of Dreams Way, Salem, tel. 503/390–2225, www.volcanoesbaseball.com.*

EUGENE EMERALDS

League: Northwest League • **Major League Affiliation:** Chicago Cubs • **Class:** Short Season A • **Stadium:** Civic Stadium • **Opened:** 1938 • **Capacity:** 6,800 • **Dimensions:** LF: 335, CF: 400, RF: 328 • **Surface:** grass • **Season:** mid-June–Labor Day

STADIUM LOCATION: 2077 Willamette St., Eugene, OR 97405.

WEB SITE: www.go-ems.com

GETTING THERE: From I–5, take I–105/Route 126 west toward downtown. Take the Coburg Road exit and go south (turn left) across the river to Broadway (Route 99). Go south (take a quick left) onto Pearl Street to the stadium at 20th Street.

PARKING: Limited free parking in the main lot north of the stadium. Parking available across Pearl Street at the First Place Family Center for $2.

TICKET INFORMATION: Box 5566, Eugene, OR 97405, tel. 541/342–5367.

PRICE RANGE: Box seats $7; general admission $4.50; reserved seating in food area on third-base side, $7 adults, $6 children; $1 discount on all tickets for senior citizens and ages 12 and under.

GAME TIME: Mon.–Sat. 7:05 PM, Sun. 6:05 PM; gates open 1 hr before game.

TIPS ON SEATING: General admission seats are close to the action. Seats down the first-base line past the base afford a great view of the field and the foothills beyond the park. Make sure your view is not blocked by pillars. The reserved seating in the food area on the third-base deck also gets you very close to the game.

SEATING FOR PEOPLE WITH DISABILITIES: On the decks on the first- and third-base side.

STADIUM FOOD: There is standard fare (hotdogs, popcorn, nachos) at three concession stands. Get specialty items (snow cones, burritos, ice cream, and pizza) from individual stands behind the grandstand on the first-base side. Grilled sandwiches ($4.25) are sold at an adjacent barbecue pit.

SMOKING POLICY: Smoking prohibited in seating areas, but allowed in the picnic deck areas.

VISITING TEAM HOTEL: Doubletree Inn (3280 Gateway Rd., Springfield, OR 97477, tel. 541/726–8181 or 800/222–8733).

TOURISM INFORMATION: Convention and Visitors Bureau of Lane County (115 W. 8th, #190, Eugene, OR 97411, tel. 541/484–5307 or 800/547–5445).

Eugene: Civic Stadium

Eugene's Civic Stadium is one of the oldest ballparks still in use in minor-league baseball. The Eugene School District joined with the federal Works Progress Administration (WPA) and civic boosters in 1938 to build a 5,000-seat multisport facility, at a cost of $12,000. Although professional baseball was always envisioned as a possible tenant, football was the primary sport in the early years. They played semi-pro baseball here in the 1940s and '50s, but when Eugene got a Northwest League franchise in 1955, the team played in the privately owned and smaller Bethel Park. Baseball came to Civic Stadium when Eugene got a Pacific Coast League franchise for the 1969 season, and the team needed a larger field. Eight hundred box seats were bought from the San Diego Padres and installed as part of the upgrade of the stadium for future Hall of Famer Mike Schmidt and his Triple A teammates. The lights were reconfigured from football to baseball. After five seasons in the PCL, Eugene went back to the Northwest League in 1974.

This is not your fancy 1990s minor-league park. Despite $250,000 worth of improvements in recent years, Civic Stadium has retained its classic WPA feel. The L-shaped grandstand, built primarily with football in mind, has its long leg down the first-base line. The general admission seats in the grandstand are wooden bench seats without backs, completely covered by the grandstand roof. Be careful not to sit where one of the ten blue pillars holding up the grandstand roof might block your view of the action. There are six or seven rows of blue plastic box seats in front of the grandstand. From the grandstand, fans see the hand-operated scoreboard in right center field. Beyond the 16-ft-high outfield wall you see houses, businesses, and sports fields, with the tree-covered Coburg Hills beyond.

You can't watch the game while you stand in line for a hot dog and a soda, as you can at many of the newer ballparks. But the atmosphere behind the grandstand on the first-base side is pure county fair and is worth the inconvenience. A half-dozen blue wooden stands dish out spe-

cialty items from grilled chicken sandwiches to burritos to snow cones. Tented picnic areas are on both the first- and third-base sides. The bullpen deck picnic area on the first-base side is reserved for pre-game parties, but is open to all once the game begins.

Since 1955, in both the PCL and the Northwest League, the team's nickname has been the Emeralds, or the "Ems" as the locals call them. The name originates from the phrase, the "Emerald Empire," used by an early 20th-century newspaper to describe the Eugene region. The name never really caught on for the newspaper's purpose, but it has worked for the baseball team.

Where to Stay

Visiting Team Hotel: Doubletree Inn. This modern, three-story white-stucco motel is just over a mile north of the ballpark at a freeway interchange. Guests receive a free Continental breakfast buffet. *3280 Gateway Rd., Springfield 97477, tel. 541/726–8181 or 800/222–8733, fax 541/747–1866. 133 rooms. Facilities: outdoor pool, hot tub, coin laundry. AE, DC, MC, V. $$*

Timbers Motel. Families visiting their college students have long used this convenient, downtown motel with a country look. There are outer corridors on both floors of the motel. Beds are either queens or kings. *1015 Pearl St., Eugene 97401, tel. 541/343–3345 or 800/643–4167, fax 541/343–3345. 54 rooms. Facilities: free parking. AE, DC, MC, V. $$*

Where to Eat

Oregon Electric Station. Eat in a former railroad station, with some tables in renovated passenger cars. This restaurant specializes in prime rib, but kids can eat lighter fare, like pasta and meatballs, quesadillas, and cheese noodles. *27 E. 5th St., Eugene, tel. 541/485–4444. AE, D, DC, MC, V. $$*

Fifth Street Public Market. A variety of restaurants and food vendors fill this downtown market. It is open 10–6 and has tables and chairs for casual meals. *296 E. Fifth Ave., Eugene, tel. 541/ 484–0383. $*

Entertainments

Museum of Natural History. It's billed as a 13,000-year-old tourist trap and this small University of Oregon museum makes good on the claim. Archaeologists explain the mystery of 90 5,000-year-old sandals found inside an ancient cave in Fort Rock, Oregon, and discuss other items of Northwest natural history. *1680 E. 15th Ave., Eugene, tel. 541/356–3024. $1 donations welcomed. Open Wed.–Sun. noon–5.*

Willamette Science and Technology Center. There are dinosaurs in Alton Baker Park, safely encompassed in this imaginative hands-on museum. It's a bonanza for finding science fair projects for your children—all the experiments are fun and approachable. The Lane Planetarium adjoins the center. *2300 Leo Harris Pkwy. Eugene, tel. 541/682–7888. Admission: $4 adults, $3 children. Planetarium admission: $3 adults, $2 children. Open Wed.–Fri. noon–5, weekends 11–5.*

Sights to See

Saturday Market. Crafts, produce, clothing, jewelry, and music make this riverfront market a lively happening. Have a walking lunch while you browse. *8th Ave. and Oak St., Eugene, tel. 541/ 686–8885. Open Apr.–Nov. Sat. 10–5.*

State Capitol. After fires destroyed the first two capitols in 1855 and 1935, the state built this formidable, classical Greek–style white marble building in 1938 to last. Large murals in the rotunda and in the House and Senate chambers illustrate important events in Oregon history. A 23-ft-high gold leaf statue of the Oregon Pioneer, reached by 121 steps spiraling up the tower, tops the Capitol. *Court and State Sts., Salem, tel. 503/986–1388. Admission: free. Guided tours mid-June–Aug., weekdays 9–3, Sat. 10–4, Sun. noon–4. Tower trips Apr.–Sept., weekdays by appointment only. Open weekdays 7:30– 5:30, Sat. 9–4, Sun. noon–4.*

JOLTIN' JOE AND MIGHTY CASEY
STOCKTON, SAN FRANCISCO, SAN JOSE

29

If you are in San Francisco to see the Giants play, make it a triple play with visits to two California League Single A teams, in Stockton and in San Jose.

If you're driving down from northern California, you can stop in Sacramento to see the sprawling and beautifully landscaped State Capitol grounds. Stockton, 40 mi to the south, is a port city, despite being 48 mi east of San Francisco. Baseball has a long tradition here. Formerly the Ports, the team is now called the Mudville Nine: the new name refers to the poem "Casey at the Bat," which originated here. In 2001, a new HOK Sport stadium is expected to open at Banner Island, home of Stockton pro baseball in the 1880s and the birthplace of the Casey legend. Stockton is a gritty city, whose charms are not obvious, but they exist. One of the country's sweetest children's parks, Pixie Woods, with a boat ride, a train, a carousel, and a wading pool, is found at Louis Park. There's also a good children's museum and an extraordinary World Wildlife Museum, with more than 3,000 preserved animals, from giraffes to an orca whale, displayed extremely close to visitors and not behind glass.

Driving west to San Francisco, you'll find a glorious new waterfront park in China Basin that replaces the wind tunnel of legendary Candlestick Park. The City by the Bay will never be accused of cookie-cutter sameness. Delight in its abundance of small, neighborhood hotels, its thriving coffeehouses and ethnic eateries, and its singular experiences, like the ferry to Alcatraz, the Japanese Tea Garden, and the fortune-cookie factory in Chinatown. More than a day can be spent simply sampling the attractions in Golden Gate Park, from Steinhart Aquarium and the California Academy of Sciences to the Children's Playground.

Forty miles south of San Francisco in San Jose is a well-kept Works Progress Administration ballpark, featuring the Santa Cruz Mountains in the distance. The San Jose park is decorated with hand-painted baseball murals and serves unusual food—grilled turkey legs and abalone steaks—in a large picnic area. The city has the most imaginative children's museum in the country, and two all-day amusement parks, Raging Waters and Paramount's Great America (in nearby Santa Clara), to entice you as well. As you drive down the coast, you can stop in Santa Cruz for its beach boardwalk with the 1924 Giant Dipper roller coaster. Another worthwhile stop is Monterey, for its extraordinary, ever-expanding aquarium and the charming, free-admission Dennis the Menace playground, donated by the comic strip's creator, Hank Ketchum.

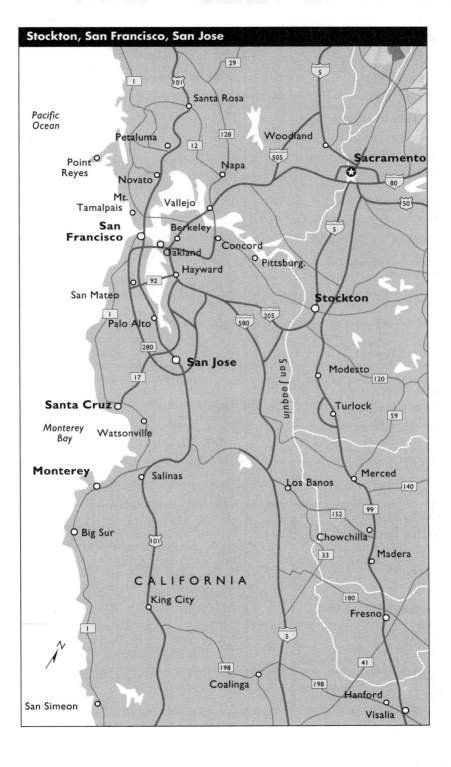

Stockton, San Francisco, San Jose

STOCKTON MUDVILLE NINE

League: California League • **Major League Affiliation:** Milwaukee Brewers • **Class:** A • **Stadium:** Billy Hebert Field • **Opened:** 1950s • **Capacity:** 3,500 • **Dimensions:** LF: 325, CF: 392, RF: 335 • **Surface:** grass • **Season:** Apr.–Labor Day

STADIUM LOCATION: Oak Park, Sutter St., and Alpine Ave., Stockton, CA 95204.

TEAM WEB SITE: www.stocktonports.com

GETTING THERE: From I–5, March Lane exit east for just over 2 mi. Right on El Dorado St. for 1 mi. Left on Alpine St. Stadium is in Oak Park on left. From State Hwy. 99, take Wilson Way exit. Right on Alpine Ave. Stadium is in Oak Park on left.

PARKING: Ample free parking.

TICKET INFORMATION: Box 8550, Stockton, CA 95208, tel. 209/944–5943, fax 209/463—4937.

PRICE RANGE: Reserved $6.50; general admission $5 adults, $3 ages under 13 and over 65, under 3 free.

GAME TIME: Mon.–Sat. 7:05 PM, Sun. 5 PM; gates open 1 hr before game.

TIPS ON SEATING: General admission seats excellent; less than 500 reserved seats. Sit on third-base side behind home-team dugout to avoid sun and smokers on first-base side.

SEATING FOR PEOPLE WITH DISABILITIES: In first row of bleachers just past dugouts on each side; access by ramps.

STADIUM FOOD: The **Casey Barbecue Area** down the third-base line has BBQ chicken and burger dinners, with watermelon wedges and a choice of beans or potato salad, for $7.50. Plain, grilled hamburgers are $4. Smaller appetites will be happy with the Junior Ports menu of hot dog, chips, and a soda for $3.75. Hot churros are $2.

SMOKING POLICY: Smoking prohibited except in bleachers on first-base side and concourse.

VISITING TEAM HOTEL: Best Western Stockton Inn (4219 E. Waterloo Rd., Stockton, CA 95215, tel. 209/931–3131 or 800/528–1234).

TOURISM INFORMATION: Stockton/San Joaquin Convention & Visitors Bureau (46 W. Fremont St., Stockton, CA 95202, tel. 209/943–1987 or 800/350–1987).

Stockton: Billy Hebert Field

They've been playing baseball in Stockton, California, since the 1870s. The current team's excellent mascot is the Mighty Casey of baseball lore. This, according to local Stockton boosters, is the Mudville in the famous poem "Casey at the Bat," by Ernest Thayer. The best baseball in Stockton in the late 1800s was played at a field on Banner Island nicknamed Mudville. The local team had players named Flynn, Blake, and Cooney, as in Thayer's poem.

In 1890, the center of Stockton's baseball activity shifted to the Oak Park Baseball Field, where

Billy Hebert learned to play baseball in Stockton's Recreation Department boys' league. He played Junior Legion ball and became a professional in the California League. He was the first player in all of organized baseball to give his life for his country when he was killed in action in the South Pacific in World War II. In 1950, the City Council renamed the Oak Park field Billy Hebert Field. In the 1950s, the wooden grandstand burned and was replaced with the stadium that now sits among the oak trees and softball fields of Oak Park.

Billy Hebert Field is a traditional-looking stadium with seating for 3,500 fans, mostly on aluminum benches with backs. There are fewer than 500 individual reserved seats. In the hot California sun, the absence of a roof is noticeable. But after the sun goes down, it can grow cool quickly. Stockton is California's most inland port—the team was originally called the Ports in tribute to the importance of the shipping industry here. A stiff breeze from the San Joaquin Delta blows into home plate from left field, making it tough on hitters and providing a delightfully cool night for spectators.

When a pitcher is pulled out of a game, keep an eye on him. More likely than not, you'll see him slip through a gate in left center field at a break between innings. That's where the showers are at Hebert Field. The locker rooms were rebuilt for the 1995 season at a cost of $250,000, but they remain in center field. It's a tradition here and one of the most unusual arrangements in professional baseball. There aren't any further plans for upgrading Hebert Field as the city and the team are building a new field as part of a downtown revitalization plan.

This is an exciting, fan-friendly place. There is a souvenir stand and a fan information booth at the main entrance. We have never seen so many contests, lucky numbers, and giveaways. The best treat at Stockton came during the seventh-inning stretch, with the traveling mascot BirdZerk hip-hop dancing with the home-plate umpire.

Where to Stay

Holiday Inn. This newly renovated motor inn off I-5 has three stories of standard rooms 1½ mi north of the ballpark. It is part of a commercial strip next to a grocery store. *111 E. March La., Stockton 95207, tel. 209/474–3301, fax 209/474–7612. 204 rooms. Facilities: coffee shop, outdoor pool, hot tub. AE, D, DC, MC, V. $$*

Days Inn. On the water, the three-story brick downtown hotel overlooks the Stockton Channel. The rooms are standard size and furnished plainly. Guests receive a free Continental breakfast. *33 N. Center St., Stockton 95202, tel. 209/948–6151 or 800/325–2525, fax 209/948–1220. 96 rooms. Facilities: indoor pool. AE, D, DC, MC, V. $*

Where to Eat

On Lock San. A family-run restaurant, it has dispensed Cantonese cuisine since founder Wong Sai Chun arrived from Guangdong Province in 1898. Don't miss the asparagus with chicken. (Stockton is known for its asparagus festival each April.) The restaurant specializes in family-style meals; its booths even have drapes for privacy. *333 S. Sutter St., Stockton, tel. 209/466–4561. AE, MC, V. $$*

Pacific Baking Company. This is a very California country restaurant, with great pastries, pasta, and wine. The tables are wooden, tiles adorn the walls, and the mood is casual. Half-orders of pasta, ample for light eaters and children, and good polenta and salads are available. *3236 Pacific Ave., at Alpine St., Stockton, tel. 209/462–7939. MC, V. $*

Ye Old Hoosier Inn. A former Hoosier turned this truck stop into a warm family restaurant filled with antiques, stained-glass windows, and marble-topped tables. The Midwestern yeast rolls and homemade sausage are especially good. *1537 N. Wilson Way, at Harding Way, Stockton, tel. 209/463–0271. MC, V. $$*

Entertainments

Children's Museum of Stockton. This is a bright, airy warehouse of make-believe. Kids get to act out many professional fantasies—working in a hospital, a bank, a grocery store, a pet shop, a fast-food restaurant, a TV station, or a factory. The police cruiser, with working lights and alarm, and the ambulance are especially popular. *402 W. Weber St., Stockton, tel. 209/465–4386. Admission: $4, under 2 free. Open Tues.–Sat. 9–4, Sun. 10–4.*

Pixie Woods at Louis Park. This sweet, small park run by the city has a boat ride, a train ride, a carousel, and a wading pool. Rides are 60¢ each. Opened in 1956, it is built around a lake. Good for younger children, it has live rabbits and goats and a play town, a toadstool theater, and an *Alice in Wonderland* playground. There's also a concession stand and a picnic area. *Occidental and Monte Diablo Aves., in Louis Park, Stockton, tel. 209/464–3534. Admission: $2 adults, $1 children. Open Feb.–May and Sept.–Oct., weekends noon–5; June–Labor Day, Wed.–Fri. 11–5, weekends 11–6.*

World Wildlife Museum. This former warehouse holds an incredible collection of 3,000 stuffed animals—thousands of bears, tigers, and wolves shot by hunters worldwide over the last century. Black jaguars, giraffes, orca whales, great white sharks, and every kind of sheep in the world are arranged by species. This is a mecca of fine taxidermy, with such tableaux as a 16-ft African crocodile lunging for a sable antelope. Many endangered or extinct species are preserved in death. Children can get very close to these animals, which are not behind glass. Some scenes, like one of a zebra and a lion fighting, are intense. *1245 W. Weber St., Stockton, tel. 209/465–2834. Admission: $5 adults, $3 children. Open Wed.–Sun. 9–5. MC, V.*

Sights to See

State Capitol. Sacramento is only 40 mi north of Stockton and well worth a visit. The State Capitol building was handsomely restored and structurally enhanced to withstand earthquakes in the late 1970s and early 1980s. Originally opened in 1869, the building is a model of how modern technology can help preserve the past. Highlights include the magnificent copper dome with a gold-leafed ball on top, the eight Corinthian columns on the front portico, the 1871 marble statue of Columbus and Queen Isabella, and the bizarre portrait of former governor Jerry Brown on the third floor. A pamphlet is available for self-guided tours. In the basement, a large, inexpensive cafeteria for state workers is open to the public. *State Capitol, at 10th and L Sts., Sacramento, tel. 916/324–0333. Open daily 9–5; free tours every hr 9–4.*

SAN FRANCISCO GIANTS

League: National • **Class:** Major League • **Stadium:** Pacific Bell Ballpark • **Opened:** 2000 • **Capacity:** 40,800 • **Dimensions:** LF: 335, CF: 404, RF: 307 • **Surface:** grass • **Season:** Apr.–early Oct.

STADIUM LOCATION: 24 Willie Mays Plaza, San Francisco, CA. 94107.

TEAM WEB SITE: www.sfgiants.com

GETTING THERE: The new downtown ballpark is at the intersection of Third and King streets, on China Basin, in the South of Market area. It is near several public transit systems serving the Bay region. It is adjacent to the Muni Metro line, within a block of five Muni bus routes, and just over one block from the Caltrain depot. It is about a 15–20 minute walk from BART and the Golden Gate, SamTrans, and AC Transit regional bus routes and the Ferry Terminal. Interstates 280, 80, and 101 provide access to the ballpark.

PARKING: The ballpark parking lots accommodate 5,000 cars and are just south of the park along Third Street (across Lefty O'Doul Bridge). Fee is $13.50. Up to 6,000 additional spaces available on streets and in lots within a 15-minute walk.

TICKET INFORMATION: Box 24 Willie Mays Plaza, San Francisco, CA 94107, tel. 415/972–2400.

PRICE RANGE: Lower box $23, arcade $18, upper box $18, upper reserved $15, bleachers $10.

GAME TIME: Night games, 7:05, 7:35 PM; day games, 12:35, 1:05 PM; gates open two hours before game.

TIPS ON SEATING: This may be the toughest ticket of the new millennium. The Giants expect to be sold out for the 2000 season before the first pitch is thrown. A limited number of bleacher seats will be available on the day of each game. Fans unable to get tickets may watch the game for free through knotholes in the right-field wall. The Giants dugout will be on the third-base side. The sun sets behind first base, with sun in the eyes of fans in the left-field seating.

SEATING FOR PEOPLE WITH DISABILITIES: The park is fully accessible to people with disabilities. There are elevators at all park entrances and ramps at Third and King Sts. and at Second and King Sts.

STADIUM FOOD: Candlestick had the best food in baseball and Pacific Bell Park continues the tradition. There are classy versions of basic stadium fare—hot dogs, sodas, popcorn, and peanuts—along with many San Francisco favorites, including clam chowder in a sourdough bowl, specialty ice creams, espresso, and garlic fries.

SMOKING POLICY: No smoking in seating areas.

TOURISM INFORMATION: San Francisco Visitor Information Center (900 Market St., lower level, San Francisco, CA 94102, tel. 415/391–2000).

San Francisco: Pacific Bell Ballpark

Mark Twain once said the coldest winter he ever spent was a summer in San Francisco. And he never watched an extra-inning game at Candlestick Park. Well, Mark Twain never met Bruce White either. White, a professor of aeronautical science and engineering at the University of California at Davis, was called in by the designers of San Francisco's 21st-century ballpark and given one really big job—stop the wind that threatened to blow baseball out of San Francisco. Apparently White and his colleagues have done it, and Pacific Bell Park is a considerably more comfortable baseball experience than its infamous predecessor.

The original ballpark design was to face the downtown San Francisco skyline. The UC Davis engineers found that prevailing winds would have blown directly into the seating bowl. The ballpark was turned 180 degrees to have the back of the ballpark absorb the wind. With the new configuration, left-handed sluggers can knock home runs over the right-field wall into the San Francisco Bay, and Giants fans can have views of the water from nearly every seat.

The $319-million ballpark was designed by HOK Sport of Kansas City, the folks who brought us Camden Yards, Coors Field, and Jacobs Field. The seats are green and the brick exterior is designed to fit into this funky waterfront, warehouse district. Fans are greeted by an 8-ft bronze statue of #24 Willie Mays blasting a ball off his bat, surrounded by 24 palm trees. And, yes, the address is 24 Willie Mays Plaza.

The whole picture is nearly perfect, and it very nearly never happened. Wind and money almost killed big-league baseball in San Fran-

cisco. When Candlestick Park opened in 1960 as the first major-league stadium built exclusively of reinforced concrete, it was hailed as a dazzling diamond palace. But the fans knew Candlestick was a mistake almost from day one. In the top of the ninth at the 1961 All-Star Game, Giants pitcher Stu Miller was blown off the mound by a wind gust and called for a balk. The Stick's reputation as baseball's wind tunnel was firmly established. The Giants failed in four attempts to get the voters to agree to fund a new ballpark to keep the Giants from bolting. Finally, the Giants owners bit the bullet and agreed to build the first privately financed major-league ballpark since Dodger Stadium in 1962. In March of 1996, the voters approved a ballpark plan for the China Basin area. And the next month, Pacific Bell stepped up to provide a big chunk of the cash for the right to put its name on the building.

After decades of failed attempts, San Francisco got it right: a privately financed ballpark in a historic downtown location with Willie Mays and palm trees to greet you at the door and Barry Bonds blasting home runs into the Bay. The only problem: how the heck to get a ticket. It's a good thing the designers included those knotholes in the right-field wall to give fans on the outside a peek at the action.

More San Francisco Baseball

Candlestick Park. Candlestick began the trend of building concrete, multi-use stadiums and locating them away from downtown. San Franciscans paid the price for four decades. This is the stadium local fans loved to hate. They built Candlestick Park on top of a landfill on Candlestick Point overlooking San Francisco Bay. The stadium was built right in the teeth of the prevailing westerly winds and would be cold even on the night of a hot summer day. They would reward fans with a pin if they lasted to the end of an extra-inning game here. The wind experts who made sure this sin would not be repeated at China Basin say the problem might have been mitigated if Candlestick had been built a few hundred yards to the north. The 1962 Giants with Willie Mays, Willie McCovey, Juan Marichal, and Orlando Cepeda took the New York Yankees to the very last out of the last inning of the seventh game of the World Series. The Beatles played here in 1966. An earthquake just before game three of the 1989 World Series did only limited damage. Now also known as 3COM Park, the stadium continues to be the home of the San Francisco 49ers of the National Football League. *From San Francisco, take the Cow Palace/Brisbane exit from U.S. 101. Go to 3rd Street and turn left over the freeway. Turn right on Jamestown Avenue to the main parking lot. Candlestick Point, tel. 415/468–3700.*

Seals Stadium. The California gold rush brought baseball to the West Coast, and organized ball playing has been here ever since. The California League was organized in 1885 with three teams from San Francisco. In 1903, San Francisco became a charter member of the Pacific Coast League and finished first in the league 12 times in the next 55 years, six times between 1915 and 1928. Many major-league-caliber ballplayers opted to stay in the Pacific Coast League during its heyday in the 1920s and 1930s because its longer, 200-plus-game schedule allowed them to make more money than major-league players. Joe DiMaggio hit in 61 consecutive games for the Seals in 1933 and led the league in runs batted in 1933 and 1934 before going east to the Yankees.

Seals owner Paul I. Fagan was a major advocate of the league's plans to be recognized as a third major league. It was a campaign that greatly changed baseball, as it brought major leagues to the West Coast. He invested heavily in turning Seals Stadium—built in 1931 and nicknamed "The Queen in Concrete"—into a first-class facility. The 1946 PCL champion Seals drew 670,563 fans, a minor-league single season record. In 1957, the New York Giants announced that they would move from the Polo Grounds to San Francisco for the 1958 season.

The Giants played in Seals Stadium in 1958 and 1959. When Candlestick Park opened in 1960, Seals Stadium was leveled.

Seats and light towers from Seals Stadium were shipped to Tacoma for that city's new Cheney Stadium in 1960. The famed ballpark was located on the northeastern edge of the Mission District at Bryant Street, 16th Street, Alameda Street, and Potrero Avenue. There is a shopping center there now without a historic marker. The Double Play bar and restaurant at 16th and Bryant has extensive photos and memorabilia from Seals Stadium.

Where to Stay

As with most major-league teams, no one hotel is used by the visiting team. Players frequently stay at the pricey Parc 55 and the Hilton in the Union Square area. If you're going to pay top dollar, consider the Marriott at 4th and Mission streets, which overlooks the beautiful Yerba Buena Gardens. But we advise you to take advantage of San Francisco's abundance of small hotels, many of them bargains. The San Francisco Lodging Guide, mailed from the Convention & Visitors Bureau (tel. 415/391–2000), includes 11 hotels with bargain package rates. Two reservation firms also offer discount lodgings: Preferred Hotel Rates (tel. 800/964–6835) and California Reservations (tel. 800/576–0003).

Britton Hotel. This pleasant bargain hotel is owned jointly with its three neighboring hotels (Best Western's Americania, Carriage House, and Flamingo Motor Inn; *see below*), and all are good deals for visiting families. The five-story brick Britton is the oldest and most expensive. Guests at any of the four hotels can use the large, tiled outdoor heated pool at the adjacent Americania Motor Lodge Best Western. The Britton has a free shuttle to the convention centers and Amtrak stations for out-of-city excursions. *112 7th St., at Mission St., San Francisco 94103, tel. 415/621–7001 or 800/444–5819, fax 415/626–3974. 79 rooms. Facilities: coffee shop, coin laundry, parking (fee). AE, D, DC, MC, V. $$*

Americania Motor Lodge Best Western. This white, salmon, and green hotel is built over the parking lot and outdoor pool. The lobby is cool, with California greenery. Most of the quiet rooms face an interior courtyard filled with hanging plants. The hotel offers a free shuttle to Union Square, where you can get the 9X express bus to 3COM/Candlestick Park. *121 7th St., San Francisco 94103, tel. 415/626–0200 or 800/444–5816, fax 415/626–3974. 142 rooms. Facilities: restaurant, pool, sauna, exercise room, coin laundry, parking (free). AE, DC, MC, V. $$*

Best Western Carriage House. This is the quietest of the quartet and includes a Continental breakfast delivered to your room. The rooms are standard size and decorated in an English-inn theme. Parking is $10 daily. *140 7th St., San Francisco 94103, tel. 415/552–8600 or 800/444–5817, fax 415/863–2529. 48 rooms. Facilities: parking (fee). AE, DC, MC, V. $$*

Best Western Flamingo Motor Inn. Everything in this Spanish-style motor lodge is small-scale. Its lobby, shared with the Britton, leads to an inner parking courtyard and two floors of rooms. Fresh flowers are put in rooms daily; the furnishings are contemporary. Guests have access to the pool and shuttle services of the Americania, across the street. The Flamingo shares the Britton's restaurant. *114 7th St., San Francisco 94103, tel. 415/621–0701 or 800/444–5818, fax 415/863–2529. 38 rooms. Facilities: parking (free). AE, DC, MC, V. $$*

Columbus Motor Inn. This 1970s-style motor lodge is along a bus route but away from the bustle of the city. Located between Fisherman's Wharf and North Beach, it has clean rooms with updated furnishings. *1075 Columbus Ave., at Francisco St., San Francisco 94133, tel. 415/885–1492, fax 415/928–2174. 45 rooms. Facilities: parking (free). AE, D, MC, V. $$*

The Grant Plaza. This clean, compact hotel is a longtime Chinatown bargain, so you'll need to reserve two months in advance for summer weekends. Its Super Saver Package includes free parking, breakfast, and a passport to the shop-filled arcades of Pier 39. The lobby is tiny and the rooms are standard size, with updated furniture, two double beds, and private baths. It's near the gate to Chinatown, but away from much of the street noise. *465 Grant St., San Francisco 94108, tel. 415/434–3883 or 800/472–6899, fax 415/434–3886. 72 rooms. Facilities: parking (fee). AE, D, MC, V. $$*

Where to Eat

Sheraton Palace Hotel's Garden Court Restaurant. Breakfast or tea at this hotel's glorious glass-domed restaurant is a rare and affordable treat. Families won't feel as comfortable at dinner. The room is massive, with crystal chandeliers, stained glass, and potted palms. Built in 1909, it is one of the lightest, prettiest places to eat in the city. The orange juice is fresh, and the hot chocolate is genuine, not a water-based mix. *2 New Montgomery St., at Market St., San Francisco, tel. 415/392–8600. AE, DC, MC, V. $$*

Lefty O'Douls. You get a flavor of old, bohemian San Francisco in this Irish cafeteria-restaurant. Lefty played for the New York Giants, Dodgers, and Yankees, and much Joe DiMaggio, Stan Musial, and Babe Ruth memorabilia, including Marilyn Monroe DiMaggio's driver's license, adorns the walls. There are old carved wooden booths and tables, and its cafeteria line includes such Irish favorites as corned beef and lamb shanks. A kid's plate for those 10 and under is $3.99. *333 Geary St., tel. 415/982–8900. MC, V. $*

Boudin Fisherman's Wharf Bakery. Boudin is one of the oldest bakeries in the country, and it turns out a terrific French sourdough bread. You can try its bread solo or as a foundation for sandwiches or an accompaniment to thick New England clam chowder. These fast-food restaurants also serve salads, pizza bread, and a few desserts. This site has outdoor seating only. Boudin's is also at tourist spots on Pier 39, Ghirardelli Square, and Macy's Cellar, all with indoor seating. *156 Jefferson St., between Mason and Taylor Sts., San Francisco, tel. 415/928–1849. AE, D, MC, V. $*

California Culinary Academy. You can eat here at the source of the city's great chefs. Dine in the Carême Room, a cavernous dining room where you watch the students work behind glass, or at the more casual Sonoma Grill downstairs, in a dark-wood-boothed pub-style room. Both serve excellent, unusual fare, with the grill concentrating on American themes and the dining room covering Continental cuisine. Reservations are suggested for the Carême Room, which accommodates bus tours. You'll have student waiters, and you'll see scores of students in their customary checked pants and white-coat uniform throughout the building. There's a take-out carrying beautiful salads, sandwiches, and desserts. *625 Polk St., San Francisco, tel. 415/771–3536 or 800/229–2433. AE, D, DC, MC, V. Closed weekends. $$*

Sears Fine Foods. This character-laden restaurant typifies old San Francisco. Waiters serve its signature silver-dollar Swedish pancakes, sourdough French toast, and baked apples in a storefront restaurant with a faded tearoom atmosphere. *439 Powell St., San Francisco, tel. 415/986–1160. No credit cards. No dinner. $*

Entertainments

Get an official San Francisco transit guide ($2) from the San Francisco Municipal Railway. It's also a good street map. You'll save money by buying one-day ($7) or three-day ($12) transit passes, good on all MUNI vehicles, including cable cars. It may save time to buy it by mail ahead of time, as most MUNI offices do not open until 9. The passes also give you discounts at various tourist destinations and museums. You can buy them at the San Francisco Visitor's Information Center (below street level at Powell and Market Sts.). Write or call MUNI (949 Presidio Ave., San Francisco 94115, tel. 415/673–6864). The map is sold at bookstores as well. San Francisco has 20 attractive green-and-gold public bathrooms throughout the city. The fee is 25¢, there's room for strollers inside, and the toilet and floor are scrubbed automatically after each use.

Cable Cars. Your children will be thrilled to use this exciting and noisy mode of transport. Don't wait in line forever with the tourists at the obvious turnarounds. Pick an intermediate stop, get collected, and help your children navigate onto the cars. The Powell-Hyde line has the best curves and hills. The cars require a token, which is available at major stops. No transfers are given. If you reach Nob Hill, you can see videos about the cars and view their operations underground at the free **Cable Car Museum** (1201 Mason St., tel. 415/474–1887; open Apr.–Oct. daily 10–6, Nov.–Mar. daily 10–5). Cable-car fare is $2, and they operate 7 AM–1 am.

Cartoon Art Museum. This visual delight is on the second floor of what was the *San Francisco Bulletin,* the city's oldest daily—now part of the *Examiner.* Teenagers with a love of *Mad* magazine and Zippy the Pinhead tend to be particularly attracted to this collection, which has art from magazines, ads, comics books, and videos displayed in one large room with a gift shop. Admission is free on the first Wednesday of the month. *814 Mission St., between 4th and 5th Sts., San Francisco, tel. 415/227–8666. Admission: $4 adults, $3 senior citizens and students, $2 ages 6 and up. Open Wed.–Fri. 11–5, Sat. 10–5, Sun. 1–5.*

Exploratorium. This wacky, imaginative hall of wondrous science experiments is in the imposing Palace of Fine Arts, at Marina Boulevard. The science center is extremely well used, to the point that many exhibits are under repair. There are bold, live demonstrations, including the dissection of cows' eyes. Major sections on sound, motion, heat, color, weather, electricity, and light are arranged throughout. Many children will not want to crawl through the Tactile Dome, which is pitch black and requires an extra fee. Much of the main floor is dim, but Angel's Cafe is cheery under the skylights. There is a great kid- and knowledge-oriented gift shop. You'll probably want to drive here or telephone for a cab, as it's not particularly convenient by public transport. Admission is free on the first Wednesday of the month. *3601 Lyon St., at Bay St., San Francisco, tel. 415/561–0360. Admission: $9 adults, $7 senior citizens and students, $5 ages 6–17, $2.50 ages 3–5. Open Labor Day–Memorial Day, Thurs.–Tues. 10–5, Wed. 10–9:30; Memorial Day–Labor Day Tues.–Sun. 10–5, Wed. 10–9:30. MC, V.*

Ferry to Alcatraz. There are wonderful views from this island of misery. The harshness of life in the prison, which held the country's toughest federal prisoners from 1934 to 1963, can awe children. Robert (the Birdman) Stroud, Al Capone, and "Machine Gun" Kelly slept here. It's a steep quarter-mile walk to the cellblocks on the self-guided tour. Those in wheelchairs or pushing strollers may want to use interactive computers to see the cellblocks by video through the Alcatraz Easy Access Program.

National Park Service rangers give short talks, and you can rent audiocassette tours ($3 adults, $1.50 ages 5–11). You'll need to reserve ferry tickets to the island at least a day in advance, as space often sells out. It's a 12-minute cruise each way. Boats depart every 45 minutes weekdays, every 30 minutes weekends. The time of the last departure to the island varies considerably during the year; call ahead to check. *Pier 41, San Francisco, tel. 415/773–1188 or 800/445–8880 (in CA). Admission: $11 adults, $5.75 children. Open daily 9:15–4:15. AE, MC, V.*

Golden Gate Ferry to Sausalito. This 30-minute ride is a great introduction to Bay living. After debarking, choose one of several restaurants with decks for a lunch overlooking Richardson Bay along Bridgeway, the city's main street. Children 12 and under ride free with a paying adult. The Red and White Fleet (tel. 415/447–0591; $5.50 adults, $2.75 children) also leaves from Pier 43½ on Fisherman's Wharf. *Ferry Bldg., foot of Market St., Embarcadero, San Francisco, tel. 415/923–2000. Fare: $5 adults, $4 children. Weekend family fares available; up to 2 children under age 13 are free, with adults paying full fare. MC, V.*

Golden Gate Park. This huge expanse of green space has dozens of attractions. Children are likely to enjoy visiting the historic **Children's Playground**, with its 1912 Herschel Spillman carousel, and watching the koi fish and drinking tea (or juice and soda) at the **Japanese Tea Garden** ($2 adults, $1.75 ages 6–12). Six varieties of tea are served at wooden tables from 10:30 to 5, and guests walk across bridges and enjoy the serene waterfalls, ponds, koi pools, and pagodas. The most convenient park entry points are at 8th and Fulton streets (north side) and 9th and Lincoln streets (south). Parking at meters is free on weekdays, $1 per hour on weekends and holidays. *Stanyan and Fulton Sts., San Francisco. tel. 415/221–1311.*

San Francisco Zoo. This impressive, large, and handsomely designed zoo is at the south end of Ocean Beach. It has a smaller feel because of its self-contained sections, such as Penguin Island, Koala Crossing, and Gorilla World. The white tiger and pygmy hippopotami are the zoo's stars. You can watch the lions eat Tuesday

through Sunday at 2. A separate **Children's Zoo** ($1; open daily June–Aug. 10:30–4:30, Sept.–May weekdays 11–4, weekends 10:30–4:30) for younger kids includes a petting park and an insect zoo. The entire zoo is free on the first Wednesday of the month. *Sloat Blvd., at Great Hwy., San Francisco, tel. 415/753–7083. Admission: $9 adults, $5 ages 12–15, $3 ages 6–11. Open daily 10–5.*

Steinhart Aquarium and California Academy of Sciences. These Golden Gate attractions are across an open amphitheater lot from the Japanese Tea Garden. The well-designed exhibition covers three wings. Fish swim around you in the peaceful blue Fish Roundabout tank, and there's a touch pool at its base, stocked with starfish. The alligator pool is fascinating. You can be on hand to watch the penguins, the seals, or the dolphins being fed. The aquarium admission also includes entry to the two buildings that make up the **Natural History Museum,** which contains a Safequake artificial earthquake. Guests stand on a floor plate that simulates the motion of a quake while viewing films and photographs of destruction caused by past quakes of similar intensity. There's also a large blow-up of a Pacific beach in the Wild California exhibit; an open, walk-through planetarium; and dinosaur reproductions. Admission is free on the first Wednesday of the month. A money-saving consideration is the $15 Explorer Pass to all Golden Gate Park attractions. *Golden Gate Park, San Francisco, tel. 415/750–7145. Admission to aquarium and museum: $8.50 adults, $5 ages 13–17 and senior citizens, $2 ages 4–12. Open June–Aug., daily 10–6, Sept.–May, daily 10–5.*

Strybing Arboretum. Children can enjoy walking through its Garden of Fragrance, testing their powers of smell. As the garden is aimed at people who are blind, visitors are permitted to touch the plants. Admission is free on the first Wednesday of the month. *Lincoln Way, at 9th Ave., San Francisco, tel. 415/661–1316. Donations appreciated. Open weekdays 8:30–4:30, weekends 10–5.*

Sights to See

Golden Gate Cookie Company. If you're in crowded, bustling Chinatown, find this alley 30 steps in from Jackson Street and step into this small storefront to watch fortune cookies being shaped by hand by two workers. (Ignore the hot-pink "FRENCH ADULT FORTUNE COOKIE" sign outside.) Most companies use automatic cookie folders, but this authentic shop does it the old-fashioned way on Rube Goldberg–like iron contraptions. Samples are given freely, and you can buy bargain bags of fortune and almond cookies for $4. *56 Ross Alley, between Jackson and Washington Sts., west of Grant Ave., San Francisco, tel. 415/781–3956. Open daily 10 AM–midnight.*

Golden Gate Bridge Walkway. You won't want to walk the entire 8,980-ft span to Marin County, but it can be exhilarating to stand over the bay. The hike across the bridge is on a pedestrian walkway that's about 1½ mi each way. It's blustery unless you get a rare, mild day. Free parking lots are at either end of the bridge, off Route 101. On the San Francisco side, take the last exit on the right (Vista Point) before the toll plaza. *Rte. 101, San Francisco, tel. 415/457–3110. Open daily 5 AM–9 PM.*

Muir Woods National Monument. You'll see the world's tallest trees in this Marin County redwood forest, with some exceeding 250 ft in height and 3,000 years in age. There are 6 mi of hiking trails here, but no picnicking. It's 17 mi northwest of San Francisco, reached by car across the Golden Gate Bridge and continuing north on S.R. 1. The Red and White ferry fleet, at Pier 41, also has boat-bus trips to Muir Woods. A free visitor center is open Memorial Day–Labor Day, daily 9–6, and Labor Day–Memorial Day, daily 9–5. *Muir Woods, tel. 415/388–2595. Open daily 8–dusk.*

Pier 39. More than 100 shops, two amusement arcades, sea lions, and a Victorian double-deck carousel ($3 per ride) attract families here. The most fun is ignoring the commercial activity and walking outside to the actual pier to watch the multitude of sea lions that have made this home since the 1989 earthquake. These huge lumps of mammal lie on wood platforms in the bay, barking and yawning. Many of the 600 sea lions migrate to the Channel Islands from June through August, but there always are some on hand. An underwater world takes visitors (for a fee) on a simulated dive through a fish-filled tank. Pier 39 is at the end of Fisherman's Wharf, which is filled with tourist shops. Adjacent parking lots are expensive—four hours for $25. If you eat at one of the pier's full-service restaurants, your waterfront parking tab is cut one hour for lunch, two hours for dinner. Pier 39 also contains a farmer's market (Friday 8–1), with California's great produce, especially its apricots and pistachios. *The Embarcadero and Beach St., San Francisco, tel. 415/981–7437. Open late June–early Sept., Mon.–Wed. 10:30–9:30, Thurs.–Sat. 10:30–10, Sun. 10:30–8:30; mid-Sept.–mid-June, Sun.–Thurs. 11–7, Fri.–Sat. 10:30–8:30.*

San Francisco Public Library. This modern main library is a beauty, with more than a million books and dozens of computers for your free use. Kids will find a special electronic discovery center and an expansive children's room. *Larkin and McAllister Sts., San Francisco, tel. 415/557–4400. Open Mon. 10–6, Tues.–Thurs. 9–8, Fri. 11–5, Sat. 9–5, Sun. noon–5.*

SAN JOSE GIANTS

League: California League • **Major League Affiliation:** San Francisco Giants • **Class:** A • **Stadium:** Municipal Stadium • **Opened:** 1942 • **Capacity:** 5,000 • **Dimensions:** LF: 340, CF: 400, RF: 340 • **Surface:** grass • **Season:** Apr.–Labor Day

STADIUM LOCATION: 588 E. Alma Ave., San Jose, CA 95112.

TEAM WEB SITE: www.sjgiants.com

GETTING THERE: From I-280, 10th St. exit to Alma Ave. Left on Alma, stadium is on left. Going north on Hwy. 101, take Tully Rd. exit east. Right on Senter Rd. and left on Alma Ave. Going south on 101, take Story Rd. exit east. Left on Senter Rd. and right on Alma Ave.

PARKING: Ample parking, $3.

TICKET INFORMATION: Box 21727, San Francisco, CA 95151, tel. 408/297–1435, fax 408/297–1453.

PRICE RANGE: Box seats $8; general admission $6 adult, $4 ages 4–10 and over 64, under 4 free.

GAME TIME: Weekdays 7:15 PM, Sat. 5 PM, Sun. 1:30 PM (Apr.–June) or 5 PM (July–Aug.); gates open 1½ hrs before game.

TIPS ON SEATING: 882 box seats; general admission seats excellent. Sit on first-base side to avoid sun in your eyes.

SEATING FOR PEOPLE WITH DISABILITIES: At field level between grandstand and bleachers on both first- and third-base sides.

STADIUM FOOD: Follow the white painted footprints out to **Turkey Mike's Baseball and BBQ** beyond third base. Here you'll find huge roast turkey drumsticks for $4 and a grilled abalone steak sandwich for $4. Pay $2 more for a dinner and add fruit, pasta, or potato salad. You can sit at the long picnic tables here and watch the game. There is chili for $2.50 and clam chowder for $3; if you want them in hollowed-out sourdough bowls, add $1.50. If you have any room left, there are ice-cream bars at $2 each.

SMOKING POLICY: Smoking prohibited in seating areas and on main concourse; allowed behind bleachers down first- and third-base lines.

VISITING TEAM HOTEL: Gateway Inn Best Western (2585 Seaboard Ave., San Jose, CA 95131, tel. 408/435–8800 or 800/528–1234).

TOURISM INFORMATION: San Jose Convention & Visitors Bureau (333 W. San Carlos St., San Jose, CA 95110, tel. 408/295–9600).

San Jose: Municipal Stadium

The art's the thing at San Jose's Municipal Stadium. Fans are greeted at the entrance by larger-than-life paintings of Babe Ruth, Brooks Robinson, and Roberto Clemente. For even more fun and a history of professional baseball in San Jose, follow the painted white footprints under the grandstand on the third-base side. As you walk the concourse, you will see the faded, painted pennants from minor-league teams of long ago. Once out from under the grandstand, you will find a huge, colorful mural with the logos of every current professional team, organized by league. A wonderful mural timeline beginning in 1891, when San Jose won the California State League, includes a list of San Jose Bees, the team nickname in the 1960s and '70s, who made it to the majors, including George Brett.

The food is as good as the art at Municipal Stadium. Just beyond the murals on the third-base side is Turkey Mike's Baseball & BBQ. "Turkey Mike" Donlin got his start in professional baseball in San Jose in the 1890s and hit .351 in 1903

for the New York Yankees before leaving baseball for Hollywood. His distinctive, turkeylike strut onto the field has been memorialized into great ballpark food, huge barbecued turkey drumsticks.

San Jose's 1942 Municipal Stadium is a fine example of the contribution the Works Progress Administration (WPA) made to baseball and municipal architecture. Municipal Stadium is typical of California League ballparks before the construction spree of the late 1980s and '90s. This is a solid, simple, WPA-era grandstand with excellent general admission seating. The dark-green benches have backs, providing comfort but limiting legroom. There are only 882 individual box seats. A modest press box sits at the top of the grandstand, with two pennants flying above. Bleacher seats stretch down both left- and right-field lines. As young families have streamed into this, the heart of the Silicon Valley, the city has upgraded Municipal Stadium to provide modern amenities to go along with the tradition this stadium represents. In recent years, the murals were added, the parking lot paved, and the bathrooms renovated. The stadium is uncovered, but a small orange canvas shades the grandstand seats on the first-base side.

There is plenty of fun here between innings as at most other minor-league ballparks. But we have never seen anything quite like the "Smash for Cash" contest at San Jose. Three players, each representing fans, throw balls and try to break the headlights of an old bread truck. Winners— both players and fans—get cash.

The setting is better than average, with a tree-covered city park across the street and behind the stadium entrance. The Santa Cruz Mountains dominate the landscape out beyond the outfield wall in center and right fields. Over the left-field fence is a huge, long-closed factory where Beechnut used to manufacture Lifesavers and baby food.

Where to Stay

Visiting Team Motel: Best Western Gateway Inn. This spacious motel offers guests Continental breakfast. The rooms are generous in size, and many face the large outdoor courtyard, which holds a large pool. The inn is a mile from the airport, but jet noise isn't a problem. Guests are shuttled free to Paramount's Great America amusement park. *2585 Seaboard Ave., San Jose 95131, tel. 408/435–8800 or 800/528–1234, fax 408/435–8879. 146 rooms. Facilities: outdoor pool, hot tub. AE, D, DC, MC, V. $$*

Airport Inn. This standard, two-story brick motel is quiet, although only a half mile from San Jose International Airport. Most rooms have two double beds. *1355 N. 4th St., San Jose 95112, tel. 408/453–5340, fax 408/453–5208. 194 rooms. Facilities: outdoor pool, coin laundry. AE, D, MC, V. $$*

Fairmont Hotel. This elegant downtown hotel has bargain weekend rates of $109 per double room. Otherwise, the 20-story deluxe high-rise is too pricey. The rooms are beautifully decorated, with thick carpets, prime city views, and free cable movies. *170 S. Market St., San Jose 95113, tel. 408/998–1900, fax 408/287–1648. 541 rooms. Facilities: 4 restaurants, pool, sauna, exercise room. AE, D, DC, MC, V. $$$*

Where to Eat

Rock 'N Tacos. Fish tacos sound weird but taste great. Healthy Mexican food is the draw at this brightly colored fast-food storefront—chicken burritos, "health-Mex" salads, and quesadillas. The tortillas and black beans are made without lard. You can get free refills on soft drinks, and the homemade chips are free. You perch on stools in the neon-decorated, green-Formica room. There's a sister restaurant (tel. 408/246–4500) across the street from the Winchester Mystery House at Town & Country Mall. *131 W. Santa Clara St., San Jose, tel. 408/993–8230. No credit cards. $*

The Old Spaghetti Factory. Part of a chain that renovates old buildings into engaging eateries, it serves typical American fare. Kids enjoy the pasta and the casual clutter of old signs and machinery in this former textile factory. There is a separate kids' menu. *51 N. San Pedro St., San Jose, tel. 408/288–7488. D, DC, MC, V. $*

Entertainments

Children's Discovery Museum of San Jose. This is among the best children's museums in the country. The bright, airy purple building has an imaginative array of hands-on games, all of which work. Children can climb on a fire truck, a Wells Fargo wagon, or a Model T, and sort mail in a post office. At the huge waterworks, children are the engineers, and they can run a Rube Goldberg contraption with tennis balls. You should plan on closing the museum, because you'll never get the kids to leave early. Parking is $2, and you should have singles or change for the automatic tellers. The museum is at the Technology Center stop of San Jose's light-rail system. *Woz Way and Auzerais St., San Jose, tel. 408/298–5437. Admission: $6 adults, $5 senior citizens, $6 ages 3–18, $5 ages 1–2. Open July–Aug., Mon.–Sat. 10–5, Sun. noon–5; Sept.–June, Tues.–Sat. 10–5, Sun. noon–5.*

Paramount's Great America. This movie-theme amusement park has five major areas, which feature five roller coasters, a *Days of Thunder* stock-car race, kiddie rides, and *Star Trek* characters roaming the grounds. You'll want to ride the 100-ft-tall double-decker

Carousel Columbia, with its 106 enameled, fiberglass replicas of classic carousel animals. You can choose a sea horse, an ostrich, a cat, or another rare carousel animal and watch scenes of American history as you whirl by. The Drop Zone 22-story free-fall ride and the 110-ft Ferris wheel are too intense for most children. There are casual restaurants, concerts, an IMAX theater, and an ice show. *2401 Agnew Rd., Santa Clara, tel. 408/988–1776. Admission: $34.99 ages 7 and up, $24.99 senior citizens, $19.99 ages 3–6; parking $6. Open Sun.–Fri. 10–9, Sat. 10 AM–11 PM. AE, MC, V.*

Raging Waters. This water park has 32 activities, with a good assortment for young children, including a lazy river. The toboggan rides, flume rides, and wave-machine "beach" require bathing suits. Cutoffs and long pants are forbidden. Nearby Lake Cunningham has windsurfing rentals, fishing, and boating. *2333 E. Tully Rd., Lake Cunningham Regional Park, San Jose, tel. 408/270–8000. Admission: $21.99 those taller than 42", $17.99 under 42". Open daily 10–7. AE, D, MC, V.*

Winchester Mystery House. This is overpriced but memorable. It's not wise to go on a hot day, as it's stuffy and kids will complain about the hour-long trek. This weird house and gardens, designed by haunted Sarah Winchester to ward off the spirits killed by Winchester rifles, can be fascinating. Guides take you through 110 of the house's 160 rooms. There is a Victorian garden, too. The tour arrangements make the gift shop and pricey concessions hard to avoid. The house is reached by Highway 280 south to Winchester Boulevard. *525 S. Winchester Blvd., San Jose, tel. 408/247–2101. Admission: $13.95 adults, $10.95 senior citizens, $9.95 ages 6–12. Open daily 9–5:30.*

Down the Coast

As you leave San Jose and drive down the coast toward Monterey, drive first to Santa Cruz (30 mi southwest) and then another 18 mi south to Castroville, which is artichoke country. Stop at a fruit stand for delicious, inexpensive strawberries and pistachio nuts. Monterey is another 15 mi south.

Santa Cruz Beach Boardwalk. Its 1924 roller coaster, Giant Dipper, is worth the ride. The boardwalk also contains a 1911 Charles I. D. Looff Carousel with expressive horses, a working brass-ring dispenser, and an 1894 pipe band organ. You can try to win a free ride by throwing a brass ring into a clown's mouth. There's a two-story miniature golf course in the Neptune's Kingdom indoor amusement center. Lot parking is $5; try for one of the quarters-only 10-hour meters on the street. After five on Monday and Tuesday in summer, "1907 Night" prices kick in, and rides are 50¢ each. *400 Beach St., Santa Cruz, tel. 831/426–5590. Admission free; rides $1.50–$3 each; all-day pass $18.95. Open daily 11–10. D, MC, V.*

Santa Cruz Mystery Spot. The attraction is hokey, but kids love it. This spot of woods appears to favor mind over matter, as odd gravity occurs here. Guides take you on a short walk into a redwood forest where you stand in a rustic cabin and feel a gravitational pull that appears to alter your ability to stand straight. Despite the signs, it can be difficult to find. *Branciforte Dr., 2½ mi north on Market St. off Rte. 17, Santa Cruz, tel. 831/423–8897. Admission: $4 adults, $2 ages 5–11. Open June–Aug., daily 9:30–8; Sept.–May, daily 9:30–5.*

Monterey Bay Aquarium. This is the largest aquarium in the nation, with a three-story underwater kelp forest. A new wing showcases sharks and barracuda in a Monterey Bay environment behind a 13-inch-thick window the size of a drive-in movie screen. You can view sea snakes, eels, and others poisonous creatures up close and personal. At the touch pool you can handle starfish, bat rays, and crabs. A jellyfish display is one of nearly 100 galleries exhibiting the world's sea life. Special tanks allow you to watch sea otters, and daily feeding shows are held for many creatures. On weekends, you may have to wait in line for tickets, which can be bought in advance from Monterey Bay hotels, for no service fee, or with a service fee from Bass ticket outlets or by calling the aquarium (in California) at 800/756–3737. The last tickets are sold at 5 daily. From the end of May through early September, WAVE shuttle buses ($1 daily) link the aquarium with parking garages and waterfront attractions. *886 Cannery Row, Monterey, tel. 831/648–4888. Admission: $15.95 adults, $12.95 senior citizens and ages 13–17, $6.95 ages 3–12. Open June 15–Sept. 2 and weekends year-round daily 9:30–6; Sept. 3–June 14, weekdays 10–6. AE, MC, V.*

Dennis the Menace Playground. Cartoonist Hank Ketchum donated the money for this wonderful free playground, just off Route 1. It has great slides, imaginative bridges, and a cushion of sand. An adjacent lake has paddleboats for rent. *El Estero, Monterey, tel. 831/372–8446. Open daily 10–dusk.*

30

DISNEYLAND AND HOLLYWOOD
LOS ANGELES, RANCHO CUCAMONGA, SAN BERNARDINO, LAKE ELSINORE

When you make the pilgrimage to Dodger Stadium in Los Angeles, don't neglect three great Single A California League parks in the outer suburbs of Rancho Cucamonga, Lake Elsinore, and San Bernardino. You may want to base yourself east of Los Angeles, in Anaheim, home of Disneyland, to take advantage of the lodging and park discounts.

Start with a Dodgers game in Chavez Ravine, where you see palm trees, the Elysian hills, and the San Gabriel Mountains in the distance. This 1962 ballpark has produced a winning franchise, packing in fans and championships ever since the Dodgers left Brooklyn's Ebbets Field for California sunshine. You'll battle traffic here, so come early. Universal Studios and Disneyland are fun, exhausting, and expensive. You can drive to Griffith Park Observatory for a close-up view of the famed HOLLYWOOD sign, or to the La Brea Tar Pits for free tours of the grounds. A stroll down Santa Monica's Municipal Pier provides endless people-watching amusement at no charge.

East 38 mi from Los Angeles on Interstate 10 is the emerging city of Rancho Cucamonga and its spectacular miniversion of Baltimore's Camden Yards stadium. This is a gorgeous tree-lined park, with handsome seating and concourse. The Quakes' mascots are clever. The fans pack this stadium in record numbers, so you'll need to buy tickets in advance.

San Bernardino is 20 mi east of Rancho Cucamonga. Proud of its Western roots, the city brought a Western theme to its stadium: the park, named the Ranch, has adobe walls adorned by red tiles, and the team is the Stampede. The management of this club has reached out to all cultures in this city, drawing a mix of fans that is the most diverse we've seen in baseball—a healthy sign.

Forty miles south of Rancho Cucamonga is Lake Elsinore, a city of 25,000 that built a $15-million stadium in the foothills of the Ortega Mountains to meet the needs of the new families moving here from Los Angeles and San Diego. The lake provides good recreation.

LOS ANGELES DODGERS

League: National League • **Class:** Major League • **Stadium:** Dodger Stadium • **Opened:** 1962 • **Capacity:** 56,000 • **Dimensions:** LF: 330, CF: 400, RF: 330 • **Surface:** grass • **Season:** Apr.-early Oct.

STADIUM LOCATION: 1000 Elysian Park Ave., Los Angeles, CA 90012.

TEAM WEB SITE: www.dodgers.com

Los Angeles, Rancho Cucamonga, San Bernadino, Lake Elsinore

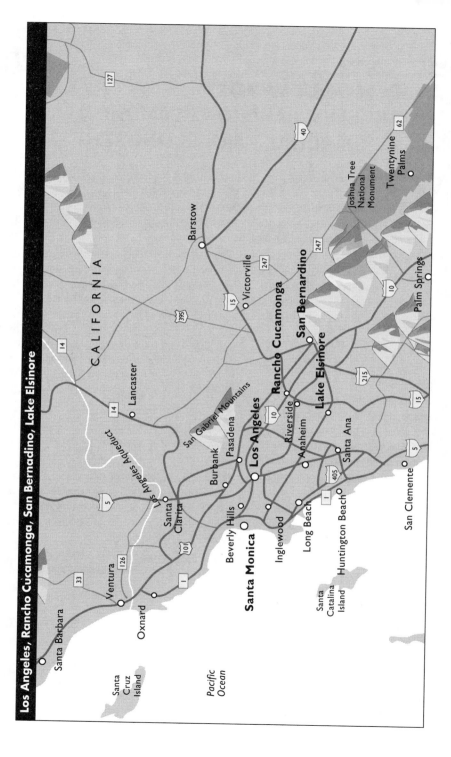

GETTING THERE: From I–5 southbound, take Stadium Way exit. Go left on Stadium Way. Take quick left onto Academy Rd. and equally quick left back onto Stadium Way. Turn left on Elysian Park Ave. From Rte. 101 northbound, take Alvarado exit and turn right. Take right on Sunset and go 2 mi. Turn left on Elysian Park Ave. and go I mi. From Rte. 110 northbound, take Dodger Stadium exit. Turn left on Stadium Way. Turn right on Elysian Park Ave. Call 800/266–6883 for bus information.

PARKING: Ample parking, $6. Color of number on baseball-shape light stand in lot should match color of level on which you sit.

TICKET INFORMATION: Box 51100, Los Angeles, CA 90051-0100, tel. 323/224–1471, fax 323/224–2609.

PRICE RANGE: Field (yellow) and loge (orange) box seats $16 and $12; blue level reserved seats $13 and $8; red level top deck $6 adults, $3 ages 4–12; pavilion (bleachers) $6 adults, $3 ages 4–12.

GAME TIME: Mon., Tues., Thurs.–Sun. 7:05 PM; Wed. 7:35 PM; day games 1:05 PM; gates open 90 min before game.

TIPS ON SEATING: In pavilion bleacher seats, no alcohol allowed. Loge seats are equivalent to club-level seats at newer stadiums at half the price.

SEATING FOR PEOPLE WITH DISABILITIES: Available on top deck (red), loge (orange), and reserved (blue) levels. Special parking in lots 2, 3, and 4.

STADIUM FOOD: The healthiest meal—the teriyaki chicken bowl at **Yoshinoya**—is the best: rice, vegetables, and chicken for $5. (There are a beef bowl and a vegetable bowl, too). Garden salads and antipasto salads are available and Buffalo wings are $4.50. There are several **Carl Jrs.** within the park for the usual fast-food fare, as well as TCBY Yogurt and Pizza Hut. The famed Dodger Dog sticks out beyond the bun by several inches on each end but isn't otherwise notable ($3). A good buy is the kid's meal at the **Dodger Dog** stands. The hot dog is full-sized and is accompanied by chips, a drink, and an activity book.

SMOKING POLICY: Smoking prohibited except in several small designated smoking areas on concourse.

TOURISM INFORMATION: Los Angeles Convention & Visitors Bureau (633 West 5th St., Suite 6000, Los Angeles, CA 90071, tel. 213/624–7300 or 800/366–6116).

Los Angeles: Dodger Stadium

When the Dodgers arrived in Los Angeles from Brooklyn in 1958, they began what has become one of the most successful franchises in baseball history. In 1978 the Dodgers were the first team to draw more than 3 million fans in a single season. Nine times the World Series has been played here, with the Dodgers' becoming World Champions five times since arriving in Los Angeles.

From the very start of the Pacific Coast League, Los Angeles had one and sometimes two top teams. In 1921, William K. Wrigley, Jr., the chewing gum executive, bought the Los Angeles Angels and built a new stadium. The $1 million double-deck Wrigley Field was opened in 1927

with capacity for 22,000 fans. After the 1956 season, the Chicago Cubs traded the Angels and Wrigley Field to Walter O'Malley, the owner of the Brooklyn Dodgers, for the Dodgers' Ft. Worth, Texas, ball club. When the Dodgers moved to California, they played in the Los Angeles Coliseum rather than Wrigley Field. Before being leveled, Wrigley Field hosted the Los Angeles Angels, the American League expansion team.

The Los Angeles Coliseum was completed in 1923 and enlarged for the 1932 Olympics. It was more suited for football and track and field than baseball. With a baseball seating capacity of 93,600, it was a shock to the Dodgers, coming from the intimate 31,497-seat Ebbets Field. Dodgers pitcher Clem Labine pretty much summed up the sentiments of his teammates: "Nobody understood those freeways, and nobody could deal with that ballpark." But almost 2 million people came to watch the Dodgers play in 1958, twice the previous year's attendance at Ebbets Field.

The Dodgers were forced to play four seasons in the Coliseum as landslides and the law stalled construction of their new stadium. This was the first major-league park built by private funds since Yankee Stadium in 1923. The massive parking lot seemed appropriate for car-crazy California, holding 16,000 cars on 21 terraced lots at five different levels. Seating levels and parking levels were color-coordinated for fan convenience.

Architect Emil Praeger designed the ballpark to seat 56,000, with the ability to enclose the outfield and raise capacity to more than 80,000. Dodger management deserves enormous credit for not succumbing to greed and turning Dodger Stadium into just another concrete doughnut.

The huge screen in left field produces a picture of spectacular quality. There is an older, more traditional scoreboard in right field. The view beyond the stadium is impressive, including palm trees and the Elysian Hills, with the San Gabriel Mountains in the distance. In memory of Ebbets Field, Dodger Stadium is located on Elysian Park Avenue.

Unlike at most major-league stadiums, especially of this era, you can get a hot dog and a drink on the concourse and still see the game.

In southern California, it's traffic, not rain, that is the major concern about whether or not you are going to see a game. The Dodgers haven't had a rain-out in Los Angeles since April 21, 1988. You'll notice many of the locals come into the park a few innings late and leave early, a practice baffling to East Coast baseball fans. Maybe it's to beat the traffic.

Where to Stay

Best Western Dragon Gate Inn. This small three-floor hotel is in Chinatown, just a mile from Dodger Stadium. There is a free Continental breakfast. Parking is inexpensive, about $2.50 per day. *818 N. Hill St., Los Angeles 90012, tel. 213/617–3077 or 800/528–1234, fax 213/*

680–3753. 50 rooms. Facilities: 2 restaurants, parking (fee). AE, D, DC, MC, V. $$

Anaheim Marriott. This fresh, California-look hotel is two blocks from Disney, with a free continuous shuttle. Its "Special to Disneyland" package is a good buy, including two adult tickets to Disneyland and free breakfast for two people. The offer is good for two adults and three children under 18. *700 W. Convention Way, Anaheim 92802, tel. 714/750–8000 or 800/228–9290, fax 714/750–9100. 1,033 rooms. Facilities: 3 restaurants, indoor and outdoor pools, hot tubs, saunas, coin laundry. AE, D, DC, MC, V. $$*

Metro Plaza Hotel. This popular four-story Chinatown hotel is a mile from Dodger Stadium. Because of its low prices, summer bookings go fast. Most rooms are standard doubles, but a few singles are available. *711 N. Main St., Los Angeles 90012, tel. 213/680–0200 or 800/223–2223, fax 213/620–0200. 82 rooms. Facilities: restaurant, free parking. AE, D, DC, MC, V. $$*

Westin Bonaventure. City travel and tourist buses frequent this huge downtown convention hotel, which is 35 stories tall. The corporate tower suites, with a king-size bed and a queen-size sofa bed, are the best for families. It's worth visiting the revolving lounge for the terrific view of the city. The hotel is 2 mi from the ballpark. *404 S. Figueroa St., Los Angeles 90071, tel. 213/624–1000 or 800/228–3000, fax 213/612–4800. 1,462 rooms. Facilities: 5 restaurants, outdoor pool, parking (fee). AE, D, DC, MC, V. $$$*

Where to Eat

Philippe's Original. An unbeatable French-dip sandwich with its own terrific mustard is the bedrock of this longtime eatery. The sliced beef sandwich is served alongside a bowl of salty beef broth for dipping. Sit at a wooden booth or table, or buy sandwiches to take out. There also are French-dip lamb, pork, and ham sandwiches and great baked apples. Coffee is 10¢. *1001 N. Alameda St., Los Angeles, tel. 213/628–3781. No credit cards. $*

Carney's. This former railroad dining car dishes out superlative hot dogs, hamburgers, and chocolate-dipped frozen bananas. There are sandwiches and tacos, but walk through the grill line and go for the $2 Chicagoan hot dog or a $2.25 hamburger. The small frozen banana ($1) is more than enough dessert. *12601 Ventura Blvd., Studio City, tel. 818/761–8300; 8351 Sunset Blvd., Hollywood, tel. 323/654–8300. No credit cards. $*

Clifton's Brookdale Cafeteria. This is one of five Clifton's cafeterias in the city, all dispensing nostalgia food and good value. The huge facility, seating 500 eaters on three floors, is decorated with a California redwood theme. Many items served today, like the coconut, raisin, and walnut "millionaire pie," were on its original menu in 1935. *648 S. Broadway, Los Angeles, tel. 213/627–1673. D, MC, V. $*

The Farmer's Market. More than 100 ethnic food stands, from Cajun to Bolivian, are sprinkled throughout Los Angeles's famed produce market. You can sample while you walk or eat at the outdoor cafés. *6333 W. 3rd St., Los Angeles, tel. 323/933–9211. $*

Nate 'n Al's. The bustling deli, decorated in 1972-era earth tones, has four rows of booths, plus table service. The blintzes, lox, and bagels are the best in their class. The corned beef sandwiches are overstuffed, and halves are available. Children like the hot dogs with baked beans and the potato pancakes. *414 N. Beverly Dr., Beverly Hills, tel. 310/274–0101. AE, MC, V. $*

Pink's Famous Chili Dogs. Chili dog and hamburger heaven have been found here since 1939, first from a pushcart and now in a restaurant under a flashing pink neon sign. There are 25 varieties of hot dogs (including Turkey dogs), plus tamales, burritos, and a pastrami Reuben dog. For vegetarians, there's a guacamole dog. Also sold are strong, nonalcoholic brewed sodas, in strawberry, black cherry, raspberry, and peach. Check out its Wall of Fame, with photos of Pink's customers such as Jay Leno and Diana Ross. *709 N. La Brea Ave., at Melrose Ave., Hollywood, tel. 323/931–4223. No credit cards. $*

Entertainments

Disneyland. Children can have a splendid day of fun if the park is done in moderation. To save time and money, pre-purchase your discount tickets at AAA. Get to the park early and head first for Fantasyland, Critter Country, and Pirates

of the Caribbean. Skip Toontown—the attractions can't handle crowds. The train around the park is a restful interlude. Eat lunch early, around 11, to avoid lines. It's hard to pull the children away, but take an afternoon break, return to your hotel for the pool and, for younger children, a nap. Go back to the park around four, finish the essential rides, and reserve a table at an outdoor restaurant on the night parade route. This gives you comfortable seating and a slight elevation. It's good to rent a stroller, even for five-year-olds. *1313 Harbor Blvd., Anaheim, tel. 714/781–4565. Admission: $39 adults, $29 ages 3–11, $37 senior citizens. Open daily 9 AM–about 10 PM; closing times vary.*

Gene Autry Western Heritage Museum. Children can dress in Western garb and ride play horses in this celebration of things Western. There are cowboy movies, photos of real pioneers, and artifacts of Americans' western trek. A children's section has saddles to play on. It's across from the zoo in Griffith Park. *4700 Western Heritage Way, Los Angeles, tel. 323/667–2000. Admission: $7.50 adults, $5 senior citizens and students; $3 ages 2–12. Open Tues.–Sun. 10–5.*

George C. Page Museum of La Brea Discoveries. You can watch fossils from the pits being cleaned and identified and a 15-minute film that explains the ice-age finds. Parking is $5 with a stamp. *5801 Wilshire Blvd., Los Angeles, tel. 323/936–2230. Admission: $6 adults, $3.50 senior citizens and students; $2 ages 5–12; free 1st Tues. of month; parking (fee). Open Tues.–Sat. 10–5.*

La Brea Tar Pits. More than 600 species of Pleistocene animals and plants have been uncovered in this section of Hancock Park. Kids are fascinated to see how the animals were caught when they tried to drink water. *Wilshire Blvd. and Curson Ave., Los Angeles, tel. 323/857–6311. Observation pit open weekends 11–2; free guided tours Wed.–Sun. at 1.*

Los Angeles Zoo. This older, sprawling zoo in Griffith Park emphasizes African animals. In the large aviary you can see a World of Birds show. The Zoo Safari Train is an extra $3 for adults and $1 for children. Throughout the park are six small restaurants, several of which offer shade. Ticket sales stop at 4 PM, and the animals are

taken from view starting at 4:30. *5333 Zoo Dr.,
Golden Gate (I–5) and Ventura Freeways (Rte.
134), Los Angeles, tel. 323/644–6400. Admission:
$8.25 adults, $3.25 ages 2–12, $5.25 senior citi-
zens; parking free. Open daily 10–5.*

Universal Studios. This park is a visual and
entertainment delight, with movie characters
and props throughout. Be warned that children
five and under may be frightened by the earthquake, King Kong, floods, avalanche, and great
white shark that threaten you on the back-lot
tram tour. The tram tours end at 4:15. Be prepared to bail out before boarding other rides,
such as "Back to the Future" and "Jurassic Park,"
which may be too scary for younger children.
The theme shows are popular, so study the
daily schedule and arrive five minutes early so
you won't be turned away. It's fun to have lunch
with Laurel and Hardy and other costumed
stars at the Studio Commissary. A warning—
you can't use credit cards at 14 of the 16
restaurants. *Lankershim Blvd. and Hollywood
Freeway (U.S. 101), Universal City, tel. 818/508–
9600. Admission: $39 adults, $29 ages 3–11,
$34 senior citizens; parking $6. Open May 25–
June 14, 9–8; June 15–June 28, 8 AM–10 PM; June
29–Aug. 18, 7 AM–11 PM; Aug. 19–May 24, 9–7.
AE, D, MC, V.*

Sights to See

Griffith Park Observatory and Planetarium. To
get a great view of the city and to see the 50-ft
HOLLYWOOD sign on Mt. Cahuenga, drive up a
hill and park in front of this observatory. You'll
recognize the Art Deco building from dozens of
movies. You can use the planetarium's telescope

or view its array of stars every summer night
from dusk to 9:45. The Hall of Science and the
observatory are free; the planetarium has daily
star and laser shows for a fee. *Los Feliz Ave., Los
Angeles, tel. 323/664–1191. Admission: planetarium $4 adults, $3 senior citizens, $2 ages 5–12;
laser shows $7 adults, $6 ages 5–12. Open Tues.–
Fri. 2–10, weekends 12:30–10.*

**Richard M. Nixon Presidential Library and
Birthplace.** Skip the Ronald Reagan museum in
Simi Valley (tel. 805/522–8444), which is cold
and unappealing. Instead, come to Yorba Linda
for an admirably honest portrayal—warts and
all—of a complex and difficult man. Children
respond to the birthplace cottage and the
grounds. The Nixon museum has a gift shop
with a sense of humor—it sells a birthplace
birdhouse—and offers baseball memorabilia.
Richard and Patricia Nixon are buried between
the museum and the cottage. *18001 Yorba
Linda Blvd., Yorba Linda, tel. 714/993–3393.
Admission: $5.95 adults, $4.95 military, $3.95
senior citizens and students, $2 ages 8–11, free
under 7. Open Mon.–Sat. 10–5, Sun. 11–5.*

Santa Monica Municipal Pier. Its restored
carousel is worth a weekend visit, but some of
the other games and rides are shabby. Several
ride housings have been rebuilt and repainted,
however, and public bathrooms have been
improved. The city's Main Street and Third
Street Promenade offer nice bookstores, street
art, and coffeehouses. The pier is about 20 mi
southwest of downtown Los Angeles. *200
Santa Monica Pier, at Colorado Ave., Santa Monica, tel. 310/458–8900. Carousel: 50¢ adults, 25¢
children; open weekends 10–5.*

RANCHO CUCAMONGA QUAKES

League: California League • **Major League Affiliation:** San Diego Padres • **Class:** A • **Stadium:**
The Epicenter • **Opened:** 1993 • **Capacity:** 6,631 • **Dimensions:** LF: 330, CF: 400, RF: 330 • **Surface:** grass • **Season:** Apr.–Labor Day

STADIUM LOCATION: 8408 Rochester Ave., Rancho Cucamonga, CA 91730

TEAM WEB SITE: www.rcquakes.com

GETTING THERE: From Los Angeles, take I–10E to I–15N to Foothill Blvd., exit left for less than 1 mi.
Take left on Rochester Ave. to parking lot. Epicenter is in Rancho Cucamonga Sports Complex.

PARKING: Available throughout Sports Complex, $3.

TICKET INFORMATION: Box 4139, Rancho Cucamonga, CA 91729, tel. 909/481–5252, fax 909/481–5005.

PRICE RANGE: Superbox $8; field box $7; box $6; view $4.50; terrace $3; café $5; club $5.

GAME TIME: Mon.–Sat. 7:15 PM, Sun. 1:15 (Apr.–mid-June) or 5:15 (mid-June–Sept.); gates open 75 min before game.

TIPS ON SEATING: Call ahead and order reserved tickets; most games sold out. $4.50 view seats are fine. $5 café seating is good.

SEATING FOR PEOPLE WITH DISABILITIES: In two superbox sections just behind dugouts and in cafés.

STADIUM FOOD: Fruit and vegetable trays are the best tickets here. For $3, your children can snack on a variety of good California fruits. For $3, try the vegetables. The chicken burrito, at $3.50, is worth it. The french fries actually are potato wedges, at $2.50. It's most pleasant to sit at one of the **outdoor cafés,** along each base line. Concession stands on the main concourse include an **espresso shop** with nine concoctions, including good hot chocolate. For bigger appetites, there's the **Sausage House** with spicy hot dogs, brats, burgers, a meatball grinder, and a sub sandwich. A chicken sandwich is relatively pricey at $5.

SMOKING POLICY: Smoking prohibited in seating areas; permitted only in main concourse behind both cafés.

VISITING TEAM HOTEL: Best Western Heritage Inn (8179 Spruce Ave., Rancho Cucamonga, CA 91730, tel. 909/466–1111 or 800/528–1234).

TOURISM INFORMATION: Ontario Convention & Visitors Bureau (421 N. Euclid Ave., Ontario, CA 91762, tel. 909/984–2450 or 800/455–5755).

Rancho Cucamonga: The Epicenter

Drive due east from Los Angeles on I-10 for about an hour. Head north on I-15 for a bit and turn off at the emerging suburban city of Rancho Cucamonga. Cucamonga is the "land of many waters" in the language of the native people who first settled here. These waters later fed some of the largest vineyards in the world. They now feed mostly suburban sprawl, but Rancho Cucamonga isn't all ticky-tacky. Here lies the Epicenter, one of the finest little baseball parks in all of America. It's a miniature of Baltimore's Camden Yards, deep green elegance and all. Trees—palm and others—line your walk from the nicely landscaped parking lot. Beautiful softball fields with aluminum bench seating surround the Epicenter.

This is California-style architecture at its best, with a handsome white stucco exterior. Designed by Grillias-Pirc-Rosier-Alves of Irvine, six large glass and dark-green tile arches flank a large, central arched entryway. As you pass through the turnstiles, you're greeted by a life-size statue of Jack Benny, complete with violin.

The Quakes, who play at the Epicenter in Cucamonga, have a huge green dinosaur mascot named Tremor, the Rallysaurus. When it turned out the 6-ft, 7-inch Tremor was too scary for some of the youngest Quake fans, the club added a smaller little brother named Aftershock. According to the coloring book sold in the excellent gift shop at the entrance to the stadium, Tremor was a baseball-playing Rallysaurus who was swallowed up during an earthquake 2 million years ago and awoke in a recent earthquake in time to be named mascot for the Quakes' inaugural season. These folks aren't afraid to have a little fun with California's number one threat.

The city-owned stadium sits in the valley with a stunning view of the towering San Gabriel Mountains in the background. The interior is every bit as good as the exterior, with dark-green tiles, fence, and hand rails nicely setting off the white stucco. The seats are all wide and close to the Class A California League action.

While the concourse access to food and bathroom facilities is wide and attractive, it is under the seating area and requires fans to miss the action when they go for food and drinks. There is a wonderful "Quakes Fun Zone" on the concourse that has games only for little kids but no large grassy area to really let off steam on. The scoreboard measures the speed of each pitch.

The main problem with the Epicenter is that this $20-million stadium was too small from the day it opened on April 8, 1993, with room for only 4,648 fans. In 1994, they added two not completely satisfactory bleacher areas out past each café. In 1995 they very successfully added almost 500 superbox seats near home plate. There are now 6,615 seats. The lesson here is clear—if you build a stadium as fine as the Epicenter, plan on the fact that people will come in big numbers.

Where to Stay

Visiting Team Motel: Best Western Heritage Inn. This attractive adobe hotel, built in 1992, has a red-tile roof and good views of the San Gabriel Mountains. The grounds are nicely landscaped, and most of the fresh, airy rooms have two queen-size beds. Guests receive a free Continental breakfast. *8719 Spruce Ave. (Rte. 66), Rancho Cucamonga 91730, tel. 909/* 466–1111 or 800/682–7829, fax 909/466–3876. 117 rooms. Facilities: outdoor pool, hot tub exercise room, spa, coin laundry. AE, D, DC, MC, V. $$

Where to Eat

Magic Lamp Inn. This family-owned restaurant specializes in beef and seafood. Its homemade soups are special and the weekday lunch buffet is a bargain. There is a children's menu. *8189 Foothill Blvd. (Rte. 66), Rancho Cucamonga, tel. 909/981–8659. AE, D, MC, V. $$*

Entertainments

Scandia Family Fun Center. There are 17 rides, 16 baseball pitching machines, miniature golf, and a speedway at this roadside amusement park. You can see the blue-and-white roller coaster from I–15. The bumper boats are fun, but the Scandia Screamer coaster is too jolting for kids under 10. The kiddie rides are more creative than usual, and the Little Dipper roller coaster is fun. You can buy individual tickets for $1 each. *1155 S. Wanamaker Ave., 1 mi south of I–10, at I–15, Ontario, tel. 909/390–3092. Admission: $17.95 persons 54" tall and over, $13.95 children under 54"; $9.95 children under 36". Open Sun.–Thurs. 10 AM–11 PM, Fri.–Sat. and holidays 10 AM–1 AM.*

SAN BERNARDINO STAMPEDE

League: California League • **Major League Affiliation:** Los Angeles Dodgers • **Class:** A • **Stadium:** The Ranch • **Opened:** 1996 • **Capacity:** 5,000 • **Dimensions:** LF: 330, CF: 410, RF: 330 • **Surface:** grass • **Season:** Apr.–Labor Day

STADIUM LOCATION: Between Mill St. and Rialto Ave. and between E and G Sts.

TEAM WEB SITE: www.stampedebaseball.com

GETTING THERE: From Los Angeles, take I–10 east to I–215 north, right on 2nd St. to G St., then right to stadium.

PARKING: Ample parking, $3.

TICKET INFORMATION: Box 1806, San Bernardino, CA 92402, tel. 909/888–9922, fax 909/888–5251.

PRICE RANGE: Superbox $7; field box $6; upper box $5; general admission $4 adults, $3 children and senior citizens.

GAME TIME: Mon.–Sat. 7:05 PM, Sun. 2:05 PM (Apr.–mid-June) and 5:05 PM (mid-June–Sept.); gates open 1 hr before game.

TIPS ON SEATING: Best bargain seats are in upper boxes. From first-base side, you can see downtown. On third-base side (home team dugout), you have sun at your back. **Boot Hill** is a grass area beyond left-field outfield fence.

SEATING FOR PEOPLE WITH DISABILITIES: Throughout stadium.

STADIUM FOOD: The roasted ears of corn are particularly great. Other best bets are the $5–$8 meals from the grill that include either a chicken or rib sandwich or hamburger, plus potato salad and baked beans. There are also pork chop sandwiches. Don't miss the home-baked extra-large chocolate chip and peanut butter cookies, for $1.50. Sunday is 2-for-1 hot dog day, and Wednesday nights are "buck beverage" nights with all 12-ounce drinks priced at $1.

SMOKING POLICY: Smoking not allowed in seating area but allowed in designated areas.

VISITING TEAM HOTEL: Radisson Hotel & Convention Center (295 N. E St., San Bernardino, CA 92401, tel. 909/381–6181 or 800/333–3333).

TOURISM INFORMATION: San Bernardino Convention & Visitors Bureau (201 N. E St., San Bernardino, CA 92401, tel. 909/889–3980 or 800/867–8366).

San Bernardino: The Ranch

Just 20 mi east of Rancho Cucamonga and in the same county is San Bernardino, a very different place. San Bernardino has roots. It has an older, more culturally and economically diverse population than the new suburban cities nearby.

You wouldn't expect to see a fancy 1990s HOK Sport–designed stadium here. And we didn't. In 1935, the federal Works Progress Administration (WPA) built a fine ballpark—Perris Hill Park—on the edge of town. In 1941 San Bernardino fielded a team in the California League. The San Bernardino team did not finish the 1941 season, and the California League did not go back to San Bernardino until 1987. The returning San Bernardino Spirit found a remodeled aluminum-bench and blue-plastic-seat stadium renamed Fiscalini Field on the site of Perris Hill Park. Ken Griffey, Jr. tore through here in 1988, batting an impressive .338 in 58 games before moving up to Double A baseball. The stadium is a standard 1980s Single A stadium, but the view is terrific, with the building surrounded by tall trees and taller hills. This was the only stadium we found with a violet neon ELKS lodge sign set against a mountain over the left-field fence.

We enjoyed Fiscalini Field, but now only local and college baseball is played on the Highland Avenue site. In 1995 San Bernardino signed on as a Los Angeles Dodgers farm team and followed the lead of several of its California League rivals, bringing in HOK Sport of Kansas City, the architects who designed Camden Yards. The $13-million stadium opened August 12, 1996. It was designed to look like the 18th-century Spanish missions that were instrumental in the settlement of this region, with the outside walls made of adobe and red tiles.

The theme is now Western. The team nickname has been changed to Stampede, and the stadium is called the Ranch. A grassy area beyond the outfield fence in left field is called Boot Hill. The mascot is a giant bug with a baseball head—the Stampede Bug.

In most places, unfortunately, baseball as a spectator sport has become largely a white person's game. We don't know what they are doing in San Bernardino, but major-league baseball should find out. The lively crowd the night we attended was the most culturally diverse we saw anywhere on our travels.

Where to Stay

Radisson Hotel & Convention Center. This imposing 12-story downtown hotel is near City Hall and across the street from the grand Harris Department Store. Parking is free, and the hotel offers family packages that include four full breakfasts for $89 in a standard-size room. *295 N. E St., San Bernardino 92401, tel. 909/381–*

6181 or 800/333–3333, fax 909/381–5288. 231 rooms. Facilities: restaurant, hot tub, health club. AE, D, DC, MC, V. $$

Comfort Inn. This two-story peach-stucco motel is in a commercial strip of hotels and restaurants. All of its rooms have refrigerators, microwave ovens, and hair dryers. Guests receive a free Continental breakfast. The inn is 8 minutes south of the ballpark. 1909 S. Business Center Dr., at the Waterman Ave. exit (north) off I–10. San Bernardino 92408, tel. 909/889–0090 or 800/424–6423, fax 909/889–0090. 50 rooms. Facilities: outdoor pool. AE, D, DC, MC, V. $

Super 8 Motel–Downtown. This ordinary beige-concrete hotel is convenient to the ballpark and offers guests free use of its laundry machines. The rooms for four have two double beds. Extra rollaways are $4 each. 777 W. 6th St., San Bernardino 92410, tel. 909/889–3561 or 800/800–8000, fax 909/884–7127. 58 rooms. Facilities: outdoor hot tub, sauna, laundry service. AE, D, DC, MC, V. $

Where to Eat

Buffalo Ranch. The decor is Old West here, with attractive cowboy artifacts, such as chaps, antlers, and saddles for children to sit on. The food is exceptional, with fresh salads, imaginative combinations, and overgenerous portions. The buffalo stew and mashed potatoes are standouts. There are also good buffalo burgers and lake trout. On the kids' menu you'll find

shrimp, ribs, and steak. The entire restaurant is no-smoking. 970 S. E St., San Bernardino, tel. 909/884–3819. AE, D, MC, V. $

El Torito. This busy Mexican restaurant has pleasant ethnic decor, with hanging flowers and stucco walls, and an extensive menu. 118 E. Hospitality La., 2 blocks northwest of I–10 from Waterman exit, San Bernardino, tel. 909/381–2316. AE, MC, V. $

Entertainments

Santa's Village. You'll find 15 rides, a children's theater, and a large gingerbread house in this amusement center in the San Bernardino Mountains. You can ride a donkey, try out a bobsled, watch live reindeer, or hike a nature trail within the park. There are pony rides and a petting zoo. The village is 30 minutes north of the ballpark. S.R. 18, Skyforest, tel. 909/336—3661. Admission: $11. Open mid-June–early Sept. and mid-Nov.–early Jan., daily 10–5; mid-Jan.–early June, weekends 10–5.

Sights to See

Rim of the World Drive. This winding, 40-mi drive leads to the Lake Arrowhead resort. You can see Big Bear Lake and Bear Canyon from Lakeview Point. Elevations on the drive range from 1,100 to 7,000 ft. There are adjacent picnic areas within the San Bernardino National Forest. S.R. 18, San Bernardino, tel. 909/383–5588.

LAKE ELSINORE STORM

League: California League • **Major League Affiliation:** Anaheim Angels • **Class:** A • **Stadium:** The Diamond • **Opened:** 1994 • **Capacity:** 7,866 • **Dimensions:** LF: 330, CF: 400, RF: 310 • **Surface:** grass • **Season:** Apr.–Labor Day

STADIUM LOCATION: 500 Diamond Dr., Lake Elsinore, CA 92530.

TEAM WEB SITE: www.stormbaseball.com

GETTING THERE: From San Diego, I–15 north, Diamond Dr. exit, west ½ mi to stadium. From Los Angeles, I–10 or Freeway 60 east to I–15 south, Diamond Dr. exit, west to stadium. From Orange County, Freeway 91 east to I–15 south, Diamond Dr. exit west.

PARKING: Ample parking, $3; lot opens 2½ hrs before game.

TICKET INFORMATION: Box 535, Lake Elsinore, CA 92531, tel. 909/245–4487, fax 909/245–0305.

PRICE RANGE: Super box seats $7; box seats $6; reserved seats $5; general admission $4 adults, $3.50 ages under 15 and over 66.

GAME TIME: Mon.–Sat. 7:05 PM, Sun. 2:05 (Apr.–early June) or 5:05 (early June–Sept.); gates open 90 min before game.

TIPS ON SEATING: General admission tickets allow you to sit on a grassy berm beyond first base. If you want a real seat, buy a reserved seat ticket.

SEATING FOR PEOPLE WITH DISABILITIES: Available on concourse in both box and reserved seating areas. Special food line at each concession stand.

STADIUM FOOD: The offerings are ordinary and overpriced. A small soda is $2.25 and a pizza slice is $2.50. Avoid the BBQ beef sandwich. You'll find a latte stand and microbrews. A better bet is the **Diamond Club,** a 400-seat sports bar and restaurant open to anyone in the stadium. Outdoor tables on two levels provide an excellent view of the game, and the menu has better choices.

SMOKING POLICY: Smoking prohibited in stadium except in small designated area in general admission area beyond first base.

VISITING TEAM HOTEL: Lake Elsinore Resort and Casino (20930 Malaga St., Lake Elsinore, CA 92530, tel. 909/674–3101).

TOURISM INFORMATION: Lake Elsinore Valley Chamber of Commerce (132 W. Graham Ave., Lake Elsinore, CA 92530, tel. 909/245–8848).

Lake Elsinore: The Diamond

When we first visited Rancho Cucamonga in its inaugural season of 1993, we thought it wasn't possible that a Single A baseball team could play in such a wonderful facility. Now, just 40 mi south on I–15 in Lake Elsinore, we found an equally spectacular stadium. What will it be like for the players who spend a summer playing baseball in these miniature Camden Yards and Jacobs Fields in Rancho Cucamonga and Lake Elsinore and then graduate to far inferior Double A stadiums the next year?

The Lake Elsinore Diamond, opened in 1994, has all the modern comfort of the Epicenter in Rancho Cucamonga, with even more character. After a couple of weeks of watching ball games in the Pioneer, Northwest, and Northern leagues, we found it literally breathtaking to approach the Diamond. As you walk up the tree-lined pathway from the parking lot, you see the marvelous pointed entryway of brick and Camden Yards green. There are nine large concrete baseballs in a circle around a wire sculpture of a baseball pitcher and an impressive clock tower. You know immediately that this is the work of people who care about baseball tradition. The architects were HNTB of Kansas City.

Once inside, you are not disappointed. The outfield wall is an irregular shape with left center 425 ft from home and right field only 310 ft but with a Fenway Park–type 36-ft-high wall. Since this is minor-league baseball, the wall is covered with 17 large ads as well as a scoreboard. Behind home plate is a 90-ft-high clock tower reminiscent of the one in the famed minor-league Wrigley Field in Los Angeles.

No benches without backs here—all the seats are real seats, maroon with plenty of legroom. The field was dug out amphitheater-style so the concourse is directly behind the seats and you don't have to miss the action to get your hot dog and soda. The concourse and the dozen skyboxes are covered with a dark-green roof. General-admission ticket holders sit on a grassy berm down the first-base line just below an arcade of speed pitch and other games. Pity the smokers here. They stand in a small fenced area above the general-admission area that evokes memories of 17th-century stocks.

There is a huge, almost major league–quality scoreboard beyond the left-field wall. Down the third-base line is the Diamond Club, a 400-seat restaurant and bar open to all fans. Three outside levels rise above left field. To see Lake Elsinore, southern California's largest natural inland lake, walk through the restaurant to the grill area before the game starts.

The excellent souvenir shop at the entrance has plenty of items celebrating the Diamond's biggest celebrity—Hamlet, the 8-ft, 4-inch sea serpent who ranges all over the stadium throughout the game urging the fans to cheer on the home team. Hamlet—a coloring book in the souvenir shop tells the story of how he traveled from Shakespeare's Castle Elsinore in the 16th century to 20th-century California—shoots the visiting-team players with a water gun after the game and then signs autographs and poses for pictures at the entranceway.

Where to Stay

Lakeview Inn. Ask for a room on the second floor, stadium side. Postgame, you'll see a spectacular view of the illuminated, empty stadium. Morning views include Lake Elsinore and the Ortega Mountains. The hotel is near the I-15 freeway but is quiet. A small heated pool is suited to children, with a maximum depth of 4½ ft. *31808 Casino Dr., Lake Elsinore 92530, tel. 909/674–9694, fax 909/245–9249. 56 rooms. Facilities: outdoor pool, hot tub, coin laundry. AE, D, DC, MC, V. $*

Where to Eat

Park Plaza Family Restaurant. This casual, family-run enterprise offers ostrich and buffalo burgers. Both taste like slightly gamier versions of beef but are much lower in fat. There are also salads, fajitas, potpies, and cobblers, served at the counter or at tables. The children's menu includes burritos and spaghetti. The restaurant is 10 minutes north of the ballpark by Lake Elsinore State Park. *31731 Riverside Dr., Lake Elsinore, tel. 909/674–5744. DC, MC, V. $*

The Family Basket. This corner restaurant has Mexican and American favorites at bargain

prices. Its kids' breakfast, for $1.59, comes with two pancakes, one egg, sausage, and a drink. Likewise, the chorizo-and-eggs platter is more than you can eat. The atmosphere is fast-food, but you'll find much more than burgers, including pork chops and fresh pies. *202 N. Main St., Lake Elsinore, tel. 909/674–8577. MC, V. $*

Entertainments

The town has a surprisingly long and interesting history. The lake was called Entengvo Wumoma—Hot Springs by the Little Sea—by its first inhabitants, the Pai-ah-che Indians. In 1797 Father Juan Santiago of the Mission San Juan Capistrano found it while searching for a new mission site. In the 1850s, it was on the stagecoach mail route between San Francisco and St. Louis, and in the 1880s it became a link in the transcontinental railroad. Developers came in the 1880s and changed the name to Lake Elsinore to celebrate Shakespeare's castle. People flocked here for the hot mineral waters. The Crescent Bath House, a historic landmark built in 1887 and visited by such notables as Grover Cleveland and Buffalo Bill, still stands in the downtown albeit in quite bad shape. In the 1920s, Lake Elsinore's baths and recreation opportunities attracted Hollywood's elite. But the boom crashed with the Depression, not to revive again until the 1980s. At night, Main Street, which is lined with an assortment of antiques stores and a Mexican bakery, is illuminated by small white lights.

Lake Elsinore Recreation Area. Rent pedal boats and aquacycles by the half hour ($9) for a closer look at Lake Elsinore. When water conditions permit, Jet Skis are available. Rowboats and fishing tackle can be rented at the adjacent West Marina. Fishing licenses are required for those 16 or older. There are swimming areas on both sides of the lake. *32040 Riverside Dr. (Hwy. 74), Lake Elsinore, tel. 909/674–3177. Open daily 7–dusk.*

THE CACTUS LEAGUE AND DESERT BASEBALL
PHOENIX, TUCSON, ARIZONA
SPRING TRAINING

31

Phoenix and Tucson are in the Valley of the Sun. Take the name seriously! With 300 days of sunshine, there is baseball from March through November in Arizona. We recommend the warm glow of spring training in March, rather than the oppressive heat of summer. Ten major-league teams train here in the Cactus League each spring, all within 90 mi of each other.

The Arizona Diamondbacks, an expansion major-league team, began playing in 1998 in a new downtown Phoenix stadium with a retractable roof and real grass. A Triple A Pacific Coast League team, the Sidewinders, plays in Tucson. In October and November of each year, six teams square off in the Arizona Fall League. There is a mix of new and old ballparks in both Phoenix and Tucson.

The big sports attraction outside of baseball here is golf, with dozens of courses throughout the valley. Both Phoenix and Tucson have exceptional zoos, and Phoenix has the downtown Heard Museum, which highlights Native American cultures with intriguing exhibits, many aimed at children. Tucson's zoo is in the same park complex at its ballpark, and the city has an imaginative children's museum in a renovated downtown library. To see life on an Indian reservation, it is worth a drive to the Mission at San Xavier south of the city.

ARIZONA DIAMONDBACKS

League: National League • **Class:** Major League • **Stadium:** Bank One Ballpark • **Opened:** 1998 • **Capacity:** 48,500 • **Dimensions:** LF: 330, CF: 405, RF: 335 • **Surface:** grass • **Season:** Apr.–early Oct.

STADIUM LOCATION: 401 E. Jefferson St., Phoenix, AZ 85004.

TEAM WEB SITE: www.azdiamondbacks.com

GETTING THERE: The ballpark is downtown, between 4th and 7th streets, across from America West Arena. It can be approached from the north on I-17, the south on I-10 to I-17, the west on I-10, and the east on Loop 202. For driving information, tel. 602/462–6607. For bus information, tel. 602/253–5000.

PARKING: There are numerous parking lots within walking distance of the stadium. For specific lots, tel. 602/462–6607. Without a parking pass, do not expect to park adjacent to the ballpark.

TICKET INFORMATION: Box 2095, Phoenix, AZ 85001, tel. 602/462–6500, fax 602/462–6600.

PRICE RANGE: Lower-level seats $55–$10, upper-level seats $15.50–$1. Two hours prior to games, 350 $1 tickets are sold at Window 24 near Gate K. Buyers must enter the park immediately.

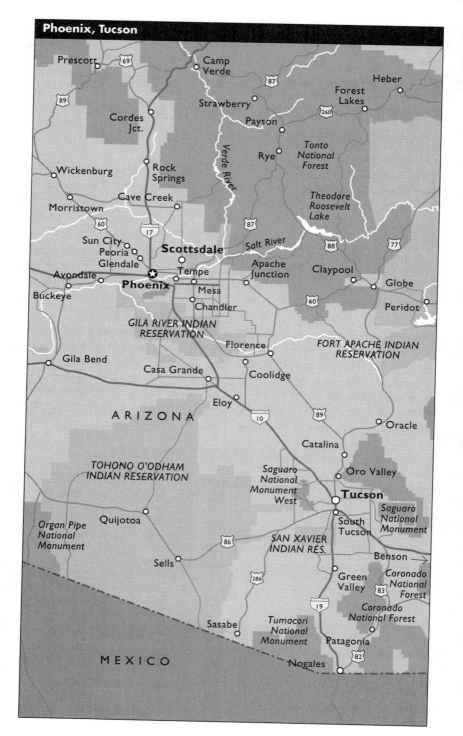

GAME TIME: Apr.–last week in Aug., Mon.–Sat. 7:05 PM, Sun. 1:05 or 5:05 PM; last week in Aug.–early Oct. Mon.–Sat. 6:35 PM, Sun. 1:35 PM; gates open two hours before game.

TIPS ON SEATING: General admission seats are aluminum benches with backs, located on the 100 level in the outfield, with a good view of the action.

SEATING FOR PEOPLE WITH DISABILITIES: Seating is throughout the park. Look for the booklet titled "Guide to Bank One Ballpark for Guests with Disabilities." tel. 602/462–6607.

STADIUM FOOD: There is a large selection here, from generous burritos at Garcia's for $6.50, to Ben & Jerry's ice cream (low fat and regular), to Indian fry bread, dipped in honey or with cinnamon and sugar. There's a fresh fruit and vegetable stand, with strawberries and cream, mixed fruit, carrots, salads, and pickles on a stick. You also can find fresh cookies and Rice Krispie treats. The **Front Row Sports Grill,** open during the game and afterward, has good views of the action, but avoid the overly large and overly sweet desserts. Its kids menu is a bargain, with $3 selections; the smoothies and potato soup are fair.

SMOKING POLICY: Smoking is not permitted in any seating area or general concourses. Smoking in designated areas only.

TOURISM INFORMATION: Greater Phoenix Convention & Visitors Bureau (400 E. Van Buren St., Ste. 600, Phoenix, AZ 85004, tel. 602/254–6500 or 877/266–5749)

Phoenix:
Bank One Ballpark

We don't usually recommend domed stadiums. But you have to give credit to the Arizona Diamondbacks and Maricopa County. They are actually growing real grass on the playing field of Phoenix's Bank One Ballpark.

The BOB's retractable roof, made from nine million pounds of steel, can fully close in just under five minutes. When the roof is retracted, the opening is almost 5.5 acres. The basketball and hockey teams play next door in the America West Arena; you could fit eight such arenas inside Bank One Ballpark. The park is cooled by 8,000 tons of air-conditioning with electric wiring that could be stretched 631 mi. Unlike Seattle's new retractable roof, the point here is not just to provide an umbrella. It gets hot here in the summertime, and the roof allows the park to be air-conditioned during games. Fans can stay after air-conditioned games on steamy summer nights and watch the roof being opened.

Bank One Ballpark opened in 1998 as the home field of the Arizona Diamondbacks, one of major league baseball's two newest teams. Tampa Bay built a horrible domed stadium and after eight years of hard work won a franchise. Phoenix pursued the more conventional route,

and its ballpark is much newer and far superior. Maricopa County owns this baseball palace, with county taxpayers footing a big portion of the $354 million it cost to build it. Ellerbe Becket, the designers of Atlanta's Turner Field, were the architects.

The playing field is 25 ft below street level, but at 1,090 ft above sea level, the BOB's elevation is second only to Denver's Coors Field. There is a swimming pool just beyond right center field. Fountains from the pool shoot up 32 ft when the Diamondbacks hit a home run. Two other charming oddities: There is a 5-ft-wide strip of grass between the warning track and the outfield fence to provide improved footing and added warning to outfielders. And there is a dirt strip between the pitcher's mound and home plate, reminiscent of baseball fields of decades past.

Above the lower-level seating, there is an open concourse where you'll find food, drink, and baseball history. There are tributes to great ballplayers and classic ballparks as well as display cases of baseball memorabilia. Take the time to walk the concourse and soak it all up. The Cox Clubhouse on the concourse level beyond center field displays vintage uniforms from all 30 major league teams and the historic women's professional league. You'll also find there a Diamondbacks logo mosaic made from

2,754 baseballs, interactive games (with a fee to play), and a Kid's Land Play Area for youngsters under 48" tall.

Don't just arrive at game time and race into this ballpark—there's superb art to see outside the gates. Our favorite is *Based on Balls,* a funky collection of colorful miniature baseballs that roll endlessly across and along blue and green ramps and pulleys, banging and bouncing and ringing gongs and bells. It sits on a main entrance court in front of the ticket windows, where you'll also find remembrances of 24 of the greatest moments in baseball. And there are other pieces of art worth seeking out. The floor of the rotunda near the entrance to the team shop is a colorful Arizona mosaic. Above on the walls is a *History of Sport* from ancient Greece to the modern Diamondbacks, by Richard Haas. The exterior along Jefferson Street includes huge colorful baseball paintings mounted high in the air. The dozen large panels can swing open, giving the ballpark a more open feel. There is a handsome metal sculpture representing baseball as a family attraction at the northeast corner of the site.

Bank One Ballpark Tours. There is so much to see here that it is well worth a return visit for a 75-minute tour. *401 E. Jefferson St., Phoenix, tel. 602/462–6799. Admission: $6 adults, $4 senior citizens and ages 7–12, $2 ages 4–6. Open nongame days. Tours: Mon.–Sat, 10:30, noon, 1:30, 3; days of night games, 10:30, noon.*

OAKLAND ATHLETICS SPRING TRAINING

League: Cactus League • **Class:** Major League Spring Training • **Stadium:** Phoenix Municipal Stadium • **Opened:** 1964 • **Capacity:** 7,975 • **Dimensions:** LF: 340, CF: 410, RF: 340 • **Surface:** grass • **Season:** Mar. spring training

STADIUM LOCATION: 5999 E. Van Buren St., Phoenix, AZ 85008.

TEAM WEB SITE: www.oaklandathletics.com

GETTING THERE: Muni Stadium is just south of the Phoenix Zoo on the Tempe-Phoenix-Scottsdale city line at the intersection of Van Buren Street and Galvin Parkway/Priest Drive. From the East Valley, it's a ½ mi north of 202 Freeway, off the Priest Drive exit. From the West Valley, it's a ½ mi east of 202 Freeway, off Van Buren Street exit.

PARKING: There is ample parking across the street from the ballpark for $5.

TICKET INFORMATION: 5999 E. Van Buren St., Phoenix, AZ 85008, tel. 602/392–0074, fax 602/392–0225.

PRICE RANGE: Field box seats $11, reserved $9, outfield $8, bleachers $5.

GAME TIME: Day games 1:05 PM, night games 7:05 PM; gates open one hour before game.

TIPS ON SEATING: The top row of the grandstand is shaded by a partial roof. The sun is behind the grandstand at 1 PM during spring training. The Athletics use the dugout on the first-base side.

SEATING FOR PEOPLE WITH DISABILITIES: Seating is along the top of the concourse.

STADIUM FOOD: There are limited choices here—hot dogs, popcorn, nachos, and lemonade. The best item is a $4 Polish dog. Candy bars are a pricey $3.

SMOKING POLICY: Smoking is not allowed in the seating bowl, but is permitted in designated areas behind the grandstand.

TEAM HOTEL: Doubletree Suites Hotel (320 N.44th St., Phoenix AZ 85008, tel. 602/225–0500 or 800/222–8733).

TOURISM INFORMATION: Phoenix & Valley of the Sun Convention & Visitors Bureau (1 Arizona Center, 400 E. Van Buren St., Suite 600, Phoenix, AZ 85004-2290, tel. 602/252–5588).

Phoenix: Municipal Stadium

Phoenix Muni still has a funky 1960s concrete wave-pattern roof over its stone grandstand, and the press box hasn't been modernized. We like it just fine the way it is. The state-of-the-art ballparks like Tucson Electric and Maryvale are great, but we appreciate the character and history of the old parks.

They have been playing spring training games in Phoenix Muni since the early 1960s, with the Oakland Athletics in residence since 1984. The World Champion A's team that trained here in 1990 included the Bash Brothers Mark McGwire and Jose Canseco, Rickey Henderson, and Dennis Eckersley.

The San Francisco Giants trained here for years, bringing the light poles with them from New York's venerated Polo Grounds. Phoenix's Triple A teams played here before moving to Scottsdale Stadium and then leaving Arizona in 1998 to make way for the Diamondbacks.

More than $4 million was spent in the mid-1990s when Oakland agreed to a 10-year contract extension. A new scoreboard in right center field arrived in 1999. For the year 2000 season, the number of top-quality seats in the grandstand has more than doubled to 3,845. By 2002, there will be a new press box.

Fans enter the ballpark on the third-base side to see an oddly shaped roof over an unusual grandstand with a stone facade. The concessions and facilities are conveniently located on the concourse above the seating bowl, where fans can stand in line and not miss a pitch. The Papago Buttes provide the scenery beyond the outfield.

One danger of the impressive wave of ballpark building in the 1990s is that the ballparks are beginning to look alike. The choice by Phoenix to spare the bulldozer and renovate this odd old ballpark adds immeasurably to the total Cactus League experience. We recommend Phoenix Muni to spring training travelers despite our stunning April Fool's Day surprise of cold, wind, and rain. So who says it's always sunny in Arizona?

CHICAGO CUBS SPRING TRAINING

League: Cactus League • **Class:** Major League Spring Training • **Stadium:** HoHoKam Park • **Opened:** 1997 • **Capacity:** 10,000 • **Dimensions:** LF: 340, CF: 410, RF: 350 • **Surface:** grass • **Season:** Mar. spring training

STADIUM LOCATION: 1235 N. Center St., Mesa, AZ 85201

TEAM WEB SITE: www.chicagocubs.com

GETTING THERE: The park is 1½ mi north of Main Street in Mesa, east of Phoenix. Take Freeway 202 to McKellips Road (exit 3). Go east to Center Street. Turn right on Center and the ballpark is on your left.

PARKING: Get there before 12:30 PM, as the $5 parking at the ballpark is limited. Overflow parking is on the local streets. The exit from the stadium lot is very slow.

TICKET INFORMATION: Box 261, Mesa, AZ 85211, tel. 480/964–4467.

PRICE RANGE: Field box $13; terrace box $12; terrace field $10; grandstand $6; lawn $5.

GAME TIME: Daily 1:05 PM; gates open 11 AM.

TIPS ON SEATING: The sun is behind the grandstand at 1 PM for spring training games. Most of the terrace box seats, especially on the first-base side, are shaded by a roof and have a great view of the mountains beyond the outfield wall. The Cubs dugout is on the first-base side. There is $5 lawn seating just beyond the outfield wall.

SEATING FOR PEOPLE WITH DISABILITIES: Seating is along the concourse at the top of the field box seating.

STADIUM FOOD: You'll find a good Polish sausage for $4, Italian ices, and fairly good pizza sold by the slice. The rest of the offerings—nachos, popcorn, hot dogs—are undistinguished. There are fresh lemonade and shaved ice, each for $4, and a chocolate-chip cookie sandwich for $3.

SMOKING POLICY: This is a smoke-free ballpark. Smoking is allowed only outside the ballpark gates.

TEAM HOTEL: Best Western Dobson Park Inn (1666 S. Dobson Rd., Mesa, AZ 85202, tel. 602/831–7000 or 800/528–1234).

TOURISM INFORMATION: Mesa Convention & Visitors Bureau (120 North Center St., Mesa, AZ 85201, tel. and fax 480/827–4700 or 800/283–6372.

Mesa: HoHoKam Park

This isn't the best ballpark in the Cactus League. There are better mountain views at other parks, the parking here is constrained, and the food selection is limited. So why is this so much fun? Let us spell it out: C-U-B-S. Loyal Cubs fans flee the icy confines of Chicago for sunny Arizona and pack this ballpark to cheer on Sammy Sosa and their other heroes.

An exceptional community support group—the HoHoKam of Mesa—deserves credit as well for the record-breaking crowds at HoHoKam Park each spring. Dwight Patterson, a local rancher and HoHoKam founder, attracted the Cubs to Mesa in 1952 for spring training at Rendezvous Park. The Cubs left for California in 1966, but Patterson was able to recruit the Oakland Athletics to Mesa in 1969. Rendezvous Park was razed in 1977 to make way for the city's community center, and the first HoHoKam Park was opened for spring training in 1978. The Cubs, not happy in California or later in Scottsdale, returned to Mesa in 1979.

The Cactus League was hurting by the early 1990s, and the possibility of losing its crown jewel—the Chicago Cubs—motivated local business and community leaders to action. A sales tax on rental cars built a pot of money that funded construction of a wave of new Cactus League ballparks in the latter half of the 1990s. In 1996, the original HoHoKam Park was completely leveled and an entirely new $17-million ballpark was built. In return, the Cubs agreed to stay in Mesa for 20 years.

Dwight W. Patterson Field at HoHoKam Park has 10,000 seats and room for 2,500 more on the grass berms beyond the outfield wall. HOK Sport designed a traditional ballpark with the trademark Southwestern sand-colored stucco style of the Cactus League. To allow room for more seats, the souvenirs, concessions, and bathrooms are under the grandstand rather than at the back of the main concourse. Beyond the left-field wall is a scoreboard that's uncharacteristically large for the Cactus League.

The HoHoKam (pronounced HO-HO-COM) were a Native American tribe that occupied the region from AD 1 until the middle of the 15th century. One of the world's most advanced civilizations of the first millennium, the tribe's name means "those who are gone." A large copper statue at the northeast corner of the park honors our Native Americans, but for some reason it's not a HoHoKam.

SAN FRANCISCO GIANTS SPRING TRAINING

League: Cactus League • **Class:** Major League Spring Training • **Stadium:** Scottsdale Stadium • **Opened:** 1992 • **Capacity:** 8,250 • **Dimensions:** LF: 360, CF: 430, RF: 340 • **Surface:** grass • **Season:** Mar. spring training

STADIUM LOCATION: 7408 E. Osborn Rd., Scottsdale, AZ 85251.

TEAM WEB SITE: www.sfgiants.com

GETTING THERE: From I–10, Broadway Rd., exit to Rural Rd.; north on Rural Rd., which becomes Scottsdale Rd., 4½ mi to Osborn Rd.; right on Osborn, stadium on left. From 202 Fwy. E, right at McDowell exit, north on Osborn to stadium. For information about spring training express shuttle, Ollie the Trolley, call 480/312–7696.

PARKING: Free around stadium on city streets and in public parking garages north of stadium.

TICKET INFORMATION: 7408 E. Osborn Rd., Scottsdale, AZ 85251, tel. 480/784-4444.

PRICE RANGE: Lower/upper box seats $13; line box seats $12; reserved grandstand $11; reserved bleachers $9; lawn seating $6.

GAME TIME: Most games 1:05 PM; gates open 2 hrs before game.

TIPS ON SEATING: Many seats behind walking concourse between first and third bases are shaded during afternoon games.

SEATING FOR PEOPLE WITH DISABILITIES: Just behind field box seats, behind home plate, and past first and third bases.

STADIUM FOOD: There is a grill behind the bleachers on the third-base side that serves barbecued chicken sandwiches, locally made Italian sausages, hamburgers, and jumbo hot dogs. To give a California flavor, iced lattes and Anchor Steam beer are served. The most refreshing drinks are lemon and strawberry frozen fruit concoctions. Fresh lemonade with grenadine is also available. Children gravitate toward the pizza, cookies, and yogurt waffle cones. Dippin' dots, the odd ice cream that comes in a mound of bits, is found here, too. A nice picnic area behind home plate is shaded by palm trees.

SMOKING POLICY: No-smoking ballpark with designated smoking areas.

TEAM HOTEL: Mountain Shadows Marriott Resort and Golf Club (5641 E. Lincoln Dr., Scottsdale, AZ 85253, tel. 480/948–7111 or 800/228–9290).

TOURISM INFORMATION: Phoenix & Valley of the Sun Convention & Visitors Bureau (1 Arizona Center, 400 E. Van Buren St., Suite 600, Phoenix, AZ 85004-2290, tel. 602/252–5588).

Phoenix:
Scottsdale Stadium

New York's loss was Phoenix's gain. The 1957 National League decision to allow the Dodgers and Giants to move from New York to California catapulted Phoenix several steps closer to its place in baseball's major leagues. The Giants' Triple A Pacific Coast League team, the San Francisco Seals, moved to Phoenix, replacing a Class C team in the Arizona-Mexico League.

As early as the 1940s, the Giants trained in Phoenix. In 1982, they moved to Scottsdale, the fancy tourist magnet next door to Phoenix. Scottsdale had hosted spring-training baseball off and on since 1956. A new stadium, designed by HOK Sport of Kansas City, was built in 12 months for $7 million and opened in 1992. They tore out the green wooden stands of the old Scottsdale Field to build this baseball beauty.

Owned and operated by the city of Scottsdale, the new stadium seats 8,250, with room for 2,500 more fans in the general admission grass-berm area beyond the outfield fence.

Scottsdale Stadium is attractive and inviting, with all seats close to the action. Eight rows of comfortable, dark-green field box seats are found along the first- and third-base lines. The food and souvenir concourse is wide and customer-friendly, but as it's behind the seats, you can't see the game while grabbing a hot dog and drink. The grass berm in the outfield is often wall-to-wall beach blankets packed with tanners. An attractive rust-colored roof with flags flying above provides some shade between first and third.

As is often the case to avoid excessive sun in the players' eyes, the stadium layout is turned so that fans in the stands miss the best natural vistas. Walk to the top of the seating area on the third-base side for the best view of Phoenix-area mountains.

Sunscreen is a must at this ballpark, as is plenty of water. Savvy fans bring water bottles and refill them at the stadium. There are also good fruit drinks, both frozen and fresh-squeezed, to keep you hydrated.

Scottsdale Stadium will remain the spring-training home of the San Francisco Giants at least through 2007.

More Phoenix Baseball

Arizona League. Michael Jordan played in Scottsdale Stadium in the 1994 Arizona Fall League as a member of the Scottsdale Scorpions. Founded in 1992 and now owned and operated by Major League Baseball, the Arizona Fall League is intended for the best major-league prospects from the Double A and Triple A minor leagues. Six teams play 45-game schedules from early October to mid-November. All teams are based in the greater Phoenix area and play at five different ballparks, including HoHoKam Park, Phoenix Municipal, and Scottsdale Stadium. For information write 10201 S. 51st St., Ste. 230, Phoenix, AZ 85044, or tel. 602/496–6700.

Where to Stay

Team Hotel (Athletics): Doubletree Suites Hotel. This business hotel is conveniently located in midtown. The six-story building is close to a busy street, but the rooms are well insulated from noise. There is not much storage space for clothes, but the furnishings are new and the rooms are bright. 320 N. 44th St., Phoenix 85008, tel. 602/225–0500 or 800/222–8733, fax 602/225–0957. 242 suites. Facilities: restaurant, outdoor pool, exercise room. AE, D, DC, MC, V. $$$

Team Hotel (Cubs): Best Western Dobson Park Inn. Guests receive a free full breakfast in this nicely landscaped two-story stucco ranch inn. There are fountains and native shrubbery on the 10 acres surrounding the facilities. Rooms are large, with contemporary Southwestern furnishings. 1666 S. Dobson Rd., Mesa 85202, tel. 602/831–7000 or 800/528–1234, fax 602/831–7000. 213 rooms. Facilities: 2 out-

door pools, 2 spas, fitness center, golf, tennis. AE, D, DC, MC, V. $$$

Team Hotel (Giants): Mountain Shadows Marriott Resort and Golf Club. This sprawling resort is expensive and built around a popular golf course at the base of Camelback Mountain. The two-story hotel was built in 1959 and has been extensively remodeled. The interiors feature reproduction antiques, large rooms, and walk-in closets; outside you'll find fountains and creeks. Guests can play night golf under the lights. 5641 E. Lincoln Dr., Scottsdale 85253, tel. 480/948–7111 or 800/228–9290, fax 480/951–5430. 337 rooms. Facilities: 3 restaurants, 3 outdoor swimming pools, fitness center, tennis courts, golf course. AE, DC, MC, V. $$$

Holiday Inn Old Town Scottsdale. This campus-style low-rise hotel complex is convenient for walks into the Old Town area, which is filled with tourist shops and restaurants. It's just one block from the San Francisco Giants' spring-training facility. The rooms are decorated in cool Southwest colors and have floor-to-ceiling windows looking onto interior courtyards. 7353 E. Indian School Rd., Scottsdale 85251, tel. 602/994–9203 or 800/465–4329, fax 602/941–2567. 206 rooms. Facilities: restaurant, outdoor pool, tennis court. AE, D, DC, MC, V. $$

San Carlos Hotel. Built in 1928, this affordable Italian Renaissance–style downtown hotel is on the National Register of Historic Places. Its lobby is small but elegant, and the cozy rooms have updated plumbing, lovely city views, and expensive furnishings. The copper elevators are vintage. Summer rates can be a bargain. 202 N. Central Ave., at Monroe St., Phoenix 85004, tel. 602/253–4121 or 800/678–8946, fax 602/253–6668. 107 rooms, 9 suites. Facilities: 2 restaurants, small outdoor pool, exercise room, parking (fee). AE, DC, MC, V. $$

Where to Eat

Carolina's Mexican Food. The floor is chipped, the windows and doors gated, but members of all economic groups converge at Carolina's for terrific, inexpensive Mexican food. There's one large dining room, and guests order at a window. An army of cooks turns out fresh tortillas, chorizo, soft tacos, and tamales. The flour tortillas are unbeatable. Combination plates are a bargain $3.95. *1202 E. Mohave St., Phoenix, tel. 602/252–1503. AE, D, MC, V. $*

Don & Charlie's. This busy, casual rib and steak house is popular with ballplayers. It serves huge entrée salads, frogs' legs, garlic cheese toast, creamed spinach, and steaks of all varieties. The children's menu is more expensive than most— $5 to $8—and the portions are large. *7501 E. Camelback Rd., Scottsdale, tel. 602/990–0900. AE, D, DC, MC, V. $$*

MacAlpine's. This 1928 drugstore soda fountain is missing the pharmacy, but everything else is here: wooden booths, overhead fans, a counter with 10 stools, and a neon clock. You can get good sandwiches, omelets, and soups, but it's the phosphates, malts, and white cows (vanilla milk shakes) that bring in loyal customers. *2303 N. 7th St., Phoenix, tel. 602/252–7282. MC, V. $*

Yoshi's. This nine-outlet Japanese restaurant chain resembles an upscale burger palace, with colorful umbrellas and oversize chopsticks on the walls and bright upholstered booths. Its menu is a welcome departure from fried food. Chicken teriyaki, cold noodle salads, sushi, rice bowls, and potstickers are the mainstay. Half-orders of teriyaki are available. The first branch listed is closest to Bank One Ballpark. *18 W. Adams St., at Central Ave., Phoenix, tel. 602/254–7174; 24th St. and E. Indian School Rd., tel. 602/468–9737; 4060 N. Central Ave., at E. Indian School Rd., tel. 602/274–6470; 4825 E. Warner, Phoenix, tel. 480/592–9320. No credit cards. $*

Entertainments

Phoenix Zoo. You enter this lovely 125-acre zoo by a bridge walkway, framed by palm trees. Inside, the zoo is arranged around separate trails, covering Arizona wildlife, desert creatures, the tropics, and Africa. There's also a children's trail with a barnyard petting zoo and a prairie-dog village. A 35-minute safari-zoo train ride with good narration costs $2 and is worth it. The desert terrain makes this a very different zoo experience. You hear and see uncaged birds throughout the grounds and can get very close to bobcats and mountain lions. There are uncommon animals, such as roadrunners, piglike javelinas, and gazelles. You'll find a

shaded area for lunch, camel rides ($3), and areas where you can pan for gold and look for gems (50¢ each). *455 N. Galvin Pkwy., Papago Park, Phoenix, tel. 602/273–1341. Admission: $8.50 adults, $4.25 ages 3–12, $7.50 senior citizens. Open May–Labor Day, daily 7–4, Labor Day–Apr., daily 9–5.*

Telephone Pioneers of America Park. In the far northern part of the city is the nation's first barrier-free park and playground, created in 1988 by engineers and employees of the Bell Telephone system. Most of the equipment is wheelchair-accessible and the overall design is aimed at those with reduced coordination. Beep baseball, which uses balls that emit noises for low-vision or sightless players, is played here. There is a wonderful climbing playground, good for children of all abilities. *1946 W. Morningside Dr., Phoenix, tel. 602/262–4543. Open daily, dawn–dusk.*

Sights to See

The Heard Museum. This beautiful downtown museum was founded in 1929 to showcase the cultural heritage of the country's native people. The permanent exhibit presents a journey through time and across the landscape of the Southwest. At the museum entrance, kids can use mano and metate stones—lava rock and sandstone grinding tools traditionally used by Native Americans—to make meal. You'll find a sidewalk café, a superb gift shop with Native American–handcrafted art, 10 galleries, and outdoor courtyards. *2301 N. Central Ave., Phoenix, tel. 602/252–8848. Admission: $7 adults, $6 senior citizens, $3 ages 4–12. Open daily 9:30–5.*

State Capitol. Arizona's capitol building has been restored to re-create its condition in 1912, the year Arizona gained statehood. Now serving as Arizona's State Capitol Museum, the building was constructed of native stone between 1898 and 1901 to serve as the territorial capitol. The highlight of the building is the 16-ft-high *Winged Victory* crowning the copper dome. Sculpted as a weather vane, the lady has a few bullet nicks in her from turn-of-the-century gunplay. *1700 W. Washington St., Phoenix, tel. 602/542–4581. Open weekdays 8–5.*

ARIZONA DIAMONDBACKS AND
CHICAGO WHITE SOX SPRING TRAINING

League: Cactus League • **Class:** Major League Spring Training • **Stadium:** Tucson Electric Park • **Opened:** 1998 • **Capacity:** 8,000 • **Dimensions:** LF: 340, CF: 405, RF: 340 • **Surface:** grass • **Season:** Mar. Spring Training

STADIUM LOCATION: Kino Veterans Memorial Sports Park, 2500 E. Ajo Way, Tucson, AZ 85713

TEAM WEB SITE: www.tucsonbaseball.com

GETTING THERE: Kino Veterans Memorial Sports Park is just south of downtown Tucson. Take the Kino Street exit north off of I–10 and turn right to go east on Ajo Way. The ballpark is on your right.

PARKING: There is ample parking for $3 at the ballpark.

TICKET INFORMATION: 2500 E. Ajo Way, Tucson, AZ 85713, tel. 520/434–1400 (AZ) or 520/434–1300, fax 520/434–1443.

PRICE RANGE: Club level $14; field level infield $12; grandstand $9; outfield bleachers $6; lawn seating $3.

GAME TIME: Day games 1:05 PM, night games 6:05 PM or 7:05 PM; gates open 90 min. before game.

TIPS ON SEATING: There are 5,600 seats with chair backs, 1,400 bleacher seats with backs, and 1,000 bleacher seats without backs. There is lawn seating for 3,000 beyond the outfield wall in left and right center. The sun is behind home plate at 1 PM for spring training games. There is a small, shaded upper deck area. The Diamondbacks dugout is on the third-base side. The White Sox dugout is on the first-base side.

SEATING FOR PEOPLE WITH DISABILITIES: Seating is located at the top of the lower bowl seating area.

STADIUM FOOD: You can bring food into the park. Local barbecue made by Bobby Deans can be found at the right-field concession stand. Pulled pork sandwiches are $4 and four ribs and a roll are $5. Grilled hamburgers are large and good. Brats and hot dogs are fine, but the mustard isn't. An unusual plus is soft-serve ice cream made by Healthy Choice. There are a concession stand and bathrooms behind the huge batter's eye in straightaway center field.

SMOKING POLICY: Smoking is allowed only behind the bleachers and behind the seats on the upper level.

TEAM HOTELS: (Diamondbacks) Doubletree Suites (6555 E. Speedway, Tucson 85710, tel. 520/721–7100 or 800/222–8733); **(White Sox) Best Western Inn–Airport** (7060 S. Tucson Blvd., Tucson 85706, tel. 520/746–0271 or 800/528–1234).

TOURISM INFORMATION: Metropolitan Tucson Convention & Visitors Bureau (130 S. Scott Ave., Tucson, AZ 85701, tel. 520/624–1817 or 800/638–8350).

Tucson: Electric Park

This $35-million spring training complex shared by the Arizona Diamondbacks and the Chicago White Sox includes a dozen practice fields. Tucson Electric Park, the centerpiece of the complex, opened in 1998 and hosts a game virtually every day each March.

A shared spring training facility is "the ideal situation," according to baseball wise man Roland Hemond of the Arizona Diamondbacks. "It helps the community, it gives the fans more games, and it is good for both teams." With spring training at Tucson Electric Park and its Triple A team in residence here from April to Labor Day, the Diamondbacks have built a strong fan base 100-plus mi from home.

The park shares many characteristics of minor-league ballparks built across America in the late 1990s. Yet it does have a regional flavor: the maroon block and sand-colored stucco evoke the Southwest, and the gorgeous Santa Catalina Mountains beyond the outfield wall more than reinforce the point.

Fans enter on the first-base side and walk down to bowl seating below a wide concourse. An attractive blue slatted sunroof runs along the top of the concourse, providing virtually the only relief from the strong Arizona sun. Colorful banners hang at each end of the concourse, telling baseball history and displaying children's paintings of the game.

If you like to shag batting-practice home runs, this is a nearly perfect place, with large grass berm seating areas beyond the outfield wall in left center and right center. The gates open at 11:30 AM, and batting practice lasts until about 12:15 PM. One of the charms of spring training is the opportunity to watch early-morning practices. The White Sox training fields are adjacent to the ballpark, and the Diamondbacks' fields are across Ajo Way. They're usually accessible to fans from dawn till dusk.

The Tucson Sidewinders, the Diamondbacks' Triple A franchise in the Pacific Coast League, play here from early April to Labor Day. For information, call 520/434–1021 or visit www .tucsonsidewinders.com.

COLORADO ROCKIES SPRING TRAINING

League: Cactus League • **Class:** Major League Spring Training • **Stadium:** US West Sports Complex at Hi Corbett Field • **Opened:** 1937 • **Capacity:** 9,500 • **Dimensions:** LF: 366, CF: 392, RF: 348 • **Surface:** grass • **Season:** Mar. Spring Training

STADIUM LOCATION: 3400 E. Camino Campestre, Tucson, AZ 85716.

TEAM WEB SITE: www.coloradorockies.com

GETTING THERE: Field is in Randolph Park. From I–10, go east on Broadway Blvd., then right on Randolph Way, where a large sign will direct you to the staduim. For information about bus system, call 520/ 792–9222.

PARKING: Free parking at ballpark and a shuttle from El Con Mall.

TICKET INFORMATION: Colorado Rockies Spring Training, Box 28830, Tucson, AZ 85775, tel. 520/327– 9467 or 800/388–7625.

PRICE RANGE: Home-plate grandstand $9; reserved grandstand $8; pavilion $7; midfield bleachers $5; outfield bleachers $4.

GAME TIME: Most games, 1:05 PM; gates open 2 hrs before game.

TIPS ON SEATING: To avoid Tucson's ever-present sun, sit under the small grandstand roof in the seats directly behind home plate. The individual seats found from behind home plate to the edge of each dugout are preferable to aluminum bleacher seats beyond the bases. The sun at afternoon spring training games is over the left field scoreboard. The Rockies dugout is on the first-base side.

SEATING FOR PEOPLE WITH DISABILITIES: The seating is in the front row of the entire grandstand.

STADIUM FOOD: The longest lines for the Rockies' concessions are at the water fountain, with fans filling bottles to drink under the Arizona sun. Eegee's $3 frozen fruit drinks are a sweet alternative, in lemon and strawberry flavors. Or try fresh lemonade, also for $3. At the Eegee stand on the first-base side are veggie subs and turkey grinders for $4.50. Personal pan pizzas are $4.50. A grill on the third-base side serves burgers, Polish dogs, and hot dogs. There are pretzels rolled in butter, cheese, and cinnamon. (One warning: some of the soft pretzels contain jalapeño peppers that are too hot for children.) There is also a Mexican food stand with great quesadillas.

SMOKING POLICY: Smoking prohibited in seating area.

TEAM HOTEL: Tucson Hilton East (7600 E. Broadway, Tucson 85710, tel. 520/721–5600 or 800/445–8667)

TOURISM INFORMATION: Metropolitan Tucson Convention & Visitors Bureau (130 S. Scott Ave., Tucson, AZ 85701, tel. 520/624–1817 or 800/638–8350).

Tucson:
Hi Corbett Field

Hi Corbett Field isn't a fancy 1990s ballpark like Tucson Electric Park. Instead, after seven decades of baseball history and several restorations, it is a splendid combination of old and new—efficient enough to please most fans while authentic enough for central casting. This prototype of an old-style spring-training stadium was featured in the 1989 movie *Major League.*

Hi Corbett played for a local railroad team in some of Tucson's first intracity games at Elysian Grove Field in 1907. Forty years later, his friendship with Cleveland Indians owner Bill Veeck led the Indians to establish their spring-training camp in Tucson. Corbett served for many years as the president of the Tucson Baseball Commission, and in 1951 the stadium was named for him.

A 1972 remodeling gave the ballpark a distinct Southwestern style, with a sand-colored stucco exterior wall. The current grandstand is a product of the 1972 renovation. A new press box, new right-field bleachers, a new clubhouse, and larger dugouts were added in 1993 to lure the Colorado Rockies to replace the departed Indians. Further improvements were made in the late 1990s, including the addition of 1,500 new seats and a handsome new entrance and souvenir shop.

Ironically, while the great thrill of spring training is the opportunity to be much closer to the players than most of us are likely to be in major-league parks, the afternoon desert breezes and glorious mountain views often are enhanced by sitting high in the grandstand. From up there you get a good view of mountains in every direction, including the Rincon, Catalina, and Santa Rita.

The ballpark is in Reid Park, near a golf course. The city zoo lies just beyond the right-field fence. Center field is only 392 ft from home plate, but the dark-green outfield fence is monster-high, and the power alleys are deep, at 410 and 405 ft. The Southwestern stucco style predominates in the wide concourse behind the grandstand, where the concessions, souvenirs, and bathrooms are located.

More Tucson Baseball

USA Baseball. USA Baseball replaced a Triple A minor league team that had played at Corbett Field, adding international competition to Arizona's already rich mix of baseball. USA Baseball is responsible for selecting, training, and supporting the U.S. Olympic team as well as National, Junior National, and Youth National teams for international competition. For information, tel. 520/327–9700 or visit www.usabaseball.com.

Elysian Grove Field. Tucson's first city-league games were played at Elysian Grove Field from 1907 to 1913 at the southwest corner of Simpson and South Main streets. Hi Corbett, Tucson's Mr. Baseball for whom Hi Corbett Field is named, played for the Southern Pacific Railroad team on this field. In 1913 the land was subdivided for development and baseball had to relocate. Today the Carrillo School, an elementary-level magnet school, occupies the ground where the ball field was. *Simpson and S. Main Sts., Tucson.*

Where to Stay

Team Hotel (Diamondbacks): Doubletree Suites. All suites have a bedroom and living room. A full breakfast is included at this beautifully landscaped five-story hotel. *6555 E. Speedway, Tucson 85710, tel. 520/721–7100 or 800/222–8733, fax 520/721–1991. 303 suites. Facilities: outdoor pool. AE, D, DC, MC, V. $$.*

Team Hotel (White Sox): Best Western Inn–Airport. There are balconies and patios built around a large, attractive heated pool in this courtyard hotel. Guests receive a free breakfast and there is a free airport shuttle. Rooms have been renovated recently and have good views. *7060 S. Tucson Blvd., Tucson 85706, tel. 520/746–0271 or 800/528–1234, fax 520/889–7391. 149 rooms. Facilities: restaurant, outdoor pool. AE, D, DC, MC, V. $$*

Team Hotel (Rockies): Tucson Hilton East. The Santa Catalina Mountains are visible from most rooms of this convenient atrium hotel. Rooms are large and comfortable. *7600 E. Broadway, Tucson 85710, tel. 520/721–5600 or 800/445–8667, fax 520/721–5696. 231 rooms. Facilities: restaurant, outdoor pool, fitness center, spa. AE, D, DC, MC, V. $$$*

Viscount Suite Hotel. This striking stucco hotel has a large central courtyard with a fountain, potted palms, and seating for breakfast and casual lunch. Local radio shows regularly host mixers and broadcast from the sports bar that adjoins the courtyard. The spacious rooms include a refrigerator and a dressing table. *4855 E. Broadway Blvd., Tucson 85711, tel. 520/745–6500 or 800/527–9666, fax 520/790–5114. 215 2-room suites. Facilities: 2 restaurants, outdoor pool, hot tub, exercise room. D, DC, MC, V. $$*

Elysian Grove Market Bed & Breakfast Inn. Near Tucson's original ball field, this handsome bed-and-breakfast is in a restored adobe market next to the downtown arts district. The kitchen is in the market's old meat locker. There are four guest suites with antique beds, tribal rugs, and Mexican tiled baths. Each suite has two bedrooms, bath, living area, and kitchen. The inn has fireplaces and a backyard garden. *400 W. Simpson St., Tucson 85701, tel. 520/628–1522 or www.bbonline.com. 4 rooms. No credit cards. $$*

Where to Eat

Carlos Murphy's. This imposing restaurant is in the former El Paso and Southwestern Railroad depot. Built in classical style in 1913, it has a stained-glass dome and a large rotunda. The restaurant is casual, serving American versions of Mexican favorites, including fish tacos and nachos. Terrific fajitas are a specialty; you can get them made with shrimp, vegetables, shark, chicken, or beef. The full children's menu includes burritos, quesadillas, burgers, and chicken fingers. *419 W. Congress St., Tucson, tel. 520/628–1956. AE, D, MC, V. $$*

Cocina. You can eat inside this wooden, mission-style restaurant in the Old Town Historic District or in its beautifully shaded courtyard. The courtyard is part of an 1850s adobe marketplace, with hanging baskets, crafts stalls, and Native American art. The simple and inexpensive food includes Southwestern pasta salads, roasted poblano chiles, sandwiches, and mesquite-grilled fish. *201 N. Court Ave., at Meyer St., Tucson, tel. 520/622–0351. AE, D, MC, V. $$*

The Good Earth Restaurant and Bakery. This lovely, casual restaurant has an atrium filled with cacti. It serves homemade soups, pasta, beef, seafood, and several types of fruit crepes. An irresistible dessert is the mangoes with crème anglaise. *6366 E. Broadway Blvd., at Wilmot St. (El Mercado), Tucson, tel. 520/745–6600. No credit cards. $*

Entertainments

Tucson Zoo and Reid Park. A two-minute walk from Hi Corbett ballpark brings you to this cool, shaded zoo threaded with streams. There are only about 300 animals, but their habitats are attractive, and visitors can get as close as 8 ft from macaws, lions, and anteaters. It's a stroller-friendly zoo, but watch for the ducks that cross your path. You may want to eat here before the ball game at the inexpensive snack bar. Reid Park also has a man-made lake with half-hour paddleboat rentals (tel. 520/791—4088; $10 deposit; four-person boats, $6; two-person boats, $4.50). *22nd St. and Country Club Rd., at Randolph Way, Tucson, tel. 520/791–4022. Admission: $4 adults, $3 senior citizens, 75¢ ages 5–14. Open daily 9–4.*

Tucson Children's Museum. This 1901 former Carnegie library has been transformed into a colorful, imaginative children's museum. You are welcomed by a large iron dinosaur in pink and green on the front lawn. The museum contains hands-on exhibits focusing on health and nature. *200 S. 6th Ave., Tucson, tel. 520/884–7511. Admission: $5.50 adults, $4.50 senior citizens, $3.50 ages 3–16, $2.50 for all after 3 PM, free on third Sun. of month. Open Tues.–Sat. 9–5, Sun. noon–5.*

Arizona State Museum. Children enjoy this free museum's display of some 20 dozen colorful Mexican masks. Located just inside the main gate of the University of Arizona, the two-story museum includes Hopi pottery, with good questions put to visitors on each display. Across the campus roadway is the Arizona Historical Society (tel. 520/628–5774), with a children's history exhibit. *949 E. 2nd St., at Park Ave., Tucson, tel. 520/628–5774. Open Mon.–Sat. 10–4, Sun. noon–4.*

Sights to See

Arizona-Sonora Desert Museum. They call it a living museum, but "zoo" and "natural habitat" fit, too—it's an exceptional display of the animals and plants of the Sonora Desert. There are 300 animal species, from mountain lions to hummingbirds, and 1,200 kinds of plants, including a colorful desert garden. Bring a hat, sunscreen, and comfortable shoes for a mostly outdoor experience with 2 mi of paths across 21 acres. It's 14 mi west of downtown Tucson. *2021 N. Kinney Rd., Tucson, tel. 520/883–2702 or www.desertmuseum.org. Admission: $8.95 adults, $1.75 ages 6–12, under 6 free. Open Mar.–Sept., daily 7:30–6; Oct.–Feb. daily 8:30–5.*

Mission at San Xavier. Approach this Spanish mission by the slower Mission Road to see life on the Indian reservation that surrounds it. There's a rural Hispanic cemetery near the mission church, which was founded in 1692. Its vivid wall paintings are under renovation by some of the same curators who did the Sistine Chapel cleaning in Rome. Rows of prayer candles are adorned with sonograms, hospital bracelets, and driver's licenses pinned to religious icons by those seeking miracles or other good fortune. Residents of the Tohonó O'odham Reservation frequently make and sell Indian fried bread outside the mission. *1950 W. San Xavier Rd., Tucson, tel. 520/294–2624. Donations appreciated. Open daily 7–5.*

ROCKY MOUNTAIN BASEBALL
DENVER, COLORADO SPRINGS, ALBUQUERQUE

32

Colorado's mile-high baseball provides many glorious views and lots of home runs flying through the thin mountain air. Start with the Colorado Rockies' Coors Field, a $215-million HOK-designed beauty in Denver's lower downtown district. While exploring the downtown area near the ballpark, make sure you find baseball's best art, a funky arched sculpture titled *The Evolution of the Ball*. Visit the U.S. Mint to see where 38 million coins are minted every day. Elich Gardens and Lakeside amusement parks, the Denver Zoo, and the State Capitol are four of Denver's other treasures.

Colorado Springs, 75 mi south of Denver on Interstate 25, is the home of the Rockies' Triple A franchise in the famed Pacific Coast League, the Colorado Springs Sky Sox. When you ride the Cog Railway to the top of Pikes Peak, you will be twice as high above sea level as Sky Sox Stadium. The Air Force Academy, the Pro Rodeo Hall of Fame, and the stately Broadmoor Hotel are among our favorites here.

Albuquerque, New Mexico, lies 280 mi south of Colorado Springs, but is worth the long haul. For the real experience of New Mexico's Native American culture, stop in Santa Fe, 60 mi north of Albuquerque. Nearly every building is adobe-style in Santa Fe, including one of the most unusual state capitol buildings you will ever visit.

The Albuquerque Dukes are the Los Angeles Dodgers' entry in the Pacific Coast League. The Dukes play in the Albuquerque Sports Stadium with its unique drive-in baseball, where 100 cars can park atop a wall of black lava beyond left field, 30 to 40 ft above the playing surface. The Indian Pueblo Cultural Center on the edge of Old Town lets children grind corn, weave baskets, and make jewelry in old-fashioned ways.

COLORADO ROCKIES

League: National League • **Class:** Major League • **Stadium:** Coors Field • **Opened:** 1995 • **Capacity:** 50,000 • **Dimensions:** LF: 347, CF: 415, RF: 350 • **Surface:** grass • **Season:** Apr.–early Oct.

STADIUM LOCATION: 2001 Blake St., Denver, CO 80205-2000.

TEAM WEB SITE: www.coloradorockies.com

GETTING THERE: From north, take I–25 south to Exit 213/Park Ave. From east and west, take I–70 to I–25 south. Take Exit 213/Park Ave. From south, take I–25 north to Exit 207A/Broadway/Lincoln. Follow downtown signs. Call 303/299–6000 for information about RockiesRide—express routes from free park-n-ride lots—and other transit alternatives. A free Mall Shuttle runs along 16th St. to Market St. Station.

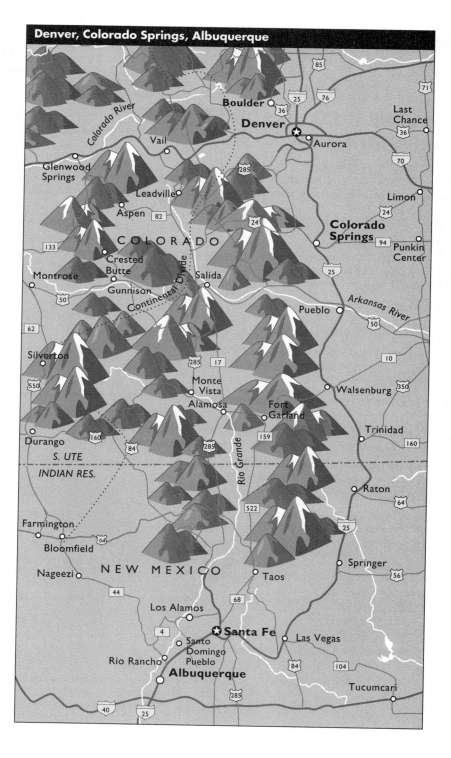

PARKING: Stadium lots ($6) have entrances on Blake St. at 23rd, 27th, and 33rd Sts.; open 3 hrs before game. At private lots within blocks of stadium, $12 is about average for 6-block walk.

TICKET INFORMATION: Box 120, Denver, CO 80201-0120, tel. 303/762–5437 or 800/388–7625, fax 303/312–2219.

PRICE RANGE: Box seats $23–$25; club level $31–$33; reserved $12–$17; pavilion $11; rockpile $4 (limit 4), $1 (limit 2; ages under 13 and over 54).

GAME TIME: Sun.–Fri. 7:05 PM, Sat. 6:05 PM, day games 1:05.

TIPS ON SEATING: Order tickets in advance; ballpark usually sold out. 2,300 seats in bleacher section on top of batter's eye in deep center field go on sale 2½ hours before each game at ticket window near gate A; line forms early. To see mountains past left-field foul pole, sit on first-base side.

SEATING FOR PEOPLE WITH DISABILITIES: Available throughout stadium. Parking behind right field, accessible from Wazee and Park Ave.

STADIUM FOOD: If you have a club-level ticket, you can get a plate of Mt. Ranch pasta ($5) or a sliced turkey sandwich on a decent roll ($6). Otherwise, there are endless repeats of the same two pizza and hot-dog stands throughout the park. The Chicago dog at $4 is passable, and Itza Pizza at $3.75 tastes fine but is overpriced. You can get Rocky Mountain oysters, which are deep-fried bull testicles, but you won't want to; they're gamey and greasy. At **Madeline's,** behind center field, there are Green River drinks for $2.75 and six flavors of Dreyer's ice cream. Columbo frozen yogurt, squishy frozen lemonade ($3), and beers of the world are also available. A deli behind section 136 has chef salads, potato and pasta salad, and sandwiches.

SMOKING POLICY: Smoking not allowed in seating areas; designated smoking areas in stadium.

TOURISM INFORMATION: Denver Metro Convention & Visitors Bureau (225 W. Colfax Ave., Denver, CO 80202, tel. 303/892–1112 or 800/645–3446).

Denver: Coors Field

When Denver won a major-league baseball franchise, the Colorado Rockies played two seasons in aging Mile High Stadium, home of the Denver Broncos of the National Football League. The baseball-starved fans of the Rocky Mountain region flocked to Mile High Stadium. They were richly rewarded for their patience in 1995 with the inaugural season of a magnificent new ballpark in Denver's downtown.

Designed by HOK of Kansas City, Coors Field was built at a cost of $215.5 million. Originally designed for 43,500 fans, it was reconfigured for 45,000 and then 50,249 because of the amazing fan support of the Rockies at Mile High Stadium. The ballpark fits neatly into the historic lower downtown area known as LoDo to locals. It is on the former site of the Denver Pacific Depot, Denver's first railroad station. The exterior red brick matches the warehouses and office buildings that surround it. A huge clock sits high atop the entranceway under the American flag and between the large silver letters spelling out Coors Field. Musical groups often welcome you into the park, and official greeters help you find your way.

The field is 21 ft below street level, providing for a 350-yard main concourse encircling the field. Workers dug up a 66-million-year-old dinosaur rib bone near home plate while building the stadium.

This is a hitter's park; the ball goes 9 percent farther at Denver's mile-high altitude, and the thin air is said to flatten out pitchers' curveballs. With a small foul territory, a ball that is an out in most parks often goes home with a fan here.

There is an old-fashioned hand-operated scoreboard in right field and a huge video screen above left center field. The field is circled by deep-reddish-colored crushed lava rock that serves as the outfield warming track. The lower-deck seats at first and third bases are as close to the action as major-league baseball will allow. Seats in the front rows of the upper deck have an excellent view of the field. The horseshoe-shape, 2,300-seat bleacher section—called the Rockpile—is high up above the batter's eye in center field.

This is a kid-friendly park with a small play-ground for children out past the left-field wall.

Our favorite piece of Denver baseball art is *The Evolution of the Ball* by Lonnie Hanzon. You will find this funky arched sculpture on the Wynkoop Street pedestrian way across the street from deep left field. Its 108 balls include a matzo ball, a spitball, Lucille Ball, and a mothball. Don't miss the 40 lovely terra-cotta tiles of the state flower—the columbine—designed by Barry Rose that appear at the top of the stadium's exterior columns. Walk around the front of the stadium on Blake Street to the opposite corner of the stadium complex at 22nd Street to see *The Bottom of the Ninth* by Erick Johnson. This neon and aluminum piece depicts a runner sliding into home with an umpire making a call.

Plan to take a walk inside the park. One of the best features of Coors Field is the concourse open to the field. You can get a hot dog or a drink without missing a pitch. For the best art inside the stadium, make sure you see the 100-ft-long mural out beyond center field. *The West, the Worker, and the Ballfield* by Matt O'Neill and Jeff Starr hits a few of the highlights of the history of this site, from the buffalo to baseball.

The very best views in Coors Field are from the upper deck on the third-base side looking away from the field to downtown and the mountains beyond. From way down the left-field side, you can see Mile High Stadium. Hike up to the top of the stadium and sit in one of the purple seats six rows from the top of the upper deck, 1 mi high at 5,280 ft above sea level. You'll need to bring windbreakers or plastic ponchos, as Denver frequently has short rainstorms.

Take a pregame tour of the park. The walking tours of Coors Field take about 60 minutes, cover 1 mi, and are excellent. Call 303/762-5437 for information on times.

Where to Stay

Holiday Inn–North/Coliseum. This four-story, mid-city hotel offers what may be the easiest way to get a ticket to the sold-out Rockies: $55 per person includes double-occupancy lodging, transportation to the game, a "premium" seat, and a full breakfast. Kids eat free with an adult. *4849 Bannock St., Exit 215 from I–25 N, Denver 80216, tel. 303/292–9500 or 800/465–4329, fax 303/295–3521. 218 rooms. Facilities: outdoor pool, health center. AE, D, DC, MC, V. $$*

Best Western Landmark Inn. The upper floors in the west tower of this nine-story high-rise have mountain views. The rooms are modern and have queen-size beds. *455 S. Colorado Blvd., Exit 240 from I–25 N, Denver 80222, tel. 303/388–5561 or 800/528–1234, fax 303/388–7936. 280 rooms. Facilities: restaurant, indoor pool, hot tub, sauna, exercise room, coin laundry. AE, D, DC, MC, V. $$*

Wyndham Garden Hotel. Ask for an upper mountain-view room in this high-rise hotel in a busy restaurant and hotel area in midtown Denver. The rooms are standard size. *1475 S. Colorado Blvd., Denver 80222, tel. 303/757–8797 or 800/996–3426, fax 303/758–0704. 240 rooms. Facilities: restaurant, indoor pool, coin laundry. AE, D, DC, MC, V. $$*

Where to Eat

Rounders at the Sandlot. You must have a ticket to the ball game to eat here. You enter through a turnstile and then step inside Rounders to see the only beer-brewing operation in a baseball stadium. The restaurant is named after a 17th-century British game that preceded baseball. Rounders has good American café food, including salads, sandwiches, burritos, pizza, and, of course, beer. *2151 Blake St., Denver, tel. 303/312–2553. AE, D, MC, V. $$*

Furr's Cafeteria. This chain of inexpensive, high-quality cafeterias is a regional institution. Decorated in a Southwest theme, the western Denver branch has a kiddie buffet bar. Families fill the booths and tables, especially after church, for its chicken and dumplings, pecan surprise pie, and tapioca pudding. *4900 Kipling St., Denver, tel. 303/423–4602. AE, D, MC, V. $*

Gunther Toody's. This bright diner is spacious enough to hold a Corvette, a motorcycle, and dozens of booths. Named after one of the hapless cops on *Car 54, Where Are You?*, the restaurant dishes out slapstick in addition to good salads, phosphates, wet fries, and lumpy mashed potatoes. There are old pinball machines, joking waitresses, and funny signs throughout. *4500 E. Alameda Ave., exit on Colorado Blvd. from I–25, Denver, tel. 303/399–1959. AE, MC, V.* $

Rocky Mountain Diner. There is a rustic cowboy theme and healthy food at this cheerful downtown restaurant. You can get a children's menu and fresh limeade and lemonade. Do you dare try the Rocky Mountain Oysters? The sandwiches are overstuffed, and the venison chili is unusual and hot. The kids will want to try sitting in the bar's saddle barstools. *800 18th St., Denver, tel. 303/293–8383. AE, D, MC, V.* $$

Entertainments

Elitch Gardens. This 110-year-old attraction, now owned by Six Flags, is America's only downtown amusement park. You can ride the huge 1926 Philadelphia Toboggan carousel and an old wooden coaster and see the lights of the city. An extensive kiddieland, a waterpark, and a 300-ft Total Tower ride keep the young ones busy. The pirate diving show is thrilling; the many juggling and magic shows are also good. *4620 W. 38th St, at I–25 and Speer Blvd., Denver, tel. 303/595–4386. Admission: $29 for over 48″, $14.50 ages 4–48″, senior citizens 70 and older free. Open mid-Apr.–Labor Day, Mon.–Thurs. 10–10, Fri.–Sat. 10–11.*

Children's Museum of Denver. This is an extensive hands-on center, with science experiments and visual games. Reserve ahead to try skiing without snow on Kidslope, where instructors give 90-minute lessons for an $8 fee. A separate theater in the museum has a $1 entry fee. The museum is just east of Mile High Stadium. Parking is $5. *2121 Children's Museum Dr., I–25 at 23rd Ave. exit, Denver, tel. 303/433–7444. Admission: $5 ages 3–59, $3 senior citizens, $2 ages 1–2; free Fri. 5:30–8. Open late May–Labor Day, daily 10–5; Labor Day–late May, Mon.–Thurs. 10–5, Fri. 10–5 and 5:30–8, Sat. 10–5, Sun. noon–5.*

Denver Museum of Natural History. The emphasis is on Botswana, Egyptian mummies, dinosaurs, bears, and sea mammals at this extensive museum. Its Hall of Life health-education center is popular, with the heart's function explained in clever graphics. The Gates Planetarium and IMAX shows require extra fees. *2001 Colorado Blvd., Denver, tel. 303/370–6357. Admission: $6 adults, $4 ages 3–13. Open Labor Day–Memorial Day, daily 9–5; Memorial Day–Labor Day, Sat.–Thurs. 9–5, Fri. 9–8.*

Denver Zoo. This nicely landscaped zoo in City Park has Primate Panorama, a 5-acre primate habitat. There's an endearing nursery for baby animals. You can watch polar bears swim underwater and attend free-flight bird shows daily in summer at 11:30, 1, or 3 in the Event Meadow. The gates close an hour before closing time. *2300 Steele St., between Colorado Blvd. and York St., Denver, tel. 303/331–4100. Admission: $8 adults, $6 senior citizens, $4 ages 4–12. Open Apr.–Sept., daily 9–6; Oct.–Mar., daily 10–5.*

Lakeside Amusement Park. Step back to 1908 at this bargain park with intact Art Deco neon signs, ticket booths, and ride buildings. There's an extensive, imaginative kiddieland with 16 rides. The vintage Cyclone wooden roller coaster starts in the darkness of a short tunnel. At night, thousands of lightbulbs and a 150-ft tower light the family-run park. The steam trains that circle the lake are from the 1904 World's Fair. The park is just two mi west of Denver. Parking is free. *4601 Sheridan Blvd., Denver, tel. 303/477–1621. Admission: $1.25 with pay-per-ride, or $12 all-day pass. Kiddieland open May–Labor Day, weekdays 1–10; major rides open 6 PM–11 PM, weekends noon–11.*

Ocean Journey. You can experience a flash flood at this terrific new aquarium that places tanks over your head and under your feet. The Colorado River and the Kampar River in Indonesia are featured, along with the appropriate birds, mammals, plants, and trees. There are also touch pools and a sea otter cove, plus a cafeteria. The aquarium is directly north of the Children's Museum. *700 Water St., Denver, tel. 303/561–4450. Admission: $14.95 adults, $12.95 ages 13–17 and senior citizens, $6.95 ages 4–12. Open daily 10–6.*

Tiny Town. Built in 1915, this vintage miniature village is a hit with younger children. It includes homes, shops, a church, newspaper office, and toy store, all constructed at one-sixth scale and in the style of the late 1800s. Guests can ride a small steam train on a mile journey throughout the 100 buildings for $1. *6249 S. Turkey Creek Rd., exit on S. Turkey Creek Rd. from Hwy. 285 S, Denver, tel. 303/697–6829. Admission: $3 adults, $2 ages 3–12. Open daily 10–5.*

Sights to See

U.S. Mint. Here 38 million coins are manufactured daily. The guides show you the stamping machines and recite some big financial numbers. Until the 1970s, many of these mounds of pennies were counted by hand. There's an old-time security guard's nest and a gift shop. Tours start every 15 minutes. Go early in the day to avoid lines for this free downtown attraction. *320 W. Colfax Ave., Denver, tel. 303/837–3582. Open weekdays 8–2:45.*

Lower Downtown Walking Tour. Don't just drive in, see the game, and leave. Coors Field has sparked an impressive revival of Denver's lower downtown, with its warehouses and ethnic neighborhoods. For a "Lower Downtown Walking Tour" brochure and information about events, call the Lower Downtown District, Inc. (tel. 303/628–5428).

The Capitol. The Colorado Capitol is based on the classic Corinthian design of the nation's Capitol in Washington. Construction began in 1886 but was not completed for 22 years, in part because of a strong commitment to using state materials. Be sure to see the stained-glass windows in the old Supreme Court chambers and *Women's Gold,* a hand-stitched wall hanging that tells the stories of Colorado's most prominent women. For a fabulous view of the Rocky Mountains, visit the observation deck in the 272-ft gold dome, up 93 winding steps from the third floor. Denver is known as the Mile High City, and there is a granite step on the west side of the Capitol identified as "ONE MILE ABOVE SEA LEVEL." In 1969 engineering students from Colorado State University found the designation inaccurate. A geodetic survey marker three steps above the original one indicates the real mile-high point. *Colfax Ave. and Lincoln St., Denver, tel. 303/829–2604. Open weekdays 7:30–5:30; tours and observation deck, weekdays 9–3:30 and Sat. June–Aug. 9:30–2:30.*

COLORADO SPRINGS SKY SOX

League: Pacific Coast League • **Major League Affiliation:** Colorado Rockies • **Class:** AAA • **Stadium:** Sky Sox Stadium • **Opened:** 1989 • **Capacity:** 6,200 • **Dimensions:** LF: 350, CF: 410, RF: 350 • **Surface:** grass • **Season:** Apr.–Labor Day

STADIUM LOCATION: 4385 Tutt Blvd., Colorado Springs, CO 80922.

TEAM WEB SITE: www.skysox.com

GETTING THERE: From Denver, I–25 S to Woodmen Rd. exit. Turn left, east on Woodmen 5 mi. Right on Powers Blvd., go 3 mi, left on Barnes Rd.

PARKING: At stadium, $3.

TICKET INFORMATION: 4385 Tutt Blvd, Colorado Springs, CO 80922, tel. 719/597–3000, fax 719/597–2491.

PRICE RANGE: Box seats $7 adults, $6 ages under 13 and over 59; upper reserved $4.75 adults, $4.25 ages under 13 and over 59.

GAME TIME: Apr.–mid-June, weekdays 6:35 PM, Sat. 1:35 PM; mid-June–Labor Day, Mon.–Sat. 7:05 PM, Sun. 1:35 PM; gates open 1 hr early.

TIPS ON SEATING: Seats on third-base side have view of Pikes Peak (behind first base) but face sun during early innings of night games.

SEATING FOR PEOPLE WITH DISABILITIES: On main concourse under canopy.

STADIUM FOOD: Mexican food is the standout here, with excellent beef and chicken burritos at the **Casa Llenas** stand for $3. The hottest food in baseball has to be the jala bumpers, deep-fried jalapeño peppers with cheese (50¢). Also on the menu are chicken wings, brats, and espresso. Once the game starts, anyone is welcome in the **Hall of Fame Bar and Restaurant**; it's worth a trip to get the chicken Caesar salad with crackers for $5.

SMOKING POLICY: General-admission section behind home plate and box seats section (section 100) near third base are no-smoking.

VISITING TEAM HOTEL: Best Western Le Baron Hotel (314 W. Bijou St., Colorado Springs, CO 80905, tel. 719/471–8680 or 800/528–1234).

TOURISM INFORMATION: Colorado Springs Convention & Visitors Bureau (104 S. Cascade Ave., Colorado Springs, CO 80901, tel. 719/635–1632 or 800/888–4747).

Colorado Springs: Sky Sox Stadium

Sky Sox Stadium, built according to a design used for several late 1980s stadiums, has three great attributes for fans: The food is on the concourse above the seats so you don't have to miss the action; the players leave up stairs just beyond the seating areas at third and first bases after batting practice, so even the shyest child can bring home a ball full of autographs; and just past these stairs on each side are grassy berms for kids to roam and chase foul balls. At Sky Sox Stadium, they have 2,200 box seats and room for 4,000 in general admission bench seating with backs. Eighteen skyboxes are built over the roof above the concourse.

The night we attended, more than 7,000 fans poured into Sky Sox Stadium to see their local heroes. It was about 1,500 fans more than the stadium handles comfortably. The food lines packed the concourse above the seating while hundreds of general-admission fans sat on the grass berms beyond first and third.

Sky Sox Stadium claims to be the highest ballpark in North America; it is a full 1,000 ft above Denver's Coors Field, and there were plenty of home runs flying through the thin mountain air—six by the Sky Sox—when we were there. Fireworks go off beyond the left-center scoreboard after the National Anthem, at the seventh-inning stretch, and after every Sox home run and victory—nine times the night we visited.

In 1901 the Colorado Springs baseball team was called the Millionaires in tribute to the local residents who had made their fortunes mining nearby hills and mountains. The current Sky Sox draw their name from the high altitude and a long association with the Chicago White Sox in the 1950s when Colorado Springs was in the now-defunct Western League.

From the seats on the third-base side, fans can see the front range of the Rocky Mountains. Pikes Peak—14,110 ft above sea level and twice as high as Sky Sox Stadium—is visible. At night, look over first base and way beyond for a light—it's at the Summit House at the top of the peak.

We were here on a gorgeous day in late July, and it was chilly. Wear long pants and take a sweater or coat. When the sun drops behind the mountains, the air cools off quickly.

We found Colorado Springs—both the city and the ballpark—an odd combination of trendy and traditional. There is a hot tub near the right-field foul pole. Eight fans pay big bucks for dinner, champagne, and baseball. You have to wonder what the attraction is on a cool Colorado Springs night.

Where to Stay

Best Western Le Baron Hotel. The back of this three-story downtown hotel is built around a courtyard, with a large pool and gazebo. Most of its rooms are standard doubles, with contemporary furnishings. *314 W. Bijou St., at Exit 142 off I–25, Colorado Springs 80905, tel. 719/471–8680 or 800/528–1234, fax 719/471–0894. 206 rooms. Facilities: restaurant, outdoor pool, coin laundry. AE, D, DC, MC, V. $$*

Dale Motel. This old-fashioned two-story bargain motel has a pool and is convenient to the freeway, downtown, and attractions. The rooms are clean, with dated furnishings, and have writing alcoves. Kitchens are available in six rooms for an extra fee. *620 W. Colorado Ave., Exit 142 off I–25, Colorado Springs 80905, tel. 719/636–3721 or 800/456–3204. 29 rooms. Facilities: outdoor pool. AE, D, DC, MC, V. $*

Where to Eat

Conway's Red Top. All three Red Tops in the city serve huge (dinner-plate-size) hamburgers, fine fries, and a good beef stew. Children should get the half-burgers. These casual restaurants with Formica booths concentrate on a few items done well. *1520 S. Nevada St., at Navaho St., Colorado Springs, tel. 719/633–2444. MC, V. $*

The Broadmoor. It's too pricey for most to stay in this sprawling Italian Renaissance–style hotel, built in 1918, in the foothills of the Rockies. You can eat lunch at the casual Grill Room (in the main golf club) or Julie's (at Broadmoor West, across the lake) or have pastries at Espresso Broadmoor (in the main lobby) and view the resort. Afternoon tea is served in the mezzanine daily from May through October from 4 to 5 and November through April on Friday and Saturday. There are ducks on a man-made lake and paddleboats for hire. Nonguests may pay to swim here. *Lake Ave. and Circle Dr., 2 mi west of I–25, Colorado Springs, tel. 719/634–7711 or 800/634–7711. AE, D, DC, MC, V. $$*

The Mason Jar. This antiques-filled family restaurant has a peaceful atmosphere. You can have chicken-fried steak, real mashed potatoes, and excellent home-style fruit cobblers. There is a children's menu. Drinks are served in mason jars. *2925 W. Colorado Ave., Colorado Springs, tel. 719/632–4820. Open daily 11–10. D, MC, V. $*

Entertainments

The Colorado Springs Visitors Bureau will give you $100 worth of discount coupons for many attractions if you stop in at the visitor center (104 S. Cascade Ave., Suite 104, Colorado Springs, tel. 800/368–4748; open weekdays 8:30–5).

Cheyenne Mountain Zoo. A wolf exhibit, 500 animals, and a merry-go-round are what you'll find here. Visitors can drive up the Tutt Scenic Highway to the Shrine of the Sun, a monument to Will Rogers. The zoo is at the base of Cheyenne Mountain. Entry gates close one hour before closing time. *4250 Cheyenne Mountain Zoo Rd., Exit 128 from I–25, Colorado Springs, tel. 719/475–9555. Admission: $7.50 adults, $4.50 ages 3–11, $6.50 senior citizens. Open Memorial Day–Labor Day, daily 9–6; Labor Day–Memorial Day, daily 9–5.*

Pikes Peak Cog Railway. You'll need to dress warmly for this three-hour journey to the 14,110-ft top of Pike's Peak. You can see the Garden of the Gods below you as well as Denver, which is 75 mi to the north. Passengers have a half hour to explore the peak before returning. There is a café at the depot. Train reservations are advised; passengers should arrive 30 minutes before departure. Trains depart every 80 minutes. *515 Ruxton Ave., Manitou Springs, tel. 719/685–5401. Admission: $22.50 adults, $11 ages 3–11; under 3 free if held on adult's lap. Open daily 8–5:20.*

Pro Rodeo Hall of Fame and Museum of the American Cowboy. Watch a clever movie with an audiovisual cowboy and climb on models of rodeo horses. This handsome museum lets you gawk at the intricate saddles and achievements of the men and women who are and were daredevils on horseback. The informative and classy Hall of Fame includes movie cowboy Gene Autry, owner of the California Angels and former semipro ballplayer. It contains a great gift shop with many imaginative and inexpensive items. *101 Pro Rodeo Dr., Colorado Springs, tel. 719/528–4764. Admission: $6 adults, $3 ages 6–12, $5 senior citizens. Open daily 9–5.*

Sights to See

Garden of the Gods. This free city park has magnificent red sandstone formations that are more than 300 million years old. Shaped by erosion, the rocks cover 1,350 acres. Visitors may hike or picnic among the unusual geology and plant life. Entry is free, but the visitor center requests donations. Take I–25 west at Garden of the Gods Road to 30th Street. *Garden of the Gods Rd., Colorado Springs, tel. 719/578–6939. Open May–Oct., daily 5 AM–11 PM; Nov.–Apr., daily 5 AM–9 PM.*

U.S. Air Force Academy. The architecture is striking and the feeling of isolation is strong at this impressive service academy. Visitors are permitted in the chapel, the field house, the planetarium, and the cadet social center. The chapel is open for services Sunday mornings at 9 and 11. Jewish services that are open to the public are held Friday at 8 PM. On Monday through Friday, visitors may watch the cadets line up in the Noon Meal Formation. The visitor center contains a theater, a gift shop, and a snack bar. I–25, Exit 156B, Colorado Springs, tel. 719/333–2025. Open daily 9–6.

U.S. Olympic Complex. Take a free guided tour of the Olympic Training Facility that serves 15,000 athletes yearly. The 90-minute tour includes a film and access to the gym, aquatic, and training centers. 1750 E. Boulder St., Colorado Springs, tel. 719/578–4644. Open Mon.–Sat. 9–5, Sun. 10–4.

World Figure Skating Hall of Fame. Nancy Kerrigan, Sonja Henie, Dick Button, and Dorothy Hamill are among those honored in this free museum, which adjoins the headquarters of the U.S. Figure Skating Association. Costumes, videos of various choreographed works, skates, and medals are on display. There is a library and archives downstairs and a small gift shop. The museum is a half mile northeast of the Broadmoor Resort. 20 1st St., Colorado Springs, tel. 719/635–5200. Open Mon.–Sat. 10–4.

ALBUQUERQUE DUKES

League: Pacific Coast League • **Major League Affiliation:** Los Angeles Dodgers • **Class:** AAA • **Stadium:** Albuquerque Sports Stadium • **Opened:** 1969 • **Capacity:** 10,510 • **Dimensions:** LF: 360, CF: 410, RF: 340 • **Surface:** grass • **Season:** Apr.–Labor Day

STADIUM LOCATION: 1601 Stadium Blvd. SE, Albuquerque, NM 87106.

GETTING THERE: I–25 to Stadium Blvd. exit. East several blocks on Stadium Blvd.

PARKING: $1 at stadium lots and free across street in parking lot of University of New Mexico football stadium

TICKET INFORMATION: 1601 Stadium Blvd. SE, Albuquerque, NM 87106, tel. 505/243–1791, fax 505/842–0561.

PRICE RANGE: Box seats $5.50; general admission $4.50 adults, $3.50 students and senior citizens, $2 ages 6–12; drive-in $3.50 adults, $2 children.

GAME TIME: Mon.–Sat. 7 PM, Sun. 1 PM; gates open 1 hr before game.

TIPS ON SEATING: General admission seats in grandstand are fine. Sit on third-base side to avoid sun in your eyes and to get a better view of mountains.

SEATING FOR PEOPLE WITH DISABILITIES: On concourse just behind box seats.

STADIUM FOOD: In this park, the servings are large, prices are low, and the selections limited. The souvenir cups are huge—$2.50 for a huge lemonade, nonalcoholic piña colada, or soda. Regular-size drinks are $1.50, including an orange whippee (like an Orange Julius). Hamburgers are a bargain at $2, hot dogs at $1.50, and burritos at $2. The always-refreshing lemon chill is $2.50. Churros and popcorn are $1 each.

SMOKING POLICY: Smoking prohibited in seating areas. Designated areas in lower concourse near rest rooms, behind left-field bleachers, and in drive-in area.

VISITING TEAM HOTEL: Plaza Inn Albuquerque (900 Medical Arts NE, Albuquerque, NM 87106, tel. 505/243–5693 or 800/237–1307).

TOURISM INFORMATION: Albuquerque Convention & Visitors Bureau (Box 26866, Albuquerque, NM 87125, tel. 505/842–9918 or 800/733–9918).

Albuquerque:
Sports Stadium

In 1705, the Viceroy of New Spain and Duque de Albuquerque, Francisco Fernández de la Cueva Enríquez, sent a temporary governor to Santa Fe. The next year, the agent founded what is now Albuquerque, New Mexico. In 1915, the Albuquerque Dukes competed in the Class D Rio Grande Association. Albuquerque began a long association with the Los Angeles Dodgers in 1963, first as a Double A Texas League team. In 1972, under the direction of manager Tommy Lasorda, the Dukes became the Dodgers' Triple A team in the Pacific Coast League.

"We're not into nuttiness. We're into baseball," Pat McKernan, the longtime Dukes president and general manager says. That pretty much sums up what you get at the Albuquerque Sports Stadium. No dizzy bat contests or mascots here. The Dukes play some of the very best baseball in the minor leagues, winning the Triple A Pacific Coast League championship six times since McKernan took over in 1980.

The Albuquerque Sports Stadium was a state-of-the-art stadium when it was built in 1969 to replace the WPA-era Tingley Field. It is showing its age. Sports Stadium—a city-owned stadium across the street from the athletic complex of the University of New Mexico—seats more than 10,000. This is a formidable baseball place in the tradition of Richmond's Diamond and Pawtucket's McCoy Stadium. The large grandstand has 2,528 box seats and 3,714 general admission seats. There is a live organist, but there aren't any skyboxes. The gray roof covers many of the general admission seats in the grandstand. Down the third-base side, there is a huge football-like bleacher area—aluminum benches without backs—with seating for 4,254 fans. The grassy area down the first-base line is not open to fans unless the crowd exceeds 10,000. The Sandia Mountains rise beyond right center field.

The bathrooms and concession stands are in the dark, not very fan-friendly concourse under the grandstand. There isn't anything fancy or innovative here—just traditional baseball food.

We did find the largest souvenir cups with the best prices for beverages anywhere in baseball.

The Albuquerque Sports Stadium offers the only drive-in baseball in the professional ranks. They dug 320,000 cubic yards of earth in 10 days to create a stadium bowl, so that the stands sit above the field, especially beyond the outfield fences. There is room for more than 100 cars to pay and park just beyond the outfield fences. People come early for tailgating and barbecue, bringing blankets, lawn chairs, and grills. No alcohol is allowed in the drive-in area. Home runs into or over the drive-in area are frequent. The 30- to 40-ft drop from the car level to the field level is a wall of black lava rock quarried from volcanoes near the city.

Another special treat is the general manager's office on the lower concourse, directly across from the main food stand. In the program, Pat McKernan invites fans to drop by to talk. And he means it. You might have to wait a few minutes—a Los Angeles Dodgers executive was arranging to bring a Duke to the majors when we knocked on McKernan's door. You will find a true baseball man in a comfortable and cluttered office with walls covered with family photos, fish, and baseball memorabilia.

Where to Stay

Visiting Team Motel: Plaza Inn Albuquerque. Children stay free at this five-story, white-brick former Howard Johnson's motel, which sits on a hilltop overlooking the West Valley. The standard-size rooms have small balconies. At night the motel is aglow in twinkling white lights. There's a restaurant next door. *900 Medical Arts Ave. NE, at I–25 and Lomas Blvd., Albuquerque 87102, tel. 505/243–5693 or 800/237–1307, fax 505/843–6229. 120 rooms. Facilities: outdoor pool, exercise room, coin laundry. AE, D, MC, V. $*

Traveler's Inn. This bargain four-story hotel is in a quiet industrial neighborhood downtown. The beds are queen-size and the rooms freshly furnished. The surroundings aren't scenic, but the price is right for this pleasant hotel. *411 McKnight Ave. NW; exit I–40 at 4th or 2nd Sts.; Albuquerque 87102, tel. 505/242–5228 or 800/633–8300, fax 505/766–9218. 100 rooms. Facilities: outdoor pool, hot tub. AE, D, DC, MC, V. $*

Where to Eat

Frontier. Across the street from the University of New Mexico, this busy student standby is known for its butter-drenched pale sweet rolls. Come for breakfast and get fresh orange juice and breakfast burritos. The food is cheap, the Formica-tabled restaurant is open 24 hours, and the clients are loyal. *2400 Central Ave. SE, at Cornell St., Albuquerque, tel. 505/266–0550. MC, V.* $

M & J Restaurant. This city favorite has a kids' menu and great burritos, sopapillas, and warm corn chips. The tortillas are wonderfully fresh, as the Sanitary Tortilla Factory is part of this smoke-free restaurant. *403 2nd St. SW, Central Ave. exit from I–25, Albuquerque, tel. 505/242–4890. No credit cards. Closed Sun.* $

Powdrell's Barbeque. A former home has been renovated into a restaurant with very good barbecue slathered with a sauce handed down in the Powdrell family since 1870. You can enjoy smoked meats of all kinds—beef, pork, chicken, ribs, and sausages. Miniplates are available for children with one meat, one side dish, and Texas toast. The cobblers are a bit too sweet, but you'll be too full to try them or the sweet-potato pie anyway. *5209 4th St. NW, Albuquerque, tel. 505/345–8086. MC, V.* $

Entertainments

Albuquerque Biological Park/Rio Grande Zoo. View an extraordinarily large number of species, from white tigers to gorillas, in one of the country's least expensive zoos. The reptiles and rainforest animals are particularly good. From April through September, a bird show is presented. There is a separate fee, $4.50 for adults and $2.50 for children, for the aquarium and botanic gardens. A combination ticket costs $8 for adults, $4 for children. *903 10th St. SW, Albuquerque, tel. 505/764–6200. Admission to zoo: $4.50 adults, $2.50 ages 3–15 and senior citizens. Open weekdays 9–5, weekends 9–6.*

Indian Pueblo Cultural Center. This museum, gallery, gift shop, and restaurant is owned by the 19 Pueblo tribes of New Mexico. Youngsters can grind corn, weave baskets, and dress in shawls, bandoliers, bells, and fox tails in the hands-on children's center. Try your hand at making heishi jewelry the pre-electric way and learn to use an Indian bow and arrow. Native dancers perform on Saturday and Sunday at 11 and 2. You can also get directions here on how to tour the existing pueblos in the area. *2401 12th St. NW, 1 block north of I–40, Albuquerque, tel. 505/843–7270 or 800/766–4405. Admission: $4 adults, $3 senior citizens, $1 students; under 5 free. Museum open daily 9–5:30; children's center, Tues. and Thurs.–Fri. 9–4, Wed. 9–12:30, occasional Sat. 10–2.*

New Mexico Museum of Natural History. This small museum in Old Town allows you to walk through a volcano, stand on a pretend earthquake, and marvel at real-size dinosaurs. Children skip through it quickly, learning about the geology of the region. Films on the hour are an extra $4 for adults, $2 for children. Cheaper combination tickets are available. *Mountain Rd. NW, at 18th St. NW, Albuquerque, tel. 505/841–2802. Admission: $5.25 adults, $4.20 senior citizens and students, $2.10 ages 3–11. Open daily 9–5.*

Sandia Peak Tramway. Travel nearly 3 mi on the world's longest aerial tramway to Sandia Peak in Cibola National Forest. Trams leave every 20 to 30 minutes; count on a round-trip time of 1½ hours. There are mountain-bike trails and rental bikes and skiing in the winter. Tramway passengers often see hang-gliders and hot-air balloonists. If you have reservations to eat at the High Finance Restaurant (tel. 505/243–9742), at the peak, or the Firehouse restaurant (tel. 505/856–3473), at the base, the adult tram fees drop to $10. There's also a sandwich shop, Yogi's, at the lower tramway terminal. *Tramway Blvd., Exit 234 off I–25, Albuquerque, tel. 505/856–7325. Admission: $14 adults, $10 ages 5–12 and senior citizens. Open Memorial–Labor Day, daily 9 AM–10 PM.*

Sights to See

Route 66. Central Avenue is one section of famous Route 66. There are Art Deco storefronts, decorative metal signposts, and the 66 Diner (1405 Central Ave. NE, Albuquerque, tel. 505/247–1421), in a former Phillips 66 gas station, with a jukebox and vintage Route 66 photographs on the walls. It's worth driving through this section of Albuquerque to learn about the

Mother Road. At night, look for the El Vado Motel's (2500 Central Ave. SW, near Old Town Plaza) neon Indian sign. It dates from 1937 and is a beauty.

Santa Fe. The state capital, just 60 mi north of Albuquerque, is well worth a visit. New Mexico's Native American culture dates back centuries. The area was a Spanish colony for more than 250 years until 1821, when Mexico declared its independence and New Mexico became a province of Mexico. It became a United States Territory in 1850, soon after the Mexican-American War, and our 47th state in 1912.

The Palace of Governors, built in 1610, was the center of Spanish, Mexican, and American governments for several centuries. The Palace, which contains the State History Museum, stands in Santa Fe's downtown on the north side of the Plaza. *Palace Ave., Santa Fe, tel. 515/827–6483.*

The New Mexico State Capitol. Completed in 1967 and renovated in 1992, this is one of the most modern capitols in the nation. As with most other buildings in Santa Fe, the building's exterior is tan stucco in the adobe style. The round structure is patterned after the Zia Indian Sun Symbol, with four entrances representing the four rays of the symbol. The columns around the building are the only accommodation to more traditional, Greek Revival capitol architecture. Look for the Great Seal of the State of New Mexico, inlaid in turquoise and brass, in the floor of the rotunda. *Old Santa Fe Terr. and Paseo de Peralta, Santa Fe, tel. 505/827–3050. Open weekdays 8–5; free tours weekdays at 10 and 3.*

Loretto Chapel. The Sisters of Loretto dedicated their chapel in 1878, but it lacked space for a staircase to the choir loft. A gray-haired carpenter arrived, built a staircase with two complete 360-degree turns, and left without being paid. See his wooden masterpiece and wonder. *207 Old Santa Fe Trail, Santa Fe, tel. 505/982–0092. Admission: $2. Open Mon.–Sat. 8–6, Sun. 10:30–5.*

COWBOYS AND OIL WELLS 33
SAN ANTONIO, ARLINGTON

Texas baseball goes back to the 1880s, when some fans packed six-shooters at the games. The best of Texas baseball is now played in brand-new ballparks that reflect the local cultures. San Antonio's Wolff Stadium is as modern as they come, but in an attractive Spanish Mission style, complete with twin bell towers at the entrance. Whether you eat a catcher's mitt pita sandwich or a beef fajita, make sure you leave room for roasted corn-on-the cob, one of baseball's best food treats. The Missions are the Dodgers' entry in the Double A Texas League.

There is too much for families to explore in a single day in spectacular San Antonio, with its signature Riverwalk and historic missions. Your children will learn history on your visit to the Alamo, the oldest and most famous of the missions, later turned into a fort, where 189 men died fighting for Texas independence from Mexico. On your 190-mi drive north on Interstate 35 to the Fort Worth–Dallas area, stop in Austin, a booming college and state-government town full of energy and history.

Arlington, Texas, is a stop on the turnpike between Dallas and Fort Worth where builders put the airport and the theme parks. In 1994, The Ballpark in Arlington opened here. Lacking the downtown location that has made the new Baltimore, Cleveland, and Denver ballparks so successful didn't seem a problem to Texans. They simply built a steel and glass office building right in the stadium. On the state fairgrounds in Dallas, you'll find activities for children, including a comprehensive science museum and a small aquarium.

SAN ANTONIO MISSIONS

League: Texas League • **Major League Affiliation:** Los Angeles Dodgers • **Class:** AA • **Stadium:** Wolff Stadium • **Opened:** 1994 • **Capacity:** 6,300 • **Dimensions:** LF: 310, CF: 402, RF: 340 • **Surface:** grass • **Season:** Apr.–Labor Day

STADIUM LOCATION: 5757 Hwy. 90 W, San Antonio, TX 78227.

TEAM WEB SITE: www.samissions.com

GETTING THERE: From downtown, I–35 south to Hwy. 90 west. 6 mi to Callaghan Rd. exit. Stadium at intersection of I–90 and Callaghan.

PARKING: Available, $3.

TICKET INFORMATION: 5757 Hwy. 90 W, San Antonio, TX 78227, tel. 210/675–7275, fax 210/670–0001.

PRICE RANGE: Lower box (first 5 rows) $8.50; box seats $7.50; upper box $6.50; reserved seats $5.50; general admission $4.50 adults, $2.50 ages 2–12.

GAME TIME: Mon.–Sat. 7:05 PM, Sun. 6:05 PM; gates open 1 hr before game.

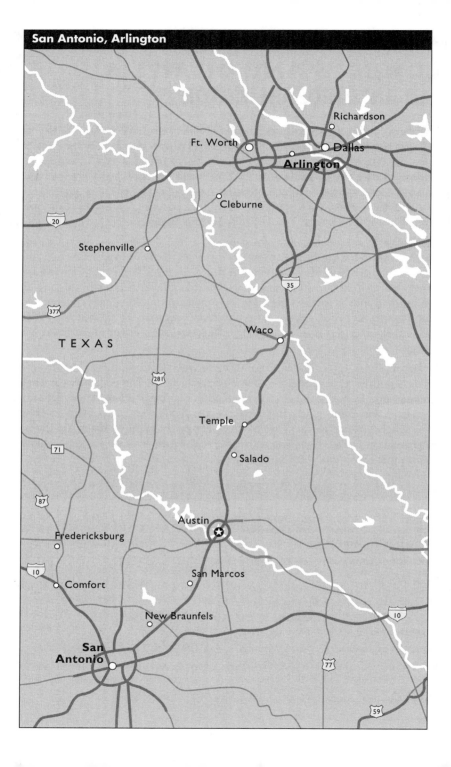

TIPS ON SEATING: Upper box seat preferable, as reserved seating is uncomfortable. Arrive early and get general-admission seats near field down first- and third-base lines.

SEATING FOR PEOPLE WITH DISABILITIES: In many sections throughout stadium.

STADIUM FOOD: There is a wide array of foods here, from excellent marinated beef and chicken fajitas ($3) to roasted corn on the cob ($2.50) and huge, fabulous pickles ($1). Roasted turkey legs are $4 and are too large for a young child to finish. A pita filled with ground beef and chili and topped with cheese is called a Catcher's Mitt ($3.50). It's messy, as is the Frito Pie, which has the same ingredients minus the pita ($2.50). There are also gyros ($3.25), which are easy for children to eat, and personal pan pizza ($4.50). The grill is on the third-base side.

SMOKING POLICY: Smoking not allowed in the seating area but allowed on the concourse.

VISITING TEAM HOTEL: Thrifty Inn–Northwest (I–10 at Wurzbach, San Antonio, TX 78230, tel. 210/696–0810 or 800/325–8300).

TOURISM INFORMATION: San Antonio Convention & Visitors Bureau (Box 2277, San Antonio, TX 78298, tel. 210/270–8700 or 800/447–3372).

San Antonio: Wolff Stadium

The Texas League was a wild and woolly affair right from its start in 1888, with teams in Austin, Dallas, Fort Worth, Galveston, Houston, and San Antonio. Wild Bill Setley, an umpire in 1910, said: "I've seen them wear six-shooters to games in the Texas League, and when a fan pulled one out in Fort Worth and took a shot at a fly ball, I was ready to check out."

Fans in the Dallas, Fort Worth, and Houston areas now cheer for major-league teams. Of the six charter members, only San Antonio remains in the Texas League. The team has gone by many different nicknames in its long history, but the one they use now—Missions—has the longest tradition and best represents San Antonio's rich history.

Wolff Stadium, opened in 1994 and named for the mayor who helped get it built, is reminiscent of the old Mission Stadium used from 1947 to 1964. This gorgeous stadium is in the Mission style, with twin bell towers at the entrance.

Designed by Ford, Carson & Powell of San Antonio, Wolff Stadium now has 6,300 permanent seats, but more than 8,000 showed up the night we were there and were plenty comfortable. The stadium—built in 194 days for $10.5 million—has a grassy berm down the left-field line. In San Antonio, the berm also goes beyond the fence in left field, serving as grass bleachers. These areas have room for 3,000 fans, but are likely to be replaced with seats within the next few years, given the popularity of the Missions. There is a large, state-of-the-art, almost-Alamo-shaped scoreboard in right field. The reserved seats at the back of the grandstand, covered by a roof, are aluminum benches with backs but not enough leg room. The general-admission seats down the baselines are really close to the action but are taken soon after the gates open.

You would pay to be a pitcher here. A stiff breeze from the Gulf blows from right center field toward home plate.

Wolff Stadium has a spectacular sound system and wonderful, eclectic taste in music. The crowd—mixed almost equally Anglos and Hispanics—was really into the music and the game as the music switched rapidly from country to Sinatra to Motown to salsa. Puffy Taco—with a tomato head and jalapeño feet—is a perfect mascot. Puffy comes out in the sixth inning and races around the bases, always letting a young fan tackle him just before home plate.

Don't miss the Wall of Fame near the Missions' souvenir shop. Hall of Famers Brooks Robinson and Joe Morgan both played their Texas League ball here. San Antonio has been a Los Angeles Dodgers farm team since 1977.

Where to Stay

This is one of the few cities with a multitude of historic hotels in a concentrated downtown area.

Visiting Team Hotel: Thrifty Inn–Northwest. This 25-year-old motel was fully renovated in 1991. Its large rooms are well kept and furnished with contemporary drapes and spreads. Guests receive a free Continental breakfast. *9806 I–10 W., at Wurzbach Rd., San Antonio, TX 78230, tel. 210/696–0810 or 800/325–8300, fax 210/696–0810. 93 rooms. Facilities: outdoor pool, wading pool. AE, D, MC, V. $$*

Best Western Historic Crockett Hotel. This is a grand, classic hotel within feet of The Alamo. Its huge atrium lobby has a waterfall. The spacious rooms have reproduction antique furniture. The grounds are nicely landscaped, and there's a seventh-floor sundeck with a Jacuzzi. *320 Bonham, San Antonio, TX 78205, tel. 210/225–6500 or 800/292–1050, fax 210/225–6251. 206 rooms. Facilities: restaurant, outdoor pool, whirlpool, coin laundry, parking (fee). AE, D, DC, MC, V. $$*

Menger Hotel. This beautiful hotel is opposite The Alamo. Built in 1859, it has five floors of luxurious rooms. *204 Alamo Plaza, San Antonio, TX 78205, tel. 210/223–4361 or 800/345–9285, fax 210/228–0022. 320 rooms. Facilities: restaurant, heated outdoor pool, sauna, whirlpool, parking (fee). AE, D, DC, MC, V. $$$*

Ramada Emily Morgan Hotel. This grand older hotel is across from The Alamo. Its 12 stories offer fine views of the city. Most of the rooms have Jacuzzi tubs. *705 E. Houston, San Antonio, TX 78205, tel. 210/225–8486 or 800/228–2828, fax 210/225–7227. 177 rooms. Facilities: outdoor pool, saunas, whirlpool, exercise room. AE, D, DC, MC, V. $$*

Where to Eat

The Pig Stand. This is the start of America's first drive-in restaurant chain. It's the originator of Texas toast, onion rings, and car hops. You can get burgers, chicken fried steak, Western omelets, black cows, and frosted root beer here. Table jukeboxes and vintage neon signs serve as wall art. *1508 Broadway, San Antonio,* *tel. 210/222–2794; 801 S. Presa St., tel. 210/227–1691; 3054 Rigsby Ave., tel. 210/333–8231. AE, D, MC, V. $*

Earl Abels. A city institution for 64 years, Abels's slogan is "Is Everything All Right?" This is American comfort food. You can sit at its long counter or have table service. There is a children's menu. *4200 Broadway, at Hildebrand Ave., San Antonio, tel. 210/822–3358. AE, D, DC, MC, V. $$*

Landry's Seafood House. The fresh fish is cooked any way you can imagine it at this cheery family restaurant. There is a children's menu, and you get free downtown parking when you eat here. *600 E. Market St., San Antonio, tel. 210/229–1010. AE, D, MC, V. $$*

Entertainments

Call or visit the **Visitor's Center** (317 Alamo Plaza, San Antonio, TX 78205, tel. 800/447–3372; open 8:30–6), to get valuable discounts to area attractions.

Riverwalk/Paseo del Rio. This system of walkways is romantic at night, bustling by day. Dozens of sidewalk restaurants and shops line the river. On sunny days you can walk, ducking under shade, rather than ride in the open river barges. Two walking-tour brochures are offered by the San Antonio Conservation Society (tel. 210/224–6163).

San Antonio Children's Museum. A gravity wall, a child-sized tour trolley, a pretend bank, a toddler play center, and a build-a-building area can all be found in this small, imaginative museum. Displays emphasize conservation, anatomy, and computers. *305 E. Houston, San Antonio. tel. 210/212–4453. Admission: $4; under 2 free. Open Mon. 9–noon, Tues.–Fri. 9–6, Sat. 9–6, Sun. noon–4.*

San Antonio Zoo. This sprawling zoo is within Brackenridge Park. An aerial ride takes you from the zoo to the park's sunken gardens. Of special note are the outdoor hippo pool and Monkey Island. There is also a petting zoo. The grounds remain open until 8 each day. Single and double strollers, wagons, and wheelchairs can be rented to cover the spacious grounds. *3903 N. St. Mary's St., San Antonio, tel. 210/734–7183. Admission: $7 adults, $5 children 3–11 and senior citizens. Open daily 9–6.*

Sea World of Texas. There are killer whales, sharks, and touch pools in this busy water world 16 mi northwest of the city. Admission includes entry to a water park with wave pool and slides. *10500 Sea World Dr., off Loop 1604, San Antonio, tel. 210/523–3611. Admission: $32.95 adults, $22.95 ages 3–11, $29.95 senior citizens. Open Memorial Day–mid-Aug. 10–10, mid-Mar.– Memorial Day and mid-Aug.–late Oct. weekends 10–6. D, MC, V.*

Six Flags Fiesta Texas Theme Park. This amusement and water park is 20 minutes from downtown. There are mariachi bands, nightly fireworks, ice skating, miniature golf, a kiddie ride area, and a laser show. The park's tall wooden roller coaster, the Rattler, is suitable for older children. Parking is $5. *17000 I–10W, Exit 555 off Loop 1604, San Antonio, tel. 210/697–5050 or 800/473–4378. Admission: $35.50 those over 48", $17.75 those under 48", $24.50 senior citizens and people with disabilities; ages 2 and under free. Open late May–Aug., daily 10–10; Apr.–May and Sept.–Oct. weekends 10–10. Closing hrs vary. AE, D, MC, V.*

Sights to See

The Alamo. This is the oldest and most famous of the city's missions. San Antonio de Valero was established in 1718 as part of an effort to convert the Native Americans and extend Spain's frontier. In 1836 the former mission site was the scene for one of the great dramas in American history. It was here—known popularly as The Alamo—that 189 men died in the cause of Texas independence. The names Travis, Bowie, and Crockett are immortalized for their efforts in slowing the advance of Santa Anna's Mexican Army. *100 Alamo Plaza, San Antonio, tel. 210/225–1391. Donations appreciated. Open Mon.–Sat. 9–5:30, Sun. and holidays 10–5:30.*

Institute of Texan Cultures. This exhibit, in HemisFair Park, tells of Texas's 27 different cultural groups. It is more appropriate for older children who can look for the life-size buffalo, a buffalo-hide tepee, and stuffed Texas longhorn cattle. A silk Chinese dragon and a two-room sharecropper's house of the 1910s are on display. The African-American section pays tribute to Hall of Fame slugger Frank Robinson, born in Beaumont, Texas, in 1936. Parking is $2. *801 S. Bowie St., San Antonio 78205, tel. 210/558–2300. Donations appreciated. Open Tues.–Sun. 9–5.*

San Antonio Mission National Historical Park. This site includes four Spanish Colonial missions that cover 835 acres. The National Park Service has preserved these missions to remember the Spanish empire's effort to colonize North America. You should begin with the Mission Concepcion, where Park Service Rangers give information and suggest driving routes along the Mission Trail. *2202 Roosevelt Ave., exit I–10 at Probandt Dr., San Antonio 78210-4919, tel. 512/ 229–5701. Open summer 9–6, winter 8–5.*

Tower of the Americas. A few blocks from The Alamo is a tall reminder of Texas's 1968 World's Fair. The observation level—579 ft high—provides a spectacular view and is reached by a glass-walled elevator. *HemisFair Plaza, Commerce and Market Sts., San Antonio, tel. 210/ 207–8615. Admission: $3 adults, $1 children 4– 11. Open 8 AM–11 PM.*

TEXAS RANGERS

League: American League • **Class:** Major League • **Stadium:** The Ballpark in Arlington • **Opened:** 1994 • **Capacity:** 49,178 • **Dimensions:** LF: 332, CF: 400, RF: 325 • **Surface:** grass • **Season:** Apr.– early Oct.

STADIUM LOCATION: 1000 Ballpark Way, Arlington, TX 76011.

TEAM WEB SITE: www.texasrangers.com

GETTING THERE: From Dallas, take I–30 west 16 mi to Ballpark Way exit. Go south off exit and follow Ballpark Way to stadium. From Ft. Worth, take I–30 east 13 mi to Nolan Ryan Expressway exit. Turn right off exit and follow Ryan Expressway to stadium.

PARKING: Stadium complex has 9 parking lots ($5) surrounding ballpark.

TICKET INFORMATION: Box 90111, Arlington, TX 76004, tel. 817/273–5100, fax 817/273–5190.

PRICE RANGE: Club box $30–$35; corner and lower box $25–$30; upper box $10–$14; home run porch $15; grandstand reserved $5–$7; bleachers $10.

GAME TIME: 7:05, 7:35, 2:05 PM; gates at first and third bases open 3 hrs before night games, 90 min before day games.

TIPS ON SEATING: Home-run porch seats in right field sound like fun and have fans, but Texas hot is too hot under that roof.

SEATING FOR PEOPLE WITH DISABILITIES: Call Fan Relations Office (tel. 817/273–5128).

STADIUM FOOD: Most of the large assortment of food is very good. The **Hall of Flame BBQ** and **Red River BBQ** have competing forms of smoked meats. Be sure to ask for mild versions for the children. The **Tex Mex Express** has great soft tacos ($3) and nachos ($3.50). The customary heat makes lemon and lime chills essential ($3). For healthy eating, try the turkey club ($5) and a bagel on a stick ($2). A park **bakery** carries average brownies ($1.75) and cookies ($1.25). **The Grill** serves good bratwurst for $4, ordinary hot dogs for $2, burgers for $3.50, and a good chicken sandwich for $4.25.

SMOKING POLICY: Smoking prohibited in seating areas but allowed in designated areas on outer concourse.

VISITING TEAM HOTEL: No hotel designated for visiting team.

TOURISM INFORMATION: Arlington Visitors Center (921 Six Flags Dr., Arlington, TX 76011, tel. 817/640–0252 or 800/342–4305).

Arlington: The Ballpark in Arlington

Dallas and Fort Worth were two of the original six teams when the Texas League began in 1888, and both continued in the league until the late 1950s. During much of the 1960s, they fielded combined Dallas–Fort Worth teams in several different leagues. In 1965 the appropriately named Turnpike Stadium was built in Arlington, midway between the two cities, and the Dallas–Forth Worth Spurs rejoined the Texas League. Built with seating for 10,000, it was doubled in capacity in 1970. It was doubled again after the 1971 season to accommodate major-league baseball as the Washington Senators moved to Texas. The park's name was changed to Arlington Stadium when the Texas Rangers played their 1972 inaugural season.

The Rangers played in this former minor-league stadium for 22 seasons until 1994, when they moved nearby to the Ballpark in Arlington. Rangers pitcher Kenny Rogers highlighted the inaugural season with a perfect game on July 28, 1994. The All-Star Game was played here in 1995. The new stadium is part of a $189-million entertainment complex.

The Ballpark is a huge beauty designed in the manner of the new stadiums in Baltimore, Cleveland, and Denver, but lacking a downtown location. It sits in the middle of a parking lot. Its neighbor is the Six Flags over Texas amusement park. Plans call for a Little League stadium, an amphitheater, and a public park with lakes and trails.

To get here, you drive on the Nolan Ryan Expressway—named in honor of the Hall of Famer who ended his extraordinary strikeout career here in Arlington. Designed by architect David Schwarz, the stadium's neo-Romanesque exterior is sunset-red granite topped by red brick and punctuated by four handsome brick corner towers. Tall brick arches stand on a base of granite arches to give the stadium an open appearance from the outside. Cast-stone carvings of 35 longhorn-steer heads and 21 Lone Star emblems adorn the spaces between the tops of the upper arches. A brick Texas Rangers Walk of Fame rings the entire stadium with a historical record of the club going back to 1972.

The almost completely enclosed interior does not match the spectacular exterior. There are enough concession stands and memorabilia shops to empty your wallet. A picnic area lies beyond the center-field wall. An art gallery and an exceptional souvenir shop sit behind that. What does not work here for us is the four-story, 138,000-square-ft office building beyond the shops. It adds too much bulk for too little architectural advantage.

There is an old-style Wrigley Field scoreboard in left field and a modern version of Detroit's Tiger Stadium home-run porch in right. The ceiling fans were hard at work on the late July night we visited, but it was 105° outside and surely hotter under the second deck. Next to the television screen is a sign inspired by Brooklyn's Ebbets Field: HIT IT HERE & WIN A FREE SUIT. 501 FEET. Fifty-minute tours of the Ballpark in Arlington are given year-round. *Tel. 817/273–5098. Admission: $5 adults, $4 senior citizens, $3 ages 4–18. Tours on the hr, weekdays 9–4, Sat. 10–4, Sun. noon–4 on nongame days; on game days, tours end at noon, none on Sun.*

Where to Stay

Arlington imposes a 90¢-per-night tax per hotel room in its entertainment district to finance no-fee trolleys and shuttle buses that take guests at the following hotels, among others, to the ballpark, Six Flags over Texas amusement park, and Hurricane Harbour water park. The trolleys (tel. 800/824–2024) run every 30 minutes daily 9:30 AM–11:30 PM or later if the ball game runs late. They're worth taking to avoid the $5–$6 parking fees at the attractions.

Courtyard by Marriott. You can walk to the ballpark from this three-story hotel, which is in an office-park setting. The rooms are modern and standard size, with dark-wood and burgundy furnishings. *1500 Pennant Dr., Arlington 76011, tel. 817/277–2774 or 800/321–2211, fax 817/277–3103. 147 rooms. Facilities: restaurant, indoor and outdoor pools, hot tub, exercise room, game room, coin laundry. AE, D, DC, MC, V. $$*

Best Western Great Southwest Inn. Less than 2 mi from the ballpark, this two-story stucco motel is close to the Six Flags amusement park.

Its standard rooms have extra-long double beds. *3501 E. Division St., Arlington 76011, tel. 817/640–7722 or 800/346–2378, fax 817/640–9043. 122 rooms. Facilities: restaurant, outdoor pool, hot tub, playground. AE, D, DC, MC, V. $$*

La Quinta Inn and Conference Center. This two-story stucco motel is in a commercial area, with several chain restaurants nearby. The rooms are standard size, with contemporary furnishings. *825 N. Watson Rd., at S.R. 360 and I-30, Arlington 76011, tel. 817/640–4142 or 800/551–5900, fax 817/649–7864. 340 rooms. Facilities: outdoor pool, wading pool, hot tub, coin laundry. AE, D, DC, MC, V. $$*

Where to Eat

Landry's Seafood House. This casual neon-marquee chain restaurant is in the same office park as the baseball stadium. It's an eight-minute walk from the park, and restaurant patrons may park free in its rear lot for baseball games. You can sit at tables, in booths, or on the patio and order all manner of broiled or fried fish. All is fresh, except the catfish, which is frozen. The dessert favorite is bananas Foster, made with Texas's incomparable Blue Bell ice cream. The children's menu includes fried shrimp, good pizza, and macaroni and cheese. *1520 Nolan Ryan Expressway, Arlington, tel. 817/261–4696. AE, D, MC, V. $$*

Luby's Cafeteria. This outstanding Southern chain cafeteria serves regional favorites, an array of salads, and hard-to-resist pies, especially its coconut and egg custard varieties. It is less than a mile from the ballpark. *701 N. Watson Rd., Arlington, tel. 817/649–5090. No breakfast. D, MC, V. $*

Paris Coffee Shop. Fifteen minutes west of Arlington is a classic Texas lunch counter. Since 1926, happy eaters have debated among the each-day's specials. A light lunch includes two vegetables, a regular lunch includes three. The mashed potatoes, fried chicken, and pies, especially cherry and custard, are great. Baseball memorabilia fill the walls. *704 W. Magnolia, Fort Worth, tel. 817/335–2041. AE, D, MC, V. No dinner Sat. Closed Sun.*

Entertainments

Dallas Aquarium. Just in front of the huge Ferris wheel at Fair Park is this small, approachable aquarium stocked with species found in local rivers, plus some tropical fish. Visitors can watch the piranhas being fed at 2:30 on Tuesday, Thursday, and Saturday and the sharks being fed at 2:30 on Wednesday, Friday, and Sunday. A scuba demonstration is held at noon daily. *1st St. and Martin Luther King Blvd., Dallas, tel. 214/ 670–8443. Admission: $2 adults, $1 ages 3–11. Open daily 9–4:30.*

Dallas World Aquarium. This large aquarium is in the city's West End District and displays both fresh- and saltwater species. There's a walk-through tunnel surrounded by fish tanks, as well as displays housing penguins and coral reefs. The world's various aquatic habitats are featured. *1801 N. Griffin St., Dallas, tel. 214/720– 1801. Admission: $11.85 adults, $6.50 ages 4–12 and senior citizens. Open daily 10–5.*

Dallas Zoo. Three miles south of downtown is a large natural-habitat zoo with many rare species. There are six African habitats, including one with lowland gorillas, and a free-flight aviary. A monorail ($1.50 for visitors ages three and up) takes you for a 1-mi ride through the Wilds of Africa exhibit. Several sit-down casual restaurants are sprinkled throughout the grounds. *621 E. Clarendon Dr., Ewing Ave. exit off I–35 E, Dallas, tel. 214/670–5656. Admission: $6 adults, $3 ages 3–11, $4 senior citizens; parking $3. Open daily 9–5.*

Hurricane Harbor. This huge water park has slides, rides, and five swimming pools. There are 48 different attractions, including a separate section with huge water guns for smaller children. The park also has 22 picnic areas, snack bars, and locker rooms. Locker rental is $4 daily; tube rental is $7 daily. *1800 E. Lamar Blvd., Ballpark Way exit off I–30 E, Arlington, tel. 817/265– 3356. Admission: $26.93 adults, $13.47 those 48" or shorter and senior citizens; parking $5. Open mid-May–mid-Sept., daily 10 AM–11 PM.*

Legends of the Game Baseball Museum & Learning Center. This is a fascinating children's museum within the ballpark. Learn about the sweet spot and ball construction, and feel the speed and intensity of a Roger Clemens or Nolan Ryan pitch through a glove. The Dugout, for younger fans, lets you put magnetic clothes on players and sign balls. The lower floors house an impressive collection of important game balls, signed gloves, uniforms, trophies, and photographs. Combination tickets with a ballpark tour are sold, $10 adults, $8 senior citizens, and $6 ages 4 to 18. *The Ballpark in Arlington, I–30 at Hwy. 157, Arlington, tel. 817/273–5600. Admission: $6 adults, $4 ages 4–18, $5 senior citizens and students. Open Mar.–Oct., Mon.–Sat. 9–6:30, Sun. noon–4.*

The Science Place. This imaginative center has many unusual features, including an area where you pay $1 and get made up with special effects, like bruises, scrapes, or gruesome cuts. A crowd-pleaser is a huge dinosaur that kids ride while watching themselves on TV. Kids seven and under can build water canals and dams; they can also play on an inflatable raft on a water bed. There's also a 79-ft domed-screen IMAX theater with separate admission that shows nature and adventure films. The center is in Dallas Fair Park, 2 mi from downtown. *Fair Park, 1st St. exit off I–30 W, Dallas, tel. 214/428–5555. Admission: $6 adults, $3 ages 3–12 and senior citizens. Open Mon.–Sat. 9:30–5:30, Sun. noon– 5:30.*

Six Flags over Texas. Yosemite Sam and other Looney Tunes characters have joined this theme park. Teens can try many extreme thrill rides, including Flashback, a coaster that turns you upside down six times each ride. There are more than 100 attractions here, including a 1926 Dentzel carousel and the Texas Giant wooden coaster. *I–30 at Hwy. 360, Dallas, tel. 817/640–8900. Admission: $40.93 adults, $20.46 those 48" or shorter and senior citizens; parking $8. Open May–Aug. daily 10–10; Apr. and Sept.–Oct., weekends 10–10.*

Sights to See

Fair Park. This 277-acre national historic landmark, with a large collection of Art Deco exposition buildings, was constructed for the 1936 Texas Centennial. Fair Park is still the home of the State Fair of Texas and boasts, in Texan style, that the Texas Star is the tallest Ferris wheel in North America. This aging Texas treasure is a welcome relief from the steel and glass of downtown Dallas. Start with the visitor center near the 1st Avenue entrance to the park.

Perhaps the most impressive building at Fair Park is the **Hall of State,** with its magnificent entrance. Tejas Warrior, a tribute in gold leaf honoring the Native Americans of Texas—set off by blue tiles representing the bluebonnet, the state flower—stands above the bronze doors. Admission is free.

The site of the annual **Cotton Bowl** football classic, on January 1 since 1936, sits just behind the Hall of State. To arrange a tour of the 72,000-capacity stadium, call the Fair Park administrative office (tel. 214/670–8400) in advance. *Fair Park, 1st or 2nd Ave. exit off I–30, tel. 214/421–4500 or 214/890–2911, or write Dallas Historical Society, Box 26038, Dallas, TX 75226. Open Tues.–Sat. 9–5, Sun. 1–5.*

SOONER BASEBALL
OKLAHOMA CITY, TULSA

Baseball came to Oklahoma City during the 1890s land rush. Native son Mickey Mantle is the most famous player from the state, and his statue greets visitors to Oklahoma City's vibrant new stadium. Sellout crowds are packing the park and enjoying restaurants and shops in the surrounding Bricktown area. The team, the Oklahoma Redhawks, represents the Texas Rangers in the AAA Pacific Coast League. Residents aren't bashful about their allegiance to oil; the State Capitol is surrounded by working oil wells. Don't miss the wonderful National Softball Hall of Fame during your visit here.

Northeast 100 mi is Tulsa, built by oil, railroads, and shipping—its dams, waterways, and lakes create an inland harbor. The Tulsa Drillers are an affiliate of the Texas Rangers and play in a large fairgrounds stadium. The city has one of the nation's best small amusement parks and an impressive collection of downtown Art Deco office buildings and churches, many built with money from the oil boom of the 1920s.

OKLAHOMA REDHAWKS

League: Pacific Coast League • **Major League Affiliation:** Texas Rangers • **Class:** AAA • **Stadium:** Southwestern Bell Bricktown Ballpark • **Opened:** 1998 • **Capacity:** 13,066 • **Dimensions:** LF: 325, CF: 400, RF: 325 • **Surface:** grass • **Season:** Apr.–Labor Day

STADIUM LOCATION: 2 South Mickey Mantle Dr., Oklahoma City, OK 73104.

TEAM WEB SITE: www.redhawksbaseball.com

GETTING THERE: The ballpark is in the Bricktown area east of downtown, at Walnut St. and Reno Ave. At I–235 and I–40, take the Reno exit and go east on Reno to the ballpark.

PARKING: Public and private lots surrounding the ballpark.

TICKET INFORMATION: 2 South Mickey Mantle Dr., Oklahoma City, OK 73104, tel. 405/218–1000, fax 405/218–1001.

PRICE RANGE: Club $12; field box $8; field bleacher and terrace reserved $6; left-field bleachers $5; general admission and standing room $4; $1 discount on reserved seats for ages 3–12, senior citizens, and military.

GAME TIME: Mon.–Sat. 7:05 PM, Sun. (Apr.–June) 2:05 PM; gates open 90 min before game.

TIPS ON SEATING: Since seats are inexpensive for a new ballpark of this quality, buy the field box seats right next to the action. The field bleacher seats, past first and third, are bench seats with backs that turn back toward home and extend almost to the foul lines. There is a second deck—a rare thing for a minor-league park. The sun sets behind third base.

SEATING FOR PEOPLE WITH DISABILITIES: Last row of the main concourse in all price categories.

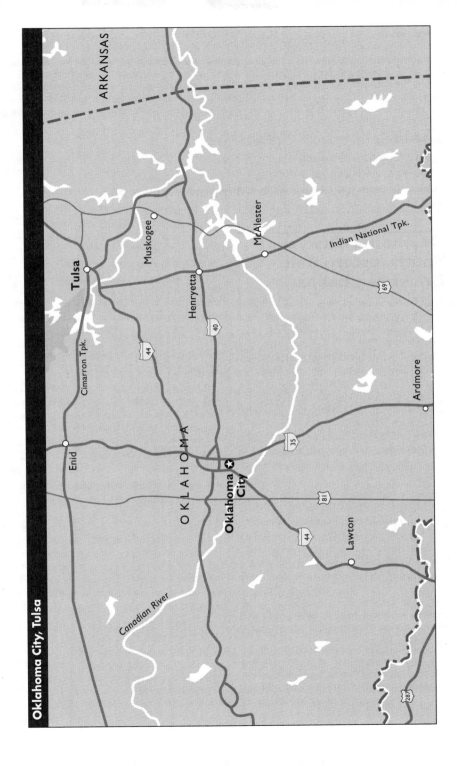

Oklahoma City, Tulsa

STADIUM FOOD: The food is unusual, good, and inexpensive. There's bargain Tex-Mex, including crisp and soft tacos and burritos. Not only are there regular gyros, but barbecued gyros, with baklava for dessert. Smoothies with nonfat yogurt are $3.50. There's a chopped beef barbecue sandwich for $4.50, along with potato salad and baked beans, and hot links, plain or salted soft pretzels, and $1 dill pickles. The Hideaway Pizza is great, at $2.50–$3 a slice or $14–$22 whole. Even the basic hot dogs, at Bar S, are exceptional.

SMOKING POLICY: Smoking allowed in designated areas only.

VISITING TEAM HOTEL: Westin Hotel (One North Broadway, Oklahoma City, OK 73102, tel. 405/235–2780 or 800/937–8461).

TOURISM INFORMATION: Oklahoma City Convention & Visitors Bureau (123 Park Ave., Oklahoma City, OK 73102, tel. 405/297–8910 or 800/225–5652).

Oklahoma City: Southwestern Bell Bricktown Ballpark

What a difference a few years can make. When we first visited Oklahoma City in 1995, the American Association Triple A team was called the Oklahoma City 89ers and they played in a somewhat shabby ballpark on the State Fairgrounds. Engines roared from the State Fair Speedway during the game we saw. The city is still the Triple A affiliate of the Texas Rangers—nearly everything else is different . . . and better. We love the old ballparks, but it was past time to retire All Sports Stadium. And Oklahoma City did it right. The new ballpark opened in 1998 in the historic Bricktown area just east of downtown.

Great care was taken to ensure that the new ballpark reminded fans of the old days. The ballpark was designed with the goal of respecting tradition and providing the most modern of amenities. It scores high on both goals. Bricktown is Oklahoma City's industrial area, and the ballpark along Mickey Mantle Drive plays nicely off the district's redbrick warehouses. The ticket booth was modeled after the old Santa Fe train station, and the third-base entrance pavilion reminds you of Oklahoma City's first ballpark, Delmar Gardens.

The field box seats and even the left-field bleachers are very close to the baseball action, providing the intimacy of the old days at amazingly modest prices. The short left-field porch and asymmetrical outfield wall evoke the special magic of the great old ballparks. The outfield wall's weird angles and the 8-ft-tall fences make for exciting outfield action. There are even knothole-like perspectives built into the ballpark. Before the game, try to watch batting practice through the wooden slat fence beyond left field. Snag a ball if you can. Out front, before you walk into the park, take time to admire the tribute to Oklahoma native son Mickey Mantle. The dramatic 9-ft-tall statue of Mantle crushing a big fly ball was sculpted by Blair Buswell.

The ballpark is the first of nine Metropolitan Area Projects slated for the Bricktown area, once the home of machine shops, candy factories, and furniture warehouses. The ballpark was designed by Architectural Design Group, Inc. of Oklahoma City and was built at a cost of $21 million.

We liked the former 89ers name, as it celebrated the pioneers who flocked here when a strip of land in Native American territory opened up in 1889. The new team name honors a fierce raptor indigenous to Oklahoma. The new mascot is Rowdy the RedHawk, a giant red bird in a baseball jersey, less fierce than its namesake. The team's handsome colors—brick, black, and silver—reflect the colors of the RedHawk and the Bricktown community.

Baseball fields sprang up east and west of Oklahoma City in the summer of the 1889 land rush. By 1904, professional baseball was played here. In 1961, the city got a Triple A franchise in the American Association, and the team began to play in All Sports Stadium on the fairgrounds. In the 1960s, the team switched to the Pacific Coast League, then back again. In 1977, Allie

Reynolds, a Native American New York Yankees pitcher from the 1940s and '50s, put together an ownership group that kept the team from leaving. In the 1998 reorganization of Triple A, Oklahoma City returned to the Pacific Coast League.

Where to Stay

Visiting Team Hotel: Westin Hotel. This fancy yet reasonable downtown hotel has 15 floors and is two blocks from the ballpark. The rooms are bright, with oversized double beds. *One North Broadway Ave., at Sheridan Blvd., Oklahoma City 73102, tel. 405/235–2780 or 800/937–8461, fax 405/272–0369. 395 rooms. Facilities: restaurant, exercise room, parking (fee). AE, D, DC, MC, V. $$*

Quality Inn West. This well-maintained two-story brick hotel offers guests a free Continental breakfast. Some rooms have love seats or recliners. It's in a commercial strip with several other hotels. *720 S. MacArthur Blvd., Oklahoma City 73128, tel. 405/943–2393 or 800/424–6423, fax 405/943–9860. 65 rooms. Facilities: outdoor pool. AE, D, DC, MC, V. $$*

Where to Eat

Abuela's. Guests sit in a cool interior courtyard at this casual Mexican restaurant with tile-topped tables. Beige adobe arches edge the room, which is airy and lighted by skylights. There are hearty portions of tamales, enchiladas, and shrimp fajitas, along with layered salads and good beans and rice. Abuela's is in Bricktown, steps from the ballpark. *17 E. Sheridan St., Oklahoma City, tel. 405/235–1422. AE, D, DC, MC, V. Closed Sun. $$*

Bricktown Brewery. The brewing kettles are on view in this two-floor restaurant in a renovated warehouse in historic Bricktown. The menu covers Mexican favorites, steak, ribs, and salads. It's a noisy place, as there are pool tables and video games upstairs. (No children are allowed upstairs after 8 PM.) Its kids' menu, with $3.95 entrées, includes a good potpie, pasta, and grilled cheese sandwiches. A bubbling cherry cobbler is the dessert standout. *1 N. Oklahoma Ave., Oklahoma City, tel. 405/232–2739. AE, D, MC, V. $$*

Coit's Root Beer. Sweet root beer in frosty mugs is the draw at this casual hangout. It's summertime heaven, with floats, whips, malts, limeades, and fried pies. There are also chicken sandwiches, burgers, hot dogs, and great onion rings. *5001 N. Portland Ave., Oklahoma City, tel. 405/946–8778. No credit cards. $*

Leo's. You can watch the pit men working at this dimly lit authentic rib joint. Skip the barbecued bologna and stick to the ribs and beef, especially the generous chopped beef dinner. There is a children's menu. You'll smell the smoke from its smoking pits before you see this converted gas station. The tables are Formica-covered; photos of local residents who have made good line the walls. *3631 N. Kelley, Oklahoma City, tel. 405/427–3254. AE, D, MC, V. $*

Entertainments

Frontier City Western Theme Park. There are staged gunfights and magic shows in addition to the 32 rides here, including 8 kiddie rides. Teens gravitate to the three roller coasters, the skycoaster bungee jump, and the go-carts. Local IGA groceries often carry a $5 coupon for ages 7–11. *11601 N.E. Expressway, 122nd St., exit off I–35, Oklahoma City, tel. 405/478–2412. Admission: $21.99 adults, $14.99 those 48" or shorter, $12.99 senior citizens; under 3 free; parking $4. Open June–Aug., Mon.–Thurs. 10:30–10, Fri.–Sat. 10:30–midnight, Sun. noon–10; Apr.–May and Sept.–Oct., various weekend hrs. AE, MC, V.*

Lazy E Arena. This arena, on a 300-acre working ranch 30 mi north of Oklahoma City, holds exciting rodeos and horse shows throughout the year. *Rte. 5, I–35 north, Seward Rd. East exit, Guthrie, tel. 405/282–3004 or 800/234–3393.*

Kirkpatrick Center and Omniplex Science Museum. You can spend a full day or two at this complex with museums, gardens, and a planetarium. Your admission gives entry to museums exploring science, air and space, photography, art, history, and Indian culture. The science center has 320 hands-on exhibits, including a crystal molecule that children enjoy crawling through. The planetarium has daily shows. *2100 N.E. 52nd St. and Martin Luther King Jr. Ave., Oklahoma City, tel. 405/427–5461. Admission: $7.60 adults, $6 ages 3–12, $6.80 senior citizens. Planetarium* *admission: $1.65 adults, $1.35 senior citizens, $1.10 ages 3–12. Open Memorial Day–Labor Day, Mon.–Sat. 9–6, Sun. noon–6; Labor Day–Memorial Day, weekdays 9:30–5, Sat. 9–6, Sun. noon–6.*

National Cowboy Hall of Fame and Western Heritage Center. Children may want to skip the art galleries and see the basement exhibits, depicting saloons, chuck wagons, and a general store. A children's hands-on section is under way. The good gift shop has Western wear. *1700 N.E. 63rd St., Oklahoma City, tel. 405/478–2250. Admission: $6.50 adults, $5.50 senior citizens, $3.25 ages 6–12. Open June–Labor Day, daily 8:30–6; Labor Day–May, daily 9–5.*

Oklahoma City Zoo. This sprawling zoo houses 2,000 animals, a children's zoo, and a Great EscApe primate center. Marine life from around the world is presented in Aquaticus, which offers dolphin and sea-lion shows several times daily ($2 fee). There's also a free-flight aviary and a herpetarium. You can make use of the sky safari overhead tram and the zoo train ($2 fee) to cover its 110 acres. *Remington Pl. and Martin Luther King Jr. Ave., Oklahoma City, tel. 405/424–3344. Admission: $6 adults, $3 ages 3–11 and senior citizens. Open Apr.–Oct., daily 9–6; Nov.–Mar., daily 9–5.*

Sights to See

National Softball Hall of Fame. This terrific small museum focuses equally on the women and men involved in softball across the country. There are films of winning teams and star athletes, current and vintage uniforms, and other memorabilia. Seeing the community and company teams that compete gives you a picture of how basic this sport is to small-town America. A 2,000-seat stadium behind the museum hosts national tournaments. The gift shop contains a variety of jerseys and equipment. *2801 N.E. 50th St., tel. 405/424–5266. Admission: $2 adults, $1 ages 6–12. Open weekdays 8–5, weekends 10–4.*

State Capitol. Even if you don't share our enthusiasm for state capitols, take a few minutes to drive by Oklahoma's. Oklahoma is famous for oil and not bashful about it. The Capitol is surrounded by working oil wells. Petunia One, set in a petunia bed near the front of the Capitol, produced up to 600 barrels of oil a day from 1941 until it ran dry in 1986.

The building itself is a quite handsome Greco-Roman structure done in white Indiana limestone on a foundation of Oklahoma pink and black granite. Completed in 1917, the Oklahoma Capitol is one of only a dozen in the nation without a dome. In the rotunda there are portraits of four great Oklahomans, including humorist Will Rogers and Jim Thorpe, one of the greatest athletes in history. Information is available at the Oklahoma Tourism and Recreation Department (Box 60789, Oklahoma City, OK 73146). *2300 Lincoln Blvd., Oklahoma City, tel. 405/521–2409 or 800/652–6552. Free guided tours. Tours weekdays on the hr. 8–3.*

State Museum of History. This free museum is just southeast of the Capitol. Operated by the Oklahoma Historical Society, it details the "Trail of Tears," the road taken by displaced Native Americans during their forced removal from their territories. *2100 N. Lincoln Blvd., at N.E. 20th St., Oklahoma City 73105, tel. 405/521–2491. Open Mon.–Sat. 8–5.*

TULSA DRILLERS

League: Texas League • **Major League Affiliation:** Texas Rangers • **Class:** AA • **Stadium:** Drillers Stadium • **Opened:** 1981 • **Capacity:** 10,955 • **Dimensions:** LF: 335 CF: 390 RF: 340 • **Surface:** grass • **Season:** Apr.–Labor Day

STADIUM LOCATION: 4802 E. 15th St., Tulsa, OK 74112.

TEAM WEB SITE: www.tulsadrillers.com

GETTING THERE: The stadium is at 15th St. and Yale Ave. on the Tulsa County Fairgrounds, 3 mi north of I–44 and 1 ½ mi south of I–244. From downtown, go north on 15th St. to Yale Ave.

TICKET INFORMATION: Box 4448, Tulsa, OK 74159, tel. 918/744–5998.

PRICE RANGE: Dugout and terrace box seats $8; field box seats $7.50; reserved seats $5.50; general admission $4.

GAME TIME: Mon.–Sat. 7:35 PM, Sun. 2:05 PM (Apr.–May), 6:05 PM (June–Aug.). Gates open 90 min before game.

TIPS ON SEATING: The reserved seats are a good buy and give you a second-deck view comparable to major-league club-level seats. The back rows of the general admission seats are shaded by a roof, but may have obstructed views. Avoid the first rows of general admission, as there is a constant flow of traffic. The sun sets behind third base, so sit on the third-base side.

SEATING FOR PEOPLE WITH DISABILITIES: In the front rows of the second deck behind first, third, and home. An elevator is available.

STADIUM FOOD: A cherry limeade is a good baseball drink, especially for washing down a Frito chili pie ($2.25) or a smoked turkey leg ($4). The **Hot Corner Cantina** has good fajita salads, burritos, and chicken and beef fajitas. There are root beer floats and Hiland Dairy hand-dipped cones, each $2.25. The grill has onion rings and a hefty chicken fingers basket. A kid's meal, named after the mascot, is $4 and includes a hot dog, chips, and small drink. It's an Oklahoma thing—the park also sells large dill pickles for $1.

SMOKING POLICY: Smoking prohibited in the seating areas, but allowed on the walkway behind the box seats.

VISITING TEAM HOTEL: Best Western Tradewinds Central (3141 E. Skelly Dr., Tulsa, OK 74105, tel. 918/749–5561 or 800/528–1234).

TOURISM INFORMATION: Tulsa Convention and Visitors Bureau (616 South Boston, Tulsa, OK 74119, tel. 800/558–3311).

Tulsa: Drillers Stadium

Tulsa's Drillers Stadium has a gaudy, patched-together, county fairgrounds kind of feel. The entranceway is red and blue with white baseball globe lights. The interior seats are blue, and there's a red press box tucked under a roof that partially covers the upper-deck general admission seats.

The concourse is a lively place appropriate for a county fairgrounds, with activities from face painting to speed pitch, and a wide variety of good foods offered at the entrance level and accessible from the box seats and the second deck. When the home team is doing well, it can get really loud: the fans stomp their feet on the second-deck aluminum bleachers. Hornsby the mascot is a blue, long-horned bull named after Hall of Famer Rogers Hornsby.

Tulsa has not followed the Oklahoma City lead of building a new ballpark downtown, but has opted to make continual improvements to the fairgrounds ballpark. The stadium was built in 1981 with a capacity of 4,843 and artificial turf. It was named Robert Sutton Stadium after the man who footed most of the bill, but the Sutton name was quickly dropped in the face of a questionable oil-pricing scheme in which Sutton was involved. The left-field bleachers were added in 1984. More seats and an enlarged press box followed in the late 1980s. The field was converted from a multi-use facility to a strictly baseball stadium in the early 1990s, and real grass replaced the plastic surface. The '90s renovation also included the addition of more seats and a large scoreboard.

The best thing about this stadium is its colorful history. Pinched on its first-base side by a former auto racetrack (now a horse racetrack), the park has a huge net above the outfield wall in left to protect cars on 15th Street. But neither wall nor net can contain some of the sluggers in the Double A Texas League. Driller Stadium lore is made on nights when the huge American flag in centerfield is blowing with the prevailing wind, away from home plate. For batting practice, sit in the second deck on the left-field side and watch the balls bounce out onto busy 15th Street and into the parking lot beyond. In 1989, Chicago Cubs home run king Sammy Sosa ended a game one night with a 12th-inning blast that landed at the foot of a shopper coming out of the neighborhood grocery store. The biggest blast came in 1983 when Rob Deer flew one out that bounced once and landed on the top of a house next to the grocery store, more than 500 ft from home plate.

Tulsa's previous fairgrounds ballpark—Texas League Park, built in the 1930s on the site of the existing parking lot—had its own amazing story. Racing to avoid a sudden spring rain shower during a Texas Rangers pre-season exhibition game in 1977, too many fans crowded into too small a space. The wooden grandstand collapsed and seventeen people fell 20 ft. The next day the stadium was condemned. They bulldozed away half of the park, but the team played there for four more seasons before moving into Drillers Stadium.

Where to Stay

Visiting Team Hotel: Best Western Tradewinds Central. This bargain two-story hotel has free Continental breakfasts. Queen-size beds are standard in double rooms. The decor is modern. It is 4 mi southwest of the ballpark. *3141 E. Skelly Dr., Tulsa, OK 74105, tel. 918/749–5561 or 800/528–1234, fax 918/749–6312. 167 rooms. Facilities: restaurant, outdoor pool, exercise room, coin laundry. AE, D, DC, MC, V. $$*

Adams Mark Tulsa at Williams Center. This downtown 15-story hotel has large rooms with balconies and upscale furnishings. There's a free shuttle to the airport. *100 E. 2nd, Tulsa 74103, tel. 918/582–9000 or 800/444–2326, fax 918/560–2232. 462 rooms. Facilities: 2 restaurants, indoor pool, exercise room, airport shuttle. AE, D, DC, MC, V. $$$*

Where to Eat

Betty Ann's Restaurant. In a busy strip mall, this storefront restaurant feels like a small-town café. The homemade cinnamon rolls satisfy, and

the Western omelet and breakfast quesadilla are good. Bowls of pinto beans accompany many lunches, and 3-way chili, fruit cobblers, and several salads are on the menu. *4401 S. Memorial, Tulsa, tel. 918/663–8269. D, MC, V. No dinner. $*

Metro Diner. Pink and blue neon illuminate this '50s diner re-creation. It has stainless tubular chairs, 45s hanging from the ceiling, and turquoise banquettes. From the short stack pancakes to grilled cheese sandwiches, meat loaf, and a variety of malts and shakes, this is the early version of fast food. There are 8 senior citizens' meals and several 99¢ dinners for children under 6. *3001 E. 11th, Tulsa, tel. 918/592–2616. AE, D, MC, V. $*

Nelson's Grill and Buffeteria. American downtowns used to have many of these efficient breakfast and lunch restaurants. Nelson's has been going strong since 1929. You can eat blue-plate specials on a red stool at the counter or at a table. Famous for its chicken fried steak ($5), this is also the place for hearty, inexpensive breakfasts with very good biscuits. *514 S. Boston Ave., Tulsa, tel. 918/584–9969. MC, V. No dinner. $*

Ruby's. The decor may be early '60s beige, with gold frosted lights, but the hearty meals of serious home-cooked food keep the place lively. The menu is the reverse of trendy—timeless breaded tomatoes, navy beans, meatloaf, and chicken fried steak. The beef stew is terrific, as are the cobblers, pies, and breads. There is a children's menu. *4634 E. 31st St., Tulsa, tel. 918/749–3270. No credit cards. $*

Entertainments

Bell's Amusement Park. It's a family-run park on the other side of the ballpark, built in 1951. There are 10 acres of rides, including the wooden Zingo roller coaster that goes under a concession stand and is brilliantly lit in white at night. White Lightning log flume and Phantasmagoria, a dark ride, are teen magnets. Also on the grounds are a Himalaya and Tilt-a-Whirl, an aerial tram, and bumper boats. Every Friday night, two people can get in for the price of one. *3901 E. 21st St. Tulsa State Fairgrounds, Tulsa, tel. 918/744–1991. Gate admission: $1,* *senior citizens free. All-day pass: $14.95, $9.70 under 36 ", senior citizens free. Open Mon.–Sat. 10–5:30.*

Tulsa Zoo and Living Museum. The jewel in this Mohawk Park zoo is the LaFortune North American Living Museum, a four-building exhibit connected by bridgewalks. Each building highlights a major region of North America. A $1.50 steam train ride is the easiest way to navigate the spacious zoo; the complex includes a shark aquarium and coral reef, as well as the Oxley Nature Center, an Elephant Center, a children's zoo, two golf courses, horse rentals, and a boat ramp on Lake Yahola. A tropical rain-forest exhibit contains 500 animals and displays on Central and South America. Sea lions and alligators have daily public feedings. *5701 E. 36th St. N., Tulsa, tel. 918/669–6600. Admission: $5 adults, $4 senior citizens, $2 ages 3–11, half price after 5 PM July–Aug. Open daily 10–5.*

Baseball Teams in the United States and Canada

To access Minor League Baseball Web sites, use this format: www.minorleaguebaseball.com/teams/NAME OF TEAM CITY/

Teams with names in **boldface** below are major league.

Alabama

Birmingham Barons (Hoover Metropolitan Stadium; AA; Southern League), 100 Ben Chapman Dr., Birmingham, AL 35244, tel. 205/988–3200

Huntsville Stars (Joe W. Davis Municipal Stadium; AA; Southern League), 3125 Leeman Ferry Rd., Huntsville, AL 35801, tel. 205/882–2562

Mobile Baybears (Hank Aaron Stadium; AA; Southern League), 755 Bolling Bros. Blvd., Mobile, AL 36606, tel. 334/479–2327

Arizona

Arizona Diamondbacks (Bank One Ballpark; National League), 401 E. Jefferson St., Phoenix, AZ 85004, tel. 602/462–6500

Tucson Sidewinders (Tucson Electric Park; AAA; Pacific Coast League), 2500 E. Ajo Way, Tucson, AZ 85713, tel. 520/434–1021

Arkansas

Arkansas Travelers (Ray Winder Field; AA; Texas League), War Memorial Park, Little Rock, AR 72205, tel. 501/664–1555

California

Anaheim Angels (Edison International Field of Anaheim; American League), 2000 Gene Autry Way, Anaheim, CA 92806, tel. 714/940–2000

Bakersfield Blaze (Sam Lynn Ballpark; A; California League), 4009 Chester Ave., Bakersfield, CA 93301, tel. 661/322–1363

Chico Heat (Nettleton Stadium; Independent; Western League), 250 Vallombrosa Ave., Chico, CA 95926, tel. 530/343–4328

Fresno Grizzlies (Beiden Field; AAA; Pacific Coast League), 700 Van Ness Ave., Fresno, CA 93721, tel. 559/442–1994

High Desert Mavericks (Mavericks Stadium; A; California League), 12000 Stadium Way, Adelanto, CA 92301, tel. 760/246–6287

Lake Elsinore Storm (Lake Elsinore Diamond; A; California League), 500 Diamond Dr., Lake Elsinore, CA 92530, tel. 909/245–4487

Lancaster Jethawks (Lancaster Municipal Stadium; A; California League), 45116 Valley Central Way, Lancaster, CA 93536, tel. 661/726–5400

Los Angeles Dodgers (Dodger Stadium, National League), 1000 Elysian Park Ave., Los Angeles, CA 90012, tel. 323/224–1500

Modesto A's (John Thurman Stadium; A; California League), 601 Neece Dr., Modesto, CA 95351, tel. 209/572–4487

Oakland Athletics (Oakland-Alameda County Coliseum; American League), 7000 Coliseum Way, Oakland, CA 94621, tel. 510/638–4900

Rancho Cucamonga Quakes (The Epicenter; A; California League), 8408 Rochester Ave., Rancho Cucamonga, CA 91730, tel. 909/481–5000

Sacramento Steelheads (Union Stadium; Independent; Western League), 2527 J St., Sacramento, CA 95816, tel. 916/553–4500

San Bernardino Stampede (The Ranch; A; California League), 280 South E St., San Bernardino, CA 92401, tel. 909/888–9922

San Diego Padres (Qualcomm Stadium; National League), 9449 Friars Rd., San Diego, CA 92108, tel. 619/881–6500

San Francisco Giants (Pacific Bell Park; National League), 24 Willie Mays Plaza, San Francisco, CA 94107, tel. 415/468–3700

San Jose Giants (Municipal Stadium; A; California League), 588 E. Alma Ave., San Jose, CA 95112, tel. 408/297–1435

Sonoma County Crushers (Rohnert Park Stadium; Independent; Western League), 5900 Labath Ave., Rohnert Park, CA 95404, tel. 707/588–8300

Stockton Mudville 9 (Billy Hebert Field; A; California League), Alpine and Sutter Sts., Stockton, CA 95204, tel. 209/944–5943

Visalia Oaks (Recreation Park; A; California League), 440 N. Giddings Ave., Visalia, CA 93291, tel. 559/625–0480

Colorado

Colorado Rockies (Coors Field; National League), 2001 Blake St., Denver, CO 80205, tel. 303/292–0200

Colorado Springs Sky Sox (Sky Sox Stadium; AAA; Pacific Coast League), 4385 Tutt Blvd., Colorado Springs, CO 80922, tel. 719/597–1449

Connecticut

Bridgeport Bluefish (Ballpark at Harbor Yard; Independent; Atlantic League), 500 Main St., Bridgeport, CT 06604, tel. 203/345–4800

New Britain Rock Cats (New Britain Stadium; AA; Eastern League), S. Main St., New Britain, CT 06051, tel. 860/224–8383

New Haven Ravens (Yale Field; AA; Eastern League), 252 Derby Ave., West Haven, CT 06515, tel. 203/782–1666

Norwich Navigators (Sen. Thomas J. Dodd Stadium; AA; Eastern League), 14 Stott Ave., Norwich, CT 06360, tel. 860/887–7962

Waterbury Spirit (Municipal Stadium; Independent; Eastern Division), 1200 Watertown Rd., Waterbury, CT 06708, tel. 203/419–0393

Delaware

Wilmington Blue Rocks (Daniel S. Frawley Stadium; A; Carolina League), 801 S. Madison St., Wilmington, DE 19801, tel. 302/888–2015

Florida

Brevard County Manatees (Space Coast Stadium; A; Florida State League), 5800 Stadium Pkwy., Melbourne, FL 32940, tel. 407/633–9200

Charlotte Rangers (Charlotte County Stadium; A; Florida State League), 2300 El Jobean Rd., Port Charlotte, FL 33948, tel. 941/625–9500

Clearwater Phillies (Jack Russell Memorial Stadium; A; Florida State League), 800 Phillies Dr., Clearwater, FL 34615, tel. 727/441–8638

Daytona Cubs (Jackie Robinson Ballpark; A; Florida State League), 105 E. Orange Ave., Daytona, FL 32114, tel. 904/257–3172

Dunedin Blue Jays (Dunedin Stadium; A; Florida State League), 311 Douglas Ave., Dunedin, FL 3469, tel. 727/733–9302

Florida Marlins (Pro Player Stadium; National League), 2257 NW 199th St., Miami, FL 33056, tel. 305/626–7400

Fort Myers Miracle (Bill Hammond Stadium; A; Florida State League), 14400 Six Mile Cypress Pkwy., Fort Myers, FL 33912, tel. 941/768–4210

Jacksonville Suns (Wolfson Park; AA; Southern League), 1201 E. Duval St., Jacksonville, FL 32202, tel. 904/358–2846

Jupiter Hammerheads (Roger Dean Stadium; A; Florida State League), 4751 Main St., Jupiter, FL 33458, tel. 561/775–1818

Kissimmee Cobras (Osceola County Stadium; A; Florida State League), 1000 Bill Beck Blvd., Kissimmee, FL 32744, tel. 407/933–5500

Lakeland Tigers (Joker Marchant Stadium; A; Florida State League), 2125 N. Lake Ave., Lakeland, FL 33805, tel. 941/688–7911

Orlando Rays (Tinker Field; AA; Southern League), 287 S. Tampa Ave., Orlando, FL 32805, tel. 407/649–7297

St. Lucie Mets (Thomas J. White Stadium; A; Florida State League), 525 NW Peacock Blvd., Port St. Lucie, FL 43986, tel. 561/871–2100

St. Petersburg Devil Rays (Florida Power Park/Al Lang Field; A; Florida State League), 180 2nd Ave. SE, St. Petersburg, FL 33701, tel. 727/822–3384

Sarasota Red Sox (Ed Smith Stadium; A; Florida State League), 2700 12th St., Sarasota, FL 34237, tel. 941/365–4460

Tampa Bay Devil Rays (Tropicana Field; American League), 1 Tropicana Dr., St. Petersburg, FL 33705, tel. 727/825–3137

Tampa Yankees (Legends Field; A; Florida State League), 3802 Martin Luther King Blvd., Tampa, FL 33614, tel. 813/875–7753

Vero Beach Dodgers (Holman Stadium; A; Florida State League), 4101 26th St., Vero Beach, FL 32960, tel. 561/569–4900

Georgia

Atlanta Braves (Turner Field; National League), 755 Hank Aaron Dr., Atlanta, GA 30315, tel. 404/522–7630

Augusta Greenjackets (Lake Olmstead Stadium; A; South Atlantic League), 78 Milledge Rd., Augusta, GA 30904; tel. 706/736–7889

Columbus Redstixx (Golden Park; A; South Atlantic League), 100 4th St., Columbus, GA 31901, tel. 706/571–8866

Macon Braves (Luther Williams Field; A; South Atlantic League), Central City Park, 7th St., Macon, GA 31201, tel. 912/745–8943

Savannah Sand Gnats (Grayson Stadium; A; South Atlantic League), 1401 E. Victory Dr., Savannah, GA 31404, tel. 912/351–9150

Idaho

Boise Hawks (Memorial Stadium; Short Season A; Northwest League), 5600 Glenwood St., Boise, ID 83714, tel. 208/322–5000

Idaho Falls Padres (McDermott Field; Rookie Short Season; Pioneer League), 568 W. Elva St., Idaho Falls, ID 83402, tel. 208/522–8363

Illinois

Chicago Cubs (Wrigley Field; National League), 1060 W. Addison St., Chicago, IL 60613, tel. 773/404–2827

Chicago White Sox (Comiskey Park; American League), 333 W. 35th St., Chicago, IL 60616, tel. 312/674–1000

Cook County Cheetahs (Hawkinson Ford Field; Independent; Frontier League), 4545 Midlothian Turnpike, Crestwood, IL 60445, tel. 708/489–2255.

Gateway Grizzlies (Gateway Field; Independent; Frontier League), 1403 Nickell St., Sauget, IL 62206, tel. 618/632–0100.

Kane County Cougars (Philip B. Elfstrom Stadium; A; Midwest League), 34W002 Cherry Ln., Geneva, IL 60134, tel. 630/232–8811

Peoria Chiefs (Pete Vonachen Stadium; A; Midwest League), 1524 W. Nebraska Ave., Peoria, IL 61604, tel. 309/688–1622

Rockford Reds (Marinelli Field; A; Midwest League), 101 15th Ave., Rockford, IL 61104, tel. 815/962–2827

Schaumburg Flyers (Schaumburg Baseball Stadium; Independent; Northern League), 1144 S. Roselle Rd., Schaumburg, IL 60193, tel. 847/891–2255

Springfield Capitals (Robin Roberts Stadium; Independent; Frontier League), 1351 N. Gand Ave., E. Springfield, IL 62702, tel. 217/525–5500

Indiana

Dubois County Dragons (Huntingburg League Stadium; Independent; Frontier League), 426 E. 4th St., Huntingburg, IN 47542, tel. 812/683–4405

Evansville Otters (Bosse Field; Independent; Frontier League), 1701 N. Main St., Evansville, IN 47711, tel. 812/435–8686

Fort Wayne Wizards (Memorial Stadium; A; Midwest League), 4000 Parnell Ave., Fort Wayne, IN 46805, tel. 219/482–6400

Indianapolis Indians (Victory Field; AAA; International League), Maryland and West Sts., Indianapolis, IN 46225, tel. 317/269–3545

Richmond Roosters (Don McBride Stadium; Independent; Frontier League), McBride Stadium, Richmond, IN 47375, tel. 765/935–7529

South Bend Silver Hawks (Stanley Coveleski Regional Stadium; A; Midwest League), 501 W. South St., South Bend, IN 46601, tel. 219/235–9988

Iowa

Burlington Bees (Community Field; A; Midwest League), 2712 Mt. Pleasant St., Burlington, IA 52601, tel. 319/754–5705

Cedar Rapids Kernels (Veterans Memorial Stadium; A; Midwest League), 950 Rockford Rd. SW, Cedar Rapids, IA 52404, tel. 319/363–3887

Clinton Lumber Kings (Riverview Stadium; A; Midwest League), 6th Ave. N and 1st St., Clinton, IA 52733, tel. 319/242–0727

Iowa Cubs (Sec Taylor Stadium; AAA; Pacific Coast League), 350 SW 1st St., Des Moines, IA 50309, tel. 515/243–6111

Quad City River Bandits (John O'Donnell Stadium; A; Midwest League), 209 S. Gaines St., Davenport, IA 52802, tel. 319/324–2032

Sioux City Explorers (Lewis & Clark Park; Independent; Northern League), 3400 Line Dr., Sioux City, IA 51106, tel. 712/277–9467

Kansas

Wichita Wranglers (Lawrence-Dumont Stadium; AA; Texas League), 300 S. Sycamore St., Wichita, KS 67213, tel. 316/267–3372

Kentucky

Louisville Riverbats (Slugger Stadium; AAA; International League), Preston and Main Sts., Louisville, KY 40202, 502/367–9121

Louisiana

Alexandria Aces (Bringhurst Field; Independent; Texas-Louisiana League), 1 Babe Ruth Dr., Alexandria, LA 71307, tel. 318/473–2237

Bayou Bullfrogs (Moore Field; Independent; Texas-Louisiana League), 801 W. Congress St., Lafayette, LA 70501, tel. 318/233–0998

New Orleans Zephyrs (Zephyr Field; AAA; Pacific Coast League), Airline Hwy. and Elise Ln., Metairie, LA 70003, tel. 504/734–5155

Shreveport Captains (Fair Grounds Field; AA; Texas League), 2901 Pershing Blvd., Shreveport, LA 71109, tel. 318/636–5555

Maine

Portland Sea Dogs (Hadlock Field; AA; Eastern League), 271 Park Ave., Portland, ME 04102, tel. 207/874–9300

Maryland

Baltimore Orioles (Oriole Park at Camden Yards; American League), 333 W. Camden St., Baltimore, MD 21201, tel. 410/685–9800

Bowie Baysox (Prince George's Stadium; AA; Eastern League), 4101 NE Crain Hwy., Bowie, MD 20716, tel. 301/805–6000

Delmarva Shorebirds (Arthur W. Perdue Stadium; A; South Atlantic League), 6400 Hobbs Rd., Salisbury, MD 21802, tel. 410/219–3112

Frederick Keys (Harry Grove Stadium; A; Carolina League), 6201 New Design Rd., Frederick, MD 21702, tel. 301/662–0013

Hagerstown Suns (Municipal Stadium; A; South Atlantic League), 274 E. Memorial Blvd., Hagerstown, MD 21740, tel. 301/791–6266

Massachusetts

Boston Red Sox (Fenway Park; American League), 4 Yawkey Way, Boston, MA 02215, tel. 617/267–9440

Lowell Spinners (Edward LeLacheur Park; Short Season A; New York–Penn League), 450 Aiken St., Lowell, MA 01854, tel. 978/459–2255

Massachusetts Mad Dogs (Fraser Field; Independent; Eastern Division), 359 Western Ave., Lynn, MA 01904, tel. 781/592–2255

Pittsfield Mets (Wahconah Park; Short Season A; New York–Penn League), 105 Wahconah St., Pittsfield, MA 01201, tel. 413/499–6387

Michigan

Detroit Tigers (Comerica Park; American League), Brush & Witherell Sts., Detroit, MI 48226, tel. 313/962–4000

Lansing Lugnuts (Oldsmobile Park; A; Midwest League), 505 E. Michigan Ave., Lansing, MI 48933, tel. 517/485–4500

Michigan Battle Cats (C.O. Brown Stadium; A; Midwest League), 1392 Capital Ave. NE, Battle Creek, MI 49017, tel. 616/660–2287

West Michigan Whitecaps (Old Kent Park; A; Midwest League), 4500 W. River Dr., Comstock Park, MI 49321, tel. 616/784–4131

Minnesota

Duluth-Superior Dukes (Wade Stadium; Independent; Northern League), 101 N. 35th Ave. W., Duluth, MN 55807, tel. 218/727–4525

Minnesota Twins (Hubert H. Humphrey Metrodome; American League), 501 Chicago Ave. S, Minneapolis, MN 55415, tel. 612/375–1366

St. Paul Saints (Midway Stadium; Independent; Northern League), 1771 Energy Park Dr., St. Paul, MN 55108, tel. 651/644–3517

Mississippi

Greenville Bluesmen (Legion Field; Independent; Texas-Louisiana League), 1040 S. Raceway Rd., Greenville, MS 38701, tel. 601/335–2583

Jackson Generals (Smith-Wills Stadium; AA; Texas League), 1200 Lakeland Dr., Jackson, MS 39216, tel. 601/981–4664

Missouri

Kansas City Royals (Kauffman Stadium; American League), 1 Royal Way, Kansas City, MO 64141, tel. 816/921–2200

Ozark Mountain Ducks (Ducks Stadium; Independent; Texas-Louisiana League), 5245 N. 17th St., Ozark, MO 65721, tel. 417/581–2868

River City Rascals (T.R. Hughes Ballpark; Independent; Frontier League), 900 Ozzie Smith Dr., O'Fallon, MO 63366, tel. 314/240–2287

St. Louis Cardinals (Busch Stadium; National League), 250 Stadium Plaza, St. Louis, MO 63102, tel. 314/421–3060

Montana

Billings Mustangs (Cobb Field; Rookie Short Season; Pioneer League), 901 N. 27th St., Billings, MT 59103, tel. 406/252–1241

Butte Copper Kings (Alumni Coliseum; Rookie Short Season; Pioneer League), Montana Tech, W. Park St., Butte, MT 59701, tel. 406/723–8206

Great Falls Dodgers (Legion Park; Rookie Short Season; Pioneer League), 11 5th St. N, Great Falls, MT 59401, tel. 406/452–5311

Helena Brewers (Kindrick Legion Field; Rookie Short Season; Pioneer League), Warren and Memorial Sts., Helena, MT 59601, tel. 406/449–7616

Missoula Osprey (Lindborg-Cregg Field; Rookie Short Season; Pioneer League), 137 E. Main St., Missoula, MT 59802, tel. 406/543–3300

Nebraska

Omaha Goldenspikes (Rosenblatt Stadium; AAA; Pacific Coast League), 1202 Bert Murphy Dr., Omaha, NE 68107, tel. 402/734–2550

Nevada

Las Vegas Stars (Cashman Field; AAA; Pacific Coast League), 850 Las Vegas Blvd. N, Las Vegas, NV 89101, tel. 702/386–7200

Reno Chukars (Moana Stadium; Independent; Western League), 249 W. Moana Ln, Reno, NV 89509, tel. 702/829–7890

New Hampshire

Nashua Pride (Holman Stadium; Independent; Atlantic League), 100 Main St., Nashua, NH 03060, tel. 603/883–2255

New Jersey

Atlantic City Surf (The Sandcastle; Independent; Atlantic League), 545 N. Albany Ave., Atlantic City, NJ 08401, tel. 609/344–8873

New Jersey Cardinals (Skylands Park; Short Season A; New York–Penn League), 94 Championship Pl., Augusta, NJ 07822, tel. 973/579–7500

New Jersey Jackals (Yogi Berra Stadium; Independent; Eastern Division), 1 Hall Dr., Little Falls, NJ 07424, tel. 973/746–7434

Newark Bears (Riverfront Stadium; Independent; Atlantic League), 10 Bridge St., Newark, NJ 07102, tel. 973/483–6900

Somerset Patriots (Somerset County Ballpark; Independent; Atlantic League), Patriots Park, Bridgewater, NJ 08807, tel. 908/252–0700

Trenton Thunder (Mercer County Waterfront Park; AA; Eastern League), 1 Thunder Rd., Trenton, NJ 08611, tel. 609/394–3300

New Mexico

Albuquerque Dukes (Albuquerque Sports Stadium; AAA; Pacific Coast League), 1601 Avenida Cesar Chavez. SE, Albuquerque, NM 87106, tel. 505/243–1791

New York

Adirondack Lumberjacks (East Field; Independent; Eastern Division), 15 Dix Ave., Glens Falls, NY 12801, tel. 518/743–9618

Albany-Colonie Diamond Dogs (Heritage Park), 780 Watervliet-Shaker Rd., Albany, NY 12211, tel. 518/869–9234

Auburn Doubledays (Falcon Park; Short Season A; New York–Penn League), 108 N. Division St., Auburn, NY 13021, tel. 315/255–2489

Batavia Muckdogs (Dwyer Stadium; Short Season A; New York–Penn League), 299 Bank St., Batavia, NY 14020, tel. 716/343–5454

Binghamton Mets (Binghamton Municipal Stadium; AA; Eastern League), 211 Henry St., Binghamton, NY 13901, tel. 607/723–6387

Buffalo Bisons (Dunn Tire Field; AAA; International League), 275 Washington St., Buffalo, NY 14203, 716/846–2000

Elmira Pioneers (Dunn Field; Independent; Eastern Division), 546 Luce St., Elmira, NY 14904, tel. 607/734–1270

Hudson Valley Renegades (Dutchess Stadium; Short Season A; New York–Penn League), Rte. 90, Wappingers Falls, NY 12590, tel. 914/838–0094

Jamestown Jammers (Russell Diethrick Park; Short Season A; New York–Penn League), 485 Falconer St., Jamestown, NY 14702, tel. 716/664–0915

New York Mets (Shea Stadium, National League), 123 Roosevelt Ave., Flushing, NY 11368, tel. 718/507–6387

New York Yankees (Yankee Stadium; American League), 161st St. and River Ave., Bronx, NY 10451, tel. 718/293–4300

Oneonta Tigers (Damaschke Field; Short Season A; New York–Penn League), 95 River St., Oneonta, NY 13820, tel. 607/432–6326

Rochester Red Wings (Frontier Field; AAA; International League), 1 Morrie Silver Way, Rochester, NY 14608, tel. 716/454–1001

Staten Island Yankees (College of Staten Island Field; Short Season A; New York-Penn League), 2025 Richmond Ave., Staten Island, NY 10314, tel. 718/698–9265

Syracuse SkyChiefs (P & C Stadium; AAA; Independent League), Hiawatha Blvd. E and 2nd St., Syracuse, NY 13208, tel. 315/474–7833

Utica Blue Sox (Donovan Stadium; Short Season A; New York–Penn League), 1700 Sunset Ave., Utica, NY 13502, tel. 315/738–0999

North Carolina

Asheville Tourists (McCormick Field; A; South Atlantic League), 30 Buchanan Pl., Asheville, NC 28801, tel. 828/258–0428

Burlington Indians (Burlington Athletic Stadium; Rookie Short Season; Appalachian League), 1450 Graham St., Burlington, NC 27215, tel. 336/222–0223

Cape Fear Crocs (J.P. Riddle Stadium; A; South Atlantic League), 2823 Legion Rd., Fayetteville, NC 28306, tel. 910/424–6500

Carolina Mudcats (Five County Stadium; AA; Southern League), 1501 Hwy. 39, Zebulon, NC 27597, tel. 919/269–2287

Durham Bulls (Durham Bulls Athletic Park; A; Carolina League), 409 Blackwell St., Durham, NC 27701, tel. 919/687–6500

Greensboro Bats (War Memorial Stadium; A; South Atlantic League), 510 Yanceyville St., Greensboro, NC 27405, tel. 336/333–2287

Hickory Crawdads (L.P. Frans Stadium; A; South Atlantic League), 2500 Clement Blvd. NW, Hickory, NC 28601, tel. 828/322–3000

Kinston Indians (Grainger Stadium; A; Carolina League), 400 E. Grainer Ave., Kinston, NC 28501, tel. 252/527–9111

Piedmont Boll Weevils (Fieldcrest Cannon Stadium; A; South Atlantic League), 2888 Moose Rd., Kannapolis, NC 28083, tel. 704/932–3267

Winston-Salem Warthogs (Ernie Shore Field; A; Carolina League), 401 Deacon Blvd., Winston-Salem, NC 27105, tel. 336/759–2233

North Dakota

Fargo-Moorhead Redhawks (Newman Outdoor Field; Independent; Northern League), 1515 15th Ave. N, Fargo, ND 58102, tel. 701/235–6161

Ohio

Akron Aeros (Canal Park; AA; Eastern League), 300 S. Main St., Akron, OH 44308, tel. 330/253–5151

Canton Crocodiles (Thurman Munson Memorial Stadium; Independent; Frontier League), 2501 Allen Av. SE, Canton, OH 44707, tel. 330/455–2255

Chillicothe Paints (V.A. Memorial Field; Independent; Frontier League), 59 N. Paint St., Chillicothe, OH 45601, tel. 740/773–8326

Cincinnati Reds (Cinergy Field; National League), 100 Cinergy Field, Cincinnati, OH 45202, tel. 513/421–4510

Cleveland Indians (Jacobs Field; American League), 2401 Ontario St., Cleveland, OH 44115, tel. 216/420–4200

Columbus Clippers (Cooper Stadium; AAA; International League), 1155 W. Mound St. Columbus, OH 43223, tel. 614/462–5250

Mahoning Valley Scrappers (Cafaro Field; Short Season A; New York-Penn League), 111 Eastwood Mall Blvd., Niles, OH 44446, tel. 330/505–0000

Toledo Mud Hens (Ned Skeldon Stadium; AAA; International League), 2901 Key St., Maumee, OH 43537, tel. 419/893–9483

Oklahoma

Oklahoma Redhawks (Southwestern Bell Bricktown Ballpark; AAA; Pacific Coast League), 2 S. Mickey Mantle Dr., Oklahoma City, OK 73104, tel. 405/218–1000

Tulsa Drillers (Drillers Stadium; AA; Texas League), 4802 E. 15th St., Tulsa, OK 74112, tel. 918/744–5998

Oregon

Eugene Emeralds (Civic Stadium; Short Season A; Northwest League), 2077 Willamette St., Eugene, OR 97405, tel. 541/342–5367

Portland Rockies (Civic Stadium; Short Season A; Northwest League), 1844 SW Morrison Portland, OR 97207, tel. 503/223–2837

Salem-Keizer Volcanoes (Volcanoes Stadium; Short Season A; Northwest League), 6700 Field of Dreams Way, Keizer, OR 97307, tel. 503/390–2225

Southern Oregon Timberjacks (Miles Field; Short Season A; Northwest League), 1801 S. Pacific Hwy. Medford, OR 97501, tel. 541/770–5364

Pennsylvania

Allentown Ambassadors (Bicentennial Park, 1511 Hamilton St., Allentown, PA 18102, tel. 610/437–6800

Altoona Curve (Altoona Ballpark; AA; Eastern League), 100 Park Ave., Altoona, PA 16602, tel. 814/943–5400

Erie Seawolves (Jerry Uht Park; Short Season A; New York-Penn League), 110 E. 10th St., Erie, PA 16507, tel. 814/456–1300

Harrisburg Senators (RiverSide Stadium; AA; Eastern League), City Island, Harrisburg, PA 17101, tel. 717/231–4444

Johnson Johnnies (Point Stadium; Independent; Frontier League), 211 Main St., Johnstown, PA 15901, tel. 814/536–8326

Lehigh Valley Black Diamonds (Lehigh Valley Sport Complex; Independent; Atlantic League), 800 Cedarville Rd., Easton, PA 18042, tel. 610/250–2273

Philadelphia Phillies (Veterans Stadium; National League), 3501 S. Broad St., Philadelphia, PA 19148, tel. 215/463–6000

Pittsburgh Pirates (Three Rivers Stadium; National League), 600 Stadium Cir., Pittsburgh, PA 15212, tel. 412/323–5000

Reading Phillies (Reading Municipal Memorial Stadium; AA; Eastern League), 1900 Centre Ave., Reading, PA 19605, tel. 610/375–8469

Scranton/Wilkes-Barre Red Barons (Lackawanna County Stadium; AAA; International League), 235 Montage Mountain Rd., Moosic, PA 18507, tel. 570/969–2255

Williamsport Crosscutters (Bowman Field; Short Season A; New York-Penn League), 1700 W. 4th St., Williamsport, PA 17701, tel. 570/326–3389

Rhode Island

Pawtucket Red Sox (McCoy Stadium; AAA; International League), 1 Columbus Av., Pawtucket, RI 02860, tel. 401/724–7300

South Carolina

Capital City Bombers (Capital City Stadium; A; South Atlantic League), 301 S. Assembly St., Columbia, SC 29201, tel. 803/256–4110

Charleston Riverdogs (Joseph P. Riley Jr. Ballpark; A; South Atlantic League), 360 Fishbourne St., Charleston, SC 29403, tel. 843/723–7241

Charlotte Knights (Knights Castle; AAA; International League), 2280 Deerfield Dr., Fort Mill, SC 29715, tel. 704/357–8071

Greenville Braves (Greenville Municipal Stadium; AA; Southern League), 1 Braves Ave., Greenville, SC 29607, tel. 864/299–3456

Myrtle Beach Pelicans (Coastal Federal Field; A; Carolina League), 1251 21st Ave. N., Myrtle Beach, SC 29577, tel. 843/918–6000

South Dakota

Sioux Falls Canaries (Sioux Falls Stadium; Independent; Northern League), 119 Main St., Sioux Falls, SD 57102, tel. 605/333–0179

Tennessee

Chattanooga Lookouts (BellSouth Park; AA; Southern League), 1 Power Alley, Chattanooga, TN 37401, tel. 423/267–2208

Elizabethton Twins (Joe O'Brien Field; Rookie Short Season; Appalachian League), 208 N. Holly Ln., Elizabethton, TN 37643, tel. 423/547–6440

Johnson City Cardinals (Howard Johnson Field; Rookie Short Season; Appalachian League), 111 Legion St., Johnson City, TN 37601, tel. 423/461–4866

Kingsport Mets (Hunter Wright Stadium; Rookie Short Season; Appalachian League), 433 E. Center St., Kingsport, TN 37660, tel. 423/378–3744

Knoxville Smokies (Bill Meyer Stadium; AA; Southern League), 633 Jessamine St., Knoxville, TN 37917, tel. 423/637–9494

Memphis Redbirds (AutoZone Park; AAA; Pacific Coast League), 3rd St. & Union Ave., Memphis, TN 38103, tel. 901/721–6000

Nashville Sounds (Herschel Greer Stadium; AAA; Pacific Coast League), 534 Chestnut St., Nashville, TN 37203, tel. 615/242–4371

West Tenn Diamond Jaxx (Pringles Park; AA; Southern League), 4 Fun Pl., Jackson, TN 38305, tel. 901/664–2020

Texas

Abilene Prairie Dogs (Crutcher-Scott Field; Independent; Texas-Louisiana League), 2249 N. Judge Ely Blvd., Abilene, TX 79601, tel. 915/673–7364

Amarillo Dillas (Potter County Memorial Stadium; Independent; Texas-Louisiana League), 3222 E. 3rd St., Amarillo, TX 79120, tel. 806/342–3455

El Paso Diablos (Cohen Stadium; AA; Texas League), 9700 Gateway N. Blvd., El Paso, TX 79924, tel. 915/755–2000

Houston Astros (Astrodome; National League), 8400 Kirby Dr., Houston, TX 77054, tel. 713/799–9500

Midland Rockhounds (Christensen Stadium; AA; Texas League), 4300 N. Lamesa Rd., Midland, TX 79705, tel. 915/683–4251

Rio Grande Valley Whitewings (Harlingen Field; Independent; Texas-Louisiana League), 1216 Fair Park Blvd., Harlingen, TX 78550, tel. 956/412–9464

San Antonio Missions (Nelson Wolff Municipal Stadium; AA; Texas League), 5757 Hwy. 90 W., San Antonio, TX 78227, tel. 210/675–7275

Texas Rangers (Ballpark in Arlington; American League), 1000 Ballpark Way, Arlington, TX 76011, tel. 817/273–5222

Utah

Ogden Raptors (Lindquist Field; Rookie Short Season; Pioneer League), 2330 Lincoln Ave., Ogden, UT 84401, tel. 801/393–2400

Salt Lake Buzz (Franklin Covey Field; AAA; Pacific Coast League), 77 W. 1300 S., Salt Lake City, UT 84115, tel. 801/485–3800

Zion Pioneerzz (Bruce Hurst Field; Independent; Western League), 1240 E. 100 S, St. George, UT 84790, tel. 435/656–9000

Vermont

Vermont Expos (Centennial Field; Short Season A; New York–Penn League), Champlain Mill, Winooski, VT 05404, tel. 802/655–4200

Virginia

Bristol Sox (DeVault Memorial Stadium; Rookie Short Season; Appalachian League), 1501 Euclid Ave., Bristol, VA 24201, tel. 540/645–7275

Danville Braves (Dan Daniel Memorial Park; Rookie Short Season Appalachian League), 302 River Park Dr., Danville, VA 24541, tel. 804/791–3346

Lynchburg Hillcats (City Stadium; A; Carolina League), Fort Ave. and Wythe Rd., Lynchburg, VA 24501, tel. 804/528–1144

Martinsville Astros (Hooker Field; Rookie Short Season; Appalachian League), Chatham Heights Rd., Martinsville, VA 24112, tel. 540/666–2000

Norfolk Tides (Harbor Park; AAA; International League), 150 Park Ave., Norfolk, VA 23510, tel. 757/622–2222

Potomac Cannons (Pfitzner Stadium; A; Carolina League), 7 County Complex, Woodbridge, VA 22192, tel. 703/590–2311

Pulaski Rangers (Calfee Park; Rookie Appalachian League), 5th St., Pulaski, VA 24301, tel. 540/980–1070

Richmond Braves (The Diamond; AAA; International League), 3001 N. Boulevard, Richmond, VA 23230, tel. 804/359–4444

Salem Avalanche (Salem Memorial Baseball Complex; A; Carolina League), 1004 Texas St., Salem, VA 24153, tel. 540/389–3333

Washington

Everett Aquasox (Everett Memorial Stadium; Short Season A; Northwest League), 2118 Broadway, Everett, WA 98201, tel. 425/258–3673

Seattle Mariners (Safeco Field; American League; 1st & Atlantic Sts., Seattle, WA 98104, tel. 206/346–4000

Spokane Indians (Seafirst Stadium; Short Season A; Northwest League), 602 N. Havana, Spokane, WA 99202, tel. 509/535–2922

Tacoma Rainiers (Cheney Stadium; AAA; Pacific Coast League), 2502 S. Tyler, Tacoma, WA 98405, tel. 253/752–7707

Tri-City Posse (Tri-Cities Stadium; Independent; Western League), 6200 Burden Rd., Pasco, WA 99301, tel. 509/547–6773

Yakima Bears (Yakima County Stadium; Short Season A; Northwest League), 810 W. Nob Hill Blvd., Yakima, WA 98902, tel. 509/457–5151

West Virginia

Bluefield Orioles (Bowen Field; Rookie Short Season; Appalachian League), Stadium Dr., Bluefield, WV 24701, tel. 540/326–1326

Charleston Alley Cats (Walt Powell Park; A; South Atlantic League), 3403 MacCorkle Ave., Charleston, WV 25304, tel. 304/344–2287

Princeton Devil Rays (Hunnicutt Field; Rookie Short Season; Appalachian League), Old Bluefield-Princeton Rd., Princeton, WV 24740, tel. 304/487–2000

Wisconsin

Beloit Snappers (Harry Pohlman Field; A; Midwest League), 2301 Skyline Dr., Beloit, WI 53511, tel. 608/362–2272

Madison Black Wolf (Warner Park; Independent; Northern League), 2920 N. Sherman Ave., Madison, WI 53704, tel. 608/244–5666

Milwaukee Brewers (County Stadium; American League), 201 S. 46th St., Milwaukee, WI 53214, tel. 414/933–4114

Wisconsin Timber Rattlers (Fox Cities Stadium; A; Midwest League), 2400 N. Casaloma Dr., Appleton, WI 54911, tel. 920/733–4152

Canada

Calgary Cannons (Burns Stadium; AAA; Pacific Coast League), 2255 Cowhild Trail NW, Calgary, Alberta T2M 4S7, tel. 403/284–1111

Edmonton Trappers (TELUS Field; AAA; Pacific Coast League), 10233 96th Ave., Edmonton, Alberta T5K 0A5, tel. 780/414–4450

Les Capitales de Quebec (La Stade de Quebec; Independent; Northern League Eastern Division), 100 rue du Cardinal Maurice-Roy, Quebec City, Quebec G1K 8Z1, tel. 418/521–2255

London Werewolves (Labatt Memorial Park; Independent; Frontier League), 25 Wilson Ave., London, Ontario N6H 1X2, tel. 519/679–7337

Medicine Hat Blue Jays (Athletic Park; Rookie Short Season; Pioneer League), 1 Birch Ave. SE, Medicine Hat, Alberta T1A 7GS, tel. 403/526–0404

Montreal Expos (Olympic Stadium; National League), 4549 Pierre-de-Coubertin Ave., Montreal, Quebec H1V 3N7, tel. 514/253–3434

Ottawa Lynx (JetForm Park; AAA; International League), 300 Chemin Coventry Rd., Ottawa, Ontario K1K 4P5, tel. 613/747–5969

St. Catherines Stompers (Community Park; Short Season A; New York–Penn League), 426 Merritt St., St. Catherines, Ontario L2P 1P3, tel. 905/641–5297

Toronto Blue Jays (SkyDome; American League), 1 Blue Jays Way, Toronto, Ontario M5V 1J1, tel. 416/341–1000

Vancouver Canadians (Nat Bailey Stadium; AAA; Pacific Coast League), 4601 Ontario St., Vancouver, British Columbia V5V 3H4, tel. 604/872–5232

Winnipeg Goldeyes (Canwest Global Park; Independent; Northern League), 200 McDermott Ave., Winnipeg, Manitoba R3B OS1, tel. 204/982–2273

Notes